FAMILY COUNSELING

PATTY HARMAN

Behavioral Theories and Treatment of Anxiety

Behavioral Theories and Treatment of Anxiety

Edited by

Samuel M. Turner

Department of Psychiatry
Western Psychiatric Institute and Clinic
University of Pittsburgh School of Medicine
Pittsburgh, Pennsylvania

Plenum Press • New York and London

Library of Congress Cataloging in Publication Data

Main entry under title:

Behavioral theories and treatment of anxiety.

Includes bibliographical references and index.
1. Anxiety — Treatment. 2. Behavioral therapy. I. Turner, Samuel M., 1944–   .
[DNLM: 1. Anxiety Disorders. 2. Anxiety Disorders — therapy. 3. Behavior. WM 172
B419]
RC531.B43   1984   616.85′22306   84-9832
ISBN 0-306-41593-3

©1984 Plenum Press, New York
A Division of Plenum Publishing Corporation
233 Spring Street, New York, N.Y. 10013

Printed in the United States of America

Contributors

David H. Barlow ● Center for Stress and Anxiety Disorders, Department of Psychology, State University of New York at Albany, Albany, New York

Alan S. Bellack ● Medical College of Pennsylvania at Eastern Pennsylvania Psychiatric Institute, Philadelphia, Pennsylvania

Dennis J. Delprato ● Department of Psychology, Eastern Michigan University, Ypsilanti, Michigan

Rolf G. Jacob ● Department of Psychiatry, Western Psychiatric Institute and Clinic, University of Pittsburgh School of Medicine, Pittsburgh, Pennsylvania

Thomas W. Lombardo ● Department of Psychology, University of Mississippi, Oxford, Mississippi

Joni A. Mayer ● Department of Psychology, Virginia Polytechnic Institute and State University, Blacksburg, Virginia

F. Dudley McGlynn ● Department of Basic Dental Sciences, University of Florida, Gainesville, Florida

Larry Michelson ● Department of Psychiatry, Western Psychiatric Institute and Clinic, University of Pittsburgh School of Medicine, Pittsburgh, Pennsylvania

Gerald T. O'Brien ● Agoraphobia and Anxiety Program, Department of Psychiatry, Temple University Medical School, Philadelphia, Pennsylvania

Thomas H. Ollendick ● Department of Psychology, Virginia Polytechnic Institute and State University, Blacksburg, Virginia

Mark D. Rapport • Department of Psychology, University of Rhode Island, Kingston, Rhode Island

Reda Scott • Psychology Service, Jackson Veterans Administration Medical Center, and Department of Psychiatry and Human Behavior, University of Mississippi Medical Center, Jackson, Mississippi

Ellie T. Sturgis • Department of Psychiatry and Human Behavior, University of Mississippi Medical Center, Jackson, Mississippi

Richard M. Suinn • Department of Psychology, Colorado State University, Ft. Collins, Colorado

Peter Trower • Department of Psychology, Leicester University, Leicester, England

David Turland • Department of Psychology, Hollymoor Hospital, Northfield, Birmingham, England

Samuel M. Turner • Department of Psychiatry, Western Psychiatric Institute and Clinic, University of Pittsburgh School of Medicine, Pittsburgh, Pennsylvania

Lawrence A. Vitulano • Greater Bridgeport Children's Services Center, Bridgeport, Connecticut

Karen C. Wells • Department of Psychiatry, Children's Hospital National Medical Center, George Washington University School of Medicine, Washington, D.C.

Foreword

When behavior therapy was first applied to what would now be labeled an anxiety disorder, a simplistic theoretical model guided the treatment of a simple phobia. Time and research have shown that the techniques of behavior therapy have been more successful than its models have been explanatory. Yet progress has been substantial in both realms, as the following volume makes patently clear. In 1980 an inventory of this progress was catalogued at an NIMH-sponsored workshop.

What both that workshop and this volume clearly show is that the behavior therapy researcher need no longer suffer the epithet "overly simplistic." One of the major strengths of this volume is its elucidation of the complexities that now attend the study of the anxiety disorders, particularly from a behavioral point of view. The researcher at times appears almost to be buried in a landslide of complexities regarding this topic.

The concept of anxiety itself has undergone a differentiation to a level of complexity that poses problems for both the conceptualization and the treatment of anxiety disorders. In virtually one voice, the several authors of this volume argue the multidimensional nature of anxiety. The "lump" view of anxiety has given way to the three-channel view of anxiety. An investigator's future research career could well be secured just by spending time puzzling out the significance of the low intercorrelations among the channels.

Another important complexity concerns the manner in which anxiety disorders may be acquired and maintained. Attractive as it was, the conditioning paradigm was found to be insufficient to explain the diverse manner by which patients acquired their phobias and other anxiety disorders. The consensus now suggests that conditioning is only one of at least three pathways for the acquisition and maintenance of fear and anxiety. Moreover, a different process may be involved in the acquisition, as opposed to the maintenance, of anxiety. Different processes are also probably involved in each of the two major components of an anxiety disorder: the experience of anxiety and the avoidance behavior that usually accompanies it. Thus in a short 2½ decades, behavior therapy researchers have moved from one paradigm applied to one symptom to a class of multicomponent disorders, expressed through three channels and acquired through at least three different pathways.

This volume also makes clear the path by which behavior therapy researchers arrived at this multifaceted view of anxiety disorders. It was achieved through the slow accretion of facts obtained from systematic empirical research. It is well known that behavior therapists have shown a greater affinity for research than therapists of other orientations and have been more willing to subject their ideas to the stern discipline of empirical testing. Compelling models of anxiety thus have dimmed in their promise as their limits were plumbed and their weaknesses exposed. In the self-correcting spirit of scientific inquiry, this is a fact to be celebrated, not lamented. The spirit and the discipline of science are most clearly honored when, as has occasionally happened within behavior therapy, the herald and detractor of a given theoretical model resides in the same person.

This timely and welcome volume provides a comprehensive consideration of the behavioral approach to research on the anxiety disorders. Included are lengthy treatments of the issues involved in the assessment and remediation of these disorders and of the now extensive range of behavioral theories on their etiology. In addition to fairly complete summaries of the research evidence, each chapter is replete with a wealth of clinical wisdom regarding the management and treatment of these disorders.

Each chapter documents the very real progress that has been made in the behavioral classification, assessment, and treatment of individual anxiety disorders. Emerging from them, however, is a kind of "thermodynamic law of research." For every question successfully resolved, there results a new question to be addressed. This excellent book amply demonstrates that the successes have been many, but the questions that remain are even more numerous.

BARRY E. WOLFE

National Institute of Mental Health
Rockville, Maryland

Preface

The past decade has witnessed increased understanding of the psychopathology of anxiety and increased refinement of treatment strategies for the anxiety disorders. This advancement in treatment has been spearheaded on two fronts: pharmacological approaches emanating from advances in biological psychiatry and psychological approaches within a behavioral framework. With respect to behavioral therapy, we have now reached a point where it can be stated that certain treatments have been demonstrated to be effective for a given condition. Moreover, we can state that specific treatments are most effective for specific conditions. This is most evident in the instances of phobic conditions (e.g., agoraphobia) and the obsessive-compulsive disorders where variants of exposure treatments have been noted to obtain approximately 75% remission rates and an even higher degree of effectiveness in treating simple phobia. On the other hand, treatment for such conditions as generalized anxiety disorder and panic states is less clear, and these conditions are poorly understood in comparison to the others. Similarly, we do not understand why there is a certain percentage of each disorder that does not appear to respond to our best treatments, and the question of how best to achieve maintenance has not totally been solved.

The present volume is designed to present an integrated view of our current knowledge regarding psychopathology, theory, and treatment of the major anxiety disorders using current DSM-III nomenclature. Particular attention is given to areas of controversy, inconsistencies, and the current status of treatment outcome. The book begins with a major review of behavioral theories of anxiety (Chapter 1), which is followed by a chapter on measurement issues (Chapter 2)—still a major problem in the anxiety area. The remaining chapters are devoted to specific anxiety conditions. Chapter 3 is concerned with simple phobia, Chapter 4 with agoraphobia, Chapter 5 with panic disorder, Chapter 6 with obsessive-compulsive disorder, Chapter 7 with generalized anxiety disorder, and Chapter 8 with social phobia. The final two chapters are concerned with problems of anxiety in children. Chapter 9 is devoted to school phobia and Chapter 10 deals with other anxiety conditions of childhood.

Many individuals have worked to make this volume a success. First and foremost are the many contributors who extended considerable time and effort to meet the specified criteria. Second, I would like to thank Deborah C. Beidel and Felicia Zack who provided technical assistance with the manuscript. Finally, I wish to express thanks to my editor at Plenum, Eliot Werner, for his encouragement and support.

SAMUEL M. TURNER

Contents

Chapter 3

Ellie T. Sturgis and Reda Scott

Chapter 4

Gerald T. O'Brien and David H. Barlow

Chapter 5

Chapter 6

Contents

1

Behavioral Theories of Anxiety Disorders

DENNIS J. DELPRATO and
F. DUDLEY McGLYNN

INTRODUCTION

In 1917, Watson and Morgan theorized that Pavlov's (1927) conditioning paradigm could account for much emotional behavior in humans. In subsequent studies Watson and Rayner (1920) and Jones (1924) supported the classical conditioning interpretation of human fear behavior. These efforts provided the first conceptual foundation for that part of behavior therapy concerned with anxiety and the neuroses (e.g., Wolpe, 1958). Hence the Pavlovian model of conditioned emotionality became part of the early behavioral orthodoxy.

As interest in behavior therapy for the neuroses has evolved, a good deal of conceptual diversification has taken place. This trend has included several attempts to extend and/or modify the orthodox analysis of fear behavior. This chapter will reiterate the major theoretical viewpoints that have evolved, review some experimental data related to them, and take note of associated conceptual issues.

THE SCOPE OF ANXIETY DISORDERS

The vernacular of the dominant American culture routinely permits at least four uses of the term anxiety that are relevant here. Anxiety sometimes

DENNIS J. DELPRATO ● Department of Psychology, Eastern Michigan University, Ypsilanti, Michigan 41897.   F. DUDLEY McGLYNN ● Department of Basic Dental Sciences, University of Florida, Gainesville, Florida 32610.

denotes an enduring and transsituational personality trait, for example, "John is an anxious person." At other times, anxiety refers to a transient and situationally specific response, for example, "John is anxious during final exams." At still other times, the casual language equates anxiety with a particular quality of affective experiencing, for example, "John feels anxious." Frequently the term anxiety does not refer to any behavior at all. Rather it labels an inference or presumptive explanation of some behavior, for example, "John studied the material because he was anxious about failing the exam."

Popular uses of anxiety are replicated within the jargon of medicine and psychiatry. DSM-III contains 208 classifications of which 54 involve anxiety or fear in some way. Generalized Anxiety Disorder (300.03) and Post-traumatic Stress Disorder, Chronic (309.81) are classifications in which anxiety amounts to an enduring and transsituational trait of the individual. Post-traumatic Stress Disorder, Acute (308.30), Simple Phobia (300.29), and Social Phobia (300.23) are classifications in which anxiety is a transient and/or situationally specific response. Much of the narrative surrounding psychiatric jargon seems to treat anxiety as a qualitative aspect of the patient's phenomenology and diverse diagnostic categories use anxiety as a gross inferential construct to explain symptomatic activities, that is, anorexia nervosa, bulimia, stuttering, depersonalization disorder, kleptomania, and avoidant personality disorder.

Following in the traditions of medicine and psychiatry, behavior therapists have used the term anxiety uncritically and in too many ways. Most behavior therapists, however, try to avoid thinking of anxiety as an enduring, transsituational "disposition" of the individual. (Opposition to monolithic dispositional constructs is uniform throughout the behavior therapy movement.) Most behavior therapists likewise try to avoid thinking of anxiety as an actual phenomenal quality in affective experiencing. Hence the diverse uses of anxiety in the behavior-therapy literature fall into one of two categories: (1) Anxiety is a label for an inferential construct used to explain symptomatic behaviors or (2) anxiety is a simple categorical concept denoting the occurrence of designated behaviors in specific situations (anxiety events).

Because behavior-therapy research has aligned itself historically with the experimental method in psychology, empirical referents for behavioral anxiety constructs typically are clearcut. Accordingly, the behavioral theorist who uses anxiety as an inferential construct *can* use it as a well-anchored intervening variable (see MacCorquodale & Meehl, 1948). This practice is validated by a half-century of theoretical functionalism in experimental psychology (e.g., Tolman, 1932) and is not to be confused with the animistic use of anxiety in psychodynamic formulations (see Spence, 1944). When anxiety is used simply to describe given classes of behaviors, it might denote verbal and/or physiological and/or motoric states of affairs (Lang, 1968; Rachman, 1978). Anxiety disorders within the verbal system typically are seen in interview- or questionnaire-elicited verbal reports of subjectively experienced apprehension, dread, and the like. (In inferential uses of anxiety constructs, verbal reports might or might not be seen as being under significant regulation from consciousness or from a "cognitive response system." The "cognitive system" thus inferred may be treated as presumptively real or as purely conventional. See Turner, 1967, pp. 7–17.) Anxiety disorders within the physiologic (autonomic) system are seen in psychophysiological recordings such as cardiac rate or skin conductance. Anxiety disorders within the motor system are seen in locomotor escape, in both active and passive avoidance, and in situationally cued performance decrements.

Even this brief overview reflects extreme diversity in casual, psychiatric, and behavioral use of the word anxiety. The theoretical task for a modern behaviorist is not one of tying together these diverse usages. Nor is it one of accounting for the subjective experience of anxiety. Rather, it is one of accounting for situationally cued verbal and/or physiologic and/or motoric *behaviors* that by convention are said to either "reflect" anxiety or to "manifest" it. For the purpose of expository clarity, this chapter deals first with behavioral theories of anxiety events and then with behavioral theories involving anxiety constructs.

BEHAVIORAL THEORIES OF ANXIETY EVENTS

The Respondent Conditioning Theory

Behavioral theories of anxiety are concerned with two issues: acquisition and maintenance. The original behavioral account (Watson & Morgan, 1917) focused on the ontogenic (acquisition) question and offered the Pavlovian conditioning procedure as the basic explanatory model. In the original statement, an unconditional stimulus (UCS) which consistently evokes anxiety as an unconditional response (UCR) follows in close temporal contiguity a conditional stimulus (CS) that does not initially elicit anxiety. With repeated CS–UCS pairings, the CS comes to elicit anxiety as a conditional response (CR). Anxiety responses to stimuli never explicitly paired with UCSs in the life history of the individual are explained by the principle of stimulus generalization, according to which feared stimuli need be only similar to some CS previously encountered.

History and Current Statement

Watson and Rayner (1920) reported the first test of Watson and Morgan's theory in their widely reiterated study with the 11-month-old child, Albert B. They reasoned that if inadvertent CS–UCS pairings in the daily lives of individuals are responsible for the development of fear reactions to innocuous stimuli, then one should be able to produce fear to a neutral stimulus within the context of an experiment. Watson and Rayner's description of the second conditioning trial administered to Albert indicates the stimuli used and their arrangement:

Instrumental learning   *operant punishment*
rather than Pavlovian

> Just as the right hand touched the rat [CS] the bar was again struck [UCS—loud sound]. Again the infant jumped violently, fell forward and began to whimper [UCR]. (p. 4)

One week following this second CS–UCS pairing, Albert displayed defensive behavior (withdrawal of hand from the rat) when the rat was presented alone. Additional CS–UCS pairings had the effect of magnifying his anxiety reaction to the rat CS. Furthermore, the experimenters demonstrated stimulus generalization when the boy exhibited emotional (crying) and avoidant reactions for the first time to certain other stimuli having characteristics similar to the rat (e.g., rabbit, dog, fur coat, cotton).

The most influential contemporary presentation of the respondent theory of anxiety is that of Wolpe (1952, 1958, 1973). In their paper offering Albert B. in the place of Freud's Little Hans model, Wolpe and Rachman (1960) state:

> Phobias are regarded as conditioned anxiety (fear) reactions. Any "neutral" stimulus, simple or complex, that happens to make an impact on an individual at about the time that a fear reaction is evoked acquires the ability to evoke fear subsequently. If the fear at the original conditioning situation is of high intensity or if the conditioning is many times repeated the conditioned fear will show the persistence that is characteristic of *neurotic* fear; and there will be generalization of fear reactions to stimuli resembling the conditioned stimulus. (pp. 145–146)

A wide variety of laboratory and clinical data has been cited supporting the respondent theory of fear acquisition. Table 1 provides a sampling of the major classes of studies that have produced emotional respondent conditioning using an aversive UCS. With the exception of the clinical-assessment studies and some of the clinical-treatment studies, this research has been procedurally orthodox (i.e., it involved controlled presentations of the CS and of the aversive UCS without regard to the concurrent behavior of the subject). Various physiologic and motoric responses have been classically conditioned. Most of these experimental responses are quite comparable to clinically encountered anxiety referents. The most and best evidence comes from laboratory investigations of nonhuman physiological (especially heart rate) and overt motor (especially response suppression) systems and from human physiological (especially electrodermal) responding.

Some Implications of the Respondent Conditioning Theory

Watson's application of the Pavlovian model to the problem of the theoretical interpretation of fears has had a robust influence on the evolution of

Table 1. *Major Classes of Aversive Respondent Conditioning Studies*

Setting	Subjects	Response system	Example(s) of UCS	Review(s)[a]
Laboratory	Nonhumans	Physiological. e.g., heart rate, blood pressure	Electric shock	b, d, e, f, g, h, p, u
Laboratory	Humans	Physiological, e.g., heart rate, electrodermal activity	Electric shock, noise	b, j, k, p, q, r, y
Laboratory	Nonhumans	Overt motor, e.g., response suppression,	Electric shock	b, g, h, i, k, l, n, o, t, u, w, x
Laboratory	Humans	Overt motor, e.g., leg flexion, finger withdrawal, eyeblink	Electric shock, air puff	b, c, k
Clinical (assessment, treatment)	Humans	Cognitive, physiological, overt motor	Nauseous pharmacological agents, aircraft accidents, dental trauma	a, m, s, v

[a] a = Bandura (1969), b = Beecroft (1966), c = Beecroft (1967), d = Black (1965), e = Black (1971), f = Black & deToledo (1972), g = Brady (1975a), h = Broadhurst (1972), i = Davis (1968), j = Grings & Dawson (1973), k = Hall (1976), l = Kamin (1965), m = Lautch (1971), n = Maier, Seligman, & Solomon (1969), o = McAllister & McAllister (1971), p = Obrist, Sutterer, & Howard (1972), q = Öhman (1979), r = Prokasy & Kumpfer (1973), s = Rachman (1978), t = Rescorla (1973), u = Schneiderman (1972), v = Sours, Ehrlich, & Phillips (1964), w = Wolpe (1952), x = Wolpe (1958), y = Zeaman & Smith (1965).

behavior therapy. However, the impact of this theory is due to considerations more fundamental than the tying together of respondent behavior and fear. In Watson's view (Watson, 1930; Watson & Morgan, 1917; Watson & Rayner, 1920), the major contribution of his theory was the idea that fear behaviors result from the organism's developmental history. It is the behavioral nature of fears and the contribution of developmental factors that allow us to take an authentic scientific approach to understanding them. Since every act has a developmental history, "is not the only correct scientific procedure to single out for study whatever act is in question and to watch and record its life history?" (Watson, 1930, p. 136). It is this metatheoretical implication of Watson's theory—an idea that goes well beyond the conditional reflex framework—that set the stage for modern behavioral approaches to anxiety.

Despite the value of Watson's statement that fears result from individual life histories, it is interesting to note that he and other early behaviorists erred by using the concept of learning as a synonym for developmental history. Without question these early behaviorists labored under the view that two fundamental types of behavior exist: unlearned (innate) and learned (acquired). If factors in the organism's life history were known to be critical for a particular behavior, then the behavior was of the learned type. It is interesting to note also that the early behaviorists compounded this error by equating "learning" with Pavlovian conditioning. The Pavlovian account of learning was chosen because no other conceptualization of learning, apart from the vaguely formulated notion of suggestion, was available to explain the ontogeny of fear. The instrumental paradigm of Thorndike (1898) was not yet seen as having anything to do with emotional behavior. Witness Watson and Rayner's (1920) application of the respondent paradigm to their experiment despite the instrumental contingency between the subject's behavior and presentation of the loud sound (see above).

As we will show later, there are good reasons to believe that clinical anxieties often do develop without any respondent interactions at all. However, some clinically presented anxieties very probably are the legacies of painful respondent interactions, at least in terms of their major clinical features. Hence, research is needed that will help behavioral clinicians identify respondently acquired fears among the myriad complaints of patients.

Should research someday give us the tools for reliably identifying respondently acquired anxieties, the clinical implications of the respondent theory will be of considerable interest. However, the articulation of such implications will not be an entirely straightforward undertaking. Even when we can agree that certain anxieties are likely to have been acquired via aversive respondent interactions, different interpretations of how respondent conditioning takes place might still lead clinicians in different directions. Typically, for just one example, conditioned respondents have been said to depend upon temporal overlap of the CS with some aversive UCS. Clinicians interested in how anxiety is acquired have, therefore, questioned their patients concerning prior occasions on which clinically focal stimuli were paired temporally with aversive circumstances. Similarly, clinicians interested in helping patients to eliminate anxiety have set about therapeutically to disrupt the pairing of the CS and its characteristic response. Rescorla (1969b, 1972, 1978) has, in this connection, argued persuasively that temporal contiguity between a CS and a UCS is insufficient to account for aversive respondent conditioning. Rather, in order to function as an aversive cue, the CS must predict the onset of an aversive UCS. Insofar as Rescorla is correct, clinicians who query patients about their histories should ask about instances in which clinically targeted CSs have functioned to permit correct anticipations of aversive UCSs. Similarly, clinicians treating anxious patients should develop therapy programs specifically to rid clinically focal stimuli of their predictive cue properties. Notwithstanding conceptual problems of the type just described, there remains one major implication of conditioning theory for the clinician. This controversial notion is a limiting one, namely that clinicians need not concern themselves with any instrumental functions (secondary gains) that anxious behaviors might serve. If the patient's anxiety is construed as a conditioned emotional respondent, then his/her motoric impairments are classically acquired and the consequences of motor acts are of little more than passing interest. The most prominent voice in this regard has been Wolpe (1971, 1976). According to Wolpe, the respondent conditioning of autonomic anxiety is adequate to account for neurotic anxiety disorders. Avoidance behavior, when found, plays but a secondary role in clinical complaints.

Revised Conditioning Theories

Both Eysenck (1968, 1976) and Rachman (1977, 1978) have offered revised conditioning formulations of how anxiety is acquired. In common these reformulations take as points of departure a number of presumptive weaknesses in a simple Pavlovian account. We will reiterate their common arguments here and comment on the relative merits of each.

Alleged Failures to Replicate Watson and Rayner (1920). Eysenck, Rachman, and a variety of other writers (Gray, 1971; Marks, 1969; Seligman, 1970, 1971) have identified studies that purportedly "failed to replicate" the Watson and Rayner (1920) results. English (1929), Valentine (1930), and Bregman (1934) are commonly cited as having failed to demonstrate fear CRs when they used CSs other than the rat used by Watson and Rayner. However, each of these three studies entailed truly poor "conditioning" procedures (e.g., no functional aversive UCS in English, 1929; excessive numbers of CS alone test trials in Bregman, 1934). Hence, empirical refutation of Watson and Rayner (1920), by appeal to these studies, cannot undermine the Pavlovian account of fear acquisition. (For a complete review see Delprato, 1980.)

Innate Fears. Misinterpretations of English (1929), Valentine (1930), and Bregman (1934) have been pivotal in a second ostensible problem with the simple respondent theory. The mistaken notion is that these three experimenters failed to replicate Watson and Rayner because their CSs (common household objects, wooden blocks) were evolutionarily "neutral" as compared to the furry rat used by Watson and Rayner. According to this view, natural selection has produced humans with the capacity to acquire quickly fear of furry objects due to the survival value of this trait. Thus, Watson and Rayner's subject was genetically predisposed (prepared) to develop a fear reaction to the furry rat, while the subjects of English, Valentine, and Bregman were not genetically prepared to become fearful of wooden blocks or other household items that posed no threat to their ancestors (e.g., Seligman, 1970, 1971).

As already noted procedural errors in the English, Valentine, and Bregman studies prevent their use as grist for any theoretical mill. However, contemporary research on a much more solid foundation than that of English, Valentine, and Bregman *has* suggested that anxiety might be biologically preprogrammed in some subtle way(s). The most relevant research is in the areas of food-aversion learning (e.g., Barker, Best, & Domjan, 1977; Milgram, Krames, & Alloway, 1977) and electrodermal conditioning to "potentially phobic" versus evolutionally "neutral" CSs (Öhman, 1979; Öhman, Fredrikson, & Hugdahl, 1978). The food-aversion literature reveals interactions between preaversive (conditional) stimuli and aversive (unconditional) stimuli in response-contingent discriminative punishment paradigms. With rats, for example, taste cues more readily acquire discriminative control when they precede interoceptive punishment (illness) while audiovisual cues are more readily conditioned when they signal exteroceptive punishment (shock). The implication is that all CSs are not equally likely to evoke fear when they signal a given aversive event. This is a complexity unaccounted for by the Pavlovian theory. The electrodermal conditioning literature suggests that electrodermal responses are more easily conditioned and more resistant to extinction when evolutionarily significant stimuli (e.g., slides of snakes and spiders) rather than evolutionarily "neutral" stimuli (e.g., houses, flowers) are used as CSs. Several experiments report this outcome along with interpretations of it in terms of biologically preprogrammed anxiety. Obviously these data also pose problems for a simple respondent theory of fear acquisition.

Some writers have suggested that the food-aversion and electrodermal-conditioning work provide support for the notion of inherited fear behavior. Actually, careful conceptualization of the food-aversion and electrodermal-conditioning paradigm shows that both fail to convincingly support the notion of inherited fear behavior (Delprato, 1980). Modern developmental psychology no longer views the ontogeny of psychological behavior in terms of the discontinuous categories inherited and learned. Following geneticists such as Jennings (1924) and Dobzhansky (1976), psychological activity, including anxiety, is to be traced to the organism's developmental history, a history in which evolved morphological structures, embryological conditions, and organism–environment interactions beginning *in utero* are all involved (Kantor & Smith, 1975; Kuo, 1967; Riegel, 1978; Schneirla, 1957). Interpretations of the food-aversion and electrodermal conditioning results in terms of inherited versus learned are residuals from the outmoded nature versus nurture model of behavioral ontogeny (see Beach, 1955). Furthermore, food-aversion and electrodermal conditioning experimenters have interpreted their results in terms of genetic predisposition even though they failed uniformly to take into account variations in subjects' developmental histories (Delprato, 1980). These data do challenge the comprehensiveness of a simple Pavlovian account of fear behavior. They do not support the contention that fear behavior is innate.

Absence of Trauma in Clinical Cases. Traumatic (aversive UCS) events are often missing from clinical anamneses. Both Eysenck and Rachman note the embarrassment this poses for a simple respondent theory. The embarrassment is especially acute for those respondent views relying on a painful UCS (e.g., electric shock) as the prototypical aversive stimulus. Even allowing for deficiencies in life-history analysis, anxiety in the absence of anything resembling painful stimulation appears commonplace.

Vicarious Transmission of Fear. The respondent conditioning theory requires, of course, that the learner directly encounter both the CS and UCS. However, observers clearly can develop fear of stimuli from watching others display fear in the presence of those stimuli (e.g., Bandura & Rosenthal, 1966; Berger, 1962; Craig & Weinstein, 1965; Venn & Short, 1973). In a retrospective study of phobic patients, phobics were significantly more likely than non-phobic controls to have had mothers with phobias and other neurotic conditions (Solyom, Beck, Solyom, & Hugel, 1974). Rachman (1977) cites additional data reflecting high positive correlations between the fears of children and those of their mothers. Transmission of fear via modeling processes, in part, would account for clinical fears in the absence of traumatic events.

Unexpected Distribution of Fears. Rachman (1977) cites surveys, epidemiological studies, and anthropological observations revealing that fears are not distributed in accordance with what would appear to be the expected ratios for traumatic interactions with objects and situations. For example, fears of snakes are considerably more prevalent than are dental and injection fears in certain populations. While such observations again should not be interpreted as evidenced for innate fears, they do pose problems for a straightforward respondent-conditioning theory.

Failures to Acquire Fear. Rachman (1977) discusses instances in which individuals who endured air-raids did not develop persistent fear reactions despite repeated exposure to traumatic stimulation. These findings, although derived from minimally controlled observations, at the very least suggest there may be more to the ontogeny of fear than CS-UCS pairings.

Extinction Failures and Incubation Effects. A vast amount of experimental evidence supports the Pavlovian law of extinction which holds that CS presentations in the absence of contingent UCS presentation result in progressive diminutions of the CR. Insofar as fears are classically conditioned respondents, unreinforced CS presentations should extinguish them as well. Eysenck has argued not only that fear responses sometimes fail to diminish with repeated CS-only presentations, but also that under certain conditions there should be incremental or enhancement (incubation) effects. According to Eysenck,

> CSs which . . . produce drives follow the law of enhancement (incubation). The reason for this . . . is quite simple. When it is anxiety . . . that is being conditioned, it is not strictly speaking true to say that the CS is not reinforced when the UCS is missing. Originally the UCS produces fear/anxiety, the CS does not. However, pairing the two leads to CR effects which are identical with UCR effects; the CS produces fear/anxiety responses, just as does the UCS! Apparently, the CS (after conditioning) produces fear/anxiety, i.e., the UCR, even though the UCS may now be absent. This process should set up a positive feedback cycle, with each presentation of the CS-only reinforcing itself, and thus continuing to increment the CR. (1976, p. 257)

Eysenck is addressing the storied persistence of clinical fears here but he cites experimental support for incubation also and, in so doing, he points to another presumptive weakness in the respondent conditioning account of fear ontogeny.

Suggested Revisions in the Respondent Conditioning Theory

As noted earlier, Rachman and Eysenck offer similar revisions of the simple respondent theory in line with the above limitations. Both theorists agree on the centrality of respondent interactions but suggest that additional considerations are necessary for a *complete* account.

Rachman's revision is comprised of three main considerations.

Three-Pathways Hypothesis. Three classes of organism–environment interaction in the individual's life history can contribute to the development of anxiety behavior. Respondent interactions are but one route to fear; the other two are modeling and those involving the transmission of information and/or instruction. We have already indicated that modeling and, of course, respondent interactions have been implicated in the ontogeny of anxiety in controlled studies. Even though he favors an informational acquisition view, Rachman admits that he is "unaware of any conventionally acceptable evidence that fear can be acquired through the transmission of information (and particularly, by instruction)" (1977, p. 384). Actually, a substantial body of experimental research with human electrodermal responding, beginning with Cook and Harris (1937), supports the conclusion that "behavior change similar to that which occurs through classical conditioning occurs through processes of verbalization and verbal instruction. . . . [and] . . . the physical act of pairing external stimulus events is not necessary for this type of learning to occur" (Grings, 1965, p. 85). Cook and Harris (1937) demonstrated increases in the magnitude and frequency of skin resistance responses to a cue after subjects were informed that the cue would be followed by a shock. Furthermore, these investigators obtained diminutions in responding to the cue after the subjects were told that the cue would no longer be followed by shock. Grings (1965) and Grings and Dawson (1973) review confirmations of these findings.

Three Systems of Fear. As a second revision of respondent theory, Rachman has adopted the recently developed view (described earlier) that fear is best not conceptualized as an integrated phenomenal unit or "lump" (Lang, 1978a). Instead, fear is viewed as a multidimensional concept that can be related to three partially independent organismic systems: language behavior, physiological activity, and overt motor performance.

Hereditary Determinants of Fear. For his third revision Rachman suggests that due to an organism's phyletic history, all stimuli are not equally likely to become cues for fear; some stimuli are evolutionarily "prepared." The foundations of modern revivals of the notion of innate fears in alleged failures to replicate Watson and Rayner (1920), in research on food-aversion learning, and so on, were criticized above and by Delprato (1980). Empirical, methodological, and conceptual considerations, along with clinical evidence (deSilva, Rachman, & Seligman, 1977; Rachman & Seligman, 1976), suggest ontogeny of fear will be more illuminated by comprehensive developmental analyses than by retreat to the genetic postulate. Rejection of this component of Rachman's theory does not prevent acceptance of his other two revisions.

Eysenck's revision of the original respondent conditioning theory also is comprised of three major considerations.

Frustration as Main UCS. In the vast majority of classical aversive conditioning studies the UCS has been either a stimulus that evokes pain or a stimulus that was paired with pain in the organism's life prior to the critical conditioning interaction (higher order conditioning). Eysenck offered the view that the most common UCSs in nonlaboratory instances of fear development are imbedded in frustration-arousing circumstances such as withdrawal of positive reinforcement and conflictual situations. Wolpe (1952, 1958) has reviewed experimental studies of anxiety in which events such as these functioned as sources of aversive stimulation, and others have concluded that cues predictive of the withdrawal of positive reinforcement evoke a variety of behaviors, including avoidance, withdrawal, and other "emotional" responding (Coughlin, 1972; Daly, 1974; Wagner, 1969). Eysenck's emphasis on UCSs that are not tied to physical pain is therefore supported.

Backward Conditioning. Conventional respondent conditioning holds that backward conditioning (conservatively defined as UCS-CS presentations with no overlap between stimuli) is impossible (e.g., Kimble, 1961). (Forward conditioning, when CS onset precedes UCS onset by a short period of time, is considered the only legitimate procedure.) Anxiety can be produced by backward conditioning, hence might be viewed by conventional thought as outside the legitimate domain of respondent learning. In order to counter this eventuality, Eysenck (1975) called attention to numerous demonstrations of backward conditioning within the experimental literature. A recent review strongly corroborates Eysenck on this (Spetch, Wilkie, & Pinel, 1981). The robustness of backward conditioning is attested to by the fact that the latter reviewers cited neither Eysenck (1975) nor any of his several references.

Revision of the Law of Extinction and the Incubation of Anxiety Reactions. We have already discussed Eysenck's claim that evidence of extinction failures and incubation affects poses serious limitations to the original conditioning view of fear acquisition. Wolpe (1973, 1976) has also warned that when unopposed high levels of anxiety are evoked to cues, anxiety responding to the cues may exacerbate. As a result of his critical analysis of the incubation hypothesis, however, Bersh (1980) concluded that "its potential for contribution . . . must remain in doubt" (p. 16). Bersh found empirical evidence for incubation to be weak. He also delineated internal problems with the theory. Perhaps Bersh's critique will stimulate careful research. Additional research might or might not lead to revisions of the law of extinction as applied to classical fear conditioning.

Some Implications of the Revised Conditioning Theories

As can be anticipated from the narrative thus far, the six theoretical revisions proposed by Eysenck and Rachman are not equally valuable in our view. Least valuable among these theoretical proposals is the idea that fear development is influenced robustly by heredity. Widespread adherence to such a contention would lead clinicians and researchers alike in directions that are likely to be unproductive. At a somewhat different level, Eysenck's notion of incubation is potentially problematic because, as Bersh (1980) has argued, there is but little unambiguous evidence to support the occurrence of incubation phenomena. As a hypothesis, the notion of incubation is potentially valuable because it does attempt to deal with the persistence shown by most anxiety reactions and this persistence must be addressed by any comprehensive theory of fear ontogeny. As a hypothesis, Eysenck's revised law of extinction is potentially valuable for the same reason. Clinicians are, however, encouraged to remember the clearly tentative status of these formulations.

The broadening of potential UCSs beyond those including physical pain and the systematic recognition of backward conditioning are likely to be of continued importance to clinicians articulating complex "conditioning" formulations of fear behavior. The frustrative UCS concept, for example, might help clinicians understand cases of clinical anxiety without evidence of physical trauma. The backward conditioning notion, in turn, extends markedly the potential origins of patient anxiety problems. In short, these proposals help clinicians take account of clinical complexities without abandoning a basic conditioning framework.

The most important among the six theoretical revisions are the three-pathways hypothesis and the three-response-systems view. Lang (1968, 1970, 1971, 1978a), Hodgson and Rachman (1974), and Rachman (1977, 1978) have discussed the empirical, theoretical, and therapeutic advantages of a three-response-systems view of anxiety. While room exists for differences in theoretical conceptions of how the three systems interact, there is agreement on the core empirical proposition that language behavior, physiological behavior, and gross motor behavior are partially independent response systems that tend to occur in specific situations.

Among the problems clarified by the three-systems concept are those implied by the reliable finding of low intercorrelations among measures tapping the different response modalities. Because fear is not a unitary state of the organism "manifested" simultaneously in verbal reports, physiological arousal, and overt motor acts, there is no basis for predicting robust correlations among measures taken from these response domains. At the same time allowance *can* be made for those patients with whom multi-channel assessment does produce concordant results.

A related problem accommodated by the three-systems idea is that of "desynchrony" of change (Hodgson & Rachman, 1974) across measurement channels. Different measures of fear do not change at the same rates over the course of therapy. Because fear is not a unitary state of the organism "manifested" diversely in varying measures, there is no basis for predicting that the measures would change at the same rates.

A third problem that is addressed by the three-systems concept of fear is that of individual differences in the fine grains of anxious symptomatology. A three systems view allows for the independent development of highly idiosyncratic anxiety behaviors at different rates and to different degrees in accordance with the individual's unique developmental histories for verbal, physiologic, and gross motor performances.

When modeling and exposure to information are added to respondent conditioning as means of acquiring fear, both the potential ranges of anxiety-cueing circumstances and the potential topographies of anxious behaviors are broadened. The theoretically allowable complexities characterizing individual anxiety complaints are augmented further when the three-pathways acquisition hypothesis is linked up with the three-channel response system view. Indeed the theoretical result of combining these ideas is quite comprehensive. Some of the implications of this type of thinking are taken up later.

Cognitive Theories of Anxiety Events

Conditioning theories of fear seem to have a uniformly "connectionist" flavor. Transcending their various particulars is the empirical notion that anxious responses are connected reliably to certain classes of cue stimuli. The means by which these empirical connections are formed have been of little interest. Rather, attention has focused on procedural considerations, that is, functional relationships between training regimens (such as modeling or instructions) and the features of behaviors designated as anxious ones.

Notwithstanding the empirical posture heretofore described, the psychological behaviorism on which behavior therapy rests does not *require* a "completely empirical" approach. As noted earlier, there is ample precedent within experimental psychology for the use of empirically anchored theoretical constructions. Furthermore, the earliest behaviorists were not themselves empirical ("black-box") connectionists. Goss (1961) has shown how Watson, Meyer, Hunter, Kantor, and Weiss made use of implicit events intervening between and welding together their peripheral S-R variables. Indeed, as Goss points out, Pavlov's well-known notion of a second-signal system is "essentially equivalent to mediating responses and stimuli" (p. 285).

As we also noted earlier, the everyday language of our culture and the jargon of psychiatry both permit the use of anxiety to describe a phenomenal state of affairs or "state of mind." Therefore, while an orthodox behavioral theorist need not deal with mental events, some theorists in responding to cultural and psychiatric traditions have found themselves doing so. The resultant "cognitive" theories of anxiety are theories in which mental events are said to intervene between recognizing an aversive cue and responding to it anxiously: functional cue stimulus → cognitive mediating process → anxiety.

Recent cognitive formulations (Bolles & Fanselow, 1980; Carr, 1979; Reiss, 1980) share, more or less, four basic assumptions.

Expectancies of Harm Mediate Anxiety Responses. Conditions that lead to anxiety do so because the individual comes to anticipate danger/harm in the presence of certain cues and, in turn, because the expectation of danger produces anxiety responses (Carr, 1979; Reiss, 1980) or anxiety states (Bolles & Fanselow, 1980). The general representation of this process is as follows: cue → expectation of harm → anxiety. In the aversive respondent-conditioning situation this process is depicted as such: CS → expectancy of UCS → anxiety. Since anxiety is viewed as an internal response or state, one must further extend this conceptualization to include dependent measures in the process. Therefore, the complete version of this aspect of the theory contains four steps: (1) cue → (2) expectation of harm → (3) anxiety → (4) "manifestation" of anxiety. In the case of aversive respondent conditioning, for example, Step 1 refers to the CS, Step 4 is the CR and intervening Constructs 2 and 3 point a relationship between them.

Aversive Respondent Conditioning is Neither Necessary nor Sufficient to Produce Fear. An expectation of danger and, in turn, anxiety can develop without traumatic interactions. Hence, aversive respondent conditioning is not necessary for fear to develop. An expectation of danger will not develop unless cue–danger (CS–UCS) pairings occur "in the subject's awareness" of their contingent relationship. Hence, aversive respondent conditioning *per se* is not sufficient for fear to develop.

Expectations of Harm Can Result from Three Learning Processes. Carr (1979) suggests that respondent conditioning, observational learning, and information transmission each provide *information* that contributes to expectancies of harm *vis à vis* particular situations. Thus, Rachman's (1977, 1978) three "pathways to fear" are endorsed, but the effects of conditioning, modeling, and information transmission are said to be mediated by their contributions toward expectancies of harm.

The Magnitude of Anxiety Covaries with the Subjective Likelihood of Harm. Since anxiety occurs in varying degrees, such variations reflect covariations in cognitive mediational processes. For example, a weak belief in danger (low subjective probability of harm) will give rise to less intense anxiety than will a strong belief in danger, all other factors being equal.

Some Implications of Cognitive Theory

As we noted early on, the initial behavioral theory of anxiety events was stated in terms of the respondent conditioning paradigm. Cognitive theory was not popular when behavior therapy was in its infancy. Tolman (1932) had offered a cognitive account of how Jones' (1924) "direct conditioning" method worked to reduce fear, but until the late 1960s cognitive theorizing usually occasioned adverse reactions from the noncognitive theorists influential within the behavior therapy movement. During the 1970s, the intellectual climate changed and as of 1981 numerous writers have incorporated cognitive theory into therapeutic programs for anxiety.

The cardinal feature of contemporary therapeutic applications of cognitive theory is their reliance on "self-activated" verbalizations as causes of anxiety (e.g., Beck, 1970; Ellis, 1962; Goldfried, Decenteceo, & Weinberg, 1974; Meichenbaum, 1977). Cognitively oriented therapists have, for example, analyzed ways in which self-statements occasion anxiety and, in turn they have articulated systematic training procedures for identifying and changing untoward self-statements.

Perhaps the major contribution of cognitive theory has been to challenge the stimulus → response (S → R) conception of anxiety, a notion that is based on a mechanical cause–effect framework now obsolete within advanced sciences (cf. Kantor, 1953; Russell, 1953). Modern field-theoretical views of causality (Jones, 1977; Kantor, 1953, 1969; Staddon, 1973) make unnecessary any adherence to causal chain determinations such as S–R sequences. Although cognitive theory has not been formulated in field-theoretical terms, it is not necessarily inconsistent with such a viewpoint.

The cognitive theorist's emphasis on an "active organism" is an important substitute for traditional conceptions of an inert organism responding solely to impinging external forces. Furthermore, cognitive theory *can* be formulated so as to recognize the participation in anxiety of complex and subtle human activities such as perceiving, thinking, expecting, imagining, and verbalizing. Inclusion of these behaviors in accounts of anxiety greatly expands the narrow S → R view.

Some Pitfalls of Cognitive Conceptions

Against the several beneficient influences of cognitive theorizing stand several significant problems: some empirical, others conceptual. The apparent robustness of backward aversive conditioning (Eysenck, 1975; Spetch *et al.*, 1981) poses one empirical difficulty for the view that respondent conditioning effects rest upon newly acquired expectancies of harm in the presence of the CS. (In the backward procedure the CS is more predictive of safety than it is of harm.) A second empirical difficulty is posed by the indicator methodology whereby self-reports, physiological activities, and overt motor performances are used to infer expectations of harm. A unitary expectancy-formation process is difficult to reconcile with routine findings of discordance within and between these presumptive indicator systems (cf. Hodgson & Rachman, 1974; Sallis, Lichstein, & McGlynn, 1980).

Some of the recent controversy surrounding cognitive interpretations of anxiety has involved the efficacy of therapy regimens derived from them. Locke (1979) maintained that successful noncognitive interventions actually rely on cognitive-mediational influence, while Phillips (1981) rejoined that effective cognitive therapies can be interpreted in noncognitive terms. Ledwidge (1978) attempted to define cognitive and noncognitive therapies and to compare their relative impacts on anxiety disorders and other problems. Rimm and Masters

(1979) reviewed several findings bearing on the clinical implications of cognitive theorizing. The most prudent empirical conclusion at present seems to be that clinical support for a cognitive account of anxiety disorders is modest in extent.

No issue in behavior therapy has aroused more controversy than has the fundamental one of how best to conceptualize cognition *per se* (e.g., Ellis, 1977; Grossberg, 1981; Ledwidge, 1978; Mahoney & Kazdin, 1979; Phillips, 1981; Rachlin, 1977; Wolpe, 1978a, 1981). Since this issue is extremely complex and is as old as the "mind–body problem" in philosophy, we will attempt no resolution here, but will argue that disclaimers notwithstanding (Mahoney & Kazdin, 1979), a spurious mental–physical dualism lies at the heart of these disputes. So long as subtle psychological actions are described as things and thinglike entities (e.g., thoughts, perceptions, images, expectations) that are possessed by individuals and that serve as causal precursors to subsequent actions, cognitive theory is likely to remain embroiled in the Gordian knot of explaining how entities of one kind can influence entities of another kind (see Ryle, 1949; Schafer, 1976). So long as cognitions are separated from behaviors, psychological understanding will be side-tracked by the search for mental forces. What is needed is a thorough-going action language, a conceptualization of all psychological phenomena in terms of action or behavior.

THEORIES INVOLVING ANXIETY CONSTRUCTS

The theories discussed to this point seek to explain anxiety as an event or set of events. As we noted earlier another class of theoretical efforts uses anxiety as a theoretical construct. In the latter case the behavioral referents for the construct are conceptualized as both active and passive avoidance reactions. Thus, theories to be reviewed in this section seek to account for avoidance behavior.

Two-Factor, Fear-Mediation Theory

During the 1930s the Yale group of psychologists began an attempt to integrate the theories of Freud, Pavlov, Watson, and Thorndike. Two outcomes of this work were the development of two-process learning theory and the application of this theory to anxiety and avoidance behavior. Classic presentations of two-factor accounts of anxiety disorders are those of Mowrer (1939, 1947, 1960), Miller (1951), and Dollard and Miller (1950). Excellent reviews of these theoretical efforts have been presented by Bolles (1972b, 1975), Herrnstein (1969), Mineka (1979), Seligman and Johnston (1973), and Solomon and Brush (1956). Two-factor avoidance theory can be applied to both active and passive avoidance paradigms. For purposes of simplicity, we will concentrate on the two-factor, fear-mediation account of active avoidance only. Basically, three assertions are made.

Respondent Conditioning of Fear. The first major premise here is that fear is acquired via respondent conditioning. This is simply the orthodox account of fear ontogeny discussed at length earlier. Fear develops as a CR to a CS that was paired with or correlated with an aversive UCS.

Fear CRs as Motivational Mediators. What is the role of conditioned fear in avoidance? Fear is assumed to be a pattern of visceral responding that functions as an acquired source of motivation or drive. As Mowrer (1947) put it, conditioned fear (autonomic arousal) occasioned by a cue for danger acts as a secondary drive calling for solution to a "problem." Following the classical homeostatic model of motivation, the fearful organism is in a state of disequilibrium (tension) and is motivated to attain equilibrium (reduced tension).

Fear Reduction as Reinforcement for the Avoidance Response. The organism motivated by fear will engage in various instrumental behaviors just as will the organism in a state of food deprivation. Those acts serving to reduce drive (fear or hunger) will be reinforced, that is, their probability of recurrence will be enhanced. Fear reduction is a secondary (acquired) reinforcer involved in developing and maintaining instrumental avoidance behaviors.

Some Clinical Implications of the Two-Factor, Fear-Mediation Theory

The two-factor, fear-mediation theory of avoidance posits two domains of clinically problematical behaviors, respondently conditioned fear behaviors and instrumentally regulated avoidance behaviors. Therapeutic efforts could, therefore, conceivably be directed at either or both facets of a clinical problem.

Some therapists have analyzed a problem in two-factor terms and then directed therapy solely to the presumptive avoidance response. Yates (1958), for example, instructed a patient exhibiting four tics to emit them under massed practice conditions. Yates reasoned, in accordance with Hullian notions, that massed practice of the tic would endow it with inhibitory properties ("not performing the tic") thereby eliminating the behavior. He reported substantial diminutions in the frequencies of tics both within and outside the treatment setting.

Most therapists, however, have heeded Eysenck's (1960) warning that "extinction of the motor response without the simultaneous extinction of the conditioned autonomic response would only be a very partial cure and could not be recommended as being sufficient" (p. 13). That is, most have focused behavior therapy on the respondent anxiety aspects of complex clinical displays under the assumption that satisfactory clinical gains would follow from the elimination of the critical source of motivation and of reinforcement for avoidance responding (see also Riccio & Sylvestri, 1973). For examples, treatments of a cat phobia by graduated exposure *in vivo* (Freeman & Kendrick, 1964), of exhibitionism by systematic desensitization (Bond & Hutchison, 1964), and of compulsive behavior by response prevention in the face of ritual cue stimuli (Rachman, Hodgson, & Marks, 1971) can all be viewed in this way.

One of the earliest clinical accounts using two-factor, fear-mediation theory was given by Dollard and Miller (1950), who interpreted phobias, compulsions, hysterical symptoms, delusions, and alcoholism as fear-motivated avoidance behavior reinforced by fear reduction. In summarizing a case of a combat pilot who developed a strong phobia of airplanes they stated:

> Under traumatic conditions of combat the intense drive of fear was learned as a response to the airplane and everything connected with it. The fear generalized from the cues of this airplane to the similar ones of other airplanes. This intense fear motivated responses of avoiding airplanes, and whenever any one of these responses was successful, it was reinforced by a reduction in the strength of the fear. (Dollard & Miller, 1950, p. 158)

Numerous writers subsequent to Dollard and Miller (1950) theorized that two-factor considerations could account for certain aspects of a wide variety of clinical complaints, including phobias (Eysenck & Rachman, 1965), compulsions (Meyer & Levy, 1973; Walton & Mather, 1964), hysterical symptoms (Eysenck & Rachman, 1965), tics (Yates, 1958), alcoholism (Conger, 1951, 1956), anorexia nervosa (Leon, 1977), obesity (Kaplan & Kaplan, 1957), opiate addiction (Isbell, 1965; Wikler, 1965), asthma (Turnbull, 1962), sexual deviance (Bond & Hutchison, 1964; Cooper, 1963), and stuttering (Brutten & Shoemaker, 1967; Johnson, 1955; Sheehan, 1975). Substantial amounts of laboratory and clinical research have been conducted with some of these problems. Support for the theory is not unequivocal for any disorder, although some impressive findings have been obtained.

The theory has fared particularly well in the case of stuttering. Controlled investigations have supported the two-fold prediction from two-factor theory that disfluencies increase under conditions that evoke anxiety and, in turn, that anxiety lowers following disfluencies. As examples of the former proposition, rates of stuttering have been shown to increase when subjects read derogatory statements about stutterers (Sheehan, 1958), when subjects were in the presence of visual cues paired with shock (Hill, 1954), and when subjects read passages to authority listeners (Sheehan, Hadley, & Gould, 1967). As an example of the latter proposition, Ickes and Pierce (1973) found an increase in blood volume (anxiety reduction) after disfluencies occurred. Indications of anxiety reduction after instances of stuttering have also been obtained with systematic self-report (Wischner, 1952) and systolic blood pressure (Dabul & Perkins, 1973) measures.

One historically prominent behavior therapy that is said to rest on two-factor theory is Stampfl's implosive therapy (Stampfl, 1970; Stampfl & Levis, 1967, 1969). Stampfl views neurotic behavior as a type of avoidance reaction that is traceable to conditioning phenomena. Following the two-factor orthodoxy, Stampfl proposes that contiguity between a "neutral" event and an aversive one generates a respondently conditioned fear response to the originally neutral event. Further, since the previously neutral pattern of stimuli now elicits fear, escape from or avoidance of the stimulus pattern is accompanied by fear reduction. Tension (fear) reduction, in turn, reinforces the act of neurotic escape/avoidance.

The core procedure of implosive therapy entails having the patient visualize as vividly as possible the various cues for his/her anxiety and encouraging the patient to respond with appropriately anxious emotionalism until he/she is no longer able to do so. Care is taken also to point out that no physical injury was actually produced by the visualized cue stimuli. The intended results of this core procedure are to present aversive CSs (scenes), to provide for diminishing CRs (anxiety behaviors), and to withhold aversive UCSs (painful experiences). In brief, Stampfl seeks to classically extinguish the respondent fear component of the two-factor etiology.

Some Problems of Two-Factor, Fear-Mediation Theory

Two-factor, fear-mediation theory has been criticized frequently in recent years (Bolles, 1970; D'Amato, 1970; Gray, 1971; Herrnstein, 1969; Rachman, 1976; Seligman & Johnston, 1973), and probably cannot be maintained in its original form. Because the criticism has been extensive we can examine only a portion of it here.

One common laboratory paradigm for studying active avoidance involves presenting a preaversive stimulus (warning signal) at the onset of each trial and programming aversive shock to turn on some time (e.g., 10 sec) after the onset of the signal. Should the subject not perform the experimentally arranged avoidance response (e.g., hurdle crossing) during the preshock period, the shock is presented. The subject then can escape the shock, usually by performing the same topographical response that is arranged to be the avoidance response. On those trials in which the avoidance response occurs during the preshock period, the response immediately terminates the warning signal and shock is omitted. The goal of the two-factor, fear-mediation theory is to account for increases in the probability of avoidance responding over successive trials.

According to the theory, fear conditioning to the preaversive stimulus comes to evoke fear of greater and greater strength over the course of multiple trials. Since fear acts as a secondary drive, the subject is increasingly motivated to reduce fear during the preshock interval. When an avoidance response occurs, the immediate termination of the preaversive stimulus leads to fear reduction and to reinforcement of the avoidance response. Avoidance is not directly evoked by the preaversive stimulus. Rather, it occurs in response to conditioned fear that is aroused by the Pavlovian preaversive stimulus.

Some criticism has been made of the assumption that avoidance requires an antecedent Pavlovian CS. A ready-made exteroceptive CS is arranged in the standard Mowrerian avoidance procedure when the warning signal precedes programmed shock. Since this signal is paired with shock onset on early escape trials, these early trials allow for signal–shock pairings comparable to the CS–UCS pairings of ordinary Pavlovian conditioning. Avoidance, in effect, amounts to escape from a Pavlovian CS. However, it is possible to obtain avoidance behavior without an exteroceptive warning signal. The Sidman (1953) avoidance procedure involves the presentation of shocks at regular "shock–shock" intervals (e.g., every 10 sec) unless the subject performs the target response, which, in turn, postpones the next shock for a fixed "response–shock" time interval (e.g., 30 sec). It is possible to preserve two-factor accounts of Sidman avoidance by postulating internal CSs such as internal clocks or proprioceptive cues (Seligman & Johnston, 1973). D'Amato (1970) and Herrnstein (1969), however, have questioned attempts to do so on grounds that such formulations are empirically vacuous. Trace conditioning raises a related problem because when the warning signal terminates well before the response is made, fear reduction (reinforcement) occurs before the avoidance response (Kamin, 1954). Seligman and Johnston (1973) are dubious regarding the viability of two-factor theory but, unlike D'Amato and Herrnstein, they do not perceive either trace conditioning or Sidman avoidance as posing insurmountable difficulties for it. They argue that testable deductions from hypotheses about interoceptive CSs can be made in both instances.

Since two-factor theory holds that fear mediates avoidance and that fear reduction reinforces avoidance responding, it should be possible to manipulate avoidance behavior by altering autonomic functioning and to produce correlations between avoidance and various fear measures. Although some studies supporting correlations between fear and stuttering behavior have been reported (e.g., Ickes & Pierce, 1973), numerous findings bring into question the hypothesized relationship between fear and avoidance behavior. Portions of this issue were discussed in the earlier section on Rachman's (1977, 1978) adoption of the three-systems view of fear.

Two classes of studies have been conducted which focused on the relationship between peripheral autonomic responses and avoidance. In experiments using various methods to block peripheral sympathetic activity, avoidance acquisition was not prevented (e.g., Auld, 1951; Wenzel & Jeffrey, 1967; Wynne & Solomon, 1955). In experiments using various methods to study autonomic and avoidance responses concurrently, far from straightforward relationships between them have been routinely found. For example, in experiments with response-produced termination of a warning signal, heart rate acceleration beginning with warning signal onset usually continued for several seconds after occurrence of the avoidance response and termination of the warning signal (Black, 1959; Stern & Word, 1962). Bersh, Notterman, and Schoenfeld (1956), for another example, found with human subjects that cardiac acceleration to a warning signal decreased to preconditioning levels even when avoidance responding was maintained. Leitenberg, Agras, Butz, and Wincze (1971), for a third example, took concurrent measures of heart rate and avoidance behavior during the treatment of several phobic cases. For some patients, heart rate varied randomly as avoidance of a phobic stimulus decreased. For others heart rate increased with decreases in avoidance of the phobic stimulus.

Dissociation between avoidance and fear has also been reported in a variety of studies using motoric rather than physiological fear measures. Maintenance of fear as measured by approach to fear cues has been found after response prevention or blocking has eliminated avoidance responding (see above, Riccio & Silvestri, 1973). Avoidance responding, likewise, has persisted in the absence of (other) motoric evidence of fear. Robinson (1961), for example, first trained rats to run to avoid signalled shock, after which they were trained to depress a lever in the same apparatus to avoid the signal. Shock was not used during acquisition of lever pressing. Hence the occurrence of pressing is compatible with the two-factor notion that the signal aroused fear. Next, the running response was extinguished to a rigorous criterion. The assumption here is that fear to the warning signal had extinguished and, consequently, two-factor theory would predict no motivation for lever pressing. However, when the rats were tested for level pressing after reaching the rigorous criterion for running extinction, lever pressing remained as likely as it had been before. Experiments have even found that fear elicited by the warning signal, as assessed with Estes and Skinner's (1941) conditioned suppression technique, substantially *diminished* under conditions of maintained avoidance (Kamin, Brimer, & Black, 1963; Mineka & Gino, 1980). Linden (1969), for example, demonstrated that avoidance training to a criterion of 40 avoidances *attenuated* previously established conditioned suppression (fear) to the warning signal.

If avoidance is motivated by respondently conditioned fear and reinforced by fear reduction, the persistence of avoidance behavior during nonshock extinction poses additional difficulties for two-factor theory. Continued presentation of the warning signal (CS) in the absence of shock amounts to Pavlovian extinction training. This training alone should and does lead to rapid diminutions in the fear CR (Annau & Kamin, 1961; Church & Black, 1958).[1] The dilemma for the theory is that respondent fear *does* diminish over the course

[1]Levis and Boyd (1979) note that the long-duration CS presentations of the typical nonhuman aversive respondent conditioning experiment lead to considerably longer durations of CS exposure per trial than is the case in avoidance experiments. Therefore, conclusions regarding the relative number of trials to fear extinction based on cross-experiment comparisons will overestimate the disparity between these two classes of experiments. Levis and Boyd's point is well taken, but one of their inferences is that difficulties posed for two-factor theory by discrepancies between avoidance performance and independent measures of fear will dissolve when duration of CS exposure is considered. This is not consistent with numerous findings, e.g., Delprato & Dreilinger, 1974; Kamin *et al.*, 1963.

of extinction while avoidance responses often persist for hundreds of trials (Black, 1958; Brush, 1957; Solomon, Kamin, & Wynne, 1953). How can the two-factor, fear-mediation theory be preserved in the face of such findings? Solomon and Wynne (1954) posit the principles of anxiety conservation and partial irreversibility of intense fear. According to the former, conditional fear is conserved (not extinguished) on avoidance trials because responding to the warning signal occurs with latencies too short to permit CS exposure durations sufficient for fear extinction to occur. The second principle simply states that *intense* conditional fear is "incapable of complete extinction" (Solomon & Wynne, 1954, p. 361). However, these principles are procrustean maneuvers designed simply to preserve the theory. They do not stand up against the evidence (discussed previously) that fear diminishes with extended avoidance performance. And in the absence of such independent corroboration they appear to be circular.

Unmodified two-factor theory also is unable to handle additional findings such as the frequently observed inverse relationship between the rate of active avoidance acquisition and shock intensity (Bolles & Warren, 1965; D'Amato & Fazzaro, 1966; Moyer & Korn, 1964) or the finding that rats choose signalled over unsignalled shock conditions (Badia, Culbertson, & Lewis 1971; Lockard, 1963).

Along with the orthodox respondent conditioning view of anxiety, the two-factor theory of avoidance played an important role in the evolution of behavior therapy; it served to prompt therapists to examine the *consequences* of their clients' fear behaviors. In short, therapists allowing for the possible role of two-factor considerations in anxiety behavior were more likely than others to ask how the disorder fits into the individual's life.

Two-factor theory also greatly aided the original respondent theory with regard to the response selection problem. By emphasizing the role of response consequences in the development of behavior, the theory made selection and performance of avoidance responses potentially more predictable than it had been until then. Even contemporary theories that truncate the empirical law of effect (Staddon & Simmelhag, 1971; Timberlake & Allison, 1974) recognize the selective effect of consequences on the differentiation of behaviors.

In the final analysis, however, two-factor, fear-mediation theory has outlived its continued usefulness. General two-factor learning theory, based as it was upon confident claims that Pavlov and Thorndike had unearthed two distinctly different learning processes, is crumbling from laboratory results that today blur even the procedural distinctions between the "processes" (Kimmel, 1974; Miller, 1969; Schoenfeld, Cole, Lang, & Mankoff, 1973).

Approach-Withdrawal Theory

Dissatisfaction with two-factor, fear-mediation theory has stimulated several theorists to address its shortcomings. Out of these revisions has arisen the view of avoidance we designate as "approach-withdrawal theory." Actually, no extant theory is known by this particular label. We use it to denote a number of largely compatible revisions in and movements away from classical two-factor theory. Approach-withdrawal theory is insufficiently developed, and as presented below, it is an amalgam of views from theorists such as D'Amato (1970), Denny (1971, 1976), Dinsmoor (1954, 1977), Gray (1971), Herrnstein (1969), Keehn (1966), and Schoenfeld (1950). Probably none of these theorists would give unqualified endorsement to the theory we outline. Nevertheless, each has made important contributions toward it. We identify four major features of approach-withdrawal theory.

Alternative View to That of Motivated Behavior. Two-factor theory is predicated on the assumption that propulsive entities or forces (drives) are necessary to activate (energize) psychological activity. Kantor (1942) and Schafer (1975, 1976) have pointed out how this assumption follows from the mechanical view of the universe in which the organism is an inert body requiring the application of forces to get it moving. Kantor (1942), Schafer (1975, 1976), and Skinner (1953) examined traditional motivational theory at length, rejected it, and proposed alternative conceptions of motivation, conceptions free of mechanistic and reductionistic suppositions. Instead of searching for hypothetical inner, "causal" forces, these theorists advocate a more descriptive approach to motivational questions. The most straightforward implication for anxiety/fear and avoidance is that these concepts can only describe behavior in relation to the conditions in which it occurs. Anxiety is not an underlying motive of behavior, since the notion that "each action must be triggered by something" (Schafer, 1976, p. 232) is rejected. Anxiety is not an entity, possessed by the individual, that stands apart from and prior to action. The term anxiety refers to the individual's actions-in-the-world and does not refer to a something contained within the individual that can be expressed. The separation of anxiety from action and situation

> implies that we are treating emotion as an independent entity that may or may not be added on to behavior or included in it; it implies as well that the presence or absence of emotion has no bearing on our definition of action and situation. Both implications are to be rejected; for this separation is inconsistent with our actual ways of arriving at such definitions. In practice, we define, or may define, both actions and situations in part by the emotional way in which the person is doing something. (Schafer, 1976, p. 340)

Lang (1978a) and Schwartz (1978), as a result of their examination of the psychobiological nature of anxiety, advance views concordant with the above. For example, Schwartz (1978) argues that to talk about physiological correlates of behavior is erroneous, since this implies that physiology and behavior are separate. It follows that to view anxiety as motivating behavior similarly segregates motivation from action and situation.

We are showing in this sketch of the motivation and anxiety/fear concepts that one can legitimately view behaviors such as avoidance reactions as *unmo-*

tivated in the traditional way. Approach–withdrawal theory is predicated on such a conception.

Avoidance as Approach and Withdrawal. Approach–withdrawal theory gets its label from its solution to the motivation problem in terms of approach and withdrawal interactions (Schneirla, 1959). It is suggested that approach and withdrawal are both implicated in avoidance. Withdrawal has often been recognized as a component of avoidance—the organism withdraws from aversive cues. Approach has not often been seen as a component of avoidance. Nonetheless, a rat learning to avoid a dangerous place is simultaneously learning to approach a place that is at least temporarily less dangerous.

Denny (1971) is one of a few theorists who has emphasized the withdrawal *and* approach components of avoidance. He argues also the corollary that behavior occurring under aversive conditions is not fundamentally different from behavior occurring under nonaversive conditions. A rat learning to approach a positively reinforcing place is simultaneously learning to withdraw from a place that is at least temporarily less reinforcing. This aspect of approach-withdrawal theory integrates aversive learning with learning in other situations and does not make avoidance a special case (see also Hineline, 1977; Schoenfeld, 1969).

Safety Signals and Relaxation as Sources of Reinforcement in Ontogeny and Maintenance of Avoidance. The suggestion that approach is critically implicated in avoidance receives much support from studies of behavior during the postshock (safe) period in aversive conditioning. The outcomes of a large number of experiments show clearly that subjects in avoidance situations actively approach cues to safety or "safety signals" (e.g., Denny & Weisman, 1964; Rescorla, 1969a; Verhave, 1962; Weisman & Litner, 1969).

Two-factor theory has been offered as one interpretation of apparent reinforcing effects of safety signals (Rescorla, 1969b; Weisman & Litner, 1972). According to the two-factor account, response contingent safety cues reduce fear via a Pavlovian inhibitory process presumably operating on and within the neural centers responsible for fear. Reduced fear thus serves as a source of reinforcement for avoidance responses. Advocates of this view have marshalled some impressive data in support of it (Rescorla, 1969b; Rescorla & Solomon, 1967; Rizley & Reppucci, 1974; Weisman & Litner, 1972). Unfortunately, it can be shown that the conceptualization of reinforcing "safety signals" as Pavlovian fear inhibitors overcomes none of the other problems of two-factor, fear-mediation theory.

An alternative view of subjects' approaches to nonshock cues emphasizes descriptive features of the behaviors that occur in the presence of such cues. Denny (1971, 1976) assumes that removal of conditional and unconditional aversive stimuli has distinct response consequences that antagonistically compete with fear behavior and simultaneously mediate approach behavior. "Relief" responses occur almost immediately following termination of an aversive stimulus. "Relaxation" responses reach a maximum approximately 2–3 min following termination of an aversive stimulus. Since these two response classes are otherwise similar, and because relaxation has been given more prominence in research, we will focus on relaxation in approach–withdrawal theory.

According to the theory, the development of avoidance responding is based on relaxation-approach behavior. Early during training, the subject escapes shock (withdraws). As trials amass each shock offset is followed by relaxing and concurrently approaching the nonshock area. Relaxation in the nonshock area renders the area "positive." As training progresses, approach backchains (generalizes) until the subject responds by approaching the non-shock area before the occurrence of shock onset (avoidance). When nonshock extinction conditions are arranged, relaxation backchains through the preshock period, and because relaxation competes with fear-related behavior (including withdrawal), it brings about extinction of the avoidance response. Denny (1971) reviewed numerous experiments that provided support for the relaxation-approach interpretation of safety signal effects.

Warning Signal (CS) as S^D. Adherence to the view that traditional motivational concepts like internal drives are not needed has also led several theorists to reconceptualize the role of the warning signal in discriminated avoidance. Within two-factor theory the warning signal serves as a classical CS for fear. In approach–withdrawal theory, the warning signal is treated as a discriminated stimulus or S^D (D'Amato, 1970; Denny, 1971, 1976; Dinsmoor, 1954, 1977; Herrnstein, 1969; Keehn, 1966; Keller & Schoenfeld, 1950). As a probabilistic S^D the warning signal "sets the occasion" for responses that produce safety signals or relaxation approach. Just as the S^D in an appetitive learning situation does not arouse hunger, thirst, or any drive, neither does the warning signal in avoidance evoke motivation in the form of fear. (This view of the warning signal as an S^D does not necessarily deny the role of respondent *procedures* in aversive learning.)

Application of Approach-Withdrawal Theory to Experimental Data

We have already outlined how approach–withdrawal theory handles the facilitative effects on avoidance of response contingent safety cues and how the warning signal functions as an S^D in this process. Two-factor, fear-mediation theorists have observed that the introduction of safety signals leads to reductions in maintained avoidance, reductions in conditioned suppression, and the like. These phenomena have been interpreted as evidence for the central fear-inhibiting properties of safety signals (Rescorla, 1969b; Rescorla & Solomon, 1967; Weisman & Litner, 1972). In the framework of approach–withdrawal theory such data are more empirically interpreted as relaxation behavior competing with fear behavior (Denny, 1976). This view of "fear inhibition" is consistent with Konorski's (1967, 1972) suggestion that notions of internal inhibition and inhibitory CRs are inadequate. Rather the inhibition of motor acts is the result of the occurrence of antagonistic acts (Henton & Iversen, 1978; Konorski, 1971).

As we have indicated, the various discordances between avoidance and both biological and other behavioral measures of fear have long posed difficulties for two-factor, fear-mediation theory. Approach–withdrawal theory accounts for some of these discordances with three conceptualizations: (a) the warning signal as S^D (not fear-arousing CS); (b) the reinforcement value of relaxation approach in the safe period or place; and (c) the cumulative back-chaining of relaxation responding to the preshock period. Since the warning signal does not have to continue evoking fear behavior for avoidance to be maintained, lack of correspondence between fear and avoidance poses no problem for the theory. Gray (1971) and Rachman and Hodgson (1974) have offered a similar interpretation that especially emphasizes the reinforcing effect of approach to safety cues.

The dilemma of persistent avoidance in the face of respondent extinction was discussed above. According to approach–withdrawal theory, avoidance is maintained by relaxation approach (or response-contingent safety cues). Therefore, the respondent fear extinction trials (warning signal → no shock) embedded in the avoidance situation are of no crucial moment. This is because performance can be maintained (without fear) by contingent approach to safety (Denny, 1971; Gray, 1971).

Some Clinical Implications of Approach-Withdrawal Theory

No doubt there are weaknesses in the theoretical coverage provided by approach–withdrawal theory. By showing how the theory can be used to handle three traditionally troublesome issues, we were not arguing necessarily for its comprehensiveness. However, the approach–withdrawal conception of avoidance is sufficiently robust empirically and sufficiently sensible internally to justify at least a cursory look at its clinical implications. It turns out that the theory does have meaningful implications for analysis and treatment of anxiety disorders. Many of these are fairly evident from the discussion above. In this section we will mention major ones.

As one major clinical implication, approach–withdrawal theory tells us that attempts to identify and/or modify fear will not always prove fruitful. In some well-practiced and longstanding avoidance behaviors, we probably are dealing with positively not negatively reinforced acts. Consider, for example, a client displaying a long history of verbally and physically aggressive outbursts. Early in the development of this behavior pattern, aggressive conduct might have been importantly involved in terminating threatening interpersonal cues, social constraints, and the like. Over time, response-produced and external feedback from the outbursts could have come to acquire approach values. Thus, the problem was once one of interpersonal anxiety but became one of socially disapproved approach behavior maintained by the "deviant attractiveness" of its consequences.

As a second noteworthy implication for the clinic, approach–withdrawal theory seems to go part of the way toward explaining the problem of so-called "free-floating anxiety." Denny (1971, 1976), for example, outlined how his punished relaxation interpretation of extremely persistent avoidance (Denny & Dmitruk, 1967; Solomon & Wynne, 1953) can be used to account for anxiety behavior that does not appear to be in response to any particular set of environmental cues. Assume a child undergoes several interactions of the following general type: (a) His history leads him to work anxiously on his mathematics problems in school; (b) on a given day by the end of the mathematics period he begins relaxing, at which time he presents his completed problems to his teacher; (c) many of the problems are incorrect and the teacher orally berates him in front of the class; (d) in addition, his plight leads to excoriative remarks from his peers. If repeated sufficiently often, interactions of this type might yield anxiety reactions conditioned to relaxation-produced feedback stimuli. Whenever the boy begins relaxing he soon behaves anxiously.

The idea that termination of aversive stimulation is followed by relaxation behavior is consistent with the independently developed rationale of aversion relief therapy (Thorpe, Schmidt, Brown, & Castell, 1964). In this treatment, the presentation of cues representing anxiety-evoking stimuli or behavior is timed so as to coincide with the termination of aversive stimulation. The assumption is that anxiety responding to the cues will be counterconditioned by coterminous aversion-relief (relaxation) behaviors occasioned by aversion cessation. Probably not too much should be made of this parallel. As yet, clinical outcome data regarding aversion-relief therapy are not overly encouraging (Kapche, 1974). Moreover, clinical effects from aversion-relief regimens would not by themselves provide unambiguous support for the occurrence of actual aversion-relief responses (Barlow, 1973).

Of course, the approach–withdrawal view that relaxation behavior is antagonistic to anxiety responding accords well with numerous clinical findings demonstrating therapeutic contributions of various types of relaxation training and relaxation-based interventions in the treatment of anxiety disorders (cf. Rimm & Masters, 1979). Additionally, the theory is in agreement with Wolpe's (1973, 1976) claim that relaxation often contributes to demonstrably therapeutic programs such as flooding and with the contention of McGlynn, Mealiea, and Landau (1981) that the very reliable fear-reducing effects of systematic desensitization do, after all, depend on some degree of "relaxation."

Finally, the approach–withdrawal theory of avoidance brings into prominence a general issue relating to the behavioral analysis and theoretical understanding of several clinical problems that are often classified as anxiety disorders. Approach–withdrawal theory is the only approach that systematically allows positive reinforcement interactions a part in the development and main-

tenance of "anxiety" and "avoidance" behavior. Other theories rule out positive reinforcement because of the assumption that autonomically mediated
responses are not influenced by their consequences and/or because positive
reinforcement is thought antithetical to avoidance. The former assumption has
by now been empirically addressed and no longer appears warranted. The latter assumption is a conceptual matter, impervious to experimental analysis. For
an everyday example of our use of positive reinforcement, consider two children
who refuse to attend school. One displays various anxiety behaviors in the
school situation and shows a history there of frustrative and emotional behavior. The other shows no such anxiety behaviors in school nor is there any history
that can be construed as aversive conditioning to school-related cues. Instead,
numerous reinforcing activities such as receipt of social attention or daytime
television viewing are contingent upon the behavior of not attending school.
Clinical analysis will reveal that the refusal behavior of both children amounts
to *avoidance* of school, but clinicians might well overlook the differing interactions reflected by it. This is so because theories other than the approach–
withdrawal view are silent regarding the second case and, in fact, might
encourage the novice therapist to "find anxiety" in it. It is, after all, a school
"phobia."

Approach–withdrawal theory recognizes what clinical observations have
always shown (and what experienced parents have always known), that in certain instances phobias are developed and maintained by factors akin to positive
reinforcement (cf. Lazarus, Davison, & Polefka, 1965). In sum, the theory
calls for an extension of Rachman's (see above, 1977, 1978) three pathways to
anxiety hypothesis. In addition to respondent interactions, modeling, and informational input, there are operant (instrumental) factors potentially at work.

Cognitive-Expectancy Theory

Before the establishment of two-factor avoidance theory, Hilgard and
Marquis (1940) gave an interpretation of signalled active avoidance that
expressed a cognitive view of the problem. They suggested that subjects must
learn (a) that the warning signal signifies a potentially "dangerous" situation,
that is, shock is likely to occur, and (b) that their performance of the target
response to the warning signal results in a lowered likelihood of shock. Note
that a (cue → expectation of danger/harm) is identical to the first assumption
of the cognitive theory of anxiety previously discussed. The expansion of that
theory is the inclusion of actions beyond those of anxiety (e.g., avoidance
behavior). This means that we have already covered much of what cognitive
theory has to say regarding anxiety disorders. What remains is to consider its
application to the phenomena of avoidance addressed by two-factor and
approach–withdrawal theories.

Mutually compatible contemporary cognitive accounts of avoidance are given by Bandura (1977a, 1977b), Bolles (1972a, 1975, 1978), Carr (1979), Reiss (1980), and Seligman and Johnston (1973). Bandura as well as Seligman and Johnston offer the most complete presentations of relevance to anxiety disorders, and we will concentrate on these. Carr's (1979) discussion of avoidance is very brief. Reiss (1980), after addressing anxiety from a cognitive perspective, deviates little from aspects of two-factor and approach–withdrawal theories to account for phobias, thus adding little new. Bolles's (1972a, 1975, 1978) theorizing has focused on nonhuman behavior. He argues that once an animal has acquired a cue → shock expectancy, avoidance is a matter of the behavioral consequence of an innate expectancy that *"running away predicts safety"* (Bolles, 1972a, p. 407). This expectancy is tantamount to the inheritance of an adaptive act—a species-specific defense reaction. If the avoidance situation does not permit running away to avoid shock, the next species-specific defense reaction in a hierarchy of such reactions will be activated. If the situation is arranged such that none of the inherited defense reactions avoids shock, avoidance is impossible or greatly retarded. According to this theory, either clinical anxiety disorders are innate responses or they should not develop (or they should be extremely fragile). As discussed above and by Delprato (1980), there is no justification for viewing clinical anxiety disorders as inherited reactions. And certainly, anxiety disorders do develop and are seldom fragile in the sense of being readily overcome. Such complete lack of accord with clinical observations prompted us to deemphasize Bolles' theorizing in the present review.

Seligman and Johnston (1973) couch their presentation in terms of the subhuman shock-avoidance-training paradigm, while Bandura's (1977a, 1977b) primary focus is on therapeutic behavioral change. Because the former provide the more detailed cognitive account of the ontogeny and maintenance of avoidance, we shall review their theory first, then turn to the view of Bandura.

Seligman and Johnston postulate two major components of avoidance: a cognitive and an emotional one. We paraphrase their four assumptions regarding the cognitive component of avoidance as follows.

Preference. The animal prefers conditions of no shock over those of shock. Acquisition will not occur if for whatever reason shock is preferred to no shock or differential preferences are not exhibited.

Performance- and Nonperformance-Outcome Expectancies. The theory contains two related expectancy assumptions. The animal learns to expect that performance of the target response in the preshock period (avoidance interval) is followed by no shock rather than shock. The animal expects that nonperformance of the target response in the preshock period is followed by shock rather than no shock.

Confirmation of Expectancies. When expectancies are confirmed they are strengthened; when they are disconfirmed they are weakened.

Probability of Performance. With preference held constant, the probability of occurrence of the target response increases monotonically as a joint function of the strengths of the performance-outcome and nonperformance-outcome expectancies.

Seligman and Johnston (1973) take a rather traditional view of fear acquisition. CS–shock and CS–no-shock pairings are assumed to produce respondent fear conditioning and extinction, respectively. Autonomic and skeletal responses to the CS are used as measures of fear. Seligman and Johnston do deviate from two-factor theory regarding the motivational and reinforcing properties of fear. Fear is assumed to elicit initial avoidance responses (following two-factor theory), but continued avoidance behavior is then maintained by preference for no shock and by the joint performance-outcome and nonperformance-outcome expectancies. Fear does not motivate well-practiced avoidance. Neither does reduction of fear reinforce avoidance at any time.

Bandura's (1977a, 1977b) theory appears to be basically compatible with Seligman and Johnston's (1973) assumptions regarding the cognitive component of defensive behavior, with the addition of a cognitive "efficacy" component. There is outright disagreement, however, regarding the role of fear or the emotional component. Bandura distinguishes between response-outcome expectancies and efficacy expectations. Efficacy expectations refer to the individual's conviction that he/she can successfully perform behaviors that produce certain outcomes. Thus, an individual may have the accurate performance-outcome expectation that giving speeches will eventuate in a passing grade in a speech class and a college degree but still may not perform the requisite behavior because of a belief that he/she is unable to effectively give a speech. Efficacy expectations regarding particular situational performances or general ranges of performances develop from the individual's successful performance history (personal mastery experiences). Vicarious experiences (seeing others perform successfully) and verbal–informational processes may also regulate the development of efficacy expectations. Furthermore, situationally evoked fear can interfere with (or lower) perceptions of self-efficacy because of an individual's history of generally unsuccessful performances when anxious. In sum, problematic efficacy expectations can foster withdrawal from, or avoidance of, situations. Indeed, according to Bandura (1977a, 1977b), a complete cognitive theory of defensive behavior must include something akin to efficacy expectations because performance- and nonperformance-outcome expectations are often not in accord with performance.

In contrast with Seligman and Johnston (1973), Bandura (1977a, 1977b) makes no compromise with the two-factor view of fear and motivation. First, he maintains that all instances of fear acquisition involve development of expectancies of danger/harm. Second, fear is not conceptualized as an energizer of behavior; rather the informational functions of fear reactions are emphasized. They signify, for example, danger and/or impeded performance. Third, anxiety and defensive behavior are regarded as coeffects rather than as causally linked.

Some Major Implications of Cognitive-Expectancy Theory

Although cognitive-expectancy accounts of defensive behavior have been available since the 1940s (Hilgard & Marquis, 1940; Osgood, 1950; Ritchie, 1951), with few exceptions (e.g., Bolles, 1978) they have served primarily as *post hoc* alternatives to two-factor theory. Cognitive theorists argue that the several findings that pose difficulties for two-factor theory can be incorporated within the cognitive-expectancy framework. Seligman and Johnston (1973), in particular, discuss this matter. By way of illustration let us survey some of the major phenomena that contribute would-be grist for the cognitive theorist's mill.

While fear may be involved in the acquisition of avoidance, either as an elicitor of responses potentially predictive of no shock (Seligman & Johnston, 1973) or as information concerning the dangerousness of the situation (Bandura, 1977a, 1977b), maintained avoidance in the absence of evident fear poses no problem. This is because avoidance requires neither fear motivation nor fear reduction as reinforcement. As long as performance of the target response is followed by no shock, the performance-outcome expectancy is confirmed and strengthened; fear is not relevant to this process. Similarly, the persistence of avoidance in nonshock extinction can in large part be accounted for by the continued confirmation of the performance-outcome expectancy and the failure for the nonperformance-outcome expectancy to be disconfirmed. (Recall that the latter refers to the expectation that failure to respond within the preshock interval will result in shock rather than no shock.) Furthermore, the numerous failures of autonomic and skeletal measures of fear to correlate with avoidance have no particular bearing on cognitive-expectancy theory. However, the views of both Seligman and Johnston (1973) and Bandura (1977a, 1977b) do allow that concordance between fear and avoidance will be greater early in training rather than late. This is because the viewpoints predict that early escape trial cue–shock pairings result either in fear conditioning (Seligman & Johnston) or in expectations of danger/harm (Bandura). Kamin *et al.* (1963) and Delprato (1974) reported results grossly consistent with the prediction of maximal fear relatively early in avoidance.

If performance-outcome and nonperformance-outcome expectancies receive continued confirmation during nonshock avoidance extinction, then avoidance performance should continue indefinitely. Obviously it does not. How is the eventual diminution of avoidance responding explained? All that is needed is for the subject to sample disconfirmation of the nonperformance-outcome expectancy. Several factors can contribute to nonperformance late in avoidance. Preexperimental response tendencies, uncontrolled environmental conditions, variables related to the particular response requirements of the task (e.g., physically difficult responses and fatigue effects), and task-induced alterations in somatic functioning are some of the more obvious sources of late response impedance. The hypothesis that conventional extinction effects result

from exposure to disconfirmations of the nonperformance-outcome expectancy
also accounts for the enhanced extinction rates produced by forced exposure to
the warning signal (Baum, 1970) and for the enhanced extinction rates produced by delaying termination of the warning signal after the avoidance
response (Delprato, 1969; Katzev, 1967). These procedures ensure nonperformance of the target response in the presence of the warning signal, hence
disconfirmations of the nonperformance-outcome expectancy.

A final experimental phenomenon that seems to accommodate reasonably
well to this perspective is that of "learned helplessness." Under certain conditions, pretraining exposure to inescapable shock impedes subsequent escape
and avoidance performance of nonhumans (Seligman, Maier, & Solomon,
1971) and humans (Hiroto & Seligman, 1975). Such pretraining might bring
this about by adversely affecting performance-outcome expectancies and/or
efficacy expectations. In the former case, shocks received following attempts to
escape/avoid could promote the performance-outcome expectancy that "avoidance attempts are followed by shock." Transfer of this expectancy to the avoidance task would, in turn, interfere with development of the "appropriate" one.
In the latter case, constant "failures" during pretraining could lower efficacy
expectations thereby lowering response initiative.

Cognitive-expectancy theory implies generally that therapeutic progress
with specific anxiety disorders will be governed by the degree to which performance-outcome, nonperformance-outcome, and efficacy expectations are
altered. In turn, the therapy techniques used in such cases should be chosen by
virtue of their expectancy-changing properties. Bandura (1977a, 1977b), for
example, classifies treatments into four classes: (a) performance accomplishments such as participant modeling and *in vivo* desensitization, (b) vicarious
experiences such as modeling, (c) emotional arousal techniques like systematic
desensitization and imaginal exposure, and (d) verbal persuasion. He then pur-
sues the implication that efficacy expectations will be most effectively changed
via performance-based programs. (We would add that performance-based
expectancies fit his structure equally well.) Since all expectations are performance oriented, the maximum amount of corrective information will accrue to
therapeutic efforts that promote high levels of effective, concrete performances
vis à vis problematic life situations. Furthermore, beneficial treatment outcomes of programs based on vicarious techniques, emotional arousal, and verbal persuasion will be directly proportional to the degree to which these strategies contribute to effectual performance attainment.

Verbal persuasion is generally associated with weak effects, because
exhortations to engage in an activity long avoided can contribute neither to
disconfirming performance-outcome expectancies of disaster nor to overcoming
degraded perceptions of self-efficacy based on years of performance failure.
Modeling that includes models gradually improving their coping efforts (Kazdin, 1973) and with distinct response outcomes, can contribute in an important
way to the communication of information bearing rather directly on both per-

formance-outcome and efficacy expectations. Nonetheless, the obvious gap between the model's mastery behavior and its contingencies and the client's actual experiences will tend to make vicarious treatments less dependable than performance-based programs.

Cognitive-expectancy theory implies a radically unorthodox view of therapeutic change from emotional-arousal procedures such as systematic desensitization and imaginal exposure. In contrast to the interpretation that these methods diminish dysfunctional behavior directly (Wolpe, 1973) or indirectly (Stampfl & Levis, 1967) by anxiety reduction, the suggestion is that anxiety reduction serves mainly to enhance perceptions of self-efficacy. The implication is that therapeutic effects of arousal-based treatments like desensitization and imaginal exposure will be augmented by procedures, such as mastery experiences or coping uses of relaxation (Goldfried, 1971), that promote efficacy expectations.

According to the cognitive expectancy view, the treatment method known as participant modeling (Bandura, 1976, 1977a) represents an ideal strategy. Under conditions that promote the lowest possible emotional arousal, the therapist models the desired behavior calmly and safely while aiding the patient in performing approximations to it. This is an ideal strategy because it includes procedures that should contribute both to changing problematic outcome expectancies and to enhancing efficacy expectations. Disconfirmations of old outcome expectancies and confirmations of positive outcome expectancies follow discrete performances of new coping skills. These processes are facilitated by observation of the model's performance. Displays of mastery by the patient will, in turn, contribute to enhanced self-efficacy. This process is facilitated by minimizing arousal during the procedure. Should momentary arousal increments occur, arrangements for numerous and varied actual competence experiences allow for speedy disconfirmation of the expectancy that arousal predicts ineffectual performance. Alternatively, arousal can come to signify positive outcomes and efficacy.

An Unresolved Issue

Although cognitive-expectancy theory of defensive behavior has a long history, it has been developed only recently along the lines reviewed here. Thus, several issues remain open to clarification and further research. Some problems of cognitive theory were noted in our earlier discussion about cognitive theories of anxiety events. Without reiterating them here, we should point out that they *do* apply also to cognitive theories of avoidance.

Thoughtful appraisals of Seligman and Johnston's (1973) versions were made by authors themselves in their 1973 presentation. The self-efficacy hypothesis was examined by several reviewers both sympathetic and less sympathetic in a single issue of *Advances in Behaviour Research and Therapy* (Kazdin, 1978; Lang, 1978b; Poser, 1978; Rosenthal, 1978; Teasdale, 1978; Wilson, 1978; Wolpe, 1978b). Instead of reiterating issues and problems already raised, we should focus on one matter of general importance—the conceptual status of expectancy in relation to the activities of assessment. Since Bandura (1977a) has proposed a specific methodology for measuring self-efficacy, his paradigm provides an excellent vehicle for examining this issue.

Efficacy judgments have heretofore been obtained in the context of behavioral avoidance tests *vis à vis* a phobic stimulus (Bandura & Adams, 1977; Bandura, Adams, & Beyer, 1977; Bandura, Adams, Hardy, & Howells, 1980). After pretreatment avoidance testing and before posttreatment testing, subjects were provided with stepwise descriptions of the approach hierarchy and requested to designate those steps they could perform at that moment. High positive correlations between the self-report and subsequent performance measures are interpreted as support for the theory that self-efficacy is a critical determinant of approach to a phobic stimulus. This assumes that efficacy judgments are "signs" of an underlying cognitive expectancy that is separate from the relevant samples of approach behavior. There is at least one alternative explanation of the data not ruled out by the assessment process. It is possible that efficacy judgments, rather than providing access to privileged internal determinants of action, represent personal descriptions of known behavioral dispositions. Subjects in Bandura's experiments are making statements similar to that of an individual who states, "I expect to play golf tomorrow." This individual means, "I have arranged my schedule to play," "John and I will be playing," "My sprained ankle has healed sufficiently for me to play," "I will play even if my wife objects," or the like. Correspondence between verbal reports of expectations to play golf and performance does not legitimize the assumption that the individual's expectation is an inner determinant or cause of a subsequent action. Similarly, correspondence between self-reports of expected approach and actual approach to phobic objects does not imply internal causes of action.

Furthermore, Bandura *et al.* (1980) place great weight on data suggesting that efficacy judgments are more reliable than past performance (during treatment) for predicting posttreatment performance on a behavioral avoidance test. The implication is that an internal mastery experience is reflected by the efficacy measure, and that this causal factor accounts for approach behavior. Again, these data are compatible with the view of efficacy judgments as reports of behavioral dispositions. The data reported by Bandura *et al.* (1980) do not justify the view that self-reports of expectancy were manifestations of psychic determinants.

FUTURE DIRECTIONS

Behavioral conceptions of anxiety disorders have advanced well beyond the early notion that anxiety results simply from aversive CS–UCS pairings.

As is often the case when theoretical interpretations of a phenomenon proliferate, we are faced with some conceptual ambiguities. We will contend, however, that the variegated developments in behavioral anxiety theory do converge into the rudimentary stages of a coherent framework for conceptualizing anxiety disorders. Fundamental to this are two complementary developments: movement toward a multidimensional model of anxiety and movement away from the use of anxiety as an explanatory entity.

The Multidimensional Nature of Anxiety Behavior

Well over a half century ago John Dewey (1922) said, "There is no one fear having diverse manifestations" (p. 145). However, Dewey's point of view had little influence over the development of anxiety theory. Quite uniformly, psychiatric and psychological writers since Freud (1936) have aspired to a unitary model of the problem.

The search for a unitary model of anxiety behavior appears to have been guided more by theoretical preconceptions than by data (events). Indeed, those empirical generalizations that are trustworthy argue against a unitary conception. The routinely low intercorrelations between measures sampling different response systems are obvious examples here. If there is one true phenomenon known as anxiety, why are its various "manifestations" not more closely interrelated? Those committed to defending a unitary notion could answer that, to some extent at least, discordance between different measures of anxiety results from measurement error within "channels." In support of this contention a unitary theorist could point to data (e.g., Lick, Sushinsky, & Malow, 1977) showing how, for example, the magnitudes of correlations between self-report and behavioral measures of fear vary as a function of the amount of information imbedded within the self-report questions. The implication is that discordance between these two measurement domains will decrease as a function of more accurate assessment within the self-report domain. In the final analysis, however, the weight of data will subdue the unitary notion of anxiety. Anxiety for the time being, is best viewed multidimensionally as entailing cognitive and/or physiological and/or motoric features.

Acceptance of the multidimensional nature of anxiety leads directly to its abandonment as an explanatory entity. The subjective, physiologic, and motoric vocabularies that would be brought to bear in elucidating the multiform construct would be the same as the vocabularies used in detailing the to-be-explained anxiety events. Hence explanatory anxiety constructs are (at least) superfluous.

Viewed multidimensionally, anxiety represents a summarizing term for complex cognitive and/or physiological and/or motoric behavior–environment interactions (see Archer, 1979; Brady, 1975a, 1975b; Davidson & Schwartz, 1976; Lang, 1968, 1970, 1971, 1978a; Rachman, 1977, 1978; Thomson, 1979).

As a summary term, it emphasizes the descriptive or intervening-variable side of the intervening-variable/hypothetical-construct continuum described by MacCorquodale and Meehl (1948) and by Marx (1963). Multidimensional anxiety is an abstractive concept without any existence postulate. It does not allow "reification" or hypostatization of entities or processes inside or outside the organism.

A Multifaceted Framework for Anxiety Disorders

The multidimensional view has already proved to be eminently conducive to research, although much clarification is needed about the interrelationships among and within the three behavioral systems and about the interactions of the systems in the ontogeny and maintenance of anxiety behavior. One of the most exciting clinical implications is that, in combination with ontogenetic and maintenance information, the multidimensional description might allow us to "match the treatment with the person" using an empirically derived theoretical basis to do so.

Several behavioral writers have discussed fairly unsystematically the possibility that therapeutic strategies might be differentially effective depending on the behavioral system most involved in the anxiety disorder. Lang (1971) sketched a "multisystem training program, tailored to the unique behavioral topography presented by the patient" (p. 109). Wolpe (1977, 1981) argued that while systematic desensitization is effective with fears resulting from direct autonomic conditioning, misconception-based (cognitive system) fears require cognitive correction that may best be supplied by filmed modeling. Davidson and Schwartz (1976) suggested that certain relaxation procedures (e.g., meditation) might be more effective with cognitive anxiety, while other relaxation methods (e.g., physical exercise) may be more effective with somatic anxiety. Therapy by system interactions have in fact already been reported by Meichenbaum, Gilmore, and Fedoravicius (1971) and Foa, Steketee, and Milby (1980).

Our view of the problem is that none of the major participating factors is likely to be unitary. That is, not only do different behavioral systems participate in anxiety, but different classes of organism-environment interactions contribute to the ontogeny and maintenance of anxiety responding. This complex picture is depicted in Figure 1. We submit that this multifaceted framework synthesizes many of the key contributions made by research and theory as of the present. As is evident in Figure 1, this work demonstrates that anxiety refers to an intricate composition of action modes, developmental origins, and maintaining conditions, all of which must be taken into account in an adequate description of a given instance. A major implication for treatment is that a particular unitary or multicomponent intervention could be maximally effective for specific combinations of response system, historical-developmental

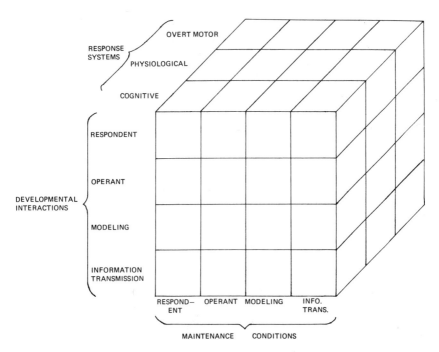

Figure 1. A multifaceted framework for anxiety disorders encompassing three major classes of factors.

origins, and maintenance conditions. Paul (1967) stated that the question addressed by outcome research should be, "*What* treatment, by *whom* is most effective for *this* individual with *that* specific problem, and under *which* set of circumstances?" (p. 111). The present model is consistent with Paul's recommendation, and it points the way toward clarifying just what is involved in specifying the problem in cases of anxiety disorders. Along the same lines, Keisler (1966) expressed concern over the limitations placed on psychotherapy research by the patient uniformity assumption. Keisler's point was that little can be concluded regarding the effects of even a well-defined intervention from studies that fail to take into account variations in patients with ostensibly the same unitary disorder.

Patient differences might be considerably more complex than anyone has heretofore admitted. For example, in cogently urging clinical-outcome researchers to subdivide subjects according to whether their fears represent respondent conditioning or cognitive learning, Wolpe (1977, 1981) implicitly assumes that primary participating response systems go hand in hand with both particular developmental origins and particular conditions of maintenance. Autonomic involvement implies respondent developmental origins *and* maintenance conditions; cognitive involvement implies informational factors in ontogeny *and* maintenance. Such response–development–maintenance consistencies very probably do occur, but this might not often be the case. Autonomic disturbance, for example, can be the outcome of *any* of the developmental interactions and can be maintained by the same or different classes of these interactions. The results of a given treatment for autonomically involved fears might, therefore, vary as a function of their pattern of development and maintenance. However, Wolpe's simplifying assumption might well be useful in the early stages of research on these questions.

As clinical analyses along the present lines will reveal, it is a rare case that involves only one response system, one developmental factor, and one maintaining condition. This state of affairs has already been recognized clinically and, indeed, is the basic rationale for using multicomponent interventions. It is to be hoped that models of the problem along the present lines will eventuate in multicomponent therapy strategies tailored very specifically to uniquely anxious patients.

SUMMARY

In this chapter six prominent classes of behavioral accounts of anxiety disorders have been reviewed, beginning with the respondent (classical) conditioning theory of Watson and Morgan (1917). Of these theories, three classes (respondent conditioning, revised conditioning, and cognitive) focus primarily on the anxiety concept itself as an event or set of events, while three other classes (two-factor, fear-mediational; approach–withdrawal; and cognitive-expectancy) treat anxiety as a theoretical construct in which the behavioral referents for the construct are conceptualized as both active and passive avoidance reactions. The latter theories seek to account for avoidance behavior, not anxiety *per se*.

It is concluded that no extant theory adequately handles the diverse environment–behavior interactions typically classified under the anxiety disorders. The two most influential behavioral theories throughout the early history of behavior therapy (respondent conditioning and two-factor, fear-mediation) are clearly deficient in numerous respects, although each contains features of continued value.

The main legacy of theoretical efforts to the present may well be the multifaceted framework in which partially independent cognitive, physiologic, and motoric action systems in various degrees participate in anxiety interactions as a function of four classes of partially independent ontogenetic and maintenance conditions: respondent, operant, modeling, and information transmission interactions.

REFERENCES

Annau, Z., & Kamin, L. J. The conditioned emotional response as a function of intensity of the US. *Journal of Comparative and Physiological Psychology,* 1961, *54,* 428–432.

Archer, J. Behavioural aspects of fear. In W. Sluckin (Ed.), *Fear in animals and man.* New York: Van Nostrand Rheinhold, 1979.

Auld, F. The effects of tetraethylammonium on a habit motivated by fear. *Journal of Comparative and Physiological Psychology,* 1951, *44,* 565–574.

Badia, P., Culbertson, S., & Lewis, P. The relative aversiveness of signalled vs. unsignalled avoidance. *Journal of the Experimental Analysis of Behavior,* 1971, *16,* 113–121.

Bandura, A. *Principles of behavior modification.* New York: Holt, Rinehart and Winston, 1969.

Bandura, A. Effecting change through participant modeling. In J. D. Krumboltz & C. E. Thoreson (Eds.), *Counseling methods.* New York: Holt, Rinehart and Winston, 1976.

Bandura, A. Self-efficacy: Toward a unifying theory of behavioral change. *Psychological Review,* 1977, *84,* 191–215. (a)

Bandura, A. *Social learning theory.* Englewood Cliffs, N.J.: Prentice-Hall, 1977. (b)

Bandura, A., & Adams, N. E. Analysis of self-efficacy theory of behavioral change. *Cognitive Therapy and Research,* 1977, *1,* 287–310.

Bandura, A., & Rosenthal, T. L. Vicarious classical conditioning as a function of arousal level. *Journal of Personality and Social Psychology,* 1966, *3,* 54–62.

Bandura, A., Adams, N. E., & Beyer, J. Cognitive processes mediating behavioral change. *Journal of Personality and Social Psychology,* 1977, *35,* 125–139.

Bandura, A., Adams, N. E., Hardy, A. B., & Howells, G. N. Tests of the generality of self-efficacy theory. *Cognitive Therapy and Research,* 1980, *4,* 39–66.

Barker, L. M., Best, M. R., & Domjan, M. *Learning mechanisms in food selection.* Waco, Tex.: Baylor University Press, 1977.

Barlow, D. H. Increasing heterosexual responsiveness in the treatment of sexual deviation: A review of the clinical and experimental evidence. *Behavior Therapy,* 1973, *4,* 655–671.

Baum, M. Extinction of avoidance responding through response prevention (flooding). *Psychological Bulletin,* 1970, *74,* 276–284.

Beach, F. A. The descent of instinct. *Psychological Review,* 1955, *62,* 401–410.

Beck, A. T. Cognitive therapy: Nature and relation to behavior therapy. *Behavior Therapy,* 1970, *1,* 184–200.

Beecroft, R. S. *Classical conditioning.* Goleta, Cal.: Psychonomic Press, 1966.

Beecroft, R. S. Emotional conditioning. *Psychonomic Monograph Supplements,* 1967, *2*(4, Whole No. 20), 45–72.

Berger, S. M. Conditioning through vicarious instigation. *Psychological Review,* 1962, *69,* 450–466.

Bersh, P. J. Eysenck's theory of incubation: A critical analysis. *Behaviour Research and Therapy,* 1980, *18,* 11–17.

Bersh, P. J., Notterman, J. M., & Schoenfeld, W. N. Extinction of human cardiac-response during avoidance-conditioning. *American Journal of Psychology,* 1956, *69,* 244–251.

Black, A. H. The extinction of avoidance responses under curare. *Journal of Comparative and Physiological Psychology,* 1958, *51,* 519–524.

Black, A. H. Heart rate changes during avoidance learning in dogs. *Canadian Journal of Psychology,* 1959, *13,* 229–242.

Black, A. H. Cardiac conditioning in curarized dogs: The relationship between heart rate and skeletal behaviour. In W. F. Prokasy (Ed.), *Classical conditioning: A symposium.* New York: Appleton-Century-Crofts, 1965.

Black, A. H. Autonomic aversive conditioning in infrahuman subjects. In F. R. Brush (Ed.), *Aversive conditioning and learning.* New York: Academic, 1971.

Black, A. H., & deToledo, L. The relationship among classically conditioned responses: Heart rate and skeletal behavior. In A. H. Black & W. F. Prokasy (Eds.), *Classical conditioning II: Current research and theory*. New York: Appleton-Century-Crofts, 1972.

Bolles, R. C. Species-specific defense reactions and avoidance learning. *Psychological Review*, 1970, *77*, 32–48.

Bolles, R. C. Reinforcement, expectancy, and learning. *Psychological Review*, 1972, *79*, 394–409. (a)

Bolles, R. C. The avoidance learning problem. In G. H. Bower (Ed.), *The psychology of learning and motivation* (Vol. 6). New York: Academic, 1972. (b)

Bolles, R. C. *Theory of motivation* (2nd ed.). New York: Harper & Row, 1975.

Bolles, R. C. The role of stimulus learning in defensive behavior. In S. H. Hulse, H. Fowler, & W. K. Honig (Eds.), *Cognitive processes in animal behavior*. Hillsdale, N. J.: Lawrence Erlbaum Associates, 1978.

Bolles, R. C., & Fanselow, M. S. A perceptual-defensive-recuperative model of fear and pain. *The Behavioral and Brain Sciences*, 1980, *3*, 291–323.

Bolles, R. C., & Warren, J. A., Jr. The acquisition of bar press avoidance as a function of shock intensity. *Psychonomic Science*, 1965, *3*, 297–298.

Bond, I. K., & Hutchison, H. C. Application of reciprocal inhibition therapy to exhibitionism. In H. J. Eysenck (Ed.), *Experiments in behaviour therapy*. Oxford: Pergamon, 1964.

Brady, J. V. Conditioning and emotion. In L. Levi (Ed.), *Emotions—Their parameters and measurement*. New York: Raven Press, 1975. (a)

Brady, J. V. Toward a behavioral biology of emotion. In L. Levi (Ed.), *Emotions—Their parameters and measurement*. New York: Raven Press, 1975. (b)

Bregman, E. O. An attempt to modify the emotional attitudes of infants by the conditioned response technique. *Journal of Genetic Psychology*, 1934, *45*, 169–198.

Broadhurst, P. Abnormal animal behaviour. In H. J. Eysenck (Ed.), *Handbook of abnormal psychology* (2nd ed.). London: Pitmans, 1972.

Brush, F. R. The effects of shock intensity on the acquisition and extinction of an avoidance response in dogs. *Journal of Comparative and Physiological Psychology*, 1957, *50*, 547–552.

Brutten, E. J., & Shoemaker, D. J. *The modification of stuttering*. Englewood Cliffs, N. J.: Prentice-Hall, 1967.

Carr, A. T. The psychopathology of fear. In W. Sluckin (Ed.), *Fear in animals and man*. New York: Van Nostrand Rheinhold, 1979.

Church, R. M., & Black, A. H. Latency of the conditioned heart rate as a function of the CS-US interval. *Journal of Comparative and Physiological Psychology*, 1958, *51*, 478–482.

Conger, J. J. The effects of alcohol on conflict behavior in the albino rat. *Quarterly Journal of Studies on Alcohol*, 1951, *12*, 1–29.

Conger, J. J. Reinforcement theory and the dynamics of alcoholism. *Quarterly Journal of Studies on Alcohol*, 1956, *17*, 296–305.

Cook, S. W., & Harris, R. E. The verbal conditioning of the galvanic skin reflex. *Journal of Experimental Psychology*, 1937, *21*, 202–210.

Cooper, A. J. A case of fetishism and impotence treated by behaviour therapy. *British Journal of Psychiatry*, 1963, *109*, 649–652.

Coughlin, R. C., Jr. The aversive properties of withdrawing positive reinforcement: A review of the recent literature. *Psychological Record*, 1972, *22*, 333–354.

Craig, K. D., & Weinstein, M. S. Conditioning vicarious affective arousal. *Psychological Reports*, 1965, *17*, 955–963.

Dabul, B., & Perkins, W. H. The effects of stuttering on systolic blood pressure. *Journal of Speech and Hearing Research*, 1973, *16*, 586–591.

Daly, H. B. Reinforcing properties of escape from frustration aroused in various learning situations. In G. H. Bower (Ed.), *The psychology of learning and motivation* (Vol. 8). New York: Academic, 1974.

D'Amato, M. R. *Experimental psychology: Methodology, psychophysics, and learning.* New York: McGraw-Hill, 1970.

D'Amato, M. R., & Fazzaro, J. Discriminated lever-press avoidance learning as a function of type and intensity of shock. *Journal of Comparative and Physiological Psychology,* 1966, *61,* 313–315.

Davidson, R. J., & Schwartz, G. E. The psychobiology of relaxation and related states: A multiprocess theory. In D. I. Mostofsky (Ed.), *Behavior control and modification of physiological activity.* Englewood Cliffs, N. J.: Prentice-Hall, 1976.

Davis, H. Conditioned suppression: A survey of the literature. *Psychonomic Monograph Supplements,* 1968, *2*(14, Whole No. 30), 283–291.

Delprato, D. J. Extinction of one-way avoidance and delayed warning-signal termination. *Journal of Experimental Psychology,* 1969, *80,* 192–193.

Delprato, D. J. Fear of the shock side as a function of acquisition criterion in one-way avoidance. *Bulletin of the Psychonomic Society,* 1974, *3,* 166–168.

Delprato, D. J. Hereditary determinants of fears and phobias: A critical review. *Behavior Therapy,* 1980, *11,* 79–103.

Delprato, D. J., & Dreilinger, C. Backchaining of relaxation in the extinction of avoidance. *Behaviour Research and Therapy,* 1974, *12,* 191–197.

Denny, M. R. Relaxation theory and experiments. In F. R. Brush (Ed.), *Aversive conditioning and learning.* New York: Academic, 1971.

Denny, M. R. Post-aversive relief and relaxation and their implications for behavior therapy. *Journal of Behavior Therapy and Experimental Psychiatry,* 1976, *7,* 315–321.

Denny, M. R., & Dmitruk, V. M. Effect of punishing a single failure to avoid. *Journal of Comparative and Physiological Psychology,* 1967, *63,* 277–281.

Denny, M. R., & Weisman, R. G. Avoidance behavior as a function of the length of nonshock confinement. *Journal of Comparative and Physiological Psychology,* 1964, *53,* 252–257.

deSilva, P., Rachman, S., & Seligman, M. E. P. Prepared phobias and obsessions: Therapeutic outcome. *Behaviour Research and Therapy,* 1977, *15,* 65–77.

Dewey, J. *Human nature and conduct.* New York: Random House, 1922.

Dinsmoor, J. A. Punishment: I. The avoidance hypothesis. *Psychological Review,* 1954, *61,* 34–46.

Dinsmoor, J. A. Escape, avoidance, punishment: Where do we stand? *Journal of the Experimental Analysis of Behavior,* 1977, *28,* 83–95.

Dobzhansky, T. The myths of genetic predestination and of tabula rasa. *Perspectives in Biology and Medicine,* 1976, *19,* 156–170.

Dollard, J., & Miller, N. E. *Personality and psychotherapy: An analysis in terms of learning, thinking, and culture.* New York: McGraw-Hill, 1950.

Ellis, A. *Reason and emotion in psychotherapy.* New York: Lyle Stuart, 1962.

Ellis, A. Can we change thoughts by reinforcement? A reply to Howard Rachlin. *Behavior Therapy,* 1977, *8,* 666–672.

English, H. B. Three cases of the "conditioned fear response." *Journal of Abnormal and Social Psychology,* 1929, *24,* 221–225.

Estes, W. K., & Skinner, B. F. Some quantitative properties of anxiety. *Journal of Experimental Psychology,* 1941, *29,* 390–400.

Eysenck, H. J. Learning theory and behaviour therapy. In H. J. Eysenck (Ed.), *Behaviour therapy and the neuroses.* Oxford: Pergamon, 1960.

Eysenck, H. J. A theory of the incubation of anxiety/fear responses. *Behaviour Research and Therapy,* 1968, *6,* 309–321.

Eysenck, H. J. A note on backward conditioning. *Behaviour Research and Therapy,* 1975, *13,* 201.

Eysenck, H. J. The learning theory model of neurosis—A new approach. *Behaviour Research and Therapy*, 1976, *14*, 251–267.

Eysenck, H. J., & Rachman, S. *The causes and cures of neurosis.* San Diego: Robert R. Knapp, 1965.

Foa, E. B., Steketee, G., & Milby, J. B. Differential effects of exposure and response prevention in obsessive-compulsive washers. *Journal of Consulting and Clinical Psychology*, 1980, *48*, 71–79.

Freeman, H. L., & Kendrick, D. C. A case of cat phobia: Treatment by a method derived from experimental psychology. In H. J. Eysenck (Ed.), *Experiments in behaviour therapy.* Oxford: Pergamon, 1964.

Freud, S. *The problem of anxiety* (H. A. Bunker, trans.). New York: W. W. Norton, 1936.

Goldfried, M. R. Systematic desensitization as training in self-control. *Journal of Consulting and Clinical Psychology*, 1971, *37*, 228–234.

Goldfried, M. R., Decenteceo, E. T., & Weinberg, L. Systematic rationale restructuring as a self-control technique. *Behavior Therapy*, 1974, *5*, 247–254.

Goss, A. E. Early behaviorism and verbal mediating responses. *American Psychologist*, 1961, *16*, 285–298.

Gray, J. *The psychology of fear and stress.* New York: McGraw-Hill, 1971.

Grings, W. W. Verbal-perceptual factors in the conditioning of autonomic responses. In W. F. Prokasy (Ed.), *Classical conditioning: A symposium.* New York: Appleton-Century-Crofts, 1965.

Grings, W. W., & Dawson, M. E. Complex variables in conditioning. In W. F. Prokasy & D. C. Raskin (Eds.), *Electrodermal activity in psychological research.* New York: Academic, 1973.

Grossberg, J. M. Comments about cognitive therapy and behavior therapy. *Journal of Behavior Therapy and Experimental Psychiatry*, 1981, *7*, 25–33.

Hall, J. F. *Classical conditioning and instrumental learning: A comparative approach.* New York: Lippincott, 1976.

Henton, W. W., & Iversen, I. H. *Classical conditioning and operant conditioning: A response pattern analysis.* New York: Springer-Verlag, 1978.

Herrnstein, R. J. Method and theory in the study of avoidance. *Psychological Review*, 1969, *76*, 49–69.

Hilgard, E. R., & Marquis, D. G. *Conditioning and learning.* New York: D. Appleton-Century, 1940.

Hill, H. E. An experimental study of disorganization of speech and manual responses in normal subjects. *Journal of Speech and Hearing Disorders*, 1954, *19*, 295–305.

Hineline, P. N. Negative reinforcement and avoidance. In W. K. Honig & J. E. R. Staddon (Eds.), *Handbook of operant behavior.* Englewood Cliffs, N. J.: Prentice-Hall, 1977.

Hiroto, D. S., & Seligman, M. E. P. Generality of learned helplessness in man. *Journal of Personality and Social Psychology*, 1975, *31*, 311–327.

Hodgson, R., & Rachman, S. II. Desynchrony in measures of fear. *Behaviour Research and Therapy*, 1974, *12*, 319–326.

Ickes, W. K., & Pierce, S. The stuttering moment: A plethysmographic study. *Journal of Communication Disorders*, 1973, *6*, 155–164.

Isbell, H. Perspectives in research in opiate addiction. In D. M. Wilner & G. G. Kassebaum (Eds.), *Narcotics.* New York: McGraw-Hill, 1965.

Jennings, H. S. Heredity and environment. *The Scientific Monthly*, 1924, *19*, 225–238.

Johnson, W. J. *Stuttering in children and adults.* Minneapolis: University of Minnesota, 1955.

Jones, D. D. Entropic models in biology: The next scientific revolution? *Perspectives in Biology and Medicine*, 1977, *20*, 285–299.

Jones, M. C. The elimination of children's fears. *Journal of Experimental Psychology*, 1924, *7*, 382–390.

Kamin, L. J. Traumatic avoidance learning: The effects of CS–US interval with a trace conditioning procedure. *Journal of Comparative and Physiological Psychology*, 1954, *47*, 65–72.

Kamin, L. J. Temporal and intensity characteristics of the conditioned stimulus. In W. F. Prokasy (Ed.), *Classical conditioning: A symposium*. New York: Appleton-Century-Crofts, 1965.

Kamin, L. J., Brimer, C. J., & Black, A. H. Conditioned suppression as a monitor of fear of the CS in the course of avoidance training. *Journal of Comparative and Physiological Psychology*, 1963, *56*, 497–501.

Kantor, J. R. Toward a scientific analysis of motivation. *Psychological Record*, 1942, *5*, 225–275.

Kantor, J. R. *The logic of modern science*. Chicago: Principia Press, 1953.

Kantor, J. R. *The scientific evolution of psychology* (Vol. 2). Chicago: Principia Press, 1969.

Kantor, J. R., & Smith, N. W. *The science of psychology: An interbehavioral survey*. Chicago: Principia Press, 1975.

Kapche, R. Aversion-relief therapy: A review of current procedures and the clinical and experimental evidence. *Psychotherapy: Theory, Research and Practice*, 1974, *11*, 156–162.

Kaplan, H. I., & Kaplan, H. S. The psychosomatic concept of obesity. *Journal of Nervous and Mental Disease*, 1957, *125*, 181–201.

Katzev, R. Extinguishing avoidance responses as a function of delayed warning signal termination. *Journal of Experimental Psychology*, 1967, *75*, 339–344.

Kazdin, A. E. Conceptual and assessment issues raised by self-efficacy theory. *Advances in Behaviour Research and Therapy*, 1978, *1*, 177–185.

Keehn, J. D. Avoidance responses as discriminated operants. *British Journal of Psychology*, 1966, *57*, 375–389.

Keisler, D. J. Some myths of psychotherapy research and the search for a paradigm. *Psychological Bulletin*, 1966, *65*, 110–136.

Keller, F. S., & Schoenfeld, W. N. *Principles of psychology: A systematic text in the science of behavior*. New York: Appleton-Century-Crofts, 1950.

Kimble, G. A. *Hilgard and Marquis' conditioning and learning*. New York: Appleton-Century-Crofts, 1961.

Kimmel, H. D. Instrumental conditioning of autonomically mediated responses in human beings. *American Psychologist*, 1974, *29*, 325–335.

Konorski, J. *Integrative activity of the brain*. Chicago: University of Chicago Press, 1967.

Konorski, J. Some ideas concerning physiological mechanisms of so-called internal inhibition. In R. A. Boakes & M. S. Halliday (Eds.), *Inhibition and learning*. New York: Academic, 1972.

Kuo, Z. Y. *The dynamics of behavior development: An epigenetic view*. New York: Random House, 1967.

Lang, P. J. Fear reduction and fear behavior: Problems in treating a construct. In J. M. Schlien (Ed.), *Research in psychotherapy*. (Vol. 3). Washington, D. C.: American Psychological Association, 1968.

Lang, P. J. Stimulus control, response control, and the desensitization of fear. In D. J. Levis (Ed.), *Learning approaches to therapeutic behavior change*. Chicago: Aldine, 1970.

Lang, P. J. The application of psychophysiological methods to the study of psychotherapy and behavior modification. In A. E. Bergin & S. L. Garfield (Eds.), *Handbook of psychotherapy and behavior change: An empirical analysis*. New York: Wiley, 1971.

Lang, P. J. Anxiety: Toward a psychophysiological definition. In H. S. Akiskal & W. L. Webb (Eds.), *Psychiatric diagnosis: Exploration of biological predictors*. New York: Spectrum, 1978. (a)

Lang, P. J. Self-efficacy theory: Thoughts on cognition and unification. *Advances in Behaviour Research and Therapy*, 1978, *1*, 187–192. (b)

Lautch, H. Dental phobia. *Brisish Journal of Psychiatry.* 1971, *119,* 151–158.

Lazarus, A. A., Davison, G. C., & Polefka, D. A. Classical and operant factors in the treatment of a school phobia. *Journal of Abnormal Psychology,* 1965, *70,* 225–229.

Ledwidge, B. Cognitive behavior modification: A step in the wrong direction? *Psychological Bulletin,* 1978, *83,* 353–375.

Leitenberg, H., Agras, S., Butz, R., & Wincze, J. Relationship between heart rate and behavioral change during the treatment of phobias. *Journal of Abnormal Psychology,* 1971, *78,* 59–68.

Leon, G. R. *Case histories of deviant behavior: An interactional perspective* (2nd ed.). Boston: Holbrook, 1977.

Levis, D. J., & Boyd, T. L. Symptom maintenance: An infrahuman analysis and extension of the conservation of anxiety principle. *Journal of Abnormal Psychology,* 1979, *88,* 107–120.

Lick, J. R., Sushinsky, L. W., & Malow, R. Specificity of fear survey schedule items and the prediction of avoidance behavior. *Behavior Modification,* 1977, *1,* 195–203.

Linden, D. R. Attenuation and reestablishment of the CER by discriminated avoidance conditioning rats. *Journal of Comparative and Physiological Psychology,* 1969, *69,* 573–578.

Lockard, J. S. Choice of warning signal or no warning signal in an unavoidable shock situation. *Journal of Comparative and Physiological Psychology,* 1963, *56,* 526–530.

Locke, E. A. Behavior modification is not cognitive—and other myths: A reply to Ledwidge. *Cognitive Therapy and Research,* 1979, *3,* 119–125.

MacCorquodale, K., & Meehl, P. E. On a distinction between hypothetical constructs and intervening variables. *Psychological Review,* 1948, *55,* 95–107.

Mahoney, M. J., & Kazdin, A. E. Cognitive behavior modification: Misconceptions and premature evacuation. *Psychological Bulletin,* 1979, *86,* 1044–1049.

Maier, S. F., Seligman, M. E. P., & Solomon, R. L. Pavlovian fear conditioning and learned helplessness: Effects on escape and avoidance behavior of (a) the CS–US contingency and (b) and independence of the US and voluntary responding. In B. A. Campbell & R. M. Church (Eds.), *Punishment and aversive behavior.* New York: Appleton-Century-Crofts, 1969.

Marks, I. M. *Fears and phobias.* New York: Academic, 1969.

Marx, M. H. The general nature of theory construction. In M. H. Marx (Ed.), *Theories in contemporary psychology.* New York: Macmillan, 1963.

McAllister, W. R., & McAllister, D. E. Behavioral measurement of conditioned fear. In F. R. Brush (Ed.), *Aversive conditioning and learning.* New York: Academic, 1971.

McGlynn, F. D., Mealiea, W. L., & Landau, D. L. The current status of systematic desensitization. *Clinical Psychology Review,* 1981, *1,* 149–179.

Meichenbaum, D. *Cognitive-behavior modification: An integrative approach.* New York: Plenum, 1977.

Meichenbaum, D., Gilmore, B., & Fedoravicius, A. Group insight versus group desensitization in treating speech anxiety. *Journal of Consulting and Clinical Psychology,* 1971, *36,* 410–421.

Meyer, V., & Levy, R. Modification of behavior in obsessive-compulsive disorders. In H. E. Adams & I. P. Unikel (Eds.), *Issues and trends in behavior therapy.* Springfield, Ill.: Charles C Thomas, 1973.

Milgram, N. W., Krames, L., & Alloway, T. M. *Food aversion learning.* New York: Plenum, 1977.

Miller, N. E. Learnable drives and rewards. In S. S. Stevens (Ed.), *Handbook of experimental psychology.* New York: Wiley, 1951.

Miller, N. E. Learning of visceral and glandular responses. *Science,* 1969, *163,* 434–445.

Mineka, S. The role of fear in theories of avoidance learning, flooding, and extinction. *Psychological Bulletin,* 1979, *86,* 985–1010.

Mineka, S., & Gino, A. Dissociation between conditioned emotional response and extended avoidance performance. *Learning and Motivation*, 1980, *11*, 476–502.

Mowrer, O. H. A stimulus-response analysis of anxiety and its role as a reinforcing agent. *Psychological Review*, 1939, *46*, 553–565.

Mowrer, O. H. On the dual nature of learning—a re-interpretation of "conditioning" and "problem-solving." *Harvard Educational Review*, 1947, *17*, 102–148.

Mowrer, O. H. *Learning theory and behavior*. New York: Wiley, 1960.

Moyer, K. E., & Korn, J. H. Effect of UCS intensity on the acquisition and extinction of an avoidance response. *Journal of Experimental Psychology*, 1964, *67*, 352–359.

Obrist, P. A., Sutterer, J. R., & Howard, J. L. Preparatory cardiac changes: A psychobiological approach. In A. H. Black & W. F. Prokasy (Eds.), *Classical conditioning II: Current research and theory*. New York: Appleton-Century-Crofts, 1972.

Öhman, A. Fear relevance, autonomic conditioning, and phobias: A laboratory model. In P.-O. Sjödén, S. Bates, & W. S. Dockens III (Eds.), *Trends in behavior therapy*. New York: Academic, 1979.

Öhman, A., Fredrikson, M., & Hugdahl, K. Towards an experimental model for simple phobic reactions. *Behaviour Analysis and Modification*, 1978, *2*, 97–114.

Osgood, C. E. Can Tolman's theory of learning handle avoidance training? *Psychological Review*, 1950, *57*, 133–137.

Paul, G. L. Strategy of outcome research in psychotherapy. *Journal of Consulting Psychology*, 1967, *31*, 109–118.

Pavlov, I. P. *Conditioned reflexes* (G. V. Anrep, trans.). London: Oxford University Press, 1927.

Phillips, L. W. Roots and branches of behavioral and cognitive practice. *Journal of Behavior Therapy and Experimental Psychiatry*, 1981, *12*, 5–17.

Poser, E. G. The self-efficacy concept: Some theoretical procedural and clinical implications. *Advances in Behaviour Research and Therapy*, 1978, *1*, 193–202.

Prokasy, W. F., & Kumpfer, K. L. Classical conditioning. In W. F. Prokasy & D. C. Raskin (Eds.), *Electrodermal activity in psychological research*. New York: Academic, 1973.

Rachlin, H. Reinforcing and punishing thoughts. *Behavior Therapy*, 1977, *8*, 659–665.

Rachman, S. The passing of the two-stage theory of fear and avoidance: Fresh possibilities. *Behaviour Research and Therapy*, 1976, *14*, 125–131.

Rachman, S. The conditioning theory of fear-acquisition. A critical examination. *Behaviour Research and Therapy*, 1977, *15*, 375–387.

Rachman, S. J. *Fear and courage*. San Francisco: W. H. Freeman, 1978.

Rachman, S., & Hodgson, R. I. Synchrony and desynchrony in fear and avoidance. *Behaviour Research and Therapy*, 1974, *12*, 311–318.

Rachman, S., & Seligman, M. E. P. Unprepared phobias: "Be prepared." *Behaviour Research and Therapy*, 1976, *14*, 333–338.

Rachman, S., Hodgson, R., & Marks, I. M. The treatment of chronic obsessive-compulsive neurosis. *Behaviour Research and Therapy*, 1971, *9*, 237–247.

Reiss, S. Pavlovian conditioning and human fear: An expectancy model. *Behavior Therapy*, 1980, *11*, 380–396.

Rescorla, R. A. Establishment of a positive reinforcer through contrast with shock. *Journal of Comparative and Physiological Psychology*, 1969, *67*, 260–263. (a)

Rescorla, R. A. Pavlovian conditioned inhibition. *Psychological Bulletin*, 1969, *72*, 77–94. (b)

Rescorla, R. A. Information variables in Pavlovian conditioning. In G. H. Bower (Ed.), *The psychology of learning and motivation* (Vol. 6). New York: Academic, 1972.

Rescorla, R. A. Second-order conditioning: Implications for theories of learning. In F. J. McGuigan & D. B. Lumsden (Eds.), *Contemporary approaches to conditioning and learning*. Washington, D. C.: V. H. Winston, 1973.

Rescorla, R. A. Some implications of a cognitive perspective on Pavlovian conditioning. In S. H.

Hulse, H. Fowler, & W. K. Honig (Eds.), *Cognitive processes in animal behavior*. Hillsdale, N. J.: Lawrence Erlbaum Associates, 1978.

Rescorla, R. A., & Solomon, R. L. Two-process learning theory: Relationships between Pavlovian conditioning and instrumental learning. *Psychological Review*, 1967, *74*, 151–182.

Riccio, D. C., & Silvestri, R. Extinction of avoidance behavior and the problem of residual fear. *Behaviour Research and Therapy*, 1973, *11*, 1–9.

Riegel, K. F. *Psychology mon amour: A countertext*. Boston: Houghton Mifflin, 1978.

Rimm. D. C., & Masters, J. C. *Behavior therapy: Techniques and empirical findings* (2nd ed.). New York: Academic, 1979.

Ritchie, B. F. Can reinforcement theory account for avoidance? *Psychological Review*, 1951, *58*, 382–386.

Rizley, R., & Reppucci, N. D. Pavlovian conditioned inhibitory processes in behavior therapy. In B. A. Maher (Ed.), *Progress in experimental personality research* (Vol. 7). New York: Academic, 1974.

Robinson, H. B. Persistence of a response in the apparent absence of motivation. *Journal of Experimental Psychology*, 1961, *61*, 480–488.

Rosenthal, T. L. Bandura's self-efficacy theory: Thought *is* father to the deed. *Advances in Behaviour Research and Therapy*, 1978, *1*, 203–209.

Russell, B. On the notion of cause, with applications to the free-will problem. In H. Feigl & M. Brodbeck (Eds.), *Readings in the philosophy of science*. New York: Appleton-Century-Crofts, 1953.

Ryle, G. *The concept of mind*. London: Hutchinson, 1949.

Sallis, J. F., Lichstein, K. L., & McGlynn, F. D. Anxiety response patterns: A comparison of clinical and analogue populations. *Journal of Behavior Therapy and Experimental Psychiatry*, 1980, *11*, 179–183.

Schafer, R. Psychoanalysis without psychodynamics. *International Journal of Psycho-Analysis*, 1975, *56*, 41–55.

Schafer, R. *A new action language for psychoanalysis*. New Haven: Yale University Press, 1976.

Schafer, R. *Language and insight*. New Haven: Yale University Press, 1978.

Schneiderman, N. Response system divergencies in aversive classical conditioning. In A. H. Black & W. F. Prokasy (Eds.), *Classical conditioning II: Current research and theory*. New York: Appleton-Century-Crofts, 1972.

Schneirla, T. C. The concept of development in comparative psychology. In D. B. Harris (Ed.), *The concept of development: An issue in the study of human behavior*. Minneapolis: University of Minnesota Press, 1957.

Schneirla, T. C. An evolutionary and developmental theory of biphasic processes underlying approach and withdrawal. In M. R. Jones (Ed.), *Nebraska symposium on motivation*. Lincoln: University of Nebraska Press, 1959.

Schoenfeld, W. N. An experimental approach to anxiety, escape, and avoidance behavior. In P. H. Hoch & J. Zubin (Eds.), *Anxiety*. New York: Grune & Stratton, 1950.

Schoenfeld, W. N. "Avoidance" in behavior theory. *Journal of the Experimental Analysis of Behavior*, 1969, *12*, 669–674.

Schoenfeld, W. N., Cole, B. K., Lang, J., & Mankoff, R. "Contingency" in behavior theory. In F. J. McGuigan & D. B. Lunsden (Eds.), *Contemporary approaches to conditioning and learning*. Washington, D. C.: V. H. Winston, 1973.

Schwartz, G. E. Psychobiological foundations of psychotherapy and behavior change. In S. L. Garfield & A. E. Bergin (Eds.), *Handbook of psychotherapy and behavior change: An empirical analysis* (2nd ed.). New York: Wiley, 1978.

Seligman, M. E. P. On the generality of the laws of learning. *Psychological Review*, 1970, *77*, 406–418.

Seligman, M. E. P. Phobias and preparedness. *Behavior Therapy*, 1971, *2*, 307–320.

Seligman, M. E. P., & Johnston, J. C. A cognitive theory of avoidance learning. In F. J. McGuigan & D. B. Lumsden (Eds.), *Contemporary approaches to conditioning and learning.* Washington, D. C.: V. H. Winston, 1973.

Seligman, M. E. P., Maier, S. F., & Solomon, R. L. Unpredictable and uncontrollable aversive events. In F. R. Brush (Ed.), *Aversive conditioning and learning.* New York: Academic, 1971.

Sheehan, J. Conflict theory of stuttering. In J. Eisenson & W. Johnson (Eds.), *Stuttering: A symposium.* New York: Harper and Row, 1958.

Sheehan, J. G. Conflict theory and avoidance-reduction therapy. In J. Eisenson (Ed.), *Stuttering: A second symposium.* New York: Harper & Row, 1975.

Sheehan, J., Hadley, R., & Gould, E. Impact of authority on stuttering. *Journal of Abnormal Psychology,* 1967, *72,* 290–293.

Sidman, M. Avoidance conditioning with brief shock and no exteroceptive warning signal. *Science,* 1953, *118,* 157–158.

Skinner, B. F. *Science and human behavior.* New York: Macmillan, 1953.

Solomon, R. L., & Brush, E. S. Experimentally derived conceptions of anxiety and avoidance. In M. R. Jones (Ed.), *Nebraska symposium on motivation.* Lincoln: University of Nebraska Press, 1956.

Solomon, R. L., & Wynne, L. C. Traumatic avoidance learning: Acquisition in normal dogs. *Psychological Monographs,* 1953, *67* (4) (Whole No. 354).

Solomon, R. L., & Wynne, L. C. Traumatic avoidance learning: The principles of anxiety conservation and partial irreversibility. *Psychological Review,* 1954, *61,* 353–385.

Solomon, R. L., Kamin, L. J., & Wynne, L. C. Traumatic avoidance learning: The outcomes of several extinction procedures with dogs. *Journal of Abnormal and Social Psychology,* 1953, *48,* 291–302.

Solyom, L., Beck, P., Solyom, C., & Hugel, R. Some etiological factors in phobic neurosis. *Canadian Psychiatric Association Journal,* 1974, *19,* 69–77.

Sours, J. E., Ehrlich, R. E., & Phillips, P. B. The fear of flying syndrome: A re-appraisal. *Aerospace Medicine,* 1964, *35,* 156–166.

Spence, K. W. The nature of theory construction in contemporary psychology. *Psychological Review,* 1944, *51,* 47–68.

Spetch, M. L., Wilkie, D. M., & Pinel, J. P. J. Backward conditioning: A reevaluation of the empirical evidence. *Psychological Bulletin,* 1981, *89,* 163–175.

Staddon, J. E. R. On the notion of cause, with applications to behaviorism. *Behaviorism,* 1973, *1,* 25–63.

Staddon, J. E. R., & Simmelhag, V. L. The "superstition" experiment: A reexamination of its implications for the principles of adaptive behavior. *Psychological Review,* 1971, *78,* 3–43.

Stampfl, T. G. Implosive therapy: An emphasis on covert stimulation. In D. J. Levis (Ed.), *Learning approaches to therapeutic behavior change.* Chicago: Aldine, 1970.

Stampfl, T. G., & Levis, D. J. Essentials of implosive therapy: A learning-theory-based therapy. *Journal of Abnormal Psychology,* 1967, *72,* 496–503.

Stampfl, T. G., & Levis, D. J. Learning theory: An aid to dynamic therapeutic practice. In L. D. Eron & R. Callahan (Eds.), *Relationship of theory to practice in psychotherapy.* Chicago: Aldine, 1969.

Stern, J. A., & Word, T. J. Heart rate changes during avoidance conditioning in the male albino rat. *Journal of Psychosomatic Research,* 1962, *6,* 167–175.

Teasdale, J. D. Self-efficacy: Toward a unifying theory of behavioural change? *Advances in Behaviour Research and Therapy,* 1978, *1,* 211–215.

Thomson, R. The concept of fear. In W. Sluckin (Ed.), *Fear in animals and man.* New York: Van Nostrand Rheinhold, 1979.

48 Dennis J. Delprato and F. Dudley McGlynn

Thorndike, E. L. *Animal intelligence.* New York: Macmillan, 1898.

Thorpe, J. G., Schmidt, E., Brown, P. T., & Castell, D. Aversion-relief therapy: A new method for general application. *Behaviour Research and Therapy,* 1964, *2,* 71–82.

Timberlake, W., & Allison, J. Response deprivation: An empirical approach to instrumental performance. *Psychological Review,* 1974, *81,* 146–164.

Tolman, E. C. *Purposive behavior in animals and men.* New York: Appleton-Century, 1932.

Turnbull, J. W. Asthma conceived as a learned response. *Journal of Psychosomatic Research,* 1962, *6,* 59–70.

Turner, M. B. *Psychology and the philosophy of science.* New York: Appleton-Century-Crofts, 1967.

Valentine, C. W. The innate bases of fear. *Journal of Genetic Psychology,* 1930, *37,* 394–420.

Venn, J. R., & Short, J. G. Vicarious classical conditioning of emotional responses in nursery school children. *Journal of Personality and Social Psychology,* 1973, *28,* 249–255.

Verhave, T. The functional properties of a time out from an avoidance schedule. *Journal of the Experimental Analysis of Behavior.* 1962, *5,* 391–422.

Wagner, A. R. Frustrative nonreward: A variety of punishment? In B. A. Campbell & R. M. Church (Eds.), *Punishment and aversive behavior.* New York: Appleton-Century-Crofts, 1969.

Walton, D., & Mather, M. D. The application of learning principles to the treatment of obsessive-compulsive states in the acute and chronic phases of illness. In H. J. Eysenck (Ed.), *Experiments in behavior therapy.* Oxford: Pergamon, 1964.

Watson, J. B. *Behaviorism* (Rev. ed.). Chicago: University of Chicago Press, 1930.

Watson, J. B., & Morgan, J. J. B. Emotional reactions and psychological experimentation. *American Journal of Psychology,* 1917, *28,* 163–174.

Watson, J. B., & Rayner, R. Conditioned emotional reactions. *Journal of Experimental Psychology,* 1920, *3,* 1–14.

Weisman, R. G., & Litner, J. S. Positive conditioned reinforcement of Sidman avoidance behavior in rats. *Journal of Comparative and Physiological Psychology,* 1969, *68,* 597–603.

Weisman, R. G., & Litner, J. S. The role of Pavlovian events in avoidance training. In R. A. Boakes & M. S. Halliday (Eds.), *Inhibition and learning.* New York: Academic, 1972.

Wenzel, B. M., & Jeffrey, D. W. The effect of immunosympathectomy on the behavior of mice in aversive situations. *Physiology and Behavior,* 1967, *2,* 193–201.

Wikler, A. Conditioning factors in opiate addiction and relapse. In D. M. Wilner & G. G. Kassebaum (Eds.), *Narcotics.* New York: McGraw-Hill, 1965.

Wilson, G. T. The importance of being theoretical: A commentary on Bandura's "Self-efficacy: Towards a unifying theory of behavioral change." *Advances in Behaviour Research and Therapy,* 1978, *1,* 217–230.

Wischner, G. J. Anxiety-reduction as reinforcement in maladaptive behavior: Evidence in stutterers' representations of the moment of difficulty. *Journal of Abnormal and Social Psychology,* 1952, *47,* 566–571.

Wolpe, J. Experimental neurosis as learned behavior. *British Journal of Psychology,* 1952, *43,* 243–268.

Wolpe, J. *Psychotherapy by reciprocal inhibition.* Stanford, Cal.: Stanford University Press, 1958.

Wolpe, J. The behavioristic conception of neurosis: A reply to two critics. *Psychological Review,* 1971, *78,* 341–343.

Wolpe, J. *The practice of behavior therapy* (2nd ed.). New York: Pergamon, 1973.

Wolpe, J. *Theme and variations: A behavior therapy casebook.* New York: Pergamon, 1976.

Wolpe, J. Inadequate behavior analysis: The Achilles heel of outcome research in behavior therapy. *Journal of Behavior Therapy and Experimental Psychiatry,* 1977, *8,* 1–3.

Wolpe, J. Cognition and causation in human behavior and its therapy. *American Psychologist,* 1978, *33,* 437–446. (a)

Wolpe, J. Self-efficacy theory and psychotherapeutic change: A square peg for a round hole. *Advances in Behaviour Research and Therapy,* 1978, *1,* 231–236. (b)

Wolpe, J. The dichotomy between classical conditioned and cognitively learned anxiety. *Journal of Behavior Therapy and Experimental Psychiatry,* 1981, *12,* 35–42.

Wolpe, J., & Rachman, S. Psychoanalytic "evidence": A critique based on Freud's case of Little Hans. *Journal of Nervous and Mental Diseases,* 1960, *131,* 135–148.

Wynne, L. C., & Solomon, R. C. Traumatic avoidance learning: Acquisition and extinction in dogs deprived of normal peripheral autonomic function. *Genetic Psychology Monographs,* 1955, *52,* 241–284.

Yates, A. J. The application of learning theory to the treatment of tics. *Journal of Abnormal and Social Psychology,* 1958, *56,* 175–182.

Zeaman, D., & Smith, R. W. Review of some recent findings in human cardiac conditioning. In W. F. Prokasy (Ed.), *Classical conditioning: A symposium.* New York: Appleton-Century-Crofts, 1965.

2

Measurement of Anxiety

ALAN S. BELLACK and
THOMAS W. LOMBARDO

Adequate assessment is integral to both clinical work and research on anxiety. Historically, assessment strategies differed between research and clinical practice. Quantitative, empirical evaluation using standardized measures was the domain of research, while more limited, idiosyncratic subjective assessments were customary in clinical practice. It is now becoming increasingly evident that idiosyncratic *and* standardized measurements of anxiety are important to both clinicians and researchers. First, there is more demand for accountability. Whether documenting the need for treatment to third party payers, substantiating treatment gains to funding agencies, or providing empirical dependent measures in research, objective data are increasingly more important.

Second, both advancement of science as well as therapeutic outcome hinge on empirical assessment. For example, clinicians using systematic, continuous, objective assessment during treatment can determine whether improvement is actually occurring. Sometimes gains are of much smaller magnitude than the patient can subjectively discriminate. More sensitive measures can serve to motivate both the therapist and patient when gains are found, and can redirect therapeutic strategies if no results are obtained. For researchers, the identification of idiosyncratic behaviors to serve as criteria for excluding subjects would help reduce variability in data (Borkovec, Weerts, & Bernstein, 1977). Wolpe (1977) describes the existing inattention to selectivity of subjects for

ALAN S. BELLACK ● Medical College of Pennsylvania at Eastern Pennsylvania Psychiatric Institute, Philadelphia, Pennsylvania 19129.   THOMAS W. LOMBARDO ● Department of Psychology, University of Mississippi, Oxford, Mississippi 38655.

clinical study as "the Achilles' heel of outcome research in behavior therapy" (p. 1).

In this chapter, we will describe assessment procedures useful to both clinicians and researchers, and some methods specific to each. First, we will discuss the conceptualization of anxiety, focusing primarily on the three response-system model, its advantages and problems. The specific procedures and instruments for assessing anxiety will be reviewed, with some attention to methods and special problems in assessment of anxiety in children. The chapter will conclude with strategies recommended for preliminary assessment and screening followed by an illustrative case study.

CONCEPTUALIZATIONS OF ANXIETY

The Anxiety Construct

The responses of a woman awakened by footsteps in her apartment might include trembling, sweaty palms, heart palpitations, a "knot in the stomach," a sense of terror, fear of impending injury, and fleeing out the back door. Provided with this description of the situation and the woman's responses, nearly all mental health professionals would label the woman's response of emotion as anxiety. Despite this common recognition of anxiety symptoms, definitions of anxiety are variable. The divergence in defining the term is a result of the fact that anxiety is a construct which is presumed to mediate certain sets of situations and responses (Lang, 1971). In other words, anxiety is an explanatory term which allows prediction from a variety of situations to a complex and variable set of reactions. Since the manner in which a construct is conceptualized will dictate the type of measures used for assessment, we will describe the anxiety construct in some detail. The following two sections will briefly review nonbehavioral views of anxiety and discuss the behavioral conceptualization of anxiety as a set of cognitive and physiological responses.

Nonbehavioral Views of Anxiety

Historically, anxiety has been described either in terms of the stimulus situation which occasions reports of anxiety, or as a trait or stable characteristic of personality. Freud used the word *Angst* to label the emotional experience of having food stuck in one's throat (Sarbin, 1964). Although the term "anxiety" was derived from this word, Freud never actually defined it. He did, however, differentiate "objective" anxiety from "neurotic" anxiety by the presence or absence, respectively, of an objectively threatening stimulus. Objective anxiety is the response to a realistic threat (e.g., a burglar, an oncoming car in the wrong lane), while neurotic anxiety is an irrational response to an internal conflict which has no basis in fact (e.g., fear of aggressive impulses).

An analogous distinction is often made between fear and anxiety, on the basis of whether the eliciting stimulus can be identified. Fear often is regarded as a response to an identifiable threat, such as height for an acrophobic or closed space for a claustrophobic. Anxiety, in contrast, can be viewed as a response, to a threat less easily pinpointed, such as when the social phobic encounters social situations. This distinction has not been useful for two reasons (Martin, 1971). First, there are no reliable differences between subjective feelings, physiological arousal, and motor behaviors that occur in response to vague and specific threats. Furthermore, an adequate assessment can (almost) always identify a specific threatening stimulus. Such stimuli are predominantly cognitive (e.g., thoughts of looking foolish, losing control), which explains why the anxiety can appear vague and diffused across a variety of situations. The concept of *anxiety* in the fear–anxiety distinction is also a fundamental component of trait theory. This nonsituational conceptualization of anxiety is exemplified by *basic anxiety*, Karen Horney's term for describing feelings of vulnerability and helplessness proposed to underlie all neuroses (Hall & Lindzey, 1970).

The Behavioral View: Anxiety as a Set of Cognitive and Physiological Responses

Anxiety, defined in terms of behavior, is a set of responses involving some combination of cognitive and physiological reactions. The responses are presumed to be elicited by some identifiable stimulus, which may include other cognitions and physiological responses as well as external stimuli and situations. The value of this definition is determined by the validity and utility of the resulting measurement. These issues will be discussed following an elaboration of what constitutes the response components.

The primary cognitive reaction is subjective distress. Such distress may take the form of vague feelings of terror or threat, or of impending catastrophe, as experienced in panic disorders or generalized anxiety disorder. Alternatively, subjective distress may involve highly specific thoughts and images. For example, snake phobics report images of being bitten during assessments requiring approach to a live snake (Wade, Malloy, & Proctor, 1977). Specific thoughts and images in nightmares may also be recalled by phobic individuals. Agoraphobic patients often report nightmares of having panic attacks in future situations they are unable to avoid.

The physiological consequences of anxiety are generally presumed to be associated with increased activation of the sympathetic pathways (SNS) of the autonomic nervous system (ANS), resulting either from direct central nervous system (CNS) stimulation or from CNS-mediated neuroendocrine activity.

For example, increased SNS activity produces cardiovascular changes (e.g., shunting of blood from extremities and visceral organs to major muscles; increased blood pressure and cardiac output due to increased cardiac contractility and stroke volume), and increased electrodermal activity, skeletal muscle tone, and respiration rate.

In addition to cognitive and physiological indices, measurements of anxiety responses typically include assessment of motor behavior, which is often termed a third response system. Changes in motoric responses are generally presumed to result from physiological arousal and fearful cognitions. Paul and Bernstein (1973) distinguish two types of motor responses: direct and indirect. Direct responses include the following (Martin & Sroufe, 1970): (1) restlessness, tics, trembling, gesturing, stuttering, and slips of the tongue occur more frequently; (2) short-term memory, perceptual discrimination ability, motor dexterity, reaction time, and learning and performance of complex tasks decrease. Fleeing from or avoidance of the anxiety eliciting stimulus are responses under voluntary control which constitute indirect motor responses. In this latter case, anxiety responses (cognitions and physiological arousal) act as discriminative stimuli or cues for further responses (e.g., escape or avoidance).

Problems and Advantages of the Response-System Conceptualization of Anxiety

Problems

A major problem for the response conceptualization is the nature of the interrelationships among the response systems. Since Lang and Lazovik's (1963) pioneering study which assessed all three response systems, investigators consistently find low, statistically nonsignificant correlations among the systems (Borkovec, Weerts, & Bernstein, 1977; Lombardo & Bellack, 1978). Rachman and Hodgson (1974) label this finding *discordance*. (A related phenomenon, termed response *system desynchrony,* is the uneven response of the systems to anxiety-reduction procedures.) Discordance is the basis for advocating measurement of all three systems in anxiety assessments (e.g., Paul & Bernstein, 1973), and is also the focus of criticism leveled at the response system conceptualization of anxiety (e.g., Hugdahl, 1981). A major type of evidence in support of the validity of a construct is the finding of significant correlations between measurements of different aspects of the construct. The behavioral anxiety construct is, therefore, not supported by discordance among response-system measurements. Although the utility of a construct is independent of its validity, a solution to the problem of discordance clearly would promote progress in the assessment and treatment of anxiety disorders.

There are three distinct interpretations of the discordance phenomenon. It is most commonly explained in terms of response system independence. Cognitive, motoric, and physiological responses are variously described as functionally independent or "co-parallel" effects of anxiety (Bandura, 1969), as a set of "loosely coupled components" (Rachman, 1978), or as "partially independent" (Hodgson & Rachman, 1974; Lang, 1971; Lang, Rice, & Sternbach, 1972). In general, these positions imply that although separate systems can be conditioned independently of each other, measurements of all three systems still reflect anxiety.

A second interpretation is that discordance may reflect problems in measurement. Although proponents of the response-system-independence hypothesis argue that measurement error is not the source of discordance (e.g., Lang, 1971; Lang *et al.,* 1972; Rachman, 1978), others suggest that acceptance of the independence hypothesis is premature (e.g., Bellack & Hersen, 1977a; Cone, 1979; Hugdahl, 1981).

There is a variety of evidence to suggest that measurement error at least contributes to discordance: First, poor agreement is often found among measurements of different aspects *within* the same system. More important, response measurements can be altered by varying the demand characteristics of the assessment. A study by Miller and Bernstein (1972) illustrates the effects of high versus low demand instructions upon response systems interrelationships. Claustrophobic subjects were told to remain in a small chamber and control their fear (high demand), or to remain until they would usually leave the situation if it happened in their daily life (low demand). Time in the chamber showed only modest correlation with heart rate and subjective distress (.42 and .56 respectively) under low demand, and near zero correlation under high demand instructions.

A third source of measurement variability may be due to the lack of consensus as to what aspects of cognition should be assessed. The typical "cognitive" assessment requires the subject to make a global evaluation of all three response systems for an answer. Such questions include "How anxious are you?" and "How uncomfortable are you?" They are rated on Likert-type scales. Questions specific to cognitive behavior, such as "Do you have self-critical thoughts?" are seldom asked. When such specific questions are employed, they are often combined with other questions requesting subjective evaluations of motor and physiological behavior. The resulting summary score of self-reported anxiety is often taken to represent cognitive anxiety.

A final argument, raised by Cone (1979), is that the methods used to compare response systems may be faulty and thus may contribute to low intercorrelations. Specifically, evaluations of interrelationships invariably vary both measurement methods (e.g., self-report, direct observation) and response modes (cognitive, physiological, and motoric behavior), thus confounding the two (Cone, 1979). For example, cognitions are typically assessed by self-report and motoric behavior by direct observations. Low intercorrelations, therefore, may be an artifact of using different measurement strategies rather than a reflection of actual relationships among response systems. It is clear, given the various potential sources of measurement error and associated methodological problems, that response system discordance should not be ascribed to system independence until further investigation into measurement issues is carried out.

A third interpretation of the discordance phenomenon is proposed by Schwartz (1978) in his psychobiological model of behavior. He suggests that response systems are interdependent, but that their dependence becomes evident only when response patterns are taken into account. Dependence cannot be made apparent from the customary method of summing across responses within systems. In Schwartz's (1978) model, cognitive and motor behavior are secondary to physiological arousal patterns, and their assessment is critical only insofar as they index the primary "psychobiological" response. Certain general conditions may be required for finding greater response system inter-correlations. For example, greater peripheral physiologic manifestations of anxiety will result in increased consistency between subjective experience and physiological responsivity. The finding that autonomic perception improves with greater ANS activity (Mandler, Mandler, & Uviller, 1958) indirectly supports this hypothesis. The most interesting aspect of the model is the hypothesis that some response patterns will yield greater concordance than others. Relevant evidence is limited to a study by Schwartz (1977). This analogue study found that subjects reported maximum anxiety only when they simultaneously generated high levels of both heart rate and frontalis-muscle activity.

Although Schwartz's model is intriguing and suggests alternative avenues for research it is clear that the discordance phenomenon is not well understood and requires much further study. It is also apparent that tacit acceptance of the response-system-independence hypothesis is unwise. Acceptance of this frequently voiced view could hinder searches for alternative explanations and alter the development of measurement technology. For example, the investigation of response patterns (versus simple individual response magnitudes) as determinants of overall response to an anxiety-provoking stimulus would be unlikely under the premise of response independence. It would be similarly unlikely that measures of specific systems would be developed in conjunction with measurements of other systems; the response-independence hypothesis discourages attempts at testing measurement validity with comparisons across response systems.

Advantages

Although certain important conceptual issues of the three-response-system model are unresolved, it has heuristic and pragmatic utility, particularly for tailoring treatments to individuals. The importance of individual differences in designing treatment strategies was first emphasized by Paul (1969) in his goal for outcome research: "What treatment, by whom, is most effective for this individual with that specific problem, under which set of circumstances and how does it come about?" (p. 44). The response-system model allows the categorization of individuals according to particular response patterns. Four patterns are of interest to clinicians: the occurrence of significant subjective/cognitive anxiety with either one or the other or both of the two response systems. Such patterns could be used to screen subjects in outcome studies in order to provide homogeneous samples. Screening to provide discrete subject groups categorized by response pattern would allow the study of response patterns in assessment or treatment research.

Unfortunately, outcome investigations have largely ignored such individual differences (Borkovec, 1976). One recent study of the efficacy of specific treatments for particular response patterns, however, highlights the potential utility of classification by response patterns (Öst, Jerremalm, & Johansson, 1981). Öst *et al.* treated two groups of clinically severe social phobics. Subjects were selected from a large pool of psychiatric outpatients for either extreme motoric responses (direct and indirect indices were used) or extreme physiological responses (heart rate) in an interpersonal test. Half of the subjects in each group received applied relaxation or social skills training. Relaxation was predicted to be differentially effective for physiologically responsive subjects, while social-skills training was expected to be better for motor responders. Results supported the predictions. Social-skills training resulted in greater improvement among motoric versus physiological responders on 6 of the 10 measures, while the opposite pattern was found with relaxation on three measures. These data suggest that treatment selected on the basis of an assessment of all three response systems may maximize therapeutic benefit.

Clearly, it will require further research to substantiate the utility of individual-difference analyses for treatment outcome. One major obstacle to this research is that the specificity of treatment is undocumented. For example, the notions that cognitive restructuring selectively affects cognitive responding, and that direct exposure techniques primarily alter motor behavior (Hugadhl, 1981), are based on intuition rather than empirical evidence. Contrary to these suppositions, a study by Odom, Nelson, and Wien (1978) found that cognitive restructuring reduced heart rate more effectively than systematic desensitization, and that guided participation was more effective than cognitive restructuring in changing self-reported anxiety. Guided participation was, however, most effective for motor responses (avoidance). These data suggest that the hypothesized specificity of various treatments may differ from their actual effects. In addition, treatment specificity may possibly vary with different anxiety disorders. In the following section we shall discuss specific anxiety-assessment methods and elucidate the difficulties encountered in attempts to reliably identify individual differences.

ANXIETY MEASUREMENT METHODS

Self-Report Measures

Behavior therapists are frequently criticized for placing too little emphasis on subject or patient self-reports. This criticism is clearly unfounded in the case of anxiety assessment. Self-report inventories and rating scales are among the most widely employed assessment strategies in this area. One reason for the ubiquity of these measures is the acknowledgment that subjective distress is central to anxiety. Spielberger (1972) states that, "in essence, if an individual reports that he feels anxious (frightened or apprehensive) this introspective report defines an anxiety state" (p. 30). Despite the importance of self-reports for anxiety assessments, collection of valid self-report data is fraught with difficulties. We will discuss these problems first, and then describe specific self-report measurement instruments and procedures.

Issues in Self-Report Assessment

Self-report information is provided by the "perceptual language system" described by Lang (1977a). This system may serve two functions. First, reports of motoric responses, physiological activity, and cognitions are elicited by questions such as Does your heart pound? Do your palms sweat? Do you have self-critical thoughts? How many times have you left or avoided going to a party due to interpersonal anxiety? The resulting data are objective in that, given adequate definition and with the exception of cognitions, they can be independently verified. The second function is the individual's subjective experience or evaluation of the three primary response components. Relevant questions here include: Do you feel anxious or tense? Do you fear attending parties? The answers to the second set of questions are not necessarily related to actual experience (i.e., the answers to the first set of questions). They are a function of a number of subjective factors, including expectations, values, and cognitive sets. Historically, the two types of self-report data have been confused. Most inventories have asked *subjective* questions in an attempt to secure *objective* data about behavior. While the lack of correspondence between such self-report data and actual behavior has been recognized, the onus has been incorrectly placed on the self-report response modality rather than on the specific assessment procedures that have been used.

There are several factors other than the source of data (i.e., written or verbal report by the subject) that could lead to a lack of correspondence between report and criterion. The form of questions asked is important. The wording of the test items is subject to interpretation by the testee (Cronbach, 1960). Terms such as anxious, afraid, and shy are all relative. The degree of distress sufficient to qualify as anxiety, as well as the response elements that are considered to be anxiety rather than anger or depression, will vary from subject to subject. The less specific and concrete the wording, the greater the probability of idiosyncratic translation of what the question is asking or what the response choices imply. The so-called "Barnum effect," the acceptance of broad, nondescript personality characterizations, reflects the latitude of interpretation possible (Dmitruk, Collins, & Clinger, 1973; Ulrich, Stachnik, & Stainton, 1963).

Verbal qualifications of degree or frequency (i.e., Likert-type scaling) are helpful in placing a restraint on responses, but still allow considerable margin for subjectivity. Simpson (1944), as reported by Cronbach (1960), found that 25% of students ascribed the term "usually" only to events occurring at least 90% of the time, 50% applied the term to events occurring between 70% and 90% of the time, and another 25% applied it to events occurring less than 70% of the time. Similar variability was found for other common frequency terms, including *often, sometimes, seldom,* and *rarely.*

Questions must be written with explicitly defined terms and with discrete objective (i.e., quantitative) response choices if accurate responses are to be secured. The following questions will all secure different information: Do you have panic attacks often? How often do you have panic attacks? How many panic attacks have you had in the past month?

Appropriate structuring of questions is a necessary, but not sufficient, condition for securing externally valid data. The information requested must be available to the subject. That is, the subject must have originally observed his behavior and be able to recall it accurately in response to the question. Whether or not either accurate observation or accurate recall occurs on a regular basis is conjectural. Observation, information storage, and recall are all subject to distortion. There is ample evidence to suggest that even ongoing self-monitoring yields unreliable and inaccurate data (Kazdin, 1974a; Lipinski & Nelson, 1974). Given that self-monitoring is typically presumed to provide more accurate information than recollection, the accuracy of self-report inventory responses must be suspect. In discussing accuracy of observation and recall, distinctions should be made among the kinds of information requested. Quantitative reports (especially of high frequency behaviors), such as reports of the number of people avoided each day or the amount of stuttering, are not likely to be highly accurate. Nonquantitative statements (e.g., "I panic whenever I see a dog running loose," or "I have nervous thoughts") and reports of low or zero frequency responses (e.g., "I have never had a date," or "I cry two or three times a week") are much more likely to be accurate.

Scale length is also important. Nine-point scales are more discriminating and reliable than 5- or 7-point scales (Horst, 1968). Teasdale, Walsh, Lancashire, and Mathews (1977) found significant pretest differences between the 0–8 phobia scale of Watson and Marks (1971) and a similar 1–5 point scale of Gelder and Marks (1966). They also found greater treatment effects on posttest with the longer scale. Also, Likert-type scales with an even number of points are generally inappropriate.

In our discussion thus far, we have emphasized *external validity*. Our focus has been on the relationship between self-reports and objective, external criteria. In that context, a self-report is valid or invalid based on the degree to which reports correspond with actual responses. When the target of assessment is the subjective experience of the subject, self-report responses are *ipso facto* valid (except in those instances where intentional distortion occurs). As Eble (1961) pointed out, all reliable tests are valid, since they are measures of themselves (i.e., the subject's response to test items). The test user must determine whether the test is valid for his criterion of interest. A subject reporting distress (e.g., anxiety, fear, depression, etc.) can be presumed to be *experiencing* distress regardless of his actual motoric, autonomic, and cognitive responses. It should be noted that while subjective responses involve cognitions, they are discrete from the cognitions associated with most target behaviors. Dollard and Miller (1950) argued that cognitions can be both responses to and stimuli for other cognitions. Self-critical, suicidal, and ruminative thoughts are just as subject to interpretation, evaluation, and affective reactions as are motoric and physiologic responses.

The *validity* of the subjective response must be distinguished from its *utility* (i.e., what the tester can do with the data). By attending to many of the same issues discussed above in relation to increasing validity, one can construct test items so as to increase utility. Generally, the more specific the questions (e.g., When and where do you feel depressed?), and the greater the extent of quantification (e.g., On a scale of 1–7, how fearful are you?), the more meaning and generality the response is likely to have.

Self-Report Methods

Self-Monitoring. Self-monitoring (Kazdin, 1974a) is the ongoing observation of one's own behavior. Clinical patients are often required to keep records, ranging from simple frequency counts to elaborate diaries, in which they detail their internal state and situational factors as well as target behaviors *per se*. Rates of avoidance or contact with specific anxiety-provoking stimuli or situations (e.g., frequency of dates, initiations in conversation with the opposite sex, panic attacks, use of elevator) are the primary targets for self-monitoring.

A major problem in the application of self-monitoring to research is that it has *reactive* effects; behavior changes as a function of self-observation (Kazdin, 1974a; Nelson, Lipinski, & Black, 1975). Such reactivity is an undesired consequence when monitoring is used for data collection, as the naturally occurring rate of the response is altered. The direction of the change is determined to a great extent by the valence of the behavior or its expected consequences (Kazdin, 1974b; Lipinski, Black, Nelson, & Ciminero, 1975). Unde-

*pre or past monitoring
weaker effects of reactivity
more reactivity when doing pre-monitoring*

sired behavior or behavior discriminative for punishment decreases, while desired behavior or behavior discriminative for positive reinforcement will increase.

Although reactivity has not been documented for self-monitoring aspects of anxiety disorders, it is plausible that certain behaviors, such as avoidance, could be affected. Research examples of self-monitoring of anxiety are limited. Lombardo and Turner (1979) instructed a patient to record both the frequency and duration of anxiety-eliciting obsessive ruminations. Thought-stopping treatment produced a marked effect which was independent of self-monitoring. Previous studies on thought-stopping confounded self-monitoring with treatment, and, thus, were unable to isolate treatment effects from monitoring reactivity. Twentyman and McFall (1975) collected self-monitored data on heterosocial interactions of shy males. The frequency and duration of interactions increased with treatment and corroborated several other measures obtained in a contrived laboratory situation. We strongly recommend the expanded use of self-monitoring as an adjunct to more standardized measures, particularly when discrete, low-frequency events are involved.

Anxiety Scales and Inventories. Anxiety scales and inventories constitute the second method of obtaining self-report data. These measures can be placed in one of three major categories, reflecting different aspects of, or types of anxiety: (1) measures of trait anxiety; (2) measures of state anxiety; or (3) measures of situation-specific anxiety (e.g., test anxiety, speech anxiety). *Trait anxiety* refers to a general and stable disposition to become anxious (Spielberger, 1972). Individuals with high trait anxiety are presumed to become anxious easily and intensely to a wide range of stimuli. Trait anxiety inventories such as the Manifest Anxiety scale (Taylor, 1953) and State-Trait Anxiety Inventory, Trait form (Spielberger, Gorsuch, & Lushene, 1970) ask subjects how they typically feel and/or how they typically respond in a variety of situations. Degree of anxiety is reflected by an overall score. The characteristic validity studies have examined correlations between trait anxiety scales (which are generally high), and compared susceptibility to stress of individuals scoring high and low. The latter form of study has involved evaluation of performance on motor and cognitive tasks (high stress should interfere with performance), and self-report of distress under laboratory stress and nonstress conditions (e.g., "ego-involving" instructions, threat of electric shock). Summarizing research on trait anxiety instruments, Sarason (1960) and Spielberger (1972) draw two similar conclusions: (1) These instruments essentially measure fear of failure and concern about one's adequacy; and (2) even for individuals with high "trait anxiety," the arousal of anxiety is primarily a function of the particular stressor or situation.

Endler and his associates (Endler & Okada, 1975; Endler, Hunt, & Rosenstein, 1962) have responded to the situational specificity of anxiety responses by developing a multidimensional test of trait anxiety—the S–R

Inventory of General Trait Anxiousness. The S–R Inventory assesses anxiety in four general types of situations: (1) interpersonal; (2) physical danger; (3) ambiguous or novel situations; and (4) routine, innocuous situations. Each situation is rated on the degree to which it is typically accompanied by each of nine response modalities (e.g., perspire, feel tense). While adequate validation has not yet been accomplished, this format appears more promising than the general, unidimensional-scale approach.

State anxiety is conceptualized as a transitory anxiety response which is situationally determined and can vary from moment to moment (Endler & Okada, 1975; Spielberger, 1972). While highly trait-anxious individuals are expected to have a low threshold for state anxiety, assessment of the two forms of anxiety is independent. Numerous state anxiety scales have been developed. The State-Trait Anxiety Inventory, State form (Spielberger, Gorsuch, & Lushene, 1970) and the Affect Adjective Check List, Today form (Zuckerman, 1960) parallel the associated trait scales, but ask subjects how they feel right at the moment or how they felt at some immediately preceding point, rather than how they generally feel. The Affect Adjective Checklist requires subjects to check 21 adjectives to indicate subjective experiences. A total anxiety score is the sum of the 11 "anxiety positive" adjectives checked and the 12 "anxiety negative" adjectives not checked. The Anxiety Differential (Husek & Alexander, 1963) employs bipolar scales of adjectives in a semantic differential format (Osgood, Suci, & Tannenbaum, 1957). Walk's (1956) Fear Thermometer (FT) simply requires checking a single 10-point Likert-type scale to indicate degree of fear. Walk (1956) correlated FT scores of parachute jump trainees and found they related to achieving correct jumping techniques earlier in training and to success in passing the course. There is no evidence that lengthier questionnaires have any advantage over the simpler FT or its variants (many studies use a 9-point version).

The various measures characteristically correlate highly with one another, and scores are generally higher during (externally defined) stress situations than during neutral situations. The possibility of bias due to expectancy and demand characteristics in this type of validation study tempers conclusions that can be drawn. However, the psychometric adequacy of these devices suggests that when bias is controlled or unlikely (as in clinical application), they should provide satisfactory data.

The third general approach to anxiety assessment has been the development of situation-specific devices. Examples include the Test Anxiety Questionnaire (Mandler & Sarason, 1952) for examination anxiety, and the Fear of Negative Evaluation Scale and Social Avoidance and Distress Scale (Watson & Friend, 1969) for interpersonal anxiety. Hersen and Bellack (1976) reviewed the profusion of self-report scales that have been constructed to assess interpersonal anxiety. They reported that most of these devices are correlated with one another and are negatively correlated with self-reports of dating frequency (e.g., social activity). These scales also reflect anxiety reduction after the application of a variety of behavioral treatments, including systematic desensitization and training in social skills. However, they do not consistently correlate with either physiological arousal in role-played interpersonal interactions or with any of a variety of behavioral components of interpersonal skill. Hersen and Bellack (1976) also reported that most of these scales were constructed for particular studies on the basis of face validity. Insufficient attention has been paid to psychometric considerations, and reliabilities are often inadequate.

Fear Survey Schedules (FSS), inventories of numerous specific fears (e.g., dogs, blood, crowds) rated for severity on Likert-type scales, can also be considered situation-specific measures. The FSS-I (Lang & Lazovik, 1963) was developed along the lines suggested by Akutagawa (1956), and included a list of 50 common fears that were presented in a seven-point Likert-scale format. Shortly after the publication of this scale, the FSS-II (Geer, 1965) and the FSS-III (Wolpe & Lang, 1964) were constructed. Even though many items in these two scales are similar, a primary difference between the two schedules is that the FSS-II is an empirically derived instrument while the FSS-III has its origin in the clinic.

In addition, many other fear survey schedules have been developed either by extending existing schedules (e.g., Gulas, McClanahan, & Poetter, 1975; Manosevitz & Lanyon, 1965), from factor analyses of an unpublished schedule by Lang (e.g., Lawlis, 1971; Rubin, Lawlis, Tasto, & Namenek, 1969), or by compiling previous schedules and omitting identical items (e.g., Braun & Reynolds, 1969). For a comprehensive review of various forms and research concerned with fear survey schedules, see Hersen (1973).

It is generally more appropriate to use inventories such as the FSS for idiographic, rather than nomothetic purposes. Summative, overall scores are statistical abstractions that presumably represent general trends and tendencies. Regardless of the terminology selected, the use of an overall score to predict or summarize behavior is a trait conception. The use of train-descriptive scores should not be expected to predict (relate to) specific response patterns in specific situations. Examination of responses to individual questions or clusters of responses are likely to be much more useful than overall fearfulness scores.

Most of the assessment measures thus far described utilize items requiring either evaluation of feeling states or of some combination of physiological sensation, motor behavior, and cognition. Although physiology and motor behavior can be independently verified, self-report is the only method for assessing cognitions. A technology for measuring cognition is sorely lacking. This is a particular shortcoming of studies evaluating therapies derived from Albert Ellis' Rational Emotive Therapy (e.g., Beck, 1976; Goldfried, Decenteceo, & Weinberg, 1974; Meichenbaum, 1977).

The importance of negative cognitions to behavioral disruption, and perhaps also to treatment, may be related to the complexity of the behavior involved. Cognitions may be less critical in specific phobias (which require simple behavior such as riding an elevator) than social phobias (e.g., fear of public speaking) and test anxiety, where actual cognitive *content* is more likely to disrupt behavior. Availability of a suitable assessment device for cognitions would promote understanding of these latter disorders, and would likely be of heuristic value.

An attempt to assess cognitions in test anxiety was recently reported by Galassi and his colleagues (Galassi, Frierson, & Sharer, 1981a, 1981b). They constructed a checklist of positive and negative thoughts for assessing "internal dialogue." Subjects check off statements (e.g., "I feel in control of my reactions on this test," "I hope other students won't notice how nervous I am") from a list if they occur as cognitions during a test. Galassi *et al.* (1981a) reported that highly test-anxious subjects (as defined by self-report) checked a significantly higher proportion of negative statements than low-anxious subjects during a college history test. Although there was no frequency or duration measure, it is logical to assume that any evaluative cognition is incompatible with the requisite on-task behavior and would have a negative effect on performance. A second assessment method is simply to have a subject monitor and record cognitions. For example, Klinger (1978) suggested the use of a portable beeper set at variable intervals to cue recording of cognitions in the natural environment. Clearly, the assessment of cognitive behavior deserves further research, and some limited technology is already available for study.

Motoric Behavior Assessment

The hallmark of behavioral assessment is the direct observation of overt behavior as it occurs in the natural environment. Resulting data are presumed to provide the most valid samples of an individual's typical behavior. However, due primarily to the low frequency of occurrence of most target behaviors, it is often extremely inconvenient, expensive, and time-consuming to collect naturalistic observations. In addition, the situational context for behavioral observation is rarely under the experimenter's control, and the inability to standardize conditions prevents making valid comparisons across subjects. Reactivity effects of the presence of an observer can also bias data (e.g., Cone, 1977; Kent, Diament, Dietz, & O'Leary, 1974). Although these problems are somewhat less critical to the clinician, they have forced researchers to devise methods for observing behavior in the laboratory under more tightly controlled conditions.

Contrived laboratory situations for assessing anxiety are based on the continuity assumption; that is, that a sample of behavior obtained under these conditions is representative of behavior in analogous situations in the natural environment. Laboratory analogue assessments involve the presentation of a phobic stimulus (e.g., snake, elevator, ladder to climb on, route to drive) in the case of agoraphobia and specific phobias, or requesting the subject to interact with confederates in the case of social phobias (e.g., dating, assertiveness, and speech anxiety). In the former case, the general focus is upon indirect measures of motor behavior and includes measuring escape or avoidance on a dimension of distance or time. Assessments of the latter disorders typically use direct measures.

Direct Measures of Motoric Anxiety

Paul (1969) pioneered the systematic measurement of direct effects of anxiety on motor behavior. In his study, speech-anxious students delivered a 4-min extemporaneous speech to two research confederates who rated anxiety on the Timed Behavioral Checklist (TBCL). The TBCL lists 20 behaviors reflecting both direct physiological effects (e.g., trembling, perspiration, pacing) and performance disruption (e.g., stuttering) which are rated for occurrence or nonoccurrence during successive 30-sec intervals of the speech. The sum of all occurrences across both behaviors and intervals yields a single motoric anxiety score. Paul reported high interrater reliabilities for the TBCL ($r = .95$), and modest but significant test–retest reliability ($r = .37$). The TBCL and its variants have been used in numerous studies of speech anxiety (e.g., Goldfried & Trier, 1974; Lombardo & Bellack, 1978; Lombardo, Zamosky, Romano, Volkin, & Bellack, 1978), for assessing social anxiety (e.g., Borkovec, Stone, O'Brien, & Kaloupek, 1974), and for evaluating snake and insect phobias (e.g., Bernstein & Nietzel, 1974; Fazio, 1972). Lombardo *et al.* (1978) used a more global measure of performance disruption in addition to the TBCL. College speech instructors rated speech content and delivery both before and after speech-anxious subjects received treatment.

A second direct measure of anxiety is Mahl's (1956) speech-dysfluency ratio, which is the proportion of non-"ah" dysfluencies (e.g., stammers, speech blocks, omissions, repetitions) among total words spoken in a speech or conversation. Mahl (1956) reported that dysfluency ratios and silence time differed significantly between high and low anxious interview segments. A related measure, speech rate, is often used to assess public speaking anxiety. However, outcome studies do not generally find significant change in speech rate following treatment. This may be due to the complex relationship between speech rate and anxiety. In this review of anxiety and speech parameters, Murray (1971) concluded that an inverted U-curve described the relationship between stress and speech rate.

Other measures of performance disruption have been devised for specific problems, such as interpersonal anxiety experienced in dating, or in responding assertively. Interpersonal anxiety is evaluated by rating the subject's performance during role-play tests. There are numerous variations but the basic strategy remains fairly constant. An interpersonal scenario is described to the subject, after which a research confederate recites a prompt line as if he or she were interacting with the subject in the scenario. The subject then responds, role playing the scene with the confederate. In some versions, the interaction ceases after the subject responds, and another scenario is presented. Other versions extend the interaction by having the confederate make two or three successive responses. Scene descriptions and prompt lines have been delivered by live experimenters, by videotape, and by audiotape in different studies. For example, Twentyman and McFall (1975) used audiotaped scenes to evaluate dating anxiety. Subjects' responses were rated for overall anxiety, adequacy, speech dysfluencies, and response latency.

Various procedures in role-play tests appear to yield different anxiety levels. For example, Galassi and Galassi (1976) found substantial differences between brief and extended interactions. They also reported that interactions with live role models were more anxiety-provoking than interactions with taped models. Our own experience suggests that the use of both audiotaped and videotaped models produces anomalous and relatively useless data.

The utility and validity of data from role-play tests is also questionable. Primary support for validity comes from studies in which "known groups" have been differentiated by their performance on role-play tests. For example, low-frequency daters have been rated as less heterosocially skillful and more anxious than high frequency daters (Arkowitz, Lichtenstein, McGovern, & Hines, 1975; Borkovec *et al.,* 1974). However, in a systematic series of criterion-validity studies examining dating skills in college students and assertiveness in psychiatric patients, Bellack and his colleagues (Bellack, Hersen, & Lamparski, 1979; Bellack, Hersen, & Turner, 1979a,b) found few significant correlations for ratings of specific behaviors and overall skills between role play and less obstrusive assessments. Those correlations which were significant were generally of modest magnitude. Assertiveness research in another laboratory corroborated these results (Christoff & Edelstein, 1981). These consistently limited relationships reported across different behaviors (assertiveness and dating skill) and populations (college students and psychiatric patients) limit any claim about utility and validity of role-play strategy.

An alternative to brief role-play tests is the use of more extended and less standardized interactions which present closer parallels to situations encountered in the natural environment. For example, Bellack, Hersen, and Lamparski (1979) unobtrusively observed college students interacting with a "stranger" of the opposite sex while waiting for an experiment. The stranger was actually an experimental confederate trained to respond in a standardized manner. Arkowitz *et al.* (1975) used two different types of interactions to assess heterosocial skill. In one task, male subjects were instructed to interact with a trained female confederate for 10 min, behaving "as if" they had just met. The second task was a simulated telephone call in which the subject was to arrange a date with a confederate.

In addition to variations in content, extended interactions vary along several other dimensions. Durations range from 3 to 10 min. Confederates respond in a warm or neutral manner, respond after silences ranging from 5 to 60 sec, and make only a limited set of specific responses or behave more spontaneously. The effects of these variations are unknown and warrant empirical evaluation. Wessberg, Marriotto, Conger, Farrell, and Conger (1979) reported subjects perform better in an "as if" context, and regard surreptitious interactions as more representative of their typical behavior. As with role-play tests, further research is needed to evaluate the external validity of both types of extended-interaction strategies. For a more complete treatment of issues regarding the validity of role play and other laboratory interaction tests, see Bellack (1979).

Indirect Measures of Motoric Anxiety

Escape and avoidance of feared situations or objects provide an additional index of anxiety magnitude. Since avoidance invariably accompanies anxiety disorders and is often more disruptive to the individual than the anxiety itself, it is strongly recommended as an adjunctive measure (Barlow & Wolfe, 1981; Hugdahl, 1981). The assessment of avoidance in cases of social anxiety is limited to self report, due to the lack of adaptability to laboratory measurement. Specific phobias and agoraphobia do not pose this problem.

Behavioral Avoidance Tests. The predominant strategy for measuring avoidance of phobic objects is the behavioral avoidance test (BAT). Lang and Lazovik (1963) pioneered the systematic use of the BAT. Snake phobics were instructed to approach, open the cage, touch, and hold a live snake. The measure of anxiety was the final distance in feet from the snake or degree of handling. Numerous studies based on this prototype appear in the literature and include other phobic objects such as cats (Whitehead, Robinson, Blackwell, & Stutz, 1978), dogs (McDonald, 1975; Kroll, 1975), and spiders (Taylor, 1977; Whitehead *et al.,* 1978). One variation of the procedure is to move the object toward the subject while seated. Levis' (1969) Phobic Test Apparatus (PTA) moves the object closer, via conveyor belt, by a fixed distance each time the subject pushes a button. Data from the PTA and standard BATs are highly correlated (Borkovec & Craighead, 1971). The PTA, however, permits simultaneous physiological measurements which generally require minimal movement of the subject. The PTA also simplifies automated recording of an additional measure of avoidance: response latency (Levis, 1969). Latency measures combined with distance correlate more highly with self-report measures than distance alone (Mac & Fazio, 1972).

The BAT procedure has been extrapolated to measure avoidance of heights and enclosed spaces and agoraphobia. Lazarus (1961) and Ritter (1970) measured distance climbed on ladders by acrophobics while duration of endurance in an elevator (Nesbitt, 1973), closet (Leitenberg, Agras, Edwards, Thomson, & Wincze, 1970), or darkened sensory-deprivation chamber (Leitenberg, Agras, Butz, & Wincze, 1971) can be used to evaluate avoidance in claustrophobics. Emmelkamp and his associates evaluate agoraphobic avoidance by measuring the time patients could spend outside their home or the hospital before becoming uncomfortable or tense (Emmelkamp & Emmelkamp-Benner, 1975; Emmelkamp & Wessels, 1975; Emmelkamp, Kuipers, & Eggeraat, 1978).

Problems of Behavioral Avoidance Tests. Despite the extremely widespread use of the BAT and its variants, two major problems limit the validity of the resulting data: susceptibility to demand characteristics and limited generalizability to *in vivo* behavior. Demand characteristics are aspects of the assessment situation which affect the subject's behavior but are irrelevant to the task. For example, social cues provide implicit demand for increased approach following treatment. Numerous studies demonstrate instruction manipulations for high and low demand (e.g., "Go as far as you feel comfortable"; "It is important you go as far as you possibly can") significantly affect approach behavior both in subclinical analogue populations (e.g., Bernstein, 1973; Bernstein & Nietzel, 1974; Kazdin, 1973) and in clinically phobic subjects (Miller & Bernstein, 1972). Borkovec (1973a,b) recommends the routine use of high demand instructions to minimize pre- and posttest demand effects.

The extent to which BAT results can be generalized to *in vivo* behavior is questionable, both on theoretical and empirical grounds. The fact that much behavior appears to be situationally specific is used by behavioral researchers to argue against traditional trait theories of behavior. However, the same phenomenon applies to behavioral assessment and suggests that the limited stimulus content of assessments may restrict generalizability (Kazdin, 1979; Lombardo & Bellack, 1978). Lick and Unger (1979) altered a single characteristic of a BAT for two clinically phobic subjects and obtained markedly different results. Both subjects were able to complete standard BATs (i.e., touch or handle a spider or snake) following treatment. However, when the animals were placed on the floor in a corner of the room, instead of in cages, the mere sight of them at a 30-foot distance elicited screaming, trembling, and pulse rates 20 beats per minute greater than when the subjects were touching the caged animals. Replication of behavior in each condition supported the finding. A subsequent study suggested that the salient situational differences may have been the unpredictability of the animal's behavior when uncaged (Lick, Condiotte, & Unger, 1978). Elucidation and incorporation of other stimulus factors which may affect BAT data are crucial for devising tests which generate behavior generalizable to the natural environment.

Physiological Assessment

Arousal of the sympathetic division of the autonomic nervous system plays a dominant role in most theories of emotion (Cannon, 1915; James, 1884;

Schachter, 1964; Schwartz, 1978) and is widely accepted as a central component of anxiety. For this reason, measurement of physiological arousal is viewed as an integral part of anxiety assessment (Barlow & Wolfe, 1981).

The various physiological responses correspond to the individual's somatic complaints during high levels of anxiety. Thus, increased muscle tone is often manifested as headaches; peripheral vasoconstriction results in cold hands; reduced gastrointestinal activity leads to constipation and dry mouth; increased sweat-gland and epidermal-membrane activity cause sweaty, "clammy" palms; and increased cardiac output and rate are perceived as a "pounding heart." Self-reports of physiological perceptions (e.g., Autonomic Perception Questionnaire; Mandler, 1972) show a variety of relationships to physiology ranging from weak (Mandler, 1972) and variable (Edelberg, 1972) to occasionally consistent (Malmo & Shagass, 1949) relationships.

Advantages of Physiological Measures

Both self-report and indirect motoric responses are under the voluntary control of the individual and therefore are easily influenced by the individual. In contrast, physiological measures are relatively free from subject bias due to the involuntary nature of the responses. For example, Andrasik, Turner, and Ollendick (1980) monitored heart rate and self-reported anxiety during flooding treatment and used heart rate as the criterion for terminating the session. Termination based on self-report would have reduced session length by aproximately 75%. Effective flooding treatment theoretically requires a reduction in anxiety following elicitation of elevated anxiety levels (Levis & Hare, 1977). Heart rate (HR), as an unbiased measure, may be a more valid and useful gauge of anxiety than self-report. Whether treatment based on HR versus self-report is more effective remains to be investigated, however (Andrasik *et al.*, 1980).

In addition to freedom from bias, physiological recordings can be completely reliable, since they are measured by objective methods. Also, with appropriate equipment, responses can be obtained on-line in hard copy form, ready for graphic presentation or analysis.

Disadvantages and Problems of Physiological Measurement

The need for expertise in psychophysiology and for equipment is a distinct disadvantage of physiological measurement. Most physiological transducers for responses provide extremely weak electronic potentials which must be filtered and highly amplified before they can be displayed. Electronic measures of HR, blood pressure, vasoconstriction, and electrodermal and electromyographic activity require cumbersome, expensive apparatus. Also, the high gain of such equipment requires that the subject remain immobile and quiescent in order to prevent artifactual responses. The generally means that simultaneous motoric and physiological measures are difficult to obtain. Furthermore, most measures must be obtained in the laboratory, thus precluding *in vivo* assessments. However, some responses can be measured without elaborate equipment and can be monitored by the experimenter or subject in the natural environment. For example, Paul (1966) and Borkovec (1973a,b) obtained HR from the radial artery pulse of speech-anxiety and snake-phobic subjects during laboratory assessments. Measurements obtained under naturalistic conditions have been reported for HR (Bell & Schwartz, 1975; Lombardo & Bellack, 1978) and auscultatory blood pressure (Lombardo & Bellack, 1978).

Despite the widely held view that physiological response measurements, being direct, are therefore an unbiased index of anxiety, these measures suffer from many of the same problems as self-report and motoric measures. Stimulus specificity affects physiology as well as motor and self-report behavior (Lick & Unger, 1975), limiting generalizability beyond assessment situations. Also, physiological measures are susceptible to demand characteristics, although possibly less so than other response modes. Smith, Diener, and Beaman (1974) reported no differences in HR among three groups of rat-phobic subjects in a BAT when given varying instructional demands. In contrast, Borkovec (1973) found that a subset of subjects with more accurate autonomic perception had significant reductions in HR between two BATs with intervening suggestions for improvement. Blom and Craighead (1974) studied demand effects in speech-anxious subjects. The public-speaking assessment setting was presented as either a speech laboratory or an anxiety clinic, and instructions labeled the assessment as either a fear-assessment or relaxation-simulation study. The manipulations affected self-report and motor behavior but not HR or electrodermal responses.

Uses of Physiological Measures

Physiological measurement can be useful at several points in assessment and therapy. Therapeutic strategy, for example, may be selected by physiological responsiveness in initial assessments. Successful outcome in extinction-based therapies, such as desensitization and flooding, may be predicted by initial physiological arousal to imaginal presentation of the anxiety-provoking stimulus. Lang, Melamed, and Hart (1974) found the effectiveness of systematic desensitization for phobics varied with physiological reactivity to fear imagery. Heart rate responses predicted the magnitude of fear reduction. Fear imagery instructions appear to be critical determinants of physiological reactions according to Lang (1977b), who maintains that fear imagery consists of both stimulus propositions (i.e., descriptions of the anxiety-provoking stimulus and situation) and response propositions (i.e., descriptions of the individual's perceptions of motor and physiological responses). Lang also found that presentation of anxiety-stimulus propositions and filler material elicited no greater HR than neutral scenes, whereas instructions to imagine both the stimulus and the response elicited significantly increased HR and skin conductance. These findings suggest that an adequate test of physiological responsiveness should include both types of stimulus imagery. Absence of a significant response might recommend coping/modeling therapy for optimum clinical effectiveness (Lang, 1977b). For research, measuring responsivity may be useful to screen or stratify subjects on an individual-difference factor.

Physiological measures may be useful during treatments directed toward reducing physiological arousal. Lang *et al.* (1974) found HR habituation during treatment predicted motoric performance in a BAT. As previously mentioned in the case of flooding, when knowledge of within-session arousal is important, physiological measures may be used to define treatment parameters, such as session length (Andrasik *et al.*, 1980). Finally, physiological responsivity can be used as a measure of treatment outcome and should be routine in research, particularly since some authors suggest that maximum therapeutic gain is realized only with changes in all three response systems (Borkovec, 1973a,b; Hodgson & Rachman, 1974).

Selection of the Response

As noted in the beginning of this section, there are several physiological responses affected by autonomic arousal. As Borkovec *et al.* (1976) point out, it would be ideal if measurement of a single response could index the other responses. Unfortunately, discordance among measures within the physiological response system is as prevalent as discordance among measures of the three response systems. For example, Lombardo and Bellack (1978) correlated HR, frequency of skin-resistance responses (SRR), and systolic and diastolic blood pressure as measured just prior to subjects' delivery of speeches in a laboratory and in a public-speaking course. None of the six correlations computed for each situation was statistically significant. Engel (1972) and Lacey, Bateman, and VanLehn (1953) identified two phenomena that account for this disparity among responses. *Response stereotype* is an idiosyncratic pattern of responding to numerous environmental stimuli. Within this idiosyncratic pattern there is a tendency for one particular system to respond maximally to a specific stimulus; this is termed *response specificity*. Although these two patterns do not occur in all individuals (Engel, 1972), they are present frequently enough to limit general statements across subjects based on one response measure.

One method of dealing with response specificity and stereotype is to measure several physiological responses. Measurements of different responses may either be combined in a summary score for each individual, or systems showing maximal response may be used. Autonomic lability scores, the standardized residuals of the arousal response measures regressed on prestimulus measurements, may be used to combine cross-system data (Lacey, 1956). The utility of this statistical equating procedure is undetermined for anxiety measurement, because its use has not been reported in the clinical literature.

An additional problem for selecting a physiological response is that the presentation of anxiety-eliciting stimuli does not always alter response systems in a direction consistent with sympathetic arousal. For example, excessive parasympathetic activation may increase intestinal activity, producing the diarrhea familiar to some, and reduce cardiac output causing syncope. Syncope appears to be particularly associated with fears of blood, illness, and injury (Cohn, Kron, & Brady, 1976; Connolly, Hallam, & Marks, 1976; Yule & Fernando, 1980).

The most common physiological responses selected for measurement are HR and electrodermal responses. Typically, only one response is assessed. HR is by far the most frequently used, primarily for technical reasons. Direct bioelectric HR recordings are relatively simple and insensitive to artifact, due to the relatively large electric potential of heart muscle. As mentioned above, indirect HR measures (e.g., pulse rate) are reliable and require no more instrumentation than a watch. Additionally, continuous *in vivo* HR measurements are feasible with a Holter Recorder, used to obtain portable electrocardiograms in cardiac patients. For example, Barlow, Mavissakalian, and Schofield (1980) measured HR continuously with a Holter Recorder while agoraphobics walked or drove a standardized course. We have assessed clinical patients less expensively using the Exersentry Heart Rate Monitor (Respironics, Inc., Monroeville, Pennsylvania) which, unlike the Holter Recorder, is free of artifact when the unit's output is read directly into digital logic equipment. A stereo tape minirecorder used with the Exersentry can provide continuously recorded heartbeat pulses on one channel and simultaneous self-reports of anxiety level and situational parameters on the second channel. Sacrificing time for equipment costs, the recorded pulses can be counted to obtain HR using a stop watch.

The reason for describing physiological recording technology is that we wish to emphasize the desirability of continuous *in vivo* measurement. Technical obstacles often dictate that physiological measurements are made just prior to rather than during exposure to the anxiety provoking stimulus. The underlying assumption, that anxiety in anticipation of the situation is representative of anxiety during exposure, has no empirical support. Consequently, anticipatory and concurrent anxiety measurements may differ widely and possibly represent two independent types of "anxieties" (Hugdahl, 1981).

There are data indicating a substantial difference in magnitude between anticipatory and concurrent HR measurements. Anticipatory HR in speech-anxious subjects seldom exceeds 95 beats per minute (bpm). For example, the mean for Paul's (1966) subjects prior to treatment was 89 bpm. Continuous recording during speeches delivered in naturalistic settings by 23 subjects not selected for speech anxiety revealed HR peaks ranging from 125–180 bpm (mean = 151) (Taggert, Carruthers, & Somerville, 1973). In this study, the anticipatory HR of one typical subject was 85 bpm. HR peaked early in his speech at 165 bpm, and was 125 bpm 20 min into the speech. Continuous *in vivo* recordings also can reveal patterns of responses during exposure. Linking peak responses to particular stimuli encountered during the course of exposure might assist in treatment and target selection.

Certain other problems may arise, depending on the form of physiological data chosen. HR data (and certain other physiological response data) are typically analyzed and reported in one of two forms: either as absolute scores (i.e., HR during anticipatory or exposure periods), or as the difference between resting baseline HR and anticipatory or exposure HR. Difference scores are used in order to reduce variability due to subjects' different resting HRs. Obtaining accurate resting baselines, then, is important to ensure against introducing additional unwarranted variability. Guidelines for baseline measurements include allowing sufficient time for adaptation to take place and providing subjects with a rationale for the adaptation period and with information on subsequent procedures for the session (Meyers & Craighead, 1978). In an earlier study, Craighead (1973) reported that resting rates for college student subjects following 10 min of adaptation without information was 85 bpm. The average resting HR for this population is usually below 70 bpm. Often in research, expedience takes precedence over precision, and "resting" baselines are taken only a matter of minutes before anticipatory anxiety measurement and exposure to the anxiety-producing situation. In these cases, values representing resting rates are actually more temporally distant anticipatory rates (Lombardo & Bellack, 1978; Marchetti, McGlynn, & Patterson, 1977).

This phenomenon is illustrated in a study we recently conducted (Lombardo & Bellack, 1978). Testing HR of speech-anxious and nonanxious subjects was recorded on two occasions: (a) shortly prior to giving subjects their speech topics in the customary manner for speech anxiety tests, and (b) in an additional assessment conducted on a nonspeech day solely to obtain baseline measurements. Resting HR during speech assessments were significantly greater than on nonspeech days. This was also the case for additional physiological responses, including systolic and diastolic blood-pressure and skin-resistance response frequency (SRR). Accurate resting physiological baselines clearly require more careful measurement than is typically reported.

Although baseline measurements are critical for precise differences scores, the difference scores themselves may not be useful, at least in analogue assessment situations. The primary purpose of the study above (Lombardo & Bellack, 1978) was to evaluate the external validity of laboratory analogue assessments of public speaking anxiety. Anxiety was assessed for two speeches delivered by subjects enrolled in public-speaking courses. One speech was evaluated in the public speaking classroom and one speech was assessed in the customary laboratory analogue situation. Correlations on physiological data between the two settings included both absolute scores and difference scores based on resting baselines obtained on nonspeech days in each setting. None of the resulting difference scores were significantly correlated across situations.

Significant correlations were obtained, however, for absolute scores of three of the four physiological responses (systolic and diastolic blood pressure and skin-resistance response frequency were significant, HR was not). Although these results may have limited generalizability, they do suggest the need for caution in interpreting difference score data.

It is noteworthy that in the Lombardo and Bellack (1978) study, HR was the only response which did not demonstrate external validity, although HR is commonly the only physiological response measured in anxiety assessments. A modest but significant correlation ($r = .56$) was obtained for skin-resistance response frequency (SRR), suggesting this measure may be more useful than HR. Katkin and his associates (Katkin, 1965; 1966; 1975; Katkin & Deitz, 1973; Lick & Katkin, 1976; Rappaport & Katkin, 1972) recommend the use of SRR (or its reciprocal, skin conductance response frequency) as an anxiety measure for two reasons. First, spontaneous or nonspecific SRRs have been reliably demonstrated to occur in response to stress or threat (Katkin, 1965; 1966; 1975; Rappaport & Katkin, 1972). Second, SRR rapidly returns to baseline rates upon offset of the threatening stimulus. Lick and Katkin (1976) point out that while the more commonly used electrodermal measure of skin resistance level shares the first feature, it does not return to baseline when the stimulus is removed. In addition much less technical expertise is needed to obtain SRR than resistance level.

One major problem with electrodermal responses is that they tend to habituate much more rapidly than other physiological responses (Lomont & Edmonds, 1967; Leitenberg, Agras, & Barlow, 1969). This is particularly critical for repeated assessments, such as in single-case designs. In these cases, a floor effect may appear before treatment effects are evident, thus obscuring results.

Measuring multiple physiological responses may circumvent several of the difficulties outlined above. Instead of combining data from different systems via methods such as autonomic lability scores, however, we concur with Schwartz (1978) and recommend examining the results response pattern. High HR alone may not be a useful index of anxiety. Leitenberg et al. (1971) found clear improvement in motoric avoidance accompanied by both increases and decreases in HR (as well as no change) for various phobic subjects. A particular pattern of HR, electrodermal and electromyographic responses might, however, be more highly associated with measurements in other response systems.

ANXIETY ASSESSMENT IN CHILDREN

The technology for behavioral assessment of anxiety in children has clearly lagged behind that for adult assessment. However, many of the anxiety measures for adults can be used to evaluate anxiety in children. Depending upon the age of the child, modification of adult procedures may prove necessary. This section will briefly highlight the adaptations of motoric, self-report, and physiological anxiety-assessment methods for children, paying particular attention to special problems of assessing anxiety in children.

The BAT can be used without modification to assess children's avoidance of phobic objects, and several examples of this are found in the literature. Problems with the BAT noted previously may be identical for children; indeed some of them may be magnified. For example, the level of demand in approach instructions may affect behavior more acutely, since a child is generally more responsive to requests from an adult. Kelley (1976) found significant increases in time remaining in a dark chamber for dark-phobic children following subtle high demand instructions. Notably, the demand instructions were markedly more effective in prolonging endurance of darkness than three sessions of therapy.

Direct measures of motoric manifestations of anxiety suitable for children include Paul's (1966) Timed Behavior Checklist and derived rating scales. Several specific rating scales and checklists have been constructed to measure anxiety in children undergoing various medical procedures such as surgery (Melamed & Siegel, 1975), dental treatment (Melamed, Hawes, Heiby, & Glick, 1975), and cancer biopsies (Katz, Kellerman, & Siegel, 1980). A specialized rating scale has also been devised for measuring separation anxiety in young children (Glennon & Weisz, 1978). Since manifestations of specific behaviors may change with age, developmental considerations appear to be critical for standardizing these various rating scales. Additionally, sex differences may be more acute than is the case with adults. Unfortunately, age and sex differences have generally been ignored in the development of rating scales for children. When such factors are considered, important differences are found. For example, Katz *et al.* (1980) validated their anxiety scale (for bone-marrow aspirations in cancer victims) on both males and females across three age groups. Younger children exhibited a greater number and longer durations of rated behaviors. They also had less bodily control and made more diffuse verbal protests. Females manifested more anxiety, more comfort-seeking behaviors, and fewer uncooperative behaviors than males. Based on these findings, it appears unwise to generalize across age and sex without relevant normative data.

Extending self-report anxiety measurements to children is a problem with younger children, whose verbal comprehension is more limited. Modifications of several standard self-report instruments have been made. Examples include the State Trait Anxiety Inventory for Children (Spielberger, 1973) and the Louisville Fear Survey Schedule (Miller, Barrett, Hamp, & Noble, 1972). In some instances, these self-report forms are used by significant others, such as teachers and parents, for rating children's anxiety. However, parent and child ratings differ significantly (Miller, Barrett, Hampe & Noble, 1971). Walk's (1956) Fear Thermometer is often used as a prototype for assessing very young children. Instead of numbers to demark anxiety levels, colors (Kelley, 1976) and faces depicting various moods are substituted.

Physiological responses in children have not frequently been measured, and are typically limited to heart rate and electrodermal responses. The primary problem in the psychophysiological assessment of children is the limited ability of children to restrain movements, which can easily introduce artifacts into the recorded data. Electrodermal measurements are particularly sensitive to movement artifact. The more recently developed devices for monitoring heart rate during exercise may be more suitable than standard polygraph measurement. The physiological assessment situation may also evoke greater arousal in children than adults, especially if the child associates electrodes and apparatus with traumatic medical procedures. Such reactivity might be reduced by giving the child a detailed explanation, demonstrating the equipment on an assistant, or other such method.

PRELIMINARY SCREENING AND ASSESSMENT PROCEDURES

The triple-response-mode assessment of an anxiety disorder typically follows a series of preliminary assessment procedures. This preliminary screening should accomplish three goals. First, it should ensure the problem (e.g., driving phobia) is not subsumed by some larger problem (e.g., agoraphobia) that should rather be the focus of assessment and intervention. Interviewing the patient is the primary method for specifying the problem. A discussion of interviewing procedures and techniques would be beyond the scope of this chapter, however; for a detailed discussion of behavioral interviewing, see Morganstern (1981).

An important component of the initial interview which has been largely ignored in the behavioral literature is the mental-status examination. The mental-status examination is a semistructured method for evaluating the patient's cognitive and motor behavior as observed in the interview. It evaluates five aspects of functioning including (1) appearance and behavior, (2) thought process, (3) mood and affect, (4) intellectual functioning, and (5) sensorium. There are several detailed outlines available for conducting these evaluations (e.g., Freedman, Kaplan, & Sadock, 1975; Wing, Cooper, & Sartorius, 1974). The examination includes such questions as "Do you ever hear voices when no one is around?" and "Do you feel you have any special powers?" A positive response to these questions is pursued to carefully define the patient's thought content. Patients frequently present with vague complaints which are rarely used as target behaviors. For example, a presenting complaint of nervousness felt in the presence of other people could indicate a social phobia. However, it could also indicate a variety of other problems, some as severe as a thought disorder in which the patient felt other people were inserting thoughts into his mind. The mental status exam is useful for defining the boundaries of the disorder.

An objective estimate of IQ is important in the consideration of treatment approaches. Although IQs based on clinical judgment can be quite accurate in many cases, the error in the minority of cases is often costly in terms of efficient and effective treatment. We have used the verbal subtests of the WAIS for screening, in order to avoid designing programs that fail to work due simply to poor comprehension by the patient.

The second task of preliminary screening is to evaluate and rule out biological factors contributing to anxiety. Although a medical examination and laboratory tests are necessary, interviewing can also sometimes reveal biological bases for complaints of anxiety. We use the Cornell Medical Index (Brodman, Erdman, Lorge, & Wolff, 1949), a 195-item questionnaire, as a gross medical screening device. The patient should be asked about health habits, particularly any changes in habits. Illicit drug use, alcohol abuse, caffeine intake, use and abuse of medication, diet, and excesses of exercise should be assessed. Also, patterns of symptoms should be evaluated, since they may be predictive of biological dysfunction. Physical problems should be suspected if, for example, fatigue preceded onset of anxiety symptoms, or if the patient suddenly developed severe anxiety between the ages of 18 and 35 without previous psychiatric history (Hall, 1980). It is important that the identification of an environmental stressor which covaries with anxiety (e.g., increased stress due to job promotion) should never be seen as a basis for excluding a complete medical evaluation. Many physical disorders fluctuate with stress. Certain medical problems precipitate anxiety by impairing higher level functioning of the individual. In such cases, anxiety responses might only appear when stressful demands are placed on the individual. A medical evaluation, including a physical examination with review of systems and blood (e.g., SMA-34 biochemical screen) and urine tests, should detect medical problems with 80% accuracy (Hall, 1980).

The third goal of preliminary assessment is to consider collateral effects of the problem. The recent research conference on anxiety disorders (NIMH, 1980) recommended assessment of the following areas in addition to the target problem: use of health services, depression, social functioning, and adjustment to work, family, and marriage (Barlow & Wolfe, 1981). These recommendations should be of interest to clinicians as well as researchers. We have assessed these areas by self-reported frequencies of relevant behaviors (e.g., use of health services, social contact, employment, and work absences) and by standardized questionnaires, such as the Beck Depression Inventory (Beck, Ward, Mendelson, Mack, & Erbaugh, 1961) and the Marital Adjustment Test (Locke & Wallace, 1959).

Although this section was written with the clinician in mind, we strongly feel that careful screening should be routine in clinical research in order to increase homogeneity of the subject sample. Subjects inappropriate for a study due to etiological anomalies, for example, may obscure results. Psychophysiological assessments are particularly likely to be influenced by drug use and medications. For example, a hypertensive subject being treated by beta-adrenergic blockade will yield invalid heart-rate measurements. Cigarette smoking and alcohol use can similarly affect physiological assessment data and should be controlled for or used as criteria for exclusion.

A CASE STUDY

To illustrate the use of the various anxiety-assessment procedures discussed, we will present a clinical case study.

The patient was a 37-year-old coal miner who presented himself as a claustrophobic. He reported that for years he felt tense in enclosed spaces. His anxiety increased, however, since he began working in the mine about 10 months ago. His anxiety recently intensified, leading to panic attacks in the mine. During the first attack, he was examined in a hospital emergency room for cardiac dysfunction. Results of a subsequent complete physical examination were negative, except for hypertension. The attacks were diagnosed as psychogenic symptoms, and Valium was prescribed to control the anxiety. When the panic attacks continued, causing significant lost work time, the company physician recommended psychological help.

For the preliminary evaluation of the patient's problem, information was sought in the following areas: historical development of the fear and coping methods; present situations avoided and consequences of avoidance or unavoidable exposure; existence of other fears, and general level of past and present functioning (e.g., marital adjustment, social contact, child rearing, work adjustment, leisure activities, intelligence). The patient was interviewed, and he completed several of the questionnaires mentioned in the previous section plus the Fear Survey Schedule (Wolpe & Lang, 1964).

Since the recent medical evaluation suggested contributing biological factors were unlikely, the initial focus of the interview was to ascertain whether anxiety was more generalized than presented by the patient. The observation that isolated, specific phobias are uncommon in clinical practice held true in this case. The man appeared highly anxious, constantly fidgeting and changing seat posture, and he chain-smoked cigarettes. Alcohol was faintly discernable on his breath. His responses to inquiries were very brief until later in the session, and eye contact was minimal throughout. Also, the receptionist noted that he had been just about to leave the waiting room when he was called to be seen. Before the interview, the patient filled out the Fear Survey Schedule, on which he indicated fears of injury, loud noises, crowds, closed spaces, and of losing control. Follow-up questioning on individual items indicated active avoidance of related situations beginning shortly after his discharge from the military. He used alcohol to reduce anxiety when these situations were unavoidable.

Mental-status questions suggested no thought disorder, but the patient experienced difficulty falling asleep, middle-sleep awakening, difficulty concentrating, chronic fatigue, irritability, and social withdrawal. His history was unremarkable through high school. Immediately after graduating college with honors he enlisted in the military and fought in Vietnam. Alcohol abuse began in Vietnam and worsened after discharge. The patient reported that he currently used alcohol only to get to sleep. He had worked at numerous jobs since his discharge, and typically had been fired or had quit after arguments with supervisors. Since he had a 1-year-old son and wife to support, he was very concerned about losing his present job. He complained that his wife "did not understand him." He often stormed out of the house when upset with her, sometimes not returning for 2 days. The patient's social withdrawal was ostensibly due to a fear that he might "lose control"—that "he might hurt someone." For the same reason, he avoided being alone with his son and never disciplined him.

When the patient admitted to frequent nightmares with military combat content, he was asked whether specific combat-related thoughts intruded during waking hours. At this, he jumped up, pounded his fist on the desk, began to cry, and eventually related several traumatic war memories. One experience seemed a plausible explanation for his claustrophobia. While hiding in a small bunker with his closest friend, they were hit by a hand grenade. The friend was killed and the patient was severely wounded and rendered briefly unconscious. He awoke hearing enemy voices and was forced to feign death for 2 days, as the enemy camped at the site. He reported that closed spaces triggered memories of this particular event.

All the interview information pointed to a combat-related posttraumatic stress syndrome (e.g., Fairbank, Langley, Jarvie, & Keane, 1981). Had the problem been limited to the simple phobia presented, much more attention would have been placed on specific eliciting situations, actual behavior, and consequences. In general, traumatic stress syndromes are conceptualized as phobias conditioned by traumatic experiences. Memories of the experience are the phobia stimuli which are avoided. The syndrome's primary features can be anxiety, depression, or a combination of these two. Treatment is directed toward reducing anxiety and depression. Among combat veterans with posttraumatic stress disorder, anxiety, depression, and other features (e.g., nightmares, and claustrophobia) appear to be secondary to the phobic memories, and tend to diminish when avoidance of the thoughts is reduced. Suitable exposure-based treatments include systematic desensitization and imaginal flooding (Keane & Kaloupek, 1982). Since the patient's hypertension was a risk in flooding, desensitization was selected.

Anxiety elicited by phobic memories was assessed using a modification of the procedure of Fairbank and Keane (in press). We first had the patient describe his most traumatic experiences. These scenes were repeated back to him, one at a time for 15 sec each, while his HR was monitored. At the end of each scene, the patient rated his anxiety on a Fear Thermometer. For a second test, we ranked a series of eight photographs from a book on the war organized from least to most combat and injury related. These were presented in a BAT format as a test of generalized motoric avoidance to combat experiences. The test procedure was analogous to the imaginal assessment. The patient viewed each photograph for 60 sec while HR was monitored, and he rated anxiety on a Fear Thermometer at the end of each minute. The patient only viewed three photographs before terminating. At this point he was trembling and tearful, and his HR was 148 bpm. Collateral assessment information was obtained with the Beck Depression Inventory, State-Trait Anxiety Inventory, and Marital Adjustment Scale. In addition, the patient self monitored his daily anxiety level, intrusion of traumatic memories, sleep duration, and nightmare occurrences for 1 week prior to and throughout treatment.

A two-tiered hierarchy of scenes for desensitization was generated. The HR data during assessment was utilized to rank the five traumatic memories for presentation in ascending order of anxiety. We felt HR was the most valid index for this purpose, despite the fact that vividness of scene could not be clearly matched, given the imaginal mode of presentation. For each memory, the patient and therapist generated a hierarchy of scenes and responses. Following relaxation training, exposure treatment began and lasted 14 sessions over four weeks (See Bellack & Hersen [1977b] for a detailed discussion of desensitization procedures and relevant research). HR was monitored during exposure to scenes. A criterion HR of 90 bpm was used to terminate scenes. Imaginal assessments were repeated weekly to gauge overall progress. The data suggested not only that treatment was working, but that generalization to higher ranked scenes was taking place according to both self-report and HR measures. The self-monitored behaviors also gradually improved and, more importantly, the patient returned to work after 2 weeks. The patient did not terminate the BAT-photograph assessment, which was repeated after 12 sessions. Administration of collateral assessment questionnaires at that time also evidenced positive changes. After three monthly follow-up assessments, no arousal was elicited by either imaginal or visual stimuli. The patient had stopped using alcohol as a sleeping medication, and he had begun to socialize with his fellow workers.

SUMMARY AND CONCLUSIONS

The advent of triple-response-mode assessments is a major technological advance for the evaluation of anxiety disorders. It provides systematic and objective means for quantifying and categorizing anxiety. Treatments can be empirically selected by evaluating which stimulus mode of presentation elicits physiological arousal or the motor behavior disruptions secondary to physiological arousal. Avoidance tests and systematic self-reports (e.g., self-monitoring) of anxiety or avoidance behavior can provide a much more finely grained analysis of progress than traditional verbal accounts of behavior occurring between treatment sessions. Researchers can increase the power of their studies either by selecting subjects with particular patterns of responses across systems, or by including patterns as a factor.

The utility of the three-response-system model is clear. Its validity is clouded, however, by the phenomenon of response-system discordance. In reviewing the literature for this chapter, we were disconcerted to find that the methodological approach to studying discordance (and desynchrony) is substantially no different today (e.g., Barlow *et al.*, 1980) from what it was a decade ago (e.g., Leitenberg *et al.*, 1971). In general, the more recent studies simply demonstrate that the phenomenon extends to additional populations.

Too little attention is paid to modifying existing measurement methods. Alternative methods include (1) assessing cognitions versus self-reported evaluations of anxiety, (2) measuring physiological response patterns versus single responses or summaries of multiple responses, and (3) measuring avoidance in multiple situations versus single laboratory or quasi-naturalistic settings. Additionally, neuroendocrine measures have been completely ignored, despite the fact that they mediate physiological reactions in anxiety. Research which expands the traditional measurement methods may help resolve the discordance phenomenon and lead to validation of the three system model of anxiety or, possibly, to a still more fruitful approach to anxiety assessment.

REFERENCES

Akutagawa, D. *A study in the construct validity of the psychoanalytic concept of latent anxiety and test of a projection hypothesis.* Unpublished dissertation, University of Pittsburgh, 1956.

Andrasik, F., Turner, S. M., & Ollendick, T. H. Self-report and physiologic responding during *in vivo* flooding. *Behaviour Research and Therapy*, 1980, *18*, 593–595.

Arkowitz, H., Lichtenstein, E., McGovern, K., & Hines, P. The behavioral assessment of social competence in males. *Behavior Therapy*, 1975, *6*, 3–13.

Bandura, A. *Principles of behavior modification.* New York: Holt, Rinehart & Winston, 1969.

Barlow, D. H., & Wolfe, B. E. Behavioral approaches to anxiety disorders: A report on the NIMH–SUNY, Albany, Research Conference. *Journal of Consulting and Clinical Psychology*, 1981, *49*, 448–459.

Barlow, D. H., Mavissakalian, M. R., & Schofield, L. D. Patterns of desynchrony in agoraphobia: A preliminary report. *Behaviour Research and Therapy*, 1980, *18*, 441–448.

Beck, A. T. *Cognitive therapy and the emotional disorders*. New York: International Universities Press, 1976.

Beck, A. T., Ward, C. H., Mendelson, M., Mack, J., & Erbaugh, J. An inventory for measuring depression. *Archives of General Psychiatry*, 1961, *4*, 561–571.

Bell, I. R., & Schwartz, G. E. Voluntary control and reactivity of the human heart rate. *Psychophysiology*, 1975, *12*, 339–348.

Bellack, A. S. A critical appraisal of strategies for assessing social skill. *Behavioral Assessment*, 1979, *1*, 157–176.

Bellack, A. S., & Hersen, M. The use of self-report inventories in behavioral assessment. In J. D. Cone & R. P. Hawkins (Eds.), *Behavioral assessment: New directions in clinical psychology*. New York: Brunner/Mazel, 1977. (a)

Bellack, A. S., & Hersen, M. *Behavior modification: An introductory textbook*. Baltimore: Williams & Wilkins, 1977. (b)

Bellack, A. S., Hersen, M., & Lamparski, D. Role play tests for assessing social skills: Are they valid? Are they useful? *Journal of Consulting and Clinical Psychology*, 1979, *47*, 335–347.

Bellack, A. S., Hersen, M., & Turner, S. M. The relationship of role playing and knowledge of appropriate behavior to assertion in the natural environment. *Journal of Consulting and Clinical Psychology*, 1979, *47*, 670–678. (a)

Bellack, A. S., Hersen, M., & Turner, S. M. Role play tests for assessing social skills: Are they valid? *Behavior Therapy*, 1979, *9*, 448–461. (b)

Bernstein, D. A. Situational factors in behavioral fear assessment: A progress report. *Behavior Therapy*, 1973, *4*, 41–48.

Bernstein, D. A., & Nietzel, M. T. Behavioral avoidance tests: The effects of demand characteristics and repeated measures of two types of subjects. *Behavior Therapy*, 1974, *5*, 183–192.

Blom, B. E., & Craighead, W. E. The effects of situational and instructional demand on indices of speech anxiety. *Journal of Abnormal Psychology*, 1974, *88*, 667–674.

Borkovec, T. D. The effects of instructional suggestion and physiological cues on analogue fear. *Behavior Therapy*, 1973, *4*, 185–192. (a)

Borkovec, T. D. The role of expectancy and physiological feedback in fear research: A review with special reference to subject characteristics. *Behavior Therapy*, 1973, *4*, 491–505. (b)

Borkovec, T. D. Physiological and cognitive processes in the regulation of anxiety. In G. E. Schwartz & D. Shapiro (Eds.), *Consciousness and self-regulation: Advances in research and theory* (Vol. 1). New York: Plenum, 1976.

Borkovec, T. D., & Craighead, W. E. The comparison of two methods of assessing fear and avoidance behavior. *Behaviour Research and Therapy*, 1971, *9*, 285–291.

Borkovec, T. D., Stone, N. M., O'Brien, G. T., & Kaloupek, D. G. Identification and measurement of a clinically relevant target behavior for analogue outcome research. *Behavior Therapy*, 1974, *5*, 503–513.

Borkovec, T. D., Weerts, T. C., & Bernstein, D. A. Assessment of anxiety. In A. R. Ciminero, K. S. Calhoun, & H. E. Adams (Eds.), *Handbook of behavioral assessment*. New York: Wiley, 1977.

Braun, P. R., & Reynolds, D. N. A factor analysis of a 100-item fear survey inventory. *Behaviour Research and Therapy*, 1969, *7*, 399–402.

Brodman, K., Erdman, A. J., Lorge, I., & Wolff, H. G. The Cornell Medical Index. I. An adjunct to medical interviews. *Journal of the American Medical Association*, 1949, *140*, 530.

Cannon, W. B. *Bodily changes in pain, hunger, fear, and rage*. New York: Appleton-Century-Crofts, 1915.

Christoff, K. A., & Edelstein, B. A. *Functional aspects of assertive and aggressive behavior: Laboratory and* in vivo *observations.* Paper presented at the meeting of the Association for Advancement of Behavior Therapy, Toronto, November 1981.

Cohn, C. K., Kron, H. D., & Brady, J. P. A case of blood-illness-injury phobia treated behaviorally. *Journal of Nervous and Mental Diseases,* 1976, *162,* 65–68.

Cone, J. D. The relevance of reliability and validity for behavioral assessment. *Behavior Therapy,* 1977, *8,* 411–426.

Cone, J. D. Confounded comparisons in triple response mode assessment research. *Behavioral Assessment,* 1979, *1,* 85–95.

Connolly, J., Hallam, R. S., & Marks, I. M. Selective association of fainting with blood-illness-injury fear. *Behavior Therapy,* 1976, *7,* 8–13.

Craighead, W. E. The assessment of avoidance responses on the Levis Phobic Test Apparatus. *Behavior Therapy,* 1973, *4,* 235–240.

Cronbach, L. J. *Essentials of psychological testing* (2nd ed.). New York: Harper & Row, 1960.

Dmitruk, O. M., Collins, K. W., & Clinger, D. L. The "Barnum Effect" and acceptance of negative personal evaluation. *Journal of Consulting and Clinical Psychology,* 1973, *41,* 192–195.

Dollard, J., & Miller, N. E. *Personality and psychotherapy: An analysis in terms of learning, thinking, and culture.* New York: McGraw-Hill, 1950.

Edelberg, R. Electrodermal recovery rate, goal orientation, and aversion. *Psychophysiology,* 1972, *9,* 512–520.

Eble, R. Must all tests be valid? *American Psychologist,* 1961, *16,* 640–647.

Emmelkamp, P. M. G., & Emmelkamp-Benner, A. Effects of historically portrayed modeling and group treatment on self-observation: A comparison with agoraphobics. *Behaviour Research and Therapy,* 1975, *13,* 135–139.

Emmelkamp, P. M. G., & Wessels, H. Flooding in imagination vs. flooding in vivo: A comparison with agoraphobics. *Behaviour Research and Therapy,* 1975, *13,* 7–15.

Emmelkamp, P. M. G., Kuipers, A. C. M., & Eggeraat, J. B. Cognitive modification versus prolonged exposure *in vivo:* A comparison with agoraphobics as subjects. *Behaviour Research and Therapy,* 1978, *16,* 33–41.

Endler, N. S., & Okada, M. A multidimensional measure of trait anxiety: The S–R Inventory of General Trait Anxiousness. *Journal of Consulting and Clinical Psychology,* 1975, *43,* 319–329.

Endler, N. S., Hunt, J. McV., & Rosenstein, A. J. An S–R inventory of anxiousness. *Psychological Monographs,* 1962, *76* (Whole No. 536).

Engel, B. T. Response specificity. In N. S. Greenfield & R. A. Sternbach (Eds.), *Handbook of psychophysiology.* New York: Holt, Rinehart & Winston, 1972.

Fairbank, J. A., & Keane, T. M. Flooding for combat-related stress disorders: Assessment of anxiety reduction across traumatic memories. *Behavior Therapy,* in press.

Fairbank, J. A., Langley, K., Jarvie, G. J., & Keane, T. M. A selected bibliography on post traumatic stress disorders in Vietnam veterans. *Professional Psychology,* 1981, *12,* 578–586.

Fazio, A. F. Implosive therapy with semiclinical phobias. *Journal of Abnormal Psychology,* 1972, *80,* 183–188.

Freedman, A. M., Kaplan, H. I., & Sadock, B. J. *Comprehensive textbook of psychiatry* (2nd ed.; Vol. 1). Baltimore: Williams & Wilkins, 1975.

Galassi, M. D., & Galassi, J. P. The effects of role playing variations on the assessment of assertive behavior. *Behavior Therapy,* 1976, *7,* 343–347.

Galassi, J. P., Frierson, H. T., & Sharer, R. Behavior of high, moderate and low test anxious students during an actual test situation. *Journal of Consulting and Clinical Psychology,* 1981, *49,* 51–62. (a)

Galassi, J. P., Frierson, H. T., & Sharer, R. Concurrent versus retrospective assessment in test anxiety research. *Journal of Consulting and Clinical Psychology,* 1981, *49,* 614–615. (b)

Geer, J. H. The development of a scale to measure fear. *Behaviour Research and Therapy,* 1965, *3,* 45–53.

Gelder, M. G., & Marks, I. M. Severe agoraphobia: A controlled prospective trial of behavior therapy. *British Journal of Psychiatry,* 1966, *112,* 309–319.

Glennon, B., & Weisz, J. R. An observational approach to the assessment of anxiety in young children. *Journal of Consulting and Clinical Psychology,* 1978, *46,* 1246–1257.

Goldfried, M. R., & Trier, C. S. Effectiveness of relaxation as an active coping skill. *Journal of Abnormal Psychology,* 1974, *83,* 348–355.

Goldfried, M. R., Decenteceo, E. T., & Weinberg, L. Systematic rational restructuring as a self-control technique. *Behavior Therapy,* 1974, *5,* 247–254.

Gulas, I., McClanahan, L. D., & Poetter, R. Phobic response factors from the fear survey schedule. *Journal of Psychology,* 1975, *90,* 19–25.

Hall, C. S., & Lindzey, G. *Theories of personality.* New York: Wiley, 1970.

Hall, R. C. Anxiety. In R. C. Hall (Ed.), *Psychiatric presentations of medical illness.* New York: S. P. Medical and Scientific Books, 1980.

Hersen, M. Self-assessment of fear. *Behavior Therapy,* 1973, *4,* 241–257.

Hersen, M., & Bellack, A. S. Social skills training for chronic psychiatric patients: Rationale, research findings, and future directions. *Comprehensive Psychiatry,* 1976, *17,* 559–580.

Hodgson, R., & Rachman, S. Desynchrony in measures of fear. *Behaviour Research and Therapy,* 1974, *12,* 319–326.

Horst, P. *Personality: Measurement of dimensions.* San Francisco: Jossey-Bass, 1968.

Hugdahl, K. The three-systems model of fear and emotion—A critical examination. *Behaviour Research and Therapy,* 1981, *19,* 75–85.

Husek, T. R., & Alexander, S. The effectiveness of the anxiety differential in examination stress situations. *Educational and Psychological Measurement,* 1963, *23,* 309–318.

James. W. What is an emotion? *Mind,* 1884, *9,* 188–205.

Katkin, E. S. Relationship between manifest anxiety and two indices of autonomic response to stress. *Journal of Personality and Social Psychology,* 1965, *2,* 324–333.

Katkin, E. S. The relationship between a measure of transitory anxiety and spontaneous autonomic activity. *Journal of Abnormal Psychology,* 1966, *71,* 142–146.

Katkin, E. S. Eletrodermal lability: A psychophysiological analysis of individual differences in response to stress. In I. G. Sarason & C. D. Spielberger (Eds.), *Stress and anxiety.* Washington, D.C.: Hemisphere Publishing Co., 1975.

Katkin, E. S., & Deitz, S. R. Systematic desensitization. In W. F. Prokasy & D. Raskin (Eds.), *Electrodermal activity and psychological research.* New York: Academic, 1973.

Katz, E. R., Kellerman, J., & Siegel, S. E. Behavioral distress in children with cancer undergoing medical procedures: Developmental considerations. *Journal of Consulting and Clinical Psychology,* 1980, *48,* 356–365.

Kazdin, A. The effect of suggestion and pretesting on avoidance reduction in fearful subjects. *Journal of Behavior Therapy and Experimental Psychiatry,* 1973, *4,* 213–222.

Kazdin, A. E. Self-monitoring and behavior change. In M. J. Mahoney & C. E. Thoresen (Eds.), *Self-control: Power to the person.* Monterey: Brooks/Cole, 1974. (a)

Kazdin, A. E. Reactive self-monitoring: The effects of response desirability, goal setting and feedback. *Journal of Consulting and Clinical Psychology,* 1974, *42,* 704–716. (b)

Kazdin, A. E. Situational specificity: The two-edged sword of behavioral assessment. *Behavioral Assessment,* 1979, *1,* 57–75.

Keane, T. M., & Kaloupek, D. G. Imaginal flooding in the treatment of a posttraumatic stress disorder. *Journal of Consulting and Clinical Psychology,* 1982, *50,* 138–140.

Kelley, C. K. Play desensitization of fear of darkness in preschool children. *Behaviour Research and Therapy,* 1976, *14,* 79–81.

Kent, R. N., Diament, C., Dietz, A., & O'Leary, K. D. Expectation biases in observational evaluation of therapeutic change. *Journal of Consulting and Clinical Psychology,* 1974, *42,* 774–780.

Klinger, E. Modes of normal conscious flow. In K. S. Pope & J. L. Singer (Eds.), *The stream of consciousness: Scientific investigations into the flow of human experience.* New York: Plenum, 1978.

Kroll, H. W. Rapid therapy of dog phobia by a feeding procedure. *Journal of Behavior Therapy and Experimental Psychiatry,* 1975, *6,* 325–326.

Lacey, J. I. The evaluation of autonomic responses: Toward a general solution. *Annals of the New York Academy of Science,* 1956, *67,* 123–164.

Lacey, J. I., Bateman, D. E., & VanLehn, R. Autonomic response specificity. *Psychosomatic Medicine,* 1953, *15,* 8–21.

Lang, P. J. The application of psychophysiological methods to the study of psychotherapy and behavior modification. In A. E. Bergin & S. L. Garfields (Eds.), *Handbook of psychotherapy and behavior change.* New York: Wiley, 1971.

Lang, P. J. The psychophysiology of anxiety. In J. Akiskal (Ed.), *Psychiatric diagnosis: Exploration of biological criteria.* New York: Spectrum, 1977. (a)

Lang, P. J. Physiological assessment of anxiety and fear. In J. D. Cone & R. P. Hawkins (Eds.), *Behavioral assessment: New directions in clinical psychology.* New York: Brunner/Mazel, 1977. (b)

Lang, P. J., & Lazovik, A. D. Experimental desensitization of a phobia. *Journal of Abnormal and Social Psychology,* 1963, *66,* 519–525.

Lang, P. J., Rice, D. G., & Sternbach, R. A. The psychophysiology of emotion. In N. S. Greenfield & R. A. Sternbach (Eds.), *Handbook of psychophysiology.* New York: Holt, Rinehart & Winston, 1972.

Lang, P. J., Melamed, B. G., & Hart, J. H. Automating the desensitization procedure: A psychophysiological analysis of fear modification. In M. J. Kietzman (Ed.), *Experimental approaches to psychopathology.* New York: Academic, 1974.

Lawlis, G. F. Response styles of a patient population on the fear survey schedule. *Behaviour Research and Therapy,* 1971, *9,* 95–102.

Lazarus, A. A. Group therapy of phobic disorders by systematic desensitization. *Journal of Abnormal and Social Psychology,* 1961, *63,* 504–510.

Leitenberg, H., Agras, W. S., & Barlow, D. H. Contribution of selective reinforcement and therapeutic instructions to systematic desensitization therapy. *Journal of Abnormal Psychology,* 1969, *74,* 113–118.

Leitenberg, H., Agras, W. S., Edwards, J. A., Thomson, L. E., & Wincze, J. P. Practice of a psychotherapeutic variable: An experimental analysis within single cases. *Journal of Psychiatric Research,* 1970, *7,* 215–225.

Leitenberg, H., Agras, W. S., Butz, R., & Wincze, J. Relationship between heart rate and behavioral change during the treatment of phobias. *Journal of Abnormal Psychology,* 1971, *78,* 59–68.

Levis, D. J. The phobic test apparatus: An objective measure of human avoidance behavior to small objects. *Behaviour Research and Therapy,* 1969, *7,* 309–315.

Levis, D. J., & Hare, N. A review of the theoretical rationale and empirical support for the extinction approach of implosive (flooding) therapy. In M. Hersen, R. M. Eisler, & P. M. Miller (Eds.), *Progress in behavior modification.* New York: Academic, 1977.

Lick, J. R., & Katkin, E. S. Assessment of anxiety and fear. In M. Hersen & A. Bellack (Eds.), *Behavioral Assessment: A practical handbook*. New York: Pergamon, 1976.

Lick, J. R., & Unger, T. E. External validity of laboratory fear assessment: Implications from two case studies. *Journal of Consulting and Clinical Psychology*, 1975, *43*, 864–866.

Lick, J., Condiotte, M., & Unger, T. Effects of uncertainty about the behavior of a phobic stimulus on subjects' fear reactions. *Journal of Consulting and Clinical Psychology*, 1978, *46*, 1559–1560.

Lipinski, D., & Nelson, R. The reactivity and unreliability of self-recording. *Journal of Consulting and Clinical Psychology*, 1974, *42*, 110–123.

Lipinski, D. P., Black, J. L., Nelson, R. O., & Ciminero, A. The influence of motivational variables on the reactivity and reliability of self-recording. *Journal of Consulting and Clinical Psychology*, 1975, *43*, 637–646.

Locke, H. J., & Wallace, K. M. Short marital adjustment and prediction tests: Their reliability and validity. *Marriage and Family Living*, 1959, *21*, 251–255.

Lombardo, T. W., & Bellack, A. S. *The external validity of laboratory analogue assessments for speech anxiety*. Paper presented at the annual meeting of the Association for Advancement of Behavior Therapy, Chicago, November 1978.

Lombardo, T. W., & Turner, S. M. Thought-stopping in the control of obsessive rumination. *Behavior Modification*, 1979, *3*, 267–272.

Lombardo, T. W., Zamosky, A., Romano, J., Volkin, J., & Bellack, A. S. *A comparative analysis of a self-control procedure for anxiety reduction*. Paper presented at the meeting of the Association for Advancement of Behavior Therapy, Chicago, November 1978.

Lomont, J. F., & Edwards, J. E. The role of relaxation in systematic desensitization. *Behaviour Research and Therapy*, 1967, *5*, 11–25.

Mac, R., & Fazio, A. F. Self-report and overt behavioral measures of fear with changes in aversive stimuli. *Behaviour Research and Therapy*, 1972, *10*, 283–285.

Mahl, G. F. Exploring emotional states by content analysis. In I. D. Pool (Ed.), *Trends in content analysis*. Urbana, Ill.: University of Illinois Press, 1959.

Malmo, R. B., & Shagass, C. Physiologic study of symptom mechanisms in psychiatric patients under stress. *Psychosomatic Medicine*, 1949, *11*, 25–29.

Mandler, G. Helplessness: Theory and research in anxiety. In C. D. Spielberger (Ed.), *Anxiety: Current trends in theory and research*. New York: Academic, 1972.

Mandler, G., & Sarason, S. B. A study of anxiety and learning. *Journal of Abnormal and Social Psychology*, 1952, *47*, 166–173.

Mandler, G., Mandler, J. M., & Uviller, E. T. Autonomic feedback: The perception of autonomic activity. *Journal of Abnormal and Social Psychology*, 1958, *56*, 367–373.

Manosevitz, M., & Lanyon, R. I. Fear survey schedule: A normative study. *Psychological Reports*, 1965, *17*, 699–703.

Marchetti, A., McGlynn, F. D., & Patterson, A. S. Effect of cue-controlled relaxation, a placebo treatment, and no treatment on changes in self-reported and psychophysiological indices of test anxiety among college students. *Behavior Modification*, 1977, *1*, 47–72.

Martin, B. *Anxiety and neurotic disorders*. New York: Wiley, 1971.

Martin, B., & Sroufe, L. A. Anxiety. In C. G. Costello (Ed.), *Symptoms of psychopathology: A handbook*. New York: Wiley, 1970.

McDonald, M. L. Multiple impact behavior therapy in a child's dog phobia. *Journal of Behavior Therapy and Experimental Psychiatry*, 1975, *6*, 317–322.

Meichenbaum, D. H. *Cognitive-behavior modification: An integrative approach*. New York: Plenum, 1977.

Melamed, B. G., & Siegel, L. S. Reduction of anxiety in children facing hospitalization and surgery by use of filmed modeling. *Journal of Consulting and Clinical Psychology,* 1975, *43*, 511–521.

Melamed, B. G., Hawes. R., Heiby, E., & Glick, J. The use of filmed modeling to reduce uncooperative behavior of children during dental treatment. *Journal of Dental Research,* 1975, *54*, 797–801.

Meyers, A. W., & Craighead, W. E. Adaptation periods in clinical psychophysiological research: A recommendation. *Behavior Therapy,* 1978, *9*, 355–362.

Miller, B. V., & Bernstein, D. A. Instructional demand in a behavioral avoidance test for claustrophobic fear. *Journal of Abnormal Psychology,* 1972, *80*, 206–210.

Miller, L. C., Barrett, C. L., Hampe, E., & Noble, H. Revised anxiety scales for the Louisville Behavior Check List. *Psychological Reports,* 1971, *29*, 503–511.

Miller, L. C., Barrett, C. L., Hampe, E., & Noble, H. Factor structure of childhood fears. *Journal of Consulting and Clinical Psychology,* 1972, *39*, 264–268.

Morganstern, K. P. Behavioral interviewing: The initial stages of assessment. In M. Hersen & A. S. Bellack (Eds.), *Behavioral assessment: A practical handbook* (2nd ed.). New York: Pergamon, 1981.

Murray, D. C. Talk, silence, and anxiety. *Psychological Bulletin,* 1971, *75*, 244–260.

Nelson, R. O., Lipinski, D. P., & Black, J. L. The effects of expectancy on the reactivity of self-recording. *Behavior Therapy,* 1975, *6*, 337–349.

Nesbitt, E. B. An escalator phobia overcome in one session of flooding in vivo. *Journal of Behavior Therapy and Experimental Psychiatry,* 1973, *4*, 405–406.

Odom, J. V., Nelson, R. O., & Wien, K. S. The differential effectiveness of five treatment procedures on three response systems in a snake phobia analogue study. *Behavior Therapy,* 1978, *9*, 936–942.

Osgood, C. E., Suci, G. J., & Tannenbaum, P. H. *The measurement of meaning.* Urbana: University of Illinois Press, 1957.

Öst L., Jerremalm, A., & Johansson, J. Individual response patterns and the effects of different behavioral methods in the treatment of social phobia. *Behaviour Research and Therapy,* 1981, *19*, 1–16.

Paul, G. L. *Insight versus desensitization in psychotherapy: An experiment in anxiety reduction.* Stanford, Cal.: Stanford University Press, 1966.

Paul, G. L. Behavior modification research: Design and tactics. In C. M. Franks (Ed.), *Behavior therapy: Appraisal and status.* New York: McGraw-Hill, 1969.

Paul, G. L., & Bernstein, D. A. *Anxiety and clinical problems: Systematic desensitization and related techniques.* New York: General Learning Press, 1973.

Rachman, S. Human fears: A three systems analysis. *Scandinavian Journal of Behavior Therapy,* 1978, *7*, 237–245.

Rachman, S., & Hodgson, R. I. Synchrony and desynchrony in fear and avoidance. *Behaviour Research and Therapy,* 1974, *12*, 311–318.

Rappaport, H., & Katkin, E. S. Relationships among manifest anxiety, response to stress and the perception of autonomic activity. *Journal of Consulting and Clinical Psychology,* 1972, *38*, 219–224.

Ritter, B. The use of contact desensitization, demonstration-plus-participation and demonstration-alone in the treatment of acrophobia. *Behaviour Research and Therapy,* 1970, *7*, 157–164.

Rubin, S. E., Lawlis, G. F., Tasto, D. L., & Namenek, T. Factor analysis of the 122-item fear survey schedule. *Behaviour Research and Therapy,* 1969, *7* 381–386.

Sarason, I. G. Empirical findings and theoretical problems in the use of anxiety scales. *Psychological Bulletin,* 1960, *57*, 405–415.

Sarbin, T. R. Anxiety: Reification of a metaphor. *Archives of General Psychiatry,* 1964, *10,* 630–633.

Schachter, S. The interaction of cognitive and physiological determinants of emotional state. In L. Berkowitz (Ed.), *Advances in experimental social psychology* (Vol. 1). New York: Academic, 1964.

Schwartz, G. E. Biofeedback and physiological patterning in human emotion and consciousness. In J. Beatty & H. Legewie (Eds.), *Biofeedback and behavior.* New York: Plenum, 1977.

Schwartz, G. E. Psychobiological foundations of psychotherapy and behavior change. In S. L. Garfield & A. E. Bergin (Eds.), *Handbook of psychotherapy and behavior change: An empirical analysis.* New York: Wiley, 1978.

Simpson, R. H. The specific meanings of certain terms indicating different degrees of frequency. *Quarterly Journal of Speech,* 1944, *30,* 328–330.

Smith, R. E., Diener, E., & Beaman, A. L. Demand characteristics and the behavioral avoidance measure of fear in behavior therapy analogue research. *Behavior Therapy,* 1974, *5,* 172–182.

Spielberger, C. D. Anxiety as an emotional state. In C. D. Spielberger (Ed.), *Anxiety: Current trends in theory and research.* New York: Wiley, 1972.

Spielberger, C. D. *Manual for the state-trait anxiety inventory for children.* Palo Alto, Cal.: Counseling Psychologist Press, 1973.

Spielberger, C. D., Gorsuch, R. L., & Lushene, R. E. *Manual for the State-Trait Anxiety Inventory.* Palo Alto, Cal.: Counseling Psychologist Press, 1970.

Taggert, P., Carruthers, M., & Somerville, W. Electrocardiogram, plasma catecholamines and lipids, and their modification by oxyprenolol when speaking before an audience. *The Lancet,* 1973, *1,* 341–346.

Taylor, C. B. Heart rate changes in improved spider-phobic patients. *Psychological Reports,* 1977, *41,* 667–671.

Taylor, J. A. A personality scale of manifest anxiety. *Journal of Abnormal Psychology,* 1953, *48,* 275–280.

Teasdale, J. D., Walsh, P. A., Lancashire, M., & Mathews, A. M. Group exposure for agoraphobics: A replication study. *British Journal of Psychiatry,* 1977, *130,* 186–193.

Twentyman, C. T., & McFall, R. M. Behavioral training of social skills in shy males. *Journal of Consulting and Clinical Psychology,* 1975, *43,* 384–495.

Ulrich, R. E., Stachnik, T. J., & Stainton, W. R. Student acceptance of generalized personality interpretations. *Psychological Reports,* 1963, *13,* 831–834.

Wade, T. C., Malloy, T. E., & Proctor, S. Imaginal correlates of self-reported fear and avoidance behavior. *Behaviour Research and Therapy,* 1977, *15,* 17–22.

Walk, R. D. Self-ratings of fear evoking situation. *Journal of Abnormal and Social Psychology,* 1956, *22,* 171–178.

Watson, D., & Friend, R. Measurement of social-evaluative anxiety. *Journal of Consulting and Clinical Psychology,* 1969, *33,* 448–457.

Watson, J. P., & Marks, I. M. Relevant and irrelevant fear in flooding—A crossover study of phobic patients. *Behavior Therapy,* 1971, *2,* 275–293.

Wessberg, H. W., Mariotto, M. J., Conger, A. J., Farrell, A. D., & Conger, J. C. The ecological validity of role-plays for assessing heterosocial anxiety and skill in college students. *Journal of Consulting and Clinical Psychology,* 1979, *47,* 525–534.

Whitehead, W., Robinson, A., Blackwell, B., & Stutz, R. Flooding treatment for phobias: Does chronic diazepam increase effectiveness? *Journal of Behavior Therapy and Experimental Psychiatry,* 1978, *9,* 219–226.

Wing, J. K., Cooper, J. E., & Sartorius, N. *The measurement and classification of psychiatric symptoms.* Cambridge, England: Cambridge University Press, 1974.

Wolpe, J. Inadequate behavior analysis: The Achilles' heel of outcome research in behavior therapy. *Journal of Behavior Therapy and Experimental Psychiatry,* 1977, *8,* 1–3.

Wolpe, J., & Lang, P. J. A fear survey schedule for use in behavior therapy. *Behaviour Research and Therapy,* 1964, *2,* 27–30.

Yule, W., & Fernando, P. Blood phobia—Beware. *Behaviour Research and Therapy,* 1980, *18,* 587–590.

Zuckerman, M. The development of an affect adjective checklist for the measurement of anxiety. *Journal of Consulting and Clinical Psychology,* 1960, *24,* 457–462.

3

Simple Phobia

ELLIE T. STURGIS and REDA SCOTT

The inclusion of a chapter on simple phobias in a book discussing the behavioral treatment of anxiety is quite appropriate, since this disorder was one of the first explained and treated from a behavioristic standpoint. The early experimental psychologists, including Watson and Raynor (1920) and Mowrer (1939) explained the development of specific fears using a conditioning model. In one of the first behavioral treatment programs, Jones extended this earlier work and demonstrated the extinction of a small-animal fear using principles of counterconditioning. The roots of behavior therapy in England and South Africa were also involved with the investigation of irrational fears and anxiety (O'Leary & Wilson, 1975). Even during the early days of behavior therapy, when the orientation was not well accepted by the majority of psychologists and psychiatrists, the simple phobia was one of the few conditions referred to the behaviorist for treatment.

Given the 60-odd-year history of research attempting to elucidate etiological factors of the simple phobias and the development of treatments for such conditions, one would expect the behaviorist to have a very comprehensive understanding of this disorder. Indeed, until the early 1970s, this appeared to be the case. More recently, however, problems have emerged with Mowrer's two-factor theory of avoidance development (1947) and Eysenck's (1967) incubation hypothesis, the two theories most commonly used to explain phobia. Although investigators have developed a number of effective treatment proce-

ELLIE T. STURGIS ● Department of Psychiatry and Human Behavior, University of Mississippi Medical Center, Jackson, Mississippi 39216.   REDA SCOTT ● Psychology Service, Jackson Veterans Administration Medical Center, and Department of Psychiatry and Human Behavior, University of Mississippi Medical Center, Jackson, Mississippi 39216.

dures for the simple phobia, a thorough understanding of the disorder and of the active ingredients involved in the treatment process has lagged behind. To date, there is no single theory which explains all aspects of simple phobia. Not surprisingly, psychologists differ in their hypotheses concerning which elements of treatment are the most potent. Treatment continues to be administered in a haphazard manner with few attempts to match the treatment with the specific symptoms of the client. Furthermore, there has been no specification of which treatment elements are most appropriate for particular types of simple phobias.

The purposes of this chapter are to review the defining characteristics of the phobic disorder, to discuss current theories of etiology, assessment, and treatment of simple phobia, to evaluate the effectiveness of current treatment procedures, and to discuss further research directions which might both clarify the understanding of simple phobia and improve the effectiveness of treatment. Throughout the chapter, an attempt will be made to integrate hypotheses with the existent data. Finally, it is hoped that this chapter will be of some utility both to the theoretician and the practicing clinician.

DEFINING CHARACTERISTICS

The *Diagnostic and Statistical Manual* (DSM-III) (American Psychiatric Association, 1980, p. 229) describes the *simple phobia*. The essential feature of the simple phobia is a persistent, irrational fear of, and compelling desire to avoid, some object or situation other than being alone or in public places away from home (agoraphobia) on the one hand, or being humiliated or embarrassed in certain social situations (social phobia) on the other. Simple phobia is thus a residual category of phobic disorder. It is a significant source of distress, and the individual recognizes that his or her fear is excessive or unreasonable. The disturbance is not due to another mental disorder.

Simple phobias are sometimes referred to as *specific phobias*. The most common simple phobias in the general population, though not necessarily among those seeking treatment, involve fear of animals, particularly dogs, snakes, insects, and mice. Other simple phobias are claustrophobia (fear of closed spaces) and acrophobia (fear of heights).

Associated Symptoms

Mavissakalian and Barlow (1981) discuss two components of phobias: phobic anxiety and phobic avoidance. Phobic anxiety is a psychophysiological response characteristic of sympathetic activation. The phobic anxiety is experienced only in the actual or imagined presence of the object, person, or situation that is feared. Phobic symptoms include a sudden onset of intense apprehension and terror, feelings of unsteadiness, feelings of unreality, feelings of impending doom, fears of dying, going crazy, or doing something uncontrolled, and psychophysiological symptoms including shortness of breath, sensations of choking and smothering, chest pain or discomfort, paresthesias, hot or cold flashes, faintness, and trembling (American Psychiatric Association, 1980).

Phobic avoidance describes the behavior or tendency of an individual to avoid contact with or exposure to a feared stimulus. As a result of the phobic anxiety, the individual typically tries to gain considerable information before entering a situation in which the phobic stimulus may be encountered. If a situation is likely to lead to such an encounter, the individual is likely to avoid that situation. Although phobic avoidance is usually demonstrated by phobic patients, there are times when an individual engages in contact with the situation despite the resulting psychophysiological and cognitive disturbances. Thus, while phobic patients are usually quite similar in terms of the psychophysiological symptoms experienced, they are often different in the avoidance patterns expressed.

Mavissakalian and Barlow (1981) reviewed the primary simple phobias, monosymptomatic fears involving animals or specific situations (e.g. fears and avoidance of dogs, cats, birds, snakes, thunderstorms, darkness, and heights) as well as fear of blood and injury. The blood and injury phobias included fear of the sight of blood, fear of going to the dentist, doctor, or hospital, and fears of certain specified illnesses. Although the blood and injury phobias are not included as simple phobias in the DSM III, they appear similar to the simple phobias in being relatively specific fears. The psychophysiological response in the blood and injury phobia is different from that of the monosymptomatic phobia (Yule & Fernando, 1980). Thus, while the monosymptomatic phobias and blood and injury phobias are all classified as simple phobias, the category is not a homogeneous one. The heterogeneity presents difficulties for individuals who attempt to determine the etiological factors involved in and the appropriate treatment for simple phobias.

Age of Onset

The age of onset for simple phobias is quite variable. The majority of animal, situation, and blood and injury phobias begin in childhood (Burns, 1980; Mavissakalian & Barlow, 1981; Rachman, 1974). Rachman observed that fears of natural manifestations such as animals, storms, and the dark typically diminish with age, while interpersonal fears or social phobias become worse over time. Agras, Sylvester, and Oliveau (1969) documented a decline in blood and injury phobias with advancing years which they attributed to the experience of repeated exposure to the feared stimuli. Burns (1980) found the peak frequency of childhood phobias to occur at 3 years of age. The frequency of new phobias gradually diminished; however, there was another peak in the incidence of new fears at ages 9–11 for boys and age 11 for girls. Agras *et al.*

(1969) found the incidence of the development of new phobias to decline with advancing age; however, the prevalence (total number of phobic cases) increased until the sixth decade of life and only then declined. In a follow-up of the earlier study, Agras, Chapin, and Oliveau (1972) found that 100% of the subjects under 20 were improved at follow-up, while 40% were asymptomatic, but that only 43% of the adults were improved, and none were asymptomatic. These data suggest that childhood phobias are more malleable and changeable than adult fears. The childhood fears, nevertheless, can persist and cause problems in adulthood.

Impairment

The impairment of life-style caused by simple phobias can also be quite variable. If the phobic situation or object is a relatively rare one and can be easily avoided, the impairment is likely to be very slight. It is considerable, however, if the phobic object is common and cannot be easily avoided. This finding relates to the earlier discussion distinguishing phobic avoidance and phobic symptoms. If the object is common, the life-style will be impaired by the circumscribed activities of the individual which result from behavioral avoidances, the intensity of the psychophysiological symptoms, and the amount of cognitive distress experienced. The greater the impairment subjectively experienced by the individual, the greater the likelihood the person will seek treatment for the phobia.

Predisposing Factors

The DSM-III provides no discussion of factors which predispose an individual to develop phobias. However, there are some data suggesting a genetic or familial component. There is a higher concordance rate for simple phobias among family members than among the general population. Whether genetic factors, differences in autonomic activity, modeling effects, or a combination of these factors contribute to this development is unclear. There do, however, seem to be individuals who are more likely to develop simple phobias than other individuals. Likewise, there are certain time periods when an individual is more likely to develop simple phobias than others. These factors will be discussed in conjunction with the theories of etiology.

Sex Ratio

The DSM-III indicates that simple phobias are diagnosed in women more often than in men. Marks (1969) hypothesized that animal phobias account for this discrepancy. He found that animal phobias are reported nine times more frequently among women than among men. Other simple phobias occurred with about equal frequency between both sexes. Burns (1980) found simple phobias to occur at a 1:1.7 male–female ratio in a study of fears and phobias from seven general medicine practices. In this study, however, social phobias were mixed with simple phobias, and a breakdown according to type of specific phobia was not reported. While it is apparent that women are much more likely than men to seek treatment for phobias, the exact difference in sex ratio for the simple phobia is unclear. If one factors out monosymptomatic animal phobias, it is possible that the sex difference is lower than has previously been hypothesized.

Prevalence of Simple Phobias

The exact prevalence of simple phobias in the general population is unknown; however, it appears that mild fears and phobias are widespread, particularly during childhood. MacFarlane, Allen, and Honzik (1954) surveyed 1096 children and found that only 10% of the total sample showed no evidence of fear reactions. In a study investigating fears in 482 children aged 6–12 years, Lapouse and Monk (1959) found 43% of the children to have seven or more fears, with more females (50%) than males (36%) exhibiting this large number of fears. While fears are quite common among children, the incidence of clinically significant phobias is much lower. In a study involving all 2000 10- and 11-year-old children on the Isle of Wight, Rutter, Tizard, and Whitmore (1968) found that only .7% of the children had clinically significant and disabling phobias. A lower prevalence was found in adult epidemiological studies. Lemkau, Tietze, and Cooper (1942) and Hollingshead and Redlich (1958) found 0.05 cases per hundred. In a more recent epidemiological survey of common fears and phobias, Agras *et al.* (1969) reported a prevalence of phobias in 7.69% of the population and a prevalence of severely disabling phobias in .22% of the population. Only .9% of the individuals had been treated for the disorder.

Early discussion of phobia classified the disorders according to the feared stimulus. Psychology students learned long lists of phobias and the object feared was considered the most significant diagnostic characteristic of the phobia. A listing of common phobias is presented in Table 1. Lang (1968) challenged this conceptualization when he proposed the three-component model of fear. The extent of involvement of three behavioral systems (the cognitive response, the motoric response, and the physiological response modes) was the most important characteristic of the behavioral abnormality. The phobic object was seen as important only because of the manner in which it activated the three systems. For the majority of the simple phobias, the behavioral components involve behavioral avoidance, activation of the sympathetic nervous system, and cognitions of fear and discomfort. Lang (1968, 1971, 1978) and Rachman (1974, 1976, 1977, 1978a,b) have shown that the three systems may

Table 1. Common Phobias and Their Definitions

Acrophobia—fear of high places
Agoraphobia—fear of open places
Ailurophobia—fear of cats
Algophobia—fear of pain
Astrapophobia—fear of storms, thunder and lightning
Claustrophobia—fear of closed spaces
Cynophobia—fear of dogs
Decidophobia—fear of making decisions
Hematophobia—fear of blood
Hydrophobia—fear of water
Monophobia—fear of being alone
Mysophobia—fear of dirt and germs
Ophidiophobia—fear of snakes
Pyrophobia—fear of fire
Xenophobia—fear of strangers

be relatively independent, contingent upon the developmental and conditioning history of the individual.

Instead of classifying phobias according to either conceptualization alone, it is possible that a consideration of both approaches is desirable. An analysis of the three-system involvement in the varied simple phobias should provide information on the commonalities and differences among the various phobic classes. There are currently no data which address the question of whether the classification according to phobic stimulus or behavioral response complex is more efficacious. This chapter will discuss the phobias from both perspectives. It is hoped that such an approach will facilitate our understanding and treatment of phobic disorder.

THEORIES

In a recent article on phobic disorder, Barendregt (1976) stated that "one fool can think of more hypotheses than ten wise men can test" (p. 137). With regard to the present topic one soon realizes that some of the most prestigious psychologists and psychiatrists of the twentieth century have been involved in research on phobias. If, as Barendregt stated, a fool can generate a plethora of theories, it is not surprising that the number of theories generated by talented scientists is even larger, and that the resultant testing of hypotheses poses a monumental task. In attempting to review the theories of phobias, it has proved impossible in a short chapter to cover all the theories currently being used to describe the etiology of phobic disorder. The authors have therefore chosen to review only those biological and psychological theories which have proved to be of greatest heuristic value.

Biological Models

The biological evidence for phobias is relatively weak. The existing biological theories include a genetic theory, a psychophysiological theory, a preparedness theory, and a tonic immobility theory. Of data involving biological conceptualizations, those supporting the preparedness theory are the strongest.

Genetic

Genetic factors affect the development of psychiatric conditions in three ways: through the action of a chromosomal anomaly, the operation of a mutant gene, or the interaction of polygenetic and environmental factors. No data suggest that chromosomes or mutant genes contribute to the development of the simple phobia. There are data, however, suggesting a familial loading in the general class of anxiety disorders. Schepank (cited in Katschnig & Shepherd 1976) reviewed 13 international studies and found the concordance rate for neurotic disorders to be 59.2% (184 pairs) for monozygotic twins and 28.2% (163 pairs) for dizygotic twins. However, no data were located which addressed the role of genetic predisposition in the simple phobia. For those cases that show a familial development trend, the modeling theory explains the trend as parsimoniously as the role of genetics. Physiological data from Lader and Mathews (1968) suggest that specific phobias are not characterized by general high levels of arousal in the autonomic nervous system—one modality through which a genetic predisposition could operate. These authors examined the frequency of spontaneous fluctuations in skin conductance and habituation rates of skin conductance for groups of agoraphobic ($N = 16$), pervasive-anxiety ($N = 16$), social-phobic ($N = 18$), specific-phobic ($N = 19$), and normal ($N = 75$) subjects. The responses of the simple-phobic group were more similar to the normal group than to the remaining three groups. Aberrant arousal patterns were phasic phenomena which occurred only when the subject was exposed to the feared stimulus. The specificity of this response weakens the assumption that the specific phobia results from a generalized level of arousal passed on to one's offspring through genetic mechanisms.

Psychophysiological Theory

In 1971, Lang hypothesized that the psychophysiological response was as important a part of the symptom complex exhibited by an individual as were the overt motor behaviors and cognitions. He maintained that tripartite or three-channel assessment of symptom patterns was fundamental to an understanding of the phenomenon under investigation. Subsequently, it was observed that changes in the systems (e.g., psychophysiological, behavioral, and cognitive) could occur concordantly (in synchrony) or discordantly (in desynchrony) (Rachman & Hodgson, 1974). While many investigators have included psychophysiological measures in their assessment and evaluation of phobic disorders, no psychophysiological theory of the disorder has emerged. Thus, current thinking regards the phobia as a phenomenon which involves psychophysiological activation but results from some other source.

Preparedness of Prepotency Theory

A marked shift in thinking concerning simple phobias occurred early in the 1970s. Until that time, the major theories of phobias were psychological theories. However, an ethological model emerged in 1971. Prior to Seligman's specification of a theory of preparedness (1971), several psychologists suggested certain fears were innate. Valentine (1946), criticizing Watson and Raynor's (1920) work, suggested that fear of rats was an innate but dormant fear. Attempting to replicate the experiment of Watson and Raynor, Valentine exposed his daughter to repeated associations of a pair of opera glasses and a loud whistle but achieved no conditioning. A repetition of the paradigm using a caterpillar stimulus yielded significant emotional conditioning which gradually faded in intensity but was quickly restored with additional association trials. Skinner (1953) strengthened the argument for an evolutionary adaptiveness of certain fears. In discussing the potential evolutionary value of selected behaviors, he indicated that an avoidance behavior of biological significance might be more readily incorporated into the response repertoire of a person or animal than one with no evolutionary significance.

Perhaps inspired by these suggestions, or by observations of either successful conditioning or of failures to condition and/or extinguish according to the typical laws of learning, Marks (1969) and Seligman (1971) proposed a prepotency or preparedness theory of simple phobias. This theory was considered superior to earlier ones since it allowed the fears to be acquired in a single conditioning trial, to be selective to certain classes of objects, and to be resistant to extinction. Seligman and Hager (1972) suggested that phobic events are all similar in that they involve a fear of objects or situations that were dangerous to pretechnological man in his natural environment. Phobias developed if the prepared stimulus was linked with an aversive outcome. The prepared association was characterized by rapid acquisition, slow extinction, and was not easily affected by voluntary cognitive activity (Hugdahl & Karker, 1981). While the phobic response would have been evaluated as a realistic or appropriate fear in pretechnological times, it has become maladaptive or irrational in a technological society. Marks (1976) described selected or prepared fear as "doing what comes naturally" (p. 124).

The concept of selected fears has received validation from several areas. First, a review of the common phobias indicates that the fears do not involve a random assortment of stimuli encountered in everyday life, but include a relatively limited number of stimuli. Common fears include fear of the dark, of snakes and spiders, reptiles, bees and wasps, small animals, thunderstorms, predators, blood and injury, crowds, and eating certain foods. DeSilva, Rachman, and Seligman (1977) had individuals evaluate whether these fears were probably or possibly dangerous to pretechnological man under certain conditions. All of the stimuli which occur as common phobic objects were rated as potentially dangerous. Fears rated as less dangerous to pretechnological man included fears of eclipses, daylight, leaves, flowers, and disconnected electrical appliances. No cases of phobias of these stimuli have been documented. A second line of evidence comes from Seligman and Hager (1972) who reviewed the conditioning literature and found that all events were not equally associable in animals. These authors constructed a continuum of preparedness. As a result of natural selection, the animal was prepared to associate certain events, unprepared to do so with others, and contraprepared in the case of still others. They hypothesized that preparedness of association influenced the laws of learning, in that prepared associations conditioned more rapidly and extinguished more slowly than unprepared or contraprepared associations.

A series of studies have examined the applicability of a preparedness hypothesis to humans. Öhman and his co-workers (Öhman, Eriksson, Fredrikson, Hugdahl, & Olofsson, 1974; Öhman, Eriksson, & Lofberg, 1975; Öhman, Eriksson, & Olofsson, 1975; Öhman, Fredrikson, Hugdahl, & Rimmö, 1976; Öhman, Fredrikson, & Hugdahl, 1978) examined the preparedness theory of phobias in students and found that skin-conductance responses conditioned more easily and extinguished more slowly to stimuli such as spiders and snakes than to neutral stimuli like houses, flowers, or geometric figures. Threat of shock or observation of another individual being shocked in association with fear relevant and irrelevant stimuli, respectively, resulted in the same behavior pattern as obtained using actual exposure to the aversive shock. Öhman and Dimberg (1978) demonstrated the existence of prepared associations to angry, but not to happy faces. More recent data have shown the development of prepared associations for stimuli phylogenetically relevant to fear such as spiders and snakes, but not for ontogenetically relevant stimuli such as guns, broken electrical cords, and damaged switches (Hugdahl & Karker, 1981; Öhman & Hugdahl, 1979). The effects of instruction upon extinction of fear relevant and irrelevant responses, respectively, were also examined by these investigators (Hugdahl, 1978). After the acquisition of a fear response to prepared and unprepared stimuli, the subjects were told the aversive stimulus would be discontinued. Subjects immediately extinguished the response to the fear-irrelevant stimulus, while the response to the fear-relevant stimulus continued. Thus, whether the fear had been induced through direct experience, threat, or observation of another's fear, the responses to fear-relevant stimuli continued, even though continuation of the response was not rational. This finding is consistent with the irrationality of many phobias (Öhman & Hugdahl, 1979).

The observations and arguments of the preparedness view of phobias are impressive. However, the majority of studies testing this concept have used college students and analogue populations. While there are arguments favoring inclusion of analogue studies (Borkovec & O'Brien, 1976; O'Leary & Borkovec, 1978), the heuristic value of a clinical theory remains limited until it can be validated in a population burdened with clinically significant fears. The evidence supporting a preparedness theory for *all* fears is not encouraging (Delprato, 1980). Rachman and Seligman (1976) examined outcome data on two individuals with unprepared fears. The symptoms included a marked fear and avoidance of chocolate and a fear of the leaves of vegetables and plants. Both fears were quite rare, had little biological significance, were characterized by a gradual acquisition curve, and showed marked generalization to other objects and a high resistance to extinction. According to the preparedness theory, limited generalization and rapid extinction would be expected.

The second clinical study incorporating the preparedness concept was carried out by de Silva, Rachman, and Seligman (1977), who reviewed the treatment outcomes of 69 clinical cases of phobias and obsessions. The fears were rated along dimensions of preparedness. Results showed a marked preponderance of prepared fears, especially for phobic subjects. A chi-square test was used to compare outcome for the least prepared and most prepared fears. There was no difference between groups in therapeutic outcome, mode of onset, severity, intensiveness of treatment, degree of generalization, age of onset, effect on life-style, or effect on reproductive capacity. These data wield a severe blow to the preparedness theory and its hypotheses. While the data have not been replicated, the consistent inability to differentiate characteristics between prepared and unprepared phobias significantly challenges this theory. The preparedness concept appears to have significant validity when used in laboratory experiments eliciting conditioned fears; however, its utility in the clinical setting as an explanation of the etiology of phobias has not been demonstrated. Further research examining the relationship of preparedness to established phobias is sorely needed.

Tonic Immobility

The final biological model of phobia is of potential applicability only to the blood and injury phobia. While typically considered a simple phobia, the blood and injury phobia appears qualitatively different from the other simple phobias. Most simple phobias are typically associated with increases in heart rate and blood pressure along with other signs of sympathetic activation. The blood and injury phobia, on the other hand, is often accompanied by decreases in heart rate upon exposure to the feared stimulus, decreases in blood pressure, and fainting, all signs of a vaso-vagal reflex (Yule & Fernando, 1980). Marks (1976) hypothesized that this response is similar to the death-feigning or tonic immobility response sometimes observed in animals lower on the phylogenetic scale. Tonic immobility or death-feigning is a catatonic-like paralysis in animals, associated with suppressions of vocal behavior, changes in heart and respiration rate, altered electroencephalographic patterns, muscle tremors in the extremities, and decreased responsiveness to external stimulation (Gallup & Maser, 1977), all of which minimize the stimuli that evoke an attack and allow the individual to escape while the predator is distracted (Sargeant & Eberhardt, 1975). Marks hypothesized that the blood phobia response is an evolutionarily preprogrammed response, triggered by the stimulus of blood, which has no adaptive function in man but which might have had survival value among man's ancestors. This highly speculative theory has received very little attention but is of potential interest to the theoretician and clinician, particularly when one considers the atypical symptom complex of the blood and injury phobia.

Psychological Theories

Psychoanalytic Theory

The psychodynamic school views phobia as a neurotic disorder primarily characterized by two defense mechanisms, repression and displacement. According to this conceptualization, during the early developmental years, particularly during the oedipal stage (3–6 years), resolution of conflicts involving sexual and aggressive drives, wishes, and desires predisposes an individual to develop deep-seated and unconscious conflicts in these areas. In later life these conflicts tend to surface, causing the individual marked discomfort. The individual therefore tends to avoid contact with the situations which elicit memories of the conflicts, and exhibits fear and avoidance (phobia) of these stimuli. He or she is thus protected against the emergence of the repressed anxiety-eliciting conflicts. In other circumstances the phobia may represent a displacement of an actual, threatening situation to another situation. Psychoanalysts hypothesized that Freud's (1909) case study of Little Hans (Wolpe & Rachman, 1960) represents an example of this displacement. Freud reported that the boy experienced feelings of sexual attraction for his mother and feelings of jealousy and hostility toward his father, all of which are frightening experiences for young children. In this case, following a frightening experience with a horse, the anxiety stemming from the feelings of attraction, jealousy, hostility, and castration were displaced to a fear of horses. However, many theoreticians have disagreed with Freud's interpretation of this case.

According to the psychoanalytic model, the unconscious must be made conscious, the original source of anxiety must be discovered, and the conflict must be resolved if the phobia is to be effectively treated (Mavissakalian & Barlow, 1981). Analysts have stressed heavily the symbolic meaning of the specific phobias. While the theory has made a significant contribution to our understanding of the characteristics of the simple phobia, a direct test of the hypothetical basis of the model is difficult if not impossible. Likewise, aside from the work of Malan (1963, 1976), evaluating short-term psychotherapy which showed a 50% improvement rate for phobics ($N = 10$), controlled statistical outcome studies on the use of psychoanalysis with simple phobias is lacking. The heuristic value of this model, therefore, is somewhat limited, although it is one espoused by a great number of practicing mental health professionals.

Conditioning Theory

Conditioning theory is the behavioral theory most commonly used to explain how individuals develop intense, irrational fears of persons, objects, or situations. This theory states that neutral stimuli (conditioned stimuli, CS) which are associated with fear, anxiety, or pain-producing events (unconditioned stimuli, UCS) develop fearful qualities and become conditioned stimuli, themselves capable of eliciting the fear response (conditioned response, CR) as a result of this association. The strength of the acquired fear is a function of the number of CS–UCS associations and the intensity of the fear experienced in the presence of the stimuli. An example of such an acquired phobia may be found in the development of the first author. At the age of 10 she was allowed to shoot her first fireworks, in this case a Roman candle. Unfortunately, as a result of ignorance of the appropriate way to handle fireworks and a malfunction in the Roman candle, the candle backfired, a coat sleeve caught fire, and the author experienced a moderately severe burn, necessitating several months of medical care. Consequences of this event included physiological activation in the presence of fireworks or loud, unexpected noises, a behavioral tendency to avoid Fourth of July celebrations, and a very negative attitude toward the sale of fireworks to nonprofessionals. This conditioning model of fear acquisition was first demonstrated by Watson and Raynor (1920), who conditioned a fear of rats and white furry objects through the temporal association of the object and loud noises.

Mowrer (1947, 1960) expanded the conditioning model to explain the fact that the phobic symptoms seldom extinguish, even if the individual has little continued contact with the phobic object or is repeatedly exposed to it in the absence of the UCS. According to the principles of Pavlovian conditioning, one would anticipate extinction of the phobic behavior under these conditions. Mowrer (1947, 1960) viewed acquisition and maintenance of the phobia as a two-stage process. Classical conditioning principles are operative during fear acquisition. However, once the fear is acquired, an operant process is involved. Imaginal or actual confrontation of the feared stimulus elicits feelings of fear and anxiety. If the individual avoids exposure to the stimulus, the anxiety response, an aversive event, is terminated. According to this model, the principles of negative reinforcement strengthen the tendency of the individual to avoid the situation. Thus, Mowrer's model explains the development of the emotional component of the fear in terms of classical conditioning and the avoidance component of the fear in terms of negative reinforcement principles.

The conditioning theory has been criticized on both experimental and clinical grounds (Herrnstein, 1969; Rachman, 1976; Seligman, 1971). Primary criticisms of the theory involve (1) the development of phobias in the absence of a traumatic conditioning event, (2) the rare occurrence of one trial conditioning in the literature, (3) the selective nature of stimuli to which phobias can be easily conditioned, and (4) the failure of the clinical data to conform to experimental predictions.

For a time, Eysenck's incubation hypothesis was used to explain the development of phobia in the absence of a traumatic conditioning event (Eysenck, 1967). According to this theory, there are phobic patients who experience an increase in fear over time. In this situation, the presence of an unassociated CS (a CS without a UCS) leads to an increased rather than decreased CR. This finding is contrary to that anticipated according to the theory of extinction. Eysenck explained this phenomenon as an example of the Napalkov effect (Napalkov, 1963), a phenomenon of ever-widening stimulus generalization. The fear grows over time as a result of such generalization. Rohrbaugh and Riccio (1970) have documented this paradoxical effect but found it to be relatively rare. They concluded that even when the phenomenon occurred, the paradoxical enhancement is reversed after a short while and extinction of the CR to the CS occurs. Again this theory appears to explain very few phobias.

While the conditioning theory assumes that phobia acquisition typically occurs during a single trial, one-trial conditioning of fear seems to be the exception rather than the rule. As laboratory studies have shown, fear conditioning usually takes six to eight pairings of the UCS and the CS (Kamin, 1969; Seligman, 1968). Phobias also fail to extinguish along the lines of conditioned responses. Mowrer's theory predicts the behavior of animals if they do not know that the CS–UCS association has been disrupted. If, however, the animal ever discovers that the CS and UCS are not linked, the CS becomes ineffective in eliciting a CR (Kamin, 1965; Rescorla & LoLordo, 1965). This is not true for phobics, however. When phobics learn that the feared object is not associated with aversive states, avoidance and physiological activation continue despite the irrationality of the fear. The conditioning theory is also a theory of equipotentiality (e.g., all stimuli should be equally conditionable). Yet, as has been illustrated in the preparedness section, stimuli show a hierarchical ability to be conditioned.

From a clinical perspective, a number of other sources of data present difficulties for the conditioning theory. First, despite repeated exposure to danger or stressful situations, most people develop very few fears or phobias (Rachman, 1976). Air raids were very commonplace occurrences in London during World War II; however, contrary to the expectation of mass panic, the great majority of people coped well with the air raids. Exposure to the bombings, while precipitating frequent short-lived fear reactions, produced surprisingly few prolonged phobic reactions (Janis, 1951; Lewis, 1942). These data are corroborated by similar reports from Japan and Germany (Rachman, 1976).

Another clinical problem for the conditioning theory is the fact that phobias often develop in the absence of specific occurrence of trauma. Many fears develop gradually. Goorney and O'Connor (1971) were able to document traumatic stimuli in only 25% of the cases they reviewed. The distribution of fears also presents problems for the conditioning theory since it contradicts the premise of equipotentiality. A survey of common fears in a small Vermont city showed the prevalence of a fear of snakes to be 390/1000 while a fear of the dentist was 198/1000 (Agras *et al.,* 1969). Since contact with the dentist is a more likely occurrence and is often associated with painful episodes, this fear should develop more readily. The finding presents a substantial problem for the conditioning theory (Rachman, 1976). Finally, fears have been found to be transmittable by vicarious means as well as through actual experience. A strong correspondence has been found between fears in parent and child. John (1941) obtained a correlation of .59 between fears in a mother and child, while Hagman (1932) found a correlation of .67 between the total number of fears experienced by a mother and her child.

Vicarious Acquisition of Phobias

With the decline in acceptance of the conditioning model of phobias and the growth of the social learning movement, some investigators concentrated on a modeling or vicarious-acquisition paradigm for phobias. According to this paradigm, if one individual observes another individual experience an aversive stimulus, the person witnessing the event may develop fears of elements in the aversive situation. The nature of the aversive experience might be positive or negative. An example of such acquisition was seen by Dr. Victor Meyer at Middlesex Hospital. He treated sisters who were phobic of birds. During childhood, one of the girls had been walking in the park and was brutally attacked by a bird. Her sister witnessed the event. Both girls thereafter developed phobias of flying birds. Interestingly, the phobia of the observing sister was more severe than that of the attacked sister (Meyer, 1977). The high concordance between fears of family members discussed earlier provides additional support for this theory, although it is not clear whether the observation of the fear response or information about the fear is what predisposes the child or sibling to develop the phobia. Rimm, Janda, Lancaster, Nanl, and Dittman (1977), assessing the phobias of 45 subjects (college students), found that only three subjects were able to relate their fears to vicarious learning conditions, while 16 related them to direct experiences.

Cognitive Factors

Behaviorists have increasingly granted cognition a role in the development and maintenance of behavior. The cognitive learning perspective of phobias emphasizes the role of overt or covert verbal instructions in the acquisition of the phobic response. This theory holds that individuals develop intense fears of objects or situations as a result of being told that the situation is dangerous. Cognitive theorists assume that after receiving such instruction, the individual subsequently rehearses the instruction whenever confronted with the phobic situation. The individual then engages in internal dialogues about the situation during which he or she can distort his or her perceptions of events through the use of personalization, arbitrary inference, and overgeneralization (Rimm & Lefebvre, 1981). There are few data testing the cognitive theories of phobias. Wade, Malloy, and Proctor (1977) examined cognitions about phobic objects in two groups of subjects with snake phobias. The groups were matched on the dimension of severity of the symptoms. Subjects with higher avoidance scores on a behavioral avoidance task reported significantly more negative imagery regarding snakes than did the low avoidance group (7% vs. 13%). The self-reports of fear during the task were higher for the negative-imagery group than for the neutral or no-imagery group (regardless of approach behavior).

Borkovec (1979) extended the two-factor theory and proposed that important cognitive and perceptual variables were functionally related to the avoidance response. In a series of experiments, Borkovec found that cognitive avoidance during imagined exposure to a task maintained the physiological fear response. Once the cognitive avoidance strategy was adopted, further exposure to an unassociated CS facilitated the maintenance of anxious behavior. He hypothesized that treatment would be effective only if it altered the cognitive avoidance response. He and his colleagues also found that attending to the physiological fear responses increased the fear experienced by the individual. Borkovec has attempted in his studies to unify the conditioning model with the cognitive model. While his data are an exciting addition to the area, the deficits of the conditioning model remain.

The preliminary data support the hypothesis of a strong cognitive component in the phobic response. Whether cognitive theories best explain this component of whether the cognitive behavior can be better explained by the other theories remains to be seen.

There is no single theory of etiology which adequately explains all phobias. The preparedness theory, a variant of the conditioning theory, and cognitive variants appear to be of greatest heuristic value. Future research which examines an integration of these theories may clarify our understanding of the simple phobic disorder.

ASSESSMENT OF SIMPLE PHOBIAS

As discussed in the introduction to this chapter, fear is presently recognized as consisting of three component response systems, subjective (or cognitive), physiological, and behavioral. It has been noted that these three systems can covary, vary inversely, or vary independently (Hodgson & Rachman, 1974;

Leitenberg, Agras, Butz, & Wincze, 1971; Rachman & Hodgson, 1974). More recently, Hugdahl (1981) has concluded that the overall impression from the literature is that the three systems do not covary, especially in the case of clinically significant emotions. Thus, these findings have important implications for assessment and treatment of phobic individuals. For example, if patients load differently on these three components, then the therapist may need to make a routine assessment of all response systems so that subsequent treatment may be individually suited for each patient (Agras & Jacob, 1981; Hugdahl, 1981; Marks, 1978; Odom, Nelson, & Wein, 1978). Moreover, the phobic individual who experiences strong physiological reactions and behavioral avoidance, but little cognitive discomfort, may show little improvement under a primarily cognitive therapy. Thus, it would be necessary to include treatment components aimed specifically toward the physiological and behavioral components.

Ideally, all aspects of the phobic response syndrome should be measured. However, since this is not possible in practice, the clinician is limited to measuring responses across several dimensions. The primary task of assessment becomes choosing the smallest number of measures which will yield the most complete information. In this section, therefore, the authors will focus primarily on various methods of assessing the three response systems. Each method will be discussed in terms of its frequency of use and sensitivity, defined by Agras and Jacob (1981) as the discrimination between treatment conditions and/or the demonstration of pre- to post-test change at or above the .05 level of significance.

Subjective/Cognitive Assessment

As can be seen in Table 2, 80% ($N = 43$) of the reviewed treatment studies employed at least some type of subjective/cognitive measure. The most frequently used measure involved the subjects' self-ratings of their fear and/or anxiety. The next most frequently used measures were forms of the Fear Survey Schedule (Barrett, 1969; Geer, 1965; Wolpe & Lang, 1969) and the Fear Thermometer (Walk, 1956), both of which were used in nine studies. The measures used least frequently included the Eysenck Personality Inventory ($N = 2$), self-competency ratings ($N = 2$), symptom checklists ($N = 2$), adjective checklists ($N = 1$), and various scales specific to the type of phobia investigated.

In terms of sensitivity, the self-ratings of fear and/or anxiety were most often sensitive to change (76%), followed by the Fear Thermometer (66%), and forms of the Fear Survey Schedule (55%). Other measures, such as questionnaires tailored to the specific fear (Denney, Sullivan, & Thiry, 1977), self-competency ratings (Smith & Coleman, 1977), Fear Inventory (Bandura, Blanchard, & Ritter, 1969; Bandura, Jeffery, & Gajdos, 1975; Smith & Coleman, 1977), and Anxiety Inventory (Barrett, 1969; D'Zurilla, Wilson, & Nelson, 1973; Odom, Nelson, & Wein, 1978) show promise, but were not included in this comparison because they were used in only four or fewer studies.

Behavioral Assessment

Eighty-three percent (N = 45) of the reviewed treatment studies employed a behavioral measure of avoidance of approach to the feared stimulus. Examples of behavioral measures include amount of distance to a caged snake for snake phobics, number of steps up a fire escape for acrophobics, amount of time spent in a closed room for claustrophobics, amount of time spent in the presence of a knife, and so forth. In most cases (96%), these behavioral measures were quite sensitive to changes made during treatment, regardless of the type of phobia examined. However, since these variations in behavioral measures cannot be equated, they highlight the problems involved in using more than one type of simple phobic in a group study.

Physiological Measures

Of the three response systems, physiological responses were measured least often. Only 22% (N = 12) of the reviewed treatment studies employed any type of physiological measure. Of these, heart rate was used most frequently (N = 9), followed by skin conductance (N = 6). The Finger Sweat Print Test and blood-flow changes in the finger were used once each. Skin-conductance measures were sensitive to change in 66% (N = 4), while heart-rate measures were sensitive to change in 55% (N = 5). While the measure of blood-flow changes in the finger was sensitive to change on the one occasion it was used, the Finger Sweat Print Test was not.

Selection of Assessment Measures for the Three Systems

In summary, behavioral measures were employed most frequently (83%), followed by subjective (80%), and physiological (22%). In addition, behavioral measures were most sensitive to change while physiological measures were the least sensitive. Twenty-four percent (N = 13) of the studies assessed only one response system; 63% (N = 34) assessed two response systems; and only 13% (N = 7) assessed all three. These findings are similar to those of Agras and Jacob (1981) who reviewed assessment measures used for all of the phobias and suggested that direct measurement was better than indirect. Agras and Jacob also suggested that few measurements are better than many since the likelihood of positive findings due to chance is higher with increases in the number of measures. Therefore, at present it seems that the most efficient assessment of the three response systems should rely upon the clients' self-ratings of anxiety or fear, a behavioral measure of approach/avoidance, and either heart rate or skin conductance. However, there is some suggestion that simply assessing across the three response systems may not be adequate. It may be crucial

Table 2. Summary of Assessment Devices and Treatment Methods with Simple Phobics

Authors	Subjects	Type of phobia	Type of symptoms	Duration	Assessment devices	Treatment conditions	Results	Follow-up
Antman, 1973.	One inpatient (24-year-old woman)	Vermiphobia (including worms, snakes, anything that wiggles)	1. Physiological	4 years	1. Walk's 10-pt. rating scale	6 sessions; 3 phases 1. *In vivo* flooding + therapist modeling (6 hr) 2. Digging in a garden for worms with a shovel (2 hr) 3. *In vivo* flooding with grass snake (2 hr)	1. Changes found within & between sessions; substantial changes within 1 week.	6 months 1. Changes on rating scale maintained

Bandura, Blanchard, Ritter, 1969.	48 fearful community & student volunteers (43 women, 5 men)	Snakes	1. Subjective
			2. Behavioral
				Mean of 27 years	1. Subjective:
					  A. Fear Ratings (10-pt. scale)
					  B. Attitudes:
					    1. 7-pt. scale
					    2. Semantic Differential
					  C. Fear Inventory
					2. Behavioral: approach to king snake
						1. Systematic Desensitization (SD)
						2. Symbolic Modeling (SM)
						3. Live Modeling + Guided Participation (LMGP)
						4. No Treatment Control (NT)
							1. A. SM & LMGP produced greatest reduction; did not differ from each other.
							B. LMGP produced greatest changes; LMGP & SM superior to SD & NT.
							C. LMGP produced most general fear reduction; SD&SM produced most specific fear reduction.
							2. All treatment groups differed from NT; LMGP produced greatest gains.
								None

Bandura, Jeffery, & Gajdos, 1975.	30 community volunteers (4 men; 26 women)	Snakes	1. Subjective
			2. Behavioral
				Not specified	1. Subjective:
					  A. Fear Arousal during approach (10-pt. scale)
					  B. Fear of Snake Encounters
					  C. Self-Competency Ratings
					  D. Personality Potency
					  E. Fear Inventory (5-pt. scale)
						1. Participant Modeling Only (PM)
						2. Participant Modeling + Self-Directed Performance (PM + SDP)
						3. Participant Modeling + Varied Self-Directed Performance (PM + VSDP)
							1. A. All 3 produced decreased arousal; PM + SDP superior.
							B. Both PM + SDP & PM + VSDP were superior to PM; PM + SDP was most improved.
							C. All 3 increased rating; PM + SDP improved the most.
							D. No differences
								1 month
								1. Changes were generally maintained.
								6 & 12 months
								2. Changes maintained.

Study	Subjects	Fear	Measures		Detailed measures	Treatment	Results	Follow-up
					2. Behavioral: Avoidance Test		E. PM + SDP & PM + VSDP were most improved in general area; PM improved only in specific areas. 2. PM + SDP & PM + VSDP produced significantly greater generalized changes than PM.	None
Barlow, Agras, Leitenberg, & Wincze, 1970. I	20 fearful undergraduate volunteers (women)	Snakes	1. Subjective 2. Behavioral	Not specified	1. Physiological: skin conductance 2. Behavioral: approach to the snake's cage	1. Systematic Desensitization (SD) 2. Shaping (S)	1. No significant differences with real or imagined scenes. 2. S produced significantly more improvement than SD	None
Barlow et al., 1970. II	30 fearful undergraduates fulfilling course requirements (women)	Snakes	1. Subjective 2. Behavioral	Not specified	1. Behavioral	Less than 10 sessions 1. Shaping without therapist present (S) 2. Shaping with therapist present (ST) 3. Shaping + therapist modeling (STM)	1. STM produced fastest change & was significantly different from S. ST not significantly different from S.	None
Barlow, Leitenberg, Agras, & Wincze, 1969.	20 fearful undergraduate volunteers (women)	Snakes	1. Subjective	Not specified	1. Physiological: GSR (during imaginal & actual presentations) 2. Behavioral: approach to harmless snakes	10 sessions or completion of hierarchy) 1. Systematic Desensitization (SD) 2. In vivo Desensitization (IVD)	1. With SD reduction of GSR to imagined scenes approached significance but little difference with real situations. With IVD, GSR was reduced significantly for both types of scenes. 2. Both groups improved, IVD produced significantly more improvement.	None
Barrett, 1969.	36 fearful volunteers (8 men; 28 females)	Snakes	1. Behavioral	Not specified	1. Subjective: A. Fear Survey Schedule (FSS III; 5-pt. scale) B. Fear Thermometer (10-pt. scale) C. S–R Inventory of Anxiousness	1. Systematic Desensitization (SD) (4 training; 11 sessions) 2. Implosive Therapy (IT) (2 interviews; 2 sessions) 3. Control	1. On all measures SD & IT more improved than C. 2. A. SD + IT had significantly more passes than C but were not significantly different from each other. b. Same trend as above.	6 months 1. Results maintained 2. Results maintained

(continued)

Table 2. Summary of Assessment Devices and Treatment Methods with Simple Phobics (Continued)

Authors	Subjects	Type of phobia	Type of symptoms	Duration	Assessment devices	Treatment conditions	Results	Follow-up
					2. Behavioral: A. Avoidance Test (requiring subject touch or hold 6-ft. black snake) B. Avoidance Test Change Score			None
Blanchard, 1970	48 fearful community & student volunteers receiving course credit (42 women; 6 men)	Snakes	1. Subjective 2. Behavioral	Not specified	1. Subjective: A. Attitudes toward snakes B. General Fear of Snakes C. Fear Arousal Ratings (11-pt. scale) 2. Behavioral: Avoidance Test	3–45 min sessions 1. Participant Modeling (PM) (Modeling + Verbal Information + Contact) 2. Modeling + Verbal Information (MVI) 3. Modeling (M) 4. No Treatment (NT)	1. On all measures, PM, MCI, & M produced significant changes. PM was superior to MVI on all measures; PM superior to M on only 1 of 3. 2. PM, MVI, & M produced significant change. PM was superior to MVI & M which did not differ.	
De Moor, 1970.	27 fearful college student volunteers (men)	Snakes	1. Subjective 2. Behavioral	Not specified	1. Subjective: Fear Thermometer 2. Physiological: Finger Sweat Print Test 3. Behavioral: Avoidance Test	5 sessions 1. Systematic Desensitization (SD) 2. Flooding (F) 3. Control (C)	1. No differences 2. No differences 3. Significant changes for all groups. Both SD & F were better than C.	6 months 1. No differences 2. No differences 3. Gains of SD remained stable; gains of F did not maintain.
Gauthier & Marshall, 1977.	60 fearful college student volunteers (men)	Snakes	1. Subjective 2. Behavioral	Not specified	1. Subjective: Anxiety Ratings (100-pt. scale) 2. Behavioral: Avoidance Test	3 45-min sessions to determine termination of flooding therapy. 1. Autonomic Group 9AG) 2. Subjective Group (SG) 3. Observers Group (OG) 4. Combined Group (CG) 5. Placebo Group (PG) 6. No Treatment Group (NTG)	1. OG was only group to differ significantly from PG & NTG. 2. OG differed significantly from PG & NTG.	9 weeks 1. Results maintained but not significant. 2. Results maintained.

Study	Subjects	Object		Follow-up	Treatment	Measures	Results
Kazdin, 1974a.	80 fearful college student volunteers (25 men; 45 women)	Snakes	1. Subjective 2. Behavioral	Not specified	2 15-min sessions of Covert Modeling 1. Similar-Coping Model (SCM) 2. Similar-Mastery Model (SMM) 3. Dissimilar-Coping Model (DCM) 4. Dissimilar-Mastery Model (DCM) 5. No Model Scene Control (C)	1. Subjective: A. Fear Survey Schedule B. Attitude measures: 1) Snake Questionnaire 2) Semantic Differential 3) Snake Attitude C. Fear ratings D. Anxiety checklist 2. Behavioral: Avoidance test	1. A. Only SCM decreased significantly in snake fear; none on general. B. 1) SCM significantly better. 2) No differences. 3) All treatment groups differed from C. C. SCM & SMM significantly less aroused. D. SCM significantly better than others. 2. SCM & SMM improved significantly more than others.	2½ weeks 1. A. Changes maintained. B. SCM significantly different on only 1. C. Only SCM consistently less aroused. D. No differences. 2. SCM was most improved; SCM & SMM improved significantly more than others
Kazdin, 1974b.	84 fearful college student volunteers (21 men; 63 women)	Snakes	1. Subjective 2. Behavioral	Not specified	2 15-min sessions of Covert Modeling 1. Self-Coping Model (SC) 2. Self-Mastery Model (SM) 3. Other-Coping Model (OC) 4. Other-Mastery Model (OM) 5. No Model Scene Control (NM)	1. Subjective A. Fear Survey Schedule B. Attitude Measures: 1) Snake Questionnaire 2) Semantic Differential 3) Attitude Survey C. Fear Arousal Ratings (10-pt. scale) D. Anxiety Checklist 2. Behavioral: Avoidance Test	1. A. SC & OC differed from NM B. 1) SC, OC, & OM differed from NM. 2) SC, OC, & OM differed from NM 3) No differences C. SC & OC differed from NM. D. SC, OC, & OM differed from NM. 2. SC, OC & OM were significantly more improved than NM.	3 weeks 1. A. No differences; all groups improved. B. 1) SC & OC differed from NM. 2) SC, OC & OM differed from NM. 3) Only OC differed from NM. C. All groups differed from NM. D. SC & OM less anxious than SM & OM. 2. Results maintained

(continued)

Table 2. Summary of Assessment Devices and Treatment Methods with Simple Phobics (Continued)

Authors	Subjects	Type of phobia	Type of symptoms	Duration	Assessment devices	Treatment conditions	Results	Follow-up

Kazdin, 1973.	64 fearful undergraduates (20 men; 44 women)	Snakes	1. Subjective
			2. Behavioral
				Not specified	1. Subjective:
					  A. Semantic Differential
					  B. Snake Attitude Survey
					  C. Adjective Checklist for Anxiety
					2. Behavioral: approach to snake
						2 sessions
						1. Covert Coping Model (CM)
						2. Covert Mastery Model (MM)
						3. No Model Scene Control (NM)
						4. Delayed Treatment Control (DT)
							1. A. CM & MM differed from NM but not DT.
							  B. Only MM differed from NM & DT.
							  C. No differences.
							2. CM & MM significantly more improved than NM & DT; CM more improved than MM.
								3 weeks on CM, MM & NM
								1. A. Changes maintained
								  B. MM improved significantly more
								  C. CM & MM improved significantly; CM no longer better than MM.

Lang & Lazovik, 1963.	24 college student volunteers (17 women; 7 men)	Snakes	1. Physiological
			2. Subjective
			3. Behavioral
				Not specified	1. Subjective:
					  A. Fear Survey Schedule
					  B. Fear Thermometer (10-pt. scale)
					  C. Anxiety Ratings (experimenter)
					2. Behavioral: approach to harmless snake
						1. Systematic Desensitization + Pretraining Test (SD + PT)
						2. Systematic Desensitization only (SD)
						3. No Treatment Control with Pretraining Test (NT + PT)
						4. No Treatment Control only (NT)
							1. A & B. SD + PT & SD show greater change; differences not significant.
							  C. No differences
							2. SD + PT & SD increased approach significantly. No pretraining effect
								6 months
								1. A & B. SD + PT & SD differed significantly from controls.
								2. C. No change.
								2. Slight increase in approach from posttest for SD + PT & SD.

Leitenberg & Callahan, 1973. III	14 fearful college students meeting course requirement (women)	Snakes	1. Subjective 2. Behavioral	Not specified	1. Behavioral: approach to harmless snake	10 sessions 1. Reinforced Practice (RP) 2. Delayed Treatment Control (DT)	1. RP significantly improved over NT.	None
Leitenberg & Callahan, 1973. II	36 fearful undergraduate volunteers (women)	Snakes	1. Behavioral	Not specified	1. Subjective: Rating Scale listing BAT items. 2. Behavioral: Avoidance Test	3 45-min sessions of flooding therapy 1. Film alone (F) 2. Tape alone (asked them to imagine touching snake, etc.) (T) 3. Film + Tape (FT) 4. Film + Tape + In vivo exposure. (FTE) 5. Placebo Control (PC) 6. No Treatment Control (NT)	1. T improved most. T changed more than F; no differences between FTE, PC, & NT. 2. F, T, FT, & FTE combined were more improved than PC & NT. FTE better than FT.	None

Study	Subjects	Phobia	Measures type	Follow-up type	Measures	Treatment/Sessions	Results	Follow-up
Marshall, Gauthier, Christie, Currie, & Gordon, 1977. I	24 fearful undergraduate volunteers (12 men; 12 women)	Snakes	1. Behavioral	Not specified	1. Subjective: Rating Scale listing BAT items. 2. Behavioral: Avoidance Test	3 40-min sessions 1. Systematic Desensitization (using slides) (SD) 2. Flooding (with slides) (F) 3. Placebo Control (neutral slides) (PC) 4. No Treatment Control (NT)	1. SD & F lower than PC & NT. 2. F significantly better than SD; SD better than PC & NT.	None
Mealiea & Nawas, 1971.	50 fearful student volunteers (women)	Snakes	1. Subjective 2. Behavioral	Not specified	1. Subjective: A. Fear Thermometer (10-pt. scale) for last step B. Fear Survey Schedule (II)–General C. Fear Survey Schedule—snakes 2. Behavioral: Avoidance Test	5 30-min sessions 1. Systematic Desensitization (SD) 2. Implosive Therapy (IT) 3. Implosive + Desensitization (IT + SD) 4. Pseudotherapy (PT) 5. No Treatment Control (NT)	1. A, B, & C: All groups showed decrease; differences not consistent. 2. SD produced more decreases than IT, IT + SD, PT; all treatment groups differed from control.	1 month 1. SD produced significantly more change on B. 2. All groups decreased; SD produced most change but no longer different from IT + SD & PT.
Odom, Nelson, & Wein, 1978.	42 fearful college volunteers (women)	Snakes	Not described	Not described	1. Subjective: A. Fear Thermometer B. Personal Reactions Questionnaire C. S–R Inventory of Anxiousness 2. Physiological: A. Heart rate (beats/sec.) 3. Behavioral: Avoidance Test	6 sessions 1. Guided Participation (GP) 2. Systematic Desensitization (SD) 3. Cognitive Restructuring (CR) 4. Verbal Extinction (VE) 5. Attention Placebo Control (PC) 6. No Treatment Control (NT)	1. A. GP decreased most; CR & VE decreased more than PC & NT. B. No differences C. GP & CR better than other groups. 2. CR significantly lower than other groups; SD lower than PC & NT. 3. GP significantly better than others; SD & CR better than VE, PC, & NT	None
Rimm, & Mahoney, 1969. I	19 fearful college students fulfilling course requirement (men & women)	Snakes	1. Subjective 2. Behavioral	Not specified	1. Subjective: Fear Ratings (10-pt scale) 2. Behavioral: Avoidance Test	1. Noncontingent Reinforcement (NR) 2. Contingent Reinforcement (CR) 3. No Treatment Control (NT)	1. No differences 2. No differences	2 weeks 1. Most subjects showed some minor decreases 2. No change except for 2 subjects.

(continued)

Table 2. Summary of Assessment Devices and Treatment Methods with Simple Phobics (Continued)

Authors	Subjects	Type of phobia	Type of symptoms	Duration	Assessment devices	Treatment conditions	Results	Follow-up
Rimm & Mahoney, 1969. II	12 of the above subjects	Snakes	1. Subjective 2. Behavioral	Not specified	1. Subjective:Fear Ratings (10-pt. scale) 2. Behavioral: Avoidance Test	1. Participant Modeling (PM) 2. No Treatment Controls (NT)	1 & 2. PM improved significantly more than NT.	None
Ritter, 1968	44 fearful children (28 girls, 16 boys)	Snakes	1. Behavioral	Not specified	1. Subjective: Fear Ratings (3-pt.) 2. Behavioral: Avoidance Test	2 35-min sessions 1. Vicarious Desensitization (VD) 2. Contact Desensitization (CD) 3. Controls (C)	1. VD & CD decreased but not significantly over C. 2. VD significantly better than CD; but both were better than C.	None
Suedfeld & Hare, 1977.	16 fearful, paid college student volunteers	Snakes	1. Subjective 2. Physiological 3. Behavioral	Not specified	1. Subjective: A. Snake Fear Questionnaire B. General Fear of Snakes 95-pt. scale) C. Fear of Approach D. Fear at Closest Pretreatment Point 2. Physiological: A. Skin Conductance B. Heart rate 3. Behavioral: Avoidance Test	8 hr 1. Sensory Deprivation (phobic self-report & physiological) (SR + P) 2. Sensory Deprivation (phobic self-report only) (SR) 3. Slide Control (SC) 4. No Treatment Control (NT)	1. SR + P superior to SC & NT on all measures; SR + P superior to SR only on A. 2. A & B. No differences; all decreased. 3. SR + P & SR significantly better than SC & NT.	None
Wieselberg, Dyckman, & Abramowitz, 1979.	17 fearful volunteers (11 women, 6 men)	Snakes	1. Behavioral	Not specified	1. Subjective: A. Fear Survey Schedule B. Attitude Toward Snakes C. Fear Ratings 2. Behavioral: Progressive Avoidance Test	5 30-min sessions 1. In vivo Desensitization (IVD) 2. Imaginal Desensitization (ID)	1 & 2. IVD superior to ID.	9 months 1 & 2. IVD no longer superior to ID.

Study	Subjects	Type	Duration	Assessment	Assessment Details	Treatment Conditions	Results	Follow-up
Ritter, 1969a.	12 fearful volunteers (2 men, 10 women)	Heights	Not specified	1. Subjective 2. Behavioral	1. Subjective A. Fear Survey Schedule II B. Fear Ratings (11 pt. scale) 2. Behavioral: Height Avoidance Test	24 min across conditions 1. Contact Desensitization (CD) 2. Non-Therapist Contact Desensitization (Non-TCD) 3. No Treatment Control (NT)	1. A. No significant differences. B. CD superior to others. 2. Only CD showed significant improvement.	None
Leitenberg & Callahan, 1973. I	18 fearful volunteers promised $15 (15 women; 3 men)	Heights	Mean duration 21 years	1. Behavioral	1. Subjective A. Rating of severity of fear in everyday life (6-pt. scale) B. Anxiety Ratings on each trial (11-pt. scale) 2. Behavioral: amount of steps patient could ascend on fire escape	6 trials; maximum of 10 sessions 1. Reinforced Practice (RP) 2. Delayed Treatment Control (DTC)	1. A. RP superior to DTC B. No change 2. RP superior to DTC	2 years 1. A. No significant differences B. Not reported 2. Some deterioration, but remained significantly better than pretest.
Ritter, 1969b.	15 fearful community volunteers (13 women, 2 men)	Heights	Not specified	1. Subjective 2. Behavioral	1. Subjective A. Fear Survey Schedule II B. Fear Ratings (11-pt. scale) 2. Behavioral: Height Avoidance Test	1 35-min session 1. Contact Desensitization (CD) 2. Demonstration + Participation (DP) 3. Live Modeling (LM)	1. A. All groups lower at posttest; no significant differences B. No differences in change; only DP ratings decreased significantly. 2. CD superior to DP & LM; DP superior to LM.	None
Denney, Sullivan, & Thiry, 1977.	72 volunteers (62 women; 10 men)	Spiders	Not specified	1. Subjective 2. Behavioral	1. Subjective A. Spider Anxiety Scale B. Fear Ratings 2. Behavioral: Avoidance Test	2 1-hr sessions 1. Modeling + Overt Rehearsal + Self-Verbalization (M + OR + SV) 2. Modeling + Overt Rehearsal (MDR) 3. Modeling + Covert	1. A. No significant differences B. All 8 treatment groups differed significantly from NT. M + OR + SV differed from Groups MCR & CR.	None

(continued)

Authors	Subjects	Type of phobia	Type of symptoms	Duration	Assessment devices	Treatment conditions	Results	Follow-up
						Rehearsal (MCR) 4. Modeling Only (M) 5. Overt Rehearsal + Self-Verbalization (OR + SV) 6. Overt Rehearsal Only (OR) 7. Covert Rehearsal Only (CR) 8. Self-Verbalization Only (SV) 9. No Treatment Control (NT)	2. M + OR + SV, MOR & OR + SV differed significantly from CR & NT. M + OR + SV also differed significantly from OR.	
Marshall, Gauthier, Christie, Currie, & Gordon, 1977.	25 fearful volunteers (women)	Spiders	1. Behavioral	Not specified	1. Subjective: Rating Scales 2. Behavioral: Avoidance Test	3 45-min. treatment sessions 1. Imaginal Flooding + Immediate Exposure (FIE) 2. Imaginal Flooding + Delayed Exposure (FDE) 3. Implosion + Immediate Exposure (IIE) 4. Implosion + Delayed Exposure (IDE) 5. No Treatment Controls (NT)	1 &2. FIE was significantly better than all other groups which were not different.	None
Rachman, 1966a.	3 fearful student volunteers (2 women, 1 man)	Spiders	1. Subjective 2. Behaviorial	Not specified	1. Subjective:Fear rating (100-pt. scale)	1. Desensitization	1. Desensitization of imaginal stimuli generalized to real-life situations	None
Rachman, 1966b.	9 fearful student volunteers (women)	Spiders	1. Subjective 2. Behavioral	Not specified	1. Subjective: Fear Ratings (100 pt. scale) 2. Behavioral: Avoidance Test	10 sessions 1. Imaginal Flooding (F) 2. Desensitization (D) 3. No Treatment (NT)	1 &2. D was significantly better than F & NT.	3 months 1. Findings maintained.

Study	Subjects	Phobic stimulus	Measures	Follow-up	Measures (detail)	Treatment/Sessions	Results	Follow-up results
D'Zurilla, Wilson, & Nelson, 1973.	73 fearful college students (women)	Dead rats	1. Subjective 2. Behavioral	Not specified	1. Subjective: A. S–R Inventory of Anxiousness (SRA) B. Expectations Scale (5 pt. scale) 2. Behavioral: Avoidance Test	6 weekly sessions 1. Systematic Desensitization (SD) 2. Graduated Prolonged Exposure (GPE) 3. Cognitive Restructuring (CR) 4. No Treatment Control (NT)	1. A. Only CR improved significantly over NT. B. No significant differences. 2. Only GPE improved significantly over NT.	None
Foa, Blau, Prout, & Latimer, 1977.	36 rat-phobic undergraduate volunteers	Rats	1. Subjective 2. Behavioral	Not specified	1. Subjective: A. Six scales of interference of daily activities (independent assessor) B. Self-rating of anxiety (1–10) 2. Behavioral: Number of steps taken in approaching cage.	1. Flooding By Tape Recorder (FTR) 2. Flooding by Therapist (FT) 3. Pleasant Imagery (PI) 4. No Treatment Control (NT)	1. A. FTR & FR were more improved than PI; all three were more improved than NT. B. No significant differences overall. 2. FTR, FT & PI increased significantly more than NT.	None
Smith & Coleman, 1977.	17 fearful volunteers (women)	Rats	1. Subjective 2. Behavioral	Not specified	1. Subjective: A. Fear Arousal Ratings (10-pt. scale) (rat generalization & pooled data) B. Attitudes regarding rat encounters in 6 situations (7-pt. scale) C. Self-Competence Ratings D. Temple Fear Survey Inventory 2. Behavioral: Approach Test	63 min total 1. Participant Modeling + Overlearning With Therapist Present (PM + OLT) 2. Participant Modeling + Self-Directed Practice With Treatment Rat (PM + TR) 3. Participant Modeling + Self-Directed Practice With Varied Rats (PM + VR) 4. Control (C)	1. A, B, & D: all 3 treatment groups better than C C. No differences 2. No differences among treatment groups; all significantly improved over C.	Length of follow-up not specified. 1. No significant differences on any measure.

(continued)

Table 2. Summary of Assessment Devices and Treatment Methods with Simple Phobics (Continued)

Authors	Subjects	Type of phobia	Type of symptoms	Duration	Assessment devices	Treatment conditions	Results	Follow-up
Willis & Edwards, 1969.	50 fearful under- graduates (women)	Mice	1. Subjective	Not specified	1. Subjective: A. Fear Survey Schedule: Mouse & Total Score B. Fear Thermom- eter (100-pt.) C. T: asked if they would touch the mouse. D. PH: asked if they would pick up & hold the mouse 2 Behavioral: Avoid- ance Test	Between 2 & 5 sessions 1. Systematic Desensitiza- tion (SD) 2. Implosive Therapy (IT) 3. Control (C)	1. On all measures except PH, SD was significantly better than IT & C which did not differ. 2. SD significantly better than IT & C.	2 months—FSS (M) only 1. No change
Leitenberg, Agras, Allen, Butz, & Edwards, 1975	56-year-old inpa- tient (woman)	Sharp Objects (knives)	1. Subjective 2. Behavioral	4 years	1. Behavioral: amount of time looking at knife	Multiple Baseline; 6 phases; 15 sessions phase except 40 in final 1. Praise (P) 2. Feedback + Praise (FP) 3. No feedback & No Praise (NFNP) 4. Praise (P) 5. Feedback + Praise (FP)	1. Little progress with P; marked improvement with addition of F.	None
Leitenberg, Agras, Thompson, & Wright, 1968.	59-year-old (woman)	Knives	1. Subjective 2. Behavioral	4 years	1. Behavioral: amount of of time knife was kept in view	Multiple Baseline; 7 phases 1. Feedback Alone (F) 2. Feedback + Praise (FP) 3. Feedback Alone (F) 4. No Feedback & No Praise (NFNP) 5. Feedback Alone (F) 6. Feedback + Praise (FP) 7. Feedback Alone (F)	1. Steady improvement with F; no apparent effect of adding and withdrawing P.	None

Authors	Subject	Fear	Duration	Assessment	Measures	Design/Treatment	Results	Follow-up
Leitenberg, Wincze, Butz, Callahan, & Agras, 1970. II	21-year-old inpatient (man)	Injury	4 years	1. Subjective 2. Behavioral	1. Behavioral: Avoidance test with: A. Fan B. Mimeograph	Multiple Baseline; 4 phases with A (20 30-min sessions) 2 with B (18 30-min sessions) A. Fan: 1. Nonreinforcement (NR) 2. Reinforcement (Praise) (R) 3. Nonreinforcement (NR) 4. Reinforcement (R) B. Mimeograph: 1. Nonreinforcement (NR) 2. Reinforcement (Praise) (R)	1. Across phases little change without R; steady increase in approach with addition of R.	None
Yule & Fernando, 1980.	16-year-old outpatient, (boy)	Blood	Not specified	1. Subjective 2. Physiological 3. Behavioral	Not specified	5 sessions 1. In Vivo Desensitization	1. Patient was about to watch blood being drawn from arm without signs of tension or fainting.	2¼ months; 5 years 1. Gains maintained according to patient's and mother's report.
Leitenberg, Agras, Thompson, & Wright, 1968.	51-year-old patient (woman)	Closed spaces	Since childhood	1. Subjective 2. Physiological 3. Behavioral	1. Behavioral: amount of time spent in closed room	Multiple Baseline; 3 phases of 22 sessions 1. Feedback (F) 2. No Feedback (NF) 3. Feedback (F)	1. Improvement in each of the phases; F superior to NF.	3 months 1. Improvement maintained in home situation according to self-report & behavioral test.
Bernstein & Beaty, 1971.	29-year-old outpatient, graduate student (woman)	Flying	2 years	1. Subjective 2. Physiological 3. Behavioral	Not described	30 sessions 1. Imaginal Desensitization + In Vivo Desensitization	1. Experienced substantial decrease in all symptoms according to self-report & therapist's observation.	None
Hamilton, Carmody, Bornstein, Rychtarik, & Trontel, 1978.	18 fearful volunteers	Ticks	Not specified	Not described	1. Subjective: A. Fear Survey Schedule B. Tick Anxiety Questionnaire C. Fear Thermometer D. Self-Rating	1. Graduated Prolonged Exposure GPE 2. Assessment Control (AC) 3. Waiting-List Control (WLC)	1. A. GPE produced most improvement B. GPE & AC differed from WLC. C. No differences. 2. GPE differed from WLC. 3. GEP performed best.	None

(continued)

Table 2. Summary of Assessment Devices and Treatment Methods with Simple Phobics (Continued)

Authors	Subjects	Type of phobia	Type of symptoms	Duration	Assessment devices	Treatment conditions	Results	Follow-up
Kolko & Milan, 1980.	31-year-old college outpatient	Self-injection	1. Subjective 2. Behavioral	26 years	2. Physiological: Heart rate 3. Behavioral: at posttest only	1. Reading relevant literature	1. Effectiveness of treatment was demonstrated in all 3 modalities.	1 year 1. Changes maintained on all 3 measures.
Leitenberg, Agras, Allen, Butz, & Edwards, 1975.	43-year-old outpatient (woman)	Thunder	1. Subjective 2. Behavioral	Not specified	1. Subjective: Anxiety rating (11-pt. scale) 2. Behavioral: Amount of time spent in simulated thunderstorm	Multiple Baseline; 8 sessions; 3 trials/session. 1. Praise (P) 2. Feedback + Praise (FP) 3. Praise (P)	1. No change until she had repeated practice meeting time-limited behavioral goal. 2. Increased time with P but improved dramatically with FP.	None
Leitenberg & Callahan, 1973. II	14 fearful children volunteered by parents (8 girls, 6 boys)	Darkness	1. Behavioral	Not specified	1. Behavioral: Time spent in dark room	2 consecutive trials of 5 min or 8 sessions 1. Reinforced Practice (RP) 2. Delayed Treatment Control (DTC)	1. RP produced more change than DTC.	None
Nesbitt, 1973.	1 student (24-year-old woman)	Escalator	1. Subjective 2. Physiological 3. Behavioral	7 years	None described	1 session 1. In Vivo Flooding: riding an escalator first with therapist then alone.	Less than 1 hr 1. Patient was able to ride the escalator alone with relative ease.	6 months 1. Patient reported changes maintained.
Boulougouris, Marks, & Marset, 1971.	16 psychiatric patients (7 men; 9 women)	Mixed (9 agoraphobics, 7 specific)	Not specified	Mean of 12 years	1. Subjective: Symptom Rating Scales (pt., therapist, & medical assessor) 2. Physiological: A. Heart Rate	Crossover Design; 6 sessions 1. Imaginal Desensitization (ID) 2. Imaginal Flooding (IF)	1. With IF, subjective anxiety decreased significantly; ID was not superior on any measure 2. A. With IF: HR decreased	1 year 1. Changes maintained & generalized across settings by self-report & relatives' report.

Study	Subjects	Type of phobia	Assessment	Chronicity	Dependent Measures	Treatment	Results	Follow-up
Crowe, Marks, Agras, & Leitenberg, 1972.	14 outpatients	Mixed (agoraphobia, noise, heights, social, study, small animals, crowds, alone at night, closed spaces)	Not described	Range from 5–35 years	B. Skin Conductance (spontaneous fluctuations & maximum deflection) 1. Subjective: A. Symptom Rating Scales (patient, therapist, & assessor) 2. Behavioral: Avoidance Test (measured in distance & time)	All received 3 treatments in randomized order: 4 50-min sessions of each 1. Systematic Desensitization (SD) 2. Imaginal Flooding (IF) 3. Shaping (Reinforced Practice; RP)	significantly during main fantasy. B. With IF; SC decreased significantly on both measures 1. No differences although RP tended to be rated lower. 2. RP was significantly superior to SD; IF was intermediate.	None
Curtis, Neese, Buxton, Wright, & Lippman, 1976.	12 volunteers (11 women, 1 man)	Mixed (snakes, spiders, birds, wasps, bees)	1. Subjective 2. Behavioral	Present since childhood	1. Subjective: Rating Scale 2. Behavioral: Contact with feared object	1. In vivo Flooding	1. All patients who remained in treatment experienced dramatic relief.	6 months–1 year 1. 1 patient maintained at 6 months, 3 at 1 year, 2 had partial relapse; 1 had full relapse.
Gelder, Marks, Wolff, & Clarke, 1967.	42 outpatients reporting 1 or more phobias	Mixed (agoraphobia, social, heights, darkness, thunder, birds)	Not specified	Average ranged from 6.3–12.2 years	1. Subjective A. Symptom Rating Scales (patient, therapist, assessor) (5-pt. scale) B. Eysenck Personality Inventory C. Symptom Checklist from Cornell Medical Index D. Checklist of Phobias & Social Anxieties	1. Systematic Desensitization (SD) (9 months) 2. Group Psychotherapy (GP) (18 months) 3. Individual Psychotherapy (12 months)	A. SD produced the fastest and largest amount of improvement. B. Scores decreased significantly with SD. C & D. No changes	7 months 1. Degree of improvement still greater with SD group, but no longer significant.
Greist, Marks, Berlin, Gournay, & Noshirvani, 1980	13 phobics & 4 obsessive-compulsive ritualizers (5 men, 8 women)	Mixed (agoraphobia, social, bowel incontinence, dogs, wasps, spiders, ants, enclosed spaces)	Not specified	All more than 1 year (Mean—9 years)	1. Subjective A. Symptom Rating Scales (patient & assessor)	Crossover Design; 6 20-min sessions, instructions for each week: 1. Expose to all fearful stimuli	1. All favored exposure; significant differences only on A. 2. Differences not significant.	None

(continued)

Table 2. Summary of Assessment Devices and Treatment Methods with Simple Phobics (Continued)

Authors	Subjects	Type of phobia	Type of symptoms	Duration	Assessment devices	Treatment conditions	Results	Follow-up
					B. Fear Questionnaire C. Expectancy Rating D. Depression Scale E. Anxiety Rating (assessor) 2. Behavioral: Avoidance Test	2. Avoid all fearful stimuli 3. Continue most helpful		
Grey, Rachman, & Sartory, 1981.	28 fearful volunteers (3 men, 25 women)	Mixed (not specified)	1. Subjective 2. Behavioral	Not specified	1. Subjective: Fear Thermometer (100-pt. scale) 2. Physiological: Heart Rate 3. Behavioral: distance predicted by subject as closest prepared to tolerate.	1 session 1. *In vivo* high demand (flooding) with massed presentation (HDM) 2. *In vivo* high demand (flooding) with distributed presentation (HDD)	1. HDM showed slightly more improvement & greater return of fear at 1 week. 2. No differences apparent. 3. No differences; both increased distance.	None
Grey, Sartory, & Rachman, 1979	27 subjects (22 fearful volunteers. 5 psychiatric patients)	Mixed (spiders, mice, snakes, worms, pigeons, toads)	1. Subjective 2. Behavioral	Not specified	1. Subjective: Fear Thermometer 2. Physiological: Heart Rate 3. Behavioral	3 sessions 1. High Demand (HD) (*In vivo* Flooding) 2. Low Demand (LD) (*In vivo* Desensitization) 3. Increasing Demand (ID)	1. HD & LD produced greater fear reduction; yet, HD & ID had return of fear between sessions.	None
Leitenberg, Agras, Allen, Butz, & Edwards, 1975	45-year-old outpatient	Multiple (injury & open spaces)	1. Subjective 2. Behavioral	2 years	1. Behavioral: time spent in hospital	Multiple Baseline; 2½ phases; 3 sessions; 2 trials/session 1. Praise (P) 2. Praise + Feedback (PF) 3. Praise (P)	1. Minimal progress with P. F improved performance dramatically.	None

Study	Subjects	Phobia	Assessment Type	Duration	Measures	Treatment	Results	Follow-up
Leitenberg, Agras, Butz, & Wincze, 1971.	9 psychiatric inpatients, outpatients & volunteers (6 women; 3 men)	Mixed (unfamiliar situations, closed spaces, injury, sharp objects, frogs)	1. Subjective 2. Physiological 3. Behavioral	Wide range	1. Subjective: Anxiety Ratings 2. Physiological: Heart Rate 3. Behavioral: different ones were used for different phobias.	9 single cases using Reinforced Practice	1. 4 of 5 had decreased anxiety ratings; 1 remained the same. 2. 7 of 9 failed to show relationship between phobic behavior and autonomic arousal. 3. 9 showed decreases	1 year, 1 subject 1. Improvement maintained by self-report.
Marks, Boulougouris, & Marset, 1971	16 psychiatric patients. (9 women; 7 men)	Mixed (open spaces, heights, pigeons, dental equipment, spiders, special gatherings)	1. Subjective	Average 11–12 years	1. Subjective: A. Clinical ratings (patient, therapist & assessor) B. Symptom Checklist C. Checklist of phobias & social anxiety. D. Eysenck Personality Inventory 2. Physiological: A. Skin Conductance (maximal deflection & spontaneous fluctuation) B. Heart Rate	6 50-min sessions 1. Systematic Desensitization (SD), Imaginal Flooding (IF) 2. Imaginal Flooding (IF), Systematic Desensitization (SD)	1. SD was not superior on any variable; IF was superior on therapist's and patient's main and total phobia. 2. Improved only with IF.	1,3,6,9,& 12 months 1. Patients continued to improve especially at 3 months; subsequent performance was static.
Watson, Gaind, & Marks, 1971.	10 adult phobic patients	Mixed (balloons, cats, feathers, water, spiders, thunder, birds)	1. Subjective 1. Behavioral	Present since childhood	1. Subjective A. Symptom Rating Scales (patient, therapist) B. Semantic Differential 2. Physiological: A. Heart Rate (HR) B. Skin Conductance (SC)	4–5 hr 1. Imaginal Flooding (IF) by tape recorder + Prolonged Exposure (PE) 2. Prolonged Exposure (PE)	1. All S improved after IF; additional improvement after PE. 2. All patients improved on HR. SC was also less prominent during phobic imagery.	3–6 months 1. Clinical improvement maintained; procedures not described.

to select a specific measure for each system on the basis of presenting symptomatology. For example, May (1977a, 1977b) gives evidence to suggest that heart rate may be sensitive to both internally and externally generated phobic stimuli, while electrodermal measures may be sensitive only to externally generated stimuli. Electrodermal measures may also show more rapid habituation than heart rate measures. Therefore, as May (1977b) suggests, clinicians may need to attend systematically to meaningful internally and externally controlling factors in their assessment.

Other Forms to Be Included in Comprehensive Assessment

In addition to the three response systems, adequate assessment should include attention to environmental contingencies. Agras and Jacob (1981) suggest that many factors, including use of alcohol and drugs and its consequences, affect the intensity of phobic behavior. Hayes (1976), emphasizing the need to assess approach contingencies, has offered as examples the snake phobic who lives in an urban area where there is little likelihood of encountering snakes and the phobic who works in a reptile house and is likely to lose his or her job. Although both these people may be classified as snake phobic, they clearly differ in degree of disruption their phobia is causing them. Thus, Hayes (1976) suggests that for treatment purposes these two people cannot be equated because of the substantial difference in approach contingencies. Moreover, it may be important to assess the incidence of phobias in significant others. In their investigation of the origins of snake fears, Murray and Foote (1979) have found that fear seems to be acquired by a variety of observational experiences and that subjects report being strongly influenced by the observation of fear in others. In addition, many investigators (Connolly, Hallam, & Marks, 1976; Yule & Fernando, 1980) have found positive family histories in a significant proportion of their patients.

VARIOUS TREATMENT APPROACHES

Since the treatment approaches for simple phobias have been described in adequate detail elsewhere (Goldfried & Davison, 1976; O'Brien, 1981), only a brief description will be provided here. Each of the major treatment approaches including systematic desensitization, implosion, flooding, graduated prolonged exposure, and shaping procedures will be described with primary emphasis on practical concerns for clinical practice.

Systematic Desensitization

Systematic desensitization is the most widely researched imagery-based approach used for the treatment of phobias. It involves three general phases including muscular-relaxation training, anxiety-hierarchy construction, and the gradual presentation of scenes in order of increasing difficulty (Goldfried & Davison, 1976; Wolpe, 1958). Thus, the procedure entails having a deeply relaxed person imagine increasingly threatening situations. Systematic desensitization has been used successfully in the treatment of simple phobias, and numerous theoretical explanations have been offered for its effectivness. Wolpe (1958) originally proposed that relaxation procedures are required to "reciprocally inhibit" anxiety responses during the exposure to the feared stimulus before improvement can occur. Marks (1978) has recently concluded that lengthy, systematic training in muscular relaxation is unnecessary for the desired change in behavior.

In vivo desensitization is a variant of the basic systematic desensitization procedure, and there is some evidence (Barlow, Leitenberg, Agras, & Wincze, 1969; Wieselberg, Dyckman, & Abramowitz, 1979) to suggest that this may be more effective than the imaginal technique across response systems with some clients. However, the preliminary findings of Wieselberg *et al.* (1979) suggest that gains of the *in vivo* technique over the imaginal may dissipate over time. In addition, for the practicing clinician *in vivo* presentation can often be time-consuming, expensive, as well as impractical in some cases. Regardless of which variation therapists chose, they should consider Rachman's (1966b) reminder to check the durability of previously desensitized items at the beginning of each treatment sessions, since fear may return between sessions.

Implosive Therapy

Although "implosive therapy" has been used interchangeably with "flooding therapy," the authors will describe these procedures separately. Implosive therapy basically involves the imaginal presentation of highly anxiety-provoking cues along with psychodynamic, catastrophic cues. As described by Levis and Hare (1977), implosive therapy involves four basic stages. Initially, the therapist identifies cues which are considered to be mediating the phobic responses. This is followed by a period of neutral imagery to determine the client's ability to imagine scenes. Then the therapist repeatedly describes the hypothesized aversive stimuli as dramatically and vividly as possible and discourages any attempt of the client to avoid these stimuli. After each session, the client is given "homework" scenes to practice between sessions. The effectiveness of this model is believed to be related to an extinction effect.

Flooding

Like implosive therapy, flooding involves the straightforward presentation of the most anxiety-producing scene without relaxation or pauses. Unlike implosion, it does not involve the presentation of psychodynamic, unrealistic cues. Instead, flooding typically involves the presentation of more realistic but, nonetheless, highly anxiety-provoking material.

For the practicing clinician, duration of sessions is a particularly crucial issue if one accepts the theoretical rationale for flooding therapy. With agoraphobics, Stern and Marks (1973) found that two hours of continuous flooding decreased phobic behavior and symptoms significantly more than four one-half hour sessions in a single afternoon. Also, during *in vivo* flooding heart rate and subjective anxiety actually decreased more during the second hour of exposure. Thus, the therapist electing to use flooding therapy for treatment of simple phobias should probably be prepared to extend it anywhere from 2 to 5 hr until the anxiety subsides.

Many authors (Levis, 1974; Stampfl & Levis, 1967) have suggested that extreme anxiety evocation is required in order for extinction to occur, and typical descriptions of flooding and implosive therapy have included accounts of horrifying scenes tailored to the simple phobia. However, some preliminary evidence from Foa, Blau, Prout, and Latimer (1977) and Marshall, Gauthier, Christie, Currie, and Gordon (1977) suggests that the presentation of terrifying scenes and the withholding of therapist comfort may not be necessary for favorable results with flooding. Indirect support for their results comes from studies where more favorable outcome has been achieved with flooding when the procedure has been carried out with the therapist present rather than by tape recorder with the therapist absent (Barrett, 1969; DeMoor, 1970; Sherry & Levine, 1980).

Finally, a number of practicing therapists have seemed hesitant about using implosion and flooding because they assume that these procedures may be harmful to their clients. Shipley and Boudewyns (1980) reviewed the literature and queried therapists who have used flooding and implosion and found little evidence to suggest that these techniques may be harmful to patients. Indirect evidence is provided by the fact that drop-out rate with implosion and flooding has been found to be low (Boudewyns & Wilson, 1972). In addition, it should be noted that there have been few controlled studies investigating the incidence of negative side effects in other treatment procedures. Thus, there seems no reason at present to believe that these procedures are potentially any more harmful than other techniques, and there is a good deal of evidence to suggest that they are highly effective in the treatment of simple phobias.

Reinforced Practice

Reinforced practice is a straightforward procedure involving the graded approach of a client toward the public object/situation with instructions to turn back whenever he or she experiences too much anxiety or discomfort. Any improvement in performance is followed by praise from the therapist. Thus, the procedure involves a combination of effective variables including graduated repeated practice, therapeutic instructions, feedback, and reinforcement (Leitenberg & Callahan, 1973). O'Brien (1981) describes the primary objective of the procedure as the shaping of appropriate behaviors through a series of successive approximations.

Modeling Procedures

With modeling techniques, the therapist initially demonstrates approach and contact with the phobic object in the presence of the client and subsequently encourages the client to do likewise. Two specific modeling techniques, participant modeling and covert modeling will be discussed here since they have been utilized most often in the treatment of simple phobias.

Participant modeling involves both modeling and behavioral rehearsal strategies, and proceeds with the use of a graded hierarchy. Like systematic desensitization, the treatment is designed so that the client's anxiety does not exceed a comfortable level during therapy. A live or filmed model performs the desired behavior, and the basic assumption is that imaginal representations of the model's behavior guide the client's subsequent performance.

The behavior-rehearsal component of participant modeling may be either covert or overt, and there is some evidence (Denney *et al.,* 1977) to suggest that these two types of rehearsal do not differ in effectiveness when combined with modeling. These results also suggest that self-verbalization may enhance the effectiveness of participant modeling, but this needs to be investigated more thoroughly.

Covert modeling, which is a variant of the modeling technique, follows from the assumption that imaginal representations of the model's behavior serve to guide the client's performance. Kazdin (1973, 1974a, 1974b) has suggested that if one accepts this assumption, then direct observation of a model may be unnecessary for changing avoidance behavior. Thus, with this procedure, the client is given verbal instructions to imagine a model interacting with the feared object on an increasingly intimate level.

With both participant and covert modeling, certain practical considerations need to be made. For example, there is evidence (Kazdin, 1973; 1974a; 1974b) to suggest that the similarity of the model in terms of age, sex, and level of initial anxiety may affect treatment outcome.

Cognitive Therapies

The cognitive therapies for the treatment of phobias are based on the assumption that thoughts and cognitions mediate phobic and nonphobic behavior. Although the therapies differ procedurally, they all share the basic assumption that cognitions must change in order for the therapeutic effect to be realized. The cognitive therapies include Meichenbaum's (1972) cognitive modification procedure, cognitive restructuring (Goldfried, Decenteceo, & Weinburg, 1974; Goldfried, Linehan, & Smith, 1978) and cognitive attentional training (Holroyd, 1976). However, since these approaches have been used primarily in the treatment of test anxiety (which the authors have not included among the simple phobias) they will not be discussed here.

TREATMENT APPROACHES FOR EACH SIMPLE PHOBIA CATEGORY

In keeping with the aim of providing a book that will be useful to practicing clinicians and graduate students, this section is organized according to categories of simple phobias. In it will be described the frequency and general effectiveness of specific treatment approaches used with each of the simple phobias, as found in the current literature.

Snake Phobia

The most frequently investigated simple phobia group is the snake phobic. Thirty-nine percent ($N = 22$) of the reviewed treatment studies investigated snake phobics. All of these studies except Antman's (1973) uncontrolled case study employed analogue populations. As can be seen from Table 1, systematic desensitization, implosive therapy, flooding therapy, reinforced practice, participant modeling, covert modeling, cognitive restructuring, and sensory deprivation have all produced significant change in at least one response system of analogue snake phobics. For the subjective response system specifically, flooding (Gauthier & Marshall, 1977; Marshall *et al.,* 1977), systematic desensitization (Bandura *et al.,* 1969; Barrett, 1969; Marshall *et al.,* 1977), participant modeling (Bandura *et al.,* 1969), implosive therapy (Barrett, 1969), sensory deprivation (Suedfeld & Hare, 1977), and convert modeling (Kazdin, 1974a, 1974b) have all produced significantly more changes than controls. In the behavioral response system, systematic desensitization (Bandura *et al.,* 1969; Barrett, 1969: DeMoor, 1970; Lang & Lazovik, 1963; Marshall *et al.,* 1977; Mealiea & Nawas, 1971; Odom *et al.,* 1978; Ritter, 1968), participant modeling (Bandura *et al.,* 1969; Blanchard, 1970; Odom *et al.,* 1978; Rimm & Mahoney, 1969; Ritter, 1968), reinforced practice (Leitenberg & Callahan, 1973), cognitive restructuring (Odom *et al.,* 1978), flooding (Gauthier & Marshall, 1977; Marshall *et al.,* 1977), implosion (Barrett, 1969; DeMoor, 1970), covert modeling (Kazdin, 1973, 1974a, 1974b), and sensory deprivation (Suedfeld & Hare, 1977) have all produced significantly more changes than controls. Finally, with reference to the physiological response system, cognitive restructuring (Odom *et al.,* 1978) and systematic desensitization (Odom *et al.,* 1978) were the only therapies to produce significantly more physiological change than controls, whereas *in vivo* desensitization produced more physiological changes than did imaginal desensitization (Barlow *et al.,* 1969). However, since there are so few studies assessing the physiological system, these results should be considered as suggestive rather than conclusive.

Acrophobia

Three of the reviewed studies (Leitenberg & Callahan, 1973; Ritter 1969a, 1969b) examined the responses of groups of height phobics to treatment. All of these studies employed volunteers, and in one study monetary remuneration was offered for participation. In these studies contact desensitization (later called participant modeling) with the therapist present (Ritter, 1969b) and reinforced practice (Leitenberg & Callahan, 1973) were effective in significantly reducing phobic symptoms across the subjective/cognitive and behavioral systems. Physiological responses were not measured in these group studies.

In addition, there were three studies employing a mixed group of phobic subjects (some of whom were acrophobics) from a clinical population. In one study (Crowe, Marks, Agras, & Leitenberg, 1972), reinforced practice was found superior to both systematic desensitization and flooding on behavioral measures, although there were no differences on subjective measures. Gelder, Marks, Wolff, and Clarke (1967) found that systematic desensitization was superior to more traditional psychotherapy on subjective measures, while Marks, Boulougouris, and Marset (1971) found flooding therapy to be superior to systematic desensitization on subjective and physiological measures. Thus, reinforced practice, participant modeling, systematic desensitization, and flooding therapy may be effective with height phobics for at least one response system.

Spider Phobia

Four of the reviewed studies (Marshall *et al.,* (III), 1977; Denney *et al.,* 1977; Rachman, 1966a, 1966b) examined the responses of spider phobics to treatment. All of these studies employed analogue subjects consisting of college and community volunteers. Imaginal flooding with immediate exposure (Marshall *et al.,* 1977), systematic desensitization (Rachman, 1966a), and various modeling procedures (Denney *et al.,* 1977) were used in effectively changing subjective and behavioral responses to phobic stimuli. Also, Rachman's (1966b) uncontrolled group study suggested that changes produced by systematic desensitization during treatment generalized to real-life situations. Physiological responses were not measured with spider phobics.

Rat Phobia

Four of the reviewed studies (D'Zurilla *et al.*, 1973; Foa *et al.*, 1977; Smith & Coleman, 1977; Willis & Edwards, 1969) examined the responses of rat phobics to treatment. All of these studies used college women volunteers as subjects. Participant modeling (Smith & Coleman, 1977), flooding (Foa *et al.*, 1977), and systematic desensitization (Willis & Edwards, 1969) produced significantly more change across subjective and behavioral response systems in these analogue subjects than the control procedures. D'Zurilla *et al.* (1973) found cognitive restructuring to be more effective only in the subjective response system, while graduated prolonged exposure was more effective with the behavioral responses. Physiological responses were not assessed in any of the studies of rat phobics.

Blood/Illness/Injury Phobia

Five of the reviewed studies (Leitenberg *et al.*, 1968; Leitenberg *et al.*, 1970; Leitenberg *et al.*, 1975, Studies 1 & 3; Yule & Fernando, 1980) examined the responses of blood/injury/illness phobics to treatment. All of these studies employed clinical subjects, and each was a single case design or case study. In addition, the study of Leitenberg *et al.* (1971) reporting nine single cases included two blood/injury/illness phobic patients. Reinforced practice, particularly the feedback component (Leitenberg *et al.*, 1968; Leitenberg *et al.*, 1975), has produced dramatic behavioral changes in the blood/injury/illness phobic. Also, Yule and Fernando's (1980) uncontrolled case study suggests that *in vivo* desensitization may be quite effective in producing behavioral changes. Finally, prolonged *in vivo* exposure (Leitenberg *et al.*, 1971) has been shown to decrease avoidance behavior but has not systematically affected physiological responses in blood/injury/illness phobics.

A special note of caution is warranted for the therapist treating a blood/injury/illness phobic since Marks (1975) noted that blood/injury/illness phobics are markedly bradycardic, whereas most phobics are tachycardic during exposure to the phobic situations. Thus, the patient presenting with these symptoms is more likely than others to faint. Marks, Connolly, and Hallam (1973) have found that blood/injury/illness phobics report frequent fainting during exposure as well as treatment containing phobic elements, whereas other phobics report infrequent fainting during exposure, and never report fainting during *in vivo* treatment. During *in vivo* exposure treatment all four of the patients reported by Connolly, Hallam, and Marks (1976) came close to or actually fainted. Similarly, in their case report, Yule and Fernando (1980) reported that their client fainted during the fourth *in vivo* treatment session after handling the first three quite well. Therefore, Yule and Fernando (1980) wisely suggest that the blood/injury/illness phobic be treated in a lying down position to decrease the likelihood of fainting. In addition, these patients should be sensitized to the physical signs that precede fainting and taught to prevent fainting by putting their heads between their knees or by lying down with their head lower than their body.

Claustrophobia

Two of the reviewed studies examined the responses of claustrophobics to treatment. Leitenbert *et al.* (1968) reported that feedback (a component of reinforced practice) produced dramatic behavior changes in their single clinical subject; no other response systems were assessed. Similarly, Leitenberg *et al.* (1971) reported that prolonged *in vivo* exposure produced consistent behavioral changes but inconsistent subjective (3 of 4) and physiological changes (2 of 4).

Other Phobias

Five of the remaining studies investigated other simple phobias including flying, ticks, self-injection, thunder, and escalators. Since each of these was examined in only one of the group studies, they will be considered together here. Hamilton, Carmody, Bornstein, Rychtarik, and Trontel (1978) found that volunteer tick phobics treated with graduated prolonged exposure improved more than the assessment control. Leitenberg and Callahan (1973) found that reinforced practice produced significant behavioral changes in a group of children reporting fears of darkness. In addition, Leitenberg *et al.* (1975) found that feedback produced significant behavior change in a thunder phobic, while Kolko and Milan (1980) found that reading relevant literature produced significant changes in all three response systems of a diabetic woman with a self-injection phobia. Finally, in uncontrolled case studies Nesbitt (1973) used *in vivo* flooding successfully with an escalator phobic while Bernstein and Beaty (1971) used imaginal plus *in vivo* desensitization successfully with a flying phobic.

Mixed Phobias

Ten of the reviewed studies examined the responses of a heterogeneous group of simple phobics to treatment. Two of these (Grey, Rachman, & Sartory, 1981; Curtis *et al.*, 1976) examined a mixed group of volunteers and patients while two others (Leitenberg *et al.*, 1971; Grey *et al.*, 1979) used volunteers only. Six of these studies (Boulougouris *et al.*, 1971; Crave *et al.*, 1972; Gelder *et al.*, 1967; Greist, Marks, Berlin, Gournay, & Noshirvani, 1980; Marks *et al.*, 1971; Watson, Gaind, & Marks, 1971) examined a heterogeneous group of patients with simple phobias. However, it is difficult to determine which treatments were effective in changing specific response systems of each phobic type. In addition, none of these studies used control groups. Thus, despite the fact that this mixed group contains the only clinical group studies reviewed, the authors will refer the reader to Table 2 rather than drawing conclusions.

Maintenance of Changes

At least 45% (N = 26) of the treatment studies employed some type of follow-up assessment. Length of follow-up ranged from 2 weeks to 5 years, and in all studies positive changes found at posttreatment were generally maintained at follow-up regardless of the length of follow-up or the treatment procedures used. Therefore, if a treatment procedure is able to produce significant improvement at the end of treatment, it might seem reasonable to assume that these changes would be maintained, and that costly follow-up assessment could be omitted. Closer inspection of the reported results, however, indicate that despite the general maintenance of treatment gains for groups, there were some individual subjects and patients who showed partial relapse and others who showed full relapse at follow-up. Marks (1971) reports similar findings in his 4-year follow-up of 65 clinical patients, with only three of these having lost all of their phobias and 52% remaining unimproved at follow-up. In addition, follow-up assessment is often not as comprehensive as posttreatment assessment and is often based only on subjects' verbal reports over the telephone. It is therefore presently unclear whether a more comprehensive, standard follow-up assessment would yield the same favorable picture. At present, moreover, there are no proven means for accurately predicting which patients will maintain improvements over time. In consequence, the authors strongly urge the use of comprehensive follow-up assessment as part of the treatment package for simple phobias.

Analogue Studies

Since the majority (66%) of the studies reviewed here can be classified as analogue in nature, it is important to mention the widely known concerns raised by reliance on nonclinical populations for evaluation of clinical treatment approaches. Analogue studies most often rely on volunteers who experience fear but would not normally seek professional help. Thus, the primary test of insuring external validity involves the selection of subjects who exhibit "clinically significant" anxiety responses to a selected stimulus (Beiman, O'Neil, Wachtel, Fruge, Johnson, & Feuerstein, 1978). In keeping with this, some researchers have selected only the most impaired from a group of volunteers, but unfortunately there is wide variation in selection criteria. Hayes (1976) has proposed that "analogue" phobias are generally weak phobias since the approach contingencies are generally minimal even if avoidance is high. Also, the duration and types of symptoms of analogue populations are only rarely described in adequate detail. This is especially important since Marks (1971) has noted that clinical impression strongly suggests that phobias with duration of less than a year have a high remission rate without special treatment. Marks (1978) also cautions that students, who are generally intelligent, middleclass, and white, represent only a small segment of the population. Similarly, Bernstein and Paul (1971) observe that the typical recruitment of such volunteers involves the presentation of the project as a research experiment involving a "payoff" such as money or extra credit for participation. Under such conditions many students may volunteer for reasons other than discomfort or anxiety, and as Bernstein and Paul (1971) observe, it is not surprising that 70% of the female college student volunteers in one study were classified as "spider phobic" on the basis of their responses on a fear rating form, while none of the 22 "phobic" subjects (selected on basis of scheduling restrictions) were eliminated on subsequent screening measures. Thus, by these criteria, 38% of the original sample were classified as "phobic."

Despite these concerns, labeling an experiment as "analogue" does not mean that the practicing clinician should routinely dismiss the results as irrelevant. Many analogue studies have employed comprehensive screening criteria which provide for a reasonably close approximation to actual clinical populations. In addition, Grey Sartory, & Rachman (1979) used psychiatric patients as well as volunteer subjects and found that psychiatric status had no influence on the outcome of their treatment.

In summary, the authors suggest that those using analogue "phobics" to investigate the efficacy of treatment approaches should select only the most impaired, and should refrain from offering a "payoff" such as course credit. The nature of the symptoms as well as the duration should be given in adequate detail so that clinicians may be able to determine similarity of analogue subjects to actual clients. Overall, clinicians should not automatically discount analogue studies, but they should exercise caution in selecting a treatment procedure that has been tested primarily on student volunteers.

CHOOSING THE APPROPRIATE TREATMENT PROCEDURES AND PARAMETERS

From this review of the literature, the authors must conclude that it is presently unclear which treatment procedure is most effective with each of the simple phobias, especially with clinical populations. For the therapist trying to treat a phobic client, it seems most important that he or she select a treatment procedure involving exposure, as this is the common variable across effective treatments. However, exposure alone may not be adequate since Marshall *et al.* (1977) have found that passive exposure alone (at least in flooding procedures) may be less effective than encouragement of active imagination of interaction with a feared object.

With reference to duration, it is unclear what the optimal length of exposure should be. However, the majority of the evidence with volunteers and animals suggests that sessions involving long exposure are generally more effective than sessions with short exposure (Stern & Marks, 1973). Similarly, many researchers (Emmelkamp & Wessels, 1975; Rachman & Hodgson, 1974) have concluded that *in vivo* exposure is more effective than imaginal exposure. Yet once again the picture is unclear. Except for the uncontrolled studies of Watson *et al.* (1971) and Gaind, Watson, and Marks (1971), most of the clinical studies comparing *in vivo* with imaginal exposure were conducted with agoraphobics and obsessive-compulsive patients, rather than with simple phobics. In addition, Wieselberg *et al.* (1979) found that the superiority of *in vivo* procedures tended to dissipate over time. Thus, the results can be no more than suggestive at present. As Marks (1978) proposes, the most salient variable may actually be self-exposure, and the most efficacious treatment procedure may be whichever one is the most persuasive in getting the client to expose him or herself to the feared stimulus. Since it remains unclear which is the most effective treatment for a specific phobia, it may seem reasonable to simply combine therapies in hopes of covering all the important parameters. However, preliminary evidence from Holroyd (1976) suggests that in some cases the combination of therapies may actually be less effective than a single therapy. Thus, it presently seems unwise to combine therapies.

It presently appears, in sum, that active, *in vivo* exposure of long duration plus encouragement for self-exposure may be the best choice for the therapist treating a simple phobic. Treatment should follow directly from the assessment and should be designed to affect the response systems most indicated by the presenting symptoms.

SUMMARY AND CONCLUSIONS

Sixty-six percent ($N = 37$) of the reviewed treatment studies were analogue in nature and utilized either college or community volunteers, 30% ($N = 17$) utilized clinical subjects, and 4% ($N = 2$) utilized both clinical and volunteer subjects. In the analogue studies, snake "phobics" were studied most frequently (38%), whereas blood/injury/illness phobics were most frequent in clinical studies. Most of the behavioral techniques reviewed were able to produce significant changes by the end of treatment, and these changes were generally maintained at follow-up. Treatment composed of active *in vivo* exposure of long duration seems to be the best approach at present. However, despite the fact that simple phobias constitute one of the most frequently researched areas of behavior therapy, the work is not yet complete. The authors were unable to review any group study of a single simple phobia in a clinical population, although they did find six clinical group studies investigating subjects with different and/or multiple phobias. In addition, the authors found only seven studies which assessed all three response systems. The ideal treatment situation would involve a comprehensive assessment of all three response modalities leading to an individualized treatment approach designed to emphasize the modality (or modalities) most affected. This type of treatment approach will be possible only if future studies routinely describe presenting symptoms in adequate detail, assess all three response systems at pre- and post-treatment as well as follow-up, and employ clinical groups selected on the basis of symptom similarity.

REFERENCES

Agras, W. S., & Jacob, R. G. Phobia: Nature and measurement. In M. Mavissakalian & D. H. Barlow (Eds.), *Phobia: Psychological and pharmacological treatment.* New York: Guilford Press, 1981.

Agras, W. S., Sylvester, D., & Oliveau, D. The epidemiology of common fears and phobias. *Comprehensive Psychiatry,* 1969, *10,* 151–156.

Agras, W. S., Chapin, H. M., & Oliveau, D. C. The natural history of phobias: Course and prognosis. *Archives of General Psychiatry,* 1972, *26,* 315–317.

American Psychiatric Association. *Diagnostic and statistical manual of mental disorders (III).* Washington: Author, 1980.

Antman, E. M. Flooding *in vivo* for a case of vermiphobia. *Journal of Behavioral Therapy and Experimental Psychiatry,* 1973, *4,* 275–277.

Bandura, A., Blanchard, E. B., & Ritter, B. The relative efficacy of desensitization and modeling approaches for inducing behavioral, affective and attitudinal changes. *Journal of Personality and Social Psychology,* 1969, *13,* 173–179.

Bandura, A., Jeffery, R. W., & Gajdos, E. Generalizing change through participant modeling with self-directed mastery. *Behaviour Research and Therapy,* 1975, *13,* 141–152.

Barendregt, J. T. Phobias and phobics. In H. M. Van Praag (Ed.), *Research in Neurosis.* Utrecht: Bohn, Scheltema, & Holkema, 1976.

Barlow, D. H., Leitenberg, H., Agras, W. S., & Wincze, J. P. The transfer gap in systematic desensitization: An analogue study. *Behaviour Research and Therapy,* 1969, *1,* 191–196.

Barlow, D. H., Agras, W. S., Leitenberg, H., & Wincze, J. P. An experimental analysis of the effectiveness of "shaping" in reducing maladaptive avoidance behavior: An analogue study. *Behaviour Research and Therapy,* 1970, *8,* 165–173.

Barrett, C. L. Systematic desensitization versus implosive therapy., *Journal of Abnormal Psychology,* 1969, *74,* 587–592.

Beiman, I., O'Neil, P. O., Wachtel, D., Fruge, E., Johnson, S., & Feuerstein, M. Validation of a self-report/behavioral subject selection procedure for analog fear research. *Behavior Therapy,* 1978, *9,* 169–177.

Bernstein, D. A., & Beaty, W. E. The use of *in vivo* desensitization as part of a total therapeutic intervention. *Journal of Behavior Therapy and Experimental Psychiatry,* 1971, *2,* 259–265.

Bernstein, D. A., & Paul, G. L. Some comments on therapy analogue research with small animal phobias. *Journal of Behavior Therapy and Experimental Psychiatry,* 1971, *2,* 225–237.

Blanchard, E. B. Relative contributions of modeling, informational influences, and physical contact in extinction of phobic behavior. *Journal of Abnormal Psychology,* 1970, *76,* 55–61.

Borkovec, T. D. Extensions of two-factor theory: Cognitive avoidance and autonomic perception. In N. Birbaumer & H. D. Kimmel (Eds.), *Biofeedback and self-regulation.* Hillsdale, N.J.: Lawrence Erlbaum Associates, 1979.

Borkovec, T. D., & O'Brien, G. T. Methodological and target behavior issues in analogue therapy outcome research. In M. Hersen, R. M. Eisler, & P. M. Miller (Eds.), *Progress in behavior modification.* New York: Academic Press, 1976.

Boudewyns, P. A., & Wilson, A. E. Implosive therapy and desensitization therapy using free association in the treatment of inpatients. *Journal of Abnormal Psychology,* 1972, *79,* 259–268.

Boulougouris, J. C., Marks, I. M., & Marset, P. Superiority of flooding to desensitization as a fear reducer. *Behavior Research and Therapy,* 1971, *9,* 7–16.

Burns, L. E. The epidemiology of fears and phobias in general practice. *Journal of International Medical Research,* 1980, *8,* 1–7.

Connolly, J., Hallam, R. S., & Marks, I. M. Selective association of fainting with blood–injury–illness fear. *Behavior Therapy,* 1976, *7,* 8–13.

Crowe, M. J., Marks, I. M., Agras, W. S., & Leitenberg, H. Time limited desensitization, implosion, and shaping for phobic patients: A crossover study. *Behaviour Research and Therapy,* 1972, *10,* 319–328.

Curtis, G., Nesse, R., Buxton, M., Wright, J., & Lippman, D. Flooding *in vivo* as a research tool and treatment method for phobias: A preliminary report. *Comprehensive Psychiatry,* 1976, *17,* 153–160.

Delprato, D. J. Hereditary determinants of fears and phobias: A critical review. *Behavior Therapy,* 1980, *11,* 79–103.

DeMoor, W. Systematic desensitization versus prolonged high intensity stimulation (flooding). *Journal of Behavior Therapy and Experimental Psychiatry,* 1970, *1,* 45–52.

Denney, D. R., Sullivan, D. J., & Thiry, M. R. Participant modeling and self-verbalization training in the reduction of spider fears. *Journal of Behavior Therapy and Experimental Psychiatry,* 1977, *8,* 247–253.

de Silva, P., Rachman, S., & Seligman, M. E. P. Prepared phobias and obsessions: Therapeutic outcome. *Behaviour Research and Therapy,* 1977, *15,* 65–77.

D'Zurilla, T. J., Wilson, G. T., & Nelson, R. O. A preliminary study of effectiveness of graduated, prolonged exposure in the treatment of irrational fear. *Behavior Therapy,* 1973, *4,* 672–685.

Emmelkamp, P. M. G., & Wessels, H. Flooding in imagination versus flooding *in vivo:* A comparison with agoraphobics. *Behaviour Research and Therapy,* 1975, *13,* 7–15.

Eysenck, H. J. Single trial conditioning, neurosis, and the Napalkov phenomenon. *Behaviour Research and Therapy,* 1967, *5,* 63–65.

Foa, E. B., Blau, J. S., Prout, M., & Latimer, P. Is horror a necessary component of flooding (implosion)? *Behaviour Research and Therapy,* 1977, 397–402.

Freud, S. Analysis of a phobia in a five-year old boy. In *Collected papers* (Vol. 3). New York: Basic Books, 1959.

Gaind, R., Watson, J. P., & Marks, J. M. Some approaches to the treatment of phobic disorders. *Proceedings of the Royal Society of Medicine,* 1971, *64,* 1118.

Gallup, G. G., & Maser, J. D. Movement, mood and madness: A biological model of schizophrenia. In J. D. Maser & M. E. P. Seligman (Eds.), *Psychopathology: Experimental methods.* San Francisco: Freeman, 1977.

Gauthier, J., & Marshall, W. L. The determination of optimal exposure to phobic stimuli in flooding therapy. *Behaviour Research and Therapy,* 1977, *15,* 403–410.

Geer, J. H. The development of a scale to measure fear. *Behaviour Research and Therapy,* 1965, *3,* 45–53.

Gelder, M. G., Marks, I. M., Wolff, H. E., & Clarke, M. Desensitization and psychotherapy in the treatment of phobic states: A controlled inquiry. *British Journal of Psychiatry,* 1967, *113,* 53–73.

Goldfried, M. R., & Davison, G. C. *Clinical behavior therapy.* New York: Holt, Rinehart & Winston, 1976.

Goldfried, M. R., Decenteceo, E. T., & Weinburg, L. Systematic rational restructuring as a self-control technique. *Behavior Therapy,* 1974, *5,* 247–254.

Goldfried, M. R., Linehan, M. M., & Smith, J. L. Reduction of test anxiety through cognitive restructuring. *Journal of Consulting and Clinical Psychology,* 1978, *46,* 32–39.

Goorney. A. B., & O'Connor, P. J. Anxiety associated with flying. *British Journal of Psychiatry,* 1971, *119,* 159–166.

Greist, J. H., Marks, I. M., Berlin, F., Gournay, K., & Noshirvani, H. Avoidance versus confrontation of fear. *Behavior Therapy,* 1980, *11,* 1–14.

Grey, S. J., Rachman, S., & Sartory, G. Return of fear: The role of inhibition. *Behaviour Research and Therapy,* 1981, *19,* 135–143.

Grey, S., Sartory, G., & Rachman, S. Synchronous and desynchronous changes during fear reduction. *Behaviour Research and Therapy,* 1979, *17,* 137–147.

Hagman, E. A study of fears of children of pre-school age. *Journal of Experimental Education,* 1932, *1,* 110–130.

Hamilton, S. B., Carmody, T. P., Bornstein, P. H., Rychtarik, R. G., & Trontel, E. H. The effects of a diagnosis/treatment expectancy manipulation upon the efficacy of graduated prolonged exposure. *Behavior Therapy,* 1978, *9,* 690–691.

Hayes, S. C. The role of approach contingencies in phobic behavior. *Behavior Therapy,* 1976, *7,* 28–36.

Herrnstein, R. J. Method and theory in the study of avoidance. *Psychological Review,* 1969, *76,* 49–69.

Hodgson, R., & Rachman, S. Desynchrony in measures of fear. *Behaviour Research and Therapy,* 1974, *12,* 319–326.

Hollingshead, A. B., & Redlich, F. C. *Social class and mental illness.* New York: Wiley, 1958.

Holroyd, K. A. Cognition and desensitization in the group treatment of test anxiety. *Journal of Consulting and Clinical Psychology,* 1976, *44,* 991–1001.

Hugdahl, K. Electrodermal conditioning to potentially phobic stimuli: Effects of instructed extinction. *Behaviour Research and Therapy,* 1978, *16,* 315–321.

Hugdahl, K. The three-systems model of fear and emotion—A critical examination. *Behaviour Research and Therapy,* 1981, *19,* 75–85.

Hugdahl, K., & Karker, A. Biological vs. experiential factors in phobic conditioning. *Behaviour Research and Therapy,* 1981, *19,* 109–115.

Janis, I. L. *Air war and emotional stress.* New York: McGraw-Hill, 1951.

John, E. A study of the effects of air raids on pre-school children. *British Journal of Education and Psychology,* 1941, *11,* 173–182.

Kamin, L. J. Temporal and intensity characteristics of the conditioned stimulus. In W. F. Prokasy (Ed.), *Classical conditioning: A symposium.* New York: Appleton-Century-Crofts, 1965.

Kamin, L. J. Predictability, surprise, attention, and conditioning. In B. A. Campbell & R. M. Church (Eds.), *Punishment and aversive behavior.* New York: Appleton-Century-Crofts, 1969.

Katschnig, H., & Shepherd, M. Neurosis: The epidemiological perspective. In H. M. Van Praag (Ed.), *Research in neurosis.* Utrecht: Bohn, Scheltema & Holkema, 1976.

Kazdin, A. E. Covert modeling and the reduction of avoidance behavior. *Journal of Abnormal Psychology,* 1973, *81,* 87–95.

Kazdin, A. E. Covert modeling, model similarity, and reduction of avoidance behavior. *Behavior Therapy,* 1974, *5,* 325–340. (a)

Kazdin, A. E. The effect of model identity and fear relevant similarity on covert modeling. *Behavior Therapy*, 1974, *5*, 624–635. (b)

Kolko, D. J., & Milan, M. A. Misconception correction through reading in the treatment of a self-injection phobia. *Journal of Behavior Therapy and Experimental Psychiatry*, 1980, *11*, 273–276.

Lader, M. H., & Mathews, A. M. A physiological model of phobic anxiety and desensitization. *Behaviour Research and Therapy*, 1968, *16*, 411–420.

Lang, P. J. Fear reduction and fear behavior: Problems in treating a construct. In J. M. Shlien (Ed.), *Research in psychotherapy* (Vol. 3). Washington, D.C.: American Psychological Association, 1968.

Lang, P. J. The application of psychophysiological methods to the study of psychotherapy and behavior change. In A. G. Bergin & S. L. Garfield (Eds.), *Handbook of psychotherapy and behavior change*. New York: Wiley, 1971.

Lang, P. J. Anxiety: Toward a psychophysiological definition. In H. S. Akiskal & W. H. Webb (Eds.), *Psychiatric diagnosis: Exploration of biological predictors*. New York: Spectrum, 1978.

Lang, P. J., & Lazovik, A. D. Experimental desensitization of a phobia. *Journal of Abnormal and Social Psychology*, 1963, *66*, 519–525.

Lapouse, R., & Monk, M. A. Fears and worries in a representative sample of children. *American Journal of Orthopsychiatry*, 1959, *29*, 803.

Leitenberg, H., & Callahan, E. J. Reinforced practice and reduction of different kinds of fear in adults and children. *Behaviour Research and Therapy*, 1973, *11*, 19–30.

Leitenberg, H., Agras, W. S., Thompson, L. E., & Wright, D. E. Feedback in behavior modification: An experimental analysis in two phobic cases. *Journal of Applied Behavior Analysis*, 1968, *1*, 131–137.

Leitenberg, H., Wincze, J. P., Butz, R. A., Callahan, E. J., & Agras, W. S. Comparison of the effects of instructions and reinforcement in the treatment of a neurotic avoidance response: A single case experiment. *Journal of Behavior Therapy and Experimental Psychiatry*, 1970, *1*, 53–58.

Leitenberg, H., Agras, W. S., Butz, R., & Wincze, J. Relationship between heart rate and behavioral change during the treatment of phobias. *Journal of Abnormal Psychology*, 1971, *78*, 59–68.

Leitenberg, H., Agras, W. S., Allen, R., Butz, R., & Edwards, J. Feedback and therapist praise during treatment of phobia. *Journal of Consulting and Clinical Psychology*, 1975, *43*, 396–404.

Lemkau, P., Tietze, C., & Cooper, M. Mental hygiene problems in an urban district. *Mental Hygiene*, 1942, *26*, 100–119.

Levis, D. J. Implosive therapy: A critical analysis of Morganstern's review. *Psychological Bulletin*, 1974, *81*, 155–158.

Levis, D. J., & Hare, N. A review of the theoretical, rational, and empirical support for the extinction approach of implosive (flooding) therapy. In M. Hersen, R. M. Eisler, & P. M. Miller (Eds.), *Progress in behavior modification* (Vol. 4). New York: Academic Press, 1977.

Lewis, A. Incidence of neurosis in England under war conditions. *Lancet*, 1942, *2*, 175–183.

MacFarlane, J. W., Allen, L., & Honzik, M. P. *A developmental study of the behavior problems of normal children between 21 months and 14 years*. Berkeley: University of California Press, 1954.

Malan, D. H. *A study of brief psychotherapy*. New York: Plenum, 1963.

Malan, D. H. *The frontier of brief psychotherapy*. New York: Plenum, 1976.

Marks, I. M. *Fears and phobias*. London: Academic Press, 1969.

Marks, I. M. Phobic disorders four years after treatment: A prospective follow up. *British Journal of Psychiatry*, 1971, *118*, 683–688.

Marks, I. Behavioural treatments of phobic and obsessive-compulsive disorders: A critical appraisal. In M. Hersen, R. M. Eisler, & A. M. Miller (Eds.)., *Progress in behaviour modification* (Vol. 1). New York: Academic Press, 1975.

Marks, I. M. Neglected factors in neurosis. In H. M. Van Praag (Ed.), *Research in neurosis.* Utrecht: Bohn, Scheltema, & Holkema, 1976.

Marks, I. M. Behavioral psychotherapy of adult neurosis. In A. E. Bergin & S. Garfield (Eds.), *Handbook of psychotherapy and behavior change.* New York: Wiley, 1978.

Marks, I. M., Boulougouris, J. C., & Marset, P. Flooding versus desensitization in treatment of phobic patients: A crossover study. *British Journal of Psychiatry,* 1971, *119,* 353–375.

Marks, I. M., Connolly, J., & Hallam, R. S. The psychiatric nurse as therapist. *British Medical Journal,* 1973, *3,* 156–160.

Marshall, W. L., Gauthier, J., Christie, M. M., Currie, S. W., & Gordon, A. Flooding therapy: Effectiveness, stimulus characteristics, and the value of brief *in vivo* exposure. *Behaviour Research and Therapy,* 1977, *15,* 79–87.

Mavissakalian, M., & Barlow, D. H. *Phobia: Psychological and pharmacological treatment.* New York: Guilford Press, 1981.

May, J. R. A psychophysiological study of self and externally regulated phobic thoughts. *Behavior Therapy,* 1977, *8,* 849–861. (a)

May, J. R. Psychophysiology of self-regulated phobic thoughts. *Behavior Therapy,* 1977, *8,* 150–159. (b)

Mealiea, W. L., & Nawas, M. M. The comparative effectiveness of systematic desensitization and implosive therapy in the treatment of snake phobia. *Journal of Behavior Therapy and Experimental Psychiatry,* 1971, *2,* 85–94.

Meichenbaum, D. H. Cognitive modification of test anxious college students. *Journal of Consulting and Clinical Psychology,* 1972, *39,* 370–380.

Meyer, V. Personal communication, 1977.

Mowrer, O. H. A stimulus-response analysis of anxiety and its role as a reinforcing agent. *Psychological Review,* 1939, *46,* 553–565.

Mowrer, O. H. On the dual nature of learning: A reinterpretation of "conditioning" and problem-solving. *Harvard Educational Review,* 1947, *17,* 102–148.

Mowrer, O. H. *Learning theory and the symbolic processes.* New York: Wiley, 1960.

Murray, E. J., & Foote, F. The origins of fear of snakes. *Behaviour Research and Therapy,* 1979, *17,* 489–493.

Napalkov, A. Information process of the brain. In N. Weiner & J. Safade (Eds.) *Progress of brain research* (Vol. 2). Amsterdam: Elsevier, 1963.

Nesbitt, E. B. An escalator phobia overcome in one session of flooding *in vivo. Journal of Behavior Therapy and Experimental Psychiatry,* 1973, *4,* 405–406.

O'Brien, G. T. Clinical treatment of specific phobias. In M. Mavissakalian & D. H. Barlow (Eds.), *Phobia: Psychological and pharmacological treatment.* New York: Guilford Press, 1981.

Odom, J. V., Nelson, R. O., & Wein, K. S. The differential effectiveness of five treatment procedures on the three response systems in a snake phobia analog study. *Behavior Therapy,* 1978, *9,* 936–942.

Öhman, A., & Dimberg, V. Facial expression as conditioned stimuli for electrodermal responses: A case of "preparedness"? *Journal of Personality and Social Psychology.* 1978, *36,* 1251–1258.

Öhman, A., & Hugdahl, K. Instructional control of autonomic respondents: Fear relevance as a critical factor. In N. Birbaumer & H. D. Kimmel (Eds.), *Biofeedback and self-regulation. Proceedings of the First International Congress.* Hillsdale, N.J.: Erlbaum, 1979.

Öhman, A., Eriksson, A., Fredrikson, M., Hugdahl, K., & Olofsson, C. Habituation of the electrodermal orienting reaction to potentially phobic and supposedly neutral stimuli in normal human subjects. *Biological Psychology,* 1974, *2,* 85–92.

Öhman, A., Eriksson, A., & Olofsson, C. One trial learning and superior resistance to extinction of autonomic responses cnditioned to potentially phobic stimuli. *Journal of Comparative and Physiological Psychology,* 1975, *88,* 619–627.

Öhman, A., Eriksson, G., & Lofberg, I. Phobias and preparedness: Phobic versus neutral pictures as conditioned stimuli for human autonomic responses. *Journal of Abnormal Psychology,* 1975, *84,* 41–45.

Öhman, A., Fredrikson, M., Hugdahl, K., & Rimmö, P. The premise of equipotentiality in human classical conditioning: Conditioned electrodermal responses to potentially phobic stimuli. *Journal of Experimental Psychology: General,* 1976, *105,* 313–337.

Öhman, A., Fredrikson, M., & Hugdahl, K. Orienting and defensive responding in the electrodermal system: Palmar–dorsal differences and recovery rate during conditioning to potentially phobic stimuli. *Psychophysiology,*1978, *15,* 93–101.

O'Leary, K. D., & Borkovec, T. D. Conceptual, methodological, and ethical problems of placebo groups in psychotherapy research. *American Psychologist,* 1978, *33,* 821–830.

O'Leary, K. D., & Wilson, G. T. *Behavior therapy: Application and outcome.* Englewood Cliffs, N.J.: Prentice-Hall, 1975.

Rachman, S. Studies in desensitization—II: Flooding. *Behaviour Research and Therapy,* 1966, *4,* 1–6.(a)

Rachman, S. Studies in desensitization—III: Speed of generalization. *Behaviour Research and Therapy,* 1966, *4,* 7–15. (b)

Rachman, S. *The meaning of fear.* Harmondsworth, Middlesex, England: Penguin Books, 1974.

Rachman, S. The passing of the two-stage theory of fear and avoidance: Fresh possibilities. *Behaviour Research and Therapy,* 1976, *14,* 125–131.

Rachman, S. The conditioning theory of fear acquisition: A critical examination. *Behaviour Research and Therapy,* 1977, *15,* 375–387.

Rachman, S. *Fear and courage.* San Francisco: Freeman, 1978(a)

Rachman, S. Human fears: A three systems analysis. *Scandanavian Journal of Behavior Therapy,* 1978, *7,* 237–245. (b)

Rachman, S., & Hodgson, R. Synchrony and desynchrony in fear and avoidance. *Behaviour Research and Therapy,* 1974, *12,* 311–318.

Rachman, E., & Seligman, M. Unprepared phobias: Be prepared. *Behaviour Research and Therapy,* 1976, *14,* 333–338.

Rescorla, R. A., & Lolordo, V. M. Inhibition of avoidance behavior. *Journal of Comparative and Physiological Psychology,* 1965, *59,* 406–412.

Rimm, D. C., & Lefebvre, R. C. Phobic disorders. In S. M. Turner, K. S. Calhoun, & H. E. Adams (Eds.), *Handbook of clinical behavior therapy.* New York: Wiley, 1981.

Rimm, D. C., & Mahoney, M. J. The application of reinforcement and participant modeling procedures in the treatment of snake phobic behaviour. *Behaviour Research and Therapy,* 1969, *1,* 369–376.

Rimm, D. C., Janda, L. H., Lancaster, D. W., Nahl, M., & Dittman, K. An exploratory investigation of the origin and maintenance of phobias. *Behaviour Research and Therapy,* 1977, *15,* 231–238.

Ritter, B. The group treatment of children's snake phobias, using vicarious and contact desensitization procedures. *Behaviour Research and Therapy,* 1968, *6,* 1–6.

Ritter, B. The use of contact desensitization, demonstration-plus-participation, and demonstration alone in the treatment of acrophobia. *Behaviour Research and Therapy,* 1969, *1,* 157–164. (a)

Ritter, B. Treatment of acrophobia with contact desensitization. *Behaviour Research and Therapy,* 1969, *1,* 41–45.(b)

Rohrbaugh, M., & Riccio, D. Paradoxical enhancement of learned fear. *Journal of Abnormal Psychology,* 1970, *75,* 210–216.

Rutter, M. Tizard, J., & Whitmore, K. *Education, health, and behavior.* London: Longmans, 1968.

Sargeant, A. B., & Eberhardt, L. E. Death feigning by ducks in response to predation by red foxes *(Vulpes fulva). American Midland Naturalist,* 1975, *94,* 108–119.

Seligman, M. E. P. Chronic fear produced by unpredictable shock. *Journal of Comparative Physiological Psychology,* 1968, *66,* 402–411.

Seligman, M. E. P. Phobias and preparedness. *Behavior Therapy,* 1971, *2,* 307–320.

Seligman, M. E. P., & Hager, J. *The biological boundaries of learning.* New York: Appleton-Century-Crofts, 1972.

Sherry, G. S., & Levine, B. A. An examination of procedural variables in flooding therapy. *Behavior Therapy,* 1980, *11,* 148–155.

Shipley, R. H., & Boudewyns, P. A. Flooding and implosive therapy: Are they harmful? *Behavior Therapy,* 1980, *11,* 503–508.

Skinner, B. F. *Science and human behavior.* Glencoe, N.Y.: Free Press, 1953.

Smith, G. P., & Coleman, R. E. Processes underlying generalization through participant modeling with self-directed practice. *Behaviour Research and Therapy,* 1977, *15,* 204–206.

Stampfl, T. G., & Levis, D. J. Essentials of implosive therapy: A learning-theory-based psychodynamic behavioral therapy. *Journal of Abnormal Psychology,* 1967, *72,* 496–503.

Stern, R., & Marks, I. Brief and prolonged flooding: A comparison in agoraphobic patients. *Archives of General Psychiatry,* 1973, *28,* 270–276.

Suedfeld, P., & Hare, R. D. Sensory deprivation in the treatment of snake phobia: Behavioral, self-report, and physiological effects. *Behavior Therapy,* 1977, *8,* 240–250.

Valentine, C. W. *The psychology of early childhood* (3rd ed.). London: Methuen, 1946.

Wade, T. C. W., Malloy, T. E., & Proctor, S. Imaginal correlates of self-reported fear and avoidance behavior. *Behaviour Research and Therapy,* 1977, *15,* 17–22.

Walk, R. D. Self-ratings of fear in a fear-invoking situation. *Journal of Abnormal and Social Psychology,* 1956, *52,* 171–178.

Watson, J., & Raynor, R. Conditioned emotional reactions. *Journal of Experimental Psychology,* 1920, *3,* 1–22.

Watson, J. P., Gaind, R., & Marks, I. M. Prolonged exposure: A rapid treatment for phobias. *British Medical Journal,* 1971, *1,* 13–15.

Watson, J. P., Gaind, R., & Marks, I. M. Physiological habituation to continuous phobic stimulation. *Behaviour Research and Therapy,* 1972, *10,* 269–278.

Wieselberg, N., Dyckman, J. M., & Abramowitz, S. I. The desensitization derby: *In vivo* down the backstretch, imaginal at the wire. *Journal of Clinical Psychology,* 1979, *35,* 647–650.

Willis, R. W., & Edwards, J. A. A study of the comparative effectiveness of systematic desensitization and implosive therapy. *Behaviour Research and Therapy,* 1969, *1,* 387–395.

Wolpe, J. *Psychotherapy by reciprocal inhibition.* Stanford, Cal.: Stanford University Press, 1958.

Wolpe, J., & Lang, P. J. A fear survey schedule for use in behavior therapy. *Behaviour Research and Therapy,* 1969, *2,* 27–30.

Wolpe, J., & Rachman, S. Psychoanalytic evidence: A critique based on Freud's case of Little Hans. *Journal of Nervous and Mental Disease,* 1960, *131,* 135–147.

Yule, W., & Fernando, P. Blood phobia—beware. *Behaviour Research and Therapy,* 1980, *18,* 587–590.

4

Agoraphobia

GERALD T. O'BRIEN and DAVID H. BARLOW

Agoraphobia is the most complex and disabling of the phobias. Agras, Sylvester, and Oliveau (1969) have estimated that the prevalence rate of agoraphobia is 6 per 1,000 people. Although agoraphobia is not the most common phobia, it is the one seen most frequently by mental health professionals, mainly because comparatively few individuals with less disabling phobias ever seek professional help (Agras, Sylvester, & Oliveau, 1969). In fact, due to increased attention to agoraphobia in both scientific and lay publications in recent years, it seems that agoraphobics are at present more likely than ever to seek and receive professional help for their handicaps.

During the last two decades, major advances have been made in the assessment and treatment of agoraphobia. In this chapter, we will discuss in detail the current state of the art and science of the behavioral assessment and treatment of this complex disorder. After some brief illustrative case examples, we will describe a two-part approach to assessment, which involves initial classification followed by a detailed behavioral assessment, including assessment of the three response systems implicated in the construct of anxiety: behavioral, somatic, and subjective-cognitive. This will be followed by a discussion of current treatments for agoraphobia and procedures involved in the clinical application of those treatments. Problems and limitations encountered in the use of exposure treatments with agoraphobics will be highlighted, as well as treatments commonly employed as adjuncts to *in vivo* exposure, together with a

GERALD T. O'BRIEN ● Agoraphobia and Anxiety Program, Department of Psychiatry, Temple University Medical School, Philadelphia, Pennsylvania 19131.   DAVID H. BARLOW ● Center for Stress and Anxiety Disorders, Department of Psychology, State University of New York at Albany, Albany, New York 12222.

discussion of evidence supporting the effectiveness of these adjunctive treatments.

DEFINITION AND DESCRIPTION

The clinical picture of agoraphobia consists of a complex cluster of fears, avoidance behavior, and other symptoms. The central feature of the disorder has been described most often as a fear of being away from a safe place or a safe person, especially in situations where incapacitation may occur. But more recently, investigators and clinicians have described agoraphobia with greater accuracy as a fear of experiencing panic or anxiety, particularly away from a safe place or person. This is termed "fear of fear." Criteria for assessment will be discussed below. First, however, we will illustrate with some brief case reports the range of difficulties experienced by agoraphobics.

Sheryl L. was a 30-year-old married agoraphobic who presented with fears and anxiety of 8 years' duration. Her major presenting fear was driving. She was unable to drive even short distances alone. On rare occasions she drove when her husband was with her, but he did most of the driving. Although able to hold down a full-time job, she was unable to drive alone to and from work. Instead, her retired father, who lived nearby, drove her and picked her up. Very infrequently, she drove home when her father was with her. Even with her husband she avoided traveling more than 20 or 30 miles from home and kept away from highways. When driving or riding, she engaged in a number of security operations, such as staying on familiar roads and continually determining how close she was to a hospital or a friend's house, in case something should happen. She also avoided travel by plane, train, or bus. She was unable to walk alone more than two blocks from her house.

In addition to traveling fears, Mrs. L. experienced periodic anxiety attacks, which she called "hyper attacks." These were characterized by tension, dizziness, and fears that she was going to pass out or go crazy. She reported "avoiding like a plague" any situations in which she might experience a panic attack. When first seen, she had avoided grocery shopping and going to shopping malls for 2 years. She also reported fears of crowds, especially of "seedy-looking" people.

Mrs. L. experienced her first panic attack when in a very high balcony in a crowded theater. However, she traced the origin of her anxiety attacks and agoraphobia to a period of time when her mother was gravely ill and eventually died. Mrs. L. was very close to her mother and experienced severe anxiety and panic attacks in going to the hospital to visit her. Her fears and anxiety gradually increased after her mother died.

Mary C. was a 33-year-old married agoraphobic whose chief complaints were frequent panic attacks and fears of being alone. She experienced panic attacks of varying severity approximately three times a week. These attacks were characterized by marked fears of fainting, as well as palpitations, chest pain, and dizziness. Although capable of driving alone for short distances (within 1½ miles of home), she could not walk alone more than a few blocks from home, and was able to go only to certain stores and churches in her immediate neighborhood. She avoided being alone as much as possible, including being alone at home, especially at night. If her husband had to work overtime or be away from home overnight, she went with her children to her mother's house or asked her mother to stay at her house. Mrs. C. also reported severe fears that she might run away and "abandon" her 3-year-old son in the midst of a panic attack.

Mrs. C. reported serious marital problems of several years' duration. She described her husband as emotionally unsupportive, critical, and impatient. He was not at all understanding about her anxiety and fears. She felt she had been recently growing more assertive, but that her husband was reacting negatively to her increased assertive behavior.

Mrs. C. had suffered from agoraphobia for approximately 7 years. She experienced her first panic attack when driving alone on the thruway at a time when she had just recovered from major surgery and started a new job that was stressful to her. Subsequently, the frequency of her panic attacks and the severity of her anxiety and avoidance behavior gradually increased.

These two cases illustrate several of the distinguishing features of agoraphobia. Both cases involved combinations of subjective anxiety, panic attacks, and avoidance behavior. Situations avoided included being alone or away from persons and/or places that represented safety. Both women were able to do more things and travel further when accompanied by their husbands than when alone. In both cases, the anxiety attacks were reported to have occurred during a stressful period in their lives. These anxiety/panic attacks apparently then led to the development of both anticipatory fears and avoidance behavior. Although limited markedly by their phobic symptoms, these women are not representative of the most severe cases of agoraphobia. In more severe cases, some individuals are unable to leave their homes unaccompanied; often they will not go anywhere even if accompanied. They fear experiencing intolerable anxiety and panic that might be precipitated by leaving the house at all. Such individuals have become virtual prisoners in their own homes and may remain housebound for years. Thus, agoraphobia is an anxiety disorder capable of disrupting most areas of the individual's functioning and one that in more severe cases can result in complete disability.

ASSESSMENT OF AGORAPHOBIA

Assessment involves many steps. In this section a comprehensive approach to assessment will be outlined, beginning with a description of current classification systems, and proceeding to an overview of the purposes of a functional behavioral analysis before describing specific assessment procedures. Assessment includes the clinical interview and systems for rating severity of avoidance behavior. We will discuss assessment procedures and provide an overview and recommendation of optimal and current measures in each of the three response systems.

Classification

The standard psychiatric classification system in the United States is the American Psychiatric Association's *Diagnostic and Statistical Manual of Mental Disorders* (DSM). The version in use until 1980, the second edition (DSM-II), specified only a single broad category of phobias, namely "phobic neurosis." This classification was quite inadequate, in that it offered a vague, poorly operationalized definition of phobia, did not subclassify phobias in any way, and explicitly accepted the controversial and unproven psychodynamic hypothesis that phobias are the result of displaced anxiety.

A greatly reivsed and expanded version of the diagnositc system—the DSM-III—was published by the American Psychiatric Association in 1980. Among other significant changes, DSM-III introduced a multiaxial system for diagnosis, provided much more specific inclusion and exclusion criteria for diagnoses, and eliminated the major classification of "neurosis," distributing the former "neurotic disorders" among a variety of other categories of disorders instead.

In the DSM-III, the phobic disorders are included under the major category of "anxiety disorders." Three types of phobic disorders are identified, namely agoraphobia, social phobia, and simple (specific) phobia.

The DSM-III diagnostic criteria for agoraphobia are as follows:

A. The individual has marked fear of and thus avoids being alone or in public places from which escape might be difficult or help not available in case of sudden incapacitation, e.g., crowds, tunnels, bridges, public transportation.

B. There is increasing constriction of normal activities until the fears or avoidance behavior dominate the individual's life.

C. Not due to a major depressive episode, Obsessive Compulsive Disorder, Paranoid Personality Disorder, or Schizophrenia.[1]

Agoraphobia itself is subdivided into two classifications, namely *agoraphobia with panic attacks* and *agoraphobia without panic attacks.* The former subclassification is used for agoraphobics who have a history of panic attacks, regardless of whether they are currently experienced; the latter is reserved for agoraphobics with no history of panic attacks.

The DSM-III's treatment of phobic disorders is vastly superior to the

---

[1] From American Psychiatric Association, *Diagnostic and Statistical Manual of Mental Disorders* (3rd Ed.), p. 227. Copyright 1980 by author, Washington D.C. Reprinted by permission.

global and superficial approach found in the DSM-II. Its increased specificity and comprehensiveness is virtually certain, for example, to improve the reliability of the diagnosis of agoraphobia. Nevertheless, evidence for reliability of the categories of anxiety disorders, including agoraphobia, is not yet available.

Despite the advantages and improvements of the DSM-III description of the criteria for agoraphobia, they are less than completely adequate. One major limitation is that no quantitative criteria are provided. For how long must the individual manifest the symptoms? How much avoidance behavior is necessary? At what point do fears and avoidance come to "dominate" an individual's life (Criterion B)? Answers to these questions are not provided in the DSM-III. Another difficulty arises in distinguishing between agoraphobia with and without panic attacks. It is often difficult to determine whether acute anxiety is in fact "spontaneous," as required by the DSM-III for diagnosing the experience as a panic attack. Indeed, it is not yet clear whether the distinction between agoraphobia with and without panic attacks is of any real use.

The differential diagnosis of agoraphobia can be problematic in some cases. Depression is common in many agoraphobic individuals and it can be difficult to determine whether the depression supercedes the agoraphobia. The most difficult differential diagnosis is to distinguish agoraphobia from other types of anxiety disorders, in particular *generalized anxiety disorder* and *panic disorder*. Although the latter two disorders are characterized primarily by disabling anxiety in the absence of avoidance behavior, this is not always clearcut. Some clients who experience generalized anxiety or panic attacks may avoid only certain types of situations or situations at certain times or on certain occasions. An individual who avoids only a specific class of stimuli (e.g., driving) may be classified under both simple phobia and generalized anxiety or panic disorder. However, some clients display a variable pattern of avoidance against a background of chronic anxiety, and it is difficult at times to decide whether the diagnosis of agoraphobia is warranted.

Functional Behavioral Analysis of Agoraphobia

Although formal psychiatric diagnosis can be valuable for clinical, research, and administrative purposes (Nathan, 1981; Nelson & Barlow, 1981), diagnosis alone is usually insufficient (Barlow, 1981). Comprehensive, multifaceted assessment is required to obtain adequate information about the individual's difficulties and problems as well as his strengths, to select appropriate treatment goals and intervention strategies, and also to evaluate the immediate and long-range effects of treatment. For these purposes, a behavioral approach to assessment (Barlow, 1981; Haynes, 1978) is highly recommended.

Behavioral assessment emphasizes an idiographic approach to assessment in which the individual's behavior is carefully observed, measured, and analyzed. Functional relationships between problem behaviors and the environmental and/or organismic variables that elicit and maintain them are sought. Behavioral assessment emphasizes quantification, specification of variables, current causal and maintaining variables, and a close association between assessment and treatment (Haynes, 1978).

Three major response modalities have been identified as having major importance in behavioral assessment, particularly in the assessment of anxiety disorders: the overt behavioral (motoric), the cognitive (or "self-report"), and the physiological (Borkovec, Weerts, & Bernstein, 1977; Hersen, 1976; Lang, 1968, 1977). Assessment within all three response modalities seems to be especially important for agoraphobia. One reason is that agoraphobia is the most complex of the phobic disorders. Agoraphobics display remarkable variability with regard to the types of fears experienced as well as the type and severity of behavioral avoidance reactions, psychophysiological arousal patterns, and cognitive processes and responses. Detailed knowledge of the specific relationships and severity of an agoraphobic's problems across all three response modalities will help in selecting the most appropriate type of behavioral treatment and the most appropriate targets on which to focus during treatment.

The assessment of all three response modalities is also important in the study and treatment of agoraphobia because the relationship between the three response modes may have important implications for treatment effectiveness and the maintenance of treatment effects (Barlow, Mavissakalian, & Schofield, 1980). Hodgson and Rachman (1974) suggested the terms synchrony and concordance to describe the relationships between response systems. *Concordance* refers to a high degree of correlation between two or more response systems, and *synchrony* refers to a high degree of covariance as response systems change over time. Some preliminary evidence and theoretical speculation (Barlow, Mavissakalian, & Schofield, 1980; Grey, Sartory, & Rachman, 1979; Rachman, 1978) suggest that desynchrony among response systems during treatment and discordance at the conclusion of treatment may be predictive of high rates of posttreatment relapse in agoraphobics and other phobics. However, since very few investigations of the treatment of phobias have included measures in all three response modes (Agras & Jacob, 1981), little empirical evidence is available to determine the relationships between desynchrony/discordance and treatment outcome and maintenance. Clearly, then, triple-response-mode assessment of agoraphobia is of crucial importance, particularly in future research efforts.

The Clinical Interview

Typically, the clinical interview is the initial step in the assessment of any client. Although it may be the primary source of information for nonbehavioral clinicians, the clinical interview should be only one component of a comprehensive behavioral assessment. It is an important component, however, because many of the clinician's initial hypotheses, formulations, and goals will be determined on the basis of information obtained during the clinical interview. Methods of conducting initial clinical interviews within a behavioral framework have been discussed in detail by several writers (Haynes, 1978; Morganstern, 1976; Peterson, 1968). Here we will discuss some recommendations specific to the interviewing of anxious and agoraphobic clients.

The initial part of the interview should consist of introduction of the client and therapist as well as preliminary discussion designed both to obtain some general information and to put the client at east. Although the initial interview is anxiety-provoking for most clients, for some agoraphobics it can be terrifying. For agoraphobics who have difficulty even leaving their house, for example, coming to a clinic or office for an evaluation can be a formidable, frightening task. Many agoraphobics anticipate upcoming stressful situations for hours, even days or weeks in advance. By the time of the initial interview, the individual may be extremely apprehensive and anxious. Indeed, some clients may report that they are experiencing a "full-blown" panic attack during the course of the interview. The clinician can help make the client feel as comfortable as possible by indicating that he is aware of how uncomfortable and anxious the client may be feeling and by conveying a combination of respect, empathy, calm, and professionalism.

Following preliminary introductions and initial establishment of rapport, the information-gathering phase begins. We recommend the graduated funnel approach (Nelson & Barlow, 1981) for obtaining information. This approach involves initially asking relatively global questions about many areas of the individual's life. Topics that should be covered include presenting complaints, existence of other problems, psychiatric history, and functioning in major areas such as family and marital relationships, career, physical health, and so on. Following the initial broad inquiry, the interviewer should gradually focus on more detailed questions about issues and problems that have been identified as requiring further information. It is not at all uncommon to discover that the client's initial complaints are not his primary concerns, or that the individual has more severe problems in other areas of functioning. By focusing immediately on the client's presenting problems, major errors can be made with regard to diagnosis, target problems, and treatment goals and strategies. Issues that are frequently problems for agoraphobics and that require special attention include depression, marital relationships, and assertiveness.

If the information obtained during the initial broad scanning phase of the interview suggests that the client's difficulties do involve anxiety, phobias, and possibly agoraphobia, then some specific variables should be explored in detail when the size of the investigative funnel is narrowed. These variables are ones that are frequently correlated with phobic and agoraphobic disorders and should be examined in addition to any other idiosyncratic areas that have been identified earlier as potential problems. One of these variables involves the specific pattern and severity of avoidance behaviors, including the degree of reliance on a "safe companion," who is usually the spouse with the occasional addition of another family member or friend. It is important to explore the pattern of avoidance behavior in detail. Some agoraphobics report a very consistent or chronic pattern, whereas others report that on "good" days they are more active and avoid fewer places and situations than they do on "bad" days. Many female clients report that they are at their worst immediately before or during menstruation.

Other important variables to be assessed include the pattern and severity of anxiety or panic. This would include the baseline level of anxiety, experience of anxiety in feared situations, the presence, pattern, and intensity of panic attacks, and the somatic symptoms associated with both anxiety and panic attacks. A panic attack is defined as the spontaneous occurrence of increased anxiety accompanied by specific physiological sensations (e.g., palpitations, difficulty breathing, paresthesias) that are presumably elicited neither by contact with phobic stimuli nor by life-threatening stress (American Psychiatric Association, 1980). It is extremely difficult to determine whether or not a panic attack occurs "spontaneously," or in the absence of any identifiable precipitant. Some panic attacks, rather than occurring spontaneously, may instead be precipitated by eliciting stimuli which are in some cases quite subtle. The identification of panic attacks is further complicated by the apparent fact that many agoraphobics are poor observers of the antecedents of emotional responses, including anxiety. Agoraphobics frequently misattribute the causes of emotional arousal (Goldstein & Chambless, 1978) or fail to recognize any reasons for the experience of anxiety or other emotions. A further complication is that for many agoraphobics, anxiety has become generalized to a broad range of stimuli.

Another variable that requires detailed assessment is the individual's cognitions with regard to anxiety and feared situations. Some clients do not understand what their problem is, believe that they are the only person in the world with such symptoms and fears, and that these symptoms mean that they are "going crazy" and/or "losing control." Other clients interpret their anxiety sensations as indicative of serious physical illness, such as heart disease or a brain tumor. Many agoraphobics report major problems with anticipation of catastrophic consequences if they were to leave their house or venture into other "dangerous" situations. They also report that frequently the anxiety produced by negative anticipation is much worse than that experienced when actually in the feared situation.

The most important part of the assessment, of course, is a determination of the functional relationship between avoidance behaviors, cognitive patterns, and the experience of anxiety on the one hand, and associated internal or external cues on the other. This "functional analysis," wherein maladaptive behaviors and feelings are related to specific events resulting in an individual and idiosyncratic pattern of responses, is the major contribution of a behavioral assessment over and above initial classification. The primary benefit of this analysis is a treatment carefully tailored to the individual even in a condition as superficially similar across clients as agoraphobia.

Clinical Rating Scales

For purposes of quantifying levels of severity of agoraphobia in a standardized way from information collected during the assessment, clinical ratings are often used. Gelder and Marks (1966) developed standardized 5-point clinical rating scales for agoraphobics' psychological symptoms and social adjustment. The symptom scales included ratings of both the client's main phobia and up to four other phobias. The rater was to consider both anxiety and avoidance in making these phobia ratings. Additional symptom rating scales included general anxiety, depression, obsessions, and depersonalization. The symptom ratings were completed periodically by clients, therapists, and an independent assessor. Social adjustment ratings (modified from Miles, Barrabee, & Finesinger, 1951) were completed by therapists and independent assessors for adjustment in areas of work, leisure activities, sexual functioning, family and non-family relationships, and self-satisfaction.

Watson and Marks (1971) revised the Gelder and Marks (1966) scales by expanding them to 9-point (0–8) scales and by obtaining separate ratings of anxiety and avoidance for the phobia ratings. Most agoraphobia researchers have used one of the above clinical rating scales. Reviews (Agras & Jacob, 1981; Emmelkamp, 1979) of the interrater reliability of these scales indicate that the level of agreement between ratings made by clients, therapists, and independent assessors have generally been acceptable. Emmelkamp (1979) reported that the evidence of interrater reliability is more consistent for the nine-point Watson and Marks (1971) scale than for the Gelder and Marks (1966) scale. Some researchers have omitted ratings by independent assessors and sometimes even by therapists, with the justification that the typically high correlations between different raters indicate that multiple raters are not necessary. Agras and Jacob (1981) pointed out, however, that in no specific study is agreement between clients, therapists and independent raters guaranteed. They recommended that investigations obtain independent ratings from all three sources, report the obtained correlations between pairs of raters, and if these correlations are high, average the independent ratings to provide a single dependent variable. This procedure will minimize error variance and decrease the number of statistical analyses, thereby reducing the probability of obtaining significant findings by chance.

Agras and Jacob (1981) also estimated the relative sensitivity of the most frequently used assessments of phobia. The concluded that the most sensitive measure of improvement appears to be *in vivo* behavioral assessment, but that a close second was clients' self-ratings of their main fears.

Standardized clinical rating scales have a number of advantages. They are quick, convenient, and therefore quite economical to administer. They appear to be sensitive to clinical improvement and are generally adequate with regard to interrater reliability. Potentially, at least, they could enable standardization of measurement across research centers. However, as Emmelkamp (1979) has pointed out, standardization has not been achieved to any extent because typically the phobias rated differ across clients. Emmelkamp recommended rating a standard series of fears for homogeneous groups of clients (e.g., agoraphobics).

Clinical rating scales have a number of disadvantages as well. They are subject to distortion due to factors such as bias, expectancy, and experimental demand (Borkovec, Weerts, & Bernstein, 1977). Ratings whose behavioral referents are difficult to identify are relatively global. Such ratings require complex judgments, and a summary rating of a possibly wide range of behaviors, situations, and fears must somehow be made. Furthermore, the quantitative level of change on a clinical rating scale provides virtually no specific information about the client's current level of functioning. Thus, although clinical rating scales have certain advantages and should not be abandoned, they should not be the sole type of measure in the assessment of agoraphobia.

Self-Report Measures

A wide variety of self-report measures have been employed in treatment outcome studies of phobias. One disadvantage of this wide variety is that different studies have used different measures, making comparisons across studies and research centers difficult (Agras & Jacob, 1981; Marks & Mathews, 1979). In this section, we will discuss briefly our recommendations concerning self-report measures. These recommendations are based on our own experience as well as on recommendations made in a recent international conference on anxiety disorder sponsored by the National Institute of Mental Health (NIMH) (Barlow & Wolfe, 1981).

One standardized self-report measure recommended by the NIMH conference (Barlow & Wolfe, 1981) as useful for all research studies on phobias is the Fear Questionnaire (Marks & Mathews, 1979). The Fear Questionnaire is a one-page instrument that is easy to administer and that provides four measures: (1) Level of avoidance of main target fear, which is described in the client's own words. (2) Global phobia rating: client's 0–8 rating of anxiety and avoidance of all phobic symptoms in general. (3) A fear questionnaire consisting of 15 items derived from factor analytic studies with clinical phobics. These items are rated by the client on a 0–8 scale with respect to avoidance behavior. The fear questionnaire provides a "Total Phobia" score as well as three subscale scores: agoraphobia, social anxiety, and blood-injury phobia. (4) Anxiety–depression scale ("Total Feelings" scale): five items of the most common nonphobic symptoms of phobic patients to assess affective problems.

Preliminary findings by Marks and Mathews (1979) support the reliability, sensitivity, and validity of the Fear Questionnaire. Although further investigation of this measure is warranted, we recommend its adoption for the time being by all phobia researchers as a standard self-report measure of clinical phobias that will permit cross-laboratory comparisons of data.

A second recommended self-report measure can provide frequent individualized assessment of clients' progress during treatment. This involves clients' ratings of phobic anxiety and avoidance of items from an individualized fear and avoidance hierarchy that can be developed prior to treatment. Typically, the items on this hierarchy include situations such as traveling to a local store or mall or waiting in line at a local bank. Before each treatment session, each client rates each item on his or her hierarchy with regard to anxiety and avoidance (combined rating) currently associated with it. We use a 10-item hierarchy and a 0–8 rating scale. Gelder and Mathews and their colleagues (Gelder, Bancroft, Gath, Johnston, Mathews, & Shaw, 1973; Mathews, Johnston, Lancashire, Munby, Shaw, & Gelder, 1976; Mathews, Teasdale, Munby, Johnston, & Shaw, 1977) have used 10- and 15-item hierarchies on which clients rate their subjective level of anxiety for each item according to a 0–10 scale. The resulting score is called the Total Phobic Anxiety (TPA) score. Since this measure has a wide scoring range and is based on personally relevant situations of increasing difficulty, it can be quite sensitive to week-by-week change in phobic anxiety and behavior.

Subjective ratings of anxiety also should be obtained in conjunction with overt behavioral measures, such as standardized walks, individualized behavioral avoidance tests, and self-monitoring of contacts with feared situations on daily diaries. Clients should be instructed to record maximum level of anxiety experience during the task or situation. Such subjective reports are inexpensive to obtain and—since they are obtained in association with assessment of overt behavior and sometimes of physiological responsiveness as well—are valuable sources of information about response concordance and synchrony.

Since depression is often associated with agoraphobia (Mavissakalian & Barlow, 1981), the Beck Depression Inventory (Beck, Ward, Mendelson, Mock, & Erbaugh, 1961) is recommended as a routine measure for screening severe depression and to assess change in depression following treatment, in addition to the usual clinical assessment. The Beck Depression Inventory is the most widely used self-report measure of depression.

Behavioral Measures

Three general types of behavioral measures of agoraphobics' approach and avoidance behaviors have been used, including standardized walks, individualized behavioral assessments, and self-monitoring of activities and traveling away from home. Each of these assessment procedures offers some unique advantages and disadvantages, which will be discussed in what follows.

One assessment procedure that provides standardized measures comparable across clients is a "structured" or standardized walk (Agras, Leitenberg, & Barlow, 1968). This usually consists of a standard walking course of a specific length. Clients are instructed to begin at a certain point, to walk alone along the course, and to return when they either reach the end of the course or they feel "unduly anxious." The course usually is divided into relatively equidistant intervals or segments. The most common dependent measure is total distance travelled or number of intervals completed by the client. Subjective reports and measures of physiological arousal also can be obtained during structured walks. Clients can carry in a purse or camera case a small tape recorder which can be used for recording subjective reports of anxiety at specified points of the walk (e.g., Barlow, Mavissakalian, & Schofield, 1980). Subjective ratings can be recorded by instructing clients to report quantitative anxiety into a small, unobtrusive lapel microphone at appropriate times. Physiological recordings of heart rate also can be obtained throughout the walk. Procedures for obtaining these recordings will be explained under "Physiological Assessment," below. Standardized walks have been employed by Agras, Leitenberg, and Barlow (1968); Watson, Mullett, and Pillay (1973); and by Crowe, Marks, Agras, and Leitenberg (1972). We also use a structured walk for agoraphobics at the Phobia and Anxiety Disorders Clinic at the State University of New York at Albany. Emmelkamp (Emmelkamp & Emmelkamp-Benner, 1975; Emmelkamp & Ultee, 1974) used a similar but less structured procedure in which clients were instructed to go outside and remain there until feeling "tense" or "uncomfortable." No specific instructions concerning walking were given to these subjects. The dependent measure was total time spent outside.

Assessment walks offer a relatively standardized measurement of walking, which is a difficult behavior for most agoraphobics. The procedure permits direct between-subject comparisons and potentially could allow for comparisons across research centers, to the extent that the walking courses are similar. As mentioned, quantitative data in all three response modalities can be obtained during structured walks.

A major disadvantage of standardized walks is that only a single behavior is assessed. For agoraphobics who have only minimal difficulties in walking alone, this assessment procedure does not seem particularly appropriate. Furthermore, data obtained from assessment walks may not be generalizable to other behaviors that often are impaired in agoraphobics (e.g., driving and shopping). An additional possible disadvantage is that clients' performance during formal behavior assessments of this type may be influenced by experimental demand and the desire to please the therapist. Although experimental demand effects have been shown to influence the behavior of mildly fearful subjects (Borkovec, Weerts, & Bernstein, 1977), empirical evidence is not available concerning the influence of demand on the behavioral assessment of agoraphobia.

Avoidance of situations selected specifically for each individual also can be assessed. Although individualized assessment of agoraphobics' behavior has been conducted infrequently, it is highly recommended since it provides important information about personally relevant behaviors in naturalistic settings.

Individualized assessments have been conducted from clients' homes by Mathews and Gelder (Gelder, Bancroft, Gath, Johnston, Mathews, & Shaw, 1973; Mathews, Teasdale, Munby, Johnston, & Shaw, 1977; Mathews, Gelder, & Johnston, 1981). Prior to treatment, these investigators developed with the client an individualized 15-item hierarchy of public situations. The hierarchy was developed with care so that no significant aspects of the phobia would be omitted, and the hierarchy items at least approached an interval measurement scale (see Mathews *et al.*, 1981, for further details of hierarchy construction). During the home-visit assessment sessions, the client first was asked to attempt the most difficult hierarchy item she felt able to try at the time. If the client completed the item successfully, she was encouraged to try increasingly difficult hierarchy items. If unable to complete the initially attempted item, she was assigned the next lowest item. The assessment was ended either when the client failed an item, having completed the one immediately below it, or when she refused to attempt a higher item. In posttreatment assessments, the client was instructed to start on the same item initially attempted at pretreatment. The score from this individualized assessment was the number of items completed successfully *during* the assessment. Credit was not given for lower hierarchy items not attempted during the assessment. Two problems with this scoring method are that the number of items completed will be influenced by the client's choice of the initial item to attempt, yet at the same time the client's performance score provides no information about the difficulty level of completed items. Mathews and his colleagues also had subjects report subjective ratings of anxiety (on a 0–10 scale) for each attempted item.

We use a somewhat different procedure for individualized home assessments of agoraphobics seen at our Phobia and Anxiety Disorders Clinic. During pretreatment assessment, an individualized 10-item fear hierarchy is developed for each client. The assessor selects from these items five to be assigned to the client during the home assessment. Items are selected that represent a range of difficulty and that are feasible for a home assessment. During the assessment, the assessor asks the client to attempt each of the five preselected items, beginning with the least difficult. The client's performance on each item is rated on a 3-point scale, on which "0" indicates that the client refused to attempt the item ("avoidance"), "1" indicates that the client attempted the task but completed it only partially ("escape"), and "2" indicates that the client completed the task successfully. Thus, the home assessment provides a scoring range from 0–10. A somewhat similar procedure for conducting individualized behavioral avoidance tests with agoraphobics was used by Hand, Lamontagne, and Marks (1974) and by Greist, Marks, Berlin, Gournay, and Noshirvani (1980).

Individualized behavioral assessments have a number of advantages. They provide quantitative data about clients' functioning on personally relevant tasks in naturalistic settings. The assessment can be tailored to the individual difficulties and fears of each client and is therefore likely to be more sensitive and generalizable than standardized assessments. Individualized assessments do have disadvantages, however. Since the assessment differs for each client, it is difficult to compare clients on the measure. Therefore, these assessments are more appropriate for within-subject comparisons than for between-group comparisons. Other limitations of individualized assessments include time and expense. We have found that a five-item individualized home behavioral approach test usually takes from 1 to 2½ hours to administer, not including the assessor's traveling time to and from the client's home.

A third general approach to the behavioral assessment of agoraphobia is client self-monitoring of activities (Haynes, 1978). Several researchers (Greist *et al.,* 1980; Jannoun, Munby, Catalan, & Gelder, 1980; Mathews *et al.,* 1977; Mathews *et al.,* 1981) have given agoraphobic clients "Behavioral Diaries" or "Weekly Records" to be used to self-monitor detailed information about such variables as total time away from home, destination and purpose of trip, whether the individual was alone or accompanied, distance traveled, anxiety level during exposure to feared situations, and use of medications. Behavioral diaries can provide the researcher with a wealth of information, unavailable through any other assessment method, about an agoraphobic's daily activities and avoidance pattern.

Behavioral diaries have not been used widely in treatment outcome studies with agoraphobics, so there is no consensus about the best procedures for collecting and interpreting such self-monitoring data. Jannoun *et al.* (1980) and Mathews *et al.* (1977) selected as their primary measure the total time out of house, other than time at work or at social engagements. They assumed that the latter two situations are less stressful for agoraphobics and that their exclusion results in a more sensitive measure of improvement. Greist *et al.* (1980) used the behavioral diary as a manipulation check of clients' compliance with instructions either to avoid or to expose themselves to feared stimuli, rather than as an outcome measure.

The major issues in the use of behavioral self-monitoring diaries are the reliability with which clients complete the forms and the validity of the data. We have used a detailed behavioral diary with agoraphobic clients for the past two years, and our experience has been that detailed self-monitoring is tedious for some clients, particularly those who are less impaired and who travel a fair amount. However, a number of steps can be taken to increase clients' compliance with self-monitoring as well as the completeness and presumably also the validity of such records. Prior to beginning self-monitoring, clients receive detailed written instructions on the purposes and procedures for the behavioral diary and examples of how to complete it. A staff member answers any questions clients may have after they go over the instructions. Throughout the treatment program and particularly during the initial few sessions, staff members carefully review all clients' daily diaries and provide clients with written feedback concerning missing data, recording errors, and any other problems. These procedures help to minimize problems with these measures and emphasize to clients the importance of the behavioral diary in the treatment program.

The measures from the diaries that we have been most concerned with are total time out of the house (including work and social situations), total time out of the house alone, and number of self-conducted exposure sessions practiced between treatment sessions. A wide range of other measures can be derived from behavioral diaries but information is not yet available as to which measures will be most useful and sensitive. We recommend that all researchers investigating agoraphobia (as well as other phobias) routinely collect behavioral diary data.

Physiological Assessment of Agoraphobia

Since psychophysiological arousal is one of the three primary response modalities of the behavioral construct of anxiety and since intense anxiety and panic as well as somatic sensations are chief complaints of many agoraphobics, psychophysiological assessment can play an important role in the comprehensive assessment of agoraphobia. Unfortunately, however, physiological assessments have often been omitted from treatment outcome studies with agoraphobics and other phobics. As a result, our knowledge of the effects of behavioral treatments on physiological arousal and of the relationships of physiological variables to behavioral and subjective variables has been limited. We highly recommend that physiological assessment be included in all research investigations on phobias and, whenever feasible, in the evaluation of clinical applications of behavioral treatment as well.

Among treatment outcome studies that have included physiological measures (e.g., Benjamin, Marks, & Huson, 1972; Marks, Boulougouris, & Marset, 1971; Mathews *et al.,* 1976; Stern & Marks, 1973), only a limited number of measures have been used. The two most frequently used are heart rate (beats per minute) and skin conductance (usually, number of "spontaneous" fluctuations and, less frequently, maximal skin conductance level). Due to recording difficulties and the need for controlled experimental conditions, most studies conducted to date have measured clients' physiological responsivitiy during imaginal visualization rather than during exposure to actual situations.

Stern and Marks (1973) conducted a relatively comprehensive physiological assessment of agoraphobics in their frequently cited study of the optimal duration of exposure. They continuously recorded heart rate and skin conductance during phobic and neutral imagery exercises and also during imaginal-exposure treatment sessions. These investigators found no differences in physiological arousal to phobic and neutral imagery. They also found minimal skin conductance or heart-rate arousal during imaginal flooding and no differences between experimental conditions on these physiological measures during imaginal flooding. These findings call into question the appropriateness of using imaginally presented stimuli during physiological assessment. However, Stern and Marks speculated that the lack of autonomic arousal during imaginal exposure might be due to their presentation of imaginal stimuli by tape recordings. Previous studies in which imaginal stimuli were presented by live therapists (e.g., Marks, Boulougouris, & Marset, 1971) found that imaginal stimuli did elicit significant levels of physiological arousal. However, Mathews, Johnston, Lancashire, Munby, Shaw, and Gelder (1976) did find differences in heart rate between visualizations of phobic and non-phobic stimuli that were presented by tape recorder.

Stern and Marks (1973) also continuously monitored heart rate during *in vivo* exposure-treatment sessions, using a portable pulsimeter worn by the client. The output from the pulsimeter (heart rate in beats per minute) was recorded on one channel of a stereo tape recorder. On the other channel, subjects' subjective anxiety ratings during exposure were recorded. The heart-rate recordings during *in vivo* exposure turned out to be the most useful physiological measure. Heart rate was substantially higher during the early stages of exposure treatment than during baseline measurement, indicating that *in vivo* exposure did elicit high levels of autonomic arousal. The finding that heart rate decreased significantly more during prolonged *in vivo* exposure than during short *in vivo* exposure was consistent with other evidence supporting the superior effectiveness of prolonged exposure.

Among the limited number of physiological measures that have been used in the assessment of phobias, heart rate has generally been found to be most sensitive to differences in stimulus conditions (phobic vs. nonphobic) as well as in detecting changes in arousal over the course of treatment. Therefore, if only one measure can be obtained, it should be heart rate. Both imaginal and *in vivo* stimulus presentations have their advantages and disadvantages. Imaginal presentation of stimuli is generally easier to conduct and can permit continuous measurement of multiple physiological variables. Clients are less likely to avoid visually presented stimuli and therefore it is possible through imaginal visualization to obtain pretreatment baseline physiological measures of stimuli that the client would avoid completely in a real-life assessment (Agras & Jacob, 1981). However, some individuals are unable to visualize situations clearly; for these individuals imagery visualization is not appropriate. In addition, the physiological arousal elicited through imaginal visualizations may not accurately reflect the level of arousal that would be elicited by exposure to the actual stimulus, which is more important to both researchers and clinicians. Therefore, *in vivo* recording of physiological measures is recommended, at least as an adjunct to physiological assessment during imagery visualization. A number of relatively inexpensive, portable devices for recording pulse rate in naturalistic surroundings are currently on the market. These can easily be modified so that the heart-rate signals can be tape recorded during assessment. Subsequently, the taped records can go into a polygraph or minicomputer for scoring. Among disadvantages of *in vivo* physiological assessment, one is that the technology is much less advanced than that available for laboratory physiological assessment. Another disadvantage is that frequently the conditions under which *in vivo* assessments are conducted lend themselves much less to adequate control than the conditions of a laboratory assessment. For example, the density of the crowd in a shopping center cannot be controlled (although it can be estimated under certain circumstances) for *in vivo* assessment, but it can be with imaginal presentations. Despite these limitations, *in vivo* physiological assessment can provide information about client's autonomic arousal during exposure to feared situations that cannot be obtained in any other way.

TREATMENT OF AGORAPHOBIA

In the 1960s, most behaviorally oriented researchers and clinicians treated agoraphobia with the then-standard behavioral treatments for phobias, namely, systematic desensitization and imaginal flooding. While the results of some controlled investigations supported the short-term effectiveness of these two treatment techniques with agoraphobics (e.g., Gelder, Bancroft, Gath, Johnston, Mathews, & Shaw, 1973), some other studies raised doubts about the effectiveness of systematic desensitization (e.g., Gelder & Marks, 1966; Marks *et al.*, 1971). Partly in an attempt to improve the effectiveness and efficiency of imagery-based treatments, some investigators began to include real-life exposure in addition to imaginal exposure (e.g., Marks *et al.*, 1971). Although these investigations did not experimentally isolate the effects of imaginal and real-life exposure, some clinical observation suggested that most of the change occurring in such studies occurred during *in vivo*, as opposed to imaginal, exposure. Further impetus for the use of real-life exposure was provided by a series of uncontrolled case reports by Watson, Gaind, and Marks (1971) in which it was shown that graduated exposure to actual phobic stimuli effectively and efficiently reduced a variety of specific phobias. During the 1970s an increasing number of studies investigated the effectiveness of *in vivo* exposure techniques. Some of these investigations will be reviewed in the following section. The consensus gradually developed that *in vivo* exposure treatments are the treatment of choice for agoraphobia and most other phobias (Barlow & Wolfe 1981; Marks, 1978; Mathews, Gelder, & Johnston, 1981). For this reason, we will focus solely on *in vivo* exposure methods in our discussion of behavioral treatments for agoraphobia. Discussion of imagery-based treatments can be found in Emmelkamp (1979), Leitenberg (1976), and Mathews, Gelder, and Johnston (1981).

Types of in Vivo *Exposure*

The essence of *in vivo* exposure is arranging contact with fear-eliciting stimuli in real-life situations. Essentially, two approaches to *in vivo* exposure have been developed, namely, prolonged exposure and graduated exposure. Although prolonged and graduated exposure can differ markedly in their procedures, a clearcut division between these two approaches does not exist. In fact, *in vivo* exposure treatments can be conceptualized as varying along two dimensions: rate and duration of exposure. Rate refers to how rapidly the client is exposed to a series of fearful stimuli. Clients can be encouraged to expose themselves to feared situations either gradually (e.g., by starting with situations that provoke minimal anxiety and/or allowing several days or more to elapse between sessions) or extremely rapidly (e.g., by starting with items at the top of a fear hierarchy and arranging daily sessions). Exposure treatments also vary with regard to the duration for which the client is instructed to maintain exposure to feared stimuli. Duration of exposure can range from about one minute up to several hours per session, occasionally even longer.

Effectiveness of in Vivo *Exposure*

No attempt will be made to review all of the investigations that have supported the effectiveness of *in vivo* exposure treatments for agoraphobia. The reader is referred to reviews by Emmelkamp (1979), Marks (1978), and Mathews, Gelder, and Johnston (1981) for more thorough reviews of the literature. We will summarize several investigations to illustrate the type of research that has been conducted in this area.

Only a few studies with agoraphobic subjects have compared *in vivo* exposure and imagery-based treatments. Working with agoraphobics, Emmelkamp and Wessels (1975) compared prolonged *in vivo* exposure first with imaginal flooding, and then with a combination of both treatments. Prolonged *in vivo* exposure was significantly superior to imaginal flooding on a behavioral measure (time out of the house alone during a single exposure trial) and on a number of clinical rating scales. Another controlled investigation supporting the superior effectiveness of *in vivo* exposure was conducted by Watson, Mullett, and Pillay (1973). Due to the use of crossover designs, neither of these studies evaluated the long-range effects of these treatments.

The results obtained by Mathews, Johnston, Lancashire, Munby, Shaw, and Gelder (1976) were inconsistent with those of the preceding two investigations. The investigators randomly assigned 36 female outpatient agoraphobics to three treatment conditions: (1) 8 sessions of imaginal flooding followed by 8 sessions of *in vivo* exposure, (2) 16 sessions of combined imaginal and *in vivo* exposure, or (3) 16 sessions of *in vivo* exposure alone. Clients in the combined-treatment condition received imaginal flooding during the first half of each treatment session and *in vivo* exposure during the second half. Self-report, behavioral and physiological measures were obtained. A midtreatment evaluation was conducted, which permitted comparison of the separate effects of imaginal and *in vivo* exposure. Although most outcome measures indicated significant improvement at posttest and at a 6-month follow-up, the three treatment conditions did not differ in effectiveness. The authors therefore concluded that real-life exposure is not superior to imaginal exposure. They also speculated (Mathews *et al.*, 1976; Mathews, Gelder & Johnston, 1981) that the difference between their findings and those of Emmelkamp and Wessels (1975) and Watson *et al.* (1973) with regard to the comparative effectiveness of imaginal and *in vivo* exposure may have been due to the fact that in their study subjects were instructed to practice self-exposure on a regular basis between treatment sessions and the longer duration of treatment.

Hand, Lamontagne, and Marks (1974) conducted prolonged *in vivo* exposure in group sessions to improve treatment efficiency and to examine the influence of social cohesiveness on treatment effectiveness. Half the groups were conducted in a structured manner to promote cohesiveness among group members, the other half in an unstructured manner to minimize group cohesiveness. In both conditions, exposure treatment resulted in dramatic improvement on an individualized behavioral avoidance test as well as marked improvement on clients', therapists', and independent assessors' ratings of phobic anxiety and avoidance. The structured and unstructured conditions did not differ in effectiveness at posttreatment. However, during the 6-month follow-up period clients in the unstructured condition showed some clinical deterioration, whereas clients in the structured condition continued to improve further. At the end of 6 months following treatment, the structured condition was significantly superior to the unstructured condition according to clients' and therapists' ratings.

Further support for the effectiveness of *in vivo* exposure treatments has been provided by studies investigating the procedural parameters of such treatments. Major findings from these studies will be reviewed next.

Procedural Parameters of in Vivo *Exposure*

All behavioral treatments for phobias involve providing clients with exposure to feared stimuli, and most researchers agree that exposure is the single most important ingredient of phobia treatments (Marks, 1978, Mavissakalian & Barlow, 1981). However, it is obvious that since exposure to feared stimuli can be arranged in numerous ways, the clinician is faced with numerous choices concerning the precise procedures to be used. Fortunately, a number of research studies have examined some of the more important parameters of exposure treatments. Although many issues have not been investigated and many questions remain, the findings from these parametric studies provide tentative guidelines for developing effective and efficient treatments. In this section, we will review parametric studies relevant to *in vivo* exposure treatment with agoraphobia.

As previously mentioned, one of the dimensions along which exposure treatments can vary is duration of exposure. Stern and Marks (1973) compared the effectiveness of brief and long imaginal and *in vivo* exposure with 16 agoraphobic clients. A Latin square design was used so that each client received two sessions of each of four treatments: (1) prolonged imaginal exposure (80 min of imaginal exposure, followed by 40 min of visualization of neutral scenes), (2) brief imaginal exposure (eight 10-min imaginal exposure trials separated by 5 min of exposure to neutral scenes), (3) prolonged *in vivo* exposure (2 hr of uninterrupted real-life exposure, with or without the therapist), and (4) brief *in vivo* exposure (four 30-min real-life exposure trials separated by 30-min "rest" intervals). Both clinical rating scales and physiological measures indicated that *in vivo* exposure was superior to imaginal treatment. More relevant to procedural parameters was the finding that the prolonged *in vivo* exposure was markedly superior to the brief *in vivo* exposure, as Stern and Marks (1973) concluded. This conclusion is consistent with findings from analogue investigations of exposure duration (see Mathews, 1978). Mathews (1978) hypothesized that the more intense the avoidance tendency, the longer exposure must be maintained to bring about lasting improvement in avoidance behavior.

Another procedural parameter that may be important is the spacing (rate) of exposure sessions. Animal research indicates that the length of the intertrial interval, that is, the time between exposure sessions, influences the speed with which extinction of fear and avoidance behavior occurs (Birch, 1965; Mackintosh, 1970; Teichner, 1952). Foa, Jameson, Turner, and Payne (1980) compared massed versus spaced prolonged *in vivo* exposure on a crossover design with 11 agoraphobics. Clients received either 10 daily sessions of exposure followed by 10 once-weekly exposure sessions, or the same two treatments in the opposite order. Subjects were not given any instructions to practice exposure between treatment sessions, in an attempt to examine the effects of only the exposure obtained during treatment sessions. Each treatment session consisted of a ½ hr discussion of symptomatology followed by 2 hr of *in vivo* exposure. Assessments were conducted at pretreatment, midtreatment (after Phase 1), and posttreatment and included only clinical ratings, by an independent rater, of phobic anxiety and avoidance. The results indicated that both massed and spaced exposure produced marked improvement in phobic anxiety and avoidance, but that massed was significantly superior to spaced practice, particularly with regard to ratings of avoidance behavior. The authors suggested that massed exposure may be superior to spaced exposure because it leaves clients fewer opportunities to experience accidental or unstructured exposure, during which they might engage in the maladaptive behavior of avoidance or escape and thus reinforce it. The authors concluded that while massed exposure is preferable to spaced exposure, the best interval between sessions and the best number of exposure sessions is still unknown.

Another variable that has been hypothesized to influence the results of exposure treatments is the level of anxiety experienced during exposure trials. Different researchers have suggested on theoretical grounds that anxiety should be maintained at either low (Wolpe, 1958, 1969) or high levels (Stampfl & Levis, 1967) during exposure. However, research is needed to determine empirically the importance of anxiety level during exposure. Unfortunately, this research is difficult to conduct and to interpret. Most studies that have attempted to manipulate anxiety level have administered either antianxiety medications or placebos during or prior to exposure. The use of medications as an adjunct to behavioral treatments will be discussed in the section on treatment adjuncts. However, Mathews (1978) has noted that state-dependent learning effects and patients' attributions about improvement cause problems of interpretation in determining from drug studies the effects of anxiety upon exposure.

Hafner and Marks (1976) conducted a study with only 12 agoraphobic clients in which they attempted to manipulate anxiety level during prolonged *in vivo* exposure without the use of antianxiety medications. Because this was a spinoff from a larger study that did investigate drug effects, all clients in this smaller investigation received before exposure a placebo that was represented to them as a drug designed to aid learning during exposure. The therapist conducted exposure treatment with half the clients so as to increase anxiety level during exposure by providing minimal reassurance, making anxiety-provoking comments, and encouraging clients to visualize themselves experiencing extreme anxiety. With the other subjects, the therapist conducted treatment in a manner to minimize anxiety level, by providing reassurance, instructing clients not to confront unpleasant feelings but to use distraction instead, and instructing clients to use relaxation techniques. Discomfort ratings during treatment indicated that the treatment manipulations were effective in producing significantly high levels of tension and anxiety in high-anxiety clients. Self-report and physiological outcome measures, however, showed no differences between the two anxiety conditions with regard to treatment effectiveness. The authors concluded that intentionally increasing anxiety during exposure does not facilitate improvement. Marks (1978) subsequently reviewed the literature concerning the relationship between anxiety and outcome in the treatment of phobics and obsessive compulsives. He concluded that anxiety level during treatment does not seem to have an important effect on the outcome of exposure treatment. He did hypothesize that level of anxiety at the end of each exposure trial may be important, in that treatment may be more effective if anxiety has decreased rather than if it remains at a high level. However, Marks' pointed out that it is difficult to evaluate this hypothesis empirically, since duration of exposure might confound studies examining end-of-session anxiety level.

Agras, Barlow, Leitenberg and their colleagues conducted systematic research to investigate the relative importance of several components of *in vivo* exposure, particularly feedback and reinforcement provided by the therapist. Both single-subject experimental designs (Hersen & Barlow, 1976) and traditional between-group designs were employed. A detailed review of these studies is not possible here and the reader is referred to the excellent, in-depth review by Leitenberg (1976). However, we will summarize some of the major findings and conclusions of this extensive research program.

Agras, Leitenberg, and Barlow (1968) found that performance-contingent social reinforcement facilitated approach behavior and that when social reinforcement was withdrawn temporarily from graduated exposure treatment, deterioration in approach behavior occurred. Leitenberg, Agras, Allen, Butz, & Edwards (1975) evaluated the relative contributions of both performance feedback and response-contingent social reinforcement in graduated exposure. Their results indicated that feedback of performance was important in getting progress started, but that once behavioral improvement was occurring on a regular basis, social reinforcement alone was sufficient to sustain the rate of improvement. An investigation by another group of researchers (Emmelkamp & Ultee, 1974) found that social praise added to performance feedback (of time spent outside) was no more effective than self-monitored feedback alone in the treatment of agoraphobic clients. These results indicate that feedback of progress seems to be particularly important in facilitating graduated *in vivo* exposure and that such feedback can be provided by either the therapist *or* the client. It is possible that feedback of other variables, such as anxiety level, and heart rate, also might facilitate prolonged exposure, but this has not been tested.

The above findings concerning procedural parameters provide valuable information concerning some of the variables involved with *in vivo* exposure treatment for agoraphobia. Obviously, much more research still is needed. Very little is known so far about the best ways of combining different procedural parameters. Unfortunately, empirical answers to many issues are likely to be slow in coming, since it would require large samples to investigate systematically the wide variety of treatment procedures and their interactions. Fortunately, however, exposure treatments seem to be powerful techniques, so that minor changes in certain procedures are likely to have little or no effect on treatment outcome.

Clinical Application of in Vivo Exposure Treatment

Most research reports on the use of exposure treatments with phobics have one limitation in common: the treatment procedures are described in such a cursory manner that it is virtually impossible to get a clear picture of how treatment was actually conducted. In the following sections, we will provide detailed descriptions for conducting both prolonged and gradual *in vivo* exposure treatment with agoraphobics.

Before any form of exposure treatment is begun, the therapist should explain in an understandable fashion the nature of agoraphobia and the manner in which agoraphobics' fears and avoidance patterns are developed, maintained, and sometimes expanded. The therapist also should present a thorough explanation of the goals, purposes, and procedures of the recommended treatment program. This initial presentation can have an important impact on clients' willingness to begin treatment as well as their compliance with treatment procedures once therapy has begun. Agoraphobic clients need to be given an optimistic but realistic expectation of what they may be able to accomplish during treatment. The three primary goals usually are decreased avoidance, decreased anxiety, and increased coping skills for dealing with anxiety. Treatment will require considerable effort and practice by clients. Clients sometimes hope or expect that they will be able to eliminate anxiety completely from their lives. Some clients seek an almost magical cure for their problems, which would require very little effort or discomfort on their part. The therapist therefore should inquire about clients' expectancies regarding treatment and educate them about reasonable expectations when this is appropriate. This will help prevent disillusionment or discouragement if clients' unrealistic expectations are not met during treatment.

In vivo exposure treatments can be conducted in a variety of settings: stores, office buildings, public transportation, and streets in the vicinity of the clinic or hospital are often ideal. Indoor shopping malls also are well-suited for exposure treatment because they provide in a single location numerous situations that present varying levels of difficult to agoraphobics. Exposure treatment also can be administered in the client's own neighborhood, either through therapist-assisted treatment (Mathews *et al.*, 1977; Mathews, Gelder, & Johnston, 1981) or instructed exposure.

We recommend that all exposure treatments be tailored as much as possible to the individual problems and needs of each client. The selection of a particular treatment can be based upon the client's primary target problems, motivation, and willingness to experience anxiety during treatment. An individualized approach can be followed in both individual as well as group exposure therapy, as long as group exposure is conducted with a manageable number (no more than 3–4 clients per therapist) of relatively homogeneous clients. During exposure treatment, clients should work on situations and tasks that have relevance for them. In group treatment, this means that different clients may at times be assigned to practice different tasks. Some clients may need minimal attention from the therapist and may practice items alone or with other group members, while other clients will need more careful therapeutic supervision and support.

It is important to note that progress in overcoming agoraphobia frequently is not linear: ups and downs are encountered by many clients. After practicing religiously and experiencing considerable initial success, clients may be surprised to discover that they are having difficulty doing something they thought they had mastered early in therapy. Or, a client whose panic attacks have almost disappeared may experience a severe attack when least expected. Clients sometimes overreact to such experiences and interpret them as indicating a relapse. Anxiety, depression, discouragement, anger, and guilt are likely to be experienced. Another relatively common pattern is that a client seems to be making definite improvement in increasing independent behavior, yet discounts all of her progress, focuses on things she still cannot do, and concludes that she is not doing better at all. These reactions should be dealt with during therapy. The therapist should explain to clients that ups and downs are common and are almost expected during the course of treatment and that they do not necessarily mean that the client is having a relapse. The best way for the client to handle these temporary "setbacks" is to accept the fact that they do occur and to work on again practicing exposure on items that cause difficulties. Clients who discount or overlook real progress should be encouraged to recognize the ways in which they are behaving and/or feeling differently from before. They should be encouraged to keep things "in perspective" and not to discount whatever gains they have made simply because there are certain things they still cannot do.

Many agoraphobics report that they have "good" and "bad" days. On good days, they are often able to do much more than they typically feel able to accomplish. Agoraphobics who will usually go nowhere unaccompanied may be able to travel alone locally and even go shopping alone. Such individuals frequently attempt to do all their out-of-home chores and errands on good days. On so-called bad days, these same individuals report that they feel anxious all day long and unable to do much at all. Clients frequently report that they "know" early in the day whether it will be a good or bad day. The precipitants or causes of such good and bad days are unknown. They may be related to hormonal changes, fluctuating patterns of depression, or sources of stress (e.g., marital conflict) that are not identified accurately by clients. Regardless of the cause, it is important for clients to recognize the importance of trying to do things on bad days as well as good days. That is, they should learn to be less controlled by internal feeling states. Activity is often helpful against negative affect anyway (Beck, Rush, Shaw, & Emery, 1979), so by working on their phobia, clients can also reduce the likelihood of having "bad days."

Prolonged in Vivo Exposure

The basic goal of prolonged *in vivo* exposure is to provide lengthy enough exposure to phobic stimuli in real-life situations for the agoraphobic individual to "become used to" the stimuli and experience a reduction of anxiety.

The primary tasks of the therapist in prolonged *in vivo* exposure are to offer directions and suggestions to clients as to what items or tasks it would be appropriate to select for exposure trials, as well as to help clients maintain exposure to fear-eliciting stimuli for as long during each session as is necessary to bring about significant reduction of anxiety. Generally, clients are encouraged to practice exposure to the most threatening stimuli that they feel capable of attempting. However, prolonged exposure procedures can be used with mildly or moderately threatening stimuli as well. This is sometimes necessary with clients who decline to expose themselves to difficult situations. It is frequently necessary for the therapist to negotiate with the client in the selection of a practice target during an exposure trial. Although clients should be encouraged to try assignments on their own as soon as possible, it is frequently necessary for the therapist to accompany the client, particularly in early exposure trials. As treatment progresses, the client should be encouraged to attempt increasingly difficult tasks and to try more tasks alone.

During exposure trials, the therapist exerts social influence to help the client maintain exposure. The primary "tools" available to the therapist include firm encouragement, reassurance, reinforcement, suggestions and reminders of treatment procedures and of the importance of maintaining exposure. Social reinforcement should be provided contingent upon completion of assigned tasks, even if anxiety level was high during exposure. Needless to say, physical force should never be used to get the client to attempt a task or to maintain exposure.

Since most agoraphobics have learned to avoid or leave situations when they experience or even anticipate experiencing anxiety, many clients find it very difficult to maintain contact with situations while experiencing marked or even extreme anxiety. Prolonged *in vivo* exposure also involves re-education about the experience of anxiety and how to cope with it. The importance of continued exposure must be stressed. Agoraphobics usually fear anxiety and any interoceptive cues that might indicate its onset. The signs and symptoms of anxiety frequently are interpreted as evidence of such catastrophes as becoming insane, having a heart attack or losing control. Clients need to be re-educated that some degree of anxiety is normal and that although anxiety may be distressing, it is not dangerous. Anxiety can be described as an exaggeration of normal bodily reactions and processes. Rather than being a catastrophe or evidence of failure, the experience of anxiety during exposure can be therapeutic, in providing the client with an opportunity to practice coping and to modify maladaptive reactions such as avoidance, escape, and catastrophic thinking.

Graduated in Vivo Exposure

Gradual exposure has a number of advantages. Some researchers maintain that the experience of high anxiety during exposure may result occassionally in sensitization of fears and deterioration rather than improvement (Wolpe, 1958, 1969). Recent theorizing about the potential causes and effects of response desynchrony implies that gradual exposure treatments may be less likely to produce desynchrony than rapid exposure treatments, and may therefore produce more stable effects (Grey, Sartory, & Rachman, 1979). Some clients who may refuse a prolonged exposure treatment and others who may drop out prematurely may tolerate a gradual approach better. Gradual exposure methods also are preferable for clients with serious medical conditions (e.g., heart disease or serious respiratory problems). Nevertheless, no controlled research has compared the effectiveness of graduated versus prolonged in vivo exposure treatments for agoraphobics.

The prototype of graduated exposure is reinforced practice or successive approximation (Agras, Leitenberg, & Barlow, 1968; Crowe, Marks, Agras, & Leitenberg, 1972; Everaerd, Rijken, & Emmelkamp, 1973; Leitenberg, 1976; Leitenberg et al., 1975). Phobic clients are instructed to enter into feared situations and to go as far as possible without becoming "unduly anxious." When unduly anxious, clients are to turn back right away and return to the starting point. Note that these instructions are markedly different from the typical instructions in prolonged in vivo exposure to remain as long as possible in feared situations even if anxiety becomes high.

The situation that has been used most often in research studies on reinforced practice with agoraphobics is walking alone outside the home or clinic, often along a specified course (e.g., Agras, Leitenberg, & Barlow, 1968). The client would be instructed to go outside, usually alone, and to walk along the route until feeling uncomfortable or unduly anxious. If the client does feel anxious she is to return immediately. The therapist then provides the client with feedback about her performance. The most common type of feedback is the amount of time spent outside, although feedback concerning distance sometimes would be appropriate instead.

A number of investigations (Agras, Leitenberg, & Barlow, 1968; Crowe, Marks, Agras, & Leitenberg, 1972; Emmelkamp & Ultee, 1974; Everaerd, Rijken, & Emmelkamp, 1973; see also Leitenberg, 1976) have supported the effectiveness of reinforced practice with agoraphobics. Parametric research indicates that performance feedback seems to be particularly important in reinforced practice, especially during the early phases of treatment (Agras, Leitenberg & Barlow, 1968; Leitenberg, 1976). Research by Emmelkamp (1974; Emmelkamp & Ultee, 1974) indicates that self-exposure, in which clients conduct exposure trials by themselves and provide their own performance feedback, also is an effective gradual exposure procedure with agoraphobics.

Andrew Mathews and his colleagues (Mathews, Teasdale, Munby, Johnston, & Shaw, 1977; Mathews, Gelder, & Johnston, 1981) recently have developed a home-based treatment program for agoraphobia that is designed to be more efficient and to have greater long-range effectiveness than other existing graduated-exposure treatment procedures. Their program, called "programmed practice," places primary responsibility for the conduct of treatment on the client, with the assistance of either a family member (usually the spouse) or a friend as a "partner." Self-exposure is the central feature of programmed practice. Detailed treatment manuals are provided to both the client and the partner. The client's manual explains the nature and development of agoraphobia, provides step-by-step instructions for practicing graduated exposure to feared situations and instructions for coping with anxiety and panic. The partner's manual explains the role of significant others in maintaining phobic fears and how the partner can help the client gradually learn to overcome dependency and avoidance. It provides instructions on how the partner can assist the client during practice exposure sessions as well as in other stressful situations. The treatment manuals emphasize the importance of daily practice. Clients are instructed to expect that they will be able to learn how to tolerate moderate levels of anxiety without overreacting to them and becoming panicky. The importance of staying in feared situations until anxiety goes down is stressed. In this respect the procedure resembles prolonged exposure, although situations are typically changed so as not to be overwhelming.

Programmed practice is conducted from the client's home. Clients are instructed to practice facing feared situations daily. It is emphasized that avoidance behavior must be changed before thoughts or feelings will change. The primary role of the professional therapist is as a consultant and an educator. The therapist typically schedules five to eight visits over a period of 4 weeks at the client's home when both the client and partner will be present. During the initial visit, the therapist discusses the treatment program and the treatment manuals, emphasizes the responsibility of the client and partner, and sets goals for initial items for graduated exposure practice. During the second visit, the therapist is present during a practice exposure session, but his role is that of an observer who offers advice as needed. Subsequently, the responsibility for daily hour-long practice is that of the client and partner, and the therapist does not routinely attend practice sessions.

During subsequent home visits, the therapist reviews with the client and partner the client's self-monitoring of all activities away from home and exposure practices since the last home visit, discusses and makes appropriate suggestions about any problems that have been encountered during exposure practices, and helps the client and partner make plans for future practices and for increasing activities.

Some initial research indicates that programmed practice has considerable potential as an effective and efficient treatment of agoraphobia. In an uncontrolled investigation, Mathews *et al.* (1977) treated 12 agoraphobics with programmed practice. Total therapist time was a mean of 9.4 hours per client (6.9 hr during treatment and 2.5 hr during a 3-month follow-up period), plus a mean of 8 hours of traveling time per client. No control condition was included, but the authors compared their outcome data with the results of some previous treatment studies. They concluded that programmed practice seemed to produce improvement, in self-report and behavioral measures as well as on clinical rating scales, equivalent or superior to results obtained in previous studies, even though total therapist time generally was much less for programmed practice.

In a subsequent controlled investigation, Jannoun, Munby, Catalan, and Gelder (1980) compared programmed practice to an alternative self-help problem-solving treatment program. The problem-solving comparison control group involved a client's and partner's manual designed to improve client's abilities to deal with everyday stressful events and to resolve problems. No specific work on exposure to feared situations was included. The results indicated that both treatment conditions produced improvement in phobic anxiety and avoidance (as assessed by clinical rating scales), but that programmed practice was significantly superior to problem solving. However, therapist differences unexpectedly appeared with the problem-solving treatment. This condition resulted in increased approach behavior when conducted by one therapist but not when conducted by the other. Although these findings are difficult to interpret, they do not diminish the fact that the programmed practice treatment was quite effective in reducing agoraphobics' anxiety and avoidance. An important point about this controlled investigation is that the time of direct contact with the therapist (not including traveling time) was reduced to an average of only 3.5 hr per client, which confirms the fact that this treatment program is quite cost-effective.

Limitations and Follow-up of in Vivo *Exposure Treatments*

In vivo exposure technique have been hailed by many researchers as the treatment of choice for phobias, including agoraphobia (e.g., Emmelkamp,

1979; Marks, 1978). Despite such optimistic claims, however, exposure treatments are not in any sense panaceas for the complex problem of agoraphobia. In fact, although it has been demonstrated to be superior to alternative treatments, the clinical outcome of *in vivo* exposure is not overly impressive if treatment refusals and dropouts, level of clinical improvement, and long-range treatment effects are taken into consideration (Barlow & Wolfe, 1981). These issues will be discussed briefly.

One determinant of the clinical usefulness of a treatment intervention is the proportion of individuals with a particular problem or disorder for whom treatment is appropriate or who will accept treatment when it is offered. The most powerful treatment is of little benefit if none of the clients for whom it is intended will accept it. Studies involving *in vivo* exposure treatments have reported drop-out rates that range from 8% to 40%, with a median of 22% (Mavissakalian & Barlow, 1981). At a recent NIMH conference on the behavioral treatment of anxiety disorders, the consensus of 20 leading clinical investigators from around the world was that approximately 25% of clients who present for behavioral treatments either refuse or drop out prematurely (National Institute of Mental Health, 1981). Preliminary indications are that the number of dropouts is considerably lower with graduated exposure than with prolonged exposure. Nevertheless, for one reason or another a large number of phobic individuals fail to receive even a fair trial of behavior therapy.

Among those individuals who do receive *in vivo* exposure treatment for agoraphobia, some do not improve at all and some others only improve partially. This fact is obscured in many research investigations because of the emphasis on statistical significance and group comparisons and the frequent neglect of data from individual clients. It has been estimated that approximately 25% of clients who do complete behavioral treatments for phobias receive little or no benefit from treatment (National Institute of Mental Health, 1981). The percentage of clients who display complete reduction of agoraphobic symptoms by the end of treatment is probably also relatively small. The majority of clients display varying levels of impairment in functioning at posttest. Some clients improve their functioning markedly but still have some residual anxiety and must still "push" themselves to go into situations that they routinely avoided. They may report that although they still have phobic symptoms, these do not interfere with their daily lives. Other clients, however, do considerably less well. Although they may have expanded the range within which they can travel, they still may be limited severely by avoidance behavior and also may be impaired by other disruptive symptoms, such as panic attacks, hypochondriacal concerns, and depression. Research that has been conducted so far to identify factors that may predict response to *in vivo* exposure treatments has not been fruitful (Mathews, Gelder, & Johnston, 1981). More research on predictor variables is needed (e.g., Norton, DiNardo, & Barlow, 1983).

In the past, many behavior therapists assumed that following formal treatment, agoraphobics would continue to expose themselves to feared situations and therefore make further progress on their own in reducing any remnants of phobic behavior (cf. Gelder, 1977). Unfortunately, the data that are now available from follow-up assessments generally do not support this optimistic assumption. It should be noted first that long-range follow-ups of the effectiveness of *in vivo* exposure treatments for agoraphobia are not very common. Many investigations have used crossover designs in which clients receive two different treatments sequentially. Such designs make it impossible to assess the long-range effects of either treatment. Other studies have not included follow-up assessments or have obtained relatively short follow-ups of only 3 to 6 months.

A number of long-range follow-ups of the effectiveness of behavioral treatments of agoraphobia have been conducted (Emmelkamp & Kuipers, 1979; McPherson, Brougham, & McLaren, 1980; Marks, 1971; Munby & Johnston, 1980). Marks (1971) conducted a 4-year follow-up of 65 phobics (55% of whom were agoraphobic) treated in several early controlled trials in which clients received systematic desensitization, hypnosis, and/or analytic therapy. Follow-up dependent measures consisted of assessors' clinical ratings, based on personal interviews with clients and in some cases with relatives as well. McPherson, Brougham, and McLaren (1980) mailed self-report rating scales to 81 agoraphobics who had displayed clinical improvement during behavioral treatment. Clients were contacted 3.0–6.3 years after treatment (mean = 4.3 years). Follow-up data were obtained from only 69% of these clients. Among the clients who were reassessed, 61% had received *in vivo* exposure, 14% systematic desensitization, and 25% other behavioral treatments. Emmelkamp and Kuipers (1979) followed up 70 agoraphobics from an original sample of 81 who had completed exposure treatment approximately four years earlier. All clients had originally received *in vivo* exposure treatment (either successive approximation or self-exposure); in addition, some clients had received other behavioral treatments, such as imaginal flooding. Follow-up measures included rating scales completed by clients and self-report questionnaires. Perhaps the most comprehensive long-range follow-up that has been conducted to date was that of Munby and Johnston (1980). From an original sample of 66 agoraphobics, 63 were interviewed and incomplete information about current status was obtained concerning two additional clients. These clients had been treated originally with systematic desensitization, imaginal flooding, *in vivo* exposure, or programmed practice. At follow-up the same dependent measures that were administered during the treatment trials were obtained, including clinical ratings by both assessors and clients, self-report measures and, for some clients, self-monitoring of time out of the house per week. Clients were followed-up 4–9 years after the end of treatment, which makes this perhaps the longest follow-up investigation reported to date.

The above four follow-up investigations provide a consistent picture concerning the long-range effects of behavioral treatments. In all four follow-ups, the data indicate that, as a group, clients had maintained the level of improvement shown at posttreatment. No evidence was obtained of either marked improvement or deterioration subsequent to the termination of treatment. The only study to find some evidence of significant improvement from posttest to follow-up was that of Emmelkamp & Kuipers (1979). Clients' anxiety ratings for secondary phobias and their Zung Self-Rating Depression Scale scores (Zung, 1965) showed significant improvement from posttest to follow-up. However, the actual level of improvement on these measures was relatively small, suggesting that the improvement may not have been clinically significant. Thus, the major finding of these follow-up studies is that improvement subsequent to various exposure-based behavioral treatments remains relatively stable over lengthy periods of time. Of course, these data provide information only about the mean performance of groups of subjects and tell us nothing about the stability of individual clients' improvement. Another point to be made is that all follow-up studies reported the majority of clients still retaining at least some level of phobic problems during the follow-up period. For example, Marks (1971) reported that only 3 out of 65 clients (4.6%) were completely free of symptoms at follow-up as determined by assessors' clinical ratings, whereas McPherson, Brougham, and McLaren (1980) reported that among clients who showed some improvement after behavioral treatment only 18% of those reached at follow-up rated themselves as completely free of agoraphobic symptoms.

In summary, although exposure treatment has been demonstrated to be highly effective for the reduction of agoraphobic anxiety and avoidance and is the treatment of choice for this disorder, we must recognize the limitations of this approach to treatment. Some agoraphobics refuse behavioral treatments, others drop out, and a proportion of those who complete treatment do not respond or respond only minimally. Few clients display complete remission of symptoms during treatment. Subsequent to treatment, clients' status generally appears to be stable. More research is needed to identify ways of improving the effectiveness of exposure-based treatments and to understand why some agoraphobics do not respond well to this treatment.

Adjuncts to the *in Vivo Exposure Treatment of Agoraphobia*

As discussed above, although *in vivo* exposure treatments are considered by many clinicians to be the treatment of choice for agoraphobia, so far these treatments have not been demonstrated to produce complete improvement in most agoraphobics. One possible method for increasing the effectiveness of behavioral treatments for agoraphobia might be to add components and procedures of different treatments to *in vivo* exposure. Three procedures that have been used as adjuncts to *in vivo* exposure are cognitive treatments, marital therapy, and pharmacotherapy. We will next discuss the application of and evidence concerning the effectiveness of these treatment adjuncts.

Cognitive Treatments

Clinical observation indicates that agoraphobics frequently report some common types of negative cognitions (Coleman, 1981). These include catastrophic cognitions about what might happen if they were to go outside or into some other feared situation alone (e.g., "I'll surely have a panic attack!" "I may freeze and get stuck!" "Something terrible is going to happen!") and irrational thoughts about and misinterpretations of the somatic sensations of anxiety (e.g., "I must be having a heart attack!" "I have a brain tumor." "I'm going to go completely out of control." "I'm losing my mind!"). Clients often report that just thinking about going outside can provoke intense anxiety and sometimes even a panic attack. If cognitions are related in some causal manner to the maintenance and exacerbation of phobic anxiety as well as to avoidance behavior, as suggested by the new field of cognitive-behavior therapy (Mahoney & Arnkoff, 1978; Meichenbaum, 1977), then treatment might be more effective if it modified phobics' cognitions as well as their behavior.

A wide variety of cognitive-behavioral treatment procedures has been developed (cf. Mahoney & Arnkoff, 1978). One of the fundamental and most thoroughly investigated forms of cognitive-behavior therapy is self-statement training (Meichenbaum, 1972, 1977). Self-statement training involves three steps: (1) identification of negative self-statements, (2) recognition of the role of self-statements in influencing behavior, mood, and cognitions, and particularly their effect on the client's presenting problem, and (3) replacing negative self-statements with incompatible positive coping self-statements (and behavior as well). For example, agoraphobics would be instructed to identify negative thoughts about going outside and about the experience of anxiety and to replace these thoughts with coping self-statements that will help them remain exposed in the phobic situation without becoming panicky (e.g., "Anxiety won't hurt me. Just accept it and let it pass. Just focus on the present and what I have to do now.").

Although self-statement training has been found effective for treating mild to moderate specific fears (Mahoney & Arnkoff, 1978; Meichenbaum, 1977), very little research has been conducted to examine its effectiveness with agoraphobics. Emmelkamp, Kuipers, & Eggeraat (1978) found that prolonged *in vivo* exposure was significantly superior to a cognitive restructuring procedure that consisted of self-statement training and a discussion of irrational beliefs (Ellis, 1962). However, as Ellis (1979) pointed out, the cognitive restructuring program in this study consisted only of cognitive components, whereas most cognitive-behavioral interventions include both cognitive and behavioral components. In addition, Emmelkamp's cognitive restructuring treatment was administered over a period of 1 week, which may not be sufficient time for cognitive change to occur.

In a more recent investigation, Emmelkamp (1980) compared *in vivo* exposure treatment with cognitive restructuring and with a combination of both treatments. At posttest, both exposure alone and the combined treatment were significantly superior to cognitive restructuring. Cognitive restructuring did not appear to add to the effectiveness of exposure alone. However, clients in the cognitive restructuring condition continued to improve over a 1-month period and ended up almost as much improved as clients in the other two conditions who received exposure during treatment.

A different form of an essentially cognitive procedure that can be incorporated within exposure treatment is paradoxical intention (Ascher, 1980, 1981; Chambless & Goldstein, 1980, 1981). Paradoxical intention basically involves instructing the agoraphobic to attempt to actually bring on feared consequences. For example, a client fearful of having a panic attack or a heart attack would be instructed to go into a moderately fearful situation and try to have a panic attack or heart attack. The rationale of using this procedure with agoraphobics is that clients usually attempt to struggle with and to prevent the experience of anxiety and of associated physiological symptoms, which frequently seems to result in increasing these very symptoms. By stopping the struggle against anxiety and actually attempting to bring on symptoms, the client can gain some control of the symptoms, which then paradoxically often decrease. Chambless and Goldstein (1980, 1981) and Ascher (1980) recommended paradoxical intention particularly for reducing clients' fear of fear. Controlled research of the effectiveness of paradoxical intention with phobics has been extremely limited. However, Ascher (1981) found that paradoxical intention was superior to graduated exposure in reducing agoraphobics' traveling restrictions. More research is needed on the effectiveness of this intriguing treatment approach.

In summary, although negative and catastrophic cognitions appear to be very common among agoraphobics and many treatment programs devote at least some time to formally or informally attempting to modify clients' beliefs and self-statements (e.g., Mathews, Gelder, & Johnston, 1981), minimal empirical evidence is available to support the incremental effectiveness of cognitive adjuncts to treatment. However, we regard it as premature to conclude that cognitive treatment adjuncts have no place in the treatment of agoraphobia. Cognitive-behavioral treatments have been found effective for a number of other less severe anxiety problems (Rachman & Wilson, 1980). A variety of cognitive-behavioral techniques have been developed; of these, the only one that has received empirical evaluation is Emmelkamp's modification of self-statement training. Yet alternative, more comprehensive, or powerful cognitive procedures may be valuable with at least some agoraphobics. Ultimately, however, controlled research will be necessary to determine the role of cognitive components in the treatment of agoraphobia.

Marital Therapy

Another form of therapy that has been recommended (Chambless & Goldstein, 1981; Hafner, 1977) for certain agoraphobics is marital therapy. Some evidence (Milton & Hafner, 1979; O'Brien, Barlow, & Last, 1982) suggests that agoraphobics who have poor marriages are less likely to improve during behavioral treatment and more likely to relapse following treatment than agoraphobics with satisfactory marriages. In addition, some evidence suggests that improvement in phobic anxiety and avoidance may sometimes be associated with deterioration in marital adjustment. This evidence is only suggestive and some recent evidence does not support it (O'Brien et al., 1982). Nevertheless, marital problems are not uncommon in married agoraphobics. This is not at all surprising, given the stress that an agoraphobic's limitations are likely to place on a marital relationship.

Chambless and Goldstein (1981) usually include the spouses of agoraphobics within the phobia treatment program. In addition, some couples are also seen for conjoint marital therapy. During marital therapy, a variety of issues pertaining to the phobia and to the marital relationship are discussed. Typical issues include each partner's personal concerns and wishes, treating the agoraphobic partner as an autonomous adult rather than as a child or an invalid, dealing with possible fears that the relationship may be threatened if the agoraphobic partner gets better, and communication between partners.

Very little research has been conducted concerning the effectiveness of marital therapy as an adjunctive or even a primary treatment for agoraphobia. A recent investigation by Cobb, McDonald, Marks, and Stern (1980) compared *in vivo* exposure treatment with behaviorally oriented marital therapy for the treatment of 11 couples with co-existing marital and mixed phobic-obsessive problems. In an unspecified number of these couples, one of the spouses was agoraphobic. Behavioral marital therapy produced significant improvement on marital target problems, which were identified individually for each couple, but no improvement on phobic-obsessive targets. However, exposure treatment produced significant improvement on phobic-obsessive targets as well as on marital therapy targets. The authors concluded that exposure treatment is the treatment of choice for phobias and obsessive-compulsive disorders, even when severe marital problems co-exist with the anxiety problems.

The investigation of Cobb et al. (1980) provides no information about the effectiveness of marital therapy employed in conjunction with or subsequent to exposure treatments. It seems more appropriate to begin with a treatment of demonstrated effectiveness for agoraphobia and to include in addition marital therapy for couples with marital adjustment problems. This is the procedure followed by Chambless and Goldstein (1980, 1981). Unfortunately, although they report that clinical evidence indicates that conjoint marital therapy is effective in improving marital adjustment and can help promote improvement in phobic problems as well, they have not reported any controlled research on the effectiveness of their conjoint marital therapy program.

Pharmacotherapy

Several classes of medications have been used, either alone or in conjunction with behavioral procedures, for the treatment of agoraphobia. In this section, since a number of excellent reviews of drug studies with agoraphobics are available (Mathews, Gelder, & Johnston, 1981; Stern, 1978; Zitrin, 1981), we will merely summarize some of the major studies and their conclusions and discuss problems encountered in the use of medications with agoraphobics.

The most frequently prescribed type of medication for agoraphobia are benzodiazepine anxiolytics, in particular, diazepam (Valium). These so-called "minor tranquilizers" can reduce the subjective experience of anxiety and may be useful for the short-term management of extreme anxiety. However, there is no controlled evidence of their effectiveness for reducing phobic avoidance when they are used alone. Many clients who are referred to phobia clinics take moderate or higher dosages of diazepam daily yet still exhibit extensive avoidance behavior.

A limited amount of controlled research has been conducted on the use of diazepam in combination with *in vivo* exposure. Marks, Viswanathan, Lipsedge, and Gardner (1972) found that diazepam administered four hours before the start of *in vivo* exposure was significantly superior to exposure treatment combined with a placebo medication for the treatment of specific phobics. Diazapam administered only 1 hr before exposure resulted in intermediate effects that generally did not differ significantly from the other two groups.

Johnston and Gath (1973) found that diazepam facilitated the effectiveness of imaginal plus *in vivo* exposure in a small sample of four agoraphobics. In contrast, Hafner and Marks (1976), in a better controlled investigation of group *in vivo* exposure with agoraphobics, found no differences either at posttreatment or in follow-up assessments between exposure combined with diazepam and exposure conducted with a placebo pill. However, diazepam did result in less subjective anxiety during exposure than the placebo. Mathews (1978) interpreted the above pattern of findings as indicating that any effects of diazepam on agoraphobia are most likely due to decreased anxiety during exposure, which results in increased exposure to phobic stimuli during exposure sessions.

Another type of antianxiety medication that has been suggested as useful for agoraphobia are the beta-adrenergic blocking agents, or beta blockers. In contrast to the benzodiazepines, the beta blockers can reduce peripheral arousal, including symptoms such a rapid pulse and palpitations. Since some agoraphobics are hypersensitive to such signs of peripheral arousal, the beta blockers might be effective for decreasing agoraphobics' peripheral arousal as well as subjective distress. No controlled evidence is available on the effectiveness of the beta blockers used by themselves with agoraphobics (Emmelkamp, 1979; Mathews, Gelder, & Johnston, 1981). Emmelkamp (1979) reviewed three studies that investigated the incremental effectiveness of three different beta blockers used in combination with exposure treatments. None of the three investigations found any incremental effects of the beta blockers. In fact, Hafner and Milton (1977) obtained evidence that one of the beta blockers, propranolol, had an adverse effect on agoraphobics both during *in vivo* exposure treatment and during a three-month follow-up period. At the present time, therefore, the evidence does not support the value of the beta blockers with agoraphobics.

Antidepressants also have been recommended as beneficial for some agoraphobics. The monoamine oxidase (MAO) inhibitors are antidepressants that have been used for the treatment of agoraphobia since at least the 1960s. Studies that have investigated the effectiveness of the MAO inhibitors for agoraphobia were reviewed by Mathews, Gelder, and Johnston (1981). The methodologies of these investigations and their findings are too complex to summarize here, but the conclusion arrived at by Mathews and his colleagues was that these studies "have not produced strong evidence that these drugs have any specific effect on phobic symptoms" (p. 56). They also concluded that relapse following termination of these medications is relatively high and that the mechanism of their action is most likely a gradual antianxiety effect. Since MAO inhibitors pose some significant health hazards and can interact negatively with a variety of foods and other medications, Mathews and his colleagues recommended that safer medications be used for the treatment of phobic disorders.

A safer class of antidepressants are the tricyclics. One of the tricyclics, imipramine (Tofranil), has been identified as showing considerable promise for the treatment of agoraphobia. Several controlled research investigations (Sheehan, Ballenger, & Jacobsen, 1980; Zitrin, Klein, & Woerner, 1978, 1980) have compared imipramine with placebo medications in conjunction with behavior therapy and/or supportive psychotherapy. These studies have been reviewed in detail by Zitrin (1981) and by Mathews, Gelder, and Johnston (1981).

Zitrin, Klein, and Woerner (1978) presented an interim report of an ongoing investigation. They presented findings for 111 adults with diagnosis of agoraphobia, simple phobia, or mixed phobia (i.e., clients with symptoms of both simple phobia and agoraphobia) and who were assigned randomly to three treatment conditions: (1) behavior therapy plus imipramine, (2) behavior therapy plus placebo, and (3) supportive psychotherapy plus imipramine. Behavior therapy involved progressive relaxation training, systematic desensitization, *in vivo* exposure homework assignments, and assertiveness training. Supportive therapy was psychodynamically oriented and nondirective. The results indicated that the majority of clients (70% to 86%, depending upon which ratings are considered) showed moderate to marked global improvement after six months of treatment.

Among the agoraphobic clients, 63% to 100% of the clients displayed moderate to marked improvement, again depending upon which type of ratings are considered. Behavior therapy plus imipramine, surprisingly, was not superior to supportive therapy plus imipramine. Behavior therapy plus imipramine was superior to behavior therapy plus placebo on clients' ratings of improvement only. However, the combined effects of the two groups that received imipramine were significantly superior to the non-imipramine group (behavior therapy plus placebo) on both therapists' and clients' ratings of improvement. Imipramine also facilitated treatment effects for mixed phobics, but not for simple phobics.

In a second investigation, Zitrin, Klein, and Woerner (1980) randomly assigned 75 female agoraphobics to group *in vivo* desensitization treatment combined with either imipramine or placebo. Treatment began with 4 weeks of medication-only treatment, followed by 10 weeks of behavioral treatment combined with medication, which was then followed by 3 months of medication alone. The results indicated that behavioral treatment combined with imipramine was significantly superior to behavioral treatment plus placebo at both the end of treatment and the 3-month drug-only period.

Zitrin, Klein, and Woerner (1978, 1980) and Zitrin (1981) concluded from their findings that imipramine facilitates the effectiveness of behavioral treatments of agoraphobia and of mixed phobics. They hypothesized that agoraphobia and mixed phobia involve a "core disorder" consisting of spontaneous panic attacks. Evidence suggests that the effects of imipramine on agoraphobia are not due to its antidepressant effects but rather to its effects on panic attacks (Zitrin, 1981). Zitrin and her colleagues contend that it is the continued experience of panic attacks among agoraphobics who are treated behaviorally without medications that results in the maintenance or recurrence of avoidance behavior. Treatment with imipramine can reduce the presumed core disorder of panic attacks. Subsequently, however, exposure treatment is likely to be necessary for helping clients modify well-learned habits of avoidance behavior.

In summary, the evidence concerning the contribution of pharmacotherapy to the behavioral treatment of agoraphobia is mixed. Little evidence is available to suggest that medications are likely to replace behavioral approaches to treatment. Further research is needed, particularly with regard to the influence of the tricyclic antidepressants on anxiety and panic attacks.

Even if antianxiety or antidepressant medications are effective for the treatment of some agoraphobics, there are numerous problems associated with drug treatments of this disorder. One problem involves the risks associated with pharmacological treatments. Some of these medications, particularly the MAO inhibitors, involve relatively high risk of medical complications. Even the ben-

zodiazepines, which are considered relatively safe, pose some risk of psychological dependence and even physical dependence at prolonged high dosages
(Tyrer, 1980). A related complication is that the MAO inhibitors, the tricyclic
antidepressants, and the beta blockers produce varying side effects in a certain
proportion of clients (Mathews, Gelder, & Johnston, 1981; Zitrin, 1981). Since
some of these side effects mimic symptoms of anxiety, agoraphobics are often
reluctant to continue taking these medications. For example, Zitrin, Klein and
Woerner (1978) reported that 18% of their agoraphobic clients exhibited an
"exquisite sensitivity" to imipramine and that the treatment dropout rate
among agoraphobics receiving imipramine was 23% (compared with a dropout
rate of 9% for the behavior therapy plus placebo condition).

There also appear to be relatively high rates of relapse when drug use is
terminated. For example, agoraphobics receiving imipramine in Zitrin's
research (Zitrin, 1981; Zitrin, Klein, & Woerner, 1978) had a relapse rate of
30% within the year following the end of treatment, compared with a relapse
rate of 14% among clients treated with behavior therapy plus placebo. Such
relatively high relapse rates suggest that medications function to reduce temporarily anxiety and panic attacks, but that they do not help clients learn how
to alter their phobic behavior. Clients who are treated with medications may
attribute their improvement to the medication rather than to improvements in
their ability to cope with stress and anxiety (Mathews, 1978). In addition,
state-dependent learning (Mathews, Gelder, & Johnston, 1981) may occur
when a client is receiving medications. This means that new skills learned when
the client is on medications may not generalize over to the nondrug state.
Alford and Williams (1980) suggested, however, that problems associated with
state-dependent learning can be minimized by gradual reduction of drug levels
during treatment.

The above difficulties with drug treatments indicate that at best only a
certain proportion of agoraphobics are likely to be suitable for pharmacological
treatment, regardless of how effective that treatment is. In addition, even if
certain medications do reduce anxiety and panic attacks, psychological treatments will be necessary to help clients change severe avoidance behavior.

CONCLUSIONS

It may surprise the reader to learn how much remains to be said. Despite
the advances that have been made in the assessment and treatment of agoraphobia during the last decade, there is at least as much left to learn. In perusing
the section on limitations of *in vivo* exposure treatments, one is struck by the
fact that very few people entirely recover from the agoraphobic syndrome,
despite the fact that the development of treatments for agoraphobia is one of
the greatest success stories the field of psychotherapy has ever seen (Barlow,

1980). Uncovering the reasons for these failures, or incomplete successes, and elucidating those factors that predict success or failure will not only make our treatments more effective and efficient, but will begin to uncover some more basic issues concerning the nature of anxiety in general. For despite the prevalence of anxiety and the variety of anxiety disorders in the general population, very little is known concerning the psychopathology of anxiety. The apparent success of both pharmacological and psychological treatments even in the face of our incomplete understanding of the mechanisms of action of these treatments raises very basic questions about the etiology of anxiety disorders and the relative contributions of biological and psychological factors. Continued treatment–assessment research should illuminate these basic processes and, in turn, spur further research into the nature of anxiety and anxiety reduction which, of course, will contribute further to our knowledge about treatment and classification. Perhaps the most positive result of the demonstrated success of *in vivo* exposure is that it is bringing the kind of research attention to anxiety disorders that has been enjoyed to date only by the major affective disorders and schizophrenia. Everyone should benefit.

REFERENCES

Agras, W. S., & Jacob, R. G. Phobia: Nature and measurement. In M. Mavissakalian & D. H. Barlow (Eds.), *Phobia: Psychological and pharmacological treatment*. New York: Guilford Press, 1981.

Agras, W. S., Leitenberg, H., & Barlow, D. H. Social reinforcement in the modification of agoraphobia. *Archives of General Psychiatry*, 1968, *19*, 423–427.

Agras, W. S., Sylvester, D., & Oliveau, D. The epidemiology of common fear and phobia. *Comprehensive Psychiatry*, 1969, *10*, 151–156.

Alford, G. S., & Williams, J. G. The role and uses of psychopharmacological agents in behavior therapy. In M. Hersen, R. M. Eisler, & P. M. Miller (Eds.), *Progress in behavior modification* (Vol. 10). New York: Academic Press, 1980.

American Psychiatric Association. *Diagnostic and statistical manual of mental disorders* (3rd ed.). Washington, D.C.: Author, 1980.

Ascher, L. M. Paradoxical intention. In A. Goldstein & E. B. Foa (Eds.), *Handbook of behavioral interventions: A clinical guide*. New York: Wiley, 1980.

Ascher, L. M. Employing paradoxical intention in the treatment of agoraphobia. *Behaviour Research and Therapy*, 1981, *19*, 533–542.

Barlow, D. H. Behavior therapy: The next decade. *Behavior Therapy*, 1980, *11*, 315–328.

Barlow, D. H. (Ed.), *Behavioral assessment of adult disorders*. New York: Guilford Press, 1981.

Barlow, D. H., & Wolfe, B. E. Behavioral approaches to anxiety disorders: A report on the NIMH–SUNY, Albany, research conference. *Journal of Consulting and Clinical Psychology*, 1981, *49*, 448–454.

Barlow, D. H., Mavissakalian, M. R., & Schofield, L. D. Patterns of desynchrony in agoraphobia: A preliminary report. *Behaviour Research and Therapy*, 1980, *18*, 441–448.

Beck, A. T., Ward, C. H., Mendelson, M., Mock, J., & Erbaugh, J. An inventory for measuring depression. *Archives of General Psychiatry*, 1961, *4*, 561–571.

Beck, A. T., Rush, A. J., Shaw, B. F., & Emery, G. *Cognitive therapy of depression*. New York: Guilford Press, 1979.

Benjamin, S., Marks, I. M., & Huson, J. Active muscular relaxation in desensitization of phobic patients. *Psychological Medicine,* 1972, *2,* 381–390.

Birch, D. Extended training extinction effect under massed and spaced extinctional trials. *Journal of Experimental Psychology,* 1965, *70,* 315–322.

Borkovec, T. D., Weerts, T. C., & Bernstein, D. A. Assessment of anxiety. In A. R. Ciminero, K. S. Calhoun, & H. E. Adams (Eds.), *Handbook of behavioral assessment.* New York: Wiley, 1977.

Chambless, D. L., & Goldstein, A. J. Agoraphobia. In A. J. Goldstein & E. B. Foa (Eds.), *Handbook of behavioral interventions.* New York: Wiley, 1980.

Chambless, D. L., & Goldstein, A. J. Clinical treatment of agoraphobia. In M. Mavissakalian & D. H. Barlow (Eds.), *Phobia: Psychological and pharmacological treatment.* New York: Guilford Press, 1981.

Cobb, J. P., McDonald, R., Marks, I. M., & Stern, R. S. Marital versus exposure therapy: Psychological treatments of co-existing marital and phobic obsessive problems. *Behavioral Analysis and Modification,* 1980, *4,* 3–16.

Coleman, R. E. Cognitive-behavioral treatment of agoraphobia. In G. Emery, S. D. Hollon, & R. C. Bedrosian (Eds.), *New directions in cognitive therapy.* New York: Guilford Press, 1981.

Crowe, M. J., Marks, I. M., Agras, W. S., & Leitenberg, H. Time-limited desensitization, implosion and shaping for phobic patients: A crossover study. *Behaviour Research and Therapy,* 1972, *10,* 319–328.

Ellis, A. *Reason and emotion in psychotherapy.* New York: Lyle Stuart, 1962.

Ellis, A. A note on the treatment of agoraphobia with cognitive modification versus prolonged exposure *in vivo. Behaviour Research and Therapy,* 1979, *17,* 162–164.

Emmelkamp, P. M. G. Self-observation versus flooding in the treatment of agoraphobia. *Behaviour Research and Therapy,* 1974, *12,* 229–237.

Emmelkamp, P. M. G. The behavioral study of clinical phobias. In M. Hersen, R. M. Eisler, & P. M. Miller (Eds.), *Progress in behavior modification* (Vol. 8). New York: Academic Press, 1979.

Emmelkamp, P. M. G. Agoraphobics' interpersonal problems: Their role in the effects of exposure in vivo therapy. *Archives of General Psychiatry,* 1980, *37,* 1303–1306.

Emmelkamp, P. M. G., & Emmelkamp-Benner, A. Effects of historically portrayed modeling and group treatment on self-observation: A comparison with agoraphobics. *Behaviour Research and Therapy,* 1975, *13,* 135–139.

Emmelkamp, P. M. G., & Kuipers, A. C. M. Agoraphobia: A follow-up study four years after treatment. *British Journal of Psychiatry,* 1979, *134,* 352–355.

Emmelkamp. P. M. G., & Ultee, K. A. A. A comparison of "successive approximation" and "self-observation" in the treatment of agoraphobia. *Behavior Therapy,* 1974, *5,* 606–613.

Emmelkamp, P. M. G., & Wessels, H. Flooding in imagination vs. flooding in vivo: A comparison with agoraphobics. *Behaviour Research and Therapy,* 1975, *13,* 7–15.

Emmelkamp, P. M. G., Kuipers, A. C. M., & Eggeraat, J. B. Cognitive modification versus prolonged exposure in vivo: A comparison with agoraphobics as subjects. *Behaviour Research and Therapy,* 1978, *16,* 33–41.

Everaerd, W. T., Rijken, H. M., & Emmelkamp, P. M. A comparison of "flooding" and "successive approximation" in the treatment of agoraphobia. *Behaviour Research and Therapy,* 1973, *11,* 105–117.

Foa, E. B., Jameson, J. S., Turner, R. M., & Payne, L. L. Massed vs. spaced exposure sessions in the treatment of agoraphobia. *Behaviour Research and Therapy,* 1980, *18,* 333–338.

Gelder, M. Behavioral treatment of agoraphobia: Some factors which restrict change after treatment. In J. C. Boulougouris & A. D. Rabavilas (Eds.), *The treatment of phobic and obsessive compulsive disorders.* Oxford: Pergamon Press, 1977.

Gelder, M. G., & Marks, I. M. Severe agoraphobia: A controlled prospective trial of behaviour therapy. *British Journal of Psychiatry*, 1966, *112*, 309–319.

Gelder, M. G., Bancroft, J. H. J., Gath, D. H., Johnston, D. W., Mathews, A. M., & Shaw, P. M. Specific and non-specific factors in behaviour therapy. *British Journal of Psychiatry*, 1973, *123*, 445–462.

Goldstein, A. J., & Chambless, D. L. A reanalysis of agoraphobia. *Behavior Therapy*, 1978, *9*, 47–59.

Greist, J. H., Marks, I. M., Berlin, F., Gournay, K., & Noshirvani, H. Avoidance versus confrontation of fear. *Behavior Therapy*, 1980, *11*, 1–14.

Grey, S., Sartory, G., & Rachman, S. Synchronous and desynchronous changes during fear reduction. *Behaviour Research and Therapy*, 1979, *17*, 137–147.

Hafner, R. J. The husbands of agoraphobic women and their influence on treatment outcome. *British Journal of Psychiatry*, 1977, *131*, 289–294.

Hafner, J., & Marks, I. Exposure *in vivo* of agoraphobics: Contributions of diazepam, group exposure, and anxiety evocation. *Psychological Medicine*, 1976, *6*, 71–88.

Hafner, J., & Milton, F. The influence of propranolol on the exposure in vivo of agoraphobics. *Psychological Medicine*, 1977, *7*, 419–425.

Hand, I., Lamontagne, Y., & Marks, I. M. Group exposure (flooding) in vivo for agoraphobics. *British Journal of Psychiatry*, 1974, *124*, 588–602.

Haynes, S. N. *Principles of behavioral assessment*. New York: Gardner Press, 1978.

Hersen, M. Historical perspectives in behavioral assessment. In M. Hersen & A. S. Bellack (Eds.), *Behavioral assessment: A practical handbook*. Oxford: Pergamon Press, 1976.

Hersen, M., & Barlow, D. H. *Single case experimental designs: Strategies for studying behavior change*. New York: Pergamon, 1976.

Hodgson, R., & Rachman, S. Desynchrony in measures of fear. *Behaviour Research and Therapy*, 1974, *12*, 319–326.

Jannoun, L., Munby, M., Catalan, J., & Gelder, M. A home-based treatment programme for agoraphobia: Replication and controlled evaluation. *Behavior Therapy*, 1980, *11*, 294–305.

Johnston, D., & Gath, D. Arousal levels and attribution effects in diazepam-assisted flooding. *British Journal of Psychiatry*, 1973, *123*, 463–466

Klein, D. F. Delineation of two drug-responsive anxiety syndromes. *Psychopharmacologia*, 1964, *5*, 397–408.

Lang, P. J. Fear reduction and fear behavior: Problems in treating a construct. In J. M. Shlien (Ed.), *Research in psychotherapy* (Vol. 3). Washington, D.C.: American Psychological Association, 1968.

Lang, P. J. Physiological assessment of anxiety and fear. In J. D. Cone & R. P. Hawkins (Eds.), *Behavioral assessment: New directions in clinical psychology*. New York: Brunner/Mazel, 1977.

Leitenberg, H. Behavioral approaches to treatment of neuroses. In H. Leitenberg (Ed.), *Handbook of behavior modification and behavior therapy*. Englewood Cliffs, N.J.: Prentice-Hall, 1976.

Leitenberg, H., Agras, W. S., Allen R., Butz, R., & Edwards, J. Feedback and therapist praise during treatment of phobia. *Journal of Consulting and Clinical Psychology*, 1975, *43*, 396–404.

MacKintosh, N. J. Distribution of trials and the partial reinforcement effect in the rat. *Journal of Comparative Physiology*, 1970, *73*, 341–348.

Mahoney, J. J., & Arnkoff, D. B. Cognitive and self-control therapies. In S. L. Garfield & A. E. Bergin (Eds.), *Handbook of psychotherapy and behavior change: An empirical analysis* (2nd ed.). New York: Wiley, 1978.

Marks, I. M. Phobic disorders four years after treatment: A prospective follow-up. *British Journal of Psychiatry*, 1971, *118*, 683–688.

Marks, I. Behavioral psychotherapy of adult neurosis. In S. L. Garfield, & A. E. Bergin (Eds.), *Handbook of psychotherapy and behavior change: An empirical analysis* (2nd ed.). New York: Wiley, 1978.

Marks, I. M., & Mathews, A. M. Brief standard self-rating for phobic patients. *Behaviour Research and Therapy*, 1979, *17*, 263–267.

Marks, I., Boulougouris, J., & Marset, P. Flooding versus desensitization in the treatment of phobic patients: A crossover study. *British Journal of Psychiatry*, 1971, *119*, 353–375.

Marks, I. M., Viswanathan, R., Lipsedge, M. S., & Gardner, R. Enhanced relief of phobias by flooding during waning diazepam effect. *British Journal of Psychiatry*, 1972, *121*, 493–505.

Mathews, A. M. Fear-reduction research and clinical phobias. *Psychological Bulletin*, 1978, *85*, 390–404.

Mathews, A. M., Gelder, M. G., & Johnston, D. W. *Agoraphobia: Nature and treatment*. New York: Guilford Press, 1981.

Mathews, A. M., Johnston, D. W., Lancashire, N., Munby, M., Shaw, P. M., & Gelder, M. G. Imaginal flooding and exposure to real phobic situations: Treatment outcome with agoraphobic patients. *British Journal of Psychiatry*, 1976, *129*, 362–371.

Mathews, A. M., Teasdale, J., Munby, M., Johnston, D., & Shaw, P. A. A home-based treatment program for agoraphobia. *Behavior Therapy*, 1977, *8*, 915–924.

Mavissakalian, M., & Barlow, D. H. Phobia: An overview. In M. Mavissakalian & D. H. Barlow (Eds.), *Phobia: Psychological and pharmacological treatment*. New York: Guilford Press, 1981.

McPherson, F. M., Brougham, L., & McLaren, S. Maintenance of improvement in agoraphobic patients treated by behavioural methods—A four-year follow-up. *Behaviour Research and Therapy*, 1980, *18*, 150–152.

Meichenbaum, D. H. Cognitive modification of test anxious college students. *Journal of Consulting and Clinical Psychology*, 1972, *39*, 370–380.

Meichenbaum, D. *Cognitive-behavior modification: An integrative approach*. New York: Plenum, 1977.

Miles, H., Barrabee, E., & Finesinger, J. Evaluation of psychotherapy, with follow-up study of 62 cases of anxiety neurosis. *Psychosomatic Medicine*, 1951, *13*, 83–105.

Milton, F., & Hafner, J. The outcome of behavior therapy for agoraphobia in relation to marital adjustment. *Archives of General Psychiatry*, 1979, *36*, 807–811.

Morganstern, K. P. Behavioral interviewing: The initial stages of assessment. In M. Hersen & A. S. Bellack (Eds.), *Behavioral assessment: A practical handbook*. Oxford: Pergamon, 1976.

Munby, J., & Johnston, D. W. Agoraphobia: The long-term follow-up of behavioural treatment. *British Journal of Psychiatry*, 1980, *137*, 418–427.

Nathan, P. E. Symptomatic diagnosis and behavioral assessment: A synthesis? In D. H. Barlow (Ed.), *Behavioral assessment of adult disorders*. New York: Guilford Press, 1981.

National Institute of Mental Health. *Final report of NIMH conference #REP NIMH ER-79-003, Behavior therapies in the treatment of anxiety disorders: Recommendations for strategies in treatment assessment research*.Bethesda, Md.: Author, 1981.

Nelson, R. O., & Barlow, D. H. Behavioral assessment: Basic strategies and initial procedures. In D. H. Barlow (Ed.), *Behavioral assessment of adult disorders*. New York: Guilford Press, 1981.

Norton, G. R., DiNardo, P. A., & Barlow, D. H. Predicting phobics' response to treatment: A consideration of subjective, physiological, and behavioral measures. *Canadian Psychologist*, 1983, *24*, 50–59.

O'Brien, G. T., Barlow, D. H., & Last, C. G. Changing marriage patterns of agoraphobics as a result of treatment. In R. DuPont (Ed.), *Phobia: A comprehensive summary of modern treatments*. New York: Brunner/Mazel, 1982.

Peterson, D. R. *The clinical study of social behavior.* New York: Appleton-Century-Crofts, 1968.

Rachman, S. J. *Fear and courage.* San Francisco: W. H. Freeman, 1978.

Rachman, S., & Hodgson, R. I. Synchrony and desynchrony in fear and avoidance. *Behaviour Research and Therapy,* 1974, *12,* 311–318.

Rachman, S. J., & Wilson, G. T. *The effects of psychological therapy* (2nd ed.). Oxford: Pergamon, 1980.

Sheehan, D., Ballenger, J., & Jacobsen, G. The treatment of endogenous anxiety with phobic, hysterical, and hypochondriacal symptoms. *Archives of General Psychiatry,* 1980, *37,* 51–59.

Stampfl, T. G., & Levis, D. J. Essentials of implosion therapy, a learning-theory-based psychodynamic behavioral therapy. *Journal of Abnormal Psychology,* 1967, *72,* 496–503.

Stern, R. S. Behavior therapy and psychotropic medication. In M. Hersen & A. S. Bellack (Eds.), *Behavior therapy in the psychiatric setting.* Baltimore: Williams & Wilkins, 1978.

Stern, R., and Marks, I. Brief and prolonged flooding: A comparison in agoraphobic patients. *Archives of General Psychiatry,* 1973, *28,* 270–276.

Teichner, W. H. Experimental extinction as a function of the intertrial intervals during conditioning and extinction. *Journal of Experimental Psychology,* 1952, *44,* 170–178.

Tyrer, P. Dependence on benzodiazepines. *British Journal of Psychotherapy,* 1980, *137,* 576–577.

Watson, J. P., & Marks, I. M. Relevant and irrelevant fear in flooding: A crossover study of phobic patients. *Behavior Therapy,* 1971, *2,* 275–293.

Watson, J. P., Gaind, R., & Marks, I. M. Prolonged exposure: A rapid treatment for phobias. *British Medical Journal,* 1971, *1,* 13–15.

Watson, J. P., Mullett, G. E., & Pillay, H. The effects of prolonged exposure to phobic situations upon agoraphobic patients treated in groups. *Behaviour Research and Therapy,* 1973, *11,* 531–545.

Wolpe, J. *Psychotherapy by reciprocal inhibition.* Stanford, Cal.: Stanford University Press, 1958.

Wolpe, J. *The practice of behavior therapy.* New York: Pergamon, 1969.

Zitrin, C. M. Combined pharmacological and psychological treatment of phobia. In M. Mavissakalian & D. H. Barlow (Eds.), *Phobia: Psychological and pharmacological treatment.* New York: Guilford Press, 1981.

Zitrin, C. M., Klein, D. F., & Woerner, M. G. Behavior therapy, supportive psychotherapy, imipramine and phobias. *Archives of General Psychiatry,* 1978, *35,* 307–316.

Zitrin, C. M., Klein, D. F., & Woerner, M. G. Treatment of agoraphobia with group exposure *in vivo* and imipramine. *Archives of General Psychiatry,* 1980, *37,* 63–72.

Zung, W. K. A self-rating depression scale. *Archives of General Psychiatry,* 1965, *12,* 63–70.

5

Panic Disorder
Medical and Psychological Parameters

ROLF G. JACOB and MARK D. RAPPORT

INTRODUCTION

Panic, as an individual experience, is an extreme form of anxiety or terror. Usually panic tends to occur in life-threatening situations, especially when it is unclear whether avenues of escape are available. An informative, subjective account of such intense anxiety was provided by Casey (1978), who described his experience of waking up from general anesthesia while remaining completely paralyzed by curare. Such experiences of panic can have profound and long-lasting effects. For example, Campbell, Sanderson, and Laverty (1964) reported a finding, later dramatized in the film *Clockwork Orange,* that stimuli classically conditioned to brief episodes of Scoline-induced respiratory paralysis produced conditioned anxiety responses that failed to habituate, even after 300 extinction trials extending over several months.

The partial independence of cognitive, physiological, and behavioral dimensions of anxiety have long been recognized (Agras & Jacob, 1981). Due to their inherent bias, behavioral theories have primarily focused on the behavioral aspects of anxiety. In the study of panic, however, one mainly has to rely on self-report. Therefore, this area is comparatively less developed from a behavioral viewpoint. This chapter will frequently draw on nonbehavioral literature and should be seen as a first attempt to juxtapose information that might be applicable to panic from a variety of fields.

ROLF G. JACOB ● Department of Psychiatry, Western Psychiatric Institute and Clinic, University of Pittsburgh School of Medicine, Pittsburgh, Pennsylvania 15213.   MARK D. RAPPORT ● Department of Psychology, University of Rhode Island, Kingston, Rhode Island 02881.

Panic attacks have occasionally been observed under "naturalistic" conditions in the laboratory. Lader and Mathews (1970) reported the physiological changes during panic attacks of three patients who happened to be attached to physiological monitoring equipment when their panic attacks occurred. A drastic increase was noted in heart rate, skin conductance, and forearm blood flow. The most common method of studying physiological changes has been to measure these parameters during induced anxiety states. For example, Hickam, Cargill, and Golden (1948), studying patients undergoing catheterization procedures and medical students undergoing examinations, found increases in cardiac output, peripheral resistance, blood pressure, and oxygen consumption in most subjects. In a publication edited by Ursin, Baade, and Levine (1978), biochemical and hormonal changes were reported for parachutist trainees before and after consecutive jumps. Especially before the first jump, there were increases in the levels of epinephrine, norepinephrine, growth hormone, glucose and fatty acids, and a decrease of testosterone. Anxiety also induces an increase in pulmonary ventilation (Dudley, Holmes, Martin, & Ripley, 1964; Garssen, 1980; Suess, Alexander, Smith, Sweeny, & Marion, 1980). This hyperventilatory response can then lead to other physiological changes, which will be discussed in the section on the hyperventilation syndrome in this chapter.

Panic and fear have also been a focus of interest for disciplines other than behavioral psychology. A neuropsychological conceptualization has recently been provided by Gray and his colleagues (1981) but will not be covered in this chapter due to space limitations. Humanistic theories have been surveyed by May (1977). Psychodynamic metapsychology grappled with the concept of anxiety throughout its formative states (Freud, 1895/1962, 1926/1959, 1933/1964—for Freud's final position, the reader is referred to the last two publications). Since Freud, the most significant advancement in the psychodynamic understanding of anxiety has been provided by Bowlby (1973). Of particular clinical relevance is his analysis of escape behavior: Bowlby points out that *escape*, by definition, will involve the approach toward something else. However, rather than being random, this approach is goal directed, the target being an attachment figure. Using this framework, Klein (1980) concluded that panic could be seen as an equivalent to the "protest" phase, the first phase of the typical sequence occurring when access to the attachment figure is cut off. This may explain why many patients are particularly distressed when left alone, and why the onset of panic attacks often seem to coincide with developmental stages of young and middle adult life in which commitments often are changed (Raskin, Peeke, Dickman, & Pinsker, 1982).

Social psychology defines panic as a group behavior occurring in response to threat or danger. By definition, the panic behavior results in increasing the danger rather than removing it (Janis, Chapman, Gillin, & Speigel, 1964). For example, in the Coconut Grove fire of 1946, pressure from the rear of the crowd toward a presumed but nonexistent exit caused people at the front to be trampled or crushed. In addition to threat, three factors are considered to contribute to producing panic: (a) partial entrapment, (b) breakdown of the escape route, and (c) front-to-rear communication failure (Janis *et al.,* 1964). Likelihood of escape is considered a key variable in determining the occurrence of panic. For example, Guten and Allen (1972), in an analogue study involving a simulated group situation, manipulated the expectaton of likelihood of escape from shock. An inverted U-shaped relationship was found between likelihood of escape and frequency of lever pressing, the operational measure of panic. In other words, *medium* likelihood of escape was associated with the highest degree of panic. Thus, panic especially tends to occur if there is ambiguity about the escape possibilities.

PANIC DISORDER AS A PSYCHIATRIC CONDITION

Only recently has panic disorder been recognized as a separate psychiatric condition. It was first defined by Spitzer, Endicott, and Robins in their *Research Diagnostic Criteria* (3rd ed., 1980) and later included in the third edition of the *Diagnostic and Statistical Manual* (DSM-III) (American Psychiatric Association, 1980) with slight modifications. The recent recognition of panic disorder, of course, does not imply that such a condition did not "exist" prior to 1977. Panic attacks have been observed for a long time but have usually been considered a symptom of anxiety neurosis. In DSM-III, anxiety neurosis was for the first time subdivided into generalized anxiety disorder and panic disorder. A consequence of the recency of recognizing panic disorder as a separate entity is that when reviewing anything but the most recent literature, it usually is not clear whether the findings might pertain to generalized anxiety disorder, panic disorder, or both.

The essential feature of panic disorder, as defined by DSM-III, is the occurrence of panic attacks. These are characterized by a sudden onset of anxious thoughts coupled with up to twelve specific symptoms of anxiety. These twelve symptoms are listed in Table 1. For a diagnosis of panic disorder, at least four of the twelve characteristic symptoms need to be present. In addition, at least three panic attacks must have occurred during the three weeks prior to the diagnostic evaluation. This latter criterion is slightly different from the Spitzer, Endicott, and Robins (1980) research diagnostic criteria, which required at least six panic attacks within a period of 6 weeks for a definite diagnosis of panic disorder. In addition, the Research Diagnostic Criteria but not the DSM-III include anxiety between attacks as a necessary criterion.

The panic attacks may occur in an unpredictable fashion, although in some cases they may be more likely to occur in certain situations. For example, when fear of dying is a prominent feature, the attacks may be more likely to

Table 1. DSM-III Criteria for Panic Disorder[a]

A. At least three panic attacks within a three-week period in circumstances other than during marked physical exertion or in a life-threatening situation. The attacks are not precipitated only by exposure to a circumscribed phobic stimulus.

B. Panic attacks are manifested by discrete periods of apprehension or fear, and at least four of the following symptoms appear during each attack:
  (1) dyspnea
  (2) palpitations
  (3) chest pain or discomfort
  (4) choking or smothering
  (5) dizziness, vertigo, or unsteady feelings
  (6) feelings of unreality
  (7) paresthesias (tingling in hands or feet)
  (8) hot and cold flashes
  (9) sweating
  (10) faintness
  (11) trembling or shaking
  (12) fear of dying, going crazy, or doing something uncontrolled during an attack

C. Not due to a physical disorder or another mental disorder, such as Major Depression, Somatization Disorder, or Schizophrenia.

D. Not associated with agoraphobia.

---

[a] From American Psychiatric Association, *Diagnostic and Statistical Manual of Mental Disorders* (3rd Ed.), p. 230. Copyright 1980 by author, Washington, D.C. Reprinted by permission.

occur in situations where there is no easy access to a hospital. Or, when fear of embarrassment is a prominent feature, the attacks may be more likely to occur in situations involving exposure to crowds and strangers. In addition, situations in which panic attacks have occurred before are probably more likely to induce new panic attacks.

The attacks may last from a few minutes up to 1 hr. Between attacks, the patient usually develops anticipatory anxiety due to fear of having another attack. Avoidance of situations associated with a higher probability of attacks may gradually develop. If so, a symptom picture consistent with agoraphobia with panic attacks will gradually emerge. It is likely that panic disorder represents an early stage of agoraphobia. The differential diagnosis of panic disorder versus agoraphobia with panic attacks is somewhat arbitrary. We would diagnose panic disorder when there is no consistent precipitating external stimulus, and when avoidance behaviors are not a consistent part of the clinical picture.

As mentioned above, panic symptoms used to be regarded as a sign of anxiety neurosis. An operational definition of anxiety neurosis was provided by Feighner, Robins, Guze, Woodruff, Winokur, and Munoz (1972). Because anxiety neurosis, according to the Feighner criteria, is sometimes considered to be equivalent to panic disorder, we need to examine these criteria. The Feighner criteria for anxiety neurosis are onset before age 40, and the presence of (a) chronic nervousness and (b) recurrent anxiety attacks. The latter are essential to the diagnosis. At least six anxiety attacks, separated from each other "by at least a week," must have occurred. Thus, the Feighner *et al.* (1972) definition of anxiety neurosis overlaps with the current criteria for panic disorder, except for the frequency of panic attacks and the requirement of anxiety between attacks.

Anxiety neurosis was first recognized as a diagnostic entity by Freud (1895/1962), who separated this condition from neurasthenia (Beard, 1869). Freud's original description of anxiety neurosis is still one of the best available and includes an excellent portrayal of the symptoms of panic disorder.

> But anxiousness—which, though mostly latent as regards consciousness, is constantly lurking in the background—has other means of finding expression besides this. It can suddenly break through into consciousness without being aroused by a train of ideas, and thus provoke an anxiety attack. An anxiety attack of this sort may consist of the feeling of anxiety, alone, without any associated idea, or accompanied by the interpretation that is nearest to hand, such as ideas of the extinction of life, or of a stroke, or of a threat of madness; or else some kind of paraesthesia (similar to the hysterical aura) may be combined with the feeling of anxiety, or, finally, the feeling of anxiety may have linked to it a disturbance of one or more of the bodily functions—such as respiration, heart action, vasomotor innervation or glandular activity. From this combination the patient picks out in particular now one, now another, factor. He complains of "spasms of the heart," "difficulty in breathing," "outbreaks of sweating," "ravenous hunger," and such like; and, in his description, the feeling of anxiety often recedes into the background or is referred to quite unrecognizably as "being unwell," "feeling uncomfortable," and so on. (p. 93)

The fact that panic disorder and generalized anxiety disorder have been united within the same diagnostic category for almost 90 years raises the question as to why the two disorders should now be considered separate entities. Walker (1959) was probably the first to provide an empirical basis for the distinction. He divided the anxiety neurotic patients under study into three groups depending on outcome: complete recovery, partial recovery, and no recovery. Patients belonging to the group that completely recovered where characterized by the onset of the anxiety being "instantaneous," unrelated to circumstances at the time, and coming "as a complete surprise to the patient." The episodes were of "sudden onset but died away more gradually" and between the attacks the patients were "relatively normal" but "tending to be irritable and morose." The reader has probably recognized by now that this description fits our criteria for panic disorder. Walker thought that this syndrome might be regarded as a depressive equivalent rather than an anxiety disorder.

The finding that was perhaps most influential in separating out panic disorder from anxiety neurosis was that episodic anxiety attacks responded to antidepressant medication, such as imipramine (Klein & Fink, 1962; McNair & Kahn, 1981) or monoamine oxidase inhibitors (King, 1962; Sargant, 1962; Sheehan, Ballenger, & Jacobson, 1980). In contrast, minor tranquilizers such as diazepam (Valium) or chlordiazepoxide (Librium) are thought to ameliorate anxiety-arousing cognitions, but not the autonomic symptoms of panic (Freedman, Dornbush, & Shapiro, 1981; Hoehn-Saric, 1982). Thus, as a result of this "pharmacological dissection," panic and generalized anxiety were considered separate.

The final discovery that may have contributed to setting aside panic disorder from generalized anxiety disorder, was the finding by Pitts and McClure (1969) that panic attacks could be induced by infusion of lactate. This gave rise to the "lactate" theory of anxiety, and made panic, perhaps more than any other manifestation of anxiety, assume a position of special interest for biologically oriented psychiatry.

DIFFERENTIAL DIAGNOSTIC PROBLEMS

Panic disorder is not very clearly delineated from other psychiatric conditions. The differential diagnosis of panic disorder versus agoraphobia was described above. Generalized anxiety disorder differs from panic disorder primarily in the absence of panic attacks. Depression, atypical anxiety disorder and the somatoform disorders constitute additional psychiatric diagnostic entities, the symptoms of which partially overlap with those of panic disorder. The differential diagnosis of these conditions may be problematic.

The differentiation between panic disorder and depression can be difficult. We will set aside the theoretical issues involved in this question (see, for example, McNair & Fisher, 1978). In current DSM-III usage, panic disorder may occur in depression. A diagnosis of depression is made if there are accompanying depressive symptoms such as weight loss, sleep disturbance, fatigue, decline of interests, difficulty concentrating, motor retardation or agitation, feelings of guilt, and suicidal ideation. If the panic attacks are considered due to the depression, a separate diagnosis of panic disorder is not made. However, at times the depressive picture may develop after the onset of panic attacks, as if it were a reaction to the social incapacitation brought on by the panic disorder. In such cases, self-blaming thoughts of having been unable to pursue various life goals due to the panic symptoms might be prominent. These patients can be diagnosed as having panic disorder as a primary diagnosis and depression as a secondary diagnosis.

In anxiety disorders, secondary depression is a common phenomenon. For example, in a study on chronic anxiety neurosis, Clancy, Noyes, Hoenk, and Slymen (1978) found a frequency of secondary depression of 44%, compared to 6% in surgical controls. Similarly, Woodruff, Guze, and Clayton (1972) found that 31 of 62 patients with anxiety neurosis qualified for an additional diagnosis of affective disorder.

Depression is even more common in patients with panic disorder than in those with generalized anxiety disorder. Dealy, Ishiki, Avery, Wilson, and Dunner (1981) recently investigated the presence of depression in anxiety patients with and without panic attacks. In males, depression was twice as common when panic attacks were present (35% vs. 17%). In females, the corresponding ratio for secondary depression was 69% vs. 42%. Thus, depression was most prevalent in females with panic attacks. Similarly, Raskin *et al.* (1982), comparing 17 panic disorder patients wth 16 generalized anxiety disorder patients, found that prior depressive episodes were twice as common in the panic disorder patients (15 vs. 7). This association between panic and depression, as well as the similarity of the psychopharmacological response of the two conditions, appear to support Walker's (1959) view that recurrent panic attacks may constitute part of a depressive disorder rather than an anxiety disorder.

The diagnostic differentiation of panic disorder from somatoform disorders such as hypochondriasis and conversion disorder is also problematic. Many patients with panic disorder do not consider themselves to be suffering from a psychiatric or psychological condition. Instead, they experience alarming physical symptoms and see their anxiety as justified worry about a possible medical condition. Consequently, when acutely distressed they often turn up in medical emergency rooms. In many cases no physical abnormality will be found, but this in no way reassures the patient. He interprets referral to a psychologist or psychiatrist as signifying that the physician does not believe in the reality of the symptom. An adversary relationship is thus set up between patient and physician. This is a picture typical for hypochondriasis as well (Turner, Jacob, & Morrison, 1984). The similarity to hypochondriasis is especially marked for what could be considered a milder form of panic disorder, with fewer than 4 of the 12 symptoms which define the full-blown variety. This variety, which we could call "subpanic disorder" (or "probable panic disorder," Spitzer *et al.,* 1980), was described by Freud (1895/1962), building upon the original description by Hecker (1893).

> Now it is an interesting fact, and an important one from a diagnostic point of view, that the proportion in which these elements are mixed in an anxiety attack varies to a remarkable degree, and that almost every accompanying symptom alone can consititue the attack just as well as can the anxiety itself. There are consequently rudimentary anxiety attacks and equivalents of anxiety attacks, all probably having the same significance, which exhibit a great wealth of forms that has as yet been little appreciated. A closer study of these larval anxiety-states (Hecker, 1893) and their diagnostic differentiation from other attacks should soon become a necessary task for neuropathologists. (p. 94)

In this case one could diagnose either generalized anxiety disorder or atypical anxiety disorder, depending on whether the other criteria for the former diagnosis are fulfilled. If preoccupation with the possibility of an underlying disease dominates the picture, a diagnosis of hypochondriasis can be made (Jacob & Turner, 1984). If the symptom appears to play a prominent role in generating gain from the social environment or in avoiding areas of conflicts, a diagnosis of conversion disorder might be made. Unfortunately, there is no independent criterion against which the validity of these diagnostic entities can be established. In addition, the reliability of these distinctions, if tested, would probably be quite low.

"Feelings of unreality"—depersonalization, derealization, *déjà vu*, and *jamais vu*—may occur during panic attacks. Brief isolated episodes of depersonalization, however, do not necessarily signify a psychiatric abnormality. They are common as a normal experience especially in adolescents and young adults (Schraberg, 1977). For example, in a questionnaire survey, Roberts (1960) found that 23 of 57 students confirmed having had such experiences. Depersonalization and other "bizarre" experiences can also be caused by substances such as LSD, either during acute ingestion or in the form of "flashbacks" (Alarcon, Dickinson, & Dohn, 1982) and can be a symptom of temporal-lobe and other types of epilepsy (Epstein, 1967; Harper & Roth, 1962). They have also been reported in simple phobics during exposure treatment (Curtis, 1981).

RELATED CONDITIONS—THE HYPERVENTILATION SYNDROME

In both the psychiatric and the medical literature, syndromes are described which appear to have been generated around particular symptoms of panic. For example, the dramatic presentation of the symptoms of panic lead to the label of "hysterical" attacks. The symptom of depersonalization was the point of origin for the "phobic depersonalization syndrome." Chest pain and palpitations was the main complaint of "neurocirculatory asthenia," the "effort syndrome," or "Da Costa's Syndrome." Finally, hyperventilation and labored breathing gave rise to the "hyperventilation syndrome." Of these, the hyperventilation syndrome appears to be very similar to panic disorder, and because the physiology of hyperventilation has been studied rather extensively, this disorder will be discussed in more detail here to further illustrate physiological changes that can occur during panic.

Hyperventilation occurs when pulmonary ventilation is excessive for satisfying the physiological needs of blood oxygenation and carbon dioxide elimination. Hyperventilation produces symptoms that most of us recognize, for example, from blowing up a balloon. The earliest sensations involve dizziness, giddiness, and faintness, proceeding to impaired ability to concentrate and lowering of consciousness. These symptoms are thought to be due to impaired oxygenation of the brain, produced by constriction of the cerebral blood vessels. Another set of symptoms include numbness and tingling sensations, especially around the mouth and hands. These symptoms are attributable to changes and excitability of the peripheral sensory nerves. If hyperventilation is continued, signs of motor neuro-irritability, such as muscular twitching and cramps, become apparent. These cramps anticipate the development of generalized tetany, which is the ultimate result of severe hyperventilation.

The effects of hyperventilation are primarily mediated via the resulting excessive elimination of carbon dioxide through the lungs. Thus, carbon dioxide tension in the blood is reduced (hypocapnia) and blood pH is increased (alkalosis) (Brown, 1953). The symptoms of hyperventilation can be reversed by breathing air with increased carbon dioxide content, for example, 30% CO_2 in oxygen (Kerr, Dalton, & Gliebe, 1937).

The hypocapnia and alkalosis resulting from hyperventilation have profound effects on several organ systems. In the blood itself, the alkaline pH shifts the hemoglobin dissociation curve so that there will be a greater tendency for oxygen to remain bound to the hemoglobin and red blood cells, rather than being delivered to the tissue cells. Thus, hyperventilation has the paradoxical effect of making oxygen delivery to the tissues more difficult. The blood vessels to the brain, heart, and skin constrict, resulting in reduced blood flow to these organs.

In the brain, the effects of vasoconstriction are quite pronounced (Raichle & Plum, 1972). In monkeys, for example, Meyer and Gotoh (1960) found that the decreased blood flow was followed by a drastic decrease in cortical oxygen concentration, from 10–35 mm Hg before hyperventilation to as low as 2 mm Hg during hyperventilation. This was associated with a slowing of the EEG rhythm. In humans, Fazekas, McHenry, Alman, and Sullivan (1961) calculated a 42% reduction in cerebral blood flow after 2 min of hyperventilation. Gotoh, Meyer, and Takagi (1965) found similar changes occurring during the first minute of hyperventilation. They also found that these changes were more pronounced in younger individuals. Hyperventilation has been reported to induce cerebrovascular accidents (strokes) in patients with sickle-cell anemia (Allen, Imbus, Powers, & Haywood, 1976; Protass, 1973). Also, hyperventilation may worsen certain types of migraine attacks (Blau, 1978).

The slowing of the EEG rhythm due to hyperventilation is a well-known phenomenon which has been shown to be associated with impairment of ability to concentrate (Engel, Ferris, & Logan, 1947). It was also found that the hyperventilation-induced slowing of the EEG was potentiated by hypoglycemia and occurred more easily in the erect position.

Hyperventilation also affects the physiology of the heart. In a catheterization study of patients with ischemic coronary artery disease, Neill and Hattenhauer (1975) reported a decrease of coronary blood flow in 9 out of 10 patients. This was compensated by the greater arterio–venous oxygen difference, so there was no change in myocardial oxygen consumption. However, these changes imply a significant reduction in the safety margin for myocardial oxygen supply. Indeed, in one patient, biochemical signs of myocardial hypoxia were found.

Hyperventilation can produce electrocardiographic changes in patients with no arteriographic evidence of coronary artery disease. Lary and Goldschlager (1974) found such changes, primarily consisting of ST-segment depressions considered to be signs of myocardial eschemia, in 7 of 46 such patients. These electrocardiographic abnormalities appear to occur more often in patients diagnosed as having hyperventilation syndrome or anxiety. Yu, Yim, and Stanfield (1959) observed no changes in 10 normal subjects after hyperventilation, whereas 15 of 20 patients diagnosed as having hyperventilation syndrome showed transient T-wave inversions, ST depressions and other changes. On the other hand, Lewis (1959) and Lewis, Seebohm, Hamilton, January, and Wheeler (1955) found changes in both normals and hyperventilators, but they tended to be more transient in the normals.

Hyperventilation may cause chest pain which is indistinguishable from that of angina pectoris. Of 95 patients examined because of cardiac symptoms, Wheatley (1975) found that in 27 cases hyperventilation syndrome was the predominent cause of symptoms. Hyperventilation can also induce cardiac arrhythmias, as demonstrated by Lamb, Dermksian, and Sarnoff (1958), Lum (1975) and Wildenthal, Fuller, and Shapiro (1968). These symptoms can then produce anxiety, resulting in further hyperventilation and more symptoms (Lewis, 1954). Thus, the patients who complain of their symptoms as being physical are certainly justified, considering all the physiological changes that hyperventilation can induce.

To reiterate, hyperventilation causes physiological changes, which can be experienced as physical symptoms. Sometimes, the only way of knowing whether a symptom is induced or augmented by hyperventilation is to perform a hyperventilation test, such as the one to which Kerr, Dalton, and Gliebe (1937) subjected a group of patients with various medical complaints. The following medical complaints could be reproduced by hyperventilation: tetany, generalized muscular irritability, convulsions, precordial pain and palpitations, Raynaud's phenomenon, epigastric pain, and dizziness with tinnitus.

The hyperventilation syndrome is recognized in two forms: acute and chronic. The acute form is well-known and not difficult to diagnose, since the hyperventilation behavior is quite obvious to anyone. However, it should be remembered that certain medical conditions, such as salicylate poisoning, diabetic acidosis, alcohol withdrawal, encephalitis, cardiac infarction, pulmonary emboli, and pulmonary insufficiency can present with acute hyperventilation. Hyperventilation will also occur in environments with low oxygen content, such as high altitude.

The chronic hyperventilation syndrome is less uniformly recognized, but a chronic hyperventilatory state was recently confirmed biochemically in patients suffering chronic back pain and cancer pain (Glynn, Lloyd, & Folkhard, 1981). In chronic hyperventilators, the excessive respiration is described as being less pronounced and frequently unrecognizable unless one pays close attention to the breathing pattern of the patient. Upper thoracic breathing, frequent sighing, yawning, sniffing and throat clearing are common varieties of "subclinical" hyperventilation (Gliebe & Auerback, 1944; Lum 1976; Rice, 1950). Indeed, hypocapnia may be present without overtly identifiable excessive breathing. Okel and Hurst (1961) observed four individuals engaging in prolonged hyperventilation. The comment was made that in three of the subjects maintenance of an alkalotic state was "surprisingly" easy and occurred without visible hyperventilation. In these individuals, two or three quick deep breaths could promptly institute symptoms.

Investigators have wondered about the mechanisms involved in maintaining a chronic state of hyperventilation. As mentioned above, Lewis (1954) postulated a vicious cycle of hyperventilation—hypocapnia—symptoms—apprehension—hyperventilation. In addition, there might be individual differences in regulation of breathing behavior. For example, Mills (1946) observed that after a hyperventilation test, certain individuals tended to continue to hyperventilate. Folgering and Colla (1978) identified a group of individuals in which lower arterial carbon dioxide levels were associated with paradoxical *increase* in ventilation. Thus, there might be a subgroup of individuals who are more prone to hyperventilation. However, it has not been established whether these are the same individuals who develop hyperventilation syndrome.

The diagnosis of hyperventilation might be confirmed by the evaluation of arterial blood gases. By the use of arterial blood CO_2 tensions, Lum (1976) separated hyperventilators from normals. However, it is unclear whether this difference was due to a hyperventilatory response to arterial catherterization, a somewhat painful procedure, or truly represented a chronic state of hyperventilation. For example, Motta, Fagiani, Dolcetti, Bellone, and Borello (1971), using local anesthesia for the arterial catheterization, found no differences in resting blood gas levels between anxious and normal patients.

The above description of hyperventilation syndrome should have made it evident to the reader that acute hyperventilation attack and panic attack are very similar conditions. At least some degree of hyperventilation with its concomitant physiological changes always occurs during a panic attack. But are the two conditions identical? If so, voluntary hyperventilation should reproduce all the symptoms of a panic attack. However, in our clinical experience this has not always been the case. Patients will often report that the feelings induced by hyperventilation are similar but "not the same." Probably, the feeling of increased arousal due to adrenaline secretion is missing. Moreover, hyperventilation is not *specific* for panic. It may also occur in other agitated psychiatric states, such as acute psychosis.

MEDICAL CONDITIONS PRESENTING WITH PANIC

When evaluating a patient with panic disorder, it is important to know that certain medical conditions mimic panic. As mentioned before, the patients themselves are often convinced that they have a medical problem. It is therefore mandatory that the therapists be familiar with the medical differential diagnosis of the condition. New medical causes for panic are still being discovered. For example, panic due to amitriptyline withdrawal (Gawin & Markoff, 1981) or to ventricular tachycardia (Brown & Kemble, 1981) have been reported only recently. Moreover, physicians often consider these patients as difficult to manage and might be tempted to discard the patients prematurely. Showing interest in the medical evaluation is one way of gaining the patient's trust and cooperation.

Following the strategy of taking the patient's concerns seriously, we have uncovered physical abnormalities in several cases. For example, otoneurological testing resulted in abnormal findings in a high percentage of cases (see below). In another case, 24-hour electrocardiographic monitoring was suggested, and episodes of second-degree heart block were discovered. The latter was, however, unrelated to his panic episodes.

Surveys have shown that physical abnormalities are more prevalent in psychiatric patients than in normal controls (Koryani, 1980). While in most cases the psychiatric and medical conditions are independent, the medical conditions were in other cases actually causative of the psychiatric symptom. Such findings have lead to an increasing awareness of the somatopsychic disorders in recent years.

The medical conditions that can present with anxiety symptoms are varied. Hall, Popkin, Devaul, Faillace, and Stickney (1978) found a wide range of medical conditions causing anxiety: pneumonia, hyperthyroidism, hypothyroidism, hyperparathyroidism, paroxysmal atrial tachycardia, hypochromic anemia, ulcerative colitis and scabies. Hall (1980) also pointed out the importance of neurological disorders, particularly transient ischemic attacks and head injuries. In general, a medical cause for anxiety is more likely in individuals whose anxiety symptoms begin before the age of 18 or after the age of 35.

In addition to medical conditions producing anxiety, there are a large number of patients with anxiety who have concomitant, although not causative, medical illness. For example, Noyes, Clancy, Hoenk, and Slymen (1978) compared the health status of patients diagnosed as anxiety neurotics with surgical controls six years after the initial diagnosis. The anxiety neurotics showed a greater frequency of health impairment, hospitalization and episodes of illness. Peptic ulcer was present in 31% of the anxiety neurotics as compared to 14% of the controls, hypertension in 27% versus 11%, and heart disease in 7% versus 4%.

The research reviewed so far pertains to the medical differential diagnosis of anxiety neurosis. Only one study has focused specifically on panic disorder

(Coryell, Noyes, & Clancy, 1982). In this study, patients with panic disorder (as identified retrospectively from hospital charts of patients discharged between 1929 and 1955), were compared with patients diagnosed as having depressive episodes and with expected morbidity data from population studies. Men with panic disorder were found to have a significantly higher mortality rate than depressives, but this difference did not hold up in a more limited comparison involving matched pairs. Both groups had a higher frequency of deaths from unnatural causes, such as suicide, than the base rate in the population. Important for the medical evaluation of patients with panic disorder was the finding of higher mortality from cardiovascular causes in panic disorder patients than in the general population. No such increase was found in the depressives, but a direct comparison between the two diagnostic groups failed to reach statistical significance.

Because it was based on inpatients, the Coryell *et al.* (1982) study may not be generalizable to all panic patients. However, it seems clear that a medical evaluation should play an important part in the assessment of patients with panic disorder. Conditions that present with episodic acute symptoms, similar to those of panic, are particularly relevant for the medical differential diagnosis. Table 2 lists some of these conditions, although it is not claimed to be exhaustive. For a more extensive treatment, the reader is referred to Hall (1980). Table 2 presupposes an individual who is not currently in treatment for any medical problem, such as diabetes, gastric surgery, or hypertension. The table also lists diagnostic tests that can be employed to confirm the suspected condition. However, we do not advocate the indiscriminate use of extensive screening batteries to replace a good history and physical examination.

Of the conditions listed in Table 2, hypoglycemia, positional vertigo, and certain cardiac conditions will be considered in somewhat more detail, either because they have received attention in the literature or because they seemed to be important according to our own clinical experience.

Idiopathic Postprandial Hypoglycemia

During the past decades, it became fashionable to explain almost any obscure symptom to the presence of reactive or postprandial hypoglycemia. This tendency to overdiagnose hypoglycemia lead Yager and Young (1974) to jokingly coin the new diagnostic label "epidemic nonhypoglycemia." Permutt (1980) estimated that in his practice, "nonhypoglycemia" was at least five times as common as verified hypoglycemia. Similarly, Ford, Bray, and Swerdloff (1976) verified the diagnosis in only 4 of 30 patients that had been previously diagnosed as having hypoglycemia.

Reactive hypoglycemia is thought to be due to excessively high secretion of insulin after ingesting carbohydrates, resulting in a rapid decline of blood sugar to hypoglycemic blood levels, and in a compensatory secretion of adrenalin and other hormones. The symptoms of reactive hypoglycemia typically

Table 2. Differential Diagnosis of Panic Disorder

Main symptoms	Condition suspected	Differentiating symptoms	Confirming test
Tremor, sweating, pallor, dizziness	Reactive hypoglycemia	Symptoms 2–4 hours after meal	5-hr glucose-tolerance tests
	Insulin-secreting tumors		Fasting blood-glucose and blood-insulin levels
Palpitations	Paroxysmal atrial tachycardia, ventricular extrasystoles	Sudden onset of rapid heart rate	24-hour electrocardiographic monitoring, event recording
	Mitral-valve prolapse	Systolic click or late systolic murmur	Echocardiogram
Dizziness	Orthostatic hypotension, anemia	Worse upon arising and exercise	Blood pressure and pulse, standing vs. sitting or lying down, blood count
	Benign positional vertigo	Triggered by rotation of head, jogging, stooping	Barany maneuver, otoneurological examination
Dyspnea, hyperventilation	Congestive heart failure	Rapid shallow breathing	Chest x-ray, EKG
	Pneumonia, pleuritis	Fever	Chest x-ray
	Asthma	Wheezing on expiration	Pulmonary function tests
	Chronic obstructive pulmonary disease	Precipitated by smoking	
	Alcohol withdrawal	History of alcohol use	
Chest pain	Angina pectoris	Precipitated by physical exercise, emotions, or heavy meals	Electrocardiogram, exercise electrocardiogram
	Myocardial infarction	Prolonged severe pain	Electrocardiogram, cardiac enzymes
	Costal chondritis	Tender spots in costochondral junctions	Normal cardiologic evaluation
	Pleuritis, pneumonia	Fever	Chest x-ray
Feelings of unreality	Temporal lobe epilepsy	Micropsia, macropsia, perceptual distortions, hallucinations	EEG with nasopharyngeal leads

Table 2. (continued)

Main symptoms	Condition suspected	Differentiating symptoms	Confirming test
	Psychedelic use or "flashback"	History of use	
Hot and cold flashes	Carcinoid syndrome		5-HIAA in 24-hr urine
	Menopause	Female sex, appropriate age	
Weakness	Multiple sclerosis	Age <40, fluctuating symptoms	Neurologic evaluation
	Transient ischemic attacks	Age >40, paralysis	
Miscellaneous	Hyperthyroidism	Rapid heart rate, warm sweaty hands	Thyroid function tests
	Hypothyroidism	Voice changes	
	Hyperparathyroidism	Varied psychiatric symptoms	Blood calcium levels
	Hypoparathyroidism	Tetany, increased sensitivity to hyperventilation	
	Pheochromocytoma	High blood pressure	Catecholamines in 24-hr urine
	Acute intermittent porphyria	History of barbituate intake	Urine porphobilinogen during attack
Drug use	Amphetamine intoxication	Paranoid feelings	Drug Screen
	Hallucinogen abuse	"Flashbacks"	
	Withdrawal from barbituates or minor tranquilizers	Agitation	
	Withdrawal from opioids	Pain, general malaise	
	Alcohol withdrawal	History of alcohol use	
	Amitriptyline withdrawal	History of amitriptyline use	

occur two to four hours after meals and are attributed to the effect of low blood sugar levels on nervous tissue, resulting in headache, mental dullness, fatigue, confusion, seizures or even unconsciousness. In addition, the compensatory secretion of adrenalin causes anxiety, irritability, sweating, palpitations, hunger sensations and tremor (Permutt, 1976). A diagnosis of reactive hypoglycemia rests on the 5-hr glucose-tolerance test, in which the lowest blood-sugar value (glucose nadir) and the rate of decline of glucose are measured. A new set of guidelines for what represents a hypoglycemic response were recently presented by Hadji-Georgopoulos, Schmidt, Margolis, and Kowarski (1980). These guidelines provided good discriminative ability between individuals who did and did not have hypoglycemic symptoms during the test. Impaired ability to concentrate, as measured by the serial sevens test, was recently demonstrated to occur when blood sugars reached hypoglycemic levels (Hale, Margen, & Rabak, 1981). In addition to changes in blood glucose, some authors require an increase in corticosteroid or insulin secretion to confirm the diagnosis of hypoglycemia (Anthony, Dippe, Hofeldt, Davis, & Forsham, 1973). In clinical practice, it is prudent to enquire for the specific criteria of the laboratory that performs the test, before drawing any diagnostic conclusions.

It should be remembered that reactive hypoglycemia is not a uniform condition. In addition to the idiopathic variety, reactive hypoglycemia can be seen in early diabetes, liver disease, after gastric surgery, carbohydrate restriction and alcohol ingestion. It is also important to differentiate between postprandial hypoglycemia and fasting hypoglycemia. The latter almost always signifies a serious disease.

Abnormalities in the MMPI have been observed in hypoglycemic patients. Anthony *et al.* (1973) found "conversion V" patterns in patients with suspected hypoglycemia. This pattern was present regardless of whether or not the diagnosis of hypoglycemia was later confirmed biochemically, and whether the hypoglycemia was idiopathic or secondary to other conditions. Control patients who had endocrine abnormalities but no hypoglycemia did not show the pattern. Similarly, Johnson, Dorr, Swenson, and Service (1980) found the conversion profile in their suspected hypoglycemic patients. The association between MMPI findings and hypoglycemia, of course, does not establish whether the relationship was a somatopsychic or a psychosomatic one. As mentioned earlier hyperventilation and hypoglycemia can potentiate each other. It would be interesting to study whether differences in tendency to hyperventilate might explain why only some patients develop symptoms of hypoglycemia at a given glucose level.

Vestibular Abnormalities

Pathological conditions in the balance organs tend to be overlooked as a diagnostic possibility for the medical work-up of panic disorder. Dizziness and vertigo are the most prominent symptoms in patients with such lesions. Upon detailed analysis, the symptom of dizziness can be categorized into the following four varieties: (a) rotational sensation, (b) loss of balance without head sensations (e.g. being pulled to the left), (c) feelings like fainting or losing consciousness, and (d) ill-defined "light-headedness" (Drachman & Hart, 1972). The first two more strongly implicate neurological or vestibular pathology, whereas the fainting variety usually signifies a vagal or cardiovascular origin.

In 125 patients referred for otological evaulation for dizziness, Drachman & Hart (1972) diagnosed vestibular problems in 38%, hyperventilation in 23% and other psychiatric problems in 9%. Thus, a large proportion of the cases were considered "psychogenic." The most common vestibular abnormality was benign paroxysmal positional vertigo. This condition is characterized by sudden onset of vertigo triggered by head rotation or sometimes linear acceleration. Driving a car is a situation characterized by frequent accelerations and decelerations, and an episode of vertigo might be triggered by this activity. Jogging, with its upward and downward accelerations, may also induce an episode (Epley, 1980). There usually is a latency of 5 sec between the triggering event and the vertigo, and the whole episode lasts about 30 sec.

In a recently completed study, we subjected 8 patients with panic disorder and 13 patients with agoraphobia with panic to a battery of vestibular and audiological tests (Jacob, Moller, Turner, & Wall, 1983). The patients all had sensations of dizziness, lightheadedness, or vertigo during their panic attacks. The results indicated that there was significant vestibular dysfunction in 14 of the 21 cases (6 of the 8 panic disorder patients). Seven of the patients with vestibular abnormalities had findings consistent with a peripheral vestibular lesion (i.e., an abnormality in the vestibular organ itself), and seven had findings which did not permit localization of the abnormality (i.e., the abnormality could be either in the vestibular organ or in the nervous system). One of the patients with peripheral vestibular lesions had benign paroxsysmal positional nystagmus. Because abnormalities in vestibular functioning also has been demonstrated in schizophrenics, the significance of the vestibular abnormalities in our panic patients is as yet unclear. In none of the patients did we discover significant neurological disorders such as eighth nerve or brain tumors. Nevertheless, input from a disordered vestibular system, resulting in unfamiliar and potentially frightening sensations, could provide the initial stimulus for the escalating fear cycle which characterizes panic (see "A Clinical Model for Panic" below).

Mitral-Valve Prolapse and Panic

Barlow and Pocock (1975) and Wooley (1976) pointed out the similarities between the symptoms of Da Costa's Syndrome (neurocirculatory asthenia) and those of a cardiac condition (the mitral-valve prolapse, MVP) that had gained increasing recognition during the preceding decade. This syndrome is known under a number of different names such as "billowing mitral-valve syndrome" or "systolic click, late systolic murmur" syndrome. The basic abnormality is an oversized mitral valve, which balloons into the right atrium during the latter part of cardiac systole.

Since the publications by Barlow and Pocock (1975) and Wooley (1976), considerable interest has been focused on the association between MVP and both anxiety and panic. Thus, Pariser, Pinta, and Jones (1978) reported a case of a 25-year-old woman with MVP, who fulfilled the Feighner diagnostic criteria for anxiety neurosis. Later, Pariser, Jones, Pinta, Young, and Fontana (1979) diagnosed MVP in six of 17 (35%) of patients with a chief complaint of panic episodes. In a controlled study, Kantor, Zitrin, and Zeldis (1980) evaluated 24 agoraphobic women selected specifically because palpitations were a prominent feature in their panic episodes. The findings were compared to those of 23 age-matched female hospital employees. Eight of the agoraphobic patients (32%) had echocardiograms diagnostic of MVP, compared to two (9%) of the controls. Similarly, Venkatesh, Pauls, Crowe, Noyes, Van Valkenburg, Martins, and Kerber (1980) reported echocardiographically verified MVP in 8 of 21 (38%) patients diagnosed as anxiety neurotics with panic, compared to 2 of 20 controls. Thus, these four studies have consistently indicated that a remarkably high proportion of patients with anxiety or panic might have mitral valve prolapse. However, a recent series with agoraphobics at this institution failed to confirm these high prevalence figures (Mavissakalian, 1982). In this latter study, the prevalence of MVP among agoraphobics was no higher than in the general population. Perhaps differences in the selection of patients can account for these conflicting data. Further studies by other investigators are needed to replicate the initial findings.

Regardless of the final status of MVP in panic disorder, a therapist dealing with anxiety disorders should be familiar with this condition (if only because many of the patients will be). It is important to know that MVP is a common finding in nonsymptomatic young adults. For example, Markiewicz, Stoner, London, Hunt, and Popp (1976) found echocardiographic findings consistent with MVP in 21 of 100 healthy young females. In 10 of these, there were also positive phonocardiographic findings, resulting in a prevalence of MVP (as measured by the convergence of these two tests) of 10%. Subjects with MVP did not differ significantly from those without MVP with regard to the presence of cardiac symptoms such as chest pain or palpitations. More recently, Darsee, Mikolich, Nicoloff, and Lesser (1979) studied 101 healthy young men. Seven percent had echocardiographic and auscultatory findings consistent with MVP. Only two of these had cardiac symptoms.

Thus, MVP is a common abnormality in healthy individuals. Most persons with this condition will not have any cardiac symptoms. This is in marked contrast with patients who are *referred* for cardiological evaluation. In such cases, symptoms such as palpitations, stabbing chest pains, and general "nervousness" are frequently described. In addition, complications such as bacterial endocarditis, sudden death, and cerebral ischemic events have been reported (Barlow & Pocock, 1975; Barnett, Boughner, Taylor, Cooper, Kostuk, & Nichol, 1980; Cheitlin & Byrd, 1981; Devereux, Perloff, Reichek, & Josephson, 1976).

The treatment for management of patients with MVP is still a matter of controversy. Some cardiologists recommend prophylactic antibiotic treatment when performing surgical procedures such as dental extractions or gynecological operations. This is done to prevent bacterial endocarditis. In addition, 24-hour electrocardiographic monitoring may be indicated in symptomatic cases to detect cardiac arrhythmias. On the other hand, the increased awareness and pursuit of the diagnosis of MVP may have as a major complication an increased incidence of "cardiac neurosis" (Cheitlin & Byrd, 1981; Forrest, 1981). The final answer as to how aggressively one should pursue the diagnosis and treatment of MVP will have to await further research.

BEHAVIORAL TREATMENT OF PANIC

A Clinical Model for Panic

We have not been able to find a single empirical study in which behavior therapy was applied specifically to the problem of panic. Perhaps one reason for this is that the results have not been encouraging. Marks (1969) listed only pharmacological treatments in his section on the treatment of panic. Gelder (1969) expressed the view that behavior therapy cannot be used unless situational elements can be identified as eliciting the anxiety attacks. These cases, however, typically also display avoidance behaviors and are thus diagnosed as agoraphobias.

In some cases, "cognitive" stimuli have been identified (Beck, Laude, & Bohnert, 1974). A logical approach would be to try flooding, implosion or desensitization with such cognitive stimuli. However, no empirical study employing this approach to panic disorders has come to our awareness.

Internal stimuli may also be involved in producing the panic attacks (Goldstein & Chambless, 1978; Marks, 1970; Weeks, 1977). Such stimuli include palpitations, dizziness, and sensations of choking. The reader will recognize these sensations as being *consequences* of anxiety as well. Thus, because the consequences of anxiety can serve as elicitors of anxiety, a vicious "fear of fear" cycle can be established, in which a spiraling increase in fear arousal ultimately results in a full-blown panic attack (Lader & Mathews, 1968). This "fear of fear" model of panic, which is depicted in Figure 1, has been postulated by many different authors, such as Evans (1972), Frankl (1975), Goldstein and Chambless (1980), Lewis (1954), Malleson (1959) and Weeks (1977).

A further expansion of the fear-of-fear model of panic will serve as a heuristic device both to guide our search for effective methods and to explain the close association between panic disorder and agoraphobia. The basic fear-of-fear spiral can be imbedded in a multitude of secondary inputs as depicted in Figure 2. Foremost among these is the association to external stimuli. If a panic attack occurred in a certain situation, similar situations will cause anticipatory anxiety, which then can set off another panic attack. Research on the "incubation effect" (Eysenck, 1968) indicates that such conditioning can occur even after a single panic episode. The individual then learns to escape or avoid these fear-producing situations, resulting in lack of extinction and reinforcement through aversion relief, thus creating the well-known vicious cycle of avoidance in agoraphobia.

The anticipatory anxiety can also result in increased vigilance, self-monitoring and self-preoccupation. As pointed out by Sarason (1979), *self-preoccupation,* which always occurs at the expense of task orientation, is a common response to overwhelming stress. Self-preoccupation is a problem because in addition to being incompatible with task-oriented behavior, it will make the patient more aware of, or "sensitized" to, fear-producing external or internal stimuli. Internal sensations, which most people probably would not have noticed, may assume threatening significance as a result of this constant self-monitoring activity.

The fear-of-fear spiral can be entered at various points. In certain cases, no doubt, medical conditions, such as benign positional vertigo, hypoglycemia, or cardiac arrhythmia can initiate a panic response. The fear can also be initiated by traumatic events or, more commonly, by current conflicts (Goldstein & Chambless, 1978). In our experience, the common denominator of such conflict seems to be either the threat of losing a source of security or the wish to

Figure 1. Basic "fear-to-fear" positive feedback loop.

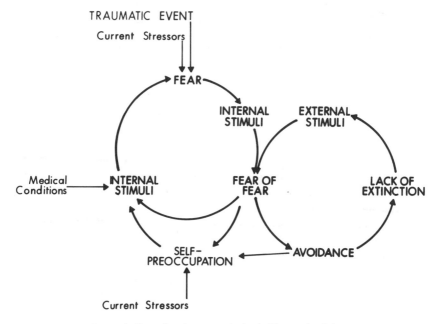

Figure 2. Secondary inputs to the basic "fear-to-fear" loop.

get out of an undesirable commitment. In many of the cases we have seen, for example, we have found issues around pregnancy seeming to elicit panic. One woman had three different episodes of recurrent panic attacks, separated by a few years. Each one of these episodes had been preceded by an unwanted pregnancy. Another male patient came to our clinic in an acute state of panic when he first found out that his wife was pregnant. Thereafter, he was not seen again until shortly after the birth of the child, when he presented with a second series of panic attacks. Both times he insisted that he was suffering from a medical condition and refused to acknowledge any significant association between the panic and the pregnancy or birth of the child.

From this model of panic, several hypotheses can be derived as to what type of treatment might be useful.

1. Treatment Needs to Attend to the Fear of Internal Stimuli. Drug treatment with antidepressant medication is claimed to have a direct effect on the primary panic loop (Zitrin, Klein, & Woerner, 1980). Just as exposure to external stimuli has been found to be a key component in the behavioral treatment of phobias, behavioral treatment of panic probably needs to include controlled exposure to the internal stimuli of anxiety. An interesting biobehavioral approach currently under investigation is desensitization from panic stimuli induced by sodium lactate (Feldman, 1980). Hyperventilation can also be employed in this fashion (Compernolle, Hoogduin, & Joele, 1979).

2. *A Positive Therapeutic Rationale Is Necessary*. To treat panic behaviorally, mere exposure to internal stimuli may not be sufficient. Most behavioral or psychological treatments include the induction of expectations for improvement. For example, Leitenberg, Agras, Barlow, and Oliveau (1969) found that treatment of snake phobics with systematic desensitization was ineffective when the subjects believed that they were merely participating in an assessment procedure rather than a treatment. Hoehn-Saric, Frank, Imber, Nash, Stone, and Battle (1964) found that a pretreatment role-induction interview, which included an induction of a "realistic expectation" for improvement, resulted in superior results for psychotherapy. Thus, if exposure to anxiety stimuli is necessary for treating panic, the therapeutic experience of these sensations should be explained as signifying a positive event which contributes to the ultimate success of treatment.

3. *Current Conflicts May Interfere with Treatment*. If there is currently an incomprehensible or insoluble conflict, the panic may be harder to treat, as the panic loop will be reactivated again and again. Difficulty in discriminating what type of aversive reinforcement contingency might be in effect has been found to significantly increase autonomic arousal in monkeys (Kimmel & Brennan, 1981). On the other hand, "spontaneous" resolution of the conflict might prevent a panic condition from becoming chronic. This is probably why many episodes of panic attacks are self-limiting. Unfortunately, the self-preoccupation resulting from the patients' continued struggle with panic will make them less likely to engage in task-oriented behavior necessary for solving the conflict. In other cases, improvement may lead to new problems, particularly in the patient's family relationship. For example, humans as well as monkeys can be led to increase their autonomic arousal if this increase is conducive to avoidance of aversive consequences (Kimmel & Brennan, 1981). As suggested by Fry (1962) and demonstrated by Hafner (1977), improvement in agoraphobia can lead to an increase in psychological distress, such as jealousy, *in the spouse*. In a similar way, operant reinforcement of panic may occur as a result of problems within the family system.

4. *"Relationship" Factors May Be an Important Variable in Treatment*. The therapist may constitute a new source of security and attachment for the patient, thus neutralizing a current conflict. This might be the reason why we sometimes see "dramatic" responses after simple reassurance or drug therapy. In the latter case, the improvement may occur even before one would expect the drug to take effect. For a more complete review of "relationship" factors in the treatment of conditions akin to panic such as agoraphobia and school phobia, the reader is referred to a review by Andrews (1966).

Empirical Studies

As mentioned earlier, the empirical literature on behavioral treatment of panic has focused on agoraphobia. We might ask, then, how does behavioral treatment affect panic in agoraphobia? One would hope the answer to this question might be generalizable to panic disorder. Most of the studies of behavioral treatment of agoraphobia have included measurements on a multitude of variables, such as ratings of phobic anxiety, phobic avoidance, psychophysiological measurements and questionnaire data (Agras & Jacob, 1981). Explicit ratings of panic were reported in only a minority. These studies are listed in Tables 3 and 4. For inclusion in these tables, the study also had to meet the methodological requirement of being a prospective study of groups of patients rather than single subjects.

Hypnosis, Imaginary Desensitization and Cognitive Behavior Modification

From our model of panic, one would expect these procedures to be ineffective in the treatment of panic, because they typically do not involve exposure to internal stimuli. Hypnosis and desensitization were compared by Marks, Gelder, and Edwards (1968). Neither treatment would produce changes in "depersonalization." However, the level of this variable was low even before treatment, so it is unlikely that panic episodes were common among the patients of this study.

Desensitization was also one of the treatments in a study by Gelder, Bancroft, Gath, Johnston, Mathews, and Shaw (1973). Using a randomized factorial design, they treated 18 agoraphobics and 18 other phobic patients with either flooding, desensitization or a control treatment called associative psychotherapy. Neither treatment resulted in a reduction of panic surpassing that of the control treatment. Presence of panic attacks was found to signify poor prognosis for desensitization. Marks, Boulougouris, and Marset (1971) used a crossover design to compare desensitization with flooding and found a correlation of $-.54$ between presence of panic attacks before treatment and improvement of main phobia after desensitization. In contrast, there was a moderately positive correlation with the outcome of flooding.

Systematic desensitization may actually increase the frequency of panic attacks. Latimer (1977) reported a case in which this occurred. Instead of getting better, the patient became more aware of stimuli that could induce panic. This problem was overcome by pairing the anxiety-producing scenes with inhalation of a carbon-dioxide mixture. The effects of this mixture is to produce an increase in heart rate and breathing rate, thereby producing sensations of palpitations and breathlessness. One might speculate that some of the internal stimuli of panic were replicated with this procedure. The treatment must have resulted in exposure to these internal stimuli. Thus, this report appears to confirm our hypothesis that exposure to internal stimuli is a necessary component for the treatment of panic.

The effect of cognitive behavior modification was assessed in one study involving a crossover comparison with prolonged exposure (Emmelkamp, Kuipers, & Eggeraat, 1978). The cognitive treatment included relabeling the situation as not "really" anxiety producing, pinpointing irrational beliefs, and the

Table 3. Behavioral Treatment of Panic in Agorophobia

Study	Population and problem	Treatment methods	Measures of panic	Results on panic measures
1. Emmelkamp & Wessels, 1975	23 agoraphobics Mean age: 34.2 years Mean duration of illness: 7.3 years 1 male, 22 females	A. Prolonged exposure *in vivo* and self-observation B. Imaginal flooding and self-observation C. Combined flooding (imaginal and *in vivo*) and self-observation	Rating on "panic" on a 0–8-point scale by therapist, independent observer	B > C = A Only patients treated with imaginal flooding plus self-observation showed significant decreases in panic ratings, but result confounded with pretreatment differences
2. Everaerd, Rijken, & Emmelkamp, 1973	14 agoraphobics Mean age: unspecified (range = 31–62 years) Mean duration of illness: unspecified (range = 2–23 years) 2 males, 12 females	A. Flooding (imaginal + *in vivo*) followed by successive approximation B. Successive approximation followed by flooding (imaginal + *in vivo*)	Ratings of "depersonalization" and "irreality" on a 1–5-point scale by independent assessor	No significant changes occurred on ratings of depersonalization or unreality by the external judge
3. Gelder, Bancroft, Gath *et al.*, 1973	18 agoraphobics 9 social phobics 6 specific phobics 3 animal phobics Mean age: 35 years Mean duration of illness: 13 years 14 males, 22 females	A. Flooding (imaginal followed by *in vivo*) B. Desensitization (imaginal followed by *in vivo*) C. Nonspecific imagery control	Ratings of panic and depersonalization on a 1–5-point scale by psychiatric assessor	A = B = C No significant differences were reported on panic measures between the three treatments
4. Marks, Boulougouris, & Marset, 1971	9 agoraphobics, 4 with panic attacks 7 specific phobics Mean age: 33.5 years Mean duration of illness: 11.5 years 7 males, 9 females	A. Desensitization followed by imaginal flooding B. Flooding (imaginal) followed by desensitization (imaginal)	Ratings of panic attacks and feelings of depersonalization on a 1–5-point scale by patient, therapist, and independent medical assessor	Results on panic not reported. Panic attacks correlated −.54 with outcome to desensitization and +.32 with outcome to flooding

Study	Sample	Treatment	Measures	Results
5. Marks, Gelder, & Edwards, 1968	12 agoraphobics 8 social phobics 8 specific phobics	A. Desensitization (followed by hypnosis) B. Hypnosis (followed by desensitization)	Ratings of depersonalization (1–5) by patient, therapist, independent assessor	No change as a result of either treatment, but pretreatment ratings very low (1.2 and 1.3)
6. Stern & Marks, 1973	13 agoraphobics 3 travel phobics	A. Tape-recorded brief imaginal flooding followed by brief *in vivo* flooding B. Tape-recorded brief imaginal flooding followed by prolonged *in vivo* flooding C. Tape-recorded prolonged imaginal flooding followed by brief *in vivo* flooding D. Tape-recorded prolonged imaginal flooding followed by prolonged *in vivo* flooding	Panic ratings by assessor and patient on a 0–8-point scale. Free flooding anxiety correlated .94 with panic attacks	Significant pooled treatment effect on panic, but panic ratings not broken down according to treatment
7. Watson & Marks, 1971	10 agoraphobics 6 specific phobics Mean age: 30.3 years Mean duration of illness: 12.3 years Males, females: unspecified	A. Imaginal flooding with relevant phobic stimuli followed by imaginal flooding with normal (irrelevant) fear stimuli B. Imaginal flooding with irrelevant (normal) fear stimuli, followed by imaginal flooding with relevant phobic stimuli	Ratings of panic attacks and feelings of depersonalization on a 0–8-point scale by patient, therapist, and independent assessor	A > B Only relevant imaginal flooding produced significant improvement of panic attacks according to therapist and assessor ratings

Table 4. Pharmacological and Behavioral Treatment of Panic Disorder

Study	Population and Problem	Treatment Methods	Measures of Panic	Outcome	Follow-Up
1. Hafner & Marks, 1976	53 agoraphobic patients Mean age: 36 years Mean duration of illness: 9 years 10 males, 43 females	A. Group *in vivo* exposure plus placebo B. Group *in vivo* exposure plus waning diazepam C. Group *in vivo* exposure plus peak diazepam D. Individual *in vivo* exposure, placebo, plus high anxiety arousal E. Individual *in vivo* exposure, placebo, plus low anxiety arousal	0–8 rating scale for panic completed by patients and blind assessor (combined results reported)	A = B > C in reducing panic attacks at 6 months' follow-up D = E. No significant difference between patients receiving individual treatment	3–6 months Patients tended to maintain treatment gains
2. Hafner & Milton, 1977	25 agoraphobic patients Mean age: 36.2 years Mean duration of illness: 8.1 years 4 males, 21 females	A. Group *in vivo* exposure plus waning propranolol (40 mg) B. Group *in vivo* exposure plus placebo	0–8 ratings of panic and "difficulty to cope with panic" compiled by patient	Week 1: A > B Week 2: B > A	4 Weeks Both groups coped more easily with panic
3. Zitrin, Klein, & Woerner, 1980	76 agoraphobic patients Mean age: 35.6 years Mean duration of illness: 8.6 years 76 females	A. Group exposure *in vivo* plus imipramine B. Group exposure *in vivo* plus placebo	Spontaneous panic scale Therapist, independent evaluator (1–7)	Both improved, but A > B. 1-point mean difference between the groups on panic ratings achieved statistical significance	6 months A. 27% relapsed B. 6% relapsed

use of positive self-statements. When given as the first treatment, cognitive restructuring was significantly *less* efficient than *in vivo* exposure and was not in itself associated with significant changes from pre- to posttreatment. While panic was not measured explicitly, a related variable, "anxious mood" did not change significantly even when the patients had undergone both treatments. Thus, cognitive therapy appears to be of limited value in agoraphobia with panic attacks. Recently, however, cognitive therapy involving positive self-statements was compared with negative self statements in patients with anxiety symptoms including panic, but not agoraphobia (Ramm, Marks, Yuksel, & Stern, 1982). The group receiving positive self-statements improved somewhat ($3.5 \rightarrow 2$ on a 0–8 scale) on frequency of panic ratings, but the difference between pre- and posttreatment ratings apparently was not statistically significant. However, the negative self-statement group became slightly worse ($3.8 \rightarrow 5.3$), resulting in a significant between-group difference after treatment. This difference did not maintain during follow-up at a statistically significant level. While this study appeared to show some effects of positive self-statements, at least compared to negative self-statements, it should be remembered that the overall conclusion was that neither treatment appeared to be particularly useful for anxiety states.

Imaginal Flooding

The results of imaginal flooding on panic have been conflicting but on the whole do not appear to be favorable. In the Gelder *et al.* (1973) study referred to in the previous section, neither flooding nor desensitization resulted in amelioration of panic. Similarly, Chambless, Foa, Groves, and Goldstein (1979), comparing flooding, Brevital-assisted flooding and attention placebo, found no difference in changes of panic between the three groups.

On the other hand, in the study by Marks *et al.* (1971), also referred to above, a moderate positive correlation between improvement in main phobia and presence of panic before treatment was found. However, no results were reported for changes in panic. Watson and Marks (1971) compared phobic stimuli with normally fear-producing cues in the flooding of 10 patients with agoraphobia and six patients with specific phobias, using a crossover design. Only flooding involving phobic stimuli resulted in statistically significant changes in the panic ratings, but the effects of the two treatments were surprisingly similar on most other variables. Because of the crossover design, the long-term effects of each of the treatments could not be evaluated. However, during follow-up 14 of the 16 patients required further treatment, indicating a poor long term result.

To summarize, the effects of imaginal flooding appear to be rather weak, and, when they are seen, only temporary. Flooding in the imagination also is considered insufficient for the treatment of other behaviors in agoraphobia, such as phobic avoidance. This has led most therapists to include *in vivo* exposure in their treatments.

In Vivo *Exposure*

In vivo exposure involves bringing the agoraphobic patients into the fear-producing situation. Because by definition there are no situations that are consistently fear-producing in patients with panic disorder, for reason of logistics alone the research on *in vivo* exposure with agoraphobics may be less generalizable to panic disorder than the research on procedures that rely on imaginary stimuli.

In vivo exposure has shown some promise in the treatment of panic, but again the results are conflicting. Everaerd, Rijken, and Emmelkamp (1973) found no significant changes in ratings of depersonalization and unreality after a combination of flooding and successive approximation. However, the pretreatment levels on this variable were rather low (1.7 and 2.2 on a 0–8 scale).

The results obtained by Stern and Marks (1973) were more encouraging. By comparing the effect of four sessions of brief versus prolonged imaginal flooding followed by brief or prolonged *in vivo* exposure, they found a significant pooled treatment effect on panic ratings. These declined from 2.0 to .9 (0–8 scale). Prolonged exposure was superior to brief exposure on a composite outcome measure, although the effect of the separate treatments on panic was not reported.

Can *in vivo* exposure alone, without imaginal procedures, result in improvement? Emmelkamp and Wessels (1975) compared the effects of self-observation preceded by four sessions of (a) prolonged exposure *in vivo,* (b) imaginal flooding, and (c) a combination of the two. Thus, the group receiving prolonged exposure *in vivo* followed by self-observation received two different exposure treatments without imaginary components. This group showed a decline in panic from 1.0 to 0 (0–8 scale), a change of no statistical significance. In contrast, the group that had begun with imaginal flooding showed a significant change from 3.7 to 1.2. However, the difference in treatment effects is confounded with the unequal pretreatment levels of panic and a possible "floor effect." The third group, beginning with a combination treatment, showed a decline from 1.0 to 0, a change that again was not statistically significant.

Exposure treatment can also be done in groups. This was done and found moderately effective on panic in a study by Zitrin, Klein, and Woerner (1980) and Hafner and Marks (1976). The former study, because it primarily involved drug treatment, will be described in the next section. In the Hafner and Marks (1976) study, group exposure coupled with placebo was found to be slightly superior to individual exposure plus placebo, although the difference apparently was of no statistical significance for panic.

Within the individual *in vivo* exposure condition of the Hafner and Marks (1976) study, some patients were subjected to high anxiety, which the therapist provoked not only by being minimally reassuring but by actively conjuring up catastrophic fantasies, and other patients were subjected to only low anxiety, because the therapist was reassuring. If our hypothesis is correct that exposure to anxiety stimuli is necessary for treating panic, the high-anxiety condition should be associated with a greater reduction in panic. Yet no difference was found between the two conditions on any of the variables. This part of the study may be criticized, however, for the low number of subjects (6 per anxiety condition) and the possibility that the high-anxiety condition might have included elements of social reinforcement for high-anxiety behaviors. If the patients became so anxious as to be close to leaving the situation, the therapists were instructed to reassure them in order to keep them from leaving. Moreover, as stated in our general principles section, the rationale for the exposure to the bodily sensation of anxiety should include a positive connotation for the anxiety experience. It is not clear whether such a rationale was given. If it was, it would seem incompatible with the simultaneous administration of placebo.

To summarize, it appears that *in vivo* exposure techniques are moderately effective on panic in agoraphobia, but the results are contradictory. This may be related to differences in pretreatment level of panic and incomplete documentation of the panic variable. Furthermore, exposure treatments typically focus on the external cues that might induce anxiety. If an exposure treatment could be designed that involved exposure specifically to the internal stimuli of anxiety, one would, according to our model of panic expect a higher rate of success.

Combinations of Pharmacological and Behavioral Treatment

Antidepressants. Antidepressants add significantly to the treatment of agoraphobia with panic attacks. Klein and Fink (1962), in an informal study, reported that imipramine alone resulted in reduction of panic, but the avoidance behaviors and anticipatory anxiety remained and had to be treated with "persuasion, direction and social support." In a more formal study, Lipsedge, Hajioff, Huggins, Napier, Pearce, Pike, and Rich (1973) compared the effect of iproniazide (a monoamine oxidase inhibitor) or placebo within each of methohexitone-assisted systematic desensitization, imaginal desensitization or relaxation, using a 3 × 2 factorial design. Consistent with the study by Klein (1962), there was a significant main effect of iproniazide in improving clinician-rated phobic anxiety, but there was no effect of the drug on avoidance behaviors.

Zitrin *et al.* (1980), referred to in the previous section, compared group *in vivo* desensitization combined with placebo medication to *in vivo* desensitization combined with imipramine. Panic measures included (a) a 1–7 spontaneous panic scale rated by the therapist and an independent evaluator, and (b) an acute panic inventory completed by the patients. Unfortunately, the results on the inventory were not reported. In the placebo group, independent evaluator ratings showed a significant improvement, with 23% showing marked improvement, 18% moderate improvement, and 59% showing minimal or no improvement. The imipramine group did better: 78% marked improvement, 4% moderate improvement, and only 18% minimal or no improvement. Thus, group exposure without imipramine did only moderately well and left a significant number of patients only minimally improved, or not improved at all. However, the follow-up data were less favorable for the imipramine group. Twenty-seven percent of the patients that had improved with imipramine relapsed, compared to 6% of the patients that had improved with placebo. This difference in relapse rate, however, was not statistically significant.

Thus, the immediate effect of the combination of imipramine plus *in vivo* exposure was superior to exposure alone. However, one should not prematurely designate this treatment as the treatment of choice for agoraphobia with panic. The use of a pharmacologically inert pill placebo in the exposure condition may have introduced an element of uncertainty and countertherapeutic expectation, which are not present in typical clinical behavioral treatment programs. This might have adversely affected the outcome for the placebo exposure group. A recent methodological review (Hollon & DuRubeis, 1981) concurs that the use of combinations of behavioral therapy with pill placebo are more problematic than was hitherto believed. In addition, long-term results indicated that maintenance for the exposure group was superior to the drug-only group, albeit not statistically significant.

Minor Tranquilizers. Minor tranquilizers have been employed acutely to facilitate *in vivo* exposure, but the evidence regarding their benefit is conflicting. On the one hand, McCormick (1973) claims that some patients simply would not have complied with exposure treatment had it not been for the drug. On the other hand, the use of the drug may take away the opportunity of exposure to internal stimuli. Hafner and Marks (1976), referred to earlier, compared group exposure combined with either placebo, waning diazepam, or peak diazepam. The rationale behind the waning diazepam treatment was that this would be specifically geared towards anticipatory anxiety, whereas peak diazepam would reduce anxiety symptoms during exposure itself. During treatment, panic was reduced in all three groups. However, at 6 months' follow-up, the peak diazepam group showed a partial relapse in panic. Chambless *et al.* (1979), in a study described briefly in the section on flooding, compared the following three treatments: (a) imaginal flooding without drugs and without *in vivo* exposure, (b) flooding plus periodic intravenous injections of methohexitone sodium, and (c) attention control (psychotherapy plus progressive relaxation). The nondrug flooding group improved significantly more than the other two groups on fear and avoidance of phobic situations. Both flooding groups improved on behavioral task. However, as the reader will remember, neither of the flooding treatments resulted in improvement of panic.

Propranolol. Freedman *et al.* (1981) recommends beta blockers such as propanolol for patients with anxiety characterized by a high degree of somatic symptoms and a comparatively low intensity of cognitive symptoms. Hafner and Milton (1977) compared waning propranolol with placebo during group exposure, following the same basic design as Hafner and Marks (1976). Propanolol was dispensed at 10:45 a.m. and the exposure exercises took place in the afternoon. Measures on panic and other variables were obtained during the exposure exercise. During exposure, severity of panic showed a decreasing trend for the placebo group but an increasing trend for the propranolol group. This increase was attributed to the waning propranolol effect during the last hour of exposure. Thus, the propranolol-treated group did receive exposure to internal stimuli that was even higher than the placebo-treated group, but because the exposure occurred during the end of a treatment session, sensitization, rather than habituation, might have taken place. Consistent with this, the placebo group became progressively more "cheerful" in the morning before the next exposure session, whereas the propranolol group became less cheerful and more tense and anxious. At posttreatment and at follow-up, the propranolol group reported fewer panic attacks during the first week, but had more severe panic attacks the second week. By the 4th week, the differences between the groups were no longer significant. Thus, this study on propranolol yielded inconclusive results on the panic measure. However, the placebo group was superior on the following variables: time spent traveling alone one and four weeks after treatment, and the general symptom scale of the Fear Survey Schedule 3 months after treatment.

To summarize, studies involving drugs offer an opportunity to experimentally manipulate internal fear stimuli. According to our hypothesis, exposure to such stimuli should facilitate treatment of panic. If this is true, most drug treatments, while temporarily effective, should show poor long-term results after the drug is discontinued. In addition, if one considers attribution theory, the same type of prediction would be made. If the patient attributes the improvement to the drugs, the gains with the treatment might not be maintained after discontinuation of the drug (cf. Davison & Valins, 1969). The literature shows some trends in this direction, but studies are needed in order to address this question specifically. In our experience, many patients, once they have found the drug helpful, are quite resistant to the very idea of discontinuing medication.

Clinical Approaches

We will devote some attention to psychological approaches that seem to be promising, according to our model of panic, but for which the empirical evidence is less established. These approaches include relaxation and breathing exercises, the self-help treatment designed by Clara Weeks, and paradoxical procedures.

Before considering these approaches, however, it should be emphasized that these treatments are meant to be applied only in cases of chronically recurring panic attacks. Not all patients who present with a first episode of panic will develop this chronic picture (Walker, 1959). Thus, initiating an extended psychological or pharmacological program would be premature when the patients have only a short history of panic attacks (less than 2 months). From a therapeutic viewpoint, it is useful to regard these transient episodes as constituting an appropriate reaction to a crisis in the patient's life, whether of an interpersonal or financial/vocational nature. This will focus the patient's attention onto the external situation and encourage task-oriented behavior, rather than self-preoccupation.

If these acute cases come to a therapist's attention, the following strategies may be useful. First of all, the patient's complaints should be taken seriously. Thus, he should be sent for a complete medical evaluation if the therapist is not a medical practitioner. In conjunction with the medical evaluation, an exploration should be made of the current life situation of the patients. Often one will find issues such as threatening loss of job, financial problems, or conflicts in the patient's personal life. We have found it useful to explore these issues at great length, ending in an overall acknowledgement of the extreme difficulty of the patient's situation, and how understandable it is that the patient should react with extreme anxiety. The positive accomplishments in the patient's coping with this situation should be highlighted. A useful way of doing this is to ask the patient, for example:

From what you are telling us, this indeed seems to be a very difficult and frightening situation. In fact, I find it remarkable how you have been able to hold things together this long. Tell me, how come we did not see you a month ago; how were you able to cope with it this long?

Finally, the patient should be informed that panic episodes of this type are often temporary and can be expected to diminish once the current stressful situation is resolved.

Breathing Exercises, Relaxation, and Biofeedback

Breathing exercises emphasizing slow abdominal breathing have been suggested for the treatment of the hyperventilation syndrome (Hill, 1979; Lum 1976; Waites, 1978). This would make sense from a physiological point of view, because the decrease of pulmonary ventilation should correct the hypocapnia and alkalosis that had been induced by hyperventilation. Moreover, slow, paced breathing has been found to reduce arousal, as evidenced by a reduced skin-resistance response during anticipation and immediate threat of electric shock (McCaul, Solomon, & Holmes, 1979). This effect was independent of the expectation whether or not the breathing procedure was a treatment to reduce stress.

The patient should be instructed to breathe through the nose, thereby increasing dead-space ventilation, and to breathe passively and not too deeply with a short pause after each exhalation. McCaul *et al.* (1979) employed a breathing rate that was half the normal rate, but initially this might be too slow for panic patients. Abdominal breathing can be taught by having the patients put one hand on the chest and one on the upper abdomen, and instructing them to breathe in a way such that the abdominal hand will move out during inspiration and in during expiration, while movements of the thoracic hand are minimal. Using breathing exercises in conjunction with relaxation with a large group of hyperventilators, Lum (1976) claimed an improvement rate of 70% becoming completely asymptomatic, and a further 25% improving considerably. However, many of these patients were "chronic" hyperventilators and probably would not be diagnosed as having panic disorder.

A further variation of breathing modification is rebreathing into a paper bag. The rationale for this is that by reinhaling the exhaled carbon-dioxide from the paper bag, the biochemical changes of hyperventilation will be corrected. A waxed paper bag has been found optimal in this regard (Riley, 1974). However, Compernolle, Hoogduin, and Joele (1979) claim this technique to be useful only after the symptoms of hyperventilation had been induced during a hyperventilation test. This treatment program will be described later.

Relaxation and biofeedback-assisted relaxation have been found useful for chronic, generalized anxiety in some cases. Raskin, Johnson, and Rodestvedt (1973) reported that four of ten cases showed moderate to marked improvement after biofeedback-assisted relaxation and daily home practice of relaxation. However, only one of these showed a "marked" effect on anxiety. Girodo (1974) tried meditation with nine anxiety-neurotic patients. Five showed a marked reduction of anxiety after eight sessions. The remaining four needed additional treatment with flooding. The patients who improved with relaxation tended to be those whose anxiety was of more recent origin. Townsend, House, and Addario (1975) found that the effect of four weeks of intensive biofeedback training and practice of relaxation resulted in a significantly greater improvement with anxious inpatients than did group therapy. Actually, however, only four of the thirteen patients treated with biofeedback-assisted relaxation improved.

A number of studies have compared relaxation or mediation with biofeedback-assisted relaxation. Raskin, Bali, and Peeke (1980) compared EMG feedback-assisted relaxation, progressive muscular relaxation and transcendental meditation in volunteers who qualified for a diagnosis of anxiety neurosis. All treatments resulted in significant improvements in anxiety symptoms as well as scores on the Taylor Manifest Anxiety Scale. Leboeuf and Lodge (1980) compared EMG feedback and progressive muscular relaxation on chronically anxious outpatients. There was no difference in the results of these treatments. Posttreatment ratings by the referring psychiatrists indicated that none of the 26 patients showed "marked" improvement, five showed "moderate" improvement, 11 had only "slight" improvement, 9 did not change, and 1 became slightly worse. Finally, Lavallee, Lamontagne, Pinard, Annable, and Tetreault (1977) compared the effect of EMG feedback versus no feedback, crossed with diazepam versus placebo, in a 2 × 2 factorial design with 40 subjects. The no-feedback groups received sessions corresponding to the biofeedback sessions, in which they were asked to relax without having been taught any specific techniques. Both the biofeedback–diazepam combination and each of the treatments separately resulted in significant reductions of anxiety, as measured by the Hamilton Anxiety Rating Scale. However, at 3 months' follow-up, only the feedback only group had maintained the treatment gains, and at 6 months, none of these three groups maintained their gains. The results for the placebo/no-feedback group were particularly surprising. Immediately after treatment, there was a nonsignificant decline, but there was a further decline during follow-up which became statistically significant. No statistical between-group comparisons were reported, but inspecting the graphs of the data leads us to believe that none of the treatments was more effective than the placebo/no-feedback condition. Indeed, at 6 months' follow-up, this latter group had the lowest anxiety scores.

It appears from these studies that relaxation or biofeedback-assisted relaxation is only moderately effective with chronic anxiety. Only one study has evaluated whether panic attacks improved with these procedures. This study compared progressive muscular relaxation with EMG feedback-assisted relaxation in 28 in- or outpatients diagnosed as anxiety neurotics. Half of these patients also had panic attacks. The results were remarkable in that all of the seven panic patients who received biofeedback and four of the seven panic patients who received progressive muscular relaxation were rated as improved. For the patients without panic, the corresponding figures were five of seven and two of seven, respectively. No statistical analysis was performed to see if these differences were significant. This study needs to be replicated with a larger sample size and more refined measurement of outcome. For example, "improvement" was not subdivided into catagories, so we do not know whether these patients improved "markedly" or only "slightly." Moreover, panic attacks were not specifically monitored. Finally, if this result is seen in the light of the study by Walker (1959) referred to earlier, the need for a control group becomes readily apparent.

To summarize, extrapolating from research on treatment of hyperventilation syndrome and anxiety neurosis, it appears that breathing exercises, relaxation and/or biofeedback-assisted relaxation may have some use as an adjunct treatment for panic disorder. This would be consistent with our model of panic and our speculations regarding the necessary conditions for treating it. What all these techniques appear to have in common is the patient is left alone to focus on bodily sensations without distraction, in a therapeutic framework. However, these techniques probably need to be integrated into a more comprehensive treatment program to be truly effective with full-blown panic disorder.

The Self-Help Approach of Clara Weeks

With a self-help program involving books, phonograph recordings and correspondence, Weeks (1977) claims a general success rate of 73% in agoraphobic patients 14 to 29 years old, 67% in patients 30 to 39 years old, 55% for patients 40 to 49 years old, and 49% for patients older than 50. Weeks is critical of relying exclusively on "exposure" treatment for agoraphobia, because of the lack of attention given to internal fear stimuli and panic. A single panic attack can undo the effects of months of carefully orchestrated exposure exercises. Instead of focusing exclusively on the avoidance aspect of agoraphobia, care is taken to teach the patient how to cope with the symptoms of panic.

Before beginning treatment, an explanation is given about the mechanism of "sensitization" in maintaining a vicious fear cycle. Sensitization is essentially equivalent to the fear-of-fear and self-preoccupation phenomena outlined in our model. The patients are also told that they cannot expect to conquer the "first fear," the first flash of anxiety that will usually set off the full-blown panic attack. This is important, because the patients typically expect never again to have a panic attack after successful treatment, an expectation that will set them up for a relapse when they experience their first panic sensation after treatment.

The patients are further told that while they will never have a completely anxiety-free existence, they can counteract the development of full-blown panic attacks by engaging in certain coping strategies. In addition, the mechanisms of various physical symptoms as they relate to anxiety are carefully explained so as to convince the patient that the symptoms do not signify physical danger. Current conflicts are also explored to some extent, provided that they are believed to contribute to the maintenance of the current panic situation, but Weeks does not engage in extensive search for hidden causes.

The coping strategies Weeks teaches are essentially geared toward preventing anticipatory anxiety and self-preoccupation. The program involves the following four steps: facing, accepting, floating, and letting time pass.

Facing involves exposure to the feared internal or external stimuli, the opposite of avoidance or escape. This will prevent the sensitization that will normally occur if the patient escaped the situation prematurely. Facing involved both physically remaining at the place of panic and avoiding the use of methods such as distraction to mentally retreat from the internal sensations of panic.

Accepting implies a resigned attitude aimed at preventing the patient from fighting the panic. The patients should not fight incipient panic attacks by reassuring themselves with self-statements such as "I am not going to let this panic overwhelm me," because by doing so, they are essentially increasing their involvement and self-preoccupation. Accepting also means resigning oneself to the idea of always having to cope with anxiety even after successful treatment.

Floating tells the patient how to go about accepting the panic when it occurs. It implies moving forward with the panic and remaining open to all the feelings and sensations that are occurring, without resisting or impatiently trying to terminate the episode. Floating lends itself to catchy self-suggestions that the patients can use during panic attack itself: "Float, Don't Fight" (Weeks, 1977) or "Float With the Fear" (Spiegel & Spiegel, 1978, tape recording accompanying the book).

Finally, *letting time pass* suggests to the patient that the body has only a limited capacity for generating and maintaining panic. Thus, every panic attack will ultimately subside. For example, if a panic attack occurs in a department store, the patient is instructed to find a place to sit down. While sitting down, facing, accepting, and floating are practiced and time is allowed to exert its curative effect. The patient has to remain in the situation until the panic attack has diminished.

The book by Weeks (1977) also contains many helpful hints on how to cope with specific symptoms. For example, patients who complain about inability to swallow are given a biscuit and asked to chew on it, without swallowing, as long as possible. The patients will be surprised to find, that when they are not trying, they swallow automatically. Patients who are fearful of not getting enough air are asked to hold their breath, and they will be surprised that their natural urge to breathe is much stronger than they thought.

Paradoxical Intention

The approach by Weeks (1977) appears to be a logical extension of our clinical model of panic. The same is true of paradoxical intention. Paradoxical procedures appear to be particularly useful in clinical situations involving vicious cycles such as panic. Unfortunately, while much of the writing on paradoxical procedures is characterized by logical elegance, the empirical foundation for these procedures is as yet scant.

Paradoxical intention, symptom prescription, symptom scheduling, and "reverse psychology" are terms applied to psychological interventions that are aimed at changing a behavior or attitude by prescribing it or encouraging it. Alternatively, desirable behaviors may be increased paradoxically by forbidding the behavior. Paradoxical interventions are employed by several schools of therapy or behavioral influence. Perhaps the earliest use was reported by Hunter (1786, cited in Marks, 1969). He advised a male patient afraid of failing with his mistress not to engage in intercourse, resulting in the prompt return of the patient's potency.

The current schools of psychotherapy that make the most extensive use of paradoxical procedures include logotherapy founded by Frankel (Fabry, Bulka, & Sahakian, 1979) and the communications–interactional school originated by

Bateson and coworkers (Watzlawick, Weakland, & Fisch, 1974). In addition, paradoxical procedures have been derived from the concept of reactive inhibition of Hullian learning theory (Yates, 1958) and from reactance theory of social psychology (Varela, 1975; Wicklund, 1974).

According to Frankel (1975), psychological problems are primarily caused by three mechanisms: (a) flight in reaction to anticipatory anxiety, (b) fight against obsessions and compulsions, and (c) fight for happiness. Paradoxical techniques are applicable particularly in the first two cases, whereas a technique called dereflection is employed in the third.

In the communications school, logical paradoxes are not only employed for the purpose of treatment, but are also considered to play a significant role in the pathogenesis of symptoms. Of particular importance is the so-called "be spontaneous paradox" (Watzlawick, Beavin, & Jackson, 1967). Such a paradox occurs, for example, when a person is requested to deliberately engage in a type of behavior, which by definition can only occur if it was not intended. "Be spontaneous!" is an example of such a request. Another example might be a demand to consciously put oneself in a condition that by definition can only exist without awareness, such as the request "don't think about pink elephants." Insomnia caused by deliberate attempts to fall asleep, lack of orgasm by trying too hard, and fear related to trying not to be afraid are examples of clinical situation in which the be spontaneous paradox is thought to assume pathogenic significance. The selection of treatment is guided by the general principle that the solutions of the problem adopted by the patient, such as avoiding fear-arousing situations or trying not to be afraid, are actually the primary cause in perpetuating the problem. A good introduction to the clinical use of these procedures, which require some technical skills and training, can be found in the books by Herr and Weakland (1979) and Watzlawick, Weakland, and Fish (1974).

The paradoxical approach to panic involves symptom prescription or symptom augmentation. Thus, it differs from the one advocated by Weeks (1977) primarily in that panic is not merely accepted, but actually *encouraged*. By doing this, the fear-of-fear cycle is stopped, since, ideally, the anticipatory anxiety is being replaced by an interest and curiosity regarding the panic attacks. It is probably important in paradoxical treatment to develop a "this is play" frame of reference (Bateson, 1972). This could be accomplished by the use of humor and exaggeration, or by encouraging an atmosphere of excitement of new discovery. Thus, the paradoxical approach does not merely involve the use of negative self-statement, as in the negative self-statement "treatment" employed by Ramm *et al.* (1982). The paradoxical approach also differs from implosion or flooding, in that it is primarily patient-paced rather than therapist-paced. However, it is similar in that each treatment involves exposure to feared stimuli.

Perhaps the earliest report of paradoxical treatment of panic was provided by Malleson (1959) in his description of the treatment of a student with test anxiety that escalated to panic episodes before a scheduled test. The treatment is described as follows:

> He was made to sit up in bed, and to try to feel his fear. He was asked to tell of the awful consequences that he felt would follow his failure—derision from his colleagues in India, disappointment from his family—financial loss. Then he was to try to imagine these things happening; try to imagine the fingers of scorn pointed at him, his wife and mother in tears. At first as he followed the instructions, his sobbings increased. But soon his trembling ceased. As the effort needed to maintain a vivid imagining increased, the emotions he could summon began to ebb. Within half an hour he was calm. Before leaving I instructed him in repeating the exercise of experiencing his fears. *Every time he felt a little wave of spontaneous alarm he was not to push it aside, but was to enhance it, to augment it, to try to experience it more profoundly and more vividly. If he did not spontaneously feel fear, every 20 or 30 minutes he was to make a special effort to try and do so, however difficult and ludicrous it might seem.* I arranged to see him twice a day over the next 2 days until his examination. He was an intelligent man, and an assiduous patient. He practiced the exercises methodically, and by the time of the examination he reported himself as almost totally unable to feel frightened. He had as it were, exhausted the affect in the whole situation. He passed his examination without apparent difficulty. (p. 225, italics added)

The first larger series of paradoxical treatment of agoraphobia was published by Gerz (1966). However, medication was also prescribed to some of these patients. Only global improvement ratings were provided. Of the 29 phobic patients treated, 22 (76%) recovered, and 5 showed "considerable" improvement. Only 2 patients showed no improvement at all.

Recently, a more systematic evaluation of paradoxical intention with agoraphobia was performed by Ascher (1981). Two groups of five patients were treated with either *in vivo* exposure plus paradoxical intention for 6 weeks, or *in vivo* exposure without paradoxical intention for 6 weeks. Following this, both groups received paradoxical intention and *in vivo* exposure to a criterion performance. The paradoxical procedure involved the patient identifying the most salient physiological sensation of anxiety, (e.g., heartbeat) and then trying to augment the intensity of this sensation, while remaining in the situation in which the anxiety occurred. After the anxiety attack subsided, the patients could either leave the situation or continue to the next exposure assignment.

After the initial 6 week period, the group that had received paradoxical intention had a significantly superior performance on a behavioral approach test than the group that had only received gradual exposure. Indeed, the improvement of the latter did not reach a statistically significant level. After the total treatment, which lasted between 13 to 28 weeks, the group that had received paradoxical intention from the beginning still showed superior results. Unfortunately, panic attacks were not measured in this study. A replication including a measure of panic would be most interesting.

The treatment of the hyperventilation syndrome advocated by Compernolle *et al.* (1979) also has paradoxical elements. During the second session, the patients are taught to bring on an attack by deliberately hyperventilating in the presence of the therapist and family members. When they succeed, they are taught to control the attack by rebreathing into an 8″ × 12″ oily paper bag. During this session, extensive explanations are also provided regarding the nature of the symptoms. The patients are instructed to practice hyperventilation and paper-bag rebreathing at home every day until the attacks cease to occur. They are instructed to carry a paper bag with them wherever they go. If there is a recurrence of attacks, the patients are to resume the exercises. The family members are involved and are asked to assist in the treatment by reminding the patient to do the exercise. The results reported appeared quite promising: One-third of the 106 patients required only two sessions and one or two follow-up visits. However, it was necessary to add family therapy to the other two-thirds. Overall, only 10% of the patients suffered recurrence of hyperventilation attacks during the 6 to 24 month follow-up period.

Clinical Cases of Paradoxical Treatment

We are currently exploring the use of paradoxical treatment of patients with mild agoraphobia and panic attacks. We will present two cases in which the patients monitored both their panic attacks and general level of anxiety on a daily basis. The patients were asked to record the time, main symptoms, and duration of each discrete panic episode. In addition, they were to record their location at the time of panic and what they were doing or what was happening before the panic. General anxiety or distress was recorded on a 0–8 point scale with 0 indicating complete calm. In both cases, paradoxical procedures were implemented only after *in vivo* exposure had resulted in behavioral improvement but failed to reduce the frequency of panic attacks. The paradoxical treatment was modeled after the Palo Alto approach. If applied to a new patient, it essentially involves two stages:

The first stage is a detailed behavioral analysis. There is a special emphasis on elaborating the following:

1. Prior unsuccessful attempts to cope with panic, including prior treatment
2. How the problem interferes with the life of the patients, particularly, their adult personal development ("getting on with life")
3. Minimal degree of improvement considered acceptable after treatment, in order to avoid setting expectations too high and considering any gains nullified by a single recurrence of panic
4. Possible disadvantages of improvement, for example, pathology in family members or having to face problems that the patient previously avoided
5. Their own view as to why they have the problem, so that, if possible, a treatment rationale can be given that fits with the patients' view

After this, a formulation is made, which may include reasons why the patients ought not to lose their panic attacks too quickly, and why it might be important for them to be able to bring on at least a mild panic attack at will. A "positive connotation" (Selvini-Palazzoli, Cecchin, Prata, & Boscolo, 1978) is provided (i.e., the significance of the panic is explored in positive terms). For example, the panic may represent an opportunity for the patients to learn something about themselves, or the panic may be expressed as an example of altruistic behavior for the benefit of certain family members. The first behavioral analysis phase usually extends over two sessions.

The second stage involves the treatment itself. As a first step, the patients are asked, as a homework exercise, to schedule two or three 30-min sessions per week in which they are to bring on a mild feeling of panic in the safety of their bedrooms. This is to be done by the use of "mind power" alone, without the help of exposure to feared situations. After or during the exercise they are asked to write down what thoughts seemed to work. Typically, the patients are unsuccessful. In the next session, alternative strategies are explored, such as hyperventilation, thoughts about death, illness, or financial disaster. At this time, the patients may discover that certain alarming panic symptoms can be brought on by hyperventilation, which itself is conducive to the realization that they have more control over their symptoms than they thought.

If the patients are able to raise their anxiety levels during the homework exercise, they are asked as a second step to "improve" their ability by gradually prolonging the experience and perhaps by raising the anxiety level even higher. Rather than improving, however, the patients typically habituate and lose their ability to become anxious. If they do not, relaxation and slow abdominal breathing exercises are employed to relieve the panic sensations. When the patients have lost their ability to panic, usually after three to four sessions of home practice, the third step consists in their going into situations in which they are likely to experience panic. This is done in order for them to obtain better ideas and fresher memories of panic-eliciting stimuli. If they experience panic in the situation, they are instructed to sit down and try to prolong the experience and possibly raise the anxiety level even higher. These instructions are also given with regard to spontaneously occurring panic attacks. The patients will often discover that by attempting to increase the panic, the attack paradoxically disappears.

In our experience, it is usually apparent after seven or eight sessions, whether or not the patient will respond to treatment. The remainder of the treatment is spent exploring more and better ways in which panic can be induced. When there are signs of improvement, the patients are warned that this might be temporary and perhaps not even desirable, thus preempting the countertherapeutic effects of unexpected "setbacks." At the end stage of treatment, the expectation is reinforced about the necessity of the continued need of having a few panic experiences and coping with them in the future.

Figure 3 shows the number of panic attacks per week and average anxiety levels during treatment for Case 1. This patient was a 27-year-old salesman in a liquor store who had suffered from a driving phobia and panic attacks for nine years. At the time of onset, the patient had had his first sexual experience which had resulted in him being fearful of contracting venereal disease. *In vivo* desensitization significantly improved the range of streets that he could drive on, and also reduced his level of general distress (Figure 3).

Because a behavioral analysis had already been performed before exposure treatment, paradoxical procedures were implemented directly in the fear-producing situations during flooding treatment. Thus, this patient started at Step 3 of Stage 2 in our treatment outline. As can be seen in the figure, weekly number of panic attacks were reduced to zero within a few weeks, but the decline in panic frequency actually began before the paradoxical phase. During the session preceding the decline, the patient had had one "insight" experience, when he realized that his panics could be traced to a fear of contracting venereal disease after his first sexual encounter many years ago.

During the last treatment session, the patient was instructed to determine how much anxiety he needed to keep for his personal needs and to "be sure not to let this moderate amount slip away" (in keeping with paradoxical intent). The treatment gains were maintained at one-month follow up. The patient was again contacted after 8 months. He reported that he had maintained treatment

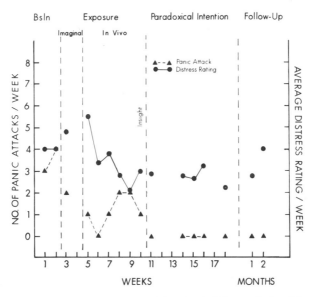

Figure 3. Number of panic attacks per week and daily level of distress (0–8 scale) averaged over 1 week for Case 1.

gains during this time period. Moderate anxiety was still experienced while driving, however discrete panic attacks were no longer occurring, and he no longer avoided situations that he had avoided before treatment.

The results of the second case are depicted in Figure 4. The patient was a 31-year-old salesman for a drug company who developed fears of driving, crowded stores, or public places, as well as panic attacks. The symptoms had begun during his honeymoon 2 years prior to treatment.

The treatment of this case was much less straightforward and further complicated by the need to change therapists after three sessions of paradoxical treatment. In order to enable the second therapist to familiarize himself with the patient, the behavioral analysis was redone. Thus, the paradoxical treatment of this case included all the stages and steps of the outline above. In the exercises of Steps 1 and 2, various current stressors were explored for their ability to raise anxiety, but this did not have much effect on the frequency of spontaneous panic attacks. A "breakthrough," however, occurred in the eleventh session. At that time, it had become apparent that the patient's sexual life was quite unsatisfactory. The assignment was given for the patient to try to have a panic attack by thinking about himself remaining sexually dissatisfied and unfulfilled the rest of his life. The following week, he reported that the exercise made him feel angry, rather than anxious, and he had several discussions with his wife. Surprisingly, there were no spontaneous panic attacks during this week. After this session, a decline was noted in his general distress level throughout the rest of treatment. The patient also claimed that his sexual enjoyment improved.

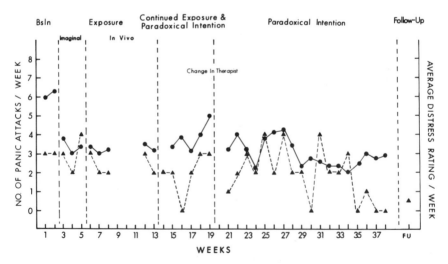

Figure 4. Number of panic attacks per week and daily level of distress averaged over one week for Case 2.

However, the panic attacks recurred and persisted despite attempts of *in vivo* exposure with anxiety "enhancement" (Step 3). The patient finally was given the exercise to try to induce panic through catastrophizing thoughts such as "what if I never ever get rid of my panic attacks?" (Session 13). In Session 14, he reported that he had not done this exercise. He was again urged to do so. At this time he did comply and managed to induce anxiety the first time he did the exercise. There were no spontaneous panic attacks that week, and the gains were essentially maintained for the following 3 weeks. At this time, he was referred for continued treatment in family therapy because it was felt that his marital issues had not been resolved. Four months later, he reported that he had had about two panic attacks per month during the intervening period.

This case illustrates that both current conflicts and self-maintaining vicious cycles (self-fulfilling speculations, such as "what if I never get rid of my panic attacks?") seemed to be operative in the maintenance of panic. Family issues were present that apparently maintained his panic attacks, and these may have been even more difficult to deal with than the panic episodes themselves. During the behavioral analysis, the patient reported pressure from his wife to add another child to the family. According to the family therapist who took over the case, the patient appeared much more comfortable limiting the discussions to his panic episodes than facing the unresolved issues in his marriage.

It should be evident, at least from the second case, that the paradoxical approach, at least as employed by us, is no panacea. The approach might be of particularly limited value when a current conflict is overlooked, or in cases in which the panic attacks are so overwhelming that the reasons for the self-generating anxiety cannot be put across to the patient. It also appears to be limited in the case of more "dependent" types of patients who expect the treatment to focus entirely on the removal of symptoms without their active participation.

A more acceptable behavioral approach in these cases might be to begin the treatment with breathing or relaxation exercises. It is also likely that family interactions need to be modified in these patients, as advocated by Compernolle *et al.* (1979). However, it should also be remembered that patients may not necessarily be committed to behavioral treatment. They may prefer a pharmacological approach, which certainly can be very successful, at least for as long as the patient may remain on the medication.

CONCLUSIONS

After reading this chapter, it should be evident to the reader that empirical data specific to panic disorder are not abundant. Instead, it was necessary to extrapolate from the literature on hyperventilation syndrome, agoraphobia, and anxiety neurosis.

Behavioral treatment of panic is at a very early stage of development and evaluation. Indeed, many therapists regard pharmacological treatment as the treatment of choice. However, it should be remembered that the long-term follow-up results after discontinuation of the medication may not be as favorable as the immediate results, leaving room for the development of alternative approaches. In addition, there will be patients who would prefer a more direct behavioral approach, either due to side-effects from the medication in the case of drugs or for philosophical reasons in the case of paradoxical intention.

Exposure treatments for agoraphobia are only moderately effective in reducing panic. In this chapter, a clinical conceptual schema was presented that might be useful in guiding the selection of appropriate behavioral treatments. Foremost among the principles of this schema was the need for controlled exposure to the somatic stimuli of panic itself. Following from this model, we believe that comprehensive programs based on relaxation and breathing exercises, the coping strategies advocated by Clara Weeks or paradoxical intention are worthy of further investigation. In addition, the interaction between behavior therapy and pharmacotherapy should be studied, particularly with regard to long-term results. Further research also needs to be directed toward uncovering medical conditions that might underlie panic disorder.

ACKNOWLEDGMENTS

The first author gratefully acknowledges his supervisory experience with Richard Fisch, Paul Watzlawick, and John Weakland, members of the Palo Alto group. Special thanks are due to Mark Graves for his intellectual input in the section on the physiology of hyperventilation, to Deborah Beidel for her editorial assistance, to Nancy Bridge for her secretarial work on the manuscript, and to Nancy Hillman for the library work necessary to update the literature review.

REFERENCES

Agras, W.S., & Jacob, R. G. Phobia: Nature and measurement. In D. H. Barlow & M. Mavissakalian (Eds.), *Phobia: Psychological and pharmacological treatment.* New York: Guilford Press, 1981.

Alarcon R., Dickinson, W., & Dohn, H. Flashback phenomena: Clinical and diagnostic dilemmas. *Journal of Nervous and Mental Disease,* 1982, *170,* 217–223.

Allen, J. P., Imbus, C. E., Powers, D. R., & Haywood, L. J. Neurological impairment induced by hyperventilation in children with sickle cell anemia. *Pediatrics,* 1976, *58,* 124–126.

American Psychiatric Association. *Diagnostic and statistical manual of mental disorders* (3rd ed.). Washington D.C.: Author, 1980.

Andrews, J. Psychotherapy of phobias. *Psychological Bulletin,* 1966, *66,* 455–480.

Anthony D., Dippe, S., Hofeldt, F. D., Davis, J. W., & Forsham, P. H. Personality disorder and reactive hypoglycemia: A quantitative study. *Diabetes,* 1973, *22,* 664–675.

Ascher, L. M. Employing paradoxical intention in the treatment of agoraphobia. *Behaviour Research and Therapy,* 1981, *19,* 533–542.

Barlow, J. B., & Pocock, W. A. Mitral valve prolapse, the specific billowing mitral leaflet syndrome, or an insignificant nonejection systolic click. *American Heart Journal,* 1975, *90,* 636–655.

Barnett, H. J. M., Boughner, D. R., Taylor, D. W., Cooper, P. E., Kostuk, W. J., & Nichol, P. M. Further evidence relating mitral valve prolapse to cerebral ischemic events. *New England Journal of Medicine,* 1980, *302,* 139–144.

Bateson, G. *Steps to an ecology of mind; Collected essays in anthropology, psychiatry, evolution and epistemology.* San Francisco: Chandler, 1972.

Beard, G. Neurasthenia, or nervous exhaustion. *The Boston Medical and Surgical Journal,* 1869, *3,* 217–221.

Beck, A. T., Laude, R., & Bohnert, M. Ideational components of anxiety neurosis. *Archives of General Psychiatry,* 1974, *31,* 319–325.

Blau, J. N. Migraine: A vasomotor instability of the meningeal circulation. *The Lancet,* 1978, 1136–1139.

Bowlby, J. Attachment and loss. In J. Bowlby (Ed.), *Psychology of attachment and loss series: Vol. 3. Separation, anxiety and anger.* London: The Hogarth Press, 1973.

Brown, E. B. Jr. Physiological effects of hyperventilation. *Psychological Reviews,* 1953, *33,* 445–471.

Brown, H. N., & Kemble, S. B. Episodic anxiety and cardiac arrhythmias. *Psychosomatics,* 1981, *22,* 907–915.

Campbell, D., Sanderson, R. E., & Laverty, S. G. Characteristics of a conditional response in human subjects during extinction trials following a single traumatic conditioning trial. *Journal of Abnormal Psychology,* 1964, *68,* 627–639.

Casey, J. F. A psychiatrist's experience of terror. *Psychiatric Annals,* 1978, *8,* 250–254.

Chambless, D., Foa, E., Groves, G., & Goldstein, A. Flooding with Brevital in the treatment of agoraphobia: Countereffective? *Behaviour Research and Therapy,* 1979, *17,* 243–251.

Cheitlin, M. D., & Byrd, R. L. The click-murmur syndrome—a clinical problem in diagnosis and treatment. *Journal of the American Medical Association,* 1981, *245,* 1357–1361.

Clancy, J., Noyes, R., Jr., Hoenk, P. R., & Slymen, D. J. Secondary depression in anxiety neurosis. *Journal of Nervous and Mental Disease,* 1978, *166,* 846–850.

Compernolle, T., Hoogduin, K., & Joele, L. Diagnosis and treatment of the hyperventilation syndrome. *Psychosomatics,* 1979, *20,* 622–625.

Coryell, W., Noyes, R., & Clancy, J. Excess mortality in panic disorder - A comparison with primary unipolar depression. *Archives of General Psychiatry,* 1982, *39,* 701–703.

Curtis, G. C. Sensory experiences during treatment of phobias by *in vivo* exposure. *American Journal of Psychiatry,* 1981, *138,* 1095–1097.

Darsee, J. R., Mikolich, J. R., Nicoloff, N. B., & Lesser, L. E. Prevalence of mitral valve prolapse in presumably healthy young men. *Circulation,* 1979, *59,* 619–622.

Davison, G. C., & Valins, S. Maintenance of self-attributed and drug-attributed behavior change. *Journal of Personality and Social Psychology,* 1969, *11,* 25–33.

Dealy, R. S., Ishiki, D. M., Avery, D. H., Wilson, L. G., & Dunner, D. C. Secondary depression in anxiety disorders. *Comprehensive Psychiatry,* 1981, *22,* 612–618.

Devereux, R. B., Perloff, J. K., Reichek, N., & Josephson, M. E., Mitral valve prolapse. *Circulation,* 1976, *54,* 3–14.

Drachman, D. A., & Hart, C. W. An approach to the dizzy patient. *Neurology,* 1972, *22,* 323–334.

Dudley, D. L., Holmes, T. H., Martin, C. J., & Ripley, H. S. Changes in respiration associated with hypnotically induced emotion. *Psychosomatic Medicine,* 1964, *26,* 46–57.

Emmelkamp, P. M. G., & Wessels, H. Flooding in imagination vs. flooding *in vivo:* A comparison with agoraphobics. *Behaviour Research and Therapy,* 1975, *13,* 7–15.

Emmelkamp, P. M. G., Kuipers, C. M., & Eggeraat, J. B. Cognitive modification versus prolonged exposure *in vivo. Behaviour Research and Therapy,* 1978, *16,* 33–41.

Engel, G. L., Ferris, E. B., & Logan, M. Hyperventilation: Analysis of clinical symptomatology. *Annuals of Internal Medicine,* 1947, *27,* 683–704.

Epstein, A. W. Body image and alterations during seizures and dreams of epileptic. *Archives of Neurology,* 1967, *16,* 613–619.

Evans, I. A conditioning model of a common neurotic pattern—fear of fear. *Psychotherapy: Theory, Research and Practice,* 1972, *9,* 238–241.

Everaerd, W. T. A. M., Rijken, H. M., & Emmelkamp, P. M. G. A comparison of flooding and successive approximation in the treatment of agoraphobia. *Behaviour Research and Therapy,* 1973, *11,* 105–117.

Eysenck, H. J. A theory of the incubation of anxiety/fear responses. *Behaviour Research and Therapy,* 1968, *6,* 309–321.

Fabry, J. B., Bulka, R. P., & Sahakian, W. S. *Logotherapy in action.* New York: Jason Aronson, Inc., 1979.

Fazekas, J. F., McHenry, L. C., Alman, R. W., & Sullivan, J. F. Cerebral hemodynamics during brief hyperventilation. *Archives of Neurology,* 1961, *4,* 132–138.

Feighner, J. P., Robins, E., Guze, S. B., Woodruff, R., Winokur, G., & Munoz, R. Diagnostic criteria for use in psychiatric research. *Archives of General Psychiatry,* 1972, *26,* 57–63.

Feldman, L. Anxiety. . . Panic, Researchers are testing new treatments. *The Emissary,* 1980, 12.

Folgering, H., & Colla, P. Some anomalies in the control of P_aCO_2 in patients with a hyperventilation syndrome. *Bulletin Europeen de Physiopathologie Respiratoire,* 1978, *14,* 503–512.

Ford, C. V., Bray, G. A., & Swerdloff, R. S. A psychiatric study of patients referred with a diagnosis of hypoglycemia. *American Journal of Psychiatry,* 1976, *133,* 290–294.

Forrest, R. D. Mitral valve prolapse syndrome in anxiety neurosis. *American Heart Journal,* 1981, *102,* 139.

Frankl, V. D. Paradoxical intention and deflection. *Psychotherapy: Theory, research and practice,* 1975, *12,* 226–236.

Freedman, A., Dornbush, R., & Shapiro, B. Anxiety: Here today and here tomorrow. *Comprehensive Psychiatry,* 1981, *22,* 44–53.

Freud, S. On the grounds for detaching a particular syndrome from neurasthenia under the description "Anxiety neurosis." In J. Strachey (Ed. & Transl.). *The standard edition of the complete psychological works of Sigmund Freud* (Vol. 3). London: The Hogarth Press, 1962 (Originally published, 1895).

Freud, S. Inhibitions, symptoms and anxiety. In J. Strachey (Ed. & Transl.), *The standard edition of the complete psychological works of Sigmund Freud* (Vol. 20). London: The Hogarth Press, 1959 (Originally published, 1926).

Freud, S. Anxiety and instinctual life; New introductory lecture #32. In J. Strachey (Ed. & Transl.), *The standard edition of the complete psychological works of Sigmund Freud* (Vol. 22). London: The Hogarth Press, 1964 (Originally published, 1933).

Fry, W. The marital context of an anxiety syndrome. *Family Process,* 1962, *1,* 245–252.

Garssen, B. Role of stress in the development of the hyperventilation syndrome. *Psychotherapy and Psychosomatics,* 1980, *33,* 214–225.

Gawin, F., & Markoff, R. Panic anxiety after abrupt discontinuation of amitriptyline. *American Journal of Psychiatry,* 1981, *138,* 117–118.

Gelder, M. Behaviour therapy for anxiety states. *British Medical Journal,* 1969, 691–694.

Gelder, M. G., Bancroft, J. H. J., Gath, D. H., Johnston, D. W., Mathews, A. M., & Shaw,

P. M. Specific and non-specific factors in behavior therapy. *British Journal of Psychiatry,* 1973, *123,* 445–462.

Gerz, H. Experience with logotherapeutic technique of paradoxical intention in the treatment of phobic and obsessive-compulsive patients. *American Journal of Psychiatry,* 1966, *123,* 548–553.

Girodo, M. Yoga meditation and flooding in the treatment of anxiety neurosis. *Journal of Behavior Therapy & Experimental Psychiatry,* 1974, *5,* 157–160.

Gliebe, P., & Auerback, A. Sighing and other forms of hyperventilation simulating organic disease. *Journal of Nervous and Mental Disease,* 1944, *99,* 600–615.

Glynn, C., Lloyd, J., & Folkhard, S. Ventilatory response to intractable pain. *Pain,* 1981, *11,* 201–211.

Goldstein, A., & Chambless, D. A reanalysis of agoraphobia. *Behavior Therapy,* 1978, *9,* 47–59.

Gotoh, F., Meyer, J., & Takagi, Y. Cerebral effects of hyperventilation in man. *Archives of Neurology,* 1965, *12,* 410.

Gray, J. A., Davis, N., Feldon, J., Nicholas, J., Rawlins, P., & Owen, S. R. Animal models of anxiety. *Progress in neuro-psychopharmacology,* 1981, *5,* 143–157.

Guten, S., & Allen, V. L. Likelihood of escape, likelihood of danger and panic behavior. *The Journal of Social Psychology,* 1972, *87,* 29–36.

Hadji-Georgopoulos, A., Schmidt, M., Margolis, S., & Kowarski, A. Elevated hypoglycemic index and late hyperinsulinism in symptomatic postprandial hypoglycemia. *Journal of Clinical Endocrinology and Metabolism,* 1980, *50,* 371–376.

Hafner, R. J. The husbands of agoraphobic women and their influence on treatment outcome. *British Journal of Psychiatry,* 1977, *131,* 289–294.

Hafner, R. J., & Marks, I. M. Exposure *in vivo* of agoraphobics; contributions of diazepam, group exposure and anxiety evocation. *Psychological Medicine,* 1976, *6,* 71–88.

Hafner, J., & Milton, F. The influence of propranolol on the exposure *in vivo* of agoraphobics. *Psychological Medicine,* 1977, *7,* 419–425.

Hale, F., Margen, S., & Rabak, D. Postprandial hypoglycemia and "psychological" symptoms. *Biological Psychiatry,* 1981, *17,* 125–130.

Hall, R., Popkin, M., Devaul, R., Faillace, L., & Stickney, S. Physical illness presenting as psychiatric disease. *Archives of General Psychiatry,* 1978, *35,* 1315–1320.

Hall, R. C. W. Anxiety. In R. C. W. Hall (Ed.), *Psychiatric presentations of medical illness.* New York: S. P. Medical and Scientific Books, 1980.

Harper, M., & Roth, M. Temporal lobe epilepsy and the phobic anxiety depersonalization syndrome. A comparative study, Parts I and II. *Comprehensive Psychiatry,* 1962, *3,* 129–151 & 215–226.

Hecker, E. Über larvirte und abortive Angstzustände bei Neurasthenie. *Zentralblatt für Nervenheilkunde,* 1893, *4,* 565.

Herr, J. J., & Weakland, J. H. *Counseling elders and their families: Practical techniques for applied geronotology.* New York: Springer, 1979.

Hickam, J. B., Cargill, W. H., & Golden, A. Cardiovascular reactions to emotional stimulus effect on cardiac output, A-V O_2 difference, arterial pressure and peripheral resistance. *Journal of Clinical Investigation,* 1948, *27,* 290–298.

Hill, O. The hyperventilation syndrome. *British Journal of Psychiatry,* 1979, *135,* 367–368.

Hoehn-Saric, R. Neurotransmitters in anxiety. *Archives of General Psychiatry,* 1982, *39,* 735–742.

Hoehn-Saric, R., Frank, J., Imber, S., Nash, E., Stone, A., & Battle, C. Systematic preparation of patients for psychotherapy—I. Effects on therapy behavior and outcome. *Journal of Psychiatric Research,* 1964, *2,* 267–281.

Hollon, S. D., & DuRubeis, R. J. Placebo–psychotherapy combinations: Inappropriate representations of psychotherapy in drug–psychotherapy comparative trials. *Psychological Bulletin,* 1981, *90,* 467–477.

Jacob, R. G., & Turner, S. M. Somatoform disorders. In S. M. Turner & M. Hersen (Eds.), *Adult Psychopathology and Diagnosis.* New York: Wiley, 1984.

Jacob, R. G., Moller, M. B., Turner, S. M., & Wall, C., III. *Otoneurological dysfunction in patients with panic disorder or agoraphobia with panic attacks.* Presented at the 17th Annual Convention, The World Congress on Behavior Therapy, Washington, D. C., Dec. 8–11, 1983.

Janis, I., Chapman, D., Gillin, J., & Speigel, J. The problem of panic. In D. P. Schultz (Ed.), *Panic behavior: Discussion and readings.* New York: Random House, 1964.

Johnson, D., Dorr, K., Swenson, W., & Service, J. Reactive hypoglycemia. *Journal of the American Medical Association,* 1980, *243,* 1151–1155.

Kantor, J. S., Zitrin, C. M., & Zeldis, S. M. Mitral valve prolapse syndrome in agoraphobic patients. *American Journal of Psychiatry,* 1980, *137,* 467–469.

Kerr, W. J., Dalton, J. W., & Gliebe, P. A. Some physical phenomena associated with anxiety states and their relation to hyperventilation. *Annals of Internal Medicine,* 1937, *11,* 961–992.

Kimmel, H., & Brennan, A. Conditioning models of anxiety. *International Journal of Psychology,* 1981, *16,* 371–387.

King, A. Penelzine treatment of Roth's calamity syndome. *Medical Journal of Australia,* 1962, *1,* 879–883.

Klein, D. F., & Fink, M. Psychiatric reaction patterns to imipramine. *American Journal of Psychiatry,* 1962, *119,* 432–438.

Koryani, E. K. Somatic illness in psychiatric patients. *Psychosomatics,* 1980, *21,* 887–891.

Lader, M., & Mathews, A. M. A physiological model of phobic anxiety and desensitization. *Behaviour Research and Therapy,* 1968, *6,* 411–421.

Lader, M., & Mathews, A. Physiological changes during spontaneous panic attacks. *Journal of Psychosomatic Research,* 1970, *14,* 377–382.

Lamb, L., Dermksian, G., & Sarnoff, C. Significant cardiac arrhythmias induced by common respiratory maneuvers. *American Journal of Cardiology,* 1958, *2,* 563–571.

Lary, D., & Goldschlager, N. Electrocardiogram changes during hyperventilation resembling myocardial ischemia in patients with normal coronary arteriograms. *American Heart Journal,* 1974, *87,* 383–390.

Latimer, P. Carbon dioxide as a reciprocal inhibitor in the treatment of neurosis. *Journal of Behavior Therapy and Experimental Psychiatry,* 1977, *8,* 83–85.

Lavallee, Y., Lamontagne, Y., Pinard, G., Annable, L., & Tetreault, L. Effects on EMG feedback, diazepam and their combination on chronic anxiety. *Journal of Psychomatic Research,* 1977, 21, 65–71.

Leboeuf, A., & Lodge, J. A comparison of frontalis EMG feedback training and progressive relaxation in the treatment of chronic anxiety. *British Journal of Psychiatry,* 1980, *137,* 279–284.

Leitenberg, H., Agras, S., Barlow, D., & Oliveau, D. Contribution of selective positive reinforcement and therapeutic instructions to systematic desensitization therapy. *Journal of Abnormal Psychology,* 1969, *74,* 114–118.

Lewis, B. I. Chronic hyperventilation syndrome. *Journal of the American Medical Association,* 1954, *14,* 1204–1208.

Lewis, B. I. Hyperventilation syndrome: A clinical and physiological evaluation. *California Medicine,* 1959, *91,* 121–126.

Lewis, B. I., Seebohm, P. M., Hamilton, W. K., January, L. E., & Wheeler, P. Continuous biophysical recording techniques in the study of cardiopulmonary phenomena accompanying psychogenic hyperventilation. *Psychosomatic Medicine,* 1955, *17,* 479.

Lipsedge, M., Hajioff, J., Huggins, P., Napier, L., Pearce, J., Pike, D., & Rich, M. The management of severe agoraphobia: A comparison of Iproniazid and systematic desensitization. *Psychopharmacologia*, 1973, *32*, 67–80.

Lum, L. C. Hyperventilation: The tip and the iceberg. *Journal of Psychosomatic Research*, 1975, *19*, 375–383.

Lum, L. C. The syndrome of habitual chronic hyperventilation. In P. Hill (Ed.), *Modern trends in psychosomatic medicine* (Vol. 3). London: Butterworths, 1976.

Malleson, N. Panic and phobia: A possible method of treatment. *The Lancet*, 1959, 225–227.

Markiewicz, W., Stoner, J., London, E., Hunt, S. A., & Popp, R. L. Mitral valve prolapse in 100 presumably healthy young females. *Circulation*, 1976, *53*, 464–473.

Marks, I. M. *Fears and phobias*. New York: Academic, 1969.

Marks, I. M. The classification of phobic disorders. *British Journal of Psychiatry*, 1970, *116*, 377–386.

Marks, I. M., Gelder, M. G., & Edwards, G. Hypnosis and desensitization for phobias: A controlled prospective trial. *British Journal of Psychiatry*, 1968, *114*, 1263–1274.

Marks, I., Boulougouris, J., & Marset, P. Flooding vs. desensitization in the treatment of phobic patients: A crossover study. *British Journal of Psychiatry*, 1971, *119*, 353–375.

Mavissakalian, M. Personal communication, 1982.

May, R. *The meaning of anxiety*. New York: Norton, 1977.

McCaul, K., Solomon, S., & Holmes, D. Effects of paced respiration and expectations on physiological and psychological responses to threat. *Journal of Personality and Social Psychology*, 1979, *37*, 564–571.

McCormick, W. O. Declining-dose drug desensitization for phobias. *Canadian Psychiatric Association Journal*, 1973, *18*, 33–40.

McNair, D. M., & Fisher, S. Separating anxiety from depression. In M. A. Lipton, A. DiMascio & K. F. Killam (Eds.), *Psychopharmacology: A generation of progress*. New York: Raven Press, 1978.

McNair, D. M., & Kahn, R. J. Imipramine compared with a benzodiazepine for agoraphobia. In D. F. Klein & J. G. Rabkin (Eds.), *Anxiety: New research and changing concepts*. New York: Raven Press, 1981.

Meyer, J. S., & Gotoh, F. Metabolic and electroencephalographic effects of hyperventilation. *Archives of Neurology*, 1960, *5*, 539–552.

Mills, J. N. Hyperapnoea induced by forced breathing. *Journal of Physiology*, 1946, *105*, 95–116.

Motta, P. E., Fagiani, M. D., Dolcetti, A., Bellone, E., & Borello, G. Modificazioni del gas nel sangue nello attacco ansioso di media gravità. *Archivo per le scienze Mediche*, 1971, *128*, 111–119.

Neill, W. A., & Hattenhauer, M. Impairment of myocardial O_2 supply due to hyperventilation. *Circulation*, 1975, *52*, 854–858.

Noyes, R., Clancy, J., Hoenk, P. R., & Sylmen, D. J. Anxeity neurosis and physical illness. *Comprehensive Psychiatry*, 1978, *19*, 407–413.

Okel, B. B., & Hurst, J. W. Prolonged hyperventilation in man. *Archives of Internal Medicine*, 1961, *108*, 757–762.

Pariser, S. F., Pinta, E. R., & Jones, B. A. Mitral valve prolapse syndrome and anxiety neurosis/panic disorder. *American Journal of Psychiatry*, 1978, *135*, 246–247.

Pariser, S. F., Jones, B. A., Pinta, E. R., Young, E. A., & Fontana, M. E. Panic attacks: Diagnostic evaluations of 17 patients. *American Journal of Psychiatry*, 1979, *136*, 105.

Permutt, M. A. Postprandial hypoglycemia. *Diabetes*, 1976, *25*, 719–733.

Permutt, M. A. Is it really hypoglycemia? If so, what should you do? *Medical Times*, 1980, *108*, 35–43.

Pitts, F. N., & McClure, J. N. Lactate metabolism in anxiety neurosis. *New England Journal of Medicine,* 1967, *277,* 1328–1336.

Protass, L. M. Possible precipitation of cerebral thrombosis in sickle cell anemia by hyperventilation. *Annals of Internal Medicine,* 1973, *79,* 451.

Raichle, M., & Plum, F. Hyperventilation and cerebral blood flow. *Stroke,* 1972, *3,* 566–575.

Ramm, E., Marks, I. M., Yuksel, S., & Stern, R. S. Anxiety management training for anxiety states: Positive compared with negative self-statements. *British Journal of Psychiatry,* 1982, *140,* 367–373.

Raskin, M., Johnson, G., & Rodestvedt, J. Chronic anxiety treated by feedback-induced muscle relaxation. *Archives of General Psychiatry,* 1973, *28,* 263–267.

Raskin, M., Bali, L., & Peeke, H. Muscle biofeedback and transcendental meditation in chronic anxiety. *Archives of General Psychiatry,* 1980, *37,* 93–97.

Raskin, M., Peeke, H., Dickman, W., & Pinsker, H. Panic and generalized anxiety disorders— development antecedents and precipitants. *Archives of General Psychiatry,* 1982, *39,* 687– 689.

Rice, R. L. Symptom patterns of the hyperventilation syndrome. *Annals of Internal Medicine,* 1950, *8,* 691–700.

Riley, D. J. The "oily" paper bag and hyperventilation. *Journal of the American Medical Association,* 1974, *229,* 638.

Roberts, W. W. Normal and abnormal depersonalization. *Journal of Mental Science,* 1960, *106,* 478–493.

Sarason, I. G. Life stress, self-preoccupation and social supports. Office of Naval Research (code 452). Organizational Effectiveness Research Program, Arlington, Virginia 22217. Contract No. N00014-75-C-0905, NR-170-804, April 15, 1979.

Sargant, W. The treatment of anxiety states and atypical depressions by the monoamine oxidase inhibitor drugs. *Journal of Neuropsychiatry,* 1962, *3,* Supp. 1, 96–103.

Selvini-Palazzoli, M., Cecchin, G., Prata, G., & Boscolo, L. *Paradox and counterparadox: A new model in the therapy of the family in schizophrenic transaction.* New York: Jason Aronson, 1978.

Sheehan, D. V., Ballenger, J., & Jacobson, G. Treatment of endogenous anxiety with phobic hysterical and hypochondrical symptons. *Archives of General Psychiatry,* 1980, *37,* 51–59.

Shraberg, D. The phobic anxiety-depersonalization syndrome. *Psychiatric Opinion,* 1977, Nov/ Dec., 35–40.

Spiegel, H. X., & Spiegel, D. *Trance and treatment: Clinical uses of hypnosis.* New York: Basic Books, 1978.

Spitzer, R. L., Endicott, J., & Robins, E. *Research diagnostic criteria.* (3rd ed.) New York: New York State Psychiatric Institute Division of Biometrics Research, 1980.

Stern, R., & Marks, I. Brief and prolonged flooding: A comparison in agoraphobic patients. *Archives of General Psychiatry,* 1973, *28,* 270–276.

Suess, W. M., Alexander, A. B., Smith, D. D., Sweeney, H. W. & Marion, R. J. The effects of psychological stress on respiration: A preliminary study of anxiety and hyperventilation. *Psychophysiology,* 1980, *17,* 535–540.

Townsend, R., House, J., & Addario, D. A comparison of biofeedback-mediated relaxation and group therapy in the treatment of chronic anxiety. *American Journal of Psychiatry,* 1975, *132,* 6.

Turner, S. M., Jacob, R. G., & Morrison, R. Somatoform and factitious disorders. In H. E. Adams & P. B. Sutker (Eds.), *Comprehensive handbook of psychopathology.* New York: Plenum Press, 1984.

Ursin, H., Baade, E., & Levine S. (Eds.), *Psychobiology of stress: A study of coping men.* New York: Academic Press, 1978.

Varela, J. A. Can social psychology be applied? In M. Deutsch and H. A. Hornstein (Eds.),

Applying social psychology: Implications for research, practice and training. New York: Halsted Press, 1975.

Venkatesh, A., Pauls, D., Crow, R., Noyes, R., Van Valkenburg, C., Martins, J. B., & Kerber, R. E. Mitral valve prolapse in anxeity neurosis. *American Heart Journal,* 1980, *100,* 302–305.

Waites, T. Hyperventilation-chronic and acute. *Archives of Internal Medicine,* 1978, *38,* 1700–1701.

Walker, L. The prognosis of affective illness with overt anxiety. *Journal of Neurology, Neurosurgery and Psychiatry,* 1959, *22,* 338–341.

Watson, J. P., & Marks, I. M. Relevant and irrelevant fear in flooding—a crossover study of phobic patients. *Behavior Therapy,* 1971, *2,* 275–293.

Watzlawick, P., Beavin, J., & Jackson, D. D. *Pragmatics of human communication.* New York: Norton, 1967.

Watzlawick, P., Weakland, J., & Fisch, R. *Change: Principles of problem formation and problem resolution.* New York: Norton, 1974.

Weeks, C. *Simple, effective treatment of agoraphobia.* New York: Hawthorn Books, 1977.

Wheatley, C. E. Hyperventilation syndrome: A frequent cause of chest pain. *Chest,* 1975, *68,* 195–199.

Wicklund, R. A. *Freedom and reactance.* Hillsdale, N. J.: Lawrence Erlbaum Associates, 1974.

Wildenthal, K., Fuller, D., & Shapiro, W. Paroxysmal atrial arrhythmias induced by hyperventilation. *The American Journal of Cardiology,* 1968, *21,* 436–441.

Woodruff, R. A., Guze, S. G., & Clayton, P. J. Anxiety neurosis among psychiatric outpatients. *Comprehensive Psychiatry,* 1972, *13,* 165–170.

Wooley, C. F. Where are the diseases of yesteryear? *Circulation,* 1976, *53,* 749–751.

Yager, J., & Young, R. J. Nonhypoglycemia is an epidemic condition. *New England Journal of Medicine,* 1974, *291,* 907–908.

Yates, A. J. The application of learning theory to the treatment of tics. *Journal of Abnormal and Social Psychology,* 1958, *36,* 175–182.

Yu, P. N., Yim, J. B., & Stanfield, C. A. Hyperventilation syndrome: Changes in electrocardiogram, blood gases, and electrolytes during voluntary hyperventilation: Possible mechanisms and clinical implications. *Archives of Internal Medicine,* 1959, *103,* 902–913.

Zitrin, C. M., Klein, D. F., & Woerner, M. G. Treatment of agoraphobia with group exposure *in vivo* and imipramine. *Archives of General Psychiatry,* 1980, *37,* 63–72.

6

Obsessive-Compulsive Disorders

SAMUEL M. TURNER and
LARRY MICHELSON

Although obsessive-compulsive disorder (OCD) is the least prevalent of the
anxiety disorders, it is often one of the more severe, extracting a heavy toll in
personal and social debilitation. As a diagnostic entity it is easily recognizable,
and Esquirol, as early as 1838, described the disorder. More systematic definitions were offered by Janet (1908), Schneider (1925), and Lewis (1966). In
this chapter, we will review and summarize the clinical syndrome, theories,
relationships to other conditions, and contemporary treatments. An exhaustive
review, however, is beyond the scope of this chapter, and the reader may refer
to Rachman and Hodgson (1980), Beech (1974), and Mavissakalian, Turner,
and Michelson (in preparation) for comprehensive critiques.

  The clinical symptoms of OCD appear to be relatively homogeneous. The
new Diagnostic and Statistical Manual (DSM-III; American Psychiatric Association, 1980) describes the essential and most commonly accepted features as

> recurrent obsessions or compulsions. Obsessions are recurrent, persistent ideas,
> thoughts, images, or impulses that are ego dystonic, that is, they are not experi-
> enced as voluntarily produced, but rather as thoughts that involve consciousness
> and are experienced as senseless or repugnant. Attempts are made to ignore or
> suppress them. Compulsions are repetitive and seemingly purposeful behaviors
> that are performed according to certain rules or in a stereotyped fashion. The
> behavior is not an end in itself, but is designed to prevent some future event or
> situation. (American Psychiatric Association, 1980, p. 234)

SAMUEL M. TURNER and LARRY MICHELSON • Department of Psychiatry, Western
Psychiatric Institute and Clinic, University of Pittsburgh School of Medicine, Pittsburgh, Pennsylvania 15213.

It should be noted that either obsessions, compulsions, or both may be present in a given case. However, the presence of any one of the two is sufficient to warrant the diagnosis of OCD, according to DSM-III criteria.

Jaspers (1963) described the disorder as an incessant preoccupation of impulses and anxieties which the individual experiences as groundless, senseless and impossible. The obsessions are intrusive, repetitive and unwanted thoughts, images, or impulses which generate resistance. The content of such thoughts is typically repulsive, consisting of blasphemous, obscene thoughts, doubts, or fears that invoke the patient's consciousness. These experiences can take the form of being plagued by thoughts of having killed someone (or fear of doing so), being contaminated (e.g., germs, cancer), worrying about one's morality, having to check names, spelling of words, or electrical appliances, and other similar cognitive intrusions.

With respect to the content of obsessions, Akhtar, Wig, Verna, Pershod, and Verna (1975) reported that the clinical content of obsessions could be meaningfully divided into five basic categories. In descending order of frequency these include (a) dirt, germs and contamination; (b) aggressive behavior; (c) orderliness of inanimate objects; (d) sexual behavior; and (e) religious matters. Although these are by far more common, the list is not necessarily exhaustive and other content might well be seen in a given patient.

Unlike obsessions, compulsions are repetitive, excessive, and unnecessary activities which are not under the person's control. Obsessions invade the consciousness without any apparent volition and despite resistance. However, the urge to carry out the compulsive act is so overwhelming that a subjective sense of reduced volition is subsequently experienced. As previously mentioned, the two primary forms of compulsive behavior are excessive cleaning/washing and checking. Thus, the compulsive cleaner may spend the vast majority of the day cleaning and recleaning his body, house, or other personal items. On the other hand, the checker may spend most of his day checking and rechecking such items as gas jets on the stove or the placement of various personal objects. Individuals so afflicted may spend most of their existence satisfying compulsive needs and have their social and vocational activities seriously impaired. In addition to obsessions and compulsions *per se,* anxiety and depression are prominent clinical features. Likewise, marital and/or family conflict as well as impairment in other interpersonal relationships are common.

EPIDEMIOLOGY

Obsessive-compulsive disorder has been estimated to account for approximately 3% to 4.6% of all psychiatric patients (Beech & Vaughan, 1978; Black,

1974). It has been estimated, in addition, that 3% of all neurotics are diagnosed as suffering from OCD (Hare, Price, & Slater, 1971). Unfortunately, there are no large-scale epidemiological studies of the major anxiety disorders, including OCD, and the evidence of new cases diagnosed according to specific objective criteria remains unknown. The above estimates, however, probably represent an underestimate given the often hidden nature of obsessional states and the reluctance of many individuals to seek treatment for fear of being diagnosed and possibly treated as "crazy."

Similarly, epidemiological data on the spontaneous recovery rate for OCD are unavailable. Cawley (1974), however, noted that with hospitalized OCD patients, approximately one-fourth recovered within 5 years, one-half showed a moderate level of improvement, and one-fourth remained the same or experienced a worsening of symptoms. With nonhospitalized OCD patients, approximately 66% improved to some extent while the other 33% reported little positive change or worsening. From our own clinical experience and other reports, these figures seem high and highlight the need for epidemiological and longitudinal studies of OCD as well as other anxiety disorders.

Despite the absence of epidemiological data, a number of sociocultural observations can be drawn when viewing the data cumulatively from the multitude of patients reported in the treatment literature. For example, interesting sex and age differences have been consistently reported. Specifically, 86% of all female OCD patients in Rachman and Hodgson's (1980) studies had cleaning compulsions. Conversely, no sex differences in incidence were found among patients experiencing compulsive checking. These data suggest as association between specific OCD symptoms and sex-role typing. However, there does not appear to be a disproportionate incidence of the disorder *per se* associated with sex.

In regard to age-related factors, it appears that OCD emerges in the late teens and during early adulthood. According to Ingram (1961) and Pollit (1957), the mean age of illness onset is in the early twenties. Black (1974) reported that over 50% of OCD patients developed their symptomatology by age 25, and 84% by age 35. These findings are consistent with data from other researchers (cf. Rachman & Hodgson, 1980) and indicate that the disorder appears to have a "window of vulnerability" associated with early adulthood.

Other sociocultural factors, including marital and sexual behavior among OCD patients, appear to be significantly impaired. For example, Hare *et al.* (1971) reported a high celibacy rate, particularly for males. Furthermore, both sexes appear to marry at an older age. Related to this, their fertility rates were quite low, less even than the rates for patients with schizophrenic disorders. Interestingly, the finding of diminished marital and sexual activity has also been associated with both severity of illness and poor therapeutic outcome (de Silva, Rachman, & Seligman, 1977).

RELATIONSHIP TO OTHER DISORDERS

The question of whether OCD is associated with other psychiatric disorders has served as an impetus for much conjecture, hypothesizing, and debate. We will now examine the relationship of OCD to other psychopathological conditions.

Schizophrenia

Although obsessions and compulsions were thought, many years ago, to have been closely associated with schizophrenia, this notion is now generally rejected by contemporary investigators. Rachman and Hodgson (1980) noted that "Whether it was fed by the fact that some schizophrenic patients at one time or another display obsessional-compulsive features (Rosen, 1957), or whether it was based on a confusion between delusions and obsessions, the belief has taken a long time to wither" (p. 87). Black (1974), examining the incidence of OCD patients who subsequently develop a schizophrenic disorder, reported probabilities which ranged from 0% to 3.3%, based upon three studies of over 300 patients. Similarly, Lo (1967) found only two out of 88 OCD patients who developed subsequent schizophrenia. More recently, Rachman and Hodgson (1980) reported that none of the 83 patients in their early series of studies subsequently developed schizophrenia. Thus, the best conclusion at this time is that OCD and schizophrenia are not closely associated. However, it is possible that an individual can suffer from both conditions.

Organic Brain Syndrome

This term is used to describe a group of disorders that have as their common feature some type of cerebral pathology, typically resulting from disease, trauma, or congenital defect. The available evidence indicates that the absolute number of OCD patients with identifiable organic impairment is quite small (Lewis, 1966; Templer, 1972). Moreover, there does not appear to be any meaningful differences between normal and OCD patients on a variety of indices including EEG abnormalities (Grimshaw, 1964; Ingram & McAdam, 1960; Rachman & Hodgson, 1980) and head injuries (Lishman, 1968). There are rare instances of OCD symptoms developing secondary to diseases such as encephalitis (Steinberg, 1974), but the majority of OCD patients cannot be differentiated from normals using neurological criteria. It has also been our clinical experience that the ritualistic behavior seen in organically impaired individuals, and sometimes in retardates, is distinctly and qualitatively different from rituals seen in OCD. Unlike obsessive-compulsives, these individuals appear to engage in stereotypic behavior for no apparent purpose. Nor is there any indication of the pressure of specific obsessive ideation, although individuals who suffer from OCD can on the contrary, identify obsessive ideation in most instances. Similarly, the ritualistic behavior characteristic of OCD seems to serve an anxiety-reducing function in most cases. Thus, while organically impaired patients engage in repetitive behavior, it does not appear to be quite the same as that seen in OCD patients.

Obsessive-Compulsive Disorder and Phobias

According to Rachman and Hodgson (1980), there is a high degree of association between phobias and OCD. Of course, it can be argued that a high degree of similarity can be observed among all the anxiety disorders listed in the new DSM-III (American Psychiatric Association, 1980). We will discuss these relationships in a later section of this chapter. Rachman and Hodgson (1980) state:

> The distinctive nature of characteristic obsessional fears, focused most often on dirt/disease and contamination, leads naturally to the execution of extensive avoidance behavior. People who are excessively frightened of dirt/disease/contamination take particular care to avoid coming into contact with disease or dirt. This is mainly a passive form of avoidance. (p. 94)

When these attempts at avoidance fail, then the person attempts to "escape." Translated into concrete examples, the obsessional phobic passively avoids dustbins, public lavatories and washrooms, door handles and telephones, sick people, and hospitals. Failure to avoid any one of these stimuli leads to escape behavior designed to remove or reduce the danger signals. The classical form of escape behavior is repetitive cleaning, hence, compulsive cleaning behavior can be construed as the natural consequence of a dirt/disease/contamination phobia. If this construction is correct, then obsessional-compulsive cleaning behavior can be seen as a subclass of the larger category of phobias.

The authors support the theory with evidence from a number of studies investigating the natural history of OCD patients. For example, Kringlen (1965) found that over half of his 91 OCD patients reported the presence of phobias. A number of other similarities emerge when comparing OCD and phobias in general. Specifically, Rachman and Hodgson (1980) identified a number of common elements. First, both OCD and phobic patients respond to anxiety-eliciting stimuli (whether imagined or real) with increases in physiological activity such as tachycardia. Similarly, phobic and OCD stimuli elicit increases in subjective distress and discomfort. Finally, both OCD and phobic responses almost invariably entail some form of phobic avoidance. After successful treatment, both OCD and phobic patients evidence decreases in psychophysiological reactivity to phobic stimuli, decreased discomfort or distress, and decreased phobic avoidance. Moreover, both disorders show an increased incidence of childhood fears, familial neuroses, and a higher incidence among females (Lo, 1967; Rosenberg 1967; Videbech, 1975).

While Mowrer's two-factor theory (Mowrer, 1939) has been used to explain phobic conditions, the failure of this theory to account for all phobias and obsessive conditions has stimulated the search for other conceptualizations which could explain the accrued data. Seligman's (1971) preparedness theory states that certain phobias, for example dirt or contamination, are more commonly reported than other fears due to the selectivity or preparedness of certain stimuli to be more easily conditioned in contrast to what would be expected on the basis of random conditioning to environmental stimuli. Specifically, the frequency with which certain types of phobias, including specific obsessive-compulsive symptoms, emerge appears to transcend what would be expected to occur from chance or random variation alone. Yet, the two-factor theory assumes that the specific unconditioned stimulus is irrelevant. This postulation has been termed the "equipotentiality premise" and has been the subject of considerable scientific criticism and debate (Seligman, 1970, 1971; Rachman, 1977; Rachman & Seligman, 1976).

In view of the disproportionate incidence of certain types of obsessions, compulsions, and fears, certain associations appear to be more easily acquired. Other stimuli may only become "conditioned" after repeated contiguous associations of the UCS with the aversive stimuli. Furthermore, as noted by Seligman (1970), the prepared phobias may be more resistant to extinction and may operate via noncognitive channels such as biological or genetic mechanisms. Seligman (1972) also noted that those situations or objects which affect the potential survival of the organism are the ones most likely to evince preparedness to become phobically conditioned.

Although there are many unresolved conceptual issues regarding preparedness theory, one of the more promising extrapolations involves the hypothesized resistance that prepared phobias would have to treatment. A major premise originating from this theory states that prepared phobias should be more resistant to treatment. However, de Silva, Rachman, and Seligman (1977) in a retrospective study of phobic and OCD patients, found that the preparedness quality of the patient's symptoms had little impact upon their resistance or extinction in clinical outcome. Although as the authors noted, the homogeneous and somewhat restricted sample of severe patients in their study may have obscured differences between the unprepared and prepared phobics, it was nevertheless concluded that the preparedness concept was not highly useful in predicting the outcome of either OCD or phobic patients.

Clearly there is much similarity between phobic disorders and OCD. It should be pointed out, however, that there are also many dissimilarities, particularly when OCD is compared with simple phobias or focal fears. The obsessional patient is continually preoccupied with disturbing, repetitive thoughts. The ritualistic behavior appears necessary despite the lack of contact with the phobic stimulus. Moreover, not all OCD patients suffer from disease/contamination fears, although this is the largest single category. There are those who suffer obsessions only, many who engage only in repetitive checking behaviors and still others who suffer from horrific images. Also, the general level of tension, irritability, self-doubt and depression seen in phobic patients is less severe than in OCD. To support this contention the results of the assessment of various anxiety disorders in our own clinic revealed that OCD patients were more severe than simple phobics on a variety of measures (See Table 1). While there are many similarities between OCD and phobic conditions, therefore, it may be premature to conclude that OCD is merely a subclass of simple phobia.

Obsessive-Compulsive Disorder and Depression

Obsessions and compulsions have also been clinically and theoretically linked to depression. Of all the symptoms associated with OCD, depression has been most highly correlated. The actual incidence of depression among OCD patients is estimated to range from 17% to 35% (Vaughan, 1976) to 66% (Solyom *et al.,* 1971). In our own study (Turner, 1983), virtually all of our OCD patients showed significant depression as measured by the Beck Depression Inventory, the depression scale of the MMPI, and the depression scale of the SCL-90 (see Table 1).

Rachman and Hodgson (1980) state that 55% of their OCD patients reported no depressive syndrome at the onset of the OCD symptoms. There were, however, numerous reports of OCD resulting in secondary depression over time. This finding has also been reported by Welner and Horowitz (1976) who found that the sequelae of OCD followed by depression occurred three times more frequently (38%) than the incidence (11%) of an initial depressive episode subsequently developing into OCD. Although the existence of the association between OCD and depression is unquestionable, its nature and etiological function remains unclear. Obviously, patients report depression as a result of the debilitating symptomatology. It is not presently known, however, whether depressive symptoms can be identified as an etiological precursor. Foa and Steketee (1977) suggest that the concomitance of OCD and depression may be due to a common factor, termed "hyperreactivity." Evidence for such over-sensitivity can be found in both depressed (Lewinsohn, Lobitz, & Wilson,

Table 1. *Assessment of Depression and Anxiety in Simple Phobia and Obsessive-Compulsive Disorder*

	Beck Depression Inventory	MMPI Depression scale	Fear Survey Schedule	Spielburger State Anxiety Inventory
Simple phobics	7.4 ($N = 19$)	55.5 ($N = 14$)	93.2 ($N = 18$)	38.4 ($N = 17$)
Obsessive-compulsives	22.3 ($N = 35$)	84.4 ($N = 18$)	147.6 ($N = 31$)	59.3 ($N = 33$)

1973) and OCD patients (Marks, 1965). Whether hyperreactivity results in, or is the cause of, these associated but quite distinguishable phenomena, awaits further study.

There are a number of clinical studies illustrating the usefulness of anti-depressant medications in treating obsessive-compulsive disorder. In particular, the drug clomipramine, a primarily serotonergic drug, has been found partic-ularly effective (Thoren, Asberg, Cronholm, Jornestedt, & Traskman, 1980; Rachman, Cobb, Grey, MacDonald, Mawson, Sartory, & Stern, 1979). The reasonable degree of success attained with clomipramine has raised the ques-tion of the role of serotonin in OCD. Serotonin has also been the subject of increasing attention among depression researchers. Preliminary data hint that serotonin may in fact be associated with OCD (Yaryura-Tobias & Neziroglu, 1975; Yaryura-Tobias, Bebirian, Neziroglu, & Bhagavam, 1977). These find-ings suggest that serotonin may be a common pathway through which both disorders are manifested and might possibly be treated on a biochemical level. Related to this have been several attempts to examine and compare OCD and depressive patients with regard to psychophysiological functioning. For exam-ple, OCD patients have been reported to experience increased rates of neuro-psychological dysfunction, typically in the form of frontal lobe dysfunction (Flor-Henry, Yudall, Koles, & Howarth 1979).

Recently, Insel, Gillin, Moore, Mendelson, Lowenstein, and Murphy (1982), recognizing the "clinical affinity" of the OCD and depressive disorders, examined the all-night-sleep EEG recordings of 14 OCD patients who had been so diagnosed according to both RDC and DSM-III criteria. In addition, they compared their sleep recordings with both normal and depressed subjects matched for both age and sex. OCD patients' sleep records differed from those of normal subjects on 8 out of 17 measures. They manifested decreased total sleep, increased awakenings, twice the amount of Stage 1 sleep, less Stage 2 sleep, and less than one-half the amount of Stage 4 sleep, decreased delta sleep, and a nearly 50% reduction in REM activity with decreased REM efficiency. Compared with depressed patients, OCD patients had more Stage 1 and Stage 3 sleep and a tendency toward lower REM density than depressed patients. The authors concluded that (a) OCD patients manifest marked abnormalities in sleep; and (b) the sleep of OCD patients had many similarities to patients hospitalized with primary depression. Although a number of methodological problems prohibit definitive conclusions from being drawn, they do raise the question of a common psychobiological link or substrate among obsessive-com-pulsive disorder and depression. Indeed, similarities in the responsivity of obsessive-compulsive and depressed patients to the dexamethasone suppression test, which is claimed to be of some diagnostic value in regard to identifying severe affective illness, provide additional support for this hypothesis (Bick, 1983). However, these hypotheses await more extensive research before they can be regarded as substantiated. Likewise, issues concerning the qualitative, nosological, and clinical variants of depression must be considered in examining the contiguity of OCD and depression. Given the wide spectrum of affective disorders in regard to varying symptom patterns, etiologies, prognoses, and treatments, further experimental and epidemiological studies are needed to permit a more careful delineation of the intricate relationship between these disorders. Unfortunately, a number of methodological problems in previous research severely limits the conclusions that can be drawn at this time. These methodological problems include

1. The absence of strict diagnostic criteria for both OCD or depressed patients
2. Measures of depression range from psychometrically validated instruments to global, unvalidated therapist ratings or impressionistic ratings performed by significant others, clinicians, or self-report
3. Absence of careful historical analysis of whether OCD preceded or followed the appearance of affective symptoms and depression
4. Paucity of data regarding the incidence, duration, and intensity of obsessive-compulsive symptoms among patients with a primary affective disorder and careful attention to the incidence of affective disorders among patients with a primary diagnosis of obsessive-compulsive disorder

With regards to the last of these problems, Rachman and Hodgson (1980) reported that 55% of their patients had no depressive symptoms prior to the onset of the disorder. Similarly, Welner *et al.* (1976) also found that over half of his 150 OCD patients reported no depressive history prior to the onset of the OCD. Thus, whereas depressive features have been shown to increase obsessive ideation, this same association has not been noteworthy with regard to increasing compulsions. Therefore, depressive symptoms may increase obsessional ideation, which is phenomenologically dissimilar to that experienced by OCD patients. That is, content for depressive patients with increased obsessional ideation typically takes the form of aggressive or suicidal thoughts (Bittleson, 1960) which differ from OCD patients whose obsessional thoughts are generally directed toward dirt, germs, contamination, sex, or religious matters and less frequently to suicidal or aggressive behavior (Rachman & Hodgson, 1980). Thus, it is very important that these two disorders be very carefully examined and differentiated in order to understand their association and possible functional relationships.

COGNITIVE FACTORS IN OBSESSIVE-COMPULSIVE DISORDER

One of the major conceptual frameworks employed to explain both the acquisition and maintenance of OCD has been Mowrer's two-stage theory

(1939), subsequently refined by Dollard and Miller (1950). According to this theory, an unconditioned stimulus initially assumes conditional aversive qualities due to a contiguous association with anxiety or discomfort. The resultant anxiety is experienced whenever the conditioned stimuli is presented in either *in vivo* or imaginal modes, and is reduced via escape or avoidance responses. These coping strategies assume a highly reinforcing character and increase dramatically over time. Although this physiologically based drive-reduction paradigm has received much attention, a number of questions remain unanswered regarding its propositions. Indeed, investigators have pointed to many of its deficiencies in explaining etiology, differential patterns of responding across patients, the various OCD stimuli which become conditioned, sex differences, and related variables that show marked individual differences. It should be noted at this point that this is not the only learning theory that has been invoked to explain ritualistic behavior (for a review see Meyer and Levy, 1973).

More recently, there has been increasing recognition of the possibility that cognitive factors such as attributions, belief systems, and expectations may play a role in mediating OCD phenomena. Clinical states including perfectionism, overestimation of harm, overvaluation of ideas, dichotomous thinking, deficient cognitive problem-solving strategies and catastrophic ideation are readily apparent to those who have worked extensively with OCD patients. Unfortunately, few studies have moved beyond this anecdotal level of observation and empirically examined the specific role of any of the cognitive mediational and/or problem-solving strategies among these individuals. Future efforts to do this may prove fruitful in two specific areas. First, a thorough assessment of OCD patients should incorporate some index of the patient's cognitive coping style, attributions, expectation of harm, and catastrophizations. This would not only provide treatment-planning data but would also serve as a baseline against which clinicians could ascertain the efficacy of their intervention. Second, the mapping of cognitive schemas and information-processing strategies might provide invaluable data leading to more effective intervention in the future.

As noted by Foa *et al.* (1974), there is growing need for the development of an effective and empirically based predictive model. Statistical techniques such as path analysis, linear regression, multivariate classification tests, and discriminant function analysis provide useful tools for determining the relative contribution of a multitude of cognitive, behavioral and physiological factors which help predict responsiveness to treatment. For example, we now suspect, based on data collected thus far as to which prognostic factors are related to outcome, that while very depressed patients are less responsive to behavioral treatment, they may be more responsive to tricyclic antidepressant interventions. Conversely, highly anxious subjects are not less apt to respond successfully to behavioral treatment. Therefore, more careful scrutiny is required of pretreatment diagnostic and historic variables which might influence outcome. In order to isolate potent predictor mechanisms, however, it is imperative that clinical researchers plan their assessment strategy *a priori* according to a tripartite model which encompasses all the major areas of functioning, namely physiology, behavior, and cognition (Turner, 1982). The absence of cognitive and psychophysiological assessments of OCD patients is readily apparent when reviewing the literature. Unfortunately, theoretical, conceptual and clinical models of etiology and treatment cannot be fully addressed as long as this omission continues. Future efforts are needed to assess OCD using a more comprehensive monitoring strategy which enables a more finely grained analysis of behavioral, physiological and cognitive dimensions of functioning. This will allow for important phenomena such as synchrony–desynchrony, concordance–disconcordance, and habituation to be more systematically studied.

OBSESSIVE-COMPULSIVE DISORDER AND ANXIETY

The new *Diagnostic and Statistical Manual* (DSM-III; American Psychiatric Association, 1980) groups most of the disorders heretofore known as neurotic under the label of anxiety disorders. These disorders, which have as their core characteristic the presence of maladaptive anxiety, include obsessive-compulsive disorder, agoraphobia, simple phobia, generalized anxiety disorder, post-traumatic stress disorder, and atypical anxiety disorder. The relationship of OCD to these disorders has been the object of considerable discussion and hypothesizing. Although the relationship of OCD to phobias was discussed earlier on in this chapter, it must have been apparent how little is actually known about the interrelationship of these conditions. Much of the lack of knowledge can be attributed to the absence of large scale epidemiological studies of the anxiety disorders based on uniform diagnostic criteria, which has prevented accurate determination of the prevalence and incidence of these disorders (Sartorius, 1980).

In examining the diagnostic criteria for anxiety disorders in DSM-III, it becomes readily apparent that there is considerable overlap in symptoms among the various categories. For example, there is much similarity in the diagnostic categories of panic disorder and agoraphobia. The category of panic disorder was created by eliminating the term anxiety neurosis and constructing two new ones: panic disorder and generalized anxiety disorder. According to DSM-III, panic disorder is characterized by "recurrent panic attacks that occur at times unpredictably" (p. 230).

Panic attack consists of spontaneous episodes of intense arousal characterized by rapid heart rate, dizziness, chest pains, choking sensation, tingling in the extremities, trembling or shaking and sometimes hyperventilation. In addition, there is a fear of death, going "crazy" or being out of control. In extreme cases, actual loss of consciousness results. These attacks appear to occur without precipitation. However, careful examination reveals that they often occur during periods of significant stress. Frequently, they occur in individuals who have high levels of general anxiety and who might well meet diagnostic criteria for generalized anxiety disorder. Avoidance typically occurs in rapid fashion following panic episodes, in which case the diagnosis becomes agoraphobia with panic attacks. Individuals with this disorder are known to avoid multiple situations, yet the central component seems to be fear of experiencing the panic episodes. Thus, the multiple phobias could be viewed as secondary phenomena. In agoraphobia without panic attacks, closer examination typically reveals panic episodes in the past or discrete episodes of anxiety not reaching panic proportions. Most of these patients are generally anxious and manifest some degree of depression. Are these conditions independent entities, or do they represent different psychological manifestations of a single anxiety disturbance?

Before following up on this question, let us now take a look at symptoms seen in OCD and how they relate to the above conditions. It is not uncommon to see "mini-panic episodes" in patients with OCD, and general anxiety and depression are common as well. The majority of OCD cases show fear of contamination which leads to the avoidance of various stimuli. However, much like patients suffering from generalized anxiety disorder, panic, and agoraphobia, they spend much of their time worrying about their bodies and their fears. The fear of panic in agoraphobia is similar to the fear of losing control seen in obsessive-compulsives. In both conditions, patients fear annihilation or similar catastrophic consequences. Much like panic episodes, obsessive thoughts are also known to occur spontaneously in some instances. In each case, the patient is found to engage in some behavior (or to refrain from some behavior) in order to restore equilibrium. Perhaps the most striking similarity is that in all of these conditions (panic, agoraphobia, OCD), there is an attempt by the individual to neutralize or prevent the occurrence of some aversive event through the process of active or passive avoidance. Although it is the OCD patient who is noted for his obsessive doubting and compulsive rituals, similar behavior can be seen in panic and agoraphobic individuals. Consider the agoraphobic who phones her husband at the office 25 times in one day for reassurance, or the patient who restricts him- or herself to a particular environment or will only travel when accompanied by a certain individual or by specified routes. The compulsive nature of these acts is clear.

In the panic disorder and agoraphobic conditions, the impetus to engage in these behaviors is panic (physiological arousal and fearful ideation concerning bodily harm), whereas in the obsessive-compulsive, it is the obsessive thought (also concerned with body integrity in many instances). In addition, OCD patients experience physiological arousal (anxiety), albeit less intense than those experiencing panic episodes (Rachman & Hodgson, 1980).

It is clear that panic disorder, agoraphobia and obsessive-compulsive disorder share some overlap in symptomatology beyond simply the experience of anxiety. Moreover, many of the symptomatic behaviors appear to be functionally equivalent. To support the contention that these disorders may represent. one basic anxiety disorder, genetic studies have shown a familial incidence of obsessive-compulsive disorder and a substantial overlap among the different anxiety disorders in the history and families of these patients (Rachman & Hodgson, 1980). Although specific genetic predisposition cannot be unequivocally demonstrated, there is considerable evidence that certain individuals exhibit a tendency toward anxiety proneness (Carey & Gottseman, 1981; Shields, 1973). The concept of *anxiety proneness* is similar to the notion of *trait anxiety* advanced by Spielberger, Pollans, and Worden (1984) and others. To further strengthen the argument for the concept of anxiety proneness in some individuals, studies employing classical conditioning paradigms have reported not only that some individuals condition much more quickly than others, but that these individuals show a much slower extinction curve. If these conceptualizations withstand the test of empirical scrutiny, important advancements in our understanding of the nature of fears and phobias might result. Specifically, we will have increased understanding of why such learning-based theories as the two-factor theory of Mowrer (Mowrer, 1951) seem to account for some acquisition of fears but not for others. It is possible that the UCS–CS pairing required to obtain conditioning could differ considerably between anxiety-prone individuals and those not anxiety prone. This line of inquiry might also contribute answers to the clinical question of why individuals are differentially reactive to stressful events in life. Likewise, ascertaining the relative contribution of biological or psychological factors to anxiety proneness would be of great benefit from both theoretical and the clinical standpoints.

If the concept of anxiety proneness is correct, there are interesting speculations to be made concerning the development of panic, agoraphobic and OCD conditions. The preparedness theory of fears (Seligman, 1970) states that there are certain stimuli to which the organism is prepared to react; there are situations or objects which are significant for the survival of the organism and these are the ones most likely to become phobically conditioned (Seligman, 1971). Fear of contamination/dirt most often seen in obsessives and fear of an autonomic nervous system out of control as seen in panic disorder and agoraphobia could be viewed as prepared stimuli because they have relevance to the survival of the organism. The experiencing of such symptoms by anxiety-prone individuals could lead to development of a specific disorder. The concept of anxiety proneness would also explain why some individuals experience panic symptoms and contamination/dirt fears but do not develop persistent disorders. Furthermore, following preparedness theory, such symptoms would be resistant to natural extinction and also to treatment. As previously noted, however, the preparedness quality of patient symptoms apparently has little impact on their rate of extinction (de Silva, Rachman, & Seligman, 1977).

While many of these conceptualizations are quite speculative, there is considerable evidence for the concept of anxiety proneness and overlap of characteristics among some of the anxiety disorders. Together with increasing evidence of familial involvement, this evidence raises the distinct possibility of one basic anxiety disturbance.

ASSESSMENT OF OBSESSIONS AND COMPULSIONS

Although readily identifiable as a syndrome, obsessive-compulsive disorder is a complex entity comprised of a myriad of behavioral, affective, cognitive, interpersonal and physiological factors. Much of our failure to understand the condition more fully is due to the limited employment of adequate assessment strategies in OCD research. This is particularly true of clinical outcome studies, where mainly self-report interviews and global rating scales have been used (Turner, 1982a). Furthermore, in light of the phenomenon of desynchrony (Rachman & Hodgson, 1974) it is imperative that a comprehensive assessment strategy be employed if we are to understand the intricate relationship of response domains and behaviors and how they affect treatment outcome. Recognizing the importance of assessment in general, and measurement of OCD in particular, we will review several of the available OCD instruments.

Self-Report Scales

Sandler and Hazari Obsessionality Scale

This instrument was developed to investigate the presence of meaningful neurotic symptoms which could be classified as either obsessive or compulsive. The 40-item scale was administered to 100 neurotic patients, ranging in age from 16 to 54. Factor analyses revealed the presence of two primary domains, following a 45-degree rotation of the centroid factor axes. The first domain depicts an individual who is systematic, methodical, punctual, meticulous in word usage, and consistent. The individual is overly concerned with minutiae, inconsequential and petty details in his/her environment. The second factor appears to describe the obsessive-compulsive disorder, in contrast to the first factor which emphasized obsessional personality traits. The domain of the second factor encompasses such symptoms as intrusive and unwanted thoughts, behavioral compulsions and persistent struggles over one's bad thoughts. Almost a decade later Sandler and Hazari's (1960) scale was utilized in a study by Reed (1969), who found no differences between patients with obsessional traits and obsessional symptoms and control patients who had neither obsessions nor compulsions. Reed (1969) obtained no significant differences using either total or subfactor scores (e.g., derived from subtotals of the first and second factor). Although the instrument served to facilitate the subsequent development of other OCD instruments, the Sandler-Hazari scale has not been widely applied as either a clinical or a research tool. Indeed, there has almost been a complete vacuum of psychometric research regarding the properties of the scale since its original development.

Hysteroid/Obsessoid Questionnaire

This 48-item self-report instrument, developed by Foulds and Caine (1958, 1959) and Foulds (1965), purports to measure obsessionality with emphasis on the constructs of hysteria and obsessional personality. The scale was administered to 93 neurotic patients in a psychiatric institution. Test–retest reliability over a 6 week period was reported as .77, and convergent validity as .68 with clinical ratings. The instrument's main weaknesses include the absence of any data regarding external validity with actual obsessive-compulsive behavior and the paucity of research supporting its ability to discriminate normals from obsessive-compulsives. Presently there are few, if any, scientific investigations citing the use of the HOQ in either clinical or research activities.

Leyton Obsessional Inventory

The Leyton Obsessional Inventory (LOI) was developed by Cooper (1970) and consists of 69 items, of which 47 relate to symptoms and 22 relate to traits associated with obsessive-compulsive disorder. The inventory provides a comprehensive assessment of typical obsessional dysfunctions, with the exception of grossly unpleasant thoughts and washing. The scale yields total trait, symptom, resistance, and interference scores. Resistance pertains to how much the person resists the obsessional behavior, be it cognitive or motoric. Interference refers to the degree of handicap experienced by the person in everyday life as a result of the symptom. Originally, the LOI required patients to card-sort items, necessitating individual supervision and, for high-scoring patients, at least one hour for administration. Even in its original time-consuming form, the LOI was one of the best known and most widely-used measures of OCD. However, the disadvantages of requiring extensive therapist supervision impeded its widespread adoption.

Recognizing this problem, Snowdon (1980) recently compared the reliability of the cumbersome card sort and a written questionnaire version, using 100 medical students as respondents. As a further experimental refinement, half the subjects received the card sort first, followed by the written questionnaire, while the other subjects received the LOI in the reverse order. In all cases respondents completed the two versions of the LOI after an 8-week interim period. This interval was included in order to ascertain the temporal stability of the LOI. The results indicate that the two versions were significantly correlated and possess acceptable temporal stability ($r = .73–.77$). Thus, it appears that the more economical and efficient paper-and-pencil form of administration is for all intents and purposes an equivalent form of the LOI.

In addition, there were no significant differences in total or subscores between the initial and subsequent testings. However, Snowdon (1980) noted that "there is a tendency to obtain lower scores on the second occasion of testing ... this effect will need to be controlled in studies where scores at different times are compared" (p. 168). Therefore, despite the absence of significant differences in scores across time, there does appear to be a slight but identifiable trend toward decreased severity over time. Although this phenomenon may not occur with actual OCD patients (given the chronicity of their symptoms), Snowdon's (1980) caution should be heeded until this effect is examined and ruled out with clinical populations of OCD patients.

With regard to the external validity of the LOI, there are some data indicating it has acceptable concurrent and discriminant validity. Specifically, Rachman, Marks, and Hodgson (1973) reported that the LOI was significantly correlated with clinical ratings of (a) severity as determined by both patient and independent judges ($r = .61-.81$); (b) Fear Thermometer ratings ($r = .47$); (c) phobic avoidance tasks ($r = .52$); and (d) semantic differential scores ($r = .53-.73$). However, these data must be tempered with earlier findings from the same authors (1973), who reported only minimal correlations with other measures of OCD.

Recently, Murray, Cooper, and Smith (1979) administered the LOI to 73 OCD patients and compared their responses to 100 normal respondents, using the card-sort technique. As predicted, OCD patients scored significantly higher than normals on all four subscales. The authors report that OCD patients scored approximately 2–4:1 the ratio of normals on the trait subscore, 3–2:1 for symptoms; 6–2:1 for resistance; and 12–5:1 for the interference subscore. Thus, the LOI does appear to differentiate normal subjects from actual OCD patients.

In summary, while the LOI has undergone a number of refinements and has been widely used in OCD clinical research (cf. Foa & Goldstein, 1978; Marks, 1975), it needs more extensive psychometric investigation. Continued efforts, such as those described in this review, to examine the reliability and validity of the LOI are clearly needed. In addition, refinement of certain items which are either sex-biased or out of date is overdue. These issues notwithstanding, the LOI can provide significant clinical and research data with which to help assess OCD and monitor therapeutic efficacy. It is the authors' experience that the LOI, if augmented with other OCD measures, can be a highly useful assessment tool which is reliable and clinically sensitive to treatment effects.

Obsessive-Compulsive Checklist

The Obsessive-Compulsive Checklist, developed by Philpott (1975), is completed at the time of a clinical interview. The interviewer rates the patients' degree of impairment for 62 different activities. The checklist yields a total impairment score, and also serves as guide for the clinical interviewer. No reliability or validity data have been reported, nor have any investigations reported its use as an outcome measure.

Maudsley Obsessional/Compulsive Inventory

The Maudsley Obsessional/Compulsive Inventory (MOC) is a 30-item instrument developed by Hodgson (1977) in an attempt to overcome the previously cited limitations evident in other obsessive-compulsive scales. The inventory was derived from a larger pool of obsessive-compulsive items on the basis of being able to discriminate obsessionals from other types of neurotics. The scale yields a total score, as well as four subfactors relating to checking, washing, doubting, and slowness. Unfortunately, it does not address the question of obsessional ruminations. The inventory is easily administered and scored and appears to be clinically sensitive to treatment effects (cf. Rachman & Hodgson, 1980). The authors report good test–retest reliability ($r = .89$), over a 4-week period. External validity with the LOI was reported as .60 for 30 obsessional patients. The scale is efficient, and can be completed without the aid of a therapist. Although it is in need of further validation, it can be employed as a concomitant measure of OCD. In regard to both psychometric and clinical characteristics, the scale appears to have been widely utilized.

Physiological Assessment

Unfortunately, little has been accomplished with respect to the physiological assessment of OCD. Yet the study of physiological arousal patterns and their relationship to symptom patterns is crucial if we are to understand the role of anxiety in the development and maintenance of the disorder. Similarly, the behavioral treatment strategies are primarily based upon the extinction of anxiety. In order, therefore, to fully understand the treatments and the effects they produce, attention to physiological variables is essential.

As in other phobic and anxiety studies, a range of psychophysiological variables has been employed. These include heart rate, skin conductance (e.g., Andrasik, Turner, & Ollendick, 1980; Boulougouris & Bassiakos, 1973; Boulougouris, Rabavilas, & Stefanic, 1977; Labavilas & Boulougouris, 1974), blood pressure (Covi, 1970), and pulse rate (Hodgson & Rachman, 1972). Presently, the heart rate response is considered most useful for OCD, just as in the other phobic disorders (Rachman & Hodgson, 1980). Psychophysiological investigations hold promise for increased understanding of the relationship of anxiety proneness to development of OCD, the relationship to other anxiety disorders, the relationship of arousal to symptom maintenance (Beech & Perigault, 1974) and in treatment outcome (Boulougouris & Bassiakos, 1973; Boulougouris *et al.,* 1977; Labavilos & Boulougouris, 1974).

Other physiological variables have been employed even more sparingly, and when included in the assessment strategy, are typically conducted to measure the effects of drugs. For example, Thoren, Asberg, Cronholm, Jornestedt, and Traskman (1980) employed biochemical measures in order to assess the pharmacological effect of the drug clomipramine in a double-blind placebo control-group study with obsessive-compulsives. Similar measures were employed by Rachman *et al.* (1979) in another blind placebo control study comparing clomipramine and behavior therapy. More recently, the dexamethasone suppression test—a biological test thought to be related to severe depression—and sleep studies have been employed with some intriguing findings (Brick, 1983). Interestingly, one patient recently treated by our group showed a positive dexamethasone test prior to treatment with response prevention and flooding. Following treatment, the test was within normal limits. No drugs were employed (Turner, Jacob, & Nathan, 1983). This suggests that the test may be an indicator of general distress rather than a particular marker for depression or OCD. Nevertheless, it has potential as a biological assessment tool in OCD and in examining the relationship of OCD to depression.

Similarly, serotonin has been implicated in the etiology of depression and OCD (Yaryura-Tobias & Neziroğlu 1975; Yaryura-Tobias *et al.,* 1977) and is thought to be the mechanism through which antidepressant drugs, particularly clomipramine (a potent serotonergic compound), achieve their beneficial effects in OCD. While the development of these measures is still in its infancy, their relevance to theoretical and clinical aspects of OCD are apparent.

Behavioral Measures

Few studies with obsessions and compulsions have employed measures of overt behavior. While obsessions are private events, the majority of compulsive behaviors (e.g., handwashing, checking) are amenable to some form of objective measurement. One means of measuring such behavior is to employ variants of the Behavior Avoidance Test (Lang & Lazovick, 1963) that has been so successfully used in studies of phobia. Rachman *et al.* (1979) employed such a test in their study of the effectiveness of clomipramine and behavior therapy. In this instance, subjects were required to make contact with phobic stimuli and rate their discomfort in doing so. Then, a behavioral index of avoidance as well as discomfort was established. In a more direct measurement strategy, Mills, Agras, Barlow, and Mills (1973) employed a "washing pen" with inpatient obsessive-compulsives. Each time the patient approached the sink to wash, he stepped on a grid that triggered a pen that recorded an instance of washing behavior. Turner, Hersen, Bellack, and Wells (1979) and Turner, Hersen, Bellack, Andrasik, and Capparell (1980) employed behavioral observation strategies to assess the level of various rituals (see Figures 1 and 2). Ward personnel were trained to observe and rate the occurrence of ritualistic behaviors in a number of time-sampling schedules. Reliability was reported to be high in both

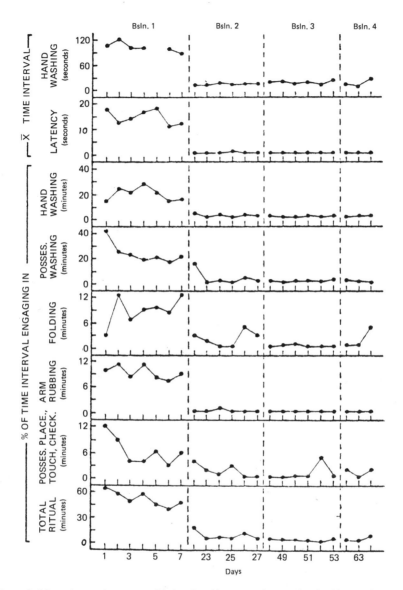

Figure 1. Mean time patient engaged in handwashing, mean latency for checking, and percentage of observation intervals patient engaged in handwashing, possession-washing, folding, arm-rubbing, possession-touching, placing, checking, and total rituals. (From "Behavioral Treatment of Obsessive-Compulsive Neurosis" by S. M. Turner, M. Hersen, A. S. Bellack, and K. C. Wells, *Behaviour Research and Therapy,* 1979, *17,* 95–106, Figure 4. Copyright 1979 by Pergamon Press, Ltd. Reprinted by permission.)

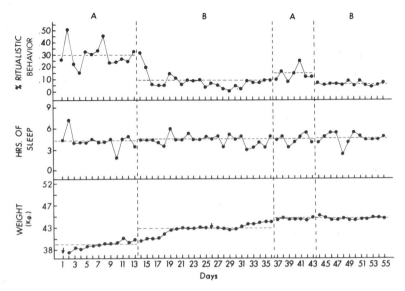

Figure 2. Percentage of time (observation periods) spent in ritualizing, hours of sleep, and weight during initial baseline, initial response prevention, withdrawal, and second response prevention treatment. (From "Behavioral Treatment of Obsessive-Compulsive Neurosis" by S. M. Turner, M. Hersen, A. S. Bellack, and K. C. Wells, *Behaviour Research and Therapy,* 1979, *17,* 95–106, Figure 3A. Copyright 1979 by Pergamon Press, Ltd. Reprinted by permission.)

studies, ranging from .87 to .99. Although such measures would be more difficult to employ on an outpatient basis, the objective measurement of rituals *per se* have taken on more importance as part of the attempt to understand the role of antidepressant drugs in the treatment of obsessions and compulsions. The drug study employing the best measurement strategy to date (Rachman *et al.,* 1979) indicated that the primary effect of the drug was on mood and not on obsessions or compulsions directly. Similar results were reported by Turner *et al.* (1980) on a smaller sample of inpatient obsessive-compulsives. Thus, in understanding the relationship of anxiety and depression in OCD as well as providing adequate assessment of treatment effects, some type of objective measurement of rituals is desirable.

TREATMENT

Obsessive-compulsive disorder has traditionally been viewed as refractory to treatment. In a sample of 90 patients treated with psychotherapy, Kringlen (1965) found that only 20% had improved 13 to 20 years after treatment. However, Grimshaw (1965) reported 40% of his sample showed much improvement over 14 years of follow-up. More recently, Sifneos (in preparation) reported that a short-term psychoanalytic procedure was effective in treating obsessive-compulsives. Little in the way of empirical data were offered as support, however, and it is questionable whether the groups of patients treated by Sifneos would meet the DSM-III criteria for obsessive-compulsive disorder. Recent reviews of behavioral intervention strategies (e.g., Rachman & Hodgson, 1980; Steketee, Foa, & Grayson, 1982) reported the effectiveness of these treatments to be in the 70% to 80% range. In a recent follow-up of 36 patients treated on an outpatient basis at Maneford Hospital in England, similar findings were reported. Subjects in this study were followed for 1–5 years, with 81% of cases requiring no additional referral (Kirk, 1983). Thus, the picture appears to have improved considerably for this relatively rare but extremely debilitating condition. Behavior therapy is not the only treatment of recent vintage to show promise in alleviating this condition. Results with pharmacotherapy, and in particular those drugs with a serotonergic effect, have been encouraging, although less clearly so than the effects of behavior therapy. There has been some suggestion that obsessive-compulsives with extreme levels of depression may be more responsive to behavior therapy if treated concurrently with anti-depressants (Foa, Steketee, & Ozarou, in preparation). If such synergistic effects are present, then a powerful treatment regimen comprised of both behavior therapy and antidepressants might be strongly considered for the most severe patients. These treatments will be discussed in some detail subsequently.

Behavioral Treatments

In many respects it is inappropriate to use the term behavior therapy when discussing treatment for obsessive-compulsive disorder. Actually, many different strategies have been employed and often times represent the application of different theoretical models (cf. Foa *et al.,* in preparation). Recall that there is no one behavior-therapy model, rather there are several models and various theoretical concepts from which a variety of treatment strategies emanate (Turner, 1982b). Major behavioral approaches will be discussed in some detail but we will not undertake an exhaustive review here inasmuch as this has been accomplished in several recent publications (Foa *et al.,* in preparation; Rachman & Hodgson, 1980; Sturgis & Meyer, 1981). Instead, the focus will be on discrepancies and areas where ambiguity still prevails.

Exposure Treatments

The rationale for the application of exposure treatment is based on the notion that the compulsive rituals are maintained because they serve an anxiety-reducing function. Anxiety is thought to be a function of the obsessive idea-tion (Ahktar, 1975). However, some investigators have questioned the anxiety-reduction hypothesis. Beech (1974), as a result of observation and interviewing of patients, maintained that rituals serve to increase anxiety. Other investiga-tors have made similar observations (Wolpe, 1958; Reed, 1969). An excellent example of an attempt to systematically investigate mood changes accompa-nying ritualistic behavior is reported by Walker and Beech (1969). Through careful, detailed interviewing, direct observation, and systematic ratings of mood (hostility, depression, and anxiety), these investigators concluded that some rituals cause mood to deteriorate and that the interruption of a ritual could have a beneficial effect on mood. Both of these findings contradicted tra-ditionally held views that compulsions have an anxiety-reducing function and that one should not interrupt the ritual for fear of an acute exacerbation of the patient's dysphoric mood.

Hodgson (1972), Roper, Rachman, and Hodgson (1973), and Roper and Rachman (1976), in a series of elegant experiments, addressed the question whether the performance of the obsessive-compulsive ritual decreases or increases the anxiety/discomfort aroused by exposing the patients to situations which provoke strong urges to perform the ritual. In the first study (Hodgson, 1972), 12 obsessive-compulsive handwashers took part in four experimental manipulations to assess the effect on subjective levels of anxiety and distress measured on standardized subjective rating scales of the following conditions: (a) touching a contaminated object; (b) handwashing immediately after the contamination; (c) delaying a handwash by 30 min; (d) handwashing after the 30-min delay; and (e) interrupting the handwashing ritual. The results showed that touching a contaminated object does produce an increase in subjective anxiety and discomfort and that the completion of the ritual produces a reduc-tion of the anxiety and discomfort to baseline precontamination levels. In addi-tion, they demonstrated that interruption of a compulsive ritual does not have an effect on anxiety and discomfort.

A second experiment (Roper *et al.,* 1973) was similarly designed and car-ried out with 12 obsessional checkers. Although the overall results replicated the findings with the washers of the previous experiment, they noted the fol-lowing differences: (a) the checkers experienced a lower level of anxiety/dis-comfort than the washers when provoked; (b) there was a significant decrease in anxiety/discomfort after the half-hour delay period following provocation with the checkers; and (c) five patients reported increases in anxiety/discom-fort after completion of the ritual on at least one occasion during the experi-ment. Because of these differences, a third experiment (Roper & Rachman, 1976) using 12 checkers was carried out in the patients' homes under two experimental conditions, one with the experimenter present and the other in his absence. The pattern of response closely followed that of compulsive wash-ers. The performance of the checking ritual produced a decrease in anxiety/

discomfort. The levels of anxiety/discomfort were higher in the experimenter-absent condition and the time taken to complete the checking ritual was also longer in this condition. These findings firmly support the anxiety-reduction hypothesis of compulsive behavior at least in the two most commonly found forms, namely compulsive handwashing and compulsive checking.

In a further experiment with eleven obsessive-compulsive checkers, Rachman (1976) studied anxiety/discomfort and urges to check over a 3-hr period immediately following provocation. In the control condition, a checking ritual immediately followed provocation, whereas in the experimental condition checking was absolutely prevented for a 3-hr period following provocation. Thus, he found that the checking ritual in the control condition resulted in a marked decrease in anxiety/discomfort and dissipation of urges to check. In the experimental condition where checking was prevented, he found a marked decline of anxiety/discomfort and dissipation of urges to check after the first hour of response prevention. In addition, a further decline, continuing during the second and third hours of response prevention, was observed. Furthermore, the decline in anxiety/discomfort and urges to perform the ritual were found to run parallel courses, with the urges dissipating slightly faster than anxiety/discomfort.

These series of experiments clearly demonstrate that in regard to obsessional washers and checkers, the performance of rituals is followed by a decline of the urges to engage in the ritual and a decrease in anxiety/discomfort caused by the obsessions. However, the fact remains that compulsions and rituals can occasionally and paradoxically produce increments in anxiety/discomfort or cause deterioration of mood, as previously mentioned (Walker & Beech, 1969; Beech, 1971; Beech & Liddell, 1974). These investigators have studied this problem very closely and offer interesting explanations hinging essentially on the obsessionals' difficulty with decision making. It would seem that if the patient cannot decide when to stop his ritual or at what point the ritual has fulfilled its purpose (been completed), he continues to perform, on and on, and it is this that may account for the deterioration of mood and increase in anxiety/discomfort.

To complicate matters, several investigators have observed that rituals can also become autonomous from underlying obsessions and have little effect on the prevailing level of anxiety/discomfort. Thus, Walton and Mather (1963) hypothesized that the disassociation of rituals from anxiety/discomfort-producing obsessions would tend to occur mainly in the chronic stages of the obsessive-compulsive illness. Marks, Crowe, Drewe, Young, and Dewhurst (1969) gave an illustration of this phenomenon when the washing rituals of a patient continued to occur despite the successful desensitization of the obsessional fear of contamination.

The bulk of the empirical evidence tends to support the anxiety-reducing function of compulsive rituals. However, anxiety elevation is clearly present in a small number of cases. In our clinical experience, we have seen a number of such instances. Interestingly, in some patients, anxiety reportedly increased due to feelings of self-contempt resulting from an inability to control the urge, and fears of going crazy because of their engaging in what the patients recognized as absurd behavior.

One of the first behavioral treatments to be used with obsessive-compulsives was systematic desensitization (Wolpe, 1958). In the largest study of this procedure, Cooper, Gelder, and Marks (1965) reported that out of 10 obsessive-compulsives treated, only 3 improved. In fact, subjects in a supportive-psychotherapy control group evinced superior gains. Numerous single-case reports exist demonstrating some indications of limited effectiveness, but they too are far from uniformly positive (e.g., Furst & Cooper, 1970; Marks, *et al.,* 1969).

It is not entirely clear why systematic desensitization is not very effective as a treatment for obsessive-compulsive disorder. Walton and Mather (1963) have suggested that the procedure is only suitable for acute disorders where conditioned anxiety is evident and there is also some indication that *in vivo* desensitization might fare a little better (Beech & Vaughan, 1978). One explanation might be the generalized nature of the anxiety and the omnipresence of the obsessions. Thus, the patient is continuously bombarded with anxiety-arousing cues between sessions. Another possibility is the level of depressions. As previously noted, depression is a common factor in most obsessive-compulsives. Recently, questions have been raised about the utility of relaxation (systematic desensitization requires relaxation) with patients who are significantly depressed (Jacob, Turner, Szekely, & Eidelman, 1983). One final and possibly most crucial explanation is that the attenuated exposure may be too short for the obsessive-compulsive patient to benefit from it. As we shall see, prolonged exposure has proved to be one of the most effective behavioral strategies for OCD.

In the initial report on response prevention, Meyer (1966) described the treatment of two female school teachers on an inpatient basis. Case 1 was a 33-year-old teacher with a 3-year history of checking behavior and fear of contamination by dirt. Strict response prevention was in effect for 4 weeks, followed by a gradual withdrawal over several weeks. Ritualistic washing and avoidance behaviors were almost completely eliminated. The effects of treatment were maintained during a 14-month follow-up, but although frequency remained low, duration and thoroughness increased.

Case 2 was a 47-year-old teacher with a 32-year history of obsessions and compulsions. These included various repetitive acts and thoughts. Strict response prevention was instituted for 3 weeks, followed by a gradual reduction over 2½ weeks. The daily number of rituals were reduced from 20 to 8. Although intrusive thoughts did not initially respond to treatment, they eventually dropped to eight thoughts per day. Treatment effects were maintained during a 22-month follow-up.

In a second report, Meyer and Levy (1973) reported the successful treatment of six chronically ill obsessive-compulsive patients with response prevention. All patients were treated on an inpatient basis and their symptoms involved a mixture of obsessions and compulsions (e.g., hand washing, ritualistic bathing, repetitive touching, fear of harm, contamination fear). Assessment was conducted at pre- and posttreatment and at follow-up by having patients, as well as an independent observer, make daily ratings. Ratings of rituals, anxiety, depression, work adjustment, sexual adjustment, and interference with leisure activities were obtained. To summarize the effects of treatment for these six patients, a large decrease in obsessive-compulsive behavior was found in all cases, and in some instances total cessation of symptoms. Anxiety and depression ratings, on the whole, tended to vary with changes in obsessive-compulsive symptoms, but there was some variation. Adjustment ratings (except for sexual adjustment) also showed improvement. A particular strong point of this study is that the follow-up period in some instances reached 5 years (range = 6–70 months). These data (ratings) showed that some patients continued to improve, others showed no further change, while two patients evidenced a return of some symptoms, but not at the level of pretreatment. Meyer and Levy pointed out that five of the six patients had previous treatment with other methods and that they all had premorbid obsessional personalities. They further concluded that the single most important element of treatment was the continuous supervision. Interestingly, they noted that Janet (1908), a half century earlier, had also observed the positive effects of supervision with 14 cases of obsessive-compulsive neurosis.

In one of the best controlled studies of response prevention, Mills *et al.* (1973) treated five obsessive-compulsive handwashers in a series of five single-case experiments. Ritualistic handwashing was measured by constructing a "washing pen" described as a railing with a single gate, completely surrounding a 6 × 8 foot board. Each time the patient approached the "pen," a switch connected to a cumulative recorder was activated. In this manner, daily recordings of duration as well as frequency of handwashing were obtained. In each instance, the results were evaluated in single-case experimental designs. Following treatment there was a "dramatic" reduction in frequency and duration of handwashing rituals in all five patients. In two experiments (3 and 4), placebo conditions were introduced to create expectancy for improvement, with no lasting effect. Thus, the results of treatment appear to be attributable to response prevention. There was no follow-up, however. Together, these studies provide impressive evidence for the effectiveness of response prevention as a treatment for OCD. It might be said that the introduction of this treatment hailed a breakthrough in the remediation of this refractory condition.

Various combinations of response prevention, flooding, modeling and other behavioral strategies have been used. Using single-case experimental designs, Turner *et al.* (1979) reported the treatment of three chronic obsessive-compulsive neurotics with response prevention, flooding, and antidepressant medication. This study employed a variety of self-report assessments as well as direct behavioral measures of response prevention. The results indicated that response prevention was effective in each instance, with no demonstrable contributions obtained from flooding or medication. In one case, treatment gains were maintained over an 18-month follow-up. Similar results were reported by Turner *et al.* (1980).

In a series of reports, Rachman and his associates (Rachman *et al.,* 1971, Hodgson & Rachman, 1972, Rachman *et al.,* 1973) described the treatment of 20 OCD patients with several behavioral strategies (exposure, modeling, response prevention) alone and in combination. According to the authors, relaxation therapy served as a control treatment. However, treatments were actually administered sequentially over a period of weeks. A positive aspect of these studies was the inclusion of a variety of assessment instruments including measures of obsessiveness, a Fear Thermometer, a Behavioral Avoidance Test, the Leyton Inventory and the Eysenck Psychoticism, Extraversion and Neuroticism Scales. Also, clinical ratings of phobic avoidance, free-floating anxiety, depression and depersonalization were obtained from patients and independent assessors.

The overall results of these studies showed a strong positive effect for all of the behavioral treatments, with no significant differences among treatments. It is difficult to fully interpret the data presented in these studies because of the designs employed. In addition, the data analyses raised as many issues as they answered. Reports of long term follow-up were quite impressive, however.

Catts and McConaghy (1975) described the treatment of six OCD patients with response prevention procedures that incorporated flooding (exposure) and modeling in the treatment. Clinical rating scales were used to evaluate compulsive behavior, phobic anxiety, avoidance behavior and social adjustment. Overall, 75% were rated much improved, 50% improved, and 25% not improved. Treatment gains were maintained over a 9- to 24-month follow-up period.

The rationale for response-prevention treatment is based on the theory that compulsive rituals persist, despite their irrationality, because they serve an anxiety-reducing function. Extinction is obtained from exposing the patient to stimuli which previously had led to rituals, but not allowing the rituals to occur, thereby extinguishing the anxiety response. According to Meyer and Levy (1973), it is also possible that a modification of expectations occurs during the course of treatment such that fear of consequences assumed to help maintain rituals are eliminated. The "modification of expectation" hypothesis embodies a cognitive explanation for some of the change achieved with response prevention. Yet, it remains to be seen how cognitive changes might occur in the absence of anxiety reduction, since the obsessions are thought to generate the high anxiety. The point being made is that it may be unlikely for changes in expectation to occur in the absence of anxiety reduction. Therefore, the change in expectation (usually concerning feared consequences) observed following response prevention might be viewed as a function of anxiety reduction *per se,* rather than as an independent event. It should be noted that the response prevention-procedure includes many elements of other behavioral treatments that have been used singly to treat obsessive-compulsives. Specifically, elements of exposure, modeling, and guidance are inherent components of the response prevention (Sturgis & Meyer, 1981). The notion of guidance is central to response prevention. In fact, response prevention has its origin in techniques designed to alter fixated behavior in animals (Maier, 1949; Maier & Ellen, 1952; Maier & Klee, 1945). Thus, it is difficult to evaluate studies in which these strategies have been used singly or as additions to response prevention. It might well be that such interventions as modeling, guided practice, and variations in the exposure paradigm are useful in individual cases. These strategies, as well as a host of others, have been used with some measure of success when applied individually.

Other Behavioral Interventions

One group of procedures used in treating OCD has been labeled *blocking procedures* by Foa *et al.* (in preparation). These include aversive strategies (Kenny, Mowbray, & Lalani, 1978; LeBoeuf, 1974; Wisocki, 1970), aversion relief (Rubin & Merbaum, 1971; Solyom, 1969), and thought stopping (Lombardo & Turner, 1979; Stern, 1970; Stern, Lipsedge, & Marks, 1973; Turner, Holzman, & Jacob, 1983). Although the use of aversive procedures has achieved a certain degree of success, some caution should be observed. Foa *et al.* (in preparation) noted that blocking of ritualistic behavior in the absence of procedures directed toward reducing anxiety, may have little effect in the long run. Moreover, Walton (1960) reported relapses in cases where only motor responses were treated.

Blocking procedures are often utilized in instances where only disturbing cognitive material is present (obsessions) in the absence of overt ritualistic behavior. A number of cases of successful use of aversive procedures for obsession have been reported (Kenny, Solyom, & Solyom, 1973; Kenny *et al.,* 1978; Mahoney, 1971).

Thought stopping has also been frequently used when only obsessional ideation was present. Thus, the Stern (1970) report employing this strategy dealt with a patient who ruminated about correctly performing certain actions. Similarly, Lombardo and Turner (1979) reported using the procedure with a 25-year-old patient who ruminated about heterosexual relationships which resulted in feelings of depression. Thus, the blocking strategies might be viewed as more appropriate in instances involving only obsessive ideation or as adjuncts to the exposure strategies. For example, Turner, Holzman, and Jacob (1983) described the use of an imaginal thought-stopping procedure to treat an intractable "looking" ritual when the patient could not experience the urge to look during *in vivo* thought-stopping sessions. This patient's ritual was highly situational and specific to her natural environment.

Biological Treatment

To some degree, almost all of the psychotropic medications in the physician's armamentarium have been used in attempts to treat obsessive-compulsive disorder (see Ananth, in preparation). In addition, various psychosurgical procedures have been used with some reports of success (Freeman & Watts, 1950; Sykes & Tredgold, 1964). These treatments have been primarily used in Europe and are not viewed as viable treatment alternatives here. Of all the pharmacological compounds, the antidepressants have been the most frequently used. These include imipramine, amitriptyline, and clomipramine. Overall, clomipramine has received the greatest amount of attention and we shall review the literature on this drug in some detail.

Clomipramine (CLI)

Clomipramine is a drug which is not presently available on the commercial market in the United States. It is an antidepressant compound with strong serotonergic effects and some adrenergic effects as well. In the initial report of its effect with obsessionals, Lopez-Ibor (1966) reported that obsessive symptoms in depressed patients improved following administration of clomipramine.

In another early report, Marshall (1971) reported moderate to marked success in 75% of a mixed diagnostic group which included phobic, obsessive-compulsive, and anxiety state patients using intervenous administration of 250 to 325 mg CLI followed by a transition to oral dosages up to 300 mg daily. Nonresponders consisted of nonobsessive patients such as manic depressives, personality disorders and patients with hysterical features. Treatment gains were maintained during a 6 month follow-up period. Although this study is plagued by problems in patient selection and objective assessment, it is of some importance that these patients had received previous therapeutic intervention with no clinical response.

Beaumont (1973) summarized the results of oral CLI treatment of 64 patients with at least some obsessional features. He reported that out of 19 patients with clear-cut obsessional disorder treated with paranteral CLI, the following response pattern was obtained: (a) 4 were rated as very much improved, (b) 13 as moderately improved, (c) 2 as fairly improved, and (e) 0 as poorly improved. Of the 45 remaining patients (with obsessional features), 2 showed very good improvement, 34 good improvement, 9 moderate improvement, and 0 poor improvement. Wide variations in dosages, ranging as high as 450 mg daily, were administered. Relapses were noted to occur rapidly, concurrent with withdrawal of CLI. Assessment in this study was conducted in a nonsystematic fashion using the Hamilton Rating Scale, the Eysenck Rating Scale, an obsessional checklist, and in some instances the Leyton Obsessional Inventory. However, no data or criteria were presented as to how the classification of patient improvement was determined.

Marshall and Micev (1973) treated 85 patients suffering from obsessional illness or phobic anxiety with intravenous CLI. Medication was initially 50 mg CLI, administered over a 2-hr period in a normal saline solution. Dosages were raised to a plateau of 300 to 350 mg with 5- to 6-hr administration time. Intravenous CLI was replaced with 50 mg oral dosages three times daily after patients had obtained maximum benefit from the infusions. Assessments were performed at pre, post, and at 3-, 6-, 12-, and 18-month follow-ups using a clinical rating scale. Clinically significant improvements were observed in 70% of the obsessional patients. Moreover, patients followed up at 18 months showed maintenance of treatment effects.

Rack (1973), reported that CLI 50 mg orally administered and then followed by intravenous infusions resulted in clinical improvements in obsessional patients. Clinical ratings in addition to the Leyton Obsessional Inventory were used as assessment measures. Out of 21 obsessional patients, 7 (33%) manifested excellent response, 5 (24%) were rated as good, slight improvement was noted in 7 cases (33%) and no improvement in 2 cases (10%). It should be noted, however, that one of the two failures reportedly engaged in compulsions associated with temporal-lobe epilepsy and probably should not have been considered a true obsessive-compulsive.

Walter (1973) treated 35 patients with intravenous CLI who had been suffering from obsessive-compulsive disorder. All patients diagnosed as having a primary obsessional illness manifested significant or marked improvement. Indeed, 100% of these patients showed continued maintenance of treatment effects over a 1-year follow-up period. In the depressive/obsessional group, the recovery rate was 75%.

Waxman (1975) describe a multi-center investigation of clomipramine among 32 patients diagnosed as either obsessional or having phobic disorders. Utilizing various scales to measure anxiety, obsessions, compulsions and associated symptomatology, patients' responses to 225 mg of CLI daily were monitored. Significant improvement in all phobic and anxiety states were reported. In addition, obsessional patients showed overall improvement in both resistance and interference scores. Since judgments of improvement in this study were made using the scale employed by Beaumont (1973), these results must be tempered with caution due to problems of inadequate reliability and validity of the measures.

Although the above-cited clinical reports suggest that CLI is effective in treating some cases of OCD, the results must be interpreted with caution. In addition to their uncontrolled nature, the studies are weakened by their use of mixed diagnostic groups, varying dose-ranges of CLI, different methods of medication administration, varying duration of treatment, and in many instances, absence of objective assessment. Although self-report, therapist and evaluator ratings are clinically valid assessment techniques, the relationship between these measures and actual performance remains unknown. Previous research suggests that these measures may be susceptible to experimental problems including subject compliance, acquiesence, therapeutic and research expectations, believability of treatment, and cognitive dissonance associated with admitting failure to respond to treatment.

Yaryura-Tobias and Neziroglu (1975) conducted one of the first controlled pilot studies of clomipramine as a treatment for obsessive-compulsive disorder. Twelve patients, diagnosed as obsessive-compulsive neurotics (DSM-II) were given oral CLI up to a maximum of 300 mg daily for 3 weeks, following a one week "wash-out" phase. Assessment included obsessive-compulsive rating scales, global evaluation, clinical psychiatric evaluations and the Hamilton Rating Scale. All of the patients (100%) showed significant reductions in anxiety, while four of seven (57%) manifested improvements in obsessive-compulsive symptomatology. Hamilton Rating Scale depression scores revealed significant reduction in overall depression as well as in subfactors of anxiety and agitation. Global evaluation ratings indicated improvement in symptomatology for six out of seven patients (86%). The success of this limited (3-week) treatment suggests that CLI may be potentially useful for OCD symptoms. The results are further strengthened by the observation that many patients treated in this study had previously received other tricyclic antidepressants without improvement.

Ananth and Van den Steen (1977) found CLI and doxepin both effective in reducing anxiety. Treatment resulted in statistically significant improvement of phobic symptoms. Twenty OCD patients were treated with CLI, 300 mg daily. In addition, 20 patients were placed on doxepin 300 mg per day. Assessments were performed on an ongoing basis and included the Leyton Obsessional Inventory, Social Adjustment Scale, Psychiatric Questionnaire for Obsessive-Compulsive Neurosis, and the Self-Analysis Rating Form. The CLI-treated group resulted in improvement in 70% of the patients, 10% showing no change and 20% getting worse. Doxepin treatment resulted in improvement in 55% of the patients; 39% did not change, and 6% deteriorated. In regard to measures of anxiety and phobia, CLI treatment led to 85% and 65% improvement rates, respectively. In contrast to CLI treatment, doxepin patients showed 65% and 69% improvement rates for anxiety and phobic ratings respectively. The Social Adjustment Scale ratings showed statistically significant differences in favor of the CLI group. The severity of the obsessive-compulsive symptomatology also showed differential improvement rates in favor or the CLI treatment.

Ananth, Solyom, Bryntwick, & Krishnappa (1979) treated 20 treatment-resistant obsessional patients using CLI. Assessment on the Leyton Obsessional Inventory, Psychiatric Questionnaire for Obsessive-Compulsive Disorder, Social Adjustment Scale, the Maudsley Personality Inventory and the Self-Analysis Form was provided. Of 20 patients receiving oral CLI (maximum dose of 300 mg) 29 showed significant improvement on obsessional scores, 14 showed improvement in depression ratings, and 17 demonstrated reductions in anxiety. Significant improvement was also obtained on the Maudsley Personality Inventory, Self-Analysis Form, and the Social Adjustment measures. Pre- versus posttreatment results on the Leyton Obsessional Inventory revealed statistically significant improvements in resistance, symptom, and interference scores.

Although it is clear from the above studies that CLI may be effective in reducing obsessions and compulsions, it is difficult to judge the special efficacy of the drug owing to the manner in which measurement has been conducted. Since it has not been common practice to provide objective assessment of rituals *per se,* the question still remains as to whether the drug achieves its effect through mood elevation (antidepressive action) or whether it affects the disorder directly. With other antidepressants, the suggestion has been made that the effects are primarily antidepressive (Turner *et al.,* 1980).

Thoren, Asberg, Cronholm, Jornestedt, and Traskman (1980) treated 24 chronic OCD patients in a double-blind placebo controlled study comparing CLI (a serotonin blocker) with nortriptyline (a norepinephrine blocker) and placebo. During the treatment period, patients were urged to resist their compulsive rituals, but no formal behavior therapy was employed. A variety of clinical rating scales and self-report inventories were used. The results showed a mean reduction of 42% on an OCD rating scale for the CLI group, 21% reduction for nortriptyline, and virtually no change in the placebo group (7%) after five weeks of treatment. However, no significant difference among treatments showed up on other assessment instruments (Leyton Obsessional Inventory, Home Incapacity Scale, Ward Incapacity Scale, Individual Self Rating Scale, Montgomery-Asberg Depression Scale). Following treatment in the study, all patients were offered extended CLI treatment, concomitant with behavior therapy. Thoren *et al.* further observed that the differences that were obtained between CLI and nortriptyline did not occur until 5 weeks into treatment, which suggests it is a slow-acting drug. Although this study is often cited as a model study demonstrating the effectiveness of CLI and its superiority over other antidepressants, a closer examination reveals that such a conclusion is premature. Clear superiority of CLI was shown on only one measure which has no known psychometric properties.

These investigators (Thoren, Asberg, Bertilsson, Mellstrom, Sjoqvist, & Traskman, 1980) also reported on extensive biochemical measures used in the above study. The rationale for clomipramine's effectiveness in obsessive-compulsive disorder is thought to be its potent serotonin-blocking action. The present study demonstrated that there was a significant reduction of cerebrospinal fluid metabolites with CLI patients but not with nortriptyline patients. There was also a significant correlation between concentration of plasma CLI and' reduction in obsessional symptom scores. Taken together, these data support the serotonin-inhibiting effects of CLI and suggest that there is an association between plasma levels of the drug and serotonin blocking, but its relationship to effectiveness remains to be demonstrated.

Perhaps the most sophisticated and best controlled study was conducted by Rachman, Cobb, Grey, MacDonald, Mawson, Sartory, and Stern (1979). This study employed a 2×2 factorial design to study the effects of CLI and behavioral treatment. Forty chronic OCD patients were randomly assigned to either CLI, placebo, CLI plus exposure, and CLI plus relaxation. Assessment included monitoring idiosyncratic and standardized obsessive-compulsive behaviors, depression ratings, anxiety, and social adjustment. Assessments were performed at pretreatment, 4, 7, 10, 36, 44, 62 and 114 weeks. Patient, therapist, and independent assessors were all blind with regard to drug condition and the assessors were blind as to the psychological treatment condition. Behavioral treatment significantly improved compulsive rituals, while CLI affected significant improvement on measures of anxiety and depression. There were no significant interaction effects between the behavioral and pharmacological treatment. Although both treatments showed statistically significant effects, it appeared that there were no potentiating effects, rather their effects were additive. As noted by Rachman *et al.* (1979), failure to find specific anti-obsessive-compulsive effects might have been due to limitations in the experimental design. The major difficulty was that assessment was performed at Week 7 which might have been premature in terms of expecting full therapeutic effects from the drug. However, Thoren *et al.* suggest effects can be seen at 5 weeks. Unfortunately, the investigators did not measure the patients actual compulsions or rituals.

In a 2-year follow-up of patients reported in the Rachman *et al.* (1979) study, Mawson, Marks, and Ramm (1982) again reported that over the 2-year period, there was substantial maintenance of improvement in rituals, mood, and social adjustment above pretreatment levels. There was no drug effect on rituals at the 2-year follow-up. Reduction of rituals was even greater in those patients who had received 30 hr than in those who had received 15 hr of exposure. Clomipramine was reported to be superior to placebo when anxiety and depression were high. The authors concluded that exposure treatment, although useful for reducing rituals, did not influence affective episodes. The affective symptoms were suppressed by CLI and other antidepressants but only as long as the drug was taken, with discontinuation resulting in relapse.

Close examination of these studies reveal that exposure treatments are most effective for reducing compulsive rituals and that there is minimal scientific support or empirical basis for CLI or other antidepressants having a specific anti-obsessive-compulsive effect. Rather such drugs apparently achieve their effects through the alleviation of affective (i.e. dysphoric) symptoms. However, a combination of the two treatments might well be advised, particularly when both significant clinical depression and marked anxiety are evident.

SUMMARY

Obsessive-compulsive disorder is the rarest among the anxiety disorders. Yet, it is one of the most socially debilitating, and highly refractory to treatment intervention. The syndrome is characterized by recurrent or persistent ideas, thoughts, images, and often overt ritualistic behaviors such as handwashing or checking. What often distinguishes it from organic and psychotic conditions is the individual's subjective discomfort and resistance to engage in the ritualistic behavior. A qualitative difference between OCD and other disorders has also been noted in ritualistic patterns. The most common fear in the disorder is fear of dirt/contamination and the most frequent ritualistic patterns are washing and checking.

The relationship of phobia, depression, and anxiety have long been the subject of theoretical and clinical interest. Although there are many similarities to phobias, there are also significant differences that warrant retention of the diagnostic distinction at this time. The relationship to depression is much more complex, and common biological substrates have been hypothesized. Yet, the selectivity of behavioral and pharmacological interventions suggests that the two disorders are distinct entities, despite significant overlap.

With respect to anxiety, an effort was made, albeit highly speculative, to show that many of the anxiety disorders have equivalent symptomatology and some suggestions of a common biological basis. Significant advancements are being made that suggest the existence of one basic anxiety disturbance and support the existence of anxiety processes among individuals who develop anxiety disorders.

Over the past decade, the treatment picture for this disorder has improved markedly. Behavioral treatments embodying exposure principles have shown themselves to be highly effective treatments, particularly on compulsive components of the disorder. These treatments have been quite useful on both an inpatient and outpatient basis. Antidepressants, and particularly clomipramine, also appear promising as adjunct treatments. Presently, the data indicate that these drugs have a primarily mood-altering effect that could prove particularly useful in OCD patients with marked affective disturbances. The best overall strategy at this time might be a combination of the two treatments, particularly when depression and anxiety are extremely high.

REFERENCES

Akhtar, S., Wig, N. H., Verna, V. K., Pershod, D., & Verna, S. K. A phenomenological analysis of symptoms in obessive-compulsive neuroses. *British Journal of Psychiatry*, 1975, *127*, 342–348.

American Psychiatric Association. *Diagnostic and statistical manual of mental disorders* (2nd ed.). Washington, D. C.: Author, 1968.

American Psychiatric Association. *Diagnostic and statistical manual of mental disorders* (3rd ed.). Washington, D. C.: Author, 1980.

Ananth, J. Clomipramine in obsessive neurosis: A review. In M. Mavissakalian, S. M. Turner, & L. Michelson (Eds.), *Obsessive-compulsive disorder: Psychological and pharmacological treatment*. New York: Plenum, in preparation.

Ananth, J. & Van den Steen, N. Systematic studies in the treatment of obsessive-compulsive neurosis with tricyclic anti-depressants. *Current Therapeutic Research*, 1977, *21*, 495–500.

Ananth, J., Solyom, L., Bryntwick, S., & Krishnappa, U. Chlorimipramine therapy for obsessive-compulsive neurosis. *American Journal of Psychiatry*, 1979, *136*, 700–701.

Andrasik, F., Turner, S. M., & Ollendick, T. H. Self-report and physiological responding during *in vivo* flooding. *Behaviour Research and Therapy*, 1980, *18*, 593–595.

Beaumont, G. Clomipramine (Anafranil) in the treatment of obsessive-compulsive disorders—A review of the work of Dr. G. A. Collins. *Journal of International Medical Research*, 1973, *1*, 423–424.

Beech, H. R. Ritualistic activity in obsessional patients. *Journal of Psychosomatic Research*, 1971, *15*, 417–422.

Beech, H. R. Approaches to understanding obsessional states. In H. R. Beech (Ed.), *Obsessional states*. London: Methuen, 1974.

Beech, H. R. & Liddell, A. Decision making, mood states and ritualistic behavior among obsessional patients. In H. R. Beech (Ed.), *Obsessional states*. London: Methuen, 1974.

Beech, H. R. & Perigault, J. Toward a theory of obsessional disorder. In H. R. Beech (Ed.), *Obsessional states*. London: Methuen, 1974.

Beech, H. R. & Vaughan, M. *Behavioral treatment of obsessional states*. New York: Wiley, 1978.

Black, A. The natural history of obsessional neurosis. In H. R. Beech (Ed.), *Obsessional states*. London: Methuen, 1974.

Boulougouris, J. & Bassiakos, L. Prolonged flooding in cases with obsessive-compulsive neurosis. *Behaviour Research and Therapy*, 1973, *11*, 227–231.

Boulougouris, J., Rabavilas, A., & Stefanis, C. Psychophysiological responses in obsessive-compulsive patients. *Behaviour Research and Therapy*, 1977, *15*, 221–230.

Bick, P. A. Obsessive-compulsive behavior associated with dexamethasone treatment. *Journal of Nervous and Mental Disease*, 1983, *171*, 253–254.

Carey, G. & Gottesman, I. I. Twin and family studies of anxiety, phobic and obsessive disorders. In D. F. Klein & J. G. Rabkin (Eds.), *Anxiety: New research and changing concepts*. New York: Raven Press, 1981.

Catts, S. & McConaghy, N. Ritual prevention in the treatment of obsessive-compulsive neurosis. *Australian and New Zealand Journal of Psychiatry*, 1975, *9*, 37–41.

Cawley, R. H. Psychotherapy and obsessional disorders. In H. R. Beech (Ed.), *Obsessional states.* London; Methuen, 1974.

Cooper, J. The Leyton Obsessional Inventory. *Psychological Medicine,* 1970, *1,* 48–64.

Cooper, J. E., Gelder, M. G., & Marks, I. M. Results of behaviour therapy in 77 psychiatric patients. *British Medical Journal,* 1965, *1,* 1222–1225.

de Silva, P., Rachman, S., & Seligman, M. E. P. Prepared phobias and obsessions: Therapeutic outcome. *Behaviour Research and Therapy,* 1977, *15,* 54–77.

Dollard, J. & Miller, N. *Personality and psychotherapy.* New York: McGraw-Hill, 1950.

Flor-Henry, P., Yeudall, L. T., Koles, Z. J., & Howarth, B. G. Neuropsychological and power spectral EEG investigations of the obsessive compulsive syndrome. *Biological Psychiatry,* 1979, *14,* 119–130.

Foa, E. B. & Goldstein, A. Continuous exposure and complete response prevention in the treatment of obsessive-compulsive neurosis. *Behavior Therapy,* 1978, *9,* 821–829.

Foa, E. B. & Steketee, G. Emergent fears during treatment of three obsessive-compulsives: Symptom substitution or de-conditioning. *Journal of Behavior Therapy and Experimental Psychiatry,* 1977, *8,* 353–358.

Foa, E. B., Steketee, G. S., & Ozarou, B. J. Behavior therapy with obsessive-compulsives: From theory to treatment. In M. Mavissakalian, S. M. Turner, & L. Michelson (Eds.), *Obsessive-compulsive disorder: Psychological and pharmacological treatment.* New York: Plenum, in preparation.

Foulds, G. A. *Personality and personal illness.* London: Tavistock, 1965.

Foulds, G. A. & Caine, T. M. Psychoneurotic symptom clusters, trail clusters and psychological tests. *Journal of Mental Science.* 1958, *104,* 722.

Foulds, G. A. & Caine, T. M. Symptom clusters and personality types among psychoneurotic men compared with women. *Journal of Mental Science,* 1959, *105,* 469.

Freeman, W. & Watts, J. W. *Psychosurgery* (2nd ed.). Oxford: Oxford University Press, 1950.

Furst, J. B. & Cooper, A. Failure of systematic desensitization in two cases of obsessive-compulsive neurosis marked by fears of insecticide. *Behaviour Research and Therapy,* 1970, *8,* 203–206.

Gittleson, N. C. The effects of obsessions on depressive psychosis. *British Journal of Psychiatry,* 1966, *112,* 253–258.

Grimshaw, L. Obsessional disorder and neurological illness. *Journal of Neurology, Neurosurgery and Psychiatry,* 1964, *27,* 229–231.

Grimshaw, L. The outcome of obsessional disorder: A follow-up study of 100 cases. *British Journal of Psychiatry,* 1965, *111,* 1051–1056.

Hare, E., Price, J., & Slater, E. Age distribution of schizophrenia and neurosis: Findings in a national sample. *British Journal of Psychiatry,* 1971, *119,* 445–458.

Hodgson, R. & Rachman, S. The effects of contamination and washing in obsessional patients. *Behaviour Research and Therapy,* 1972, *10,* 111–117.

Hodgson, R. J., & Rachman, S. Obsessional-compulsive complaints. *Behaviour Research and Therapy,* 1977, *15,* 389–395.

Ingram, I. M. Obsessional illness in mental hospital patients. *Journal of Mental Science,* 1961, *197,* 382–402.

Ingram, I. & McAdam, W. EEG, obsessional illness and obsessional personality. *Journal of Mental Science,* 1960, *106,* 686–691.

Insel, T. R., Gillin, C., Moore, A., Mendelson, W. B., Lowenstein, R. J., & Murphy, D. J. The sleep of patients. *Archives of General Psychiatry,* 1982, *39,* 1372–1377.

Jacob, R. G., Turner, S. M., Szekely, B. C., & Eidelman, B. H. Predicting outcome of relaxation therapy in headaches: The role of "depression." *Behavior Therapy,* 1983, *14,* 457–465.

Janet, P. *Les obsessions et la psychasthénie* (2nd ed.). Paris: Paillière, 1908.

Jaspers, K. *General psychopathology.* Chicago: University of Chicago, 1963.

Kenny, F. T., Solyom, L., & Solyom, C. Faradic disruption of obsessive ideation in the treatment of obsessive neurosis. *Behavior Therapy,* 1973, *4,* 448–451.

Kenny, F. T., Mowbray, & Lalani, S. Faradic disruption of obsessive ideation in the treatment of obsessive neurosis: A controlled study. *Behavior Therapy,* 1978, *9,* 209–221.

Kirk, J. Behavioural treatment of obsessional-compulsive patients in routine clinical practice. *Behaviour Research and Therapy,* 1983, *21,* 57–62.

Kringlen, E. Obsessional neurotics: A long-term follow-up. *British Journal of Psychiatry,* 1965, *111,* 709–722.

Lang, P. J., & Lazovick, A. D. Experimental desensitization of a phobia. *Journal of Abnormal and Social Psychology,* 1963, *66,* 519–525.

LeBoeuf, A. An automated aversion device in the treatment of a compulsive hand-washing ritual. *Journal of Behavior Therapy and Experimental Psychiatry,* 1974, *5,* 267–270.

Lewinsohn, P. M., Lobitz, C., & Wilson, S. Sensitivity of depressed individuals to adversive psychology. *Journal of Abnormal Psychology,* 1973, *81,* 259–263.

Lewis, A. J. Obsessional disorder. In R. Scott (Ed.), *Price's textbook of the practice of medicine.* (10th Ed.). London: Oxford University Press, 1966.

Lishman, W. A. Brain damage in relation to psychiatric disability after head injury. *British Journal of Psychiatry,* 1968, *114,* 373–410.

Lo, W. A follow-up study of obsessional neurotics in Hong Kong Chinese. *British Journal of Psychiatry,* 1967, *113,* 823–832.

Lombardo, T. W., & Turner, S. M. Use of thought-stopping to control obsessive rumination in a chronic schizophrenic patient. *Behavior Modification,* 1979, *3,* 267–272.

Lopez-Ibor, J. J. *Ensayo clínico, la monoclomi prámina* (Paper read at the Fourth World Congress of Psychiatry, Madrid, 1966). *Congress Proceedings,* 1966, *3,* 2159–2161.

Mahoney, J. M. The self-management of covert behavior: A case study. *Behavior Therapy,* 1971, *2,* 575–578.

Maier, N. R. F. *Frustration: The study of behaviour without a goal.* New York: McGraw-Hill, 1949.

Maier. N. R. F., & Ellen, P. Studies of abnormal behaviour in the rat: The prophylactic effects of guidance in reducing rigid behaviour. *Journal of Abnormal and Social Psychology,* 1952, *47,* 109–116.

Maier, N. R. F., & Klee, I. B. Studies of abnormal behaviour in the rat: XVII. Guidance versus trial and error in the alterations of habits and fixations. *Journal of Psychology,* 1945, *19,* 133–163.

Marks, I. M. *Patterns of meaning in psychiatric patients.* New York: Oxford University Press, 1965.

Marks, I. Behavioral treatment of phobic and obsessive-compulsive disorders: A critical appraisal. In M. Hersen, R. M. Eisler, & P. M. Miller (Eds.), *Progress in Behavior Modification.* New York: Academic, 1975.

Marks, I. M., Crowe, M., Drewe, E., Young, J., & Dewhurst, W. G. Obsessive-compulsive neurosis in identical twins. *British Journal of Psychiatry,* 1969, *115,* 991–998.

Marks, I. M., Hodgson, R., & Rachman, S. Treatment of chronic obsessive-compulsive neurosis by *in vivo* exposure. *British Journal of Psychiatry.* 1975, *127,* 349–364.

Marshall, W. K. Treatment of obsessional illnesses and phobic anxiety state with clomipramine. *British Journal of Psychiatry,* 1971, *119,* 467–468.

Marshall, W. K., & Micev, V. The role of intravenous clomipramine in the treatment of obsessional and phobic disorders. *Scottish Medical Journal,* 1973, *20,* 49–53.

Mavissakalian, M., Turner, S. M., & Michelson, L. M. (Eds.). *Obsessive-compulsive disorder: Psychological and pharmacological treatment.* New York: Plenum, in preparation.

Mawson, D., Marks, I. M., & Ramm, L. Clomipramine and exposure for chronic obsessive-compulsive rituals: III. Two year follow up and further findings. *British Journal of Psychiatry,* 1982, *140,* 11–18.

Meyer, V. Modification of expectancies in a case with obsessional rituals. *Behaviour Research and Therapy*, 1966, *4*, 273–280.

Meyer, V. & Levy, R. Modification of behavior in obsessive-compulsive disorders. In H. E. Adams & P. Unikel (Eds.), *Issues and trends in behavior therapy*. Springfield, Ill.: Charles C Thomas, 1973.

Mills, H., Agras, S., Barlow, D., & Mills, J. Compulsive rituals by response prevention. *Archives of General Psychiatry*, 1973, *28*, 524–529.

Mowrer, O. H. A stimulus response theory of anxiety. *Psychological Review*, 1939, *46*, 553–565.

Mowrer, O. H. Two-factor learning theory: Summary and comment. *Psychological Reports*, 1951, *58*, 350–354.

Murray, R. M., Cooper, S. E., & Smith, A. The Leyton Obsessional Inventory: An analysis of the response of 73 obsessional patients. *Psychological Medicine*, 1979, *9*, 305–311.

Philpott, R. Recent advances in the behavioral measurement of obsessional illness: Difficulties common to these and other measures. *Scottish Medical Journal*, 1975, *20*, 33–40.

Pollitt, J. Natural history of obsessional states. *British Medical Journal*, 1957, *1*, 195–198.

Rabavilas, A., & Boulougouris, J. Physiological accompaniments of ruminations, flooding and thought-stopping in obsessive patients. *Behaviour Research and Therapy*, 1974, *12*, 239–244.

Rachman, S. Obsessional-compulsive checking. *Behaviour Research and Therapy*, 1976, *14*, 269–277.

Rachman, S. The conditioning theory of fear acquisition. A critical examination. *Behaviour Research and Therapy*, 1977, *15*, 375–387.

Rachman, S. & Hodgson, R. Synchrony and desynchrony in fear and avoidance. *Behaviour Research and Therapy*, 1974, *12*, 311–318.

Rachman, S. & Hodgson, R. *Obsessions and compulsions*. Englewood Cliffs, N. J.: Prentice-Hall, 1980.

Rachman, S. & Seligman, M. E. P. Unprepared phobias: "Be prepared." *Behaviour Research and Therapy*, 1976, *14*, 333–338.

Rachman, S., Hodgson, R., & Marks, I. The treatment of chronic obsessional neurosis. *Behaviour Research and Therapy*, 1971, *9*, 237–247.

Rachman, S., Marks, I., & Hodgson, R. The treatment of chronic obsessive-compulsive neurosis by modeling and flooding *in vivo*. *Behaviour Research and Therapy*, 1973, *11*, 467–471.

Rachman, S., Cobb, J., Grey, S., MacDonald, B., Mawson, D., Sartory, G., & Stern, R. The behavior treatment of obsessive-compulsive disorders, with and without clomipramine. *Behaviour Research and Therapy*, 1979, *17*, 467–478.

Rack, P. Clomipramine in the treatment of obsessive states. *Journal of International Medical Research*, 1973, *1*, 397–399.

Reed, G. F. Some formal qualities of obsessional thinking. *Psychiatric Clinic*, 1968, *1*, 382–392.

Reed, G. F. Obsessionality and self-appraisal questionnaires. *British Journal of Psychiatry*, 1969, *115*, 205–209.

Roper, G. & Rachman, S. Obsessional-compulsive checking: Experimental replication and development. *Behaviour Research and Therapy*, 1976, *14*, 25–32.

Roper, G., Rachman, S., & Hodgson, R. An experiment on obsessional checking. *Behaviour Research and Therapy*, 1973, *11*, 271–277.

Rosen, I. A clinical significance of obsessions in schizophrenia. *Journal of Mental Science*, 1957, *103*, 773–786.

Rosenberg, C. Familial aspects of obsessional neurosis. *British Journal of Psychiatry*, 1967, *113*, 405–413.

Rubin, R. D., & Merbaum, M. Self-imposed punishment versus desensitization. In R. D. Rubin,

H. Fensterheim, A. A. Lazarus, & C. M. Franks (Eds.), *Advances in behaviour therapy.* New York: Academic, 1971.

Sandler, J. & Hazari, A. The obsessional: Or the psychological classification of obsessional character traits and symptoms. *British Journal of Medical Psychology,* 1960, *33,* 113–122.

Sheilds, J. Heredity and psychological abnormality. In H. J. Eysenck (Ed.), *Handbook of abnormal psychology* (2nd ed.). London: Pitmans, 1973.

Schneider, K. Schwangszustände in Schizophrenie. *Archiv Für Psychiatrie und Nervenkrankheiten,* 1925, *74,* 93–107.

Seligman, M. E. P. On generality of the law of learning. *Psychological Review,* 1970, *77,* 406–418.

Seligman, M. E. P. Phobias and preparedness. *Behavior Therapy,* 1971, *2,* 307–320.

Sifneos, P. Psychotherapeutic interventions in obsessive disorders. In M. Mavissakalian, S. M. Turner, & L. Michelson (Eds.), *Obsessive-compulsive disorder: Psychological and pharmacological treatment.* New York: Plenum, in preparation.

Snowdon, J. A comparison of written and postbox forms of the Leyton Obsessional Inventory. *Psychological Medicine,* 1980, *10,* 165–170.

Solyom, L. A case of obsessive neurosis treated by aversion relief. *Canadian Psychiatric Association Journal,* 1969, *14,* 623–626.

Solyom, L., Zamanyadeh, D., Ledwich, B., & Kenny, F. Aversion relief treatment of obsessional neurosis. In R. Rubin (Ed.), *Advances in behavior therapy.* New York: Academic Press, 1971.

Spielberger, C. D., Pollans, C. H., & Worden, T. J. Anxiety disorders. In S. M. Turner & M. Hersen (Eds.), *Adult psychopathology and diagnosis.* New York: Wiley, 1984.

Steinberg, M. Physical treatments in obsessional disorders. In H. R. Beech (Ed.), *Obsessional states.* London: Methuen, 1974.

Steketee, G., Foa, E. B., & Grayson, J. B. Recent advances in the behavioral treatment of obsessive-compulsives. *Archives of General Psychiatry,* 1982, *39,* 1365–1371.

Stern, R. Treatment of a case of obsessional neurosis using thought-stopping technique. *British Journal of Psychiatry,* 1970, *117,* 441–442.

Stern, R. S., Lipsedge, M., & Marks, I. Obsessive ruminations: A controlled trial of a thought-stopping technique. *Behaviour Research and Therapy,* 1973, *11,* 659–662.

Sturgis, E. & Meyer, V. Obsessive-compulsive disorder. In S. M. Turner, K. S. Calhoun, & H. E. Adams (Eds.), *Handbook of clinical behavior therapy.* New York: Wiley, 1981.

Sykes, M. & Tredgold, R. Restricted orbital undercutting. *British Journal of Psychiatry,* 1964, *110,* 609–640.

Templer, D. I. The obsessive compulsive neurosis: Review of research findings. *Comprehensive Psychiatry,* 1972, *13,* 375–383.

Thoren, P., Asberg, M., Bertilsson, L., Mellstrom, B., Sjoqvist, F., & Traskman, L. Clomipramine treatment of obsessive-compulsive disorder: II. Biochemical aspects. *Archives of General Psychiatry,* 1980, *37,* 1289–1294.

Thoren, P., Asberg, M., Cronholm, B., Jorhestedt, L., & Traskman, L. Clomipramine treatment of obsessive-compulsive disorder. *Archives of General Psychiatry,* 1980, *37,* 1281–1285.

Turner, S. M. Behavioral assessment of drug effects in obsessive-compulsive disorders. *Psychopharmacology Bulletin,* 1982, *18,* 41–43. (a)

Turner, S. M. Behavior modification and black populations. In S. M. Turner and R. T. Jones (Eds.), *Behavior modification in black populations: Psychosocial issues and empirical findings.* New York: Plenum, 1982. (b)

Turner, S. M. *Patterns of depression and anxiety in patients with anxiety disorders.* Unpublished manuscript, University of Pittsburgh, 1983.

Turner, S. M., Hersen, M., Bellack, A. S., & Wells, K. C. Behavioral treatment of obsessive-compulsive neurosis. *Behaviour Research and Therapy,* 1979, *17,* 95–106.

Turner, S. M., Hersen, M., Bellack, A. S., Andrasik, F., & Capparell, H. V. Behavioral and pharmacological treatment of obsessive-compulsive disorders. *Journal of Nervous and Mental Disease,* 1980, *168,* 651–657.

Turner, S. M., Holzman, A., & Jacob, R. G. Treatment of compulsive looking by imaginal thought-stopping. *Behavior Modification,* 1983, *7,* 576–582.

Turner, S. M., Jacob, R. G., & Nathan, R. S. *Dexamethasone suppression test in obsessive-compulsive disorder.* Unpublished manuscript, University of Pittsburgh, 1983.

Vaughan, M. The relationships between obsessional personality, obsessions and depression and symptoms of depression. *British Journal of Psychiatry,* 1976, *129,* 36–39.

Videbech, T. Psychopathology of anancastic endogenous depression. *Acta Psychiatrica Scandinavia,* 1975, *52,* 336–373.

Walker, V. J. & Beech, H. R. Mood states and the ritualistic behavior of obsessional patients. *British Journal of Psychiatry,* 1969, *115,* 1261–1268.

Walter, C. J. S. Clinical impressions on treatment of obsessional states with intravenous clomipramine. *Journal of International Medical Research,* 1973, *1,* 413–416.

Walton, D. The relevance of learning theory to treatment of an obsessive-compulsive state. In H. J. Eysenck (Ed.), *Behavior therapy and the neuroses.* Oxford: Pergamon, 1960.

Walton, D. & Mather, M. D. The application of learning principles to the treatment of obsessive-compulsive states in the acute and chronic phases of illness. *Behaviour Research and Therapy,* 1963, *1,* 163–174.

Waxman, D. An investigation into the use of anafranil in phobic and obsessional disorders. *Scottish Medical Journal,* 1975, *20,* 61–66.

Welner, N. & Harwitz, M. Intrusive and repetitive thoughts after a depressing experience. *Psychological Reports,* 1975, *37,* 135–138.

Wisocki, P. A. Treatment of obsessive-compulsive behavior by covert sensitization and covert reinforcement: A case report. *Journal of Behavior Therapy and Experimental Psychiatry,* 1970, *1,* 233–239.

Wolpe, J. *Psychotherapy by reciprocal inhibition.* Stanford, Cal.: Stanford Univerity Press, 1958.

Yaryura-Tobias & Neziroglu, J. A. The action of clomipramine in obsessive-compulsive neurosis: A pilot study. *Current Therapeutic Research,* 1975, *17,* 111–116.

Yaryura-Tobias, Bebirian, R., Neziroglu, F. A., & Bhagavarn, H. N. Obsessive-compulsive disorders as a serotogenic effect. *Research Communications in Psychology, Psychiatry, and Behavior,* 1977, *2,* 279–286.

7

Generalized Anxiety Disorder

RICHARD M. SUINN

INTRODUCTION

Generalized anxiety disorder is the human disorder previously referred to as *anxiety neurosis* and sometimes described as free-floating or pervasive anxiety. One estimate is that such anxiety disorders occur in 2% to 5% of the population in the United States and Britain (Marks & Lader, 1973). Generalized anxiety disorder differs from panic disorder in being a more persistent, chronic condition of tension, while panic disorder appears to be characterized by recurring experiences of extreme tension. Hence there are differences in duration and in intensity. A person suffering from generalized anxiety disorder often complains, "I'm constantly tense and jumpy all the time . . . it's like I know something dreadful is going to happen . . . my hands are clammy, I can't concentrate . . . it's affecting my whole life." In contrast, one client diagnosed as suffering from panic disorder reported, "I was riding my bicycle . . . and suddenly . . . my heart was going so fast I was sure I was having a heart attack. I wanted to hide somewhere . . . I was petrified . . . I thought . . . I'm going mad . . . the fright . . . made me want to scream" (Suinn, 1981a). A distinction should be made between the generalized anxiety disorder and the phobic disorder since both are characterized by similar patterns of responses, such as autonomic arousal, somatic-behavioral disruptions such as trembling, and cognitive responses such as worrying. A major distinction is that phobic disorders are characterized according to the stimulus aspects of the disorders. Phobic disorders are associated with distinctive cue conditions which, when present, pre-

RICHARD M. SUINN • Department of Psychology, Colorado State University, Ft. Collins, Colorado 80523.

cipitate the fear reaction. In contrast, it is likely that persons suffering from either a generalized anxiety disorder or a panic disorder will not be able to identify clearly the stimulus conditions associated with their anxiety responses. Another distinction is that the reactions the phobic person tends to show to the feared stimulus involve either escape or avoidance behaviors; in fact the two-factor theory of fear acquisition emphasizes the role of such avoidance behaviors in the maintenance of the phobia (Eysenck & Rachman, 1965).

SYMPTOM EXPRESSION

It is useful to examine the three response channels through which anxiety is expressed: the affective-autonomic, the somatic-behavioral, and the cognitive. Although persons with a generalized anxiety disorder tend to show symptoms in each of these response domains, there is evidence that different people may have different expressions of anxiety (Lang, 1971). For example, one client may demonstrate heightened autonomic arousal yet fail to show escape or avoidance behaviors (Leitenberg, Agras, Butz, & Wincze, 1971). In comparison, another person may report much worrying and subjective anxiety, yet show only modest physiological symptoms and no behavioral disruption. It is useful, therefore, to characterize the various specific ways in which an anxiety state may be identified. These will be grouped by the major response channels of affective, somatic, and cognitive (see Table 1).

Affective-Autonomic

The affective-autonomic domain may be the dominant mode for expression of anxiety, showing up in three possible symptoms. The first includes

Table 1. Multichannel Symptom Expressions of Anxiety[a]

    I. Affective-Autonomic Response Channel
      A. Heightened autonomic arousal
      B. Subjective feelings of distress
      C. Presence of anxiety-related psychophysiologic disorders
   II. Somatic-Behavioral Response Channel
      A. High muscular tension
      B. Performance disruptions
      C. Increased vigilance and scanning
  III. Cognitive Response Channel
      A. Disruption of attention or concentration
      B. Interferences with cognitive performances
      C. Presence of worrisome ruminations

---

[a] Adapted from J. Deffenbacher & R. Suinn, 1982.

heightened autonomic arousal. This is evidenced in physiological responses such as increased heart rate or respiration, gastric sensations, feelings of nausea, sweating, cold and clammy hands, or lightheadedness. Assessment information may readily be obtained via psychophysiological instruments, such as blood pressure, digital temperature, or heart rate measuring devices while the client is under stress.

To the degree that the autonomic changes are experienced more diffusely, a second index may be subjective feelings of distress. Instead of noting respiration itself, a patient might be more vaguely aware of "a constricting feeling around the chest"; rather than specifically reporting increased heart rate, the person may speak of "hearing my heart pound in my ears"; and instead of identifying muscle spasms, the individual may talk about "lumps in my throat," or "butterflies in my stomach."

A third evidence of affective-autonomic responses is the appearance of certain anxiety-related psychophysiological disorders. Examples of these include difficulty in falling asleep, interrupted sleep, fatigue, tension headaches, diarrhea, frequent urination, and some dermatological disorders. It should be noted that there are other medical problems which can also lead to these symptoms, as well as environmental causes (for example, change of time zones, change of work routines, environmental noise). Hence medical consultation and careful assessment of life and work routines are essential to avoid misdiagnosis.

Somatic-Behavioral

Among the somatic-behavioral signs of anxiety are evidences of muscular tension, performance disruption, and vigilance and scanning. Muscular tension is a direct effect of the increased autonomic activation, and can be seen in muscle rigidity, cramping in areas such as the neck and shoulders, trembling, muscle aches, shakiness, furrowed brow, restless movements, jumpiness, and a heightened startle response. The chronic nature of generalized anxiety disorder can also lead to fatigue due to continuous muscle tension over long periods.

Performance disruption may appear as another type of expression of anxiety, such as in speech dysfluencies or disturbances of motor coordination. In those cases where the anxiety seems to be limited to events such as public speaking, musical performances, and athletic competition, then performance anxiety is easily recognized. It should be noted that removal of the anxiety does not necessarily guarantee improvement in performance, inasmuch as such behavioral outcomes are influenced by variables other than anxiety, for example, aptitude, skill level, and ability to transfer learning. However, if performance deterioration is observed, then the role of anxiety may be inferred to be of greater importance in explaining the poorer performance.

Vigilance and scanning are behaviors involving hyperattentiveness to the environment. The anxious individual may be prompted to continuously search the environment based on the feeling that "something is going to happen." The heightened awareness (vigilance) and search (scanning) are not focused since the individual is not certain about what specifically to expect. Because the person's energies are bound up however, the ability to attend to or concentrate on other events that are occurring may be impaired.

Cognitive

There are three ways in which anxiety may be expressed in cognitive activities: disruption of attention or concentration skills, interferences with cognitive performances, and preoccupation with worrisome ruminations. Examples of the first, disruption of attention or concentration, would include distractibility, the inability to focus in a sustained way, or inappropriate narrowing of focus. The person might express these problems by saying, "I can't seem to pay attention to even simple things any more," or "My mind wanders." Or the patient might admit to becoming locked into some parts of the environment or interactions, and failing even to notice other aspects. If this is in the context of problem solving, the person tends to perseverate in talking about the feelings, or repeatedly describes the problem, or sees only a single solution rather than alternatives. The perseveration may be the continued expression of a fantasied hope for solution, "If only I could. . . ." Both this type of narrowing of focus, or the more general distractibility or failure to concentrate, may also relate to the vigilance and scanning mentioned earlier.

In considering interferences with cognitive performances, we are looking at evidence such as problems with learning and memory. An anxious person faced with acquiring new information, especially complex material, may exhibit difficulty in comprehension or recall. Interference with short-term memory might be attributable to poor information processing, which in turn might be related to the problem of attention or concentration mentioned earlier. Long-term memory might also be disrupted, as in the person who becomes "so nervous I forgot my own address", or an individual whose "mind goes completely blank" during times of stress.

During preoccupation with worrisome ruminations, the person is plagued with catastrophic thoughts. These "gloom and doom" obsessions are centered either on anticipated consequences or on unreasonable self-evaluation. Hence, the client may continue to expect the worse is going to occur, "I'm not going to have enough time to prepare properly," or may prejudge a personal action, "I'm just not good enough to succeed." In some cases, the person also exaggerates the level of the personal emotional impact of an event, "I just know I'll be mortified if this doesn't turn out right!" or "I won't be able to face anyone ever again." Anticipatory ruminations are common in an obsessional way ("What if . . .".) and are based upon an extreme statement of what might happen, instead of a reality-based expectation of what probably will happen (Beck, Laude, & Bohnert, 1974).

SYMPTOM SEVERITY

We can evaluate the severity of anxiety experiences by examining time and magnitude information. In looking at time, we would conclude that the experiences are of higher-level severity if

1. the anxiety reactions appear more often per unit time, that is, are of high frequency;
2. the anxiety reactions last for longer periods once initiated, that is, recovery time is slower; and
3. the period elapsing before the next anxiety reaction appears is shorter, that is, periods free of anxiety are less frequent.

Since generalized anxiety disorder involves the chronic occurrence of anxiety reactions, time is also important in the original diagnosis. As a rule of thumb, there should be evidence that the generalized anxiety has persisted for at least one month's duration (American Psychiatric Association, 1980).

The assessment of magnitude can be accomplished through examining each of the symptom-response channels mentioned previously (affective, somatic, cognitive). The disorder is considered more severe if

1. the symptoms within any response channel are of severe magnitude, for example, extremely high heart rate (affective channel), severe speech disruption (somatic channel), or extreme distractibility (cognitive channel);
2. there are numerous severe symptoms within or across several response channels, for example, severe diarrhea, nausea plus extremely elevated blood pressure and heart rate (high-magnitude somatic symptoms), or all-consuming worrisome ruminations, severe muscle fatigue, and continuous headaches (high-magnitude symptoms involving cognitive and affective channels); and
3. the symptoms are assessed as having a severe overall effect on life adjustment. This recognizes the unique client who may be experiencing severe symptoms (such as a feeling that a catastrophe is imminent, or the heart pounding) but who seems to function somehow in spite of the symptoms.

TYPES OF ANXIETY MANAGEMENT PROGRAMS

The next section of this chapter will identify various behavioral programs for the treatment of generalized anxiety disorder. In keeping with the preceding section, the programs will be classified as affective-autonomic, somatic-behavioral, and cognitive therapies.

Affective-Autonomic Treatment

A variety of behavioral programs are applicable to persons suffering from generalized anxiety disorder, emphasizing either relaxation training (as in applied relaxation therapy, relaxation self-control therapy, or progressive relaxation or biofeedback relaxation training), anxiety induction (as in flooding, or implosive therapy), or a combination of induced anxiety with relaxation (as in anxiety-management training). Of the various approaches, anxiety management training (AMT) (Suinn, 1977a) has been most studied as a procedure for generalized anxiety disorder clients. We will describe the technique and research findings on AMT first, then comment on some of the other affective-autonomic treatment programs.

Anxiety Management Training (AMT)

AMT was developed primarily for control over pervasive anxiety, although it is also applicable for single or multiple phobias. The theory and method of AMT acknowledges that clients with generalized anxiety disorder are aware of their anxiety reactions, but not able to identify the source of the anxiety. AMT theory is based on the belief that these anxiety responses can be made to acquire cue or drive properties, which in turn can then become associated with coping behaviors via training. In practice, AMT teaches the clients to notice the specific symptom channels in which they are experiencing anxiety, for example, dryness of the throat, neck and shoulder tensing, clenched fists, or catastrophic thoughts. The clients are then trained to use these cues to prompt calmative coping skills, thereby aborting the anxiety before it builds too severely. As will be noted, the AMT procedure emphasizes objectives of self-control training, control over automatic reactions, and transfer of self-management skills to diverse real life settings.

It would be useful to comment a little on these objectives. Regarding self-control training, there is evidence for the central role of self-management skills in therapy (Deffenbacher & Suinn, 1982). The therapy process has greater impact where the client does not simply have a problem resolved, but also learns the skill of problem-solving itself. Therapy must be more than a situation in which something is done by an expert to the client, but rather a setting where the client is able to learn new coping behaviors. Towards this end, AMT incorporates steps for self-management through a gradual process of fading out therapist control and increasing client control.

The emphasis on autonomic reactions gives recognition to the fact that heightened arousal can not only be directly distressing but can also disrupt behaviors and influence cognitions. In the early steps of AMT, anxiety arousal is initiated and attention is given to the autonomic cues, such as throat dryness, heart rate, and palmar sweating. However, other symptomatic expressions are also included, such as the somatic-behavioral cues of neck or shoulder tensing, and the cognitive cues such as worrisome thoughts.

Finally, the emphasis on transfer of training acknowledges that even behavioral skills learned in a treatment setting do not always generalize to real life circumstances (Hersen & Bellack, 1976). Therefore, the AMT program actively involves the client in homework (*in vivo* applications of anxiety management).

The actual steps of AMT cover several phases, some concurrently: (1) rationale and relaxation training, (2) guided rehearsal for anxiety arousal and control, (3) cue-discrimination training, (4) graduated self-control training, and (5) transfer to real life applications. In the first phase, AMT is briefly explained as a means of using relaxation as an active, general coping skill to achieve self-control over anxiety. Jacobsen relaxation training is then initiated along with homework to practice the relaxation method. In this phase the client also describes a recent, especially descriptive example of the heightened anxiety experience to form the basis for later guided rehearsal. One such scene is described below:

> It's a Friday evening, I'm just dragging home from work . . . my neck hurts, I'm feeling emotionally drained because it's been a hectic day, I come in the door and my wife is looking upset. The thought flashes through my mind, "I can't stand another problem to deal with." Then the argument begins: "Why didn't you call home when you promised! I've had to deal with these bills, rush to get to the bank, handle the boys, and you didn't lift a finger to help . . ." I'm feeling . . . a combination of sick and anxious . . . knot in my stomach, kind of guilty, but like I want to hide. I know I'm getting a headache, just tense inside.

Once the client has gained some control over the ability to initiate relaxation, then the anxiety scene is used to recreate anxiety arousal in the second phase of AMT. The client visualizes the scene, relying upon affective, somatic, or cognitive cues to reelicit the anxiety. The therapist guides the client in recapturing the scene, reexperiencing the anxiety, then guides the client in terminating the scene and retrieving the relaxation. The guided rehearsal therefore aims at providing the client with practice in anxiety control via relaxation. In the third phase of AMT, the client is instructed to attend to the cues that are indicative of anxiety arousal, for example, the feeling of a knot in the stomach of the prior case. The idea is to enable the client to quickly perceive early signs of anxiety, and to then introduce relaxation before the anxiety has a chance to build to the point of being out of control.

In the self-control training phase of AMT, the client is gradually given more responsibility for regaining the relaxation and eliminating the anxiety. So in an earlier stage, the therapist would give the signal to "stop the anxiety scene, turn it off," and give the instruction to "now return to relaxation, by first focusing on relaxing the hands, then concentrate on the arms . . ." (actually reviewing each muscle group in detail). However, by Phase 4 the client is given primary responsibility, for example, by being told only, "When you're ready, switch off the anxiety scene, and return to relaxation, using whatever method works best for you to retrieve the relaxation."[1]

The transfer of self-control over anxiety is the objective of Phase 5 of AMT. This is accomplished by a two-step procedure. First, the in-session guided rehearsal recognizes that a client normally cannot escape the situation in which the anxiety is being experienced. Therefore, training involves rehearsal of pairing relaxation with specific anxiety-arousing scenes. For example, "Stay in that anxiety scene, and while you're still involved in that situation, initiate the relaxation to gain control over yourself . . . using whatever method best works for you to control the anxiety and regain the relaxation. . . ." The second procedure involves the routine assignment of homework outside the therapy setting. Initially, the client practices relaxing in a quiet place; as skill develops, the client practices relaxing in a more active environment such as in a waiting room or on the bus; later the client practices using relaxation to reduce anxiety in minor stress circumstances; and finally the client uses relaxation to cope with more severe anxiety levels. Throughout the sessions, the client is also taught to recognize his or her own "stress profile," that is, early body cues of the build-up of anxiety, such as the clenching of the fist or shoulder tightening. By being aware of these "early warning signs," the client can then abort any further anxiety through the relaxation coping.

Although the original purpose of AMT was to treat generalized anxiety, the early research focused on specific anxieties. For example, Suinn and Richardson (1971) demonstrated that AMT reduced mathematics anxiety and increased mathematics performance. Other specific anxieties successfully treated by AMT include test anxiety (Deffenbacher & Shelton, 1978; Richardson & Suinn, 1973), public speaking anxiety (Deffenbacher, Michaels, Daley, & Michaels, 1980; Nicoletti, 1972), and performance anxiety (Mathis, 1978). Later research on AMT has tested its efficacy for general anxiety in a number of ways: first, through changes in outcome measures assessing general or trait anxiety following intervention; secondly through assessing improvements among clients diagnosed as suffering from generalized anxiety disorder; and finally through determining improvements among patients with symptoms considered to be associated with anxiety (such as hypertension). An example of the first type of research is that of Hutchings, Denney, Basgall, and Houston

---

[1] Exact instructions are cited in Suinn, 1977a.

(1980). A total of 70 persons who scored above the upper 15th percentile on the Taylor Manifest Anxiety Scale and the Eysenck Personality Inventory were treated with AMT. Subjects were also given the State-Trait Anxiety Inventory, State and Trait forms (STAI-Trait, STAI-State), and were evaluated under a condition of a laboratory-induced stress. In general, the AMT group showed higher improvements on self-report measures of anxiety (such as the STAI-Trait), lower self-reported anxiety during laboratory stress, and greater gains on a performance task during stress, than a placebo group. Interestingly, although physiological measures did not differentiate, AMT subjects showed a greater reduction of disturbing cognitive preoccupations than either the placebo or another treatment (applied relaxation) group. Other studies have provided added support to the conclusion that AMT leads to reduction in general anxiety measures (Edie, 1972; Suinn & Bloom, 1978). In a variation in research design, Deffenbacher and Shelton (1978) used AMT to treat a targeted anxiety, that is, test anxiety, then examined the additional effect of AMT in reducing nontargeted anxieties (as measured by the Fear Inventory or the STAI-Trait). Results in a number of studies suggest that AMT apparently does teach clients self-coping skills which generalize to nontargeted anxieties (Deffenbacher, Michaels, Daley, & Michaels, 1980; Deffenbacher, Michaels, Michaels, & Daley, 1980), and these gains are retained over 12 and 15 months' follow-up (Deffenbacher & Michaels, 1981a, b). When emotionality (autonomic distress) was measured, AMT appeared to lower such responses; and there was also a nonsignificant trend for worrisome ruminations to decrease (Deffenbacher, Michaels, Daley, & Michaels, 1980).

In the second type of research studies, the patients receiving AMT are those persons diagnosed as suffering from generalized anxiety disorder (or anxiety neurotics). Shoemaker (1976) provided either AMT, implosive therapy (another form of anxiety arousal therapy) (Stampfl, 1967), relaxation only, or a placebo, to community mental health clients diagnosed as anxiety neurotics. AMT patients showed greater reductions on three self-report anxiety measures than the other groups, with these improvements being retained during one month follow-up. Shoemaker reports an interesting clinical observation discovered during his interviews of patients returning for follow-up. Some clients had returned for further treatment, not for general anxiety attacks, but instead for more specific problems such as deficits of interpersonal skills. Shoemaker speculates that the AMT success enabled the clients to reduce the extreme anxiety that had blocked efforts to develop adaptive behaviors. Once this anxiety was controlled, the clients were able either to identify other, lesser problems needing help or to finally be able to confront problems that had originally contributed to the prior anxiety. Without the threat of uncontrollable anxiety recurring, the clients could more directly deal with deficiencies. We have also occasionally seen a client reporting "free-floating anxiety" who was able to identify the specific cue conditions triggering the anxiety in later AMT sessions. It is as though the task of describing an anxiety scene and the homework involving self-monitoring lead to greater insight.

In the final type of research reports, AMT is used with patients with symptoms associated with anxiety. Bloom and Cantrell (1978) and Houston, Jorgensen, and Zurawski (1980) applied AMT to reduce hypertension. Suinn and Bloom (1978) and Nally (1975) assumed that anxiety was linked respectively to Type A behavioral patterns or to delinquency behaviors, and demonstrated that both types of behaviors seemed to decline following AMT for anxiety control. King (1981) reported that AMT-treated medical outpatients showed not only decreases in anxiety and heart rate, but also in hostility and depression. Brooks and Richardson (1980) offered AMT and assertiveness training to patients with duodenal ulcers. They discovered that the program led to lower anxiety, decrease in severity of ulcer, and decrease in rate of return of ulcers.

Overall, it would appear that AMT shows value for treatment of generalized anxiety disorder, with gains being maintained during long-term follow-up. In addition to the stability seen in follow-up, the gains in studies of non-targeted anxiety suggest that AMT has additional value when contrasted with non-self-control behavior therapies, such as desensitization (Deffenbacher & Shelton, 1978), which do not seem to have the same level of efficacy. Though the evidence is less complete, AMT also seems to have favorable impact on all three anxiety response channels: autonomic, somatic, and cognitive, with reductions in blood pressure, improvements in performances, and declines in disruptive cognitions. The finding by Nally that AMT-treated delinquents showed improvements in self-esteem also raises the possibility that increased self-control may help feelings of self-efficacy as well.

Other Affective-Autonomic Treatment Programs

A variety of other programs are available for anxiety; however, since the research on their applications to general anxiety disorder is not as extensive, they will be only briefly covered. Among these are the relaxation programs and certain anxiety arousal programs.

Relaxation training has been examined on the logical assumption that maintaining a relaxed state would counteract the aroused state of being anxious. Initial efforts centered around training in muscle relaxation, through exercises or assisted by biofeedback. Among the exercises, the Jacobsen deep muscle or progressive relaxation (Jacobsen, 1938) method is the most common. This procedure is a type of isometric training, with tensing of muscles followed by relaxation. The exercise moves across muscle groups (for example, hands, biceps, forehead, and shoulders). The client focuses attention on the contrast between feelings when the muscles are tensed and when they are relaxed. Later, the tensing aspect is omitted and the client concentrates on simply relaxing the muscles. Relaxation scenes may be used in imagery as an adjunct to the process. In biofeedback-assisted relaxation, the client is given muscle or temperature feedback through either an auditory or visual display. The evidence is that relaxing certain muscles (e.g., those of the forehead) or increasing peripheral body temperature (e.g., at the fingertips) both lead to increased overall relaxation. Unlike the progressive relaxation exercise, clients on biofeedback are not always told exactly how to relax or to change body temperature but may be instructed to try different methods, with the auditory/visual feedback indicating how successful these methods are.

Studies on the value of relaxation for generalized anxiety reflects the various different approaches to achieving relaxation, with some studies using the Jacobsen exercise and other relying upon biofeedback. There are only a small number of pertinent studies using the same relaxation method, and even a smaller number involving patient populations. Lehrer (1978) worked with 20 patients referred by therapists from the Rutgers Mental Health Center or the Department of Psychiatry. "Most of the anxious subjects were diagnosed as anxiety neurotic" (p. 392). Both physiological and psychometric measures of anxiety were employed. The physiological measures included skin conductance and heart rate; the psychometric measure was the STAI-State scale. The physiological measures were taken during a resting period, during the presentation of loud aversive tones, and during a reaction time task with a tone as the discriminative stimulus. Although the patient group was of primary interest, a nonpatient volunteer group was also tested and trained. Relaxation training involved either a brief Jacobsen method or alpha-wave biofeedback ("relax by staying in your alpha state . . . the flashing light means you're in alpha"). Results were mixed. On the STAI-State instrument, only the nonpatients showed improvements from relaxation training; however, on heart rate data and skin conductance data, the patients did show improvements associated with relaxation. Jacobsen progressive relaxation showed a trend leading to greater improvements than alpha-based relaxation training. A final finding of interest was the fact that relaxation training had more pronounced effects on indices of physiological reactivity (e.g., skin conductance following the loud tone) than on indices of physiological activity (e.g., skin conductance during a resting state). This last data plus the results of the STAI-State could be interpreted to mean that relaxation training does benefit chronically anxious patients under some conditions of stress. It is also consistent with our earlier premise that changes in one symptomatic channel are not always accompanied by changes in all other channels in which anxiety is expressed. It is unfortunate that the Lehrer study did not include a postassessment using the STAI-Trait scale, since it was administered as a premeasure. It might have been possible to examine the results in terms of acute-chronic dimensions had this been done.

Two other studies have been reported which also deal with patient groups, although it is even less clear whether the subjects were actually diagnosed as suffering from generalized anxiety disorder, since both studies identified the patients simply as psychiatric patients where anxiety was a "primary factor." Townsend, House, and Addario (1975) matched 30 patients on the STAI, frontalis electromyograph (EMG), and the Profile of Mood States (POMS) measures. Relaxation training relied upon EMG feedback, whereby the frontalis muscle of the forehead is connected to biofeedback readouts showing tension levels. The comparison group was a group experiencing short-term group therapy aimed at anxiety reduction, including coverage of coping methods. Results showed reduction in STAI-State and STAI-Trait values and POMS scores for the relaxation group. However, the posttreatment STAI results were both still higher than the mean values for normal subjects; and the POMS values were not significantly different from those of control subjects. Correlations between the amount of change in EMG level and change in STAI-state, and POMS scores did reach statistical significance ($r = .61$ for EMG and STAI; $r = .60$ for EMG and POMS). Another factor which makes proper interpretation of the study difficult is the fact that the patients were on medication at the time of the study, and were not matched to control for the possible influence of such drugs.

A research study by Raskin, Johnson, and Rondestveldt (1973) was an earlier attempt to use EMG relaxation training for anxiety treatment. The patients were ten "chronically anxious patients" (p. 263) being seen as outpatients. All were on medication and showed "strong desire for symptomatic relief" (p. 264). The EMG-based relaxation training averaged 6 weeks, and included 1 hour daily training, followed by 8 weeks of homework practice. Results showed improvement in anxiety symptoms as rated by therapists, including observations that using relaxation at home could terminate episodes of anxiety attacks. However, the researchers found no transfer of the benefits of relaxation to settings other than the home, to other areas of anxiety, or to relaxing under other postures—the patients always had to induce relaxation lying down and with their eyes closed. There was a low, nonsignificant correlation between EMG changes and level of anxiety. There are a number of aspects of this report which prevent it from being of more than historical interest. The high motivational level of the patients to view relaxation as working, the fact that the therapists rated the patients on subjective information, and the lack of a control group, were all research-design issues limiting the conclusions that might be desired from this study. Of final interest is the Shoemaker (1976) study cited earlier in our discussion of Anxiety Management Training. It will be recalled that the study included progressive relaxation as one of the treatments for the anxiety neurotic psychiatric sample. His results failed to confirm any benefits of relaxation training on the IPAT, STAI-Trait, or STAI-State measures.

The influence of relaxation training methods on anxiety has also been examined using a sample other than psychiatric patients. In these studies, non-psychiatric volunteers are selected who score high on various measures of general anxiety. In effect, these are persons who complain of being anxious but whose anxieties are not severe enough to require treatment or hospitalization. Sherman and Plummer (1973) provided relaxation training based upon the Jacobsen method to 28 students, while another 28 volunteers comprised a wait-list control. All students had volunteered for the project based upon an explanation of the benefits of relaxation, and hence their expectations were positive. A number of instruments were used, including the IPAT Anxiety Scale, the Fear Survey Schedule, and the Willoughby Neuroticism Schedule. Results showed that the relaxation-trained subjects improved significantly on the measure of general anxiety, the IPAT, and reported reductions in specific fears as assessed by the Fear Survey Schedule. No significant differences occurred on Willoughby scores for the trained versus the untrained group. Two years later, Sherman (1975) obtained follow-up data on 19 of the trained subjects. These data suggested that subjects continued to report use of relaxation to control anxiety, to reduce fatigue or insomnia, and to cope with specific stressors such as examinations or social anxiety. It is especially interesting to note that about half of those surveyed reported using the relaxation experience as a means of learning to become more "aware of tension," a cognitive skill. One assumes that by identifying the presence of tension, the students were then better able to initiate relaxation to reduce the anxiety. Sherman and Plummer consider their results consistent with their original premise that the relaxation could be a self-control skill that could be applied by each subject in everyday life. However, some caution should be taken, given some of the follow-up data which indicated that subjects did show significant loss in their abilities to "relax at will" or achieve the same depth of relaxation as that immediately following training.

Another study using volunteer students is reported by Lewis, Biglan, and Steinbock (1978). The study used a combination of self-administered relaxation training plus money deposits, since its main objective was to determine whether a deposit would increase compliance in practicing relaxation. Of interest are the results comparing deep muscle relaxation with two control groups. One control group did not receive any relaxation-training instructions at all; a second control group were told that they should devise their own method for relaxing since "practicing relaxing itself, regardless of the method ... is the key element in feeling more relaxed and at ease" (p. 1276). On pretesting, the combined sample showed STAI-Trait results at the 90th percentile and STAI-State results at the 73rd percentile; in other words, the volunteers did report very high levels of anxiety on undergraduate norms. In fact, 39 of the 61 subjects had sought treatment. Following relaxation training, the students using progressive relaxation showed decreases in both STAI-Trait and STAI-State scores to levels within the normal range. On the other hand, the control group without relaxation training showed slight increases in STAI-State scores, and a reduction in STAI-Trait values, with this latter reduction being less than that achieved by the progressive-relaxation subjects. The control group that devised their own relaxation method surprisingly enough did not differ from the subjects systematically trained with progressive relaxation on either STAI instrument. However, subjects using progressive relaxation did report that they were able to relax at will to a significantly greater extent than subjects who devised their own training.

From a slightly different perspective, a variety of studies have used relaxation training with patients whose physical symptoms are assumed to be associated with anxiety. Therefore, improvements in such symptoms following relaxation training can be interpreted as evidence of the value of such training for anxiety reduction. Briefly, relaxation training with or without biofeedback has been reported to aid in essential hypertension (Brauer, Horlick, Nelson, Farquhar, & Agras, 1979; Patel, 1975), spastic colon (Tarler-Benlolo & Love, 1977), functional diarrhea (Weinstock, 1976), primary dysmenorrhea (Chesney & Tasto, 1975), and insomnia (Borkovec, Kaloupek, & Slama, 1975; Lick & Heffler, 1977; Nicassio & Bootzin, 1974). Since tension headaches are presumed to relate to increased muscle tension around the neck and shoulders (Dalessio, 1972), various relaxation methods have been used for this problem. The following case study demonstrates the successful use of relaxation for tension headaches.

Mr. Payne was a 53-year-old, married sales manager for a family business. Tension headaches first appeared 12 years before treatment and appeared every day. Medical examination ruled out any organic cause, and Mr. Payne had been placed on numerous medications without success, but eventually leading to addiction to Valium. The intensity of the headaches was revealed in the patient's ratings, using a 6-point scale, with Level 5 meaning the headache is so severe it is "almost impossible to do anything until it is over" and Level 0 meaning the absence of headaches. Over a one week period, Mr. Payne reported headaches averaging at the Level 4 intensity, a severity such that he could perform "only simple tasks" because of the headache.

Treatment involved progressive relaxation, aided by frontalis EMG information to show the patient his progress in learning to relax. Relaxation instructions were all on audio tape, lasting about twenty minutes. In addition, he was instructed to practice relaxation at home, and to initiate relaxation when he detected a Level 1 headache beginning, in order to prevent it from reaching Level 5. In this way, the training involved both relaxation skill development, but also instructions on how to use the relaxation as a coping response to signs of tension. After only three sessions across thirteen days, plus homework practice two or three times daily, Mr. Payne reported his headaches to have reduced to about a Level 2 intensity, that is, strong enough that it cannot be ignored, but not interfering with work. Six months after therapy had begun, the headaches were now reaching intensity levels of less than 1; that is, very slight headaches that could be ignored. There was also a reduction in the frequency of headaches, "with many no-headache days." It is interesting that Mr. Payne had originally complained about having a poor relationship with his brother, for whom he worked. Although this did not change after treatment, Mr. Payne did report that he was better able to handle criticisms from his brother. (Epstein, Webster, & Abel, 1976)

It is somewhat difficult to draw firm conclusions about the impact of relaxation training for persons suffering from generalized anxiety disorder. There are only a few studies of patients with a clear diagnosis of anxiety neurosis, the earlier term for generalized anxiety disorder. In addition, research-design issues or inconsistent results were present. Furthermore, in examining other studies using either nonpsychiatric volunteers who score high on anxiety tests, or nonpsychiatric patients with psychophysiological symptoms, there has been an added complication of the diversity of relaxation procedures used. Some rely upon therapist-presented progressive relaxation while others use audio tapes; some have given the subjects the positive expectation that relaxation will be helpful for reducing anxiety; some have augmented or substituted biofeedback for progressive relaxation; some have introduced a self-control instruction; and finally some have used homework assignments while others have not. Tentatively, relaxation training does seem to have some promise for the control of anxiety and its symptoms, especially if the symptoms are measured through self-report instruments such as the IPAT or the STAI. There also appears to be greater support for the value of relaxation, even without biofeedback, for reducing autonomic expressions of anxiety, such as in tension headaches and essential hypertension (Silver & Blanchard, 1978).

Evidence is mounting that relaxation training is enhanced where a self-control component is built in (Deffenbacher & Suinn, 1981). This orientation starts by introducing clients to the rationale that they must not only learn how to relax, but also how to use this relaxation to cope with anxieties. Learning to relax includes being able to "relax at will," without having to rely upon biofeedback instruments or even the lengthier tension-relaxation early steps of progressive relaxation. In effect, being able to relax at will can be taken as confirmation that some level of self-control has been developed. Coping with anxiety is further separated into two phases, discriminating anxiety arousal and using relaxation to reduce the anxiety. Many clients are unaware of the presence of tensions that are building. In the case of Mr. Payne, he was taught not only to recognize the onset of the tension headache, but to identify the level of the pain, in order to discriminate early signs of anxiety's effects. By developing this awareness, the client can acquire skill in using the relaxation as a coping method. Once again, in Mr. Payne's case, he was instructed to initiate bodily relaxation immediately upon his becoming aware that a Level 1 headache was appearing. Thus, relaxation training is more than teaching persons how to relax, since it is unlikely that persons suffering from chronic anxiety can achieve a less activated state through relaxation alone. As the Lehrer study showed, anxious patients were not able to reduce their tonic physiological activity by relaxing. On the other hand, such patients were able to use relaxation to cope with reactivity to stress. In the context of self-control, this means that the role of relaxation may consist in having a skill which the patient can rely upon to reduce or abort anxiety. In an early study, Goldfried and Trier (1974) demonstrated that relaxation training involving self-control aspects was superior to relaxation training without self-control. Under the self-control approach, speech-anxious subjects received instruction on the active self-application of relaxation to control anxiety. In the relaxation-without-self-control training, subjects were led to understand that simply being relaxed would help reduce anxiety. Not only did the results show that self-control relaxation led to greater reduction in speech anxiety than the relaxation-only method, but this difference was more pronounced at follow-up. Similar support has been found by Deffenbacher and his colleagues in their finding that AMT reduced trait anxiety while desensitization did not (Deffenbacher & Shelton, 1978); however, when desensitization was modified to include self-control procedures, then this version of desensitization was as effective as AMT in trait anxiety (Deffenbacher, Michaels, Michaels, & Daley, 1980).

Anxiety arousal behavioral methods are those which emphasize inducing the client to experience high levels of anxiety as a major component in treatment. Primary examples are flooding and implosion, which share a common rationale but differ somewhat in procedures. The rationale starts with the belief that the acquisition of fear follows a two-factor or two-step model: the fear is first generated through aversive experiences, and this is then followed by the person learning behaviors aimed at avoiding situations now associated with such fear. More specifically, it is believed that a form of classical conditioning may have initiated the fear, but that the maintenance of phobic responses are due to avoidance behaviors (Mowrer, 1960). As long as the person avoids confronting the feared situations, extinction is prevented, since successful avoidance reduces the anxiety, and this anxiety reduction in turn serves to reinforce future avoidance behaviors. In fact, even if the original source of the aversive fear experience is no longer present, the avoidance behaviors make it impossible for the person to learn this. Consider what might happen if a child learns to fear a certain house because of being frightened by a dog in the yard. The child picks a different route to get to school to avoid the feared animal, but suppose in the meantime the dog has been given away. Unless the child's avoidance is prevented and the child returns to the house, there is no opportunity for the child's fear to extinguish. In the two anxiety-arousal behavioral methods, the client is prevented from avoidance of the feared stimuli; in fact, flooding has also been called *response prevention*.

The major difference between flooding and implosion is in the procedure. Implosive therapists believe that part of the fear derives from psychodynamic associations symbolized by the situation, such as rejection over sexual, aggressive, or guilt conflicts (Stampfl & Levis, 1967). Hence, the technique involves using imagery to confront the client with the feared stimulus, including psy-

chodynamic themes in the fantasy: "Imagine yourself [an agoraphobic] standing in a crowd . . . everyone is staring at you, blaming you for having done
wrong . . . they see through your sham and know your shameful acts and
thoughts . . . you're agonized over this public embarrassment, and you want to
get away, to leave and hide, but you can't because your way is blocked, and
people you know are pushing you back to the platform to be placed on public
view . . ." In contrast, flooding tends to limit the presentation to more realistic
fantasies: "Imagine yourself [an agoraphobic] having to be outdoors, in the
streets, far away from your home and your privacy . . . you are walking rapidly
because you feel anxious and afraid and don't know why, but now you must
cross an open plaza, an open space without cover . . . and your palms are sweating, your heart racing, and you'd like to be safe at home indoors again, but you
must enter and cross the open plaza even though your body is frightened . . ."
In addition, flooding may involve having clients actually exposed to feared
stimuli in reality, instead of in imagination. For example, the agoraphobic person may be asked to spend time outdoors, and to resist the desire to rush back
inside.

We have been referring to flooding and implosion as methods useful in
treating fears even though this chapter involves the treatment of generalized
anxiety rather than specific fears or phobias. Nevertheless, these anxiety-
arousal techniques deserve discussion since some of the expressions of phobias
overlap with generalized anxiety. In fact, a simple working distinction between
phobias and generalized anxiety involves the clarity of stimulus dimensions.
Where the anxiety response patterns are triggered by a common class of stimuli
(e.g., small animals, open spaces, enclosed spaces), it is convenient to label
these as "phobias." Where the cue conditions are diffuse, or involve a large
number of diverse stimuli, such that the client is unable to identify the stimuli
cognitively, then the term "generalized anxiety" might be used (Suinn, 1977b).
In general, research on flooding and implosion have examined their value in
the treatment of phobias, although some data in work on phobias have relevance for generalized anxiety. Two studies obtained extra data on the IPAT as
a measure of possible changes in general anxiety. Rudenstam and Bedrosian
(1977) compared desensitization therapy and flooding with 16 persons suffering from specific phobias and 16 persons with social fears. Values on the IPAT
showed no significant changes for the groups treated with flooding, although
physiological measures showed more improvement with flooding than desensitization. Both client and therapist ratings favored desensitization over flooding.
Horne and Matson (1977) provided a variety of behavior therapies to 100 students for the target problem of test anxiety. Both IPAT and physiological data
were also obtained. Consistent with the Rudenstam and Bedrosian report, no
changes on the IPAT were found; however, in contrast to the previous study,
Horne and Matson found increases rather than decreases in pulse rate during
stress from flooding. In addition, feedback from the subjects indicated that the

flooding sample said they "would not recommend" this form of therapy to their friends. Weinberger and Engelhart (1976) offered flooding to students experiencing speech anxiety, and included the STAI-State and STAI-Trait measures. Results showed no changes on either State or Trait scale scores following treatment. Finally, as reported earlier, Shoemaker (1976) used a modified version of implosion adapted for general anxiety on his group of anxiety neurotic patients, and found no significant changes on IPAT, STAI-Trait, or STAI-State scores following therapy or at one month follow-up.

In brief, the anxiety arousal treatments, such as flooding and implosion, seem to have limited application for general anxiety in studies to date. The information derives from studies on phobias where measures of general anxiety were collected additionally, rather than from direct use of such treatment with a patient population. Shipley and Boudewyns (1980) raised the question through a mail survey of practitioners as to whether flooding and implosion are potentially harmful to patients. Responses from 70 private therapists led the researchers to the conclusion that these anxiety-arousal treatment methods were "relatively 'safe' procedures" (p. 503). They noted, however, that severe negative side effects appeared in nine clients (.26% of those treated), involving acute psychotic reactions or acute panic reactions. Additionally, 13% of the practitioners offered the opinion that implosion or flooding produced more side effects than other treatments, whereas 21% felt that they produced fewer side effects. Clearly, there is a discrepancy in these opinions on possible side effects, and whether other therapies may be more desirable on this dimension. Equally important is the implication of the survey, which showed that nearly 3,500 patients were treated by flooding or implosion; the implication being that therapists have some confidence in the procedures. What is sorely needed are more controlled research studies to determine the degree to which these treatments might be applicable to the specific population of general anxiety disorders, and to confirm the absence of risk.

Somatic-Behavioral Treatment

This section will summarize a variety of somatic-behavioral approaches to anxiety. These are treatments which basically aim at changing the somatic expressions of anxiety through promoting more adaptive behaviors. Unlike response prevention (flooding), which emphasizes preventing the undesirable avoidance behaviors, the somatic-behavioral approaches tend to promote the desirable coping responses that are being avoided. And whereas flooding involves prolonged exposure to anxiety arousal as part of response prevention, the somatic-behavioral treatments do not intentionally work with the autonomic expressions of anxiety. In a simplified sense, the principle is that the adoption of coping behaviors will allow the anxiety experience to be eliminated; or, if a person is taught nonanxious behaviors, then the anxiety will dissipate.

Recall the model of anxiety expression which we proposed in the first section of this chapter: tensional states may find expression in three response channels: affective-autonomic, somatic-behavioral, or cognitive. We would now propose that improvements derived from successful treatment in one of these response channels can 'spill over' to benefit the other channels (Hugdahl, 1981; Suinn, 1981b). Therefore, somatic-behavioral treatments may be useful not only when somatic-behavioral symptoms dominate, but also for the possible spillover benefits. Among the treatments are included: reinforced practice and modeling.

Reinforced Practice

If a person appears unable to cope, and if coping can be operationally specified as the presence of certain behaviors, then the entire field of operant learning becomes appropriate. Data from operant learning has demonstrated that it is possible to shape new behaviors through reinforced practice. Studies using this principle in therapy have been aimed at anxieties associated with definable stimuli, that is, phobias. In the Vermont Project, Leitenberg (1976) and his colleagues decided that the primary response in phobias was avoidance; hence to reverse this would mean increasing nonavoidance behaviors. For example, a claustrophobic would be asked to practice remaining in closed places; an agoraphobic would be asked to walk a planned route involving open spaces; and a woman whose phobia of knives involved a fear that she would hurt someone was required to practice looking at a knife in a box. In each case, successful practice is followed by reinforcement from the therapist, such as high praise. A sample illustration of this method is shown by the following case study:

> The patient, a 51-year-old woman with claustrophobia, had experienced the fear of closed spaces since childhood. This fear had become even worse after her husband died 7 years prior to her seeking therapy. Among her terrors were a fear of being left in any room with the doors closed, anxiety about remaining in a house alone, and fright at staying inside a car for a distance of over 3 or 4 miles. Such fears were so powerful that she enlisted the aid of her son, whom she stationed outside ladies' rooms to hold the door ajar to prevent her claustrophobia. She also had a fear of choking to death, and reported that this was strengthened by the occasional "throat spasms" she experienced.
>
> The reinforced practice treatment involved providing praise, positive feedback, and encouragement for remaining alone in a closed room. An innovation in this treatment was the providing of a specific means for the client to observe her own progress. She was given a stopwatch with which she could time her gains in terms of staying for longer and longer periods. The room in which she sat was 4 feet wide and 6 feet long, illumined only with a 100 watt shaded bulb.
>
> Treatment involved several stages, the first being praise as she was able to increase her remaining in the room, with a therapist just outside the door. Through this, she was able to increase her tolerance. In a further stage, the patient was provided

with the stopwatch and told, "You have been improving nicely. In order to further reduce your fears we will continue this repeated practice with a slight change. Larry [the therapist] will no longer remain just outside the room. Instead, he will be in the recording room at the other end of the corridor. Remember, you are to come out of the room as soon as you feel the slightest discomfort or anxiety, and you are to go back only after you rest a while."

Through this treatment, the patient was able to increase her ability to remain without anxiety from a time of 25 sec to about 9 min. Three months later, she was still reporting the same level of improvement in closed rooms and in cars. (Leitenberg, Agras, Thomson, & Wright, 1968)

A number of aspects characterized reinforced practice treatment programs used by the Vermont Project. The behaviors practiced are chosen on the basis of being adaptive and demonstrative of fear reduction rather than fear avoidance. The treatment also gradually increases the requirements of what is being practiced, so that the client is asked to assume activities that are more and more like those of normal persons. For example, the agoraphobic would stay out for longer periods of time; and a dog-phobic person would initially be required to be in the same room as the animal, but later to approach the dog, and finally to hold the dog. This method of successive approximations is a well-known procedure in operant learning. Finally, it appears that both praise and feedback, in the context of encouragement, lead to improvements in patients. However, feedback whereby the patients receive precise information on their progress may have somewhat more impact than praise. Once the patients reach a level of showing regular improvements, then the presence of general praise serves the role of sustaining this rate of improvement.

The research support for reinforced practice has centered on the works of the Vermont Project through Leitenberg, Agras, Barlow, and their colleagues (Agras, Leitenberg, & Barlow, 1968; Agras, Leitenberg, Barlow, & Thomson, 1969; Leitenberg, Agras, Edwards, Thomson, & Wincze, 1970; Leitenberg, Agras, Allen, Butz, & Edwards, 1975). The research design has tended to be a series of single-case experiments, whereby the progress of a patient is followed as different experimental conditions are changed. For example, the role of praise versus feedback was studied through first determining the level of improvement of a patient when praise was used alone, then feedback and praise are presented simultaneously, then praise alone, then neither praise nor feedback, then praise alone, and finally feedback and praise. During each of these conditions, the patient is carefully observed in order to draw final conclusions about the relative contributions of praise alone, and praise augmented by feedback, as compared with neither praise nor feedback. Further research using groups might be hoped for in order to confirm these early findings.

Modeling

Modeling therapies are those where nonanxious or coping behaviors are displayed by a model to the anxious or phobic patient. The basic premise is that a person can learn adaptive behaviors and eliminate maladaptive behaviors through observation. Unlike reinforced practice, the learning can therefore take place without a direct experience, although some modeling programs may include a practice component. In a typical treatment program, the client views another person dealing with anxiety situations in a nonanxious way. This model generally is of the same age and sex as the client, in order to encourage the client to identify with the model. Often the situatons modeled are graduated samples of adapting to more and more severe threat. For example, children afraid of dogs were presented with a peer who progressively came into closer and closer contact with a dog. The model began with patting the dog in an enclosed cage, but eventually ended up climbing into the pen to play with the dog. Modeling can be presented live or symbolically, for example through a film or videotape.

The activities and the characteristics of the model are carefully programmed on a number of dimensions. First, negative consequences to model actions do not occur since in reality such consequences are improbable. This enhances the observational learning since observers are affected by the anticipation of what might happen as a result of the model's actions (Bandura, 1965). If the model shows coping behaviors, but this leads to adverse results, then the client is unlikely to adopt the coping behaviors. Secondly, the model will enact certain desirable mood and behavioral responses. Some treatment programs have relied upon creating a nonanxious mood, in that the model faces the situation with confidence (a "mastery model"). However, data suggest that a more valuable model is one who initially manifests some signs of being anxious, but who then overcomes the anxiety and copes (a "coping model") (Meichenbaum, 1971). The coping behaviors that are modeled can vary depending upon the goals of the therapist and the characteristics of the client. The behaviors may be based upon certain basic information, for example, how to properly approach and pet a dog without scaring the dog into growling. In test-taking anxiety, the information may involve useful approaches in dealing with multiple choice or essay questions. The coping behaviors modeled might, on the other hand, be aimed at methods for reducing the impact of the threatening event. For example, a child might learn to cope with an injection by substituting distracting imagery for attention to the actions of the physician (Lazarus & Abramovitz, 1962). Finally, the coping behavior exhibited by the model may include skills associated with affective-autonomic control or cognitive control. For example, the model might say, "All right, I'm feeling jittery now, so I'll take a slow, deep breath, and relax my muscles as I exhale . . . nice and easy . . . there, I'm feeling more under control. I'll do this once more. . . ." or "I'm getting all excited about anticipating the worst, that's why I'm anxious, I'm making myself worry without any reason at all . . . now, what is a more realistic way to approach this, let me straighten out my thoughts. . . ." Of final interest is the inclusion of models who may have special influence for the observer. Peterson and Shigetomi (1981) provided children in a hospital pediatrics ward with the character Big Bird from the television program "Sesame Street" as the model showing coping behaviors.

When the client is asked to participate in activities following live modeling, this approach is called *participant modeling* (Ritter, 1968). First, the patient observes a model demonstrating the desired behaviors in graduated steps. The patient is then encouraged to repeat what the model showed, with physical help if necessary (the therapist may jointly hold a snake with a snake-phobic client). Eventually, the patient continues to practice without the therapist's help, although with the therapist's presence. In participant modeling, the therapist-model serves several functions. First, basic instruction and information is modeled, such as how to hold the snake and what to do in each step of the graduated sequence. Secondly, the therapist-model provides much reassurance and praise as the patient is able to make progress. Finally, the therapist-model acts as a motivator to reduce avoidance and to spur the patient to attempt the next step. Evidence suggests that the addition of the live participation component to modeling increases the effect of modeling, and may in fact be the single most effective modeling procedure (Rosenthal & Bandura, 1978).

Live or symbolic modeling might have their effects through capitalizing on various objects achievable through the technique (Bandura, 1977). Through modeling, patients may be taught new coping behaviors not previously in their repertoires. This is *response acquisition.* Secondly, modeling may have the effect of cueing in behaviors which the clients possess, but had not considered using. This is *response facilitation.* A third possible objective is the elimination of conditions which are inhibiting a response. Seeing that a model's handling of the animal does not lead to aversive consequences results in eliminating the anticipatory fears, thereby allowing clients to no longer have to inhibit approach behaviors. This is *response disinhibition.* Finally, modeling may enable persons to question their self-critical standards. Some clients experience anxiety because they impose too stringent self-critical evaluations on their own behaviors. This could be significantly changed through exposure to a model who sets realistic and reasonable performance standards, with appropriate self-reinforcement. This involves acquisition of reality standards for self-regulation.

Although the literature on live and symbolic modeling has been extensive (Rosenthal & Bandura, 1978), the efforts have been limited to phobias or anxieties associated with specific situations. An exciting possibility is the use of modeling as a preventative program before anxiety appears, rather than as a therapy program to resolve anxiety that is already present. In this way, modeling may have further relevance for general anxiety disorders. A series of studies have aimed at helping prevent anxiety among persons by preparing them for medical or dental experiences (Kleinknecht & Bernstein, in press; Peterson & Ridley-Johnson, 1980; Peterson & Shigetomi, 1981). Typically, the modeling is provided through films, showing a peer going through the dental or medical procedures. Since children are seen as more vulnerable, most of the films have been aimed at pediatric audiences. As with modeling to treat phobias, these modeling films offer the viewer basic information on what will happen, prototypes for coping with stress, and an opportunity to vicariously experience what the dental or medical event may feel like. It is interesting to note that those children who already have lower levels of anxiety come from families with parents who have used positive reinforcement, modeling, and reassurance in past stresses (Melamed & Siegel, 1980).

An effort by Melamed and Siegel (1975) is illustrative of the approach. The film specially designed for this project covered a surgical experience and was entitled *Ethan Has an Operation*. Ethan, a 7-year-old, is depicted in the hospital from the time of admission, to the induction of anesthesia, the awakening in the recovery room, and rejoining his parents. Drawing from the prior literature, the film emphasizes a coping rather than a master model, with Ethan hesitatingly approaching the various events but ultimately managing. To replicate reality, following the surgery he is seen wakening in the recovery room with some feelings of discomfort; however, he is comforted by a caring nurse and the presence of his parents. Through a first-person format (the film is narrated by a child), the child-viewers are further encouraged to identify with the model's experiences. In their research, Melamed and Siegel showed the film to children entering the hospital for tonsillectomies, hernia repairs, or urinary–genital tract surgery. In addition, the children had talks with the surgeon and anesthesiologist, had demonstrations of the anesthetic mask, and looked through a photographic album showing other children at various stages of the hospitalization. Results showed lower behavioral and autonomic signs of anxiety, and somewhat lower postsurgical complications (such as nausea or the need for pain medication) among children viewing the coping film than those who viewed a control film. It is notable that these anxiety measures were situation specific; on measures of general or trait anxiety, no significant differences were found. What this suggests is that it is possible to train persons to cope with a stressful event through modeling specific to that event; however, the coping skills that are learned may not generalize to other life stresses. An explanation might be found in our earlier discussion of AMT and desensitization, namely, that the inclusion of training in self-control can enhance generalization. It would appear that anxiety training or coping-skills modeling will take a client only as far as the program's objectives. If the objective is to deal with anxiety related to a specific event, then the client learns a situation-specific skill. On the other hand, if the objective is to learn coping skills for general application, then the client is able to transfer the skills of self-regulation.

In summary, the somatic-behavioral approaches have demonstrated their value in the alteration of behavioral expressions of anxiety. The evidence comes from work with phobias or situation-specific anxieties, but efforts made to prepare persons to cope with medical-dental events show great promise as preventative treatment. The somatic-behavioral approaches view anxiety management as a skill-training task, rather than as a task of emotional (affective/autonomic) control. As such, the orientation has different implications. The focus is less on "How does disruption feel?" and more on "What are you not doing that you need to do?" The orientation lends itself more logically to steps relating to prevention than remediation, and in this way is closer to self-control treatment programs. The emphasis also is more closely associated with coping than simply with control.

There are limitations, however, in the application of these approaches to generalized anxiety disorder. First, somatic-behavioral methods require precise identification of the behavioral symptoms in order for structured retraining to occur. Some somatic-behavioral symptoms can be more readily placed in a training context than others. For example, the cases of phobias have used training in approach behaviors to eliminate the behavioral symptoms of avoidance behaviors. However, if the behavioral expression is loss of motor coordination, this may be harder to convert into a reinforced practice or modeling paradigm. Of course, if the somatic-behavioral symptom is simply muscle tension, then relaxation training would seem a straightforward approach.[2] A second limitation is the general reliance of reinforced practice or modeling programs on a situational context within which the anxiety behaviors are expected to occur. Phobias are by definition clearly stimulus specific, and programs preparing persons for medical-dental events also have identifiable situation-specific experiences. In generalized anxiety disorder, the cue conditions are not all that clear and may not fall into convenient categories. It may be impossible for the person to identify concrete environmental, internal, interpersonal, or even time cues that relate to the anxiety experience. The challenge will be for somatic-behavioral therapists and researchers to design structured learning involving a more general context. This might be accomplished by exposing the clients to a set of stress situations in order to rehearse differing coping strategies. A program known as *stress inoculation* follows this model and will be described in the next section. A final limitation on the structured learning approach of the somatic-behavioral methods is the practical problem facing reinforced practice or live modeling. Even with some phobias, it may not be easy to present a controlled environment for practice. Phobias with stationary environmental features (such as claustrophobia), or with stimuli which can be brought under laboratory control (for example, through putting the animal in a cage), or where the events themselves can be programmed or are routine (such as steps in dental treatment or in hospital with a cooperative staff) are all amenable to rehearsal or modeling techniques. However, with more complex situations subject to unpredictable change (such as interpersonal anxieties), it may be more difficult to arrange the necessary conditions for behavioral change.

---

[2]Relaxation training methods were discussed in the prior section as affective-autonomic treatments since the theoretical emphasis by practitioners has been on its affective benefits.

Cognitive Treatment

This section will cover cognitive approaches to anxiety. These are aimed at changing the cognitive expressions of anxiety such as worrisome ruminations or distracting cognitions. Cognitive treatments have generally developed from a belief that not only can cognitions be symptoms of anxiety, but also that cognitions may in fact serve to precipitate or further maintain anxiety. In its simplest form, the idea is that certain words or thoughts are automatically anxiety-arousing through past learning and experiences. If I think, "That dental examination is going to hurt me again," then I am likely to become anxious. In a more sophisticated version, cognitive therapists propose that persons may adopt and accept as truth certain cognitions, even though current experiences do not support these beliefs. Hence, a peson who thinks, "If I don't perform flawlessly, this audience will be very dissatisfied with me, and I have failed as a person," may be entertaining a very inappropriate cognition not based in reality. Nevertheless, such a belief would engender anxiety, which will reappear whenever the individual views a situation in this manner, regardless of the true characteristics of the situation. The condition prompting the anxiety is therefore less situation-specific and more cognition-specific. Cognitive treatments can aim at blocking the thoughts as they appear, or at altering the content of the thoughts to be better oriented to reality. Among the cognitive therapies to be reviewed next will be thought-stopping, cognitive restructuring methods, and stress inoculation.

Thought-Stopping

This procedure builds on the premise that preventing thoughts from occurring can be a learned response. If thoughts are involved in an anxiety sequence, blocking them could then break one link in the chain and thereby possibly terminate the sequence. A typical training program starts with having the patient intentionally begin the undesired thoughts, saying them aloud, for example, "My close friend went bankrupt from a fire; I'm worried now about whether *my* store building is burning; I wonder if the electrical wiring is safe . . ." When the client is immersed in these thoughts, the therapist will suddenly shout, "STOP!" Startled, the client will discover that indeed the thoughts have ceased, and the client is told that this is as expected (Wolpe, 1973). From this demonstration, the client is instructed to practice the sequence of first permitting the negative thoughts to appear, then verbalizing these aloud as they occur, then loudly shouting "Stop!" and noticing the effects. If the client does not obtain results with self-verbalizations, then the therapist again takes over the verbal disruption. The client is warned that the thoughts will return, but that they must be interrupted each time. Later, the client shifts from overtly saying "Stop!" to covertly thinking this command. Finally, the client initiates the command even before the thoughts take hold, but at the stage at which they threaten to appear. A variant of this method has been to add a mild shock accompanying the command. For example, Mahoney (1971) had a client give himself a pain by snapping a heavy rubber band on his wrist. Although the technique is reported in some case studies as useful, one review concludes that thought-stopping has not proven to be a dependable therapeutic method (Mahoney & Arnkoff, 1978).

Cognitive Restructuring

Cognitive restructuring methods aim at actually altering the undesirable thoughts themselves, instead of stifling or blocking them out. Typically, clients are directed to directly examine their thoughts and to evaluate their sensibility, accuracy, and appropriateness. The cognitive therapist aims at helping the clients become aware of their dysfunctional cognitive patterns, learn how to evaluate them, discover alternative cognitions that are more appropriate, and achieve practice in applying these new skills in anxiety-arousing situations. Among the prominent cognitive restructuring methods are *rational emotive therapy* (RET) (Ellis, 1962) and *systematic rational restructuring* (SRR) (Goldfried, Decenteceo, & Weinberg, 1974). The rational emotive therapy of Albert Ellis gives the rationale but provides few details on steps for promoting cognitive change beyond therapist confrontation of client beliefs. Systematic rational restructuring was able to organize rational emotive therapy into more systematic steps and includes a self-control orientation. Because of the overlap, these two procedures will be discussed together.

In RET and SRR, the first step requires the patients to monitor and write down their thoughts, for example, during periods of anxiety. The patients log thoughts that occurred before, during, and after the anxious periods, in order to more fully capture the context and possible sequence of the cognitions. Patients are then trained to evaluate the content of their thoughts, with a view to classifying those which are irrational and inappropriate. The thoughts tend to be distortions involving catastrophic anticipations, including gloom and doom ruminations ("What if I forget my lines" or "I'll probably do poorly") and absolutistic views ("I'll never . . ." or "They'll always . . ."). In a next step in treatment, the patients are helped to identify the particular ways in which their thoughts are distorted. This may be through a discussion of the distorted assumptions underlying the thought processes. For example, Ellis (1962) has pointed out a number of beliefs commonly held as truths, but which are really irrational. One theme, "that there is invariably a right, precise, and perfect solution to human problems and that it is catastrophic if this correct solution is not found" (p. 87), leads a person to anxious dissatisfaction with any actions that fall short of being "perfect." One procedure in RET and SRR therefore focuses on clients' searching out such assumptions behind undesirable thoughts, and questioning the validity of such assumptions. In many cases, the thoughts themselves are questionable and are not only accepted, but prompt imagery. For example, one young college student experienced anxiety whenever entering a class, triggered by visual fantasies of stumbling, falling, and being laughed at by the instructor. In a next step, the cognitive therapist helps the patients to appreciate just how invalid and irrational the beliefs or thoughts really are. This often occurs through mutual discussion and a Socratic-style exploration: "You say you often think that you'll forget your lines. Has that actually ever happened? How likely is it that this would ever happen? How do your preparatory activities before class help make it unlikely? Is there any true reason you can think of that would make this happen? Are there good reasons to believe that it will remain unlikely to happen? What can you do to continue to insure that it won't happen?" It is in this stage that RET and SRR show some major differences in procedure despite their similarity in objectives. Ellis, as a therapist, tends to forcefully challenge the patient's false beliefs, relying heavily upon formal analysis of the rationality of these beliefs: "You say it's awful that you failed and did not succeed. *Why* is it awful? Who says you *must* succeed? This is another of those common beliefs that you must learn to dispute. Is there any logic to your conclusions from what you've said?" On the other hand, in SRR the therapist engages the client more in mutually testing out the rationality of the thoughts, in the context of reality testing, authenticating observations, validating assumptions, and taking on an objective perspective (distancing). A final step, which often occurs in RET and always is planned in SRR, is the development of alternate, realistic, cognitions which facilitate coping. In this step the patients learn to modify their thoughts as they occur and before they become problems. For example, an individual may now think, "Oh, there I go, expecting the worse. But actually, everyone is so busy getting settled that even if I stumbled, no one would even notice, much less the instructor. So, I'll just slide into my seat like I always do and look around to see if my friend is here instead of worrying." In SRR, the therapist also requires some practice and rehearsal from the patients, and may rely upon some modeling to facilitate the progress. The practice starts with imaginal rehearsal of scenes of increasingly higher levels of anxiety, during which the patients rationally re-evaluate their thoughts and practice more reasonable cognitions. Later, the rehearsal takes the form of real life homework practice in the same methodology.

A sample case drawn from Burns and Beck (1978) illustrates the various aspects of cognitive therapy:

> The patient was a university student who initially experienced mainly test anxiety, even though he had achieved a 3.5 grade average. In preparing for a specific exam, he panicked and began to think, "I can't concentrate. I'm losing my mind. I'll blow the exam," and become even more intensely anxious. Consequently he stopped studying, refused to take the test, and received an incomplete. Now he began to think, "I must really be going downhill" and withdrew from school; this prompted the belief, "I'm just a dropout now. That proves that there is something wrong with my mind." His life became further complicated as he tried marijuana, did not like it, and believed

that this confirmed his pathology since all his friends enjoyed marijuana smoking. This discomfort led to withdrawing from social events and friends, and soon he thought, "I must really be insane. I'm a social reject as well as an academic failure."

The therapist focused on thoughts relating to social interactions, since these anxieties were now dominant. The patient was asked to record the "automatic thoughts" that flowed uncontrollably through his mind when he had been invited to attend a former friend's party, an experience which he rated as evoking an extremely high level of anxiety. He also wrote down his degree of belief in these thoughts (using a scale of 0 to 100%). Among his list were (1) They will smoke pot at the party—90% belief, (2) They will put pressure on everyone to smoke pot with them—80%, (3) If I don't smoke pot, I will be ostracized—100%, (4) Because I will be anxious, I will not be able to think of anything to say—100%, and (5) If I am quiet, they will conclude I'm peculiar—100%.

The patient was then asked to realistically reassess these thoughts, generate "rational responses" for each, and rate his belief in these new responses. To the automatic thoughts (1) and (2), he wrote "They may not smoke pot, and if they do they may not insist that everyone do so. I have the right to say I don't care for pot—100%; to (3) he wrote "There are probably many people who don't smoke pot and who are accepted by others. Since they are not ostracized, there is no reason to think I will be—90%; to (4) he had "Even though I am anxious, I can talk to some people if I choose. Anxiety makes me uncomfortable but doesn't make it impossible to speak—80%; and to (5) he listed "Quiet people are not necessarily peculiar. Some people look up to people who are quiet."

Following his recognition of the irrationality of his automatic thoughts, the patient was then asked to "perform an experiment" by actually attending this party. The therapist then had the patient set certain behavioral goals. Among these were to carry out a conversation with one other person and learn as much about that person as possible in order to write a brief biographical sketch for the next therapy session; if marijuana is present, to politely decline but ask the host if this nonparticipation creates any discomfort for the others; to keep track of any automatic thoughts associated with any experiences of discomfort during the party.

The patient's actual experiences at the party were clearly different from his catastrophic initial expectations. A few individuals smoked pot, but they were in the minority. His lengthy conversation with the wife of the host led to her sharing her own feelings of anxiety in a way that was reassuring. Not only did the patient enjoy the party beyond his expectations, but he was one of the last guests to leave. (Burns & Beck, 1978)

The research on cognitive therapy is still building. Although a number of case studies have been reported, and major books have appeared, at least one reviewer has observed that the amount of controlled research on cognitive treatment methods lags behind those completed on other behavior therapies (Ledwidge, 1978). However, there have been some very interesting studies relevant to anxiety management. In perhaps the only research to use a clinical population, Lipsky, Kassinove, and Miller (1980) provided rational emotive therapy treatment in various ways to 50 persons seen in an outpatient community mental-health center. Although the exact diagnosis for each patient was not revealed, patients were accepted for the study only if they were diagnosed either as suffering from "one of the ... neuroses ... or ... adjustment reaction" (p. 368). Such categories would mean that persons with generalized anxiety disorder might have been among those receiving treatment. The various RET procedures offered were RET alone, or RET plus a behavioral exercise, or RET plus an imaginal rehearsal exercise. The control groups received either relaxation training combined with supportive therapy (ST) or no treatment (WL). The first results involving the *Idea Inventory* confirmed the expectation that RET training and its modifications did lead to changes in the patients' level of rationality. These patients showed an increase in their rational cognitions and a decrease in their endorsement of irrational beliefs. The crucial question was whether signs of general anxiety, mood disturbances, or general neuroticism would change following cognitive therapy. In general, RET alone did appear to have some impact on measures such as the STAI-Trait anxiety, the Multiple Affect Adjective Check List, and the Eysenck Personality Inventory (Neuroticism Scale), when compared with the control groups. However, there was a consistent trend for the groups receiving RET enhanced by either the behavioral or imaginal exercises to show greater improvement than RET alone. This finding becomes important when viewed in the context of other research.

A number of other studies, either on RET or SRR support the hypothesis that using an active practice component is valuable. Miller and Kassinove (1978) found that a rationale emotive therapy approach which included role-playing practice led to greater reductions in trait anxiety than RET alone. Furthermore, RET alone did not lead to significant changes in trait anxiety compared to no treatment among this group of fourth-grade youngsters. Two studies on SRR, which followed the usual SRR steps including homework practice, discovered reductions in general anxiety measures although the SRR therapy had been applied for other target problems among the clients. Thus, Linehan, Goldfried, and Goldfried (1979) applied SRR to women complaining of being unassertive. This cognitive therapy not only led to reductions in general anxiety as measured by the S–R Inventory of Anxiousness, but also to an increase in assertiveness skills. These improvements were retained on 8–10 weeks' follow-up. Working with test-anxious patients, Goldfried, Linehan, and Smith (1978) found that SRR not only led to reductions in test anxiety but also generalized to some other situational anxieties (social anxiety, evaluational anxiety). However, no changes on STAI-Trait anxiety scores were obtained. Finally, Emmelkamp, Kuipers, and Eggeraat (1978) treated agoraphobics with either a version of cognitive therapy or a form of behavioral practice. The cognitive therapy involved the initial steps of SRR and RET, that is, logging of undesirable thoughts, and identifying the irrational basis of distorted cognitions. Imaginal rehearsal involving substituting positive thoughts for negative self-statements completed the training. The behavioral practice treatment, on the other hand, involved prolonged exposure *in vivo* to the phobic situation of being outdoors. The patients and therapists walked together to the center of town, or traveled to other settings considered frightening. In this sense, the technique was a combination of response prevention, reinforced practice, and participant modeling. Prolonged exposure led to greater improvements than cognitive therapy as shown by reductions in agoraphobia. In addition, prolonged exposure also showed some generalization to other situational fears as measured by the Fear Survey Schedule, whereas cognitive therapy showed no such effects. It should be noted that the cognitive therapy did not have the homework *in vivo* practice assignments which are part of SRR training. In fact, the patients receiving cognitive treatment in this study commented that it was difficult to turn on the positive self-statements when they were outside the therapy room confronting a real life circumstance.

Stress Inoculation

From the previous discussion, it is possible to hypothesize that training in identifying and challenging the rationality of undesirable thoughts may lead persons to become more reasonable, but this guarantees neither that the reasonableness will transfer to other settings, nor that the reasonableness will remove more generalized anxieties. From his review, Ledwidge (1978) even concluded that cognitions may be changed by cognitive therapy methods, but behaviors (or anxieties) may not necessarily change; hence he would rather refer to the methods as cognitive therapy rather than cognitive behavior modification. A possible solution would be to adapt the basic concepts of RET or SRR to train the patients in general strategies instead of focusing on specific irrational beliefs, and always to include *in vivo* behavior-rehearsal training in order to produce greater transfer and behavior change. Stress inoculation (SI) (Meichenbaum, 1977) is a technique which not only includes these aspects of cognitive therapy, but also adds an affective/autonomic coping step as well (relaxation training).

In the first stage of SI, patients learn the role of cognitions in the production or expression of anxiety. Several objectives of skill training are then made clear, specifically skill in preparing for a stressor, skill in confronting or handling a stressor, skill in coping with feelings of being overwhelmed, and skill in reinforcing oneself for having coped. In the second stage, patients acquire a variety of coping skills to reach the various objectives. Two general categories of coping skills are covered: direct action and cognitive coping. Among the direct actions are developing information on phobic objects, identifying escape routes, and relaxation training. Progressive relaxation training with an emphasis on breathing control is often used. Among the cognitive coping techniques is the multiplex use of thoughts to stimulate coping, to inhibit negative or distorted cognitions, to relabel anxiety-arousal (instead of being viewed as a destructive experience the arousal becomes a signal for positive action), and to provide self-praise. Meichenbaum (1977) gives some examples of these various types of uses of cognitions:

> Cognitions for preparing for a stressor:
> "What is it you have to do now?"
> "Just focus on what you can do about it instead of getting anxious."
> "No negative thoughts, just think rationally."
> Cognitions for confronting a stressor:
> "One step at a time."
> "This is the anxiety appearing, use your coping exercises."
> "Relax, you're in control. Take a deep breath."
> Cognitions for coping with feeling overwhelmed:
> "O.K. when fear mounts, just pause."
> "Label your fear from 0 to 10 and watch it change."
> "No need to eliminate the fear completely, just manage it."
> Cognitions for reinforcing self-statements:
> "It worked. You did it!"
> "See, you can control your thoughts, and through them your anxieties."
> "It's getting better every time you face another stress."

The final stage in SI is application training, whereby patients test out their new coping skills and add more practice in real life situations. The initial practice may be during the regular therapy hour through laboratory stressors, such as mild electric shock or observing a stress-inducing movie. Imagery rehearsal may also be employed to enable the patients to practice coping with a variety of life circumstances. Varied and extensive practice is encouraged until the patients have developed a general learning set, or strategies, or as Meichenbaum states, "a general way of talking to (oneself) in order to cope" (p. 182).

Despite the obvious relevance to general anxiety problems of SI's emphasis on coping strategies, the research appropriate for generalized anxiety disorder is quite sparse. As with many other behavioral therapies for anxiety control, SI has mainly been used with situation-specific anxieties instead of diffuse or general anxiety. Thus, SI has been found effective in treatment of test anxiety (Deffenbacher & Hahnloser, 1981; Meichenbaum, 1972), speech anxiety (Meichenbaum, Gilmore & Fedoravicius, 1971), fear of flying (Girodo & Roehl, 1978), and social-evaluative anxiety (Hammen, Jacobs, Mayol, & Cochran, 1980). Weissberg (1977) provided SI training to speech-anxious students and compared the effects on public-speaking anxiety measures and on the Taylor Manifest Anxiety Scale (MAS), a test of general anxiety. Both desensitization and SI were equivalent in reducing evidences of speech anxiety. On general anxiety, neither treatment approach led to lower reductions on MAS scores in comparison to a control group. However, by the time of an 11-week follow-up both treatment groups had shown sufficient further reductions in general anxiety scores as to now be at levels significantly lower than that of the control group. Once again, however, the improvements in MAS scores were equivalent for each of the two therapeutic approaches. Hussian and Lawrence (1978) hypothesized that the SI cognitive training step could be divided into two possibly different approaches: a generalized and a phobic-specific training approach. In the generalized approach, the self-statements which patients would rehearse would be of the type, "One step at a time, I can handle this," and "When fear builds up, just pause a moment." In the phobic-specific approach, the thoughts would be highly specific to the nature of the phobia of the patients (in this study, test anxiety) and would be of the form, "If I see several test items I cannot answer, I'll take a deep breath and relax," "O.K. so I'm drawing a blank on this item, just go on to the next one." Both the generalized and phobic-specific training led to higher reductions in test anxiety than a wait-list control group. By the time of an 8-month follow-up, these treated groups showed some relapse in increases in reported test-anxiety scores. The two treatment groups still reported less test anxiety than the wait-list controls but the treated groups scores were now at the level of a placebo-treatment group. Trait anxiety scores also decreased for both treatment groups; however, once again the amount of decrease was equivalent to that achieved by the placebo-treatment group. Furthermore, by the time of an 8-month follow-up, a major part of the gains were lost. Thus, in two studies the issue of the value of SI for trait anxiety is unresolved, and regrettably there have been as yet no reports using SI with persons diagnosed as suffering from generalized anxiety disorder.

MODEL OF GENERALIZED ANXIETY

Conceptualizing the expression of anxiety as involving three possible response channels can be useful in understanding the unique characteristics of each patient. Although generalized anxiety disorder might encompass affective-autonomic, somatic-behavioral, and cognitive symptoms concurrently, individual patients might show a dominance of symptom expression in one or another channel. It is also useful for diagnosis, to determine the relationships across these expressions as they might chain together sequentially. Unlike phobic disorders where the anxiety source is easily identified as the phobic stimulus, generalized anxiety disorder is diffuse. One reason may well be that the patient reacts to multiple stimuli in such a way that no single pattern of cues appears evident. Another reason may be that internal sequencing of arousal occurs which prompt, exacerbate, or further maintain the anxiety state, thereby assuring its chronicity. For example, remember the case of the university dropout who originally panicked on one examination, took the step of withdrawing from the university, cognitively interpreted this action as evidence of a breakdown, responded to these thoughts by way of anticipating the worst from others (interpreting the environment now as threatening), and became even more general in his anxiety. Thus, affective-autonomic arousal may have formed a chain of internal events whereby each anxiety channel influenced the other. Still a third reason for the diffuseness is the possible presence of other deficiencies interacting with the anxiety. Recall Shoemaker's finding that patients suffering from generalized anxiety disorder sometimes returned for further therapy following successful treatment of the anxiety condition. In some cases, the return was prompted by the patients' now being able to recognize behavioral deficits that could well have been underlying initial anxieties before such anxieties became overwhelming and a source of problems in themselves.

The choice of behavior therapy can be made from the above diagnostic analyses. The various therapies can be conveniently grouped into affective-autonomic, somatic-behavioral, and cognitive. It seems useful to begin treatment with the therapeutic approach which best matches the patients' dominant symptom pattern. There are two practical exceptions to this rule. First, it is sometimes sensible to begin with the symptomatology which is easiest to control, in the case of patients who have low esteem for and little confidence in behavior intervention, or who may be suffering so intensely as to need immediate relief. Quick relief from relaxation training in the session can form the base for higher motivation and patient compliance. A second practical exception derives from the varied pragmatic and research information on the various approaches. As pointed out, reinforced practice and modeling work best when there is some situational context and identifiable behaviors to be practiced, and this may present a significant limitation in some cases. Anxiety management training works with the anxiety expressions themselves, as does flooding and implosion, but currently more research based on patient populations is available on AMT. Of the cognitive methods, SRR provides more diverse methods for stimulating patients to challenge their cognitions (reality testing, direct observation, distancing) than provided by RET (which relies heavily on therapist-challenges to logic). Since there are data suggesting that therapists' characteristics can influence patient-outcome in therapy (Jannoun, Munby, Catalan, & Gelder, 1980), SRR may be more suitable since it relies less on the therapist's skills for its effect than the RET-challenging style.

The choice of which therapy to use will also be influenced by the broader diagnostic picture and the immediate goals of treatment. One therapy will be selected where no skill deficits are present, another when serious deficits complicate the issue. Even with deficits present, treatment goals can affect decisions. In students with study-skill deficits, for example, Mitchell and Ng (1973) found that desensitization reduced test anxiety substantially, but was of no help on academic performance. In other words, although the students were more comfortable in preparing for examinations, they did not prepare any better!

However, an immediate goal for a student may well be to achieve control over test anxiety as a first step toward academic problem-solving. Once the anxieties that might interfere with learning new skills are removed, the next step could then be training the student in study skills. Along these lines, a conceptual model regarding type of behavior therapy chosen, presence or absence of other deficits, anxiety channel targeted, and the anticipated outcomes is presented in Figures 1 and 2. According to this model, patients might first differ on the presence of skill deficits which interact with anxiety to lead to performance deficiencies. Patients might also differ in the major contributor to anxiety as well as in their dominant anxiety response channel. Here we are adding the concept that the dominant link in anxiety sequences might also follow the affective-autonomic, somatic-behavioral, or cognitive dimensions used to describe the major channels of symptom expression. As a specific example, whereas a patient might express anxiety predominately through ruminating thoughts ("Why do I always fail?"), this same patient may also have had the initial anxiety precipitated because of irrational cognitions ("I'm not prepared enough, I'm *going* to fail"). Here, distorted cognitions are not only a symptomatic response to anxiety, but also may be a causal stimulant. Another aspect of the model acknowledges that some events are neutral and do not prompt anxiety in normal persons; however, for some patients, the events precipitate anxiety because of past learning. The learning may be the direct conditioning of affective-autonomic reactions, or the association of distorted cognitions to the events. In the former, presenting the events automatically prompts affective-autonomic anxiety responses (e.g., increased heart rate to the sight of a final examination). In the latter, the events prompt the automatic thoughts (e.g., worrying about failing the test). It is also acknowledged that some events are not neutral but represent reality threats, and hence most persons will respond with anxiety. The initial anxiety response pattern, however, can be further exacerbated by past learning, for example, if the patient has failed to cope in the past and hence overreacts to new threat with anticipatory failure. Another facet of the model distinguishes between behavioral performance and distress. It acknowledges that therapy may reduce distress but not improve on performance and vice versa; this will be elaborated upon later. Finally, the model identifies different targets for the various behavioral interventions along with the differing outcomes.

To illustrate this model, Figure 1 assumes a patient whose dominant characteristic is distorted cognitions in reaction either to environmental events or as interpretations of internal events. The illustration starts with an event that has no reality basis as a threat but which is perceived as threatening (an irrational cognition). From this perception, the patient experiences an autonomic response associated with being threatened, namely a condition of arousal or activation. As the model shows, the arousal may in turn be interpreted with the cognition of being "harmful anxiety," or as an irrelevant state of "excita-

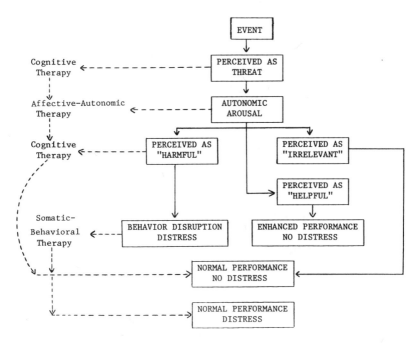

Figure 1. Conceptual model for behavior therapy where anxiety derives from perceived threat.

bility," or even as an emotional state that is helpful such as being "psyched up." Such cognitive interpretations of the autonomic condition can then precipitate differing outcomes: distress and disruption if the patient feels "anxious," no distress or disruption if the activation is viewed as irrelevant, and no distress or disruption and possibly even enhanced performance if the activation is perceived as helpful. Behavior therapy may be applied at different points with this patient. Starting at the beginning of this sequence, cognitive therapy may be aimed at helping the patient reassess the perception of the event as a threat and to substitute reality testing for the irrational belief. If this is successful, then the rest of the sequence would be aborted, such as the autonomic response, the distress, and the behavioral disruption. As an alternative, affective-autonomic therapy may be used to eliminate the autonomic response, thereby eliminating the arousal and its consequences, although not changing the patient's view of the event as a threat ("I know I feel the need to do well on this test and realize it's an important exam, but it doesn't get to me any more"). A third alternative would be to provide cognitive therapy, this time aimed at the autonomic response. Instead of the cognition that the arousal is harmful, cognitive restructuring might defuse this attitude ("You've had this experience of anxiousness before and managed well" or "When fear builds, just pause a moment"). This alternative neither changes the belief about the initial event nor removes the autonomic arousal, but directs the person to cognitive steps for coping with the stress. A final alternative is to introduce somatic-behavioral therapy in the final stage in the illustrated sequence, that is, the behavioral disruption occurring after the perception of the arousal as harmful. Such treatment might be expected to lead to the elimination of disruptions, while having no immediate effects on the distress.

Figure 2 presents the more complex example, hypothesizing an event that in reality is a threat, and in the presence of a behavioral deficit as well. This might be the case where a person is required to pass a test in order to remain in school, but the person has study-skills deficits. Another example would be where evidence of severe personal and school problems make it necessary for a parent to confront a child, but the parent has poor parent-effectiveness skills. As before, we are presenting a person in whom cognitions play a dominant role, and as before, the figure illustrates the various points for intervention. Starting with the event, the person may add to the anxiety reaction associated with the reality threat through irrational beliefs. The distorted belief may be, "If I fail this test, I will be a failure in life and no good for anything" or "I can't deal

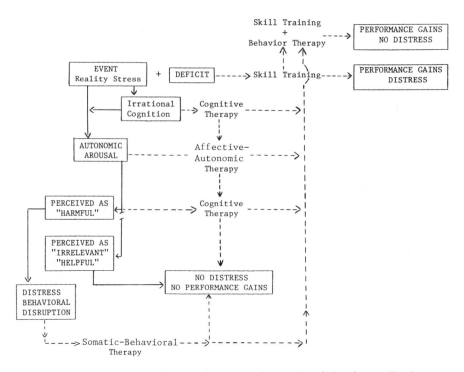

Figure 2. Conceptual model for behavior therapy where anxiety derives from reality threat.

with my child, it's all my fault that I haven't been a more loving parent, otherwise this wouldn't have happened." Such cognitions could further exacerbate the autonomic arousal which would be expected to occur in reaction to the reality threat anyway. As illustrated in Figure 1, the autonomic arousal can be perceived in a variety of ways with differing consequences. Unlike Figure 1, however, the presence of an ability deficit makes it important to recognize the difference between distress and performance gains. Although cognitive therapy can be used to change the initial irrational beliefs that follow the event or are associated with the autonomic response, and although affective-autonomic training can be directed towards the autonomic arousal and somatic-behavioral treatment may be used with the disruption following arousal, none of these alone would be expected to achieve anything more than the reduction of distress. They would not be expected to lead to performance gains, inasmuch as the behavioral deficit still exists. "Skill training" as highlighted in Figure 2 involves those training programs which increase the acquisition of new skills to alter the behavioral deficit. The training, for example, might be in study skills, parent–child relations, or assertiveness, budget management, communications skills, or any other life skill that impacts directly on the reality stress. But although such training (as Figure 2 also brings out) may lead to performance gains, it may still leave the person distressed. Therefore, to go back to the example in this illustration, it would take skill training together with behavior therapy for anxiety to achieve the outcome of eliminating distress and increasing performance. To summarize, this model of diagnosis can help a therapist in determining the various behavior therapies for an individual case as well as the likely outcomes to be expected, in order to plan case management more systematically.

A concluding statement should take into account two final factors in decisions about therapy, based upon research trends. First, some version of behavioral practice *in vivo* appears to be necessary to insure transfer of therapy from the treatment environment to the real world and follow-up. Secondly, self-control models of therapy appear to generalize better to nontargeted problems and show more continued gains during follow-up. In these self-control approaches, therapy aims at training the patients to apply the skills in order to help themselves. Such skills may be varied, ranging from discrimination learning in order to recognize the early signs of anxiety to grasping and rehearsing general coping strategies. Within such a framework, patients suffering from generalized anxiety disorder can more fruitfully benefit from behavioral therapy.

REFERENCES

Agras, W., Leitenberg, H., & Barlow, D. Social reinforcement in the modification of agoraphobia. *Archives of General Psychiatry*, 1968, *19*, 423–427.

Agras, W., Leitenberg, H., Barlow, D., & Thomson, L. Instructions and reinforcement in the modification of neurotic behavior. *American Journal of Psychiatry*, 1969, *125*, 1435–1439.

American Psychiatric Association. *Diagnostic and statistical manual of mental disorders* (3rd ed.). Washington, D.C.: Author, 1980.

Bandura, A. Influence of model's reinforcement contingencies on the acquisition of imitative responses. *Journal of Personality and Social Psychology*, 1965, *1*, 589–595.

Bandura, A. *Social learning theory*. Englewood Cliffs, N.J.: Prentice-Hall, 1977.

Beck, A., Laude, R., & Bohnert, M. Ideation components of anxiety neurosis. *Archives of General Psychiatry*, 1974, *31*, 319–325.

Bloom, L., & Cantrell, D. Anxiety management training for essential hypertension in pregnancy. *Behavior Therapy*, 1978, *9*, 377–382.

Borkovec, T., Kaloupek, D., & Slama, K. The facilitative effect of muscle tension-release in the relaxation treatment of sleep disturbance. *Behavior Therapy*, 1975, *6*, 301–309.

Brauer, A., Horlick, L., Nelson, E., Farquhar, J., & Agras, W. Relaxation therapy for essential hypertension: A Veterans' Administration outpatient study. *Journal of Behavioral Medicine*, 1979, *2*, 21–29.

Brooks, G., & Richardson, F. Emotional skills training: A treatment program for duodenal ulcer. *Behavior Therapy*, 1980, *11*, 198–207.

Burns, D., & Beck, A. Cognitive behavior modification of mood disorders. In J. P. Foreyt & D. P. Rathjen (Eds.), *Cognitive behavior therapy: Research and application*. New York: Plenum, 1978.

Chesney, M., & Tasto, D. The effectiveness of behavior modification with spasmodic and congestive dysmenorrhea. *Behaviour Research and Therapy*, 1975, *13*, 245–253.

Dalessio, D. *Wolff's headache and other head pain*. New York: Oxford University Press, 1972.

Deffenbacher, J., & Hahnloser, R. Cognitive and relaxation coping skills in stress inoculation. *Cognitive Therapy and Research*, 1981, *5*, 211–216.

Deffenbacher, J., & Michaels, A. A twelve-month follow-up of homogeneous and heterogeneous anxiety management training. *Journal of Counseling Psychology*, 1981, *28*, 463–466. (a)

Deffenbacher, J., & Michaels, A. Anxiety management training and self-control desensitization—15 months later. *Journal of Counseling Psychology*, 1981, *28*, 459–462. (b)

Deffenbacher, J., & Shelton, J. A comparison of anxiety management training and desensitization in reducing test and other anxieties. *Journal of Counseling Psychology*, 1978, *25*, 277–282.

Deffenbacher, J., & Suinn, R. The self-control of anxiety. In P. Karoly & F. H. Kanfer (Eds.), *The psychology of self-management: From theory to practice*. Elmsford, New York: Pergamon, 1982.

Deffenbacher, J., Michaels, A., Daley, P., & Michaels, T. A comparison of homogeneous and heterogeneous anxiety management training. *Journal of Counseling Psychology*, 1980, *27*, 630–634.

Deffenbacher, J., Michaels, A., Michaels, T., & Daley, P. Comparison of anxiety management training and self-control desensitization. *Journal of Counseling Psychology*, 1980, *27*, 232–239.

Edie, C. *Uses of AMT in treating trait anxiety*. Unpublished doctoral dissertation, Colorado State University, Fort Collins, Col., 1972.

Ellis, A. *Reason and emotion in psychotherapy*. New York: Lyle Stuart, 1962.

Emmelkamp, P., Kuipers, A., & Eggeraat, J. Cognitive modification versus prolonged exposure *in vivo*: A comparison with agoraphobics as subjects. *Behaviour Research and Therapy*, 1978, *16*, 33–41.

Epstein, L., Webster, J., & Abel, G. Self-managed relaxation in the treatment of tension headaches. In J. Krumboltz & C. Thoresen (Eds.), *Counseling methods*. New York: Holt, Rinehart & Winston, 1976.

Eysenck, H., & Rachman, S. *The causes and cures of neurosis.* London: Routledge & Kegan, 1965.

Girodo, M., & Roehl, J. Cognitive preparation and coping self-talk: Anxiety management during the stress of flying. *Journal of Consulting and Clinical Psychology,* 1978, *46,* 978–989.

Goldfried, M., & Trier, C. Effectiveness of relaxation as an active coping skill. *Journal of Abnormal Psychology,* 1974, *83,* 348–355.

Goldfried, M., Decenteceo, E., & Weinberg, L. Systematic rational restructuring as a self-control technique. *Behavior Therapy,* 1974, *5,* 247–254.

Goldfried, M., Linehan, M., & Smith, J. Reduction of test anxiety through cognitive restructuring. *Journal of Consulting and Clinical Psychology,* 1978, *46,* 32–39.

Hammen, C., Jacobs, M., Mayol, A., & Cochran, S. Dysfunctional cognitions and the effectiveness of skills and cognitive-behavioral assertion training. *Journal of Consulting and Clinical Psychology,* 1980, *48,* 685–695.

Hersen, M., & Bellack, A. Social skills training for chronic psychiatric patients: Rationale, research findings and future directions. *Comparative Psychiatry,* 1976, *17,* 559–580.

Horne, A., & Matson, J. A comparison of modeling, desensitization, flooding, study skills, and control groups for reducing test anxiety. *Behavior Therapy,* 1977, *8,* 1–8.

Houston, B., Jorgensen, R., & Zurawski, R. The effectiveness of anxiety management training in reducing hypertensives' blood pressure at rest and following stress. In *Program abstracts and meeting information.* Society of Behavioral Medicine, Second Annual Meeting, New York, 1980.

Hugdahl, K. The three-systems-model of fear and emotion—a critical examination. *Behaviour Research and Therapy,* 1981, *19,* 75–85.

Hussian, R., & Lawrence, P. The reduction of test, state, and trait anxiety by test-specific and generalized stress inoculation training. *Cognitive Therapy and Research,* 1978, *2,* 25–37.

Hutchings, D., Denney, D., Basgall, J., & Houston, B. Anxiety management and applied relaxation in reducing general anxiety. *Behaviour Research and Therapy,* 1980, *18,* 181–190.

Jacobsen, F. *Progressive relaxation.* Chicago, Ill.: University of Chicago Press, 1938.

Jannoun, L., Munby, M., Catalan, J., & Gelder, M. A home-based treatment program for agoraphobia: Replication and controlled evaluation. *Behavior Therapy,* 1980, *11,* 294–305.

King, M. *Anxiety management training for general medical patients.* Unpublished doctoral dissertation, Colorado State University, Fort Collins, 1981.

Kleinknecht, R., & Bernstein, D. Short-term treatment of dental avoidance. *Journal of Behavior Therapy and Experimental Psychiatry,* in press.

Lang, P. The application of psychophysiological methods to the study of psychotherapy and behavior change. In A. Bergin & S. Garfield (Eds.), *Handbook of psychotherapy and behavior change.* New York: Wiley, 1971.

Lazarus, A., & Abramovitz, A. The use of "emotive imagery" in the treatment of children's phobias. *Journal of Mental Science,* 1962, *108,* 191–195.

Ledwidge, B. Cognitive behavior modification: A step in the wrong direction? *Psychological Bulletin,* 1978, *85,* 353–375.

Lehrer, P. Psychophysiological effects of progressive relaxation in anxiety neurotic patients and of progressive relaxation and alpha feedback in nonpatients. *Journal of Consulting and Clinical Psychology,* 1978, *46,* 389–404.

Leitenberg, H. Behavioral approaches to the treatment of neuroses. In H. Leitenberg (Ed.), *Handbook of behavior modification and behavior therapy.* Englewood Cliffs, N.J.: Prentice-Hall, 1976.

Leitenberg, H., Agras, W., Thomson, L., & Wright, D. Feedback in behavior modification: An experimental analysis in two phobic cases. *Journal of Applied Behavior Analysis,* 1968, *1,* 131–137.

Leitenberg, H., Agras, W., Edwards, J., Thomson, L., & Wincze, J. Practice as a psychotherapeutic variable. An experimental analysis within single cases. *Journal of Psychiatric Research,* 1970, *7,* 215–225.

Leitenberg, H., Agras, W., Butz, R., & Wincze, J. Relationship between heart rate and behavior change during the treatment of phobias. *Journal of Abnormal Psychology,* 1971, *78,* 59–68.

Leitenberg, H., Agras, W., Allen, R., Butz, R., & Edwards, J. Feedback and therapist praise during treatment of phobia. *Journal of Consulting and Clinical Psychology,* 1975, *43,* 396–404.

Lewis, C., Biglan, A., & Steinbock, E. Self-administered relaxation training and money deposits in the treatment of recurrent anxiety. *Journal of Consulting and Clinical Psychology,* 1978, *46,* 1274–1283.

Lick, J., & Heffler, D. Relaxation training and a tension placebo in the treatment of severe insomnia. *Journal of Consulting and Psychology,* 1977, *45,* 153–161.

Linehan, M., Goldfried, M., & Goldfried, A. Assertion therapy: Skill training or cognitive restructuring. *Behavior Therapy,* 1979, *10,* 372–388.

Lipsky, M., Kassinove, H., & Miller, N. Effects of rational-emotive imagery on the emotional adjustment of community mental health center patients. *Journal of Consulting and Clinical Psychology,* 1980, *48,* 366–374.

Mahoney, M. The self management of covert behavior: A case study. *Behavior Therapy,* 1971, *2,* 575–578.

Marks, I., & Lader, M. Anxiety states (anxiety neurosis): A review. *Journal of Nervous and Mental Disorders,* 1973, *156,* 3–18.

Mathis, H. *The effects of anxiety management training on musical performance anxiety.* Unpublished master's thesis, Colorado State University, Fort Collins, 1978.

Meichenbaum, D. Examination of model characteristics in reducing avoidance behavior. *Journal of Personality and Social Psychology,* 1971, *17,* 298–307.

Meichenbaum, D. Cognitive modification of test anxious college students. *Journal of Consulting and Clinical Psychology,* 1972, *39,* 370–380.

Meichenbaum, D. *Cognitive-behavior modification: An integrative approach.* New York: Plenum, 1977.

Meichenbaum, D., Gilmore, J., & Fedoravicius, A. Group insight versus group desensitization in treating speech anxiety. *Journal of Consulting and Clinical Psychology,* 1971, *36,* 410–421.

Melamed, B., & Siegel, L. Reduction of anxiety in children facing hospitalization and surgery by use of filmed modeling. *Journal of Consulting and Clinical Psychology,* 1975, *43,* 511–521.

Melamed, B., & Siegel, L. *Behavioral medicine, practical applications in health care.* New York: Springer, 1980.

Miller, N., & Kassinove, H. Effects of lecture, rehearsal, written homework, and IG on the efficacy of a rational emotive school mental health program. *Journal of Community Psychology,* 1978, *6,* 366–373.

Mitchell, K., & Ng, K. Effects of group counseling and behavior therapy on the academic achievement of test-anxious students. *Journal of Counseling Psychology,* 1973, *19,* 491–497.

Mowrer, O. *Learning theory and the symbolic process.* New York: Wiley, 1960.

Nally, M. *AMT: A treatment for delinquents.* Unpublished doctoral dissertation, Colorado State University, Fort Collins, 1975.

Nicassio, P., & Bootzin, R. A comparison of progressive relaxation and autogenic training as treatments for insomnia. *Journal of Abnormal and Social Psychology,* 1974, *83,* 253–260.

Nicoletti, J. *Anxiety management training.* Unpublished doctoral dissertation, Colorado State University, Fort Collins, 1972.

Patel, C. 12-month follow-up of yoga and biofeedback in the management of hypertension. *Lancet*, 1975, *1*, 62–67.

Peterson, L., & Ridley-Johnson, R. Pediatric hospital response to survey on prehospital preparation for children. *Journal of Pediatric Psychology*, 1980, *5*, 1–7.

Peterson, L., & Shigetomi, C. The use of coping techniques to minimize anxiety in hospitalized children. *Behavior Therapy*, 1981, *12*, 1–14.

Raskin, M., Johnson, G., & Rondestveldt, J. Chronic anxiety treated by feedback-induced muscle relaxation. *Archives of General Psychiatry*, 1973, *28*, 263–267.

Richardson, F., & Suinn, R. The mathematics anxiety rating scale: Psychometric data. *Journal of Counseling Psychology*, 1973, *19*, 551–554.

Ritter, B. The group desensitization of children's snake phobias using vicarious and contact desensitization procedures. *Behaviour Research and Therapy*, 1968, *6*, 1–6.

Rosenthal, T., & Bandura, A. Psychological modeling: Theory and practice. In S. Garfield & A. Bergin (Eds.), *Handbook of psychotherapy and behavior change: An empirical analysis* (2nd ed.) New York: Wiley, 1978.

Rudenstam, K., & Bedrosian, R. An investigation of the effectiveness of desensitization and flooding with two types of phobia. *Behaviour Research and Therapy*, 1977, *15*, 23–30.

Sherman, A. Two-year follow-up of training in relaxation as a behavioral self-management skill. *Behavior Therapy*, 1975, *6*, 419–420.

Sherman, A., & Plummer, I. Training in relaxation as a behavioral self-management skill: An exploratory investigation. *Behavior Therapy*, 1973, *4*, 543–550.

Shipley, R., & Boudewyns, P. Flooding and implosive therapy: Are they harmful? *Behavior Therapy*, 1980, *11*, 503–508.

Shoemaker, J. *Treatments for anxiety neurosis.* Unpublished doctoral dissertation, Colorado State University, Fort Collins, 1976.

Silver, B., & Blanchard, E. Biofeedback and relaxation training in the treatment of psychophysiological disorders: Or are the machines really necessary? *Journal of Behavioral Medicine*, 1978, *1*, 217–239.

Stampfl, T. Implosive therapy: The theory, the subhuman analogue, the strategy, and the technique: Part I: The theory. In S. G. Armitage (Ed.), *Behavior modification techniques in the treatment of emotional disorders*. Battle Creek, Mich.: V. A. Publication, 1967.

Stampfl, T., & Levis, D. Essential of implosive therapy: A learning-theory-based psychodynamic behavioral therapy. *Journal of Abnormal Psychology*, 1967, *72*, 496–503.

Suinn, R. *Manual for anxiety management training (AMT)*. Fort Collins, Colorado: Rocky Mountain Behavioral Science Institute, 1977 (Available from publisher [P.O. Box 1066, Fort Collins, Col., 90522]). (a)

Suinn, R. Treatment of phobias. In G. Harris (Ed.), *The group treatment of human problems.* New York: Grune & Stratton, 1977. (b)

Suinn, R. *Fundamentals of behavior pathology* (3rd ed.). Menlo Park, Cal.: Benjamin/Cummings, 1981. (a)

Suinn, R. *Stress management studies: Remedies for alphabet soup.* Address presented at Rocky Mountain Psychological Association Convention, Denver, May, 1981. (b)

Suinn, R., & Bloom, L. Anxiety management training for Type A persons. *Journal of Behavioral Medicine*, 1978, *1*, 25–35.

Tarler-Benlolo, L., & Love, W. *EMG-biofeedback treatment of spastic colon: A case report.* Paper presented to the meeting of the Biofeedback Society of America, Orlando, Fla., March 1977.

Townsend, R., House, J., & Addario, D. A comparison of biofeedback-mediated relaxation and group therapy in the treatment of chronic anxiety. *American Journal of Psychiatry*, 1975, *132*, 598–601.

Weinberger, A., & Engelhart, R. Three group treatments for reduction of speech anxiety among students. *Perceptual Motor Skills*, 1976, *43*, 1317–1318.

Weinstock, S. *The reestablishment of intestinal control in functional colitis.* Paper presented at the meeting of the Biofeedback Research Society, Colorado Springs, Col., February, 1976.

Weissberg, M. A comparison of direct and vicarious treatments of speech anxiety: Desensitization, desensitization with coping imagery, and cognitive modification. *Behavior Therapy,* 1977, *8,* 606–620.

Wolpe, J. *The practice of behavior therapy* (2nd ed.). New York: Pergamon, 1973.

8

Social Phobia

PETER TROWER and DAVID TURLAND

THE NATURE AND PREVALENCE OF SOCIAL PHOBIA

Miss G., a well-groomed 23-year-old, was referred to a psychiatric clinic when she sought help from her family doctor for the discomfort she felt in certain social situations. She was one of six siblings and recalled her childhood as being happy, although she had always been shy and lacking in self-confidence and had never developed close friendships outside the family. She left school at 18 having obtained qualifications to proceed to higher education, but elected instead to start work and left home to work for an advertising agency in a large city. Although she enjoyed most of what this job entailed, Miss G. found it difficult to deal with clients. She would sometimes have to participate in working lunches, for example, and while this did not disturb her so long as the conversation focused on the job in hand, it would usually turn at some point to more social topics. She would then become uncomfortable, feeling tense and shaky, perspiring excessively. Worrying that her companions might think her dull, uninteresting, and not much fun, she would find herself unable to think of things to say. Eventually these reactions became so unpleasant that she had to quit this job. Returning to her parents' home, Miss G. obtained a job in the ticket office of a cinema. She claimed that if anyone visited the home, including relatives, she would usually retire to her bedroom rather than endure the discomfort of their presence. There was no discomfort in the presence of her immediate family, however. Miss G. had no hobbies other than reading and was isolated from any social contact with her own age group. She had consulted her doctor because she believed that these reactions were apt to restrict her future vocational prospects greatly. During clinical interviews, both a psychiatrist and a psychologist were impressed by her vivacity, apparent sense of being at ease, and fluent verbal style. When this was mentioned, she explained that she

PETER TROWER ● Department of Psychology, Leicester University, Leicester LE1 7RH, England.   DAVID TURLAND ● Department of Psychology, Hollymoor Hospital, Northfield, Birmingham B31 5EX, England.

always tended to feel more comfortable with "strangers" than with people whom she had gotten to know slightly, and that in the context of speaking to people who might understand her difficulties from a professional standpoint she was able to remain calm.

The foregoing is a typical example of a prominent social problem which has only recently begun to receive much-needed research and clinical investigation (Barlow & Wolfe, 1981). The problem is generally classified as social phobia—a term which has developed within the framework of medical diagnosis and is intended to summarize the clinical features of the disorder, and possibly to refer to its etiology and prognosis. Accordingly the diagnosis implies, at the descriptive level, an abnormal fear in connection with social situations. The purpose of this chapter is to review, from the standpoint of the behavioral clinician, the syndrome of social phobia in the light of developments which have taken place over the last decade or so. An attempt is made to integrate a number of related topics within a social-learning model of fear development, and to derive principles for the treatment of the various components of social phobia.

Fear, Anxiety, Phobia

Although attempts have been made to differentiate between fear and anxiety on the grounds that the former emotion occurs in response to a specifiable external stimulus and the latter occurs without apparent cause (e.g., Marks, 1969, p. 6), current usage tends to avoid this distinction and in this chapter the terms are used interchangeably. The term *phobia* implies that a fear or anxiety fulfills these four criteria: it (1) is out of proportion to the demands of the situation, (2) cannot be explained or reasoned away, (3) is beyond voluntary control, and (4) is associated with avoidance of the feared situation (Marks, 1969, p. 3).

Social Phobia

Social phobia can develop in response to a diverse range of situations, and in the past, with other phobic disorders, no classification of social phobia as such was utilized. Thus, phobias were specified by a prefix—usually in Greek or Latin—to designate the situation or object which produced fear, so that rubraphobia would refer to fear of blushing and scriptophobia to fear of writing while being watched. Current taxonomic practice recognizes that certain specific fears are related in both correlational and descriptive sense, and thus a more compact system of classification is favored (Marks, 1969, p. 104). This practice has a heuristic value for research purposes and is supported by a number of factor-analytic studies.

When nonpatient subjects are asked to indicate which on a list of items make them fearful, a proportion of responses always relate to situations involving contact with other people. Thus, such items as (a) speaking in public, (b) being watched or stared at, (c) talking to people in authority, (d) eating or drinking with other people, and (e) looking foolish typically receive a high rate of endorsement. It will be noted that such situations usually imply a sense of the subject's performance being monitored, regarded critically, or disapproved by others. Further, subjects who report fear of such situations usually endorse several items of this sort rather than just one or two, so that factor analyses of various fear schedules usually identify a cluster of social items which are inter-correlated (Braun & Reynolds, 1969; Lang & Lazovik, 1963; Rubin, Lawlis, Tasto, & Namenek, 1969; Wolpe & Lang, 1964). As well as this social-inter-action cluster, other factors which have been frequently identified refer to fears of small animals, fears associated with death or body-tissue damage, fears of noise, and fears of isolation or loneliness.

Similar patterns of fearfulness—always including a cluster of items refer-ring to social disapproval—have been found in studies of fear schedules com-pleted by samples of neurotic inpatients (Bates, 1971), mixed psychiatric patients (Dixon, DeMonchaux, & Sandler, 1957; Lawlis, 1971; Rothstein, Holmes, & Boblitt, 1972), and phobic patients (Arrindell, 1980; Hallam & Hafner, 1978). Trower (in press) reports a principle-components analysis of the responses of social phobics to the Social Situations Questionnaire (Bryant & Trower, 1974). The first component (31% of the variance) identified on its positive pole situations which were characterized by public exposure (public places, large numbers, relative strangers) and by the carrying out of some activity (e.g., eating). Smith (1972) reported that highly socially anxious indi-viduals were much concerned about the evaluation of others, were strongly motivated to avoid disapproval, and possessed a generalized need to be liked. Lawlis (1971) in his survey of psychiatric samples found that a major fear related to loss of approval, feelings of rejection by others, loss of status, and humiliation. In a few studies, a cluster of "agoraphobic" items show up prom-inently—a type of fear which is not apparent in nonclinical or even in nonpho-bic psychiatric patients, and which has social elements.

Thus, the foregoing shows that fearfulness of situations involving the pres-ence of other people—especially where the individual has to carry out some activity which may be evaluated and/or be subject to critical appraisal by oth-ers—is claimed to be experienced by both psychiatric patients and nonpa-tients—at least when they are requested to complete a self-report inventory.

Social Anxiety in Nonclinical Populations

In a review of major factor analytic studies of personality structure, Cro-zier (1979) draws attention to the occurrence of a factor which he terms "shy-ness." This factor has features of both introversion—quietness, keeping in the background, and a preference to be alone—and neuroticism—emotional arousal and worrying about appearing foolish. But while it is correlated with both of these dimensions, it can be distinguished from them empirically and conceptually. Pilkonis and his associates (Pilkonis, 1977a, 1977b; Pilkonis & Zimbardo, 1979; Zimbardo, Pilkonis, & Norwood, 1974) define shyness as "a tendency to avoid social situations, to fail to participate appropriately in social encounters and to feel anxious, distressed and burdened during interpersonal interactions." It is clear that this concept corresponds very closely to the social-phobia scale that emerges from fear-schedule analyses and to the clinical concept of social phobia. These workers not only report that in samples of high school and college students, 42% of the subjects described themselves as "shy persons" in disposition (Zimbardo *et al,* 1974), but also quote cross-cultural studies showing prevalence rates between 31% and 60% for different cultural groups (Pilkonis & Zimbardo, 1979).

Bryant and Trower (1974) studied social difficulty in a sample of 223 second-year undergraduates at Oxford University who completed a postal questionnaire indicating the degree of difficulty they experienced in 30 specified situations representative of those which are reported as presenting difficulties to psychiatric patients. The following results emerged:

1. More than a quarter of the sample reported either "moderate" or "great" difficulty or avoidance of situations which involved actively seeking contact with relative strangers such as "going to dances," "approaching others," or "taking the initiative in conversation."

2. Almost 10% reported similar levels of difficulty in such situations as "being in a mixed sex group," "being in a same sex group," or "people standing or sitting very close" and about 3% found "going into restaurants or cafés" or "being with just one other person" of at least "moderate" difficulty.

3. Approximately 10% reported "great difficulty" or complete avoidance of at least 4 of the 30 situations.

4. There was evidence that one group of subjects found most difficulty in social contacts of the casual, public type, while another group was more disturbed by situations where a deeper, more personal relationship was implied (as in the case history described above).

These studies illustrate that anxiety generated by exposure to various types of social situations is quite common, and obviously most people who experience social anxiety do not come to the attention of treatment agencies, although that is not to say that this majority do not experience some degree of handicap or disadvantage as a result of these problems. (For an account of the "associated pathologies of shyness" see Pilkonis & Zimbardo, 1979.)

Further research is needed to elucidate the factors which differentiate between these "normal" fears and those which become objects of therapeutic attention. Although it is unlikely that any single factor will prove universally relevant, potential sources of difference include (a) the intensity or duration of anxiety, or its pattern of effects; (b) the degree of interference with an individual's goals or aspirations resulting from social dysfunction; (c) the availability of treatment services and their perceived acceptability; (d) the coexistence of other psychological or physical-health problems; (e) the existence of secondary-gain factors reinforcing the phobic state; (f) the individual's personality resources, an issue which we shall discuss at greater length in a later section.

Characteristics of Clinical Samples

In an analysis of different sorts of phobics who had attended the Maudsley Hospital in the previous decade, Marks (1969) describes a group of 25 social phobics, representing 8% of the total monosymptomatic phobic patients (compared with 60% of this total who were agoraphobics, 3% with animal phobias, 14% with miscellaneous specific phobias, and 15% with illness phobias) (Marks & Gelder, 1966). Four social phobias developed before age 10, but the age of onset was usually after puberty with a peak in the late teens, and only about 15% developed after age 25. Sixty percent of the sample were female, but this was a smaller proportion than for agoraphobia or animal phobias; social phobias were thus one of the commonest kinds among men. Most social phobias were very specific, but a minority of patients had other phobias, usually agoraphobia, and gave evidence of depressed mood. As a group, on the Eysenck Personality Inventory (EPI) their neuroticism scores were high and they were slightly introverted, resembling the agoraphobics on these measures. Also like agoraphobics, the social phobics showed a high rate of spontaneous fluctuation in the galvanic skin response (GSR) and a slow rate of habituation to auditory stimuli compared with normal controls (Lader, 1967), but they acquired conditioned eye-blink responses more rapidly (Martin, Marks & Gelder, 1969) than agoraphobics, normal controls or anxiety-state patients.

Shaw (1976) reported a detailed comparison of 87 social phobics with 57 agoraphobics who had been referred for treatment by general practitioners or psychiatrists. In the social phobia group 61% were male compared with only 13% of agoraphobics. Sixty percent of social phobics and 20% of agoraphobics had developed their complaint by the age of 20. The onset was rated as acute in 53% of agoraphobics and only 19% of social phobics. On a symptom check list, agoraphobics reported significantly greater frequencies of difficulty in breathing, weakness, dizziness, and buzzing in the ears, whereas social phobics reported more blushing and twitching. There was, however, some overlap of the situations in which the two groups reported fear, with 51% of agoraphobics also reporting problems typical of social phobia but only 23% of social phobics reporting agoraphobic difficulties. On the EPI, both groups were significantly more neurotic than controls (acute orthopedic patients, matched for age and sex) and social phobics were significantly more introverted than agoraphobics.

Parker (1979) subsequently contacted 132 of Shaw's sample and obtained responses from 40 agoraphobics and 41 social phobics on the Parental Bonding

Instrument (Parker, Tupling, & Brown, 1979), a 25-item questionnaire measuring two principle dimensions of parental behaviors and attitudes, care and over-protection. The social phobics scored both their mothers and fathers as less caring and as more overprotective than matched controls, whereas the only significant difference for the agoraphobics was that their mothers were seen as less caring than controls. It should be noted, however, that since these results refer to the retrospectively *perceived* qualities of parental behavior rather than to any independently assessed features of the phobic's childhood environment, the question of the direction of any causality could not be determined.

A few investigators have looked at the social behavior of social phobics. Marzillier & Lambert (1976) examined the behavioral elements in a patient sample which contributed to impressions of social anxiety. "The subject is perceived as anxious if there is less speech in the interaction generally, he looks little at the stooge, shows a lot of fiddling movements, hesitates a lot in speech, speaks little himself and asks few questions" (p. 9). Conger and Farrell (1981) also found low amounts of talking and gaze to be predictive of anxiety impressions (and skill). Pilkonis (1977b) found that shy males talked and looked less, and Daly (1978) found that anxious high school students spent less time in unsolicited talks and looked for less time and in shorter bursts than unanxious peers.

The Presenting Features of Social Phobia

The mode of presentation whereby the social phobic comes to the attention of a treatment agency may vary considerably. It is not known what proportion of those who receive treatment have come directly as a result of self-recognition of their problem and self-initiated referral. It is probable that a majority of those with social anxiety of phobic degree never seek treatment. Among those in whom the phobia is recognized, many will have been referred initially for some other problem to the development of which the effects of the social phobia may have been a contributing factor. Thus, pervasive social anxiety may have provoked excessive alcohol consumption, and the eventual dependence on alcohol may be the presenting problem, or attempted self-harm may have brought the individual to an assessment interview, as in the following case:

Mr. C., aged 20, was admitted to a general hospital following an overdose of analgesics and was later referred to a psychiatric clinic for depression. Eventually it emerged that, having successfully studied part-time to obtain qualifications for a university course, he became very frightened at the prospect of the greater degree of social interaction with fellow students which a full-time course would involve. Although he had worked in a busy office, he had never felt comfortable in talking to his colleagues and felt completely unable to engage in social conversation or "to make people laugh." He lived with his parents and had no leisure activities other than listening to records and reading.

In a study of 92 consecutive patients with neurosis or personality disorder, Bryant *et al.* (1976) found that 27% of the sample showed social inadequacy (defined in terms of social isolation, difficulty in forming relationships, feelings of incompetence and observed inadequate social behavior). These workers also found evidence to distinguish between two types of social failure (Trower *et al.,* 1978): (a) primary, where failure resulted from inadequate social skills, and (b) secondary, where social skills were judged to have been acquired, but their effectiveness or implementation was reduced by other problems such as social anxiety; social phobia was one form of secondary failure. For present purposes, as has been noted with other phobias (Marks, 1969), these studies illustrate that social phobia can exist concurrently with many other psychological disorders, including depression, compulsive disorders, sexual dysfunction, and even psychotic states. The nature of the relationship between these other disorders and social phobia will need careful exploration, and the question of whether treatment of the phobia should take priority over the associated disorder, whether it should be deferred until other problems have been dealt with, or whether it can be dealt with simultaneously, cannot be prescribed by general rules. Even where the phobic disorder is judged to have led directly to the other problems, it may be that the associated disorder must be treated before the social phobia can be tackled. But in many cases, the phobic disorder will demand attention in order to achieve resolution of secondary problems, even though it may have been the latter that originally precipitated therapeutic contact.

Environmental Settings

The social phobic may respond anxiously to a wide range of situations and settings, or to one specific setting only, for example, eating in public, attending a conference, writing a check in public, or making relationships with the opposite sex. The terms "social phobia," therefore, accommodates a continuum from general to specific in the range of feared situations.

The Variability of Fear Responses

In addition to the fact that different social phobics may have differential sensitivity to the *settings* which provoke phobic anxiety, it is now recognized that the pattern of anxiety seen in different subjects shows variation as well, and also that this pattern can vary within a single subject over a period of time.

The variability between subjects is illustrated in a study by Pilkonis (1977a) who required subjects to rank the "importance" of five separate elements of behavior: (1) internal discomfort in social situations, (2) fear of negative evaluation, (3) avoidance of social situations, (4) failure to respond appropriately (e.g., a reluctance to talk, an avoidance of eye contact), and (5) awkward behaviors arising from attempts to respond (e.g., an inability to be fluent or articulate, physical clumsiness).

The first two of these categories refer to "private" events, and the last three describe public behaviors or the lack of behavior. The responses of subjects who had rated themselves as "shy" were found to fall into four clusters, on the basis of which the authors proposed the following typology of shyness:

1. A small group (about 8% of the sample) who reported avoidance of social situations and failure to respond
2. A group (about 40% of the sample) for which performance deficits (awkward behavior and failure to respond) were reported to present the greatest problems
3. A group (29%) who reported subjective discomfort (internal arousal and fear of negative evaluation) as their greatest difficulty
4. A group which had features of both Groups 2 and 3 and which represented about 23% of the total

Group 2 was designated as "publicly shy" and Groups 3 and 4 as "privately shy." The validity of the distinction was supported by members of the "private cluster" obtaining higher scores on the Self-Consciousness Scale (Fenigstein, Scheier, & Buss, 1975), whereas those in the "publicly shy" cluster rated their shyness as more of a problem.

Lang (1968, 1971) and Lang *et al.* (1972) have proposed that human emotion in general, and anxiety in particular, involves responses in three expressive systems: verbal, gross motor, and physiological. As propounded elsewhere (Rachman, 1978a), this view holds that the three most important components of fear are avoidance behavior, physiological reactivity, and verbal/cognitive reports of subjective fear (Rachman, 1978a, p. 239). These components are partially independent and they can best be regarded as "loosely coupled."

This view, which can be contrasted with earlier accounts which have treated fear as a global concept or "lump" (Lang, 1970), has become known as the *three-system model* of fear and emotion and has been claimed to provide a "better construal of our present knowledge of fear and . . . [to be] . . . capable of providing the basis for generating new hypotheses of fear (Rachman, 1978a, p. 239).

Although in the original formulation of the model (e.g., Lang, 1968), the three components of fear were merely referred to as *type of response* or co-effects, other workers have considered the interaction between components. In the model of social phobia which we shall develop, we have based our conceptualization of fear on the six assumptions that follow:

1. It refers to a constellation of events: physiological, cognitive and behavioral.

2. "Physiological events" include alterations in level of activity of several physiological functions, for example, alterations in heart rate, sweat-gland activity, muscle tone, respiration, and visceral activity. The specific pattern of

alteration will vary considerably between subjects, and within subjects over time, and, at least in the case of subjects who are referred for treatment (i.e., "phobics"), will be experienced as unpleasant.

3. "Cognitive events" cover all those psychological experiences which relate to the individual's perception and evaluation of social events including the performance of himself and others. They include memories of previous social encounters, usually with emphasis on failure and embarrassment. They may take the form of self-statements and visual images (e.g., of themselves being unable to think of topics of conversation or of looking and feeling uncomfortable). These experiences are not synonymous with verbal expression of problems but can be partly accessible to verbal expression with appropriate inquiry.

4. The most usual type of "behavioral event" is avoidance of the social situations, but the term can also designate other types of behavior including low frequency of speaking or eye contact, submissive posture, excessive gesturing, or even over-talkativeness. These behaviors may sometimes be construed as "inhibited" or, more generally, "defensive."

5. There are low correlations among the physiological, cognitive, and behavioral components of fear across groups of subjects. Thus, each subject will show an idiosyncratic pattern of fear, and this pattern varies over time.

6. Complex functional relationships develop between the three components within each subject. This is especially apparent in the case of physiological and cognitive events, each of which may serve as a stimulus for the other, as well as in some circumstances both being co-effects. Thus, exposure to a social stiuation may provoke either cognitive or physiological discomfort, or both, but either response can then act as a stimulus for increased activity in the other system. Similarly, *anticipation* of a social situation (i.e., a cognitive representation of the stiuation itself) can provoke either cognitive or physiological discomfort, or both. The gross behavioral consequences of these events— what the individual does to reduce the discomfort—will depend on further evaluation of potential responses in that situation as well as subjective evaluation of how available or feasible those responses are. The availability of responses will depend, in turn, on the individual's perception of his skill repertoire and his perception of the outcome of engaging in a particular kind of behavior in terms of its ability to reduce discomfort. Behavior which has previously been effective in reducing discomfort, whether it be total avoidance, or keeping well to the periphery of a social group, or engaging in excessive talking, will tend to become a stable, high-probability response in those situations—or it may be that no effective coping response is available at all.

Such a model is of the "feedback-loop" rather than the "linear-causality" type (Coyne & Lazarus, 1980), and is also consistent with the view that behavioral treatments should be tailored to the individual profile of responding (Hugdahl, 1981; Shahar & Merbaum, 1981).

EXPLANATION OF SOCIAL PHOBIA: ITS CAUSE AND MAINTENANCE

So far, some aspects of the phenomenon or "syndrome" of social phobia have been described, and an attempt made to distinguish it conceptually from other types of anxiety at this descriptive level. It is now important to proceed to an *explanatory* level of analysis, since this will not only help sharpen the distinction from other types of phobia, but also help us understand its causes and maintenance. Such understanding is important in guiding assessment and therapy.

Social phobia is not a lump—to extend Lang's statement—and social phobics are not such a homogeneous group as the diagnostic label might imply. We have seen that the *person variables* that may contribute to social as to other anxieties may be physiological (e.g., level of autonomic reactivity), cognitive (e.g., selective perception, mode of cognitive processing, self-awareness tendencies), and behavioral (behavioral avoidance tendencies), and there are further subdivisions to be made within these, especially within the cognitive component (Hugdahl, 1981; Kihlstrom & Nasby, 1981). On top of these are the *situation and setting variables,* some situations being intrinsically more anxiety-arousing than others (Trower, in press), and to complicate the picture still further are the *interactions* between the person variables themselves (e.g., arousal symptoms become cues for further anxiety in the fear cycle) and between person and situation (e.g., avoidance behavior may atually produce feared rejection responses in a p–s cycle).

Rather than review all possible theories that might or might not accommodate these complexities, we shall focus on cognitive-behavioral theories, since these are favored by a majority of authorities (e.g., Wilson & O'Leary, 1980). One theory we shall utilize—social learning theory—has so far proved robust in current conceptual and empirical critiques (e.g., Rachman, 1978), and productive in stimulating new and much-needed therapeutic options (e.g., Goldfried & Robins, 1981) and research.

Drawing from a number of sources, particularly social learning theory, the theory of emotion by Lazarus and Opton (1966), and Carver's self-control theory (Carver, 1979), we offer the following model and a set of terms to help organize the subsequent discussion (see Figure 1). A broad distinction is made between expectancies and effects. Expectancies are of two kinds: stimulus-outcome (predictions from social cues about likely changes in the environment) and behavior-outcome (predictions that certain actions will produce certain environmental changes) (Mischel, 1973). As a result of such expectancies about the environment, certain effects are produced in the individual. These are of three kinds: changes in physiological arousal, changes in cognitions, and changes in behavior (i.e., the three responses discussed earlier).

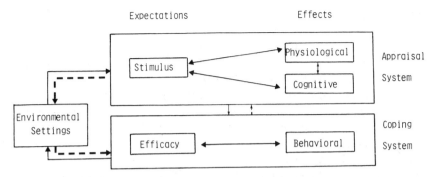

Figure 1. A feedback model of anxiety, incorporating two interdependent systems, each of which contains further components relating to various facets of anxiety. The model is offered as an organizing framework for assessment and therapy (see page 330).

Within this framework we suggest the operation of two interdependent systems that interact with the environment: an *appraisal* system for assessing a given state of affairs, and a *coping system* (our terms) for responding to that state of affairs. First of all, by means of perceived correlation and association, certain neutral stimuli set up *stimulus expectancies* for negative or positive outcomes or *social consequences,* that is, stimulus-outcome expectancies are established. Stimulus cues then elicit *anxiety experiences,* defined in terms of *autonomic arousal* and *subjective apprehension.* More formally, stimulus-outcome expectancies establish stimulus effects. This acts as a kind of early-warning system which we term the *appraisal system,* equivalent in function to Lazarus's primary appraisal which he defines as "evaluation by the individual of the harmful significance of some event" (Lazarus & Opton, 1966, p. 244). Secondly, by virtue of information gained through the appraisal system, the individual selects certain *coping responses,* that is, approach or avoidance responses (not exclusively behaviors), on the basis of perceived *outcome expectations* (the anticipated effects of a given response and *efficacy expectations* (ability to implement the response). This system acts as a way of dealing with appraised danger, and we term it the *coping system* (equivalent to Lazarus's secondary appraisal). The systems are taken to have common functional components, operating interdependently, continuously, and sequentially, and to operate like a TOTE (test–operate–test–exit) (Miller, Galanter, & Pribram, 1960).

In a nutshell, "a person is able to act realistically and effectively in a stressful situation only if he knows the nature and seriousness of the threat, knows what to do and is able to do it" (Haggard, 1949, p. 209).

In the next section we discuss the social environment and the appraisal and coping systems of the individual.

The Social Environment

Societies contain systems of rules and conventions which influence and shape, by means of rewards and punishments, the behavior of individuals. Goffman (1972) refers to these as the ground rules by which the "social order" is maintained, and he describes those (nonlegal) conventions that operate in face-to-face interaction to affirm and support some actions and those that penalize and impose sanctions on others. Harré (1979) also develops the principle of a respect–contempt continuum, with its implications of moral judgment, which deeply affects the behavior of people in daily life. In this chapter, we are mainly concerned with that end of the continuum related to social coercion and control, which is experienced as punishment.

Punishment is here understood as the punishing consequences which evoke subjective fear, physiological arousal, and behavioral avoidance and defensiveness in the individual. Indeed, all anxiety has basically to do with anticipation of the possible harm (punishment) that objects, events, or other individuals may reflect on people. In the strictly nonsocial phobias, the harm is generally taken to be of a physical nature—damage or extreme discomfort to the body. In social phobia, however, the harmful element is generally taken to be of a psychological nature, though physical threat may be present and may interact with psychological threat (e.g., as in sexual phobia which may combine fear of pain with fear of sexual inadequacy).

Negative evaluation and social failure are generally accepted as key concepts in the understanding of social phobia, but need to be further defined. Both necessarily imply social standards or yardsticks by which such judgments are made. For example, an evaluation necessarily involves a relative judgment on a good–bad scale, in which an event or action is compared with some other event or action which has been taken, or defined as a standard of either excellence or the reverse. Often such standards are implicit rather than stated, as when judges are required to judge the social-skills level of an individual from a video sample. Generally speaking, however, events or actions are evaluated as good or bad depending on their approximation to a standard, and ratings are calibrated in terms of their distance from such standards, along some dimension. This idea is familiar if restated in terms of goals. Once goals are set, individuals are praised and rewarded for successive approximations, and criticized, ridiculed, and otherwise punished for failing to progress towards them. The idea of social punishment as described here is perhaps most clearly brought out in test anxiety (Sarason, 1978).

Standards in terms of tests are rather easily defined, and levels set with some precision. Social standards, however, are more difficult to specify. Many of these include roles which are clearly circumscribed, such as work roles, in which efficiency and effectiveness can be gauged by such criteria as the amount of selling done. But although some forms of social phobia may indeed relate to failure to achieve such specifiable goals in the work situation, many and probably most forms have to do with the day-to-day, face-to-face, casual forms of social interaction and performance standards which exist somewhat vaguely and implicitly, but all the same strongly, in these settings. We hope to gain some idea of these standards from semantic differentials, often used in social skills research, which ask for ratings on such dimensions as warm/cold, assertive/submissive, anxious/calm, and more generally, skilled/unskilled.

Is it possible to be more precise about these social standards? Recently, Mischel and his co-workers identified a number of "personality prototypes," by which they mean the typical conceptual forms or "schematic representations" that average individuals use to categorize people in their social environments (Cantor & Mischel, 1979). Elaborating much earlier ideas (e.g., Bruner, 1957), Mischel *et al.* show that people judge from behavioral characteristics whether others fall into a prototypical category, and it is clear that some of these personality prototypes are regarded as socially undesirable; for example, they found an "emotionally unstable" category made up, at a lower level, of categories called "phobic" and "criminal madman." Other workers have named various behaviors and personality traits that traditionally receive negative evaluations (Buss, 1980), but here we suggest a basic twofold classification to encompass most of these: one category concerns inadequacy or incompetence (i.e., failure to reach certain approved standards of performance or ability, and would roughly correspond to Osgood's "potency" dimension); the second concerns badness or failure to reach standards of moral worth, and would correspond to the Osgood dimension of "evaluation" (Osgood, Suci, & Tannenbaum, 1957).

In addition to these rules and standards for good and bad "personalities," there are also rules and standards (and allied sanctions) for situations. More difficult situations contain formal prescriptive rules, rules that are implicit rather than explicit, rules that are complex and require great social skill, or rules that evoke self-consciousness (Trower, in press).

There are numerous behavioral routines by means of which people impose sanctions on rule-breakers or nonconformers, some linguistic, others non-verbal. (For more information on this large topic the reader is referred to Goffman, 1959/1971, 1972; Scheflen and Scheflen, 1972; and Henley, 1977.)

No doubt one of the most powerful social cues is facial expression. The face is the strongest communicator of affect (Ekman, 1972), and observers are often aroused empathically by the affect which is expressed. Particular expressions (e.g., fear or annoyance) are associated with particular classes of expected outcomes (aversive events). Lanzetta and Orr (1981) have shown the intrinsic conditioning power of fear expressions, as opposed to other stimuli, when paired with an unconditioned stimulus (UCS).

The Appraisal System

In classical conditioning, certain neutral stimuli are deemed to become conditioned (conditioned stimuli or CS) by the process of association with certain other unconditioned stimuli, so named because of their inherent capacity to elicit spontaneously certain autonomic responses (unconditioned response or UCR). After this bonding, the CS alone can automatically elicit what has now become a conditioned response (CR). This familiar theory, which forms the first part of the conditioning theory of fear acquisition, does not allow cognitive mediation as a way of explaining the bonding. However, social learning theorists assert, on the basis of experimental evidence, that the individual's recognition of and inferences about the correlation between such events is the crucial factor in the learning process. Previously neutral cues now seem to predict certain painful or pleasant outcomes. In fear acquisition, such anticipatory cues arouse anxiety experiences (autonomic arousal and subjective apprehension) simply because they are predictive of painful consequences (stimulus-outcome expectancies)—in this case social punishment. In daily social life, the cues that function in this way are usually the social behavior of others, and of the subject himself in particular contexts, while the negative consequences are usually disapproval/negative evaluation.[1]

However, people develop expectations about stimulus-outcome relations that are exaggerated or wrong, that certain looks signify hostile intent. False though the expectation may be, an anxiety reaction can nonetheless occur even in the absence of real negative consequences, and these reactions will continue to be evoked until such time as the individual's false assumptions about stimulus-outcome relations are disconfirmed. In addition, phobic individuals have strong reactions, both autonomic and cognitive, to even mild forms of punishment (perceived or real). We now need to examine in some detail each of the components of the appraisal system in social phobia in order to understand its cause and maintenance.

Stimulus Expectancies

Social cues have an informative and incentive/disincentive value because they enable one to predict events, reactions, and other potentially rewarding or punishing outcomes. Such meanings are often represented cognitively in the

---

[1]In the case of the subject's own behaviors, some may see these as operants or responses rather than stimuli. However, many behaviors are not instrumental (e.g., sweating, shaking) and others are likewise not intended or planned (e.g., silences, stuttering, *faux pas*). In addition, social behaviors function simultaneously as stimuli and responses (Bandura, 1978, 1981) and are so treated in a systems-based model such as the one presented. In a sequence of behaviors A–B–C, B is a response to A and a stimulus for C. In this section we examine behavior in its role as stimulus, in stimulus-outcome expectancies, and in a later section we examine behavior in its role as a response in behavior-outcome and efficacy-outcome expectancies.

form of verbal propositions or premises, which have been called contingency rules. To put this another way, people make causal inferences of the "if . . . then . . ." kind. Often these inferences form a chain wherein one consequence forms the premise for another inference, but the chain will eventually end with an evaluative conclusion; for example, one socially phobic patient followed this chain:

> If I lift a cup, I'll shake.
> If I shake, people will look at me.
> If they look, they will know I'm anxious.
> If they know I'm anxious, they'll think I'm inferior.

We shall see later that such inferences eventually lead to evaluative conclusions about self.

Clearly the first items in the chain may have little apparent relationship to evaluative conclusions, and indeed may be neutral to most other people. Sensitization to such cues may have occured by way of direct experience, observing the experiences of others, or from information acquired, for example, through the media, and may have developed gradually over time, or suddenly by way of trauma (Rachman, 1976).

Anticipatory cues can vary greatly. They may be objects, events, or situations; they may be the behaviors of others (particularly the potentially evaluating others) or the behaviors of the anxious individual himself. Several types of cues may be involved in an inference chain—in the above example they included a cup, the subject's behavior, and other people's behavior. It is inevitable, however, that the subject's own behavior will be the focal one, since this is what is being evaluated (i.e., some aspect of the subject's social performance).

There has been considerable research on the theory that social anxiety is a reaction to faulty social performance—faulty performances providing the stimulus cues for anticipated rejection and negative evaluation. This idea is called the skills-deficit hypothesis (Curran, 1977). Some studies show differences in behavioral skill between high- and low-anxiety subjects (Clark & Arkowitz, 1975; Glasgow & Arkowitz, 1975; O'Banion & Arkowitz, 1977; Twentyman & McFall, 1975). We saw earlier what forms some of these "skill deficits" take. Support is also claimed for the skills-deficit hypothesis from the fact that social skills training (SST) has led to reduced social anxiety (Curran, 1977; Emmelkamp, 1979); but as we shall see later, "skilled" phobics are equally helped by SST.

One of the main characteristics of phobias is that they alert people to dangers that barely exist, that is, phobics make faulty inferences from stimuli to negative consequences. This is equally true in social phobia; people react to *perceived* deficits when, in fact, few such deficits exist, or at least they are far less serious than perceived. A body of research, including some of the studies already cited, finds that these subjects perceive themselves as less skilled than they actually are. Clark and Arkowitz (1975) found that, though their high- and low-anxiety subjects had the same feedback, the highs thought their behavior had evoked more negative reactions. Alden and Cappe (1981) found that while their "unassertive" and anxious subjects perceived themselves as less effective, they demonstrated competence equal to that of an "assertive" group.

Researchers often wrongly generalize their findings to all social phobics, whereas different social phobias may have different origins and maintenance factors (Curran 1977), and some may have a combination. It seems likely that many social phobics not only are socially deficient, but also have faulty stimulus expectancies (inferences), as many of the previously cited studies have found.

How do these inferential processes work, and how do they go wrong? As noted above, it has long been recognized in the person-perception literature that people make inferences from perceptual cues by way of social stereotypes recently termed *cognitive* schemata, which serve to categorize social information. Following Kelly (1955), Mischel (1973) developed the notions of encoding strategies and personal constructs, by means of which people make personality judgments—one type of social category—about self and others on the basis of behavioral, physical and other cues; that is, people make inferences from events and actions to "underlying" traits and dispositions. In addition to personality, the observer will also make inferences about the other's emotional state ("Is he angry, amused?") and interpersonal attitude, for example, liking versus rejection, dominance versus submission (Argyle, 1969), and a host of other features not only about individuals (e.g., race, sex, age, class, religion) but also situations and settings.

According to cognitive psychologists, this "social knowledge," once developed, is represented cognitively in the form of recognitory schemata (Carver, 1979) or constructs (Mischel, 1973), and perception is a process in which new, incoming information is compared with or matched against such pre-existing schemata and thereby "recognized." Schemata function in this sense as standards or prototypes. Once activated, such schemata can affect what the observer attends to and cause selective filtering and interpretation of information to fit the construct, a process which Snyder (1980) calls *cognitive bolstering*. People try to predict events in the above way, on one hand, by means of their beliefs or constructs, and on the other, by means of cues in the situation. Attributing theorists have considered both kinds of influence, the classical view of Kelley (1967) seeing the attributer as a data processor applying a statistical covariation principle to derive the most likely cause of events, the personality theorists seeing the attributer as applying idiosyncratic beliefs in his perception of causes. Metalsky and Abramson (1981) neatly combine both influences, suggesting that individuals vary in the extent to which they are influenced by their own generalized beliefs, as against situational information, in making a particular attribution. Clearly, belief-based attributers are most likely to possess distorted perceptions of events, and the evidence shows this to be characteristic of people who are depressed and anxious (Metalsky & Abramson, 1981).

Not only do people infer attributes from behavioral cues but they also evaluate them (Tajfel, 1978). It becomes desirable to possess some traits (e.g., extraversion), condemnable to possess others (e.g., neuroticism), and social cues that infer such traits will elicit such evaluations. Clearly, individuals know that this process applies to themselves—aspects of their own appearance and behavior will elicit evaluative judgments from others. For instance, the social phobic in our example may assume that his "shaking" will elicit the evaluative label "weak," or "nervous."

Candidates for censure will include any behavioral cue that the potential social phobic considers a public sign of something evaluatively bad or weak, or a failure to match up to some cognitively represented exemplar (e.g., where shaking fails to match a standard of "masculine" or "confident"). The greater the discrepancy from the desirable standard, the stronger will be the presumed negative evaluation (Carver, 1979). Anticipatory cues have their main value in informing individuals of likely social consequences. However, such cues must be valid predictors of events if they are to fulfill this role. In social as well as other phobias this is usually not the case, and individuals become misinformed about events and aroused to dangers that do not exist or are, at most, minimal. Beck (1976) lists some of the cognitive distortions that commonly invalidate inferential judgments in the affective disorders. These include selective abstraction—the predisposition to perceive certain cues but to be impervious to others (also Ross, 1977); arbitrary inference—drawing unjustified or false conclusions from inadequate evidence; overgeneralization—generalizing from a single incident to the general case; personalization—chronic overestimation by a person of the extent to which particular events are related to him; polarized thinking—sorting events into dichotomous categories (e.g., totally good or bad, accepted or rejected); magnification and exaggeration—tendency to see extremely bad consequences following with high probability or certainty. On this last point, for example, Halford and Foddy (1982) showed that socially anxious students endorsed significantly more negative expectations about their behavior and others' reactions (e.g., "This person probably thinks I am boring . . . a bit strange," "This person seems to think what I have said is stupid").

The discussion so far has assumed that the objects of perception are actually present social events occurring in the immediate situation. But individuals, recalling such events in thoughts and images, can also become anxious in the absence of these cues, a point emphasized in social learning theory (Bandura, 1977). Clearly, all the processes that have been discussed for actually present social stimuli would operate equally with symbolically represented equivalents.

We turn now from the external to the internal environment, from the way the individual perceives the objective world to the way he experiences and subjectively reacts to that world as perceived. Two variables are distinguished, as suggested earlier—physiological arousal and cognitive apprehension.

Physiological Arousal

We described earlier some of the characteristics of arousal seen in social phobics. Our interest here is the way such arousal functions in the appraisal system. Arousal contributes the feeling of emotion, the actual bodily discomfort. James (1893) wrote of emotion, "Without the bodily states following on the perception, the latter would be purely cognitive in form, pale, colorless, destitute of emotional warmth . . . we should not actually *feel* afraid or angry" (p. 450). When, in experiments, participants are asked to report their subjective level of anxiety, it is presumably the intensity of this "bodily state" that they are being asked to rate, namely their autonomic perception, but this is not clear (Hugdahl, 1981). However, being asked to rate anxiety in this way rather begs the question since, to reverse James's point, having *only* arousal experiences without a cognitive label will leave the subject wondering what his emotion is (Schachter, 1964).

It is well known that there are large individual differences in autonomic reaction. The particular type of autonomic arousal is of special importance in social phobia because of its feedback into the appraisal system (see below). In other words, fear-produced autonomic reactions become fear-producing cues in a fear-of-fear cycle (Beck & Emery, 1979). Candidates for this cycle include those reactions that are publicly obvious—shaking and other muscular reactions provoke fear of situations that involve writing, lifting cups, and other tasks for which dexterity is required; gastrointestinal reactions produce fear of vomiting, eating difficulties, urinating, and defecating; cardiovascular reactions produce fear of blushing and fainting. Such difference in responding are partly due to biological differences between people (e.g., blushing may be an innate tendency due to a rich capillary base or a translucent skin; Buss, 1980).

The interaction of arousal and cognition to produce emotion, which will be discussed next, is a two-way process. While emotions are initially identified from situation cues, those same emotions, once identified, can subsequently affect perceptual processing, forming a vicious cycle (e.g., anxiety may lead to selective perception of negative information). Studies show, for example, that happy or sad moods lead to selective remembering of happy or sad information (Kihlstrom & Nasby, 1981).

Cognitive Apprehension

In this section we shall discuss the way information is processed to derive conclusions about the subjective state of the individual. There are two aspects to this; the first concerns the state of *emotionality,* which refers to the identification, by means of internal arousal and external cues, of the emotion being experienced and of its intensity. The second concerns the *self*, in particular self-focus, self-perception, and attribution. In phobias, both emotionality and the self are linked, since the definition of anxiety entails threat to self—social self in the case of social phobia, physical self in the case of most simple phobias.

Emotional Experience. In order to experience an *emotion* fully, an individual needs two types of information: internal information, namely physiological arousal, and external information, derived from situational cues. Together these define the nature of the arousal. This classic view was developed by Schachter (1964), who defined emotion as consisting of these two parts termed the *autonomic* and the *cognitive*. The early experiments consisted in holding arousal constant and varying the situation, and showed that the arousal was labelled euphoria, anger, or anxiety depending on the situation. Other research shows that autonomic arousal is not a necessary condition for emotion, though the quality may be altered in its absence (Buck, 1976) and other centers in the CNS may be involved.

In earlier sections, we looked at some social cues likely to elicit a social-anxiety "cognitive" label. However, there are several kinds of social anxiety, each with its own cluster of environmental cues, and there is *some* variation in physiological reaction. Buss (1980) distinguishes four kinds, and we draw upon Buss, with some modification, in the description of each of these and the attendant research.

The first is embarrassment. Sattler (1965) clustered subjects' responses as to the causes of embarrassment under three headings: impropriety, concerned with improper dress or talk; lack of competences (e.g., slips of speech, public clumsiness, forgetting someone's name); conspicuousness (e.g., being looked at by the opposite sex or displaying excessive emotion in public). All of these would probably be triggered off by a sudden and embarrassing awareness of leakage-cues to emotions which the individual is trying to conceal (Ekman & Friesen, 1974). Buss (1980) adds breaches of privacy (e.g., into spatial intimacy zones) and over-praise. Modigliani (1968) found that the types of situations which caused embarrassment were, in order of severity, accidental foolishness, inability to respond, being the passive center of attention, watching someone else fail, and inappropriate sexual encounters. The physiological characteristics of embarrassment is not only *lowered* heart rate, but more importantly blushing, which becomes a further stimulus in an embarrassment cycle.

The second emotion distinguished by Buss is called shame, and the main type of external cue to shame identity is failure to achieve a standard of performance, whether by the individual or an important social group. Such failure can range from failure to achieve standards of academic performance, sexual performance, masculinity/femininity, and immorality such as proscribed sexual acts, lying, cheating, stealing, and murder. Another major cause is stigma due to a social or physical deficit. Whereas Buss suggests the realization of shame as a form of social anxiety, we suggest that it is the anticipation of future shame that should be considered here.

The third social anxiety distinguished is audience anxiety. Various researchers have identified behavioral features of audience anxiety, all of which involve a deterioration of performance. Mulac and Sherman (1974) observed marked alterations in verbal fluency, voice, facial expressions, use of arms and hands, and body movement. Kinds of situations which increase audience anxiety include conspicuousness and novelty, and large, high-status audiences which show signs of disinterest. Unlike embarrassment, the physiological response is full-blown: sweating, rapid breathing, high blood pressure, increased heart rate (Behnke & Carlile, 1971).

The last reaction identified by Buss is shyness, which we have already discussed.

The Self. Earlier we dealt with the perceptual categorizing processes by which social stimuli become anticipatory signals of negative evaluation. We also noted that at some point the individual's own appearance or behavior serves as the anxiety-provoking cue (Curran, 1977). However, while such behavioral cues are necessary, they are not sufficient cause for social anxiety. People commonly behave in disapproved ways without experiencing concomitant anxiety. If the cause of the negative behavior is attributed entirely to the situation or other ("I failed because the examiner was unfair"), the individual will not feel himself responsible, will not be the focus of criticism, and anxiety will be minimal. If the negative behavior is attributed entirely to the person ("I failed because I am stupid"), the individual will blame himself, will be the object of his own disapproval, and this anticipation will evoke high anxiety. The processes by which behavior is attributed to the situation or the person, a crucial factor in social anxiety as well as depression, has a long history in attribution theory. Heider (1958) asserted that the amount of personal causality attributed to an actor would depend upon the observer's estimate of the balance between personal compared with environmental forces. Jones and Nisbett (1971) showed that individuals tended to attribute the cause of their own behavior to the situation but the behavior of observed others to their personalities. This is because they "perceive" others, but not themselves, as objects in the environment. Ross (1977) uses the term "fundamental attribution error" to describe the tendency people have of inferring dispositional causes even when the evidence clearly indicates situational causes.

What is of interest to the student of social anxiety are those conditions under which people will attribute their behavior to their *own* personalities, rather than to the situation. A body of research shows that the Jones and Nisbett effect is modified by a motive to enhance self-esteem. This work reveals that people generally tend to attribute their successes to their own efforts, abilities or other dispositions, but their failures to bad luck, task difficulty, or other extenuating circumstances (Bradley, 1978). This is termed the *self-serving bias.* However, Arkin, Appelman, and Burger (1980), among others, found that high socially anxious subjects showed a *reverse* bias, assuming more personal responsibility for failure than for success, which, the authors argue, "may derive from their severely debilitating reactions to evaluative social situations" (p. 33). Similar findings were obtained by Sutton-Simon and Goldfried (1981). In their review and analysis of attributional styles, Metalsky and Abramson (1981) found a number of studies showing that socially anxious and test-anxious subjects tend to blame themselves for failure (i.e., they attribute it to stable, global, and internal factors). In this connection, the investigators go on to discuss the logical flaws that typify such belief-based, as opposed to evidence-based, styles.

Another group of researchers has examined the role played by direction of attention in altering the direction of attribution. This research in the main shows that when attention is external, people perceive others as objects in the environment, "personalities" or "selves" with describable behavioral attributes. When focus is internal, people perceive *themselves* as objects, as a personality or "self" with attributes. This is the basic idea of objective self-awareness theory (Duval & Wicklund, 1972). When the focus of attention is shifted from others to self, the attribution process described by Jones and Nisbett (1971) is reversed, resulting in self-attribution. A number of experiments have shown this effect (cf. Storms, 1973).

Self-focus also makes the individual aware of a discrepancy between his actual performance and his standards or goals—a real versus ideal self-discrepancy. When this is large, the resulting negative self-evaluation reduces self-esteem (Duval & Wicklund, 1972) and often results in impaired performance and increased avoidance (Brockner & Hulton, 1978).

Self-focus is another term for self-consciousness, a common feature of social anxiety, but one that—with notable exceptions such as Pilkonis (1977b) discussed earlier, and Buss 1980)—has been rather neglected. Buss proposed that some individuals may have a "trait" of self-consciousness, part of which is the tendency to focus on one's own appearance and performance (public self-consciousness), resulting in awareness of self-ideal discrepancies, reduced self-esteem, and increased attribution to self (Fenigstein, 1979). Self-focus can be evoked by any social situation where the individual is being observed by others, such as in front of audiences or in interviews. In addition, it can be evoked by "any distinctive dysfunctional behavior" (Storms & McCaul, 1976), including social skill deficits (Curran, 1977).

The self-ideal discrepancy will be largest and the risks, *ergo* the anxiety, greatest when the goal or standard is high, as in those with perfectionist tendencies, but performance is low, as in the socialy unskilled. A number of studies have shown that the socially anxious have high, perfectionist social standards (Alden & Cappe, 1981; Alden & Safran, 1978; Goldfried & Sobocinski, 1975; Sutton-Simon & Goldfried, 1979), as measured by Ellis's "classic twelve irrational beliefs" (Ellis, 1962). Alden and Safran (1978) comment: "The individual actualizes such beliefs in overt behavior, often striving to attain impossible goals. The person not only ensures failure by establishing impossible standards for himself *but then over-reacts to such "failures" with excessive anxiety, hostility, guilt and self-blame*" (p. 358) (our italics). They found their high-anxious, low-assertive subjects endorsing two beliefs in particular: "I believe I should be competent at everything I attempt," and "I become more upset than I should about other people's problems and disturbances."

A final step in the exacerbation of anxiety and other emotions is to take a self-attributed failure as evidence of failure of the total person—an illogical generalization from a sample of behavior to the whole self. In terms of rational emotional therapy (RET), the irrational beliefs function as propositions about self-worth, so that, for example, X *must* do or achieve Y at all times in order to have worth. These form premises from which certain conclusions are drawn: "If I make a mistake (causing disapproval, etc.), I will be useless." Such beliefs also function as unconditional imperatives; a single failure in such a system is sufficient to give rise to catastrophic conclusions (of worthlessness, etc.). For further discussion see Ellis (1962).

The Coping System

The appraisal system asked the questions "Is it dangerous?" and "How dangerous is it?" If the situation is found to be dangerous, the coping system asks the question "What can I do about it?" and proceeds with some kind of coping action such as a socially skilled response or some kind of avoidance action—a socially failed response. In other words, people do not wait passively for anticipated social rewards and punishments to come to them. Rather, they actively seek the former and try to cope with or avoid the latter by either deploying effective social skills or withdrawing. Behaviors are selected which the individuals believe will produce anticipated effects. Whereas the operant view is that behavior is under the control of and reinforced by its consequences, the social-learning view is that reinforcement acts as an antecedent rather than consequent influence, thus affecting attentional, organizational, and rehearsal processes. As with stimulus–outcome relations, therefore, it is the individual's recognition or interpretation of behavior–outcome relations that are crucial in learning. In fear situations, people may deploy those behaviors that they expect will reduce or remove them from anticipated danger (coping or avoidance behavior). Commonly, however, people deploy avoidance behaviors even if the punishing consequences no longer exist, or in some cases never existed, and such defensive behavior may be seen as failure to adapt to the new behavior–outcome relations.

Efficacy Expectations

In his self-efficacy theory, Bandura (1977) recently elaborated a distinction between two types of behavior-outcome expectations. The first type, called behavior–outcome expectation, is defined as a person's estimate that a given behavior will lead to certain outcomes. The second, called efficacy expectation, is the conviction that one can successfully execute the behavior required to produce the outcome. We shall discuss efficacy expectation, the strength of which determines whether or not someone will even try to cope with difficult situations (i.e., whether he will approach or avoid). It also determines the amount of effort expended and the degree of persistence. In sum, efficacy expectations play a major part in the initiation, generalization, and maintenance of coping behaviors. The presence and the strength of efficacy expectations are based on several sources of information. These are, in brief, past performance accomplishments by the individual, vicarious experiences (the successes and failures of observed others), verbal persuasion, and emotional arousal (because high arousal debilitates performance) (Bandura, 1977).

The value of self-efficacy theory lies on its prediction that those low in perceived self-efficacy will withdraw, and thereby fail socially, irrespective of their actual skill efficacy. However, it is equally true that those low in actual skill efficacy will fail socially irrespective of their perceived skill efficacy. In other words, a distinction can be made between primary social failure, where the individual lacks the skills in his repertoire, and secondary social failure where the individual has the skill but cannot deploy it, due to low perceived self-efficacy. Trower (1980) showed that, despite highly significant differences in their levels of social skill, primaries and secondaries both exhibited high levels of social anxiety and social avoidance. It is important for theoretical and therapeutic purposes to distinguish these two sources of social failure, perceived versus actual level of skill efficacy, and to specify cases where they converge and cases where they diverge.

This is shown diagrammatically in Figure 2 and is also presented in an essentially similar form by Curran (1979). Cell 1 represents a competent group (perceived and actually skilled), Cells 2 and 4 represent two forms of social-anxiety problems (perceived and actually unskilled, perceived unskilled and actually skilled) and Cell 3 represents a low anxious but unskilled group (perceived skilled, actually unskilled). Of course these groups are by no means so dichotomous as shown here.

Skill efficacy—perceived or actual—depends on the difficulty of the task, in addition to the level of deployable skills, or in other words the discrepancy between the standard demanded or required and the skills available. In his control theory (Carver, 1979; Carver & Scheier, 1984), Carver asserts that when the discrepancy is seen as large (standards high, skills low) the individual

PERCEIVED

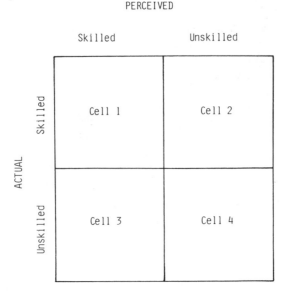

Figure 2. Diagram showing ways that individuals may react to their own levels of skill. The outcome of actual versus perceived skill has implications for assessment and treatment (see page 343).

may predict a failure to match-to-standard, and on the basis of that prediction, no matching-to-standard will be attempted. We have seen a tendency in the social phobic's appraisal system to evaluate against unrealistically high standards. It is to be expected equally that they will set unrealistically high goals for instrumental skill responses, and we have reviewed some of the evidence that they have, or believe they have, poor levels of skill. Such conditions will inevitably produce low efficacy expectations.

Few studies have directly examined social phobics' efficacy expectations immediately prior to, and consequent behavioral choices during the course of, social interaction tasks. Fiedler & Beach (1978) found that the difference between participants who chose an assertive response, and those who did not, lay in the former's assessment of the probabilities that bad consequences would occur and good consequences would not—a type of efficacy judgment. However, they did not find this to be related to standard measures of anxiety. Cacioppo, Glass, and Merluzzi (1977) found that while waiting to interact with an unfamiliar woman, men of high social anxiety generated more negative self-statements, rated both the impending discussion and themselves more negatively, rated themselves less potent and less active, and reported more state anxiety than did men of low social anxiety.

Mandel and Shrauger (1980) had shy and non-shy men receive either self-enhancing (SE) or self-critical (SC) statements to concentrate on. The SC group took longer to initiate a conversation, spent less time conversing, avoided eye contact, smiled less, and were less facially expressive—behaviors that could all be described as avoidant. There were similar differences between the shy and non-shy subjects, though it could have been that the shy subjects were merely unskilled, rather than negative thinkers.

On the basis of the above studies, there is some evidence that social phobics have low efficacy expectations and consequently make avoidant behavioral choices, but now we have the interesting possibility that avoidant behaviors of the Mandel and Shrauger kind will function as aversive stimuli for others, producing negative reactions from others of the kind that triggered the avoidance behaviors in the first place—a vicious cycle. Givens (1978) noted that contact avoidance cues, commonplace between strangers, can be construed as rejection cues. This is an important point, and can be summarized as follows: On the basis of perceived threat, the phobic client chooses a strategy which he can implement to reduce or deal with the threat, namely avoidance behavior. The avoidance strategy he chooses, however, can increase or even create the very same negative responses from others that his action aimed to deal with. Anxiety-generated avoidant behaviors like gaze aversion, long latencies, reduced talking, and facial inexpressiveness, are perceived as aversive, and are likely to produce rejecting responses. The interesting speculation here is that the client is unaware of the true contingencies—the phobic is unaware of his own behavior as an aversive stimulus—but is nonetheless responsible for producing self-confirming evidence in a self-fulfilling prophecy cycle. Such a cycle may camouflage our earlier primary/secondary distinction, since the skilled and the unskilled alike may behave in unskilled and unrewarding ways, the former because of the way negative beliefs operate on behavior.

The behavioral decisions that the client makes on the basis of his efficacy expectations (and appraisals) are not made once and for all in social interactions, but are constantly being remade in the light of continuous feedback (appraisal) from the ongoing interactions with others.

In a series of studies, Steffen and his colleagues have charted the patterns of prior thoughts and consequent steps taken in the ongoing interaction. Steffen and Lucas (1981) found their low-competent and socially anxious subjects judging their strategies (plans to influence others) as ineffective, and taking a pessimistic attitude about pauses in the conversation. Steffen and Redden (1977) found that their low-competent subjects had longer reaction times after negative feedback (i.e., pauses), and putting the two studies together we may speculate that low-efficacy judgments were interfering with performance as it proceeded. It is easy to see how this may develop into a self-fulfilling-prophecy cycle.

A number of perceptual processes, cognitive processes, and physiological arousals already considered in the appraisal system will also affect self-efficacy expectations. Owing to selective perception, for example, socially anxious clients fail to benefit from success experiences because of their tendency to overlook or ignore them (Clark & Arkowitz, 1975; Glasgow & Arkowitz, 1975). Attributions to external, specific, and unstable causes for success, and attributions to internal, global, and stable dispositions (Weiner, 1974) for failure, will lead to lowered self-efficacy (Bandura, 1977). These attributional styles have been found to be related to social anxiety (Sutton-Simon & Goldfried, 1981). Finally, high arousal may lead to expectations of disrupted performance, hence low efficacy.

Behavioral Responses

We now turn to the behavioral responses chosen as a result of appraisal of the situation and efficacy expectancies. In classic phobias, the behavioral response is usually avoidance, and this is no less true of social phobia, except that in this case the avoidance may be far more subtle than simple withdrawal. This is marked by a reduction of verbal and nonverbal behavior such as gaze avoidance. There is little research on social avoidance behavior, as such, viewed as a defensive consequence of social phobia, although the findings reported earlier can be viewed in this way. Findings also exist under related headings, in particular self-presentation and unassertiveness.

Arkin (1981) reviews evidence for what he terms "protective self-presentation style" which is designed mainly to avoid the disapproval of others. At its most extreme, this would be complete social avoidance and withdrawal, a relatively uncommon manifestation (Watson & Friend, 1969). The most common orientation is composed of diverse behaviors that serve to "forestall challenges" or create an impression that is "unassailable" (Arkin, 1981, p. 316). Among these he includes modest self-portrayals, neutral, uncertain or qualified expressions of some judgment, and conformity and compliance. For evidence in support of this view, readers are referred to Arkin (1981).

One group that could be described as socially avoiding are the publicly shy, discussed above (Pilkonis, 1977a). Another group are the *unassertive*, about whom there is now a very large literature. A number of these studies have shown that unassertive subjects were social phobics in the sense defined in this chapter, in that they are variously reported to exhibit perceptions, cognitive levels, and arousal levels similar to social phobics (where such measures have been taken), and a number of authors have long argued that unassertiveness is due to inhibitions caused by anxiety (Wolpe, 1958).

In their review of the "assertive" literature, Galassi and Galassi (1978) found the following common behavioral dimensions of assertion: standing up for one's rights, initiating and refusing requests, giving and receiving compliments, initiating, maintaining, and terminating conversations, expressing love and affection, expressing personal opinions, including disagreement, and expressing justified anger and annoyance. Unassertive subjects were found to exhibit low levels of performance on these dimensions. More specific elements of behavior and their relation to complex interacting variables have been delineated by a number of authors (Eisler, Miller, & Hersen, 1973; Eisler, Hersen, Miller, & Blanchard, 1975).

THERAPY

In this chapter we have presented a model of social phobia containing different processes and elements, any of which may give rise to faulty functioning. The aim of therapy is, therefore, to bring about change in that element or combination of elements which are responsible for the malfunctioning of the system as a whole. In other words, therapy aims at destabilizing and restructuring the relationship between perceptions, cognitions and physiological reactions. In the individual case, the specific change required will depend on the detailed specification of a problem-producing pattern of relationships between these elements.

The most effective treatment, therefore, is likely to be the one that is able to specify personal variables, stimulus variables, and therapy variables (Gurman & Razin, 1977; Paul, 1969) and the case for such specification has been underscored by a number of recent studies, albeit with less complex models of dysfunction than that presented here. Thus, Öst, Jerremalm, and Johannsson (1981) divided their social phobics, on the basis of their response patterns, into two groups, behavioral reactors and physiological reactors, and looked at their response to two forms of treatment, a behavioral method (social skills training) and a physiological method (applied relaxation). They found that the behavioral method worked best for the behavioral reactors, the physiological method for the physiological reactors. Marshall, Keltner, and Marshall (1981) also found specific treatment effects. Assertiveness training led to increased assertion but did not decrease social fear, while an anxiety-reduction procedure achieved the reverse result. Safran, Alden, and Davidson (1980) found that skills training improved behavior, and cognitive restructuring improved cognitions, in socially anxious subjects—a specific effect. This is just a sample of studies showing specific effects, and it must be said that there are other studies which show more generalized effects.

Important though specificity is, in many clinical practice settings it needs to be tempered by another therapeutic principle, that of cost-effectiveness. In an ideal world, the therapist would design anew for each client a comprehensive treatment program in which a sequence of therapy techniques would be carefully matched to a range of problems. Unfortunately, in clinical practice the available resources—time, money, equipment and the expertise and number of support personnel—are often strictly limited, and do not allow the implementation of the ideal approach. What the therapist needs in practice is a simple, straightforward routine of treatment that will indeed generalize across individuals and component problems.

There is impressive evidence that nonsocial phobias respond favorably to procedures which contain the common active ingredient of prolonged exposure to the feared stimulus (Marks, 1978), and that the effects of such procedures are noted in cognitive and physiological improvements as well as reduced avoidance (Bandura, 1977). Is social phobia a condition which would also yield to such an approach? There is some empirical evidence in favor of attempting such a strategy (e.g., Arkowitz, Lichtenstein, McGovern, & Hines, 1975; Emmelkamp, 1979), but it cannot be relied upon to produce change in all subjects. In some cases, a behavioral change is produced, but no cognitive or physiological change, and there is a failure of generalization and durability. For example, Biran, Augusto, and Wilson (1981) found participant modeling superior to cognitive therapy in those suffering from "scriptophobia"—fear of writing in front of others—but this superiority was confined to overt behavior alone. Subjective anxiety levels remained high, and the initial benefits were not well maintained.

At a theoretical level, predictions regarding the efficacy of exposure treatments for social phobias are far from straightforward. On the other hand, social phobia, in common with other phobias, may be due to an exaggerated and faulty assessment of danger (a failure of the appraisal system) or to a perceived or actual inability to cope (a failure of the coping system). While each system may fail independently, they often interact in a mutual exacerbation of phobia. In particular, avoidance behavior (failure in coping) maintains and exacerbates faulty appraisal by shielding the patient from disconfirming evidence. Treating the behavioral component should therefore not only improve coping ability, including efficacy expectations, but also bring beneficial changes in the appraisal system.

Disconfirming evidence comes mainly from exposure to relatively "static" situations, favoring eventual acknowledgment that risks are not only minimal but unvarying. However, social situations, by their very nature, involve a constantly changing stream of interactions in which the risk of rejection and negative evaluation is always present and always variable. In addition, the continuing revival of perceived threat is often brought on by the patient himself, since his own defensive and/or unskilled behavior will often act as a negative stimulus, producing negative responses from others. The reciprocally determined nature of such interactions (Bandura, 1977) means that the patient often brings about precisely the negative consequences that he predicts and dreads (Trower, 1981). Even if the patient does not actually produce behavioral confirmation of his beliefs (Snyder, 1980), he may well selectively perceive and distort the evidence and thereby bolster his beliefs this way. Such a process of self-fulfilling prophecy implies that the patient will not change, because the evidence he confronts by means of exposure *in vivo* provides confirmation rather than discomfirmation. In these circumstance, effective therapy is unlikely to result from simple exposure *in vivo,* but may require on the one hand response training *in vivo,* and on the other hand, changes in cognitions (the evaluation of evidence).

Emmelkamp (1979) concluded from his review of social-phobia treatment-outcome studies that cognitive therapy combined with skills training, construed as a kind of *in vivo* procedure and used to test the newly acquired cognitions, could prove to be the treatment of choice. This combined treatment approach goes part way toward meeting the requirements of our model of social phobia. We now go on to pay closer attention to the design of a more comprehensive approach to treatment.

Assessment

The process of assessment involves the formulation of hypotheses concerning the generating and maintaining conditions associated with a disorder, and the model we have presented constitutes the framework within which those hypotheses can be made. As well as being the crucial prerequisite for planning treatment, assessment also serves the function of providing a baseline for detecting change.

There have been many studies on the process of assessment, a few specifically on social anxiety (e.g., Glass & Merluzzi, 1981), and several useful general sources exist (Beck & Emery, 1979; Curran & Monti, 1982; Kendall & Hollon, 1981; Lazarus, 1976; Trower, Bryant, & Argyle, 1978). The global clinical interview, supplemented by existing background reports or interviews with friends and relatives of the client, should provide material for development of preliminary hypotheses, although we would caution against basing even this level of assessment on a single interview. But these hypotheses can be further extended and subjected to test, by a range of other techniques, including questionnaires, rating scales, diaries and other self-monitoring records, role-play, observation of typical social interactions and physiological assessments. Further references to specific assessment techniques are made in the following sections.

The Appraisal System

Social phobia may be due to a faulty appraisal of danger, to a perceived or actual inability to cope, or both. We shall consider therapeutic strategies in each case, bearing in mind that each system closely interacts and has common components.

The aim of therapy is to help the client achieve a realistic appraisal of the existence, intensity, and nature of potential threat. The client's exaggerated fear may be due to faulty perception of cues, overreactive autonomic or CNS arousal, exaggerated assessment of anxiety experiences, and distorted evaluations of threat to self. There will be variable contributions from each, and we consider each in turn.

Stimulus Expectancies

Clients are prone to infer that "catastrophic" consequences will follow from certain social cues to threatening outcomes, or to selectively perceive negative rather than positive information. Therapy aims at helping the client discover the stimulus–outcomes that exist in reality. The favored approach is to expose the client to "reality"—almost always the actual feared situation—thus breaking the avoidance cycle that customarily protects the client from ever discovering the true contingencies. For example, a client feared that if she blushed and went "blotchy" her husband would find her unattractive and reject her. However, she always left the situation before this happened. After cognitive therapy, she was able to bring herself to stay in the presence of her husband while blushing, failed to get the expected reaction, and found that the blushing rapidly diminished.

In such cases, clients predict that certain negative events will occur ("I will just go to pieces"), or that certain catastrophic consequences will follow ("people will think I'm insane/stupid"). Therapy shows that in reality these events and outcomes usually do not occur, and that even if they do, they are much milder than predicted. The power of *in vivo* exposure is that the evidence that disproves such expectancies is real and irrefutable. The problem, however, is often that clients fail to take such evidence into account, or distort it when subsequently making predictions, because by habit they switch back into their previous pattern of thinking. A number of steps can be taken to try to ensure that the client makes the most use of exposure in altering his inferences.

1. Therapist reminds the client by such questions as "What did you learn from the situation?" "What happened (or rather *did not* happen)?"
2. To cue himself at appropriate times in future, the client writes down the answers to Step 1 on a card.
3. The client writes down his catastrophic predictions and notes down how often it is disproved. The evidence should take the form of a daily diary of events that can be used as data (Beck & Emery, 1979).

Among cognitive therapies, a technique termed systematic rational restructuring has been found effective (Kanter & Goldfried, 1979). This gets clients to replace unrealistic predictions with realistic ones—from certainty to a low probability of disapproval and from expecting severe disapproval to predicting only mild levels of such disapproval. Clients are taught to visualize scenes from a hierarchy, to use anxiety as a signal for identifying unrealistic thoughts, and to challenge these thoughts and substitute more reasonable ones.

The therapist helps the client "decatastrophize" by using "guided fantasy" to go through the worst that can happen, blow by blow, unpacking global labels into behavioral and factual elements, and coupling this with Lazarus's time-projection method. This procedure is also useful for getting at "automatic thoughts" (Beck & Emery, 1979) in cases where the client cannot retrieve his fear-provoking inferences. The therapist helps the client distinguish beliefs from facts, as in a case where, for example, the client says, "She rejected me," whereas in fact she said she was working that night. Wessler's assessment method (Wessler & Wessler, 1980) can be used for laying out inference chains, starting with the facts and laying out each inferential layer. Also Beck's "triple column" method can be used in a similar way to retrieve fear-provoking inferences. These techniques and many others suggested by Beck and Emery (1979) are used to alter inferences and are all forms of hypothesis-testing and disputing for the client: the therapist and client can generate further ideas from this principle. Once existing inferences are undermined, new beliefs are developed and used, systematically and *in vivo,* as self-instructions (Meichenbaum, 1977).

Physiological Arousal

Individuals vary considerably in the pattern of their autonomic reactivity (Lacey, 1950). Therapy aims to reduce abnormally high arousal levels in those patients who are "physiological responders" (Öst *et al.,* 1981). In social phobias, as well as the self-perception of high arousal—that is, unpleasant experiences tending to provoke avoidance—there is additionally an awareness of the possibility that physiologically mediated responses, such as blushing or shaking, may be perceived by others; and this anticipatory component has additional aversive qualities.

The choice of method for reducing this arousal will depend on the pattern of physiological response, the characteristics of the client (whether they are more likely to respond to a self-control procedure, or a more "passive" technique, such as systematic desensitization), and the resources and expertise of the therapist. Self-control, or coping-skill training aims at teaching clients an active skill such as relaxation which can be applied to a range of real-life situations; a useful review is provided by Barrios and Shigetomi (1979).

Relaxation training can be carried out by a variety of techniques: Jacobson's deep muscle-relaxation training and variants thereof, hypnosis, autogenic training, biofeedback, distraction and focusing exercises, and breathing exercises. Often a combination of methods will be found useful, especially where prominent responses are resistant to control by global, that is, nonspecific, training methods.

Although in general, pharmacological methods for the reduction of the physiological components of phobic disorders are either not effective at controlling the response peaks in the feared situations, or, if effective, are administered at dosage levels sufficient to provoke side-effects, there are many situations where concurrent anxiolytic medication can protect the client from the intense discomfort which would otherwise make progress with behavioral treatments impossible. Scope undoubtedly exists for the matching of specific agents to the pattern of physiological responding, such as the use of beta-blockers in relation to palpitations, tachycardia, or tremor. For a fuller discussion the reader is referred to Hicks, Okonek, and Davis (1980), and Hollon and Beck (1978).

Emotional Experience. Systematic desensitization aims to break the "conditioned" link between physiological arousal and situation cues (counter-conditioning) in order to help a person "redefine" his emotion. In other words, systematic desensitization and anxiety-management training can be used to alter the emotional relationship between arousal and perceptual information.

Individuals vary in their tolerance for negative information, both perceptual and physiological, and react differentially to a given intensity of emotional experience. In RET, this is termed *discomfort anxiety* and the procedure recommended by Wessler and Wessler (1980) is designed to help the client recalibrate his subjective rating scale in such a way that levels of discomfort previously rated 100 (worst possible) are re-rated at much lower levels. Moreover, he is shown how to change self-instructing cognitions from "I can't" to "I can" (e.g., I can stand x level of discomfort).

The Self. In Bandura's social learning theory (and other theories such as that of Carver, 1979), the self-system plays a central role in perceiving, evaluating, and regulating behavior (Bandura, 1978), and therapy aimed at modifying maladaptive self-cognitions has a special importance in emotional disorders. Following our earlier discussion, we are concerned with modifying mistaken attributions (blaming self for failure), with changing perfectionistic criteria in making evaluative judgments, with reducing self-consciousness, and with changing total self-worth evaluations.

Attribution retraining has received increasing attention recently. Dweck (1975), for example, helped school children attribute their failures to lack of effort rather than incompetence. Metalsky and Abramson (1981) suggest evaluating old and new evidence, close attention to situational information plus assertion and social-skills training. Beach, Abramson, and Levine (1981), Seligman (1981), and Ickes and Layden (1978) all suggest attribution retraining programs.

All these features of self-conception are dealt with in more general, comprehensive cognitive behavior-therapy programs. In particular, we might name such treatment strategies as those of Beck and Emery (1979), Goldfried and Davison (1976), Grieger and Boyd (1980), Walen, DiGuiseppe, and Wessler (1980), and Wessler and Wessler (1980). In one of these procedures, concerned with "self-downing" or negative evaluations of the total self, therapy consists of challenging this on empirical and logical grounds, by both disputation (in the form of Socratic dialogue), and disproof (by means of risk or "shame-attacking" homework assignments). The aim is to help the patient "work through," get the insight, and then put this into practice *in vivo* with the help of new self-instructions.

The Coping System

Failure in the coping system consists of avoidance, maintained both by perceived low efficacy and perceived high threat. We have considered therapeutic methods for changing threat evaluation (the appraisal system). In this section, we review techniques for improving perceived efficacy, and in the next section, methods for improving actual efficacy (i.e., social skills), both of which are aimed at the main therapeutic goal: eradication of social avoidance behavior and/or instigating skilled coping behavior.

Efficacy Expectations

Earlier we described two types of phobics: skilled and unskilled (Cells 2 and 3). They both shared low efficacy expectations, the first unrealistically, the second more realistically. Therapy is aimed at altering the underlying faulty inferences, but the process will differ somewhat in each case. We begin with the competent phobic.

Such clients are prone to wrongly infer severe and certain punishing outcomes for behavioral initiatives, and believe they lack the skills to avoid such outcomes. As with stimulus expectancies, the potentially most effective intervention for the competent phobic is *in vivo* exposure, though imaginal versions also help. In his review of outcome studies, Emmelkamp (1979) found that SST was one of the more effective techniques for reducing anxiety in social phobics because SST operates as an *in vivo* exposure procedure (though for competent clients the skill-acquisition component is somewhat redundant). However, SST sometimes fails to reduce anxiety (Marshall *et al.,* 1981) and often produces only marginal changes in behavior. This may be because some clients have not altered their efficacy expectations, and the "reality-testing" benefits and potential success experience of *in vivo* responding are thus lost due to existing cognitive distortion processes (O'Banion & Arkowitz, 1977; Smith, 1972; Smith & Sarason, 1975). Safran, Alden, and Davidson (1980) found that even when skills training was effective in changing behavior in socially anxious subjects, it neither reduced their anxiety nor improved their self-concepts. In fact, there was a nonsignificant trend for cognitive restructuring to produce greater change. They concluded that behavior change may be insufficent to modify cognitions. Therefore, effective therapy will combine *in vivo* responding with congnitive restructuring, which directly focuses on changing faulty expectations and helps the client perceive accurately. Emmelkamp (1979) finds encouraging evidence to support cognitive therapy in the treatment of social anxiety as opposed to other forms of anxiety, and suggests cognitions may turn out to be more important in mediating anxiety reactions in social phobics than in agoraphobics and obsessive-compulsives.

A number of studies have shown that various forms of cognitive restructuring actually result in increased social behavior. Wolfe and Fodor (1977), and Alden and Safran (1978) found that cognitive techniques equalled skill training in increasing assertiveness. Glass, Gottman, and Shmurak (1976) found that treatment emphasizing the use of rational self-statements was significantly more effective in improving heterosocial interaction than was a procedure emphasizing skills training. Thorpe (1975) reported that training individuals to rationally re-evaluate the consequences of their assertive behavior was more effective than desensitization and just as effective as behavior rehearsal. Hammen, Jacobs, Mayol, and Cochran (1980) found cognitive therapy equalled behavior rehearsal in increasing assertion, although cognitive therapy appeared to contain elements of behavior rehearsal. Linehan, Goldfried, and Goldfried (1979) found that cognitive therapy helped women to make assertive responses, and that a combination of cognitive therapy and behavior rehearsal was the most effective treatment.

Another method of improving efficacy expectation is to use modeling as a response facilitator. "Exposure to models performing feared activities without any harmful effects weakens defensive behavior, reduces fears, and creates favorable changes in attitude . . . the modelled actions function simply as social prompts" (Bandura, 1977).

The studies so far cited put forward useful techniques for changing efficacy inferences and evaluations, and those methods already listed earlier in the "Stimulus Expectancies" section will also be applicable, with minor modification. However, these can be augmented by techniques that are more specifically designed to help clients re-evaluate the effects of their instrumental behavior.

Goldfried and Robins (1982) suggest four ways to help clients re-evaluate their behavior: (1) discrimination between past and present to help patients detect change by reference to reliable, but overlooked, evidence; (2) adding an objective vantage point to patients' subjective outlook in order to bring about change in attributions, in this way enabling them to see self as cause of successful behaviors; (3) retrieval of past successes by record-keeping and use of such successes to help guide future actions; and (4) aligning expectancies, anticipatory feelings, behaviors, objective consequences, and self-evaluation. This helps clients generalize change in one component to others (see Goldfried & Robins, 1982 for more details).

Another useful method is to get patients to set relative, rather than absolute, goals and to judge performances by such relative criteria (e.g., Point 1 in Goldfried & Robins; see also Goldfried & Davison, 1976). Finally, patients need to learn to rate their behavior, not themselves, thereby limiting a failure to a single performance, rather than having it generalize to all possible performances via the "self." Lazarus's "little *i*" technique is useful in this regard

(Lazarus, 1976), or one of the RET manuals (Wessler & Wessler, 1980) will provide guidance.

To summarize, the optimal treatment for altering efficacy expectations in socially competent phobics is probably a combination of exposure *in vivo* and cognitive methods aimed at changing inferences and evaluations.

In dealing with the noncompetent phobic, we are presented with a case where the expectation is not necessarily false, the patient may indeed behave incompetently in some way and may well receive criticism or rejection. Exposure *in vivo* may fail in this case because the patient continues to behave unskillfully and needs training in response skills. The therapist would also have to be careful which cognitive technique he uses, since methods aimed at altering inferences would certainly be misplaced wherever these inferences were valid. Other methods listed would be useful, however, especially those aimed at self-evaluations rather than inferences, or in RET terms, those aimed at beliefs rather than activating events (see, for example, Walen, DiGuiseppe, & Wessler, 1980).

Behavioral Responses

Perceived high threat and low efficacy combine to produce defensive behaviors. Often downright avoidance is evident, but degrees of inhibited behavior or even behavioral excesses such as over-talkativeness can be observed. This in turn maintains and exacerbates failure experiences and faulty inferences. Therapy aimed at altering these behavioral responses is one of the most powerful ways of breaking into this vicious and self-sustaining cycle of events. In considering the modification of these behavioral dysfunctions, we must examine two questions: First, how do we bring the patient into the feared situations and keep him there (achieve prolonged exposure *in vivo*), and, second, how do we ensure that the patient behaves appropriately in the situation (skilled responding *in vivo*)?

Exposure in vivo. Great care is needed to ensure that the situations the client is exposed to do not provoke degrees of arousal that will overwhelm him and disrupt the learning of coping responses. We envisage that only in the case of the very competent client will it be fruitful to arrange for unsupervised introduction into existing community activities, such as social clubs and dances, and even in such cases the behavioral targets that the client is expected to achieve should be specified in detail and subject to previous rehearsal. Techniques such as modeling, role-play, and videotaped feedback are all relevant in this context.

In other cases, where coping responses are deficient, protected exposure settings are required initially, with progression to more threatening social environments *pari passu* with skills acquisition. Specially designed group-based treatments which combine both therapeutic and social functions can provide a crucial stepping-stone to more naturalistic settings (Jackson, 1981). In addition to these behavior-based procedures, imaginal methods such as covert modeling, which has been effective with socially anxious, unassertive patients (Kazdin, 1974, 1975, 1976; Rosenthal & Reese, 1976), are of value as an easily arranged induction procedure for *in vivo* homework assignments.

Social Skills Training. The second behavioral objective of therapy is to help the patient perform skillfully once in a situation. By skillful, we mean the deployment of sequences of verbal and nonverbal behaviors designed to achieve a specified social target or goal desired by the patient (Argyle, 1969) within the limits or constraints allowed by any given situation. From previous discussion, it is clear that the targets at the most global level will include such variables as friendliness, assertiveness, and persuasiveness. The particular form that these expressions take will depend on the rules of the situation in which the skill is to be attempted.

Social skills training may be said to have two main requirements in order to be effective: (1) a technology of behavior acquisition and (2) access to social behavior norms and situation rules for assessment and training. One behavior-acquisition technique is modeling, in which the client observes (and later imitates) others performing a skill sequence. Modeling helps clients acquire knowledge of complex interaction skills which would be difficult if not impossible to teach singly. A second popular technique is behavior rehearsal, in which the client repeats a behavioral sequence until it reaches a given criterion. A third is coaching, in which a sequence is broken down into components and used as verbal information to guide the client. Fourth, there is feedback, which can be given by audio or videotape playback, by comments on the effect of responses, or during interaction by means of a "bug in the ear" device. Reinforcement is also used to motivate patients. Finally, structured homework assignments are essential if skills are to be maintained and utilized *in vivo*.

Less attention has been given to the appropriate behavioral components and validation of their effectiveness in achieving desired effects. This and other problems has hampered progress in the assessment of social skills (Bellack, 1979). Few normative components have been established, but trainers can utilize peer "models" who possess the relevant skills, and who can also act as assessors, using various published rating scales. These and other issues have been critically reviewed (Bellack & Hersen, 1979; Twentyman & Zimering, 1979). There are also a number of training manuals (e.g., Goldstein, Sprafkin, & Gershaw, 1976; Liberman, King, De Risi, & McCann, 1975; Trower, Bryant, & Argyle, 1978).

Most publications on SST have emphasized training clients in particular elements of social skill which they purportedly lack. Only a few have emphasized an equally important task, which is to help clients acquire the processing or cognitive skills to generate appropriate social skills: perception of cues, monitoring behavior, and synchronizing with the other (Lange & Jakubowski, 1976; Spivack, Platt & Shure, 1976; Trower, 1980; Wallace, 1982). A number of authors from various disciplines have recently addressed the task of integrating cognitive and social skills techniques into a unified therapy (Trower, 1984).

To help the client focus on his dual task of dealing with his anxiety in the situation and planning his skills, the cognitive induction aid known as stress inoculation (Meichenbaum, 1977) should be invaluable. The central component is the application, in stressful situations, of two types of coping self-statements—applied relaxation and task-oriented instructions. This procedure has been found successful in interpersonal anxiety (Glass, Gottman, & Shmurak, 1976). Task-focusing instructions have been shown to improve performances of anxious, low self-esteem subjects, and to partially offset the effects of self-consciousness (Brockner & Hulton, 1978). Many techniques already described will clearly help in induction, particularly those that reduce perceived threat and emotional reaction and those that increase self-efficacy expectations. One method found to be effective from clinical experience is the RET method of reduction of discomfort anxiety (see Grieger & Boyd, 1980).

SUMMARY

The once-acceptable notion that social phobia can be construed merely in terms of conditioned fear responses acquired fortuitously in "social situations" is now widely discredited. The need for a more complex model is confirmed by several lines of recent research: the findings of more considerable differences in subject characteristics than is the case with other phobias, the understanding that anxiety is not a "lump," our ability to conceptualize the interaction of cognitive and physiological behavior, and impressive developments in our knowledge about social-learning mechanisms, social perception, and attribution.

We have attempted to integrate some of these developments, drawing in particular on social learning theory, the Lazarus and Opton (1966) theory of emotion, and Carver's (1979) theory of self-control, to provide a framework which can describe the features of social phobia and which can guide the practitioner who has responsibilities for assessment and treatment. This framework is offered as an organizing heuristic, rather than a rigorous, theory.

The framework proposed contains two main elements: an appraisal system and a coping system. The appraisal system is concerned with the way in which the patient evaluates threat, and how this is related to his state of physiological arousal and to cognitive processing characteristics. The coping system is concerned with the individual's capacity to perform certain instrumental behaviors, as well as with his self-efficacy expectations and his response repertoire. The main implications of this conception are that the practitioner should assess on the one hand the way the patient perceives and evaluates, and on the other hand the way the patient copes, or fails to cope, with perceived dangers.

Therapy demands a careful appraisal of these elements of the model and the implementation of appropriate change strategies. We have reviewed the possibilities in terms of (a) the structure of the model and (b) existing treatment research. We have tried to organize the literature within this framework, although much research obviously cuts across the conceptual boundaries drawn here.

REFERENCES

Alden, L., & Cappe, R. Nonassertiveness: Skill deficit or selective self-evaluation? *Behavior Therapy*, 1981, *12*, 107–114.

Alden, L., & Safran, J. Irrational beliefs and nonassertive behavior. *Cognitive Therapy and Research*, 1978, *2*, 357–364.

Alden, L., Safran, J., & Weideman, R. A comparison of cognitive and skills training strategies in the treatment of unassertive clients. *Behavior Therapy*, 1979, *9*, 843–846.

Argyle, M. *Social interaction*. London: Methuen, 1969.

Arkin, R. M. Self-presentation styles. In J. T. Tedeschi (Ed.), *Impression management theory and social psychological theory*. New York: Academic Press, 1981.

Arkin, R. M., Appelman, A. J., & Burger, J. M. Social anxiety, self-presentation, and the self-serving bias in causal attribution. *Journal of Personality and Social Psychology*, 1980. *38*, 23–25.

Arkowitz, H., Lichtenstein, E., McGovern, K., & Hines, P. The behavioral assessment of social competence in males. *Behavior Therapy*, 1975, *6*, 3–13.

Arrindell, W. A. Dimensional structure and psychopathology correlates of the Fear Survey Schedule (FSS-III) in a phobic population: A factorial definition of agoraphobia. *Behaviour Research and Therapy*, 1980, *18*, 229–242.

Bandura, A. The self-system in reciprocal determinism. *American Psychologist*, 1978, April, 344–358.

Bandura, A. *Social learning theory*. Englewood Cliffs, N.J.: Prentice-Hall, 1977.

Bandura, A. In search of pure unidirectional determinants of behavior. *Behavior Therapy*, 1981, *12*, 30–40.

Barlow, D. H., & Wolfe, B. E. Behavioral approaches to anxiety disorders: A report on the NIMH–SUNY, Albany Research Conference. *Journal of Consulting and Clinical Psychology*, 1981, *49*, 448–454.

Barrios, B. A., Shigetomi, C. C. Coping-skills training for the management of anxiety: A critical review. *Behavior Therapy*, 1979, *10*, 491–522.

Bates, H. D. Factorial structure and MMPI correlates of a Fear Survey Schedule in a clinical population. *Behaviour Research and Therapy*, 1971, *9*, 355–360.

Beach, S. R. H., Abramson, L. Y., & Levine, F. M. The attributional reformulation of learned helplessness: Therapeutic implications. In J. Clarkin & H. Glazer (Eds.), *Depression: Behavioral and directive intervention strategies*. New York: Garland, 1981.

Beck, A. T. *Cognitive therapy and the emotional disorders*. New York: International Universities Press, 1976.

Beck, A. T., & Emery, G. *Cognitive therapy of anxiety and phobic disorders*. Philadelphia: Center for Cognitive Therapy, 1979.

Behnke, R. R., & Carlile, L. W. Heart rate as an index of speech anxiety. *Speech Monographs*, 1971, *38*, 65–69.

Bellack, A. S. Behavioral assessment of social skills. In A. S. Bellack & M. Hersen (Eds.), *Research and practice in social skills training*. New York: Plenum, 1979.

Bellack, A. S., & Hersen, M. *Research and practice in social skills training.* New York: Plenum Press, 1979.

Biran, M., Augusto, F., & Wilson, G., T. *In vivo* exposure versus cognitive restructuring in the treatment of scriptophobia. *Behaviour Research and Therapy,* 1981, *19,* 525–532.

Bradley, G. W. Self-serving biases in the attribution process: A re-examination of the fact or fiction question. *Journal of Personality and Social Psychology,* 1978, *36,* 56–71.

Braun, P. R., & Reynolds, D. J. A factor analysis of a 100-item fear survey inventory. *Behaviour Research and Therapy,* 1969, *7,* 399–402.

Brockner, J., & Hulton, A. J. B. How to reverse the vicious cycle of low self-esteem: The importance of attentional focus. *Journal of Experimental Social Psychology,* 1978, *14,* 564–578.

Bruner, J. S. Going beyond the information given. In J. S. Bruner, E. Brunswik, L. Festinger, F. Heider, K. F. Muenzinger, C. E. Osgood, & D. Rapaport (Eds.), *Contemporary approaches to cognition.* Cambridge, Mass.: Harvard University Press, 1957.

Bryant, B., & Trower, P. E. Social difficulty in a student sample. *British Journal of Educational Psychology,* 1974, *44,* 13–21.

Bryant, B. M., Trower, P. E., Yardley, K., Urbeita, H., Letemendia, F. J. J. A survey of social inadequacy among psychiatric outpatients. *Psychological Medicine,* 1976, *6,* 101–112.

Buck, R. *Human motivation and emotion.* New York: Wiley, 1976.

Buss, A. H. *Self-consciousness and social anxiety.* San Francisco: W. H. Freeman, 1980.

Cacioppo, J. T., Glass, C. R., and Merluzzi, T. V. Self-statements are self-evaluations: A cognitive response analysis of heterosexual society anxiety. *Cognitive Therapy and Research,* 1979, *3,* 249–262.

Cantor, N., & Mischel, W. Prototypes in person perception. In L. Berkowitz (Ed.), *Advances in experimental social psychology,* 1979, *12,* 3–51.

Carver, C. S. A cybernetic model of self-attention processes. *Journal of Personality and Social Psychology,* 1979, *37,* 1251–1281.

Carver, C. S. & Scheier, M. F. A control-theory approach to behavior, and some implications for social skills training. In P. Trower (Ed.), *Radical approaches to social skills training.* London: Croom Helm, 1984.

Clark, J. V., & Arkowitz, H. Social anxiety and self-evaluation of interpersonal performance. *Psychological Reports,* 1975, *36,* 211–221.

Conger, J. C., & Farrell, A. D. Behavioral components of heterosocial skills. *Behavior Therapy,* 1981, *12,* 41–55.

Coyne, J. C., & Lazarus, R. S. Cognitive style, stress perception, and coping. In I. L. Kutash, L. B. Schlesinger, & Associates, *Handbook on stress and anxiety.* San Francisco: Jossey-Bass, 1980.

Crozier, W. R. Shyness as a dimension of personality. *British Journal of Social and Clinical Psychology,* 1979, *18,* 121–128.

Curran, J. P. Skills training as an approach to the treatment of heterosexual-social anxiety: A review. *Psychological Bulletin,* 1977, *84,* 140–157.

Curran, J. P. Pandora's box reopened? The assessment of social skills. *Journal of Behavioral Assessment,* 1979, *1,* 55–71.

Curran, J. P., & Monti, P. (Eds.), *Social skills training: A pratical handbook for assessment and treatment.* New York: Guilford Press, 1982.

Daly, S. Behavioural correlates of social anxiety. *British Journal of Social and Clinical Psychology,* 1978, *17,* 117–120.

Dixon, J. J., DeMonchaux, C., & Sandler, J. Patterns of anxiety: The phobias. *British Journal of Medical Psychology,* 1957, *30,* 34–40.

Duval, S., & Wicklund, R. A. *A theory of objective self awareness.* New York: Academic Press, 1972.

Dweck, C. S. The role of expectations and attributions in the alleviation of learned helplessness. *Journal of Personality and Social Psychology,* 1975, *31,* 674–685.

Eisler, R. M., Miller, P. M., & Hersen, M. Components of assertive behavior. *Journal of Clinical Psychology,* 1973, *29,* 295–299.

Eisler, R. M., Hersen, M., Miller, P. M., & Blanchard, E. B. Situational determinants of assertive behavior. *Journal of Consulting and Clinical Psychology.* 1975, *43,* 330–340.

Ekman, P. Universals and cultural differences in facial expressions of emotion. In J. Cole (Ed.), *Nebraska Symposium on Motivation, 1971.* Lincoln: University of Nebraska Press, 1972.

Ekman, P., & Friesen, W. V. Nonverbal leakage and clues to deception. In S. Weitz (Ed.), *Nonverbal communication: Readings with commentary.* New York: Oxford University Press, 1974.

Ellis, A. *Reason and emotion in psychotherapy.* New York: Lyle Stuart, 1962.

Emmelkamp. P. M. G. The behavioral study of clinical phobias. In M. Hersen, R. M. Eisler, & P. M. Miller (Eds.), *Progress in behavior modification* (Vol. 8). New York: Academic Press, 1979.

Fenigstein, A. Self-consciousness, self-attention, and social interaction. *Journal of Personality and Social Psychology,* 1979, *37,* 75–86.

Fenigstein, A., Scheier, M. F., & Buss, A. H. Public and private self-consciousness: Assessment and theory. *Journal of Consulting and Clinical Psychology,* 1975, *43,* 522–527.

Fiedler, D., & Beach, L. R. On the decision to be assertive. *Journal of Consulting and Clinical Psychology,* 1978, *46,* 537–546.

Galassi, M. D., & Galassi, J. P. Assertion: A critical review. *Psychotherapy: Theory, Research, and Practice,* 1978, *15,* 16–29.

Givens, D. Greeting a stranger: Some commonly used nonverbal signals of aversiveness. *Semiotica,* 1978, *22,* 351–367.

Glasgow, R., & Arkowitz, H. The behavioral assessment of male and female social competence in dyadic heterosexual interactions. *Behavior Therapy,* 1975, *6,* 488–498.

Glass, C. R., & Merluzzi, T. V. Cognitive assessment of social-evaluative anxiety. In T. V. Merluzzi, C. R. Glass, & M. Genest (Eds.), *Cognitive assessment.* New York: Guilford Press, 1981.

Glass, C. R., Gottman, J. M., & Shmurak, S. H. Response acquisition and cognitive self-statement modification approaches to dating skills training. *Journal of Counseling Psychology,* 1976, *23,* 520–526.

Goffman, E. *The presentation of self in everyday life.* Harmondsworth, Middlesex: Penguin, 1971. (Originally published 1959).

Goffman, E. *Relations in public: Micro-studies of the public order.* Harmondsworth, Middlesex: Penguin 1972.

Goldfried, M. R., & Davison, G. C. *Clinical behavior therapy.* New York: Holt, Rinehart and Winston, 1976.

Goldfried, M. R., & Robins, C. On the facilitation of self-efficacy. *Cognitive Therapy and Research,* 1982, *6,* 361–379.

Goldfried, M. R., & Sobocinski, D. Effect of irrational beliefs on emotional arousal. *Journal of Consulting and Clinical Psychology,* 1975, *43,* 504–510.

Goldstein, A. P., Sprafkin, R. P., & Gershaw, N. J. *Skill training for community living.* Oxford: Pergamon, 1976.

Gormally, J., Sipps. G., Raphael, R., Edwin, D., & Varvil-Weld, D. The relationship between maladaptive cognitions and social anxiety. *Journal of Consulting and Clinical Psychology,* 1981, *49,* 300–301.

Grieger, R., & Boyd, J. Rational-emotive therapy: A skills-based approach. New York: Van Nostrand Reinhold, 1980.

Gurman, A. S., & Razin, A. M. *Effective psychotherapy: A handbook of research.* Oxford: Pergamon, 1977.

Haggard, E. Psychological causes and results of stress. In D. Lindsley (Ed.), *Human factors in undersea warfare.* Washington: National Research Council Press, 1949.

Halford, K., & Foddy, M. Cognitive and social skills correlates of social anxiety. *British Journal of Clinical Psychology*, 1982, *21*, 17–28.

Hallam, R. S., & Hafner, R. J. Fears of phobic patients: Factor analyses of self-report data. *Behaviour Research and Therapy*, 1978, *16*, 1–6.

Hammen, C. C., Jacobs, M., Mayol, A., & Cochran, S. D. Dysfunctional cognitions and the effectiveness of skills and cognitive-behavioral assertion training. *Journal of Consulting and Clinical Psychology*, 1980, *48*, 685–695.

Harré, R. *Social being: A theory for social psychology*. Oxford: Blackwell, 1979.

Heider, F. *The psychology of interpersonal relations*. New York: Wiley, 1958.

Henley, N. M. *Body politics: Power, sex and nonverbal communication*. Englewood Cliffs, N.J.: Prentice-Hall, 1977.

Hicks, R., Okonek, A., & Davis, J. M. The psychopharmacological approach. In I. L. Kutash, L. B. Schlesinger, & Associates, *Handbook on stress and anxiety*. San Francisco: Jossey-Bass, 1980.

Hollon, S. D., & Beck, A. T. Psychotherapy and drug therapy: Comparisons and combinations. In S. L. Garfield & A. E. Bergin (Eds.), *Handbook of psychotherapy and behavior change* (2nd ed.). New York: Wiley, 1978.

Hugdahl, K. The three-systems-model of fear and emotion—a critical examination. *Behaviour Research and Therapy*, 1981, *19*, 75–86.

Ickes, W., & Layden, M. A. Attributional styles. In J. H. Harvey, W. Ickes, & R. F. Kidd (Eds.), *New directions in attributional research* (Vol. 2). Hillsdale, N.J.: Erlbaum, 1978.

Jackson, M. F. *A socal skills youth club—Outpatient treatment of adolescents with social difficulty*. Paper presented to the Annual Conference of the British Association for Behavioural Psychotherapy, Bristol, England, July 1981.

James, W. *The principles of psychology* (Vol. 2). New York: Henry Holt & Co., 1893.

Jones, E. E., & Nisbett, R. E. *The actor and the observer: Divergent perceptions of the causes of behavior*. Morristown, N.J.: General Learning, 1971.

Kanter, N. J., & Goldfried, M. R. Relative effectiveness of rational restructuring and self-control desensitization in the reduction of interpersonal anxiety. *Behavior therapy*, 1979, *10*, 472–490.

Kazdin, A. E. Effects of covert modeling and model reinforcement on assertive behavior. *Journal of Abnormal Psychology*, 1974, *83*, 240–252.

Kazdin, A. E. Covert modeling, imagery assessment, and assertive behavior. *Journal of Consulting and Clinical Psychology*, 1975, *43*, 716–724.

Kazdin, A. E. Effects of covert modeling, multiple models, and model reinforcement on assertive behavior. *Behavior Therapy*, 1976, *7*, 211–222.

Kelley, H. H. Attribution theory in social psychology. In D. Levine (Ed.), *Nebraska Symposium on Motivation*. Lincoln: University of Nebraska Press, 1967.

Kelly, G. A. *The psychology of personal constructs* (Vols. 1 and 2). New York: Norton, 1955.

Kendall, P. C., & Hollon, S. D. *Assessment strategies for cognitive-behavioral interventions*. New York: Academic Press, 1981.

Kihlstrom, J. F., & Nasby, W. Cognitive tasks in clinical assessment: An exercise in applied psychology. In P. C. Kendall & S. D. Hollon (Eds.), *Assessment strategies for cognitive-behavioral interventions*. New York: Academic, 1981.

Kozak, M. J., & Miller, G. A. Hypothetical constructs vs. intervening variables: A re-appraisal of the three-systems model of anxiety assessment. *Behavioral Assessment*, 1982, *4*, 347–358.

Lacey, J. I. Individual differences in somatic response patterns. *Journal of Comparative and Physiological Psychology*, 1950, *113*, 338–350.

Lader, M. H. Palmar skin conductance measures in anxiety and phobic states. *Journal of Psychosomatic Research*, 1967, *11*, 271–281.

Lang, P. J. Fear reduction and fear behavior: Problems in treating a construct. In J. M. Shlien

(Ed.), *Research in psychotherapy* (Vol. 3). Washington, D.C.: American Psychological Association, 1968.

Lang, P. J. Stimulus control, response control and desensitization of fear. In D. Levis (Ed.), *Learning approaches to therapeutic behavior change.* Chicago: Aldine Press, 1970.

Lang, P.J. The application of psychophysiological methods to the study of psychotherapy and behavior change. In A. E. Bergin & S. L. Garfield (Eds.), *Handbook of psychotherapy and behavior change.* New York: Wiley, 1971.

Lang, P. J., & Lazovik, A. D. Experimental desensitisation of a phobia. *Journal of Abnormal and Social Psychology,* 1963, *66,* 519–525.

Lang, P. J., Rice, D. G., & Sternbach, R. A. The psychophysiology of emotion. In N. S. Greenfield and R. A. Sternbach (Eds.), *Handbook of psychophysiology.* New York: Holt, Rinehart and Winston, 1972.

Lang, A. J., & Jakubowski, P. *Responsible assertive behavior.* Champaign, Ill.: Research Press, 1976.

Lanzetta, J. T., & Orr, S. P. Influence of facial expressions on the classical conditioning of fear. *Journal of Personality and Social Psychology,* 1981, *39,* 1081–1087.

Lawlis, G. F. Response styles of a patient population on the Fear Survey Schedule. *Behaviour Research and Therapy,* 1971, *9,* 95–102.

Lazarus, A. A. *Multimodal behavior therapy.* New York: Springer, 1976.

Lazarus, R., & Opton, E. The study of psychological stress: A summary of theoretical formulations and experimental findings. In C. Spielberger (Ed.), *Anxiety and behavior.* New York: Academic, 1966.

Liberman, R. P., King, L. W., De Risi, W. J., & McCann, M. *Personal effectiveness.* Champaign, Ill.: Research Press, 1975.

Linehan, M. M., Goldfried, M. R., & Goldfried, A. P. Assertion therapy: Skill training or cognitive restructuring. *Behavior Therapy,* 1979, *10,* 372–388.

Mandel, N. M., & Shrauger, J. S. The effects of self-evaluative statements on heterosocial approach in shy and non-shy males. *Cognitive Therapy & Research,* 1980, *4,* 369–382.

Marks, I. M. *Fears and phobias.* London: Heinemann, 1969.

Marks, I. M. Behavioral psychotherapy of adult neurosis. In S. L. Garfield & A. E. Bergin (Eds.), *Handbook of psychotherapy and behavior change* (2nd Ed.). New York: Wiley, 1978.

Marks, I. M., & Gelder, M. G. Different onset ages in varieties of phobia. *American Journal of Psychiatry,* 1966, *123,* 218–221.

Marshall, P. G., Keltner, A. A., & Marshall, W. L. Anxiety reduction, assertive training, and enactment of consequences. *Behavior Modification,* 1981, *5,* 85–102.

Martin, I., Marks, I. M., & Gelder, M. G. Conditioned eyelid responses in phobic patients. *Behaviour Research and Therapy,* 1969, *7,* 115–124.

Marzillier, J. S., & Lambert, C. *The components of conversational skills: Talking to a stranger.* Unpublished manuscript, Birmingham University, 1976.

Meichenbaum, D. *Cognitive-behavior modification.* New York: Plenum, 1977.

Metalsky, G. I., & Abramson, L. Y. Attributional styles: Towards a framework for conceptualization and assessment. In P. C. Kendall & S. D. Hollon (Eds.), *Assessment strategies for cognitive-behavioral interventions.* New York: Academic Press, 1981.

Miller, G. A., Galanter, E., & Pribram, K. H. *Plans and the structure of behavior.* New York: Holt, 1960.

Mischel, W. Toward a cognitive social learning reconceptualization of personality. *Psychological Review,* 1973, *80,* 252–283.

Modigliani, A. Embarrassment and embarrassability. *Sociometry,* 1968, *31,* 313–326.

Mulac, A., & Sherman, A. R. Behavioral assessment of speech anxiety. *Quarterly Journal of Speech,* 1974, *60,* 134–143.

O'Banion, K., & Arkowitz, H. Social anxiety and selective memory for affective information about the self. *Social behavior and personality*, 1977, *5*, 321–328.

Osgood, C. E., Suci, G. J., & Tannenbaum, P. H. *The measurement of meaning.* Urbana: University of Illinois Press, 1957.

Öst, L.-G., Jerremalm, A., & Johansson, J. Individual response patterns and the effects of different behavioral methods in the treatment of social phobia. *Behaviour Research and Therapy*, 1981, *19*, 1–16.

Parker, G. Reported parental characteristics of agoraphobics and social phobics. *British Journal of Psychiatry*, 1979, *135*, 555–560.

Parker, G., Tupling, H., & Brown, L. B. A parental bonding instrument. *British Journal of Medical Psychology*, 1979, *52*, 1–11.

Paul, G. L. Behavior modification research: Design and tactics. In C. M. Franks (Ed.), *Behavior therapy: Design and tactics*. New York: McGraw Hill, 1969.

Pilkonis, P. A. Shyness, public and private, and its relationship to other measures of social behavior. *Journal of Personality*, 1977, *45*, 585–595. (a)

Pilkonis, P. A. The behavioral consequences of shyness. *Journal of Personality*, 1977, *45*, 596–611. (b)

Pilkonis, P. A., & Zimbardo, P. G. The personal and social dynamics of shyness. In C. E. Izard (Ed.), *Emotions in personality and psychopathology*. New York: Plenum Press, 1979.

Rachman, S. The passing of the two-stage theory of fear and avoidance: Fresh possibilities. *Behaviour Research and Therapy*, 1976, *14*, 125–131.

Rachman, S. J. Human fears: a three-system analysis. *Scandinavian Journal of Behavior Therapy*, 1978, *7*, 237–245 (cited by Hugdahl, 1981). (a)

Rachman, S. Perceived self-efficacy: Analyses of Bandura's theory of behavioral change. In H. J. Eysenck & S. Rachman, *Advances in behaviour research and therapy* (Vol. 1, Pt. 1). Elmsford Park, N.Y.: Pergamon, 1978. (b)

Rosenthal, T. L., & Reese, S. L. The effects of covert and overt modeling on assertive behavior. *Behaviour Research and Therapy*, 1976, *14*, 463–469.

Ross, L. The intuitive psychologist and his shortcomings: Distortions in the attribution process. *Advances in experimental social psychology*, 1977, *10*, 173–220.

Rothstein, W., Holmes, G. R., & Boblitt, W. E. A factor analysis of the Fear Survey Schedule with a psychiatric population. *Journal of Clinical Psychology*, 1972, *28*, 78–80.

Rubin, S. E., Lawlis, G. F., Tasto, D. L., & Namenek, T. Factor analysis of the 122-item Fear Survey Schedule. *Behaviour Research and Therapy*, 1969, *7*, 381–386.

Safran, J. D., Alden, L. E., & Davidson, P. O. Client anxiety level as a moderator variable in assertion training. *Cognitive Therapy and Research*, 1980, *4*, 189–200.

Sarason, I. G. The test-anxiety scale: Concept and research. In C. D. Spielberger & I. G. Sarason (Eds.), *Stress and anxiety*. Washington D.C.: Hemisphere, 1978.

Sattler, J. A. A theoretical development and clinical investigation of embarrassment. *Genetic Psychology Monographs*, 1965, *71*, 19–59.

Schachter, S. The interaction of cognitive and physiological determinants of emotional state. *Advances in Experimental Social Psychology*, 1964, *1*, 49–80.

Scheflen, A. E., & Scheflen, A. *Body language and the social order*. Englewood Cliffs, N.J.: Prentice-Hall, 1972.

Seligman, M. E. P. A learned helplessness point of view. In L. P. Rehm (Ed.), *Behaviour therapy for depression*. New York: Academic, 1981.

Shahar, A., & Merbaum, M. The interaction between subject characteristics and self-control procedures in the treatment of interpersonal anxiety. *Cognitive Therapy and Research*, 1981, *5*, 221–224.

Shaw, P. M. *The nature of social phobia*. Paper delivered to the Annual Conference of the British Psychological Society, York, April 1976.

Smith, R. E. Social anxiety as a moderator variable in the attitude similarity–attraction relationship. *Journal of Experimental Research in Personality,* 1972, *6,* 22–28.

Smith, R. E., & Sarason I. G. Social anxiety and the evaluation of negative interpersonal feedback. *Journal of Consulting and Clinical Psychology,* 1975, *43,* 429.

Snyder, M. On the self-perpetuating nature of social stereotypes. In D. L. Hamilton (Ed.), *Cognitive processes in stereotyping and inter-group behavior.* Hillsdale, N.J.: Erlbaum, 1980.

Spivack, G., Platt, J. J., & Shure, M. B. *The problem solving approach to adjustment.* San Francisco: Jossey-Bass, 1976.

Steffen, J. J., & Lucas, J. *Social strategies and expectations as components of social competence.* Unpublished manuscript, University of Cincinnati, 1981.

Steffen, J. J., & Redden, J. Assessment of social competence in an evaluation–interaction analogue. *Human Communication Research,* 1977, *4,* 30–37.

Storms, M. D. Videotape and the attribution process: Reversing actors' and observers' points of view. *Journal of Personality and Social Psychology,* 1973, *27,* 165–175.

Storms, M. D., & McCaul, K. D. Attribution processes and the emotional exacerbation of dysfunctional behavior. In J. H. Harvey, W. J. Ickes, and R. F. Kidd (Eds.), *New directions in attribution research* (Vol. 1). Hillsdale, N.J.: Erlbaum, 1976.

Sutton-Simon, K., & Goldfried, M. R. Faulty thinking patterns in two types of anxiety. *Cognitive Therapy and Research,* 1979, *3,* 193–203.

Sutton-Simon, K., & Goldfried, M. R. *A task analysis of cognitive processes in social anxiety.* Unpublished manuscript, Oberlin College, 1981.

Tajfel, H. The structure of our views about society. In H. Tajfel and C. Fraser (Eds.), *Introducing social psychology.* Harmondsworth, Middlesex: Penguin, 1978.

Thorpe, G. L. Densitization, behavior rehearsal, self-instructional training and placebo effects on assertive-refusal behavior. *European Journal of Behavioural Analysis and Modification,* 1975, *1,* 30–44.

Trower, P. Situational analysis of the components and processes of behavior of socially skilled and unskilled patients. *Journal of Consulting and Clinical Psychology,* 1980, *48,* 327–339.

Trower, P. E. Social skill disorder: Mechanisms of failure. In R. Gilmour and S. Duck (Eds.), *Personal relationships in disorder.* London: Academic Press, 1981.

Trower, P. Towards a generative model of social skills: A critique and synthesis. In J. Curran & P. Monti (Eds.), *Social skills training: A practical handbook for assessment and treatment.* New York: Guilford Press, 1982.

Trower, P. (Ed.), *Radical approaches to social skills training.* London: Croom Helm, 1984.

Trower, P. Social fit and misfit. An interactional account of social difficulty. In A. Furnham (Ed.), *Social behavior in context.* Boston: Allyn and Bacon, in press.

Trower, P., Bryant, B. M., & Argyle, M. *Social skills and mental health.* London: Methuen, 1978.

Trower, P., Yardley, K., Bryant, B. M., & Shaw, P. The treatment of social failure: A comparison of anxiety-reduction and skills-acquisition procedures on two social problems. *Behavior Modification,* 1978, *2,* 41–60.

Twentyman, C. T., & McFall, R. M. Behavioral training of social skills in shy males. *Journal of Consulting and Clinical Psychology,* 1975, *43,* 384–395.

Twentyman, C. T., and Zimering, R. T. Behavioral training of social skills: A critical review. In M. Hersen, R. M. Eisler, & P. M. Miller (Eds.), *Progress in behavior modification* (Vol 7). New York: Academic Press, 1979.

Walen, S. R., DiGuiseppe, R., & Wessler, R. L. *A practitioner's guide to rational-emotive therapy.* New York: Oxford University Press, 1980.

Wallace, C. J. The social training project of the mental health clinical research center for the study of schizophrenia. In J. P. Curran & P. M. Monti (Eds.), *Social skills training: A practical handbook for assessment and treatment.* New York: Guilford Press, 1982.

Watson, D. & Friend, R. Measurement of social-evaluative anxiety. *Journal of Consulting and Clinical Psychology,* 1969, *33,* 448–457.

Weiner, B. *Achievement, motivation and attribution theory.* Morristown, N.J.: General Learning Press, 1974.

Wessler, R. A., & Wessler, R. L. *The principles and practice of rational-emotive therapy.* San Francisco: Jossey-Bass, 1980.

Wilson, G. T., & O'Leary, K. D. *Principles of behavior therapy.* Englewood Cliffs, N.J.: Prentice-Hall, 1980.

Wolfe, J., & Fodor, I. Modifying assertive behavior in women: A comparison of three approaches. *Behavior Therapy,* 1977, *8,* 567–574.

Wolpe, J. *Psychotherapy by reciprocal inhibition.* Stanford, Cal.: Stanford University Press, 1958.

Wolpe, J., & Lang, P. J. A Fear Survey Schedule for use in behavior therapy. *Behaviour Research and Therapy,* 1964, *2,* 27–30.

Zimbardo, P. G., Pilkonis, P. A., & Norwood, R. M. The silent prison of shyness. Office of Naval Research, Technical Report No. Z-17. Stanford, Calif.: Stanford University, November, 1974.

9

School Phobia

THOMAS H. OLLENDICK and JONI A. MAYER

The purpose of this chapter is to examine the current status of school phobia from a learning-based perspective. In pursuing this goal, issues related to diagnosis, incidence, etiology, assessment, treatment, and prevention will be addressed. Quite obviously, a chapter such as this cannot claim to provide an index to all of the literature or issues in this area. Rather, our objective has been to present an overview of major considerations, trends, and points of view that lead to an awareness of the complexity of school phobia and that suggest new and meaningful research directions.

Prior to examining school phobia *per se,* distinction must be made between those mild fears and anxieties of childhood which are "normal" and those fears and phobias which are excessive and maladaptive (Ollendick, 1979a). As has been affirmed by a number of researchers, it is quite common for children to display a surprisingly large number of mild fears and anxieties (e.g., Hagman, 1932; Jersild & Holmes, 1935; Lapouse & Monk, 1959; MacFarlane, Allen, & Honzik, 1954; Miller, Barrett, Hampe, & Noble, 1973a; Zeligs, 1939). Jersild and Holmes (1935), for example, reported that the average child exhibits 4.6 fears while Lapouse and Monk (1959) indicated that 43% of all children evince 7 or more fears. The incidence of these mild childhood fears is not necessary reason for alarm, however; in fact, several authors have commented upon the developmental importance and the later adaptive value which these fears serve (e.g., Bauer, 1980; Graziano, DeGiovanni, & Garcia, 1979; Miller, Barrett, & Hampe, 1974).

THOMAS H. OLLENDICK and JONI A. MAYER ● Department of Psychology, Virginia Polytechnic Institute and State University, Blacksburg, Virginia 24060.

Excessive fears and phobias in children, on the other hand, are more problematic, are frequently related to other "emotional" problems, and are oftentimes associated with maladaptive behavior in adulthood. The following characteristics proposed originally by Marks (1969) and elaborated upon by Miller
et al. (1974) typify excessive fears and phobias in children: (1) they are out of
proportion to demands of the situation, (2) they cannot be explained or reasoned away, (3) they are beyond voluntary control, (4) they lead to avoidance
of the feared situation, (5) they persist over an extended period of time, (6)
they are unadaptive, and (7) they are not age- or stage-specific. Thus, whereas
mild fears and anxieties may be adaptive and appropriate, excessive fears and
phobias are unrealistic, inappropriate, and persistent. Since they are not age-
or stage-specific and are extended in duration, they can be distinguished more
readily from common, transitory childhood fears.

The primary concern in this chapter will be with school phobia: a fear of
school which is unrealistic, inappropriate, and persistent. This unwarranted
fear leads to an avoidance of the school situation and to subsequent refusal to
voluntarily attend school. Although this definition of school phobia appears
straightforward, we shall see shortly that several theoretical and practical
issues are raised by it. Toward resolution of these issues, the next section will
explore diagnostic problems while subsequent sections will address broader
issues related to incidence, etiology, assessment, treatment, and prevention of
school phobia.

DIAGNOSTIC ISSUES

The term *school phobia* was first used in the professional literature by
Johnson and her co-workers in 1941 (Johnson, Falstein, Szurek, & Svendsen,
1941). Quite obviously, children who experienced anxiety or fear about attending school were known to professionals prior to this time. In fact, even before
mandatory education became prominent, Shakespeare wrote of "the whining
schoolboy with his satchel and shining morning face creeping like a snail
unwillingly to school" (*As You Like It,* Act II). More recently, but also prior
to 1941, Broadwin described a form of "truancy" in which the

> reason for the truancy is incomprehensible to the parents and the school. The child
> may say that it is afraid to go to school, afraid of the teacher, or say that it does
> not know why it will not go to school. When at home, it is happy and apparently
> carefree. When dragged to school, it is miserable, fearful, and at the first oppor-
> tunity runs home despite the certainty of corporal punishment. (Broadwin, 1932,
> p. 254)

In 1939, Partridge labeled this reluctance to go to school "psychoneurotic
truancy" and described it as a form of the "mother-following syndrome."
Finally, in their classic paper, Johnson *et al.* (1941) called more direct atten-

tion to mutual anxiety between mother and child resulting from "poorly resolved early dependency."

These early accounts of school phobia were psychodynamically based, positing that the child suffered from "deep-seated neuroses of the obsessional type." School-phobic children were said to be obsessed by thoughts of harm or death to their mother. Only by returning home from school could the child be assured that no tragedy had befallen mother and that she was all right. From this perspective, school phobia was viewed as a form of clinical anxiety, precipitated by fear of leaving home rather than fear of school *per se.* In fact, Johnson and her co-workers (Estes, Haylett, & Johnson, 1956) later coined the term *separation anxiety* to provide a diagnostic label that more accurately reflected the locus of pathology from their psychodynamic perspective. The child's fear of school was said to mask what was in large part the child's anxiety about leaving mother, as well as mother's anxieties about separating from the child.

This early work is of more than historical importance. Given these developments, early attention centered upon examination of parent–child relationships and their subsequent impact on school phobia. As a result, considerable definitional and diagnostic problems became evident. Is the child's "phobia" due to separation anxiety from mother or to a real fear of some aspect of the school situation? Is the child afraid to leave home *or* to go to school? Or both? The resolution of these issues is of extreme importance because of the need to determine whether treatment should be directed primarily toward returning the child to school, to resolving parent–child relationships in the home, or both (Yates, 1970).

Unfortunately, school phobia is not a unitary syndrome. Historically, and even into the present, it is a term used to denote both anxiety about separation from mother (e.g., Gittelman-Klein & Klein, 1980; Waller & Eisenberg, 1980) and/or excessive fear about attending school (e.g., Berg, Nichols, & Pritchard, 1969; Yule, Hersov, & Treseder, 1980). In general, lines seem to be drawn round philosophical and theoretical leanings, with psychodynamically oriented clinicians preferring a separation-anxiety hypothesis and behaviorally oriented clinicians favoring a fear-of-school hypothesis. Of course, lines ar not clearly drawn and the actual state of affairs may well fall somewhere between the "turfs" of these two camps. It is evident to the present authors that a child may repeatedly fail to attend school for any number of reasons, including fear of separation from mother and fear of some aspect of the school situation itself. Quite simply, the etiology of school phobia varies from child to child; heterogeneity, rather than homogeneity, prevails. Children evince school phobia for a variety of reasons.

This conclusion is amply borne out by an early study by Hersov (1960), a review of the literature, and our own clinical experience. In a study of 50 cases of school phobia seen in the Children's Department of the Maudsley Hospital, Hersov (1960) reported that the most common precipitating factor was a change to a new school, followed by the death, departure, or illness of a parent (usually the mother), and then by an illness, accident, or operation which led to the child's spending a period of time in the hospital or at home. The children in this study provided personal, firsthand accounts of the school refusal, including fear of a sarcastic teacher, fear of ridicule, bullying, or harm from other children, fear of academic failure, and fear of harm befalling mother while the child was at school. In addition, fears about menstruation in girls and concerns about puberty and masturbation in boys were evident.

Our review of the literature affirms Hersov's findings and further elaborates upon them. Illnesses and operations, including bronchial infections, appendectomies, and tooth infections, are oftentimes cited as precipitating events. Mother's beginning work, her hospitalization, or her departure are also cited as are more specific fears such as fear of entering a new school, fear of vomiting, fear of interpersonal interaction, or fear of undressing for showers. Clearly, a variety of precipitating events may lead to school phobia and have been well documented in the literature. Our clinical experience is consistent with these more empirical findings. Over the past 11 years, we have worked with a total of 37 school-phobic children; of these cases, 13 were judged as primarily due to "separation" problems (as defined above), 15 appeared to be related to fears of specific aspects of the school situation (i.e., new school, failure, examinations, showers, teachers), and the remaining 9 occurred following absence from schol due to illnesses and associated anticipatory anxiety about returning to school. Further, several of these cases shared elements of these three primary categories; for example, it was not uncommon for a child to express fear of mother's health and a fear of entering a new school (or grade) following relocation. Although we were generally able to sort out primary from secondary precipitants, this was by no means a straightforward or an easy task.

Although children evidence school phobia for a variety of reasons, it is necessary to develop an agreed-upon set of criteria for diagnostic and treatment purposes. Again, such criteria do not currently exist. Definitions vary from the vague "deep-seated neurosis of an obsessional type" originally proposed by Johnson *et al.* (1941) to the rather narrow operant definition of "zero or low probability of school attendance" proposed by Ayllon, Smith, and Rogers (1970). For our own clinical and research purposes, we recommend the guidelines set forth by Berg *et al.* (1969):

1. Severe difficulty attending school often resulting in prolonged absence;
2. Severe emotional upset including excessive fearfulness, temper outbursts, or complaints of feeling ill when faced with the prospect of going to school;
3. Staying at home with knowledge of the parent when the youngster should be at school; and
4. Absence of antisocial characteristics such as stealing, lying, and destructiveness.

It is important to note that these criteria maintain the distinction between school truancy, which is often associated with conduct disorders, and school phobia, which is frequently associated wth anxiety disorders (Ollendick & Hersen, 1983; Quay & Werry, 1979), a distinction first offered by Broadwin (1932) and Partridge (1939). Further, the criteria call for evidence of prolonged absence, excessive fearfulness, somatic complaints, and adamant refusal to attend school—all characteristics which are commonly observed in school-phobic children. What is equally important, the criteria do not prejudge etiology; rather, they allow for a multiplicity of causal patterns. In our own work, we have elaborated upon these criteria by operationalizing prolonged absence as at least two weeks in duration and by employing self-report, other-report, and behavioral indices of fear. It is this expanded definition and set of criteria that will be used in the present chapter.

In addition to these primary features which characterize all school-phobic children, several authors have described associated features which may help to delineate various subtypes of school phobia. Coolidge, Hahn, and Peck (1957) first offered a distinction between two basic subtypes of school phobia: neurotic and characterological. This distinction, repeated by these same investigators (Waldfogel, Coolidge, & Hahn, 1957), was later adopted by other workers (e.g., Baker & Willis, 1978; Kahn & Nursten, 1962; Kennedy, 1965, 1971). In essence, it discriminates between what has come to be known as Type I and Type II school phobias. Type I, or the neurotic variety, is characterized by the following features (Kennedy, 1965): (1) the present episode is the first; (2) Monday onset, following an illness the previous Thursday or Friday; (3) an acute onset; (4) more prevalent in early elementary grades; (5) concern about death; (6) mother's physical health in question—or at least child fears so; (7) generally good communication between parents; (8) mother and father well adjusted; (9) father involved in household management and child-rearing; and (10) parents easy to work with and have basic understanding of what child is experiencing. In contrast, Type II or characterological phobia, is characterized by an obverse pattern: gradual, insidious onset in an older child in whom death themes are not present and whose parents are considerably more difficult to work with, showing little insight into the child's behavior. As is apparent from characteristics of both Type I and Type II school phobia, emphasis is placed upon "neuroticism" in the child and faulty "parenting" as general characteristics. In contrast, Hersov (1960) has identified a different set of subtypes based on "family relationships." In this schema, three subtypes are delineated: Type I—mother is overindulgent, father is passive, and child is demanding at home but passive in school; Type II—mother is overcontrolling, father is passive, and child is obedient at home but timid in school; and Type III—mother is overindulgent, father is firm, and the child is wilful at school but friendly at home. In a similar vein, Weiss and Cain (1964) identified two basic subtypes: the overdependent child with a rejecting mother. Although differences exist among these systems of classification, it appears that the neurotic type of Coolidge *et al.* (1957) is conceptually similar to Kennedy's (1965) Type I, Hersov's (1960) Type I and Type II, and Weiss and Cain's (1964) Type I. Similarly, the characterological type of Coolidge *et al.* is like Kennedy's Type II, Hersov's Type III, and Weiss and Cain's Type II. The primary distinction resides in whether the proposed systems are dealing with basic personality characteristics of the child (Coolidge *et al.*, 1957; Kennedy, 1965), or with the constellation of family relationships (Hersov, 1960; Weiss & Cain, 1964).

Although these subtypes have been reported frequently in the literature, there are little or no data available regarding their reliability, validity, or clinical utility. For example, while Kennedy (1965) found the distinction between Type I and Type II school phobia to be differentially predictive of child-parent characteristics and treatment outcome, Berg *et al.* (1969) failed to support such distinctions. Further, in a comparison between school-phobic children and their parents on the one hand and a matched group of nonphobic but neurotic youngsters and their parents on the other, Waldron (1976) reported that although children who were phobic differed on certain dimensions (e.g., more dependent and inhibited) parents of the two groups of children did not. Thus, differential parent characteristics were not substantiated, casting doubt on the validity of delineating subtypes on the basis of parental characteristics alone. Clearly, more research is required before the reliability and validity of "subtyping" can be established and before such conceptual distinctions can be meaningfully used in clinical practice. Certainly, our own experience would suggest that these children and their parents do not present themselves as neat and packaged "subtypes." Nonetheless, continued research in this direction is warranted. It may well be the case that subtyping based on primary etiology (e.g., separation anxiety, school situations, absence following illness) and/or on the topographic characteristics of the phobia (e.g., frequency, intensity, and duration) will be more fruitful. Obviously, this awaits further investigation.

In summary, this extended overview of definitional and diagnostic issues was undertaken because of the considerable confusion and lack of clarity that surrounds the construct *school phobia*. It is hoped that we have clarified some of the relevant issues. For purposes of the remainder of this chapter, criteria set forth by Berg *et al.* (1969) and expanded upon by us will be used to designate school phobia. While we shall occasionally make reference to different "types" of school phobia, the reader should keep in mind the limitations inherent in these classifications.

INCIDENCE

The incidence of school phobia depends to a large extent on the explicit criteria used to define it. As noted earlier, it is quite common for children to evidence a surprisingly large number of fears, including an initial fear of attending school and separating from one's parents. In fact, as recently restated by Bauer (1980) and Gittelman-Klein and Klein (1980), the distress experienced by a child when separated from the person who cares for him or her is a normal developmental phenomenon. For most children, this fear of separation occurs after the age of 6–8 months and persists, in varying degrees, until the child is 2 or 3 years of age. Generally, this fear subsides as the child develops the cognitive properties to "grasp" the meaning of mother's absence and as the child is gradually exposed to increasingly longer periods of separation (i.e., from a few minutes to a few hours). Similarly, it is a normal developmental phenomenon for the child to be fearful of imaginary creatures, being alone, and strange places (Ollendick, 1979a). For many children, school is a strange place—large, awesome, and foreboding—inhabited by imaginary creatures and characterized by "unknown" dimensions. As with fear of separation, this fear generally diminishes as the child becomes cognitively able to assimilate what was unknown and strange and as he or she becomes gradually desensitized to feared aspects of the school situation. Clearly, such initial fears are mild and not at all uncommon for a majority of children.

However, when these fears persist and develop into phobic proportion, they are no longer a part of normal social development. By utilizing the criteria of Berg *et al.* (1969), it can be seen that school phobia is a more extensive, persistent, and maladaptive fear than that indicated above. Judged according to these criteria, the incidence of school phobia is generally considered small but nonetheless highly significant. Kennedy (1965) has estimated the incidence of school phobia to be 1.7% of school-aged children while Kahn and Nursten (1962) estimated it to be between 5% and 8%. However, the accuracy of these estimates is unknown due to unclear or nonexacting definitions of school phobia. In a recent survey conducted by us in southwestern Virginia, we were able to document an incidence rate of only .4% in school-aged children, using the criteria of Berg *et al.* (1969). Nonetheless, Eisenberg (1958) has reported that children with school phobia are being referred for psychiatric services with increasing frequency. In a survey of admissions to his clinic, the incidence was noted to have risen from 3 cases per 1,000 to 17 cases per 1,000 over an 8-year period. These rates appear to be supported by other workers who have reported that the incidence rate of school phobia for psychiatrically referred youngsters has increased and ranges from about 1% (Chazan, 1962) to 3.8% (Smith, 1970).

Even though school phobia does not occur frequently in the general population and accounts for only 1% to 4% of psychiatric referrals, its clinical significance is affirmed by its frequent representation in the professional literature. In this regard, Graziano and DeGiovanni (1979) recently reviewed all behavioral studies on *all* childhood fears published since 1924. Somewhat surprisingly, they found that 86% of behavioral case studies published since 1924 addressed school phobia. Clearly, school phobia is of clinical interest. Part of this interest may well be related to its potential relationship to agoraphobia and other adulthood fears (e.g., Berg, 1976; Berg, Marks, McGuire, & Lipsedge, 1974; Hallam, 1978).

While boys outnumber girls for most types of child behavior disorders (Ollendick & Hersen, 1983; Quay & Werry, 1979; Ross, 1980), school phobia tends to be equally common in both sexes (e.g., Berg *et al.,* 1969; Johnson, 1979; Kennedy, 1965). As noted earlier, the phobia most often originates during the elementary school years and has an acute onset. Occasionally, however, it does occur during the secondary years; if so, it is typically accompanied by associated difficulties centering around family conflict and, possibly, truancy. Further, one report (Hodgman & Braiman, 1965) has described "college phobia," which was suggested to account for early college dropout and to be conceptually related to childhood school phobia. Generally, however, school phobia is thought to occur most frequently between 5–6 and 10–11 years of age and to be more of a problem with children of this age group than of any other.

Finally, while it might be expected that school phobia would appear more often in children of lower intellectual ability or those who show "learning disabilities," this has not been found to be so. In fact, children of high, intermediate, and low intelligence have been found to be equally represented, although any one study may report disproportionate frequencies. Similarly, so-called "learning-disabled" children are not disproportionately represented. As noted by Davids (1973), "it is not the child who is destined to school failure who seems to acquire school phobia, but rather the child who is sufficiently intelligent to do good work but who is unable to do so because of the unbearable anxiety engendered by the school setting" (p. 139).

In sum, school phobia occurs in a small proportion of the general population; yet it is disproportionately represented in psychiatric referrals for fear-related difficulties. In addition to its immediate detrimental effects on the child and his/her environment, it may well possess long-term consequences associated with adult phobic behavior. It appears to occur primarily in younger children and to be evident in both boys and girls. Children of varying levels of intelligence and diverse levels of academic achievement are equally represented.

ETIOLOGICAL CONSIDERATIONS

As stated from the onset, our primary concern here will be with the development and maintenance of school-phobic behavior from a learning-based perspective. While a variety of other accounts have been put forth, it is beyond the intent or scope of this chapter to review them. Several authors have commented upon these alternate theories and have contrasted them with the behavioral approach (e.g., Franks & Susskind, 1968; Miller *et al.,* 1974; Rachman & Costello, 1961; Yates, 1970). Suffice it to say that one of the most prevalent theories, in addition to the behavioral one, is the psychodynamic theory. Prior to the 1960s and even up to the present time, this theory and its formulation of school phobia have attracted several followers. Basically, psychoanalytic theory suggests that school phobia is the result of an unresolved mother–child dependency relationship which leads to anxiety in both child and mother when separation is imminent. This heightened anxiety occurs becausd the child is basically "disturbed" and lives in a family characterized by "disturbed" relationships. As we noted earlier, Johnson and her co-workers (Johnson *et al.,* 1941; Waldfogel *et al.,* 1956) proposed that school phobia was due to "deep-seated neurosis of the obsessional type" and that fear of school represented a form of "displacement" of anxiety from its real source (separation from mother) to a source more palatable to the child (the school). Further, from this perspective, the mother of the school-phobic child was thought to "unconsciously" support the child's fear by strongly sympathizing with complaints about school. The mother herself was thought to view school as an impersonal and unpleasant place, and indirectly communicated the message that she wished the child to remain at home with her. From this perspective, school phobia was, and continues to be, viewed as a clinical variant of separation anxiety.

In addition to psychoanalytic theory, learning-based theories have been used with increasing frequency in the description of the genesis and maintenance of school phobia. In general, the specific principles of operant, classical, and vicarious conditioning have been employed (Miller *et al.,* 1974; Ollendick, 1979a; Rachman, 1968). Such principles have been used to account for problems in separation as well as specific fears about the school situation itself. In fact, in his early review of etiology from a behavioral perspective, Yates (1970) acknowledged the potential importance of separation anxiety in determining school phobia. He viewed anxiety about mother–child relationships as one of many factors likely to contribute to school phobia, stating, "the genesis of a school phobia may be complexly determined by one or more of the following factors: separation anxiety leading to overdependence on the home as a safe refuge; insufficient rewards or actual anxiety-arousing experiences at school; and possibly, of course, actual traumatic events at school" (Yates, 1970, p. 152). The value of Yates' position resides in its attention to, and admission of, a variety of precipitating factors—a position compatible with our earlier comments on the diversity and complexity of the clinical variants of school phobia.

In explicating the utility of learning theory based on operant principles, Yates (1970) aptly illustrated how a child might learn to fear separation from his or her parents. During a child's preschool years, parents (especially the mother) serve as strongly reinforcing stimuli, meeting many of the child's needs as well as providing safe refuge to which the child can turn when uncertain or afraid. When separated from parents at this earlier age, he may well experience fear, which leads in turn, to intrumental acts (i.e., operants) that return the child to the parent. Insofar as the child is reassured, comforted, or in some way reinforced following return to the parent, he learns to repeat this behavior when confronted with fear or anxiety in the future. Most children "grow out of" this pattern as they learn that rewards are encountered from other sources (e.g., peers, constructive activities, etc.) and that they are safe even when not accompanied by mother. For some children, however, anxiety may become even more strongly linked to separation situations. In certain cases, this may be due to the lack of exposure to more rewarding situations (e.g., being exposed to peers); while in others, it can be generated and reinforced by a parent who may be overly concerned about the child's safety when away from home (e.g., continually "checking" to see how the child is doing and warning the child to be careful and not to get lost). Thus, from an operant perspective, a child may learn to fear separation from mother in a rather straightforward way. Further, it does not become necessary to view a school-phobic child as possessing a deep-seated neurosis or, for that matter, to impugn unconscious processes on the part of the child's mother. Like other behaviors, fear of separation can be learned and maintained through powerful reinforcers that are associated with it.

Even if separation anxiety is not a contributing factor to the etiology of school phobia, operant principles may still be useful in understanding the development and maintenance of school phobia. For example, some children may make negative statements about school, complain about how bad they are made to feel in school, and subsequently opt to stay home. Parents and significant others in the child's environment may inadvertently reinforce such statements and behaviors, contributing to the child's resolve not to return to school. In such circumstances, the child probably does not possess an excessive "fear" of school; rather, he or she has probably found it simply more reinforcing at home (parental attention and affection) than at school (perceived criticism, failure, etc.). Of course, the child's reluctance to go to school may be genuine and reflect what the child perceives as a punishing environment. That is, the child who is continuously subject to ridicule and criticism from peers or teachers may have legitimate cause for avoiding school. Oftentimes, however, such complaints are exaggerated. In such cases, the child learns that parents are sensitive to such complaints and that they respond with much attention and preoccupation. A little "fear" leads to intense and frequent responses from significant others. The more fear and avoidance behavior the child reports, the more attention he or she receives. Several published studies support the development and maintenance of school phobic behavior along the lines suggested by this operant analysis (e.g., Ayllon *et al.,* 1970; Hersen, 1970, 1971).

In addition to operant principles, classical conditioning and vicarious conditioning principles have also been frequently invoked to account for the development of school phobia. Some children indeed may become school phobic following actual traumatic events at school, while others may become phobic—in the absence of actual traumatic events—by observing other children's phobic behavior and its consequences for them. Illustrations of school-phobic behavior acquired through these principles can be found in reviews by Johnson (1979), Jones and Kazdin (1981), and Miller *et al.* (1974).

In a more general view, Rachman (1968, p. 31) has outlined the various conditioning principles involved in the acquisition and maintenance of phobic behavior:

1. Phobias are learned responses.
2. Stimuli develop phobic qualities when they are associated temporally and spatially with a fear-producing state of affairs.
3. Neutral stimuli which are of relevance in the fear-producing situation and/or make an impact on the person in the situation are more likely to develop phobic qualities than weak or irrelevant stimuli.
4. Repetition of the association between the fear situation and the new phobic stimuli will strengthen the phobia.
5. Association between high-intensity fear situations and neutral stimuli are more likely to produce phobic reactions.
6. Generalization from the original phobic stimulus to stimuli of a similar nature will occur.
7. Noxious experiences which occur under conditions of excessive confinement are more likely to produce phobic reactions.
8. Neutral stimuli which are associated with a noxious experience may develop (secondary) motivating properties. This acquired drive is termed the fear drive.
9. Responses (such as avoidance) which reduce the fear drive are reinforced.
10. Phobic reactions can be acquired vicariously.

Although fears and phobias may be learned according to the specific principles of classical, vicarious, and operant conditioning as suggested by Rachman (1968) and others, they are probably maintained by a complex, interactive process that involves each of the principles (Ollendick, 1979a; Ollendick & Ollendick, 1982). Once a fear like school phobia is learned, it might be maintained if the child suffers periodic traumatic events (classical conditioning), observes another child's phobic behavior (vicarious conditioning), and/or receives an inordinate amount of attention for the phobic behaviors (operant conditioning). Of course, it is possible that the phobia was acquired from multiple sources of conditioning as well. The important conlusion to be drawn here is that school phobia may be acquired and maintained through an interactive combination of conditioning processes.

In summary, the etiology of school phobia is complex. It may well involve elements of separation anxiety as well as intense fear of the school situation. Although the psychoanalytic orientation postulates deep-seated and unconscious processes as causative, the behavioral model suggests the influence of classical, vicarious, and operant conditioning processes. Such processes are frequently intertwined; sorting out relevant contributing factors is not an easy task. Nonetheless, the behavioral model essentially suggests that school phobia is learned and that it is responsive to treatments derived from the learning model. Such treatments will be examined in a later section.

ASSESSMENT ISSUES

It is evident from our earlier discussion that school phobia is not a unitary syndrome. It may result from a variety of causes and may be "explained" by a variety of theoretical accounts. The factors which are considered relevant to a thorough assessment of school-phobic behavior vary according to one's theoretical persuasion. The psychodynamic orientation relies primarily upon objective and projective personality tests to determine the underlying traits or unconscious motives which contribute to the development and maintenance of school phobic behavior. The behavioral orientation, on the other hand, relies less on personality tests and more on direct observation of the child in the home and school setting (or contrived settings which simulate these natural settings). Mischel (1973) has most succinctly summarized the difference between these two approaches: "The focus shifts from describing situation-free people with broad trait adjectives to analyzing the specific interactions between conditions and the cognitions and behaviors of interest" (p. 265). In effect, behavioral assessment attempts to understand and predict antecedent and consequent conditions under which phobic behavior occurs. Although underlying asumptions and assessment practices clearly differ, psychodynamic and behavioral perspectives share common features. For example, both rely to some extent on information obtained from interviews with the child and his or her parents to supplement data obtained from personality tests or direct observations. Further, they both frequently use self-report and observational rating forms completed by the child and the child's parents, teachers, or significant others. Finally, they both place emphasis on the child's return to school as the primary criterion of successful intervention (e.g., Ayllon *et al.* 1970; Eisenberg, 1958). As note by the psychodynamically oriented Eisenberg (1958), it is

> essential that the paralyzing force of the school phobia on the child's whole life be recognized. The *symptom* itself serves to isolate him from normal experience and makes further psychological growth almost impossible. If we do no more than check this central *symptom*, we have nonetheless done a great deal. (p. 718, emphasis added)

While behaviorally oriented clinicians might disagree with Eisenberg's labeling of school phobia as a *symptom* (an overt expression of some underlying conflict), they would hardly disagree with his conclusion. Clearly, from both perspectives, return to school is primary and assessment of school attendance is critical.

In the sections that follow, we shall examine assessment of the school-phobic child from a behavioral perspective, according to three specific strategies: the behavioral interview, self-report and other report rating forms, and behavioral observation procedures. Although physiological assessment has been used frequently in the measurement of anxiety and fear in adult populations, it has been used less freqently with fearful and phobic children, and not at all with school-phobic children. Accordingly use of this measure will not be reviewed here. The utility of physiological measurements for assessment and treatment of school phobia awaits additional research.

The Behavioral Interview

In general, the behavioral interview has two primary functons: to establish a positive relationship between the child and the clinician, and to obtain specific information about the phobic behavior and its antecedent and consequent conditions. As noted by Truax and Carkhuff (1967) and affirmed by Lazarus (1971), the development of a positive relationship helps to increase the likelihood of the child and his/her family willingly and candidly sharing their problems so that accurate information can be obtained. Basic helping skills, including empathy, warmth, and genuineness, appear to facilitate rapport and to make the interview less threatening.

In working with children and their families, special problms may arise during the interview because of the child's limited verbal abilities (especially younger children), frequent fear of strangers (i.e., "doctors"), and embarrassment about "the problem." Oftentimes parents, as well as clinicians, ignore, or at least fail to attend to, the child's own observations. Statements like "he's too young to know what's really going on" and "let's not discuss it in front of her, it will probably only make matters worse" unnecessarily prevail. In our own practice, we routinely interview the child (regardless of age) *prior* to requesting parents and teachers to complete rating forms, or prior to observing the child in the home or school setting. We use this procedure for ethical reasons and to obtain the explicit cooperation of the child. Although iatrogenic effects occasionally occur as a result of this practice, we prefer to address such problems as they develop rather than jeopardize cooperation of the child and family (see Ollendick & Cerny, 1981, for a fuller discussion of this issue).

When interviewing young children, it is frequently necessary to simplify questions and to make them concrete and specific. Such a strategy requires skill and patience; skill in using words the child will understand and patience in clarifying and restating questions until they are understood. In those cases where the child is seemingly unable to describe the fear-producing events, instructing the child to image what "goes on" when he or she is afraid may be helpful. Such a procedure was used by Smith and Sharpe (1970) in their assessment of a school-phobic child. The child was asked to image in minute detail a school day, from the time he wakes up to his return home from school.

He was assisted in this process by specific questions about concrete events, such as what he was wearing, whom he was with, and where he was. During this process he was carefully observed for behavioral indices of fear: flushing of the skin, increased body movements, vocal tremors, and crying. Based on this process, it was surmised that certain school classes produced greatest anxiety. In particular, the child apparently was afraid of being called on in these classes and being made fun of by his teacher and peers. This procedure was also helpful in ruling out separation from mother as a source of intense anxiety; visualizing leaving mother evoked no indices of anxiety, a finding later confirmed by parents and by direct observation.

During the interview, verbal and nonverbal behaviors of the family members are observed and used to formulate a description of the context in which the school phobia occurs. In addition, parent-report, sibling-report (when siblings are included in the interview), and self-report data are gathered. Such information generally contains firsthand observations about antecedent and consequent conditions, and is oftentimes useful in determining the presence of separation anxiety. During the interview, an opportunity is also provided to assess resources within the family which might be invoked to assist in treatment programming. In general, a detailed interview should provide information about the topographic characteristics (duration, intensity, frequency) of the phobic behavior, the sociocultural-familial context in which it occurs, and the family resources available to deal with it. This information should be viewed as tentative, however, and used primarily to formulate hypotheses about the etiology of the school avoidance behavior and to suggest additional assessment methods (e.g., rating scales, school observations, or more standardized testing like intellectual or achievement assessment). The clinical interview is the beginning phase of the assessment process.

As with other assessment strategies, clinical interviews have their share of problems related to reliability and validity (Linehan, 1977; Morganstern, 1976). Quite obviously, full treatment of these issues is beyond the scope of this chapter. Two precautions are necessary, however. *First,* several authors have noted that retrospective recollections by parent or child may be distorted (e.g., Chess, Thomas, & Birch, 1966; Yarrow, Campbell, & Burton, 1970; Evans & Nelson, 1977), and may be lacking in reliability and validity. For example, Yarrow *et al.* (1970) advised that

> investigators intending to obtain subjective recall of years ago—or only yesterday—would do well to reflect on the perspectives of their informants. Many of the respondents... have been indoctrinated in theories of development and behavior. The interviewer knows what is believed to be "good" in behavior and what are accepted as antecedents and consequences in behavior relations. This knowledge can enter into his observing, retaining and reporting on behaviors. (p. 72)

In a similar vein, as Chess *et al.* (1966) indicated, parents may inaccurately recall that certain behavior problems emerged at times which coincided with those predicted by popular theories. These observations have direct bearing on the utility of information obtained during the interview. If, for example, parents "know" that school phobia is supposed to be related to a specific event in school or to separation/dependency issues, they might well "recall" events in support of such hypotheses. Clearly, interview data are in need of consensual and empirical verification.

A second precaution regarding interview data relates to the specificity of the information requested. While the reliability and validity of general information is suspect (as indicated above), recent evidence suggests that parents and children can be dependable and accurate reporters of current and specific information about problematic behaviors (e.g., Graham & Rutter, 1968; Herjanic, Herjanic, Brown, & Wheatt, 1975; Rutter & Graham, 1968). Thus, specification of precise behaviors that are occurring, and the conditions under which they are occurring, are likely to be more reliable and valid than general description or recollections of earlier events.

In sum, the behavioral interview is viewed as an important and nesessary first step in the assessment process. Although problems exist with the reliability and validity of the information obtained, such problems can be partially offset by fostering a positive relationship with the child and his or her parents and by focusing the interview on specific, current events. When conducted along these lines, the interview can be useful in developing a positive, therapeutic relationship and specifying antecedent and consequent conditions under which school phobic behavior occurs.

Rating Forms

In general, two types of rating instruments have been used to assess fear and anxiety in children: (1) self-report of attitudes, feelings, and behaviors; and (2) other-report of ongoing behavior. Although both types of ratings have distinct limitations, self-report instruments provide specific information about felt or perceived fear from the child's perspective while other-report forms provide valuable supplemental information from those persons in the child's milieu. Since young children are unable to understand and complete complex rating forms, other-reports may be the primary source of information in these cases. As we have noted elsewhere (Ollendick & Ollendick, 1982), an advantage of both forms is that they allow a comparison of the individual child to group norms. Such norms provide information about the level and degree of fear in the average child at various ages, and allow the clinician to determine the severity of the phobic behavior. Another advantage of these forms is related to their utility as outcome measures of treatment efficacy. These questionnaires can be administered prior to intervention, postintervention, and at designated follow-up intervals to assess both specific and generalized change. A further potential advantage of these forms is that future research might determine that response to specific treatments (e.g., systematic desensitization, self-instructional training, positive reinforcement) is related to "types" of children as described on these scales (Ciminero & Drabman,1977; Ollendick & Cerny, 1981). This latter function, though largely unexplored at this time, is an especially important function in the search for the "best" treatment.

A variety of self-report measures of anxiety and fear have been used with children and adults (e.g., Barrios, Hartmann, & Shigetomi, 1981; Lick & Katkin, 1976; Ollendick, 1979a). The most frequently used self-report scales for children are the Children's Manifest Anxiety Scale (Castaneda, McCandless, & Palermo, 1956), the State-Trait Anxiety Inventory for Children (Spielberger, 1973), the Fear Survey Schedule for Children (Scherer & Nakamura, 1968), and the Children's Fear Survey Schedule recently developed by Ryall and Dietiker (1979). The two anxiety scales are primarily useful in identifying overall levels of anxiety, while the two fear survey schedules are instrumental in determining specific fear stimuli as well as providing an index of overall "fearfulness." We shall limit our discussion here to fear schedules.

Surprisingly, we were able to find *no* published studies which included use of self-report measures of fear for school-phobic children. This was surprising since these scales appear to possess reasonably good reliability and validity and provide substantive information about the intensity and extensity of the child's fear behavior. The absence of these scales may well be related to prevailing notions which suggest that the child "really doesn't know what he or she is afraid of" and the predilection of behaviorally oriented clinicians to limit data collection to behavioral observations alone. If so, we suggest that both of these notions are unnecessarily delimiting.

In the interest of conveying the potential utility of such instruments, we recently completed an analysis of responses from school-phobic children to a modified form of Scherer and Nakamura's Fear Survey Schedule for Children. In the original scale, devised for 9- to 12-year-old children, the child was instructed to rate his or her fear level on each of 80 items according to a five-point scale. We have adapted this scale for younger children by reducing the complexity of the response format to a three-point scale and by using the word "frightens" in the instructions (Ollendick, 1978). Thus, children are asked to indicate whether a specific item (e.g., having to go to school, getting sick at school, being punished by mother, snakes, and sharp objects) frightens them "none at all, " "a little bit, " or "a lot." Although this variant of the scale is still in its experimental form, initial results indicate acceptable test–retest reliability, internal consistency, and construct validity. In a retrospective analysis of 25 school-phobic children seen over the past 10 years (fear schedules were not available for 12 of the 37 children, see "Diagnostic Issues," pp. 370–371 for a description of these children), we found that their mean level of fear was significantly greater than that of non-school-phobic children matched for sex, age, IQ, and socioeconomic status. In addition, specific fear items differentiated phobic from nonphobic children. Perhaps of even greater interest, specific fear items differentiated phobic youngsters whose etiology appeared to be related to separation anxiety (e.g., ghosts, death, getting lost, my parents criticizing me, having my parents argue, being alone, closed places, and dark places) from those whose etiology appeared to be due to specific aspects of school or recent illness (e.g., taking a test, sharp objects, having to go to the hospital, having to go to school, being teased, and making mistakes). The two subgroups did not differ on overall level of self-reported fear, however. Although only suggestive, it was also observed that treatment (a combined reinforcement plus desensitization program; see "Treatment Issues," p. 386–399 was somewhat less effective for those children in both subgroups whose overall level of fear was greatest. Obviously, these findings await prospective confirmation.

Thus, although it is evident that self-report scales have not been routinely used, our initial results appear promising. Such scales provide information about the severity of the phobia, and provide the child an opportunity to express his or her own idiosyncratic set of concerns and fears. Further, they may be useful in identifying causal patterns and in determining response to differential treatments.

As with self-report, other-report rating forms have not been consistently used when working with school-phobic children. Again, this is surprising given the potential utility of such instruments. In this approach, members of the family or significant others (e.g., teachers) fill out checklists or rating forms regarding the child's level of fear. The most frequently used scale with children has been the Louisville Fear Survey Schedule for Children (Miller, Barrett, Hampe, & Noble, 1972b), an 81-item inventory that covers an extensive range of fears found in children and adolescents. Each item is rated on a 3-point scale: no fear, normal or reasonable fear, and unrealistic fear. Unlike the self-report scales, parents or teachers respond to items on this other-report survey. In their study of school phobic children, Miller *et al.* (1972a) utilized this scale and found that 32 of their 46 children had a primary fear of some aspect of school, while 14 of the 46 had a primary fear of separation. Acknowledging that this breakdown was determined by parental report, it remains of interest to note that the instrument might well be useful in "subtyping" school phobic children and in examining differential response to treatment. Unfortunately, Miller *et al.* (1972a) did not explore these possibilities in their study.

Gittelman-Klein and Klein (1973) have described two additional rating forms that may be useful. The first, completed by the mother, is a simple form assessing return to school. In response to the question "How well has child been doing for the past week?" mother rates the child on a 7-point scale (ranging from "Attends classes regularly" to "Frequent refusal to go to school—about 2 days a week" to "Complete school refusal"). This simple rating might be especially useful as a measure of school refusal throughout treatment. Reliability and validity data are not provided, however. These authors have also described the Psychiatric Interview Rating Form which is to be used by a mental health professional to assess various aspects of school phobia on an ongoing basis. Again, however, reliability and validity data are not presented.

In summary, both self-report and other-report questionnaires or rating forms can be used to assess perceived fears and anxieties. Though much research remains to be carried out on the reliablity and validity of these measures, they appear to provide important information and appear highly promising. Those instruments which measure specific fears as well as provide direct information about school attendance are especially welcome.

Behavioral Observation

Direct observation of the child's behavior in the setting in which the fear occurs is the hallmark of behavioral assessment. Within this tradition, assessment has ranged from unobtrusive observation in the child's home or school to direct observation in laboratory settings which simulate these environments (Lick & Katkin, 1976). Such observation provides a direct sample of the child's behavior and is the least inferential of data-collection methods (Goldfried & Kent, 1972). As we have suggested elsewhere, however, information obtained from behavioral observation should not necessarily be viewed as "better" than that obtained from behavioral interview or behavioral rating methods (Ollendick & Cerny, 1981). Rather, such observations should be viewed as part of an integrated and comprehensive assessment. The various sources of information should complement one another with each providing valuable data about the etiology and possible treatment of the phobic behavior.

In behavioral observation systems, a behavior or set of behaviors which is indicative of fear is operationally defined, observed, and recorded in a systematic fashion. In addition, the antecedents and the consequents to the designated behaviors are observed and subsequently used in formulating a treatment strategy. This approach is well illustrated in Neisworth, Madle, and Goecke's (1975) assessment of a young girl who displayed separation anxiety in a preschool setting. When left at school, she began to cry, sob, and scream until her mother returned to retrieve her. These behaviors (crying, screaming, and sobbing) were operationally defined and their intensity and duration were monitored in the preschool setting throughout baseline, treatment, and follow-up phases. Treatment, based on differential reinforcement and shaping procedures, was highly successful. More importantly, for our purposes here, school avoidance behavior (labeled separation anxiety) was defined as a set of observable behaviors. These fearful behaviors occurred only in school where mother, as well as the preschool staff, found it difficult to endure the child's distress without attending to her. Neisworth *et al.* (1975) indicated that records and additional observations supported the notion that this attention played a role in the maintenance and development of "separation anxiety." Thus, in this case, specific behaviors were identified and observed; further, these observations suggested a specific treatment based on the antecedent (preschool setting only) and consequent (attention) conditions under which the behaviors occurred.

Somewhat similarly, Ayllon *et al.* (1970) conduted systematic behavioral observations in the home of a school-phobic girl, who had been absent from school for a prolonged period of time. In this case, mother left for work approximately 1 hr after the girl (Valerie) and her siblings were to set off for school. Although her siblings went to school on time, Valerie was observed to sleep late and then to "cling" to mother until she left for work. "Valerie typically followed her mother around the house, from room to room, spending approximately 80 percent of her time within 10 feet of her mother. During these times, there was little or no conversation" (p. 128). Upon leaving for work, mother took Valerie to a neighbor's apartment to stay until she returned from work (mother had long abandoned any hope of Valerie's going to school). When mother left the neighbor's apartment, Valerie would follow. Observations indicated that this pattern continued with Valerie "following her mother at a 10-foot distance." Frequently, mother had to return Valerie to the neighbor's apartment. This daily pattern was usually concluded with mother "literally running to get out of sight of Valerie" so that she would not follow her into traffic.

At the neighbor's apartment, observations revealed that Valerie was free to do whatever she pleased for the remainder of the day. As noted by Ayllon *et al.,* "Her day was one which would be considered ideal by many grade children—she could be outdoors and play as she chose all day long. No demands of any type were made on her" (p. 129). Since Valerie was not attending school, the authors devised a simulated school setting to determine the extent of fear associated with academically related materials. Much to their surprise, Valerie exhibited little or no fear in the presence of these materials. Based on these observations, the authors hypothesized that Valerie's refusal to attend school was maintained by attention from mother and pleasant and undemanding characteristics of the neighbor's apartment where she stayed throughout the day. Accordingly, a shaping and differential reinforcement program, similar to that used by Neisworth *et al.* (1975), was implemented. Although treatment effects were not immediate, within 45 days Valerie was attending school on a full-time basis, and continued to do so at six months' follow-up. As with Neisworth *et al.,* behavioral observations led directly to a specific and effective intervention.

While the utility of direct behavioral observation in the home and school is evident, very few behaviorally oriented studies have actually incorporated this practice. Most studies have defined school phobia simply as "refusal to attend school" and have used school attendance as the sole criterion of behavior change. This, we suggest, is too narrow a criterion for change; many children may actually go to school but still exhibit inordinate amounts of fear. Further, simply knowing that a child is not in school tells us little about the antecedents or consequents to that behavior.

In our work with school-phobic children, we have attempted to incorporate all three sources of information: behavioral interviews, behavioral ratings, and behavioral observations. Typically, observations are initiated after the child and family have been interviewed and specific rating forms have been completed. Oftentimes, these earlier sources of information are useful in pinpointing the situation and interactions which might be most productively observed. In a retrospective analysis of our efforts, we have found a high degree of correspondence between behavioral observations and information obtained from interviews and ratings. That is, for those school-phobic children whose fear seems to be primarily associated with leaving mother, home observations are maximally useful. For those children whose fear seems to be related to a specific aspect of school, school observations are most productive. Of course, such correspondence is not always obtained.

As with other types of assessment, behavioral observation procedures must possess adequate reliability and validity before their routine use can be endorsed. Although early behaviorists tended to accept behavioral observation data on the basis of its deceptively simple surface validity, more recent investigators have enumerated a variety of problems related to its use (e.g., Johnson & Bolstad, 1973; Kazdin, 1979). Among these issues are the complexity of the observation code, observer bias, observer drift, and the reactive nature of the observation process itself. It is beyond the scope of this chapter to address these issues. Suffice it to indicate, however, that when these issues are adequately controlled for, direct observation represents one of the most elegant assessment strategies. Once the behaviors associated with school phobia are operationally defined, they can be observed and recorded in a systematic fashion.

In sum, behavioral observation in the home or school setting, represents the hallmark of behavioral assessment of school phobia. These observations, which are not without their own special set of limitations, are a welcome complement to behavioral interviews and behavioral rating forms. However, as we noted, such procedures should not be viewed as "better" than other methods. They provide valuable information, which, when combined with that obtained from other sources, yield a potentially comprehensive as well as integrated "picture" of school-phobic behavior.

TREATMENT ISSUES

As previously mentioned, both behavioral and psychodynamic orientations emphasize early return to school as the primary goal of treatment. In the present section, behaviorally based strategies that are commonly used in achieving this goal will be delineated. Conceptually, these strategies parallel etiological and maintenance factors thought to be present in school phobia, and are based on principles of classical, operant, and vicarious conditioning. Although studies which emphasize each of these principles in intervention will be described, it should be understood from the onset that most treatment strategies entail a complex interaction of these learning principles.

Classical Conditioning

Treatments based on classical conditioning principles have utilized two primary strategies for fear reduction: counterconditioning and extinction. During counterconditioning procedures, specific feared stimuli are presented in the presence of stimuli which elicit responses incompatible with anxiety. In this manner, anxiety is counterconditioned and the individual is said to acquire a competing response, most frequently the relaxation response. During extinction, on the other hand, the conditioned fear stimuli are repeatedly presented in the absence of the original unconditioned stimuli. In this manner, the individual learns that there is really nothing to be afraid of and the anxiety response is said to dissipate.

The first and most frequently cited account of the treatment of childhood phobias by counterconditioning was published by Mary Cover Jones in 1924. Jones successfully treated a rabbit phobia in a young child, Peter, by exposing him to the feared rabbit in the presence of food, a stimulus which elicited a positive response. The pairing of a fear-eliciting stimulus with a stimulus that elicits a competing (or positive) response is the crux of systematic desensitization (Wolpe, 1958). Used successfully with both adults and children for the treatment of fear and anxiety, systematic desensitization consists of three basic components: progressive relaxation, development of a stimulus hierarchy, and counterposing items in the hierarchy with relaxation. Generally, the fear-producing stimuli are presented imaginally while the individual is deeply relaxed. Although results of recent studies have questioned the active and necessary components of systematic desensitization, there is little doubt that it is an effective treatment procedure (Rimm & Masters, 1974).

Variants of systematic desensitization, including *in vivo* desensitization (e.g., Garvey & Hegrenes, 1966) and emotive imagery (Lazarus & Abramovitz, 1962) have been used frequently in treating childhood phobias (Hatzenbuehler & Schroeder, 1978). In several studies examining school phobia, imaginal and *in vivo* procedures have been employed concurrently. For example, a school-phobic child might be instructed while in a relaxed state to imagine approaching the door of the school building (as well as additional items on a fear hierarchy). In addition, to help insure that treatment will generalize to the actual situation, the child may be instructed to actually approach the school in increasingly closer approximations. She or he may begin by sitting in the school parking lot on a weekend with the therapist and progress to attending classes alone on a graduated basis. Emotive imagery (Lazarus & Abramovitz, 1962) is a form of desensitization in which an anxiety-antagonistic response other than relaxation is paired with the fear-evoking stimuli, either imaginally or *in vivo*. Anxiety-antagonistic responses include feelings of self-assertion, pride, affection, and mirth. The school phobic child may be asked to imagine playing with a favored "hero" or participating in a favorite activity, interspersed with imagining aspects of the school situation.

Numerous case studies which utilized systematic desensitization and its variants have appeared in the literature (e.g., Chapel, 1967; Garvey & Hegrenes, 1966; Lazarus, 1960; Lazarus & Abramovitz, 1962; Lazarus, Davison, & Polefka, 1965; Miller, 1972; Ney, 1967; Olsen & Coleman, 1967; Tahmisian & McReynolds, 1971; van der Ploeg, 1975). However, only one group research design study has been reported (Miller, Barrett, Hampe, & Noble, 1972a). This study compared the relative efficacies of systematic desensitization, traditional psychotherapy, and a waiting-list control, with children who for the most part displayed school-phobic behavior. Both systematic desensitization and psychotherapy groups received 24 sessions of individual treatment over a three-month period. Muscle relaxation training and construction of fear hierarchies were completed during the first four sessions of the systematic desensitization group. In the following sessions, the child was instructed to imagine progressively greater fear-eliciting stimuli while remaining relaxed. When all items of the hierarchy could be imagined without fear, an *in vivo* assessment was scheduled. If the results of this assessment were negative, imaginal desensitization was resumed. In the psychotherapy group, young children were seen for play therapy while older children were seen for interview therapy. Both older and younger children were encouraged to explore their hopes, fears, and dependency needs. Additionally, the children were "encouraged to examine and formulate both behavioral strategies for coping with stress and the affect accompanying these efforts" (p. 271). Further, intervention with families of children in this group was "essentially the same" as for children in the systematic desensitization group: "where parent–child interaction patterns appeared to reinforce fear behavior, behavior therapy principles were employed to restructure contingency schedules, for example, eliminating television during school hours for a school phobic who stayed home" (p. 271). Thus, the "psychotherapy" treatment contained many factors of "behavioral" treatment even though children did not specifically undergo systematic desensitization. The child's fear was evaluated by a clinician and by two other-report instruments completed by the parents: The Louisville Behavior Checklist (Miller, Barrett, Hampe, & Noble, 1971) and the Louisville Fear Survey for Children (Miller *et al.,* 1972b). The evaluations were completed prior to treatment, following treatment, and at a 6-week follow-up. Parents of children in the two treatment groups reported a greater reduction in fear in their children than did parents in the waiting-list group; the two treatment groups did not differ, however. Moreover, the clinician's evaluation failed to support parental judgments and, in fact, revealed no differences among the three groups at posttreatment or follow-up. Unfortunately, behavioral observations of the children were not reported and as a consequence it is difficult to determine the reliability of the findings. Had such a measure been included, one would be in a better position to answer the question about the comparative efficacy of these strategies.

In an uncontrolled case study, Garvey and Hegrenes (1966) used *in vivo* desensitization to treat Jimmy, a 10-year-old boy who had refused to attend school for approximately 1 month prior to referral. Jimmy's school refusal was precipitated by an illness which followed the Christmas holidays. In addition, he reported being afraid that some harm would befall his mother. His symptoms included feeling afraid and vomiting when he thought about going to school each morning. He also had begun to avoid his peers and friends outside of school. Jimmy received traditional psychotherapy for 6 months. At the end of this period, he reported being more self-confident. However, on the day he was to return to school he was unable to do so. Therefore, a desensitization procedure was implemented. During this intervention, which lasted 20 consecutive days, the therapist accompanied Jimmy in carrying out the following steps:

1. Sitting in a car in front of school
2. Getting out of the car and approaching the curb
3. Going to the sidewalk
4. Going to the bottom of the steps of the school
5. Going to the top of the steps
6. Going to the door
7. Entering the school
8. Approaching the classroom a certain distance each day down the hall
9. Entering the classroom
10. Being present in the classroom with the teacher
11. Being present in the classroom with the teacher and one or two classmates
12. Being present in the classroom with a full class

Jimmy, upon completing one step in the absence of self-reported anxiety, proceeded to the subsequent step. He had completed all steps in 20 days and was then able to remain in the classroom without the therapist. Altogether, treatment required only 10–12 hr of the therapist's time. The authors reported no recurrence of the school-phobic behaviors at 2-year follow-up.

This case study illustrates a relatively efficient procedure for treating school phobia. While *in vivo* desensitization was the primary treatment strategy, vicarious and operant components were also present. It should be noted that therapist- and peer-modeling were prevalent throughout treatment and that Jimmy was systematically praised by the therapist for completing each subsequent step. Therefore, it is difficult to determine whether Jimmy's approach behavior was facilitated most by deconditioning, operant, or vicarious processes. More probably it resulted from an interaction of all three.

As briefly mentioned above, several treatments for fears that utilize classical conditioning strategies are based on principles of extinction. Extinction of the fear response is said to occur as the result of continuous presentation of the fear-producing stimuli in the absence of the actual feared stimuli. Further, an avoidance response is usually present which serves to reduce the fear and to subsequently reinforce it. Implosive therapy (Stampfl & Levis, 1967; Ollendick & Gruen, 1972) is an example of an extinction-based treatment. Instead of minimizing the cognitive and physiological components of anxiety (as is the goal of counterconditioning procedures), these components are intensified while the client is exposed in imagination to the phobic stimuli. The fear images used in implosive therapy are those that are highest in the fear hierarchy. The therapist may elaborate on these images by incorporating psychodynamic themes. Thus, the therapist, when presenting the school-phobic child with images of standing up in front of the class, may also attempt to elicit feelings of being laughed at or rejected by everyone (including the mother) (e.g., Smith & Sharpe, 1970).

The use of implosive therapy in the treatment of school phobia is well illustrated by the case study described below (Smith & Sharpe, 1970). More specifically, treatment was instituted with a 13-year-old male, Billy, who had been absent from school for 7 weeks. His school phobia symptoms, which included extreme anxiety, inability to eat breakfast, chest pains when faced with going to school, and trembling and crying on arriving at school, were preceded by a 3-week absence from school due to illness. Tranquilizers, force, and bribes were reportedly ineffective in getting him to return to school.

Initially, anxiety-evoking cues were identified by visually observing his physiological responses (e.g., flushing, vocal tremors) as he described, step by step, a typical day at school. This procedure was used because Billy seemed to be unaware of the stimuli that made him anxious. Once the scenes were developed, they were presented to Billy in six consecutive daily sessions. Each scene was presented until his anxiety was visibly reduced. Additionally, he was asked to describe details associated with each scene and his feelings at the moment to help him focus on the scenes. Two of the nine scenes follow:

> While on (the auditorium) stage, Billy, with spotlights in his face, is examined by each of his teachers, who asked him questions which he cannot begin to answer. He is being examined to find out what he has learned on his vacation. The gym teacher removes Billy's shirt from his frail body and demands 30 push-ups, which he is unable to complete. The audience jeers, chants, and stares at him with hate-filled, menacing eyes while he is on stage.

> The patient boards his school bus for the first time since his absence began. The bus driver is described as thick-skinned, ape-like, sinister and evil looking. The students on the bus stare silently and malignantly at the patient as the bus veers from its normal route and enters a forest. When the bus stops, the silent students slowly move forward toward the patient and begin to jostle him. (Smith & Sharpe, 1970, p. 52)

Concurrent with the implosive therapy sessions, Billy was instructed to make increasingly closer approximations to attending school for a full day. For example, the day after the first session he attended his feared math class; after the second and third sessions, he attended half-day sessions of school, and following the fourth session, he attended school full time.

After the first implosive session, Billy was able to eat breakfast and to willingly attend his previously feared math class. The day before the first session he had blatantly refused to attend school, locking himself in the bathroom. By the time of his fourth session he was speaking positively about school and seemed to evince little anxiety. At a 13-week follow-up, his school attendance was regular and he reported no anxiety. There was an improvement in his grades and he was interacting more with his peers.

This treatment package, which also included an operant component (Billy was no longer allowed to watch television during school hours), was found to be effective. Apparently, the anxiety reduction which occurred during the first treatment session was necessary *before* Billy could start the *in vivo* desensitization procedure. For those children who are highly anxious, treatment in imagination may indeed be preferred before attempting either forced school attendance or a gradual approach procedure. Similarly, Lazarus *et al.* (1965) recommended use of classical conditioning techniques when school avoidance behavior is motivated by high levels of anxiety, and operant techniques when anxiety is minimal.

In summary, application of respondent-based strategies for the treatment of school phobia has varied in terms of the specific techniques used. We have attempted to elucidate this flexibility, as well as detail the particular steps that are employed in implementing these specific techniques. Although the added use of vicarious and operant procedures probably enhances the overall effectiveness of respondent-based strategies, the inclusion of these strategies makes it extremely difficult to isolate the necessary and sufficient treatment components. Nonetheless, at our current state of knowledge, such comprehensive programs are probably preferred (Ollendick, 1979a).

Operant Conditioning

As noted in the section on etiology, operant components are frequently postulated to be responsible for both the genesis and maintenance of school phobia. Essentially, strategies based on the operant model attempt to increase the reinforcement value of school attendance (e.g., increased peer acceptance, teacher and parental approval) as well as decrease the reinforcement value of staying at home (e.g., withdrawal of parental attention, prohibiting the watching of television). Until "natural" consequences (i.e., good grades, improved peer relations) associated with regular school attendance are realized by the school-phobic child, material or social reinforcers in the form of preferred objects and social praise may be required. The administration of reinforcers has varied in terms of who administers the reinforcers and how frequently they are administered. Contingency management programs have been utilized in several studies, and have been both home-based (Ayllon *et al.,* 1970; Cooper, 1973; Doleys & Williams, 1977; Edlund, 1971; Hersen, 1970; Kennedy, 1965; Tahmisian & McReynolds, 1971; Vaal, 1973), and school-based (Brown, Copeland, & Hall, 1974; Hersen, 1970; Rines, 1973; Weinberger, Leventhal, & Beckman, 1973). In addition, behavioral shaping has been implemented within the clinic (Hersen, 1970; Patterson, 1965). Finally, operant components can be valuable when implementing classical conditioning procedures with children. For example, during systematic desensitization, a child can be rewarded as he or she relaxes specific body parts on cue and reports his or her images in detail.

Illustratively, Ayllon *et al.* (1970) treated Valerie, an 8-year-old female, through diverse, home-based operant procedures. Valerie had gradually stopped attending school in the second grade and continued this refusal into the third grade. As noted above (p. 385), Ayllon *et al.* defined school phobia as a low frequency of school attendance. Therefore, the major goal of intervention was to increase this low frequency behavior. After a 10-day baseline period in which extensive behavioral observations were made in Valerie's home, her neighbor's home (where she stayed while her mother was at work), and at school (where Valerie's principal and teachers were interviewed), treatment began. Table 1 presents the sequence of procedures used as well as Valerie's consequential behavior. Initially, a shaping procedure was implemented. Valerie was taken to school toward the end of the school day by the therapist's

Table 1. Procedural and Behavioral Progression during the Treatment of School Phobia[a]

Temporal sequence	Procedure	Valerie's behavior
Baseline observations Day 1–10	Observations taken at home and at the neighbor's apartment where Val spent her day.	Valerie stayed at home when siblings left for school. Mother took Val to neighbor's apartment as she left for work.
Behavioral assessment Day 11–13	Assistant showed school materials to Val and prompted academic work.	Val reacted well to books; she colored pictures and copied numbers and letters.
Behavioral assessment Day 13	Assistant invited Val for a car ride after completing academic work at neighbor's apartment.	Val readily accepted car ride and on way back to neighbor's apartment she also accepted hamburger offered her.
Procedure 1 Day 14–20	Taken by assistant to school. Assistant stayed with her in classroom. Attendance made progressively earlier while assistant's stay in classroom progressively lessens.	Val attended school with assistant, performed school work, and left school with siblings at closing time.

(continued)

Table 1. (Continued)

Temporal sequence	Procedure	Valerie's behavior
Day 21	Assistant did not take Val to school.	Val and siblings attended school on their own.
Procedure 1 Day 22	Val taken by assistant to school.	Val attended school with assistant, performed school work, and left with siblings at school closing time.
Return to baseline observations Day 23–27	Observations taken at home.	Val stayed at home when siblings left for school. Mother took Val to neighbor's apartment as she left for work.
Procedure 2 Day 28–29	Mother left for work when children left for school.	Val stayed at home when children left for school. Mother took her to neighbor's apartment as she left for work.
Procedure 3 Day 40–49	Taken by mother to school. Home-based motivational system.	Val stayed at home when siblings left for school, and followed mother quietly when taken to school.
Procedure 4 Day 50–59	On Day 50, mother left for school *before* children left home. Home-based motivational system.	Siblings met mother at school door. Val stayed at home.
	After 15 min of waiting in school, mother returned home and took Val to school.	Val meekly followed her mother.
	On Day 51, mother left for school *before* children left home.	Val and siblings met mother at school door.
	On Day 52, mother left for school *before* children left home.	Siblings met mother at school door. Valerie stayed at home.
	After 15 min of waiting in school, mother returned home and physically hit and dragged Valerie to school.	Valerie cried and pleaded with her mother not to hit her. She cried all the way to school.
	On Day 53–59, mother left for school *before* children left home.	Val and siblings met mother at school door.
Fading Procedure Day 60–69	Mother discontinued going to school before children. Mother maintained home-based motivational system.	Val and siblings attended school on their own.
Fading Procedure Day 70	Mother discontinued home-based motivational system.	Val and siblings attended school on their own.

[a] From "Behavioral Management of School Phobia" by T. Ayllon, D. Smith, and M. Rogers, *Journal of Behaviour Therapy and Experimental Psychiatry,* 1970, *1*, 125–133.
Copyright 1970 by Pergamon Press. Reprinted by permission.

assistant, who remained with her in the classroom until school was dismissed. Each day she was taken to school earlier. By the 7th day of this procedure, she was able to remain in school all day without the presence of the assistant. Unfortunately, while this treatment helped to initiate Valerie's school attendance, it did not maintain it. Valerie still refused to get dressed in the morning and walk to school with her three siblings. A functional analysis indicated that Valerie was able to spend an hour alone with her mother when she did not go to school and that perhaps this was reinforcing to the child. Therefore, to remove this consequence, mother was instructed to leave for work at the same time her children left for school. However, Valerie continued her school refusal and attempted to follow mother to work.

To increase Valerie's "motivation" for attending school, mother (instructed by the therapist) implemented a reward system for all four children in which the opportunity to receive candy was made contingent on school attendance. Additionally, when Valerie did not leave for school voluntarily, mother was instructed to take her. Although Valerie willingly accompanied her mother, she still refused to go to school alone. Therefore, a contingency was placed on mother so that Valerie's not leaving for school with siblings resulted in mother having to walk back home from school (where she was waiting with rewards for the children) to retrieve Valerie and accompany her to school once again. It was of no small consequence that this meant walking 3 miles. After 2 days of this negative consequence, mother altered her behavior (became firmer, stricter) so that Valerie began to go to school with her siblings. She continued to be rewarded for voluntary school attendance, and 100% attendance was maintained at 9-month follow-up. Her pattern of voluntary attendance is presented in Figure 1.

The overall treatment strategy described here has several noteworthy strengths. First of all, comprehensive behavioral observations during baseline and treatment were invaluable in selecting and specifying the treatment procedures used. Secondly, the therapist closely observed Valerie's behavior and were relatively flexible in their approach to treating the problem. Although "school phobia" in this case was defined quite narrowly, the behaviors antecedent and consequent to low school attendance were thoroughly examined and eventually dealt with. Finally, altering mother's contingencies, as well as the child's, proved to be instrumental in improving the child's compliance.

In a similar vein, Rines (1973) presented a case study in which a school-based contingency-management program was implemented with a 12-year-old female who was on the verge of being institutionalized because of "unmanageable" behavior. Although the girl did not refuse to attend school entirely, she made numerous phone calls from school to her mother who consequently made arrangements to have her sent home from school. Accordingly, school personnel were instructed not to allow the girl to call home. On the first day of treatment, she was limited to four phone calls and then allowed to make one less

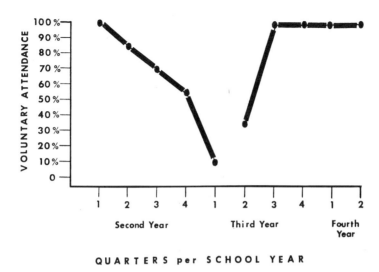

Figure 1. Valerie's voluntary school attendance. Each dot represents the percentage of voluntary attendance per school quarter (45 days). The behavioral intervention was initiated during the second quarter of the third year of school. (From "Behavioral Management of School Phobia" by T. Ayllon, D. Smith, and M. Rogers, *Journal of Behaviour Therapy and Experimental Psychiatry,* 1970, *1,* 125–133. Copyright 1970 by Pergamon Press. Reprinted by permission.)

each subsequent day. She complied with this. Her crying behavior within the classroom was ignored by the teachers, extinguishing it. Additionally, the teachers were instructed to reinforce positive behaviors. A telephone follow-up conducted at the end of the school year indicated that the child had regular school attendance and was achieving high grades; however, the long-standing family pathology and the girl's deviant behavior with peers was still present. Nevertheless, institutionalization had been avoided.

This case study was examined primarily because it illustrates an operant-based treatment applied to a relatively disturbed (Type II) school-phobic child (see "Etiological Considerations" pp. 374–378), and because school personnel were instrumental in implementing treatment. The lack of quantifiable data, however, affirms the need to collect and report baseline rates of both positive and negative behaviors, as well as their antecedents and consequences. Additionally, as long as both parents and school personnel are amenable to being "behavioral engineers," a combined cooperative effort in utilizing contingency contracting would be recommended in terms of greater consistency in the treatment of the child, and generalizability of treatment effects.

Using the broad-based operant approach mentioned above, Hersen (1970) demonstrated its utility in helping Bruce, a 12½-year-old school phobic boy. Operant strategies were used in the home, school, and clinic situation. First, an interview with mother indicated that she was inadvertently reinforcing his crying behaviors and complaints about school. She was subsequently instructed to ignore these behaviors so that they would extinguish, and to praise his coping responses. Second, during the initial intake session, Bruce's school guidance counselor had been identified as possibly reinforcing Bruce's crying behavior in school. Specifically, when Bruce cried in class, he consequently spent 2–3 hr in the counselor's office. The counselor was instructed by the therapist to be supportive but firm in having Bruce return to class and to limit any contacts with Bruce to 5 min. Third, Bruce was seen individually by the therapist who verbally reinforced his coping responses, ignored his malaptive responses, and offered social support. The entire treatment program lasted 15 weeks. Crying and complaining ceased in all three of these settings and Bruce returned to school without incident.

The comprehensive approach utilized in Hersen's study was both successful and relatively short-term. Again, a thorough functional analysis of the problem behavior facilitated development of an effective treatment plan. It is interesting to note that although Bruce evidenced relatively high levels of anxiety, a respondent-based strategy *per se* was not used; instead his crying and complaining behaviors were extinguished by ignoring them. This could indicate one of several possibilities: (1) that Bruce's school-avoidant tendencies developed in accordance with an operant model, (2) that his behaviors were actually not manifestations of anxiety, (3) that his behaviors, although manifestations of anxiety, were not strong enough to be maintained once the environmental contingencies were removed, or (4) that counterconditioning components were inadvertently included in the treatment plan. While an operant approach appeared on the surface to be a sufficient strategy, the possibility of the fourth hypothesis should not be discounted.

In summary, operant approaches employed in the home, school, and clinic, have shown success in the treatment of school phobia. Moreover, there have been specific components that have enhanced the utility of these approaches across settings. These components include: (1) conducting a thorough functional analysis *within* the particular setting, (2) procuring cooperation of significant others (e.g., parents, siblings, teachers), and (3) continuing assessment throughout treatment in order to evaluate the need for its continuation or modification.

Vicarious Conditioning (Modeling)

Controlled studies of treatments which utilize modeling principles are relatively prevalent in the child literature (Graziano *et al.,* 1979). However, accounts of modeling procedures as the primary treatment for school phobia are nonexistent. Nonetheless, several studies have employed modeling procedures indirectly. For example, in interventions that use *in vivo* desensitization procedures, the child is usually accompanied to school by either a parent, the therapist, or the therapist's assistant (Ayllon *et al.,* 1970; Doleys & Williams, 1977; Garvey & Hegrenes, 1966; Lazarus *et al.,* 1965; Smith & Sharpe, 1970; Tahmisian & McReynolds, 1971). Successive approximations are made until the child remains in the classroom with the adult model. Gradually, the adult model is removed from the classroom so that the child can remain alone for the full day unaccompanied. Once initial fears of entering the classroom are overcome, and the child's attendance is more regular, he is able to observe and model himself on behavior of peers.

The treatment of Jimmy (Garvey & Hegrenes, 1966) described in detail above, exemplifies the ancillary use of adult modeling. Specifically, the therapist accompanied Jimmy in completing 12 steps which composed the *in vivo* desensitization hierarchy. At the end of 20 days when all steps in the hierarchy were successfully completed, Jimmy was able to remain in the standard classroom situation without the therapist.

A similar school-approach hierarchy was utilized in the treatment of Carol, a 13-year-old school-phobic girl (Tahmisian & McReynolds, 1971). Prior to implementation of *in vivo* desensitization, Carol had been seen by a social worker and had also been prescribed tranquilizers. Both were reported to be ineffective, and she had been absent from school on 80 consecutive days.

In this study, parents, rather than the therapist, accompanied the client in executing the following steps:

First week:
  1. Walk around school after classes are dismissed 15 minutes accompanied by parent
  2. Same as Step 1, alone
  3. Same as Step 1, 30 min, accompanied by parent
  4. Same as Step 1, 30 min, alone
  5. Same as Step 1, 60 min, alone
Second week:
  6. Walk around school while classes in session for 30 min, accompanied by parent
  7. Same as Step 6, alone
  8. Same as Step 6, 60 min, alone
  9. Attend first class period (60 min) with parent in hall
  10. Same as Step 9, parent in car
Third week:
  11. Attend first class period (60 min), parent gone
  12. Attend class periods (160 min), alone
  13. Attend 3 class periods (180 min), alone
  14. Attend class all morning, alone
  15. Attend class all day, alone

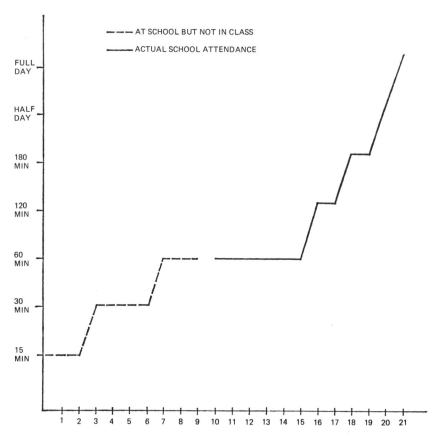

Figure 2. Time at school over 3 weeks of treatment. (From "Use of Parents as Behavioral Engineers in the Treatment of a School-Phobic Girl" by J. A. Tahmisian and W. T. McReynolds, *Journal of Counseling Psychology,* 1971, *18,* 225–228. Copyright 1971 by the American Psychological Association. Reprinted by permission.)

Carol was attending school normally by the end of the third week of treatment and reported that she was no longer afraid. A 4-week follow-up indicated that her school attendance was still regular. Her progress during the 3 weeks of intervention is depicted in Figure 2.

As can be seen, the parent was faded out of the stimulus situation intermittently rather than at the termination of treatment. Thus, while the child had the opportunity to model herself on the parent's behavior, she also had the opportunity to perform each step in the hierarchy alone. This would be particularly important if being alone was a salient cue within the complex of fear stimuli. In addition, periodic removal of the adult model helped prevent Carol's performance from becoming contingent on the presence of an adult.

The most lucid example of peer modeling can be seen in the operant-based study of Ayllon *et al.* (1970). Specifically, Valerie was prompted to walk to school with her siblings by using a backwards shaping procedure. She initially visited school toward the end of the school day, and to insure that she received social praise for attending, "the assistant gave Valerie some candy to share with the siblings and left her to walk home with them" (p. 130). As she was brought to school increasingly earlier in the day, the siblings continued to accompany her home. Additionally, the siblings were included in the contingency management program and Valerie had the opportunity to watch them be rewarded for voluntary school attendance.

The efficacy of parent and/or peer modeling remains to be empirically validated in the treatment of school phobia; however, given its effectiveness with other childhood adjustment problems including fear and anxieties (Barrios *et al.*, 1981; Gelfand, 1978; Ollendick, 1979a), we are optimistic about its potential utility. Symbolic modeling procedures, if proven effective for school phobia, would be particular cost-effective and relatively easy to deliver both individually and in groups. Finally, the large-scale "delivery" of modeling films to entire classrooms represents a potentially effective preventive measure for school phobia (prevention will be discussed in more detail below).

As noted, although vicarious procedures hold promise, neither case studies nor controlled experiments have examined them as primary strategies for treatment of school phobia. Therefore, it will be the task of future researchers to conduct sharply focused studies in this area.

Evaluative Issues

Recent reviews of the school phobia literature indicate that a majority of these studies are uncontrolled case reports (Gelfand, 1978; Hersen, 1971; Jones & Kazdin, 1981; Yule, Hersov, & Treseder, 1980). This is unfortunate, since threats to internal validity cannot be ruled out; that is, there is no way of determining whether treatment *per se* was responsible for observed changes in behavior. Because the prognosis for untreated school phobia is presently unknown, the limitations of uncontrolled case studies are particularly unsettling.

The value of utilizing controlled single-case experimental designs has been discussed in detail in the literature (Hersen & Barlow, 1976; Kazdin, 1980). However, specific factors *can* be used to maximize the utility of case reports. These factors, elucidated in a recent article by Kazdin (1981), include use of objective data, use of more than two assessment periods, and reporting the progress of more than one client. In the treatment of school phobia, objective measures are relatively easy to obtain since the target behavior of major interest is school attendance. These data can be reported qualitatively (e.g., present versus absent) and/or quantitatively (e.g., time spent in classroom) and the child's as well as significant other's report can be validated by school attendance records and by behavioral observations. As previously noted, the child's fear can be evaluated by various methods, including rating scales and behavioral observations. Ayllon *et al.* (1970) were meticulous in operationalizing their behavioral measures and in assessing these measures throughout baseline and treatment phases. Numerous assessment periods helped to better establish the course of the problem throughout treatment, as well as pre- and posttreatment.

Unfortunately, only one study (Kennedy, 1965) included the treatment results of multiple clients. Once threats to internal validity can be minimized, reporting the successful results of more than one subject can strengthen the implications of the treatment effects.

Although, as noted, the value of case studies can be enhanced, the utilization of controlled studies is strongly preferred. For example, in reversal or withdrawal designs, the controlling effects of the independent variables can be established and thus single case studies can yield more valid information. However, use of these designs may be unfeasible in studying respondent-based treatments. For example, in systematic desensitization, once progression through a fear hierarchy has been completed, termination of treatment would probably not reverse therapeutic gains. On the other hand, a reversal design may be useful in evaluating operant procedures employed in the treatment of school phobia. After the treatment phase, contingencies (at school and/or at home) could be withdrawn and reinstated. However, at the time the back-to-baseline phase begins, it is highly probable that the natural reinforcers of attending school (e.g., peer interactions, teacher approval, increased self-confidence) may be in effect. Additionally, the ethics of reversing possible treatment gains, particularly with children, must be strongly considered. Reversing the contingencies that facilitated a school-phobic child's progress could have far-reaching consequences, including strengthening of subjective anxiety, further disruption of age-appropriate learning and of peer relationships, and triggering of frustration in child, parents, and school personnel. Finally, the relief experienced by parents and teachers as the school-phobic child re-enters school most probably would obviate their cooperation in returning to baseline conditions.

The issues mentioned above could be partially offset by utilization of multiple-baseline designs. In a multiple-baseline design across subjects, two or more children in the same environment could be sequentially administered a particular treatment. This design requires that at least two children are available simultaneously in the same (or similar) environment. It should be noted, however, that this procedure may be impractical given the relatively low incidence of school phobia at any one time and in any one location. When only one school-phobic child is available, a multiple-baseline design across setting might be preferred. In this procedure, a treatment could be applied sequentially to the same behaviors across different settings (e.g., home and school).

As noted, single-case designs are of limited use in comprehensively evaluating behavioral treatments for school phobia. Ideally, clinical outcome studies would be used to compare the efficacies of various treatment packages for school phobia. Thus far, only one such study has been conducted (Miller *et al.*, 1972a). Although this was an ambitious, large-scale project, several methodological weaknesses were evident: (1) the treatment groups shared procedures (e.g., behaviorally based techniques were used in both systematic desensitization and psychotherapy groups); (2) within treatment groups, there was variability in the administration of certain components (e.g., in the systematic desensitization group, special breathing-control techniques were used for one subject while some subjects were given assertive training); and (3) behavioral assessment of the school-phobic behavior was not reported. While the relatively low incidence of school-phobic children may make group outcome studies impractical, the conduct of group studies using mixed phobics remains a viable alternative. It is to be hoped that future studies will remedy some of the weaknesses mentioned above, in order that more valid conclusions can be drawn about treatment effects.

Although there is a paucity of controlled studies examining behavioral treatments for school phobia, outcomes of diverse case reports suggest that specific operant- and respondent-based procedures contribute to efficacious treatments. In viewing the studies, however, it is evident that specific procedures are not implemented in isolation. For example, in most studies, treatments included operant and respondent (as well as vicarious) components. As noted earlier, the presence of complex interactive treatments may well be dictated by the complicated etiological factors present in school phobia.

In our own work, we have attempted to design treatment programs that utilize all the conditioning principles and that are responsive to specific information obtained during assessment. Thus, for children who are phobic largely due to "separation" problems, we have used systematic desensitization procedures aimed at reducing anxiety associated with leaving mother. Further, we have used operant principles to reinforce the child for leaving mother and approaching the school or other desired locations. In addition, modeling is used to display appropriate approach behavior. Similarly, for children who are fearful of a specific aspect of the school situation, we use a treatment program consisting of both imaginal and *in vivo* desensitization, reinforced practice for attending school, and participant modeling. Whether or not all of these components are necessary is an empirical question. Nonetheless, use of such a complex, interactive treatment program has resulted in return to school, reduced fear, and enhanced self-concept in a majority of our children (32 of the 37 cases we have worked with over the past 11 years). Clearly, systematic and well controlled research is required to affirm these findings obtained from our uncontrolled clinical efforts.

In summary, a variety of methodological issues remain in the behavioral treatment of school phobia. Nonetheless, the findings of numerous case reports have been encouraging. Treatments which combine classical, operant, and vicarious conditioning procedures have promoted school re-entry and have reduced concomitant anxieties about leaving home and returning to school. However, the majority of investigations evaluating treatment for school phobia have used uncontrolled single-case designs. Controlled studies are clearly warranted; however, commonly used single-case designs pose both methodological and ethical problems. Potentially, these problems could be alleviated through group design strategies. In this way, the complex interactive treatment strategies which we have recommended, could be evaluated more closely.

PREVENTION

In this chapter, we have examined a variety of issues related to diagnosis, incidence, etiology, assessment, and treatment of school phobia. Up to this point, our efforts have been focused upon school phobia after it occurs, not in preventing its occurrence. Caplan (1970) has labeled this approach *tertiary* prevention: the implementation of programs which are designed to eliminate problems in individuals who are currently school phobic. In addition, Caplan has described two other types of intervention which are more truly preventative in scope: *secondary* prevention and *primary* prevention. Secondary prevention programs are designed to reduce the prevalence of specific behavioral problems by reducing their duration. Such programs are aimed at children who show early "signs" of problematic behavior, and the goal of intervention is to short-circuit problem behaviors by early and prompt treatment. Primary prevention programs, on the other hand, are aimed at preventing behavioral problems *before* they occur. In primary prevention, the emphasis is placed upon identifying antecedent conditions related to the development of behavioral problems and delineating those specific conditions that promote more healthy behavior. Thus, primary prevention efforts are focused upon designing activities and events that prevent behavioral problems from occurring in the first place (Caplan, 1970; Price, Bader, & Ketterer, 1980). Obviously, space does not permit a full articulation of prevention-oriented approaches in this chapter; nonetheless, we should like briefly to address the issues involved and describe representative programs.

Jason (1980) has described four distinct types of primary prevention programs, which we shall apply to prevention of school phobia. The first type is directed toward children who are "at risk" for the development of school phobia. Based on our earlier review, high-risk target groups for school phobia include children of agoraphobics (e.g., Berg *et al.,* 1974; Hallam, 1978), children who are moderately anxious and/or fearful in specific school situations (e.g., Hersov, 1960), and children who have unusually close or dependent relationships with their parents (e.g., Eisenberg, 1958; Johnson *et al.,* 1941). The second type of primary prevention program described by Jason is directed toward defining antecedent and consequent conditions that are likely to result in problematic behavior. In reference to school phobia, such programs would be aimed at altering specific antecedent events (e.g., failure in the classroom, undressing for physical education) and consequent events (e.g., attention from teachers, being able to stay home from school) associated with development of school phobia. Such efforts might well entail environmental engineering related to organization-level interventions aimed at physical parameters of the situation, the social climate, and the characteristics of those interacting in the environment (e.g., Jason, 1980). The third type of primary prevention is oriented toward providing children with experiences to ease their transition into potentially stressful situations. Applied to school phobia, this approach suggests that children about to enter school (or a new school) be prepared for this event by visiting school, and talking with teachers. Further, for those children who are fearful of leaving parents, planned separation for gradually increasing durations could be arranged. The final type of primary prevention described by Jason is directed toward the development of affective (e.g., affect recognition, sensitivity), cognitive (e.g., problem-solving abilities), and behavioral (e.g., modalities of social-interactive skills) competencies. Clearly, the emphasis in this latter approach is upon building and strengthening health-promotion skills which preclude development of problematic behaviors like school phobia.

As noted by Jason, procedures based upon the principles of classical, operant, and vicarious conditioning can be productively employed in primary prevention programs (in addition to tertiary treatment programs, as we have detailed above under "Treatment Issues," pp. 386–399). For example, Poser (1970) has proposed a preventive model based upon classical conditioning. He has suggested that children be systematically exposed to potentially stressful and anxiety-producing situations in order to prevent the development of conditioned-avoidance responses. As we noted earlier, children about to enter school might be provided a tour of the school, visit classrooms, the library, and the gymnasium, and talk with teachers, peers, and principals. Such experiences, if graded so as not to be overly anxiety arousing, may well prevent fear from developing into phobic proportions. Poser describes this process as "antecedent systematic desensitization" and views it as a form of immunization. Although this approach has been used to prevent dental and snake fears in young children (Poser & King, 1975), it has not been systematically evaluated in the prevention of school phobia. Nonetheless, many school systems routinely incorporate such an approach in their "school-orientation" programs.

Operant techniques have also been used in a wide variety of settings to prepare parents and children to cope with potentially stressful events. These programs have ranged from childrearing programs (e.g., Matese, Shorr, & Jason, 1980; Patterson, 1971) to specific school-based preventive programs (e.g., Allen, Chinsky, Larcen, Lochman, & Selinger, 1976; Cowen, Dorr, Izzo, Madonia, & Trost, 1971; Spivack & Shure, 1974). Although general in scope, these programs have used operant technology to teach child-rearing skills, positive social interactions, and problem-solving abilities. In a similar vein, Ollendick (1979b) has proposed an immunization model based on operant principles for assisting children to cope with frustration and failure in school. In this program, efforts are made to show children how to handle frustration and failure by programming into their learning environment "doses" of success and failure experiences. In this program, we have found that varying success and failure experiences increase persistence and tolerance to stress. Through increasingly greater exposure to frustrating events associated with failure, tolerance is progressively enhanced and the child is able to perservere in difficult situations that are not immediately reinforcing. Again, although these findings show considerable promise, they have not been directly investigated *vis à vis* school phobia. However, they are directly related to Jason's (1980) formulation regarding development of adaptive competencies that potentially serve a preventive function.

Finally, modeling and cognitive procedures have also been employed as primary prevention strategies. Most thoroughly researched in Melamed and Siegel's (1975) work with dental anxiety and Jaremko's (1979) efforts in anger control, these strategies have also been used by Jason and his colleagues for school transition difficulties (Bogat, Jones, & Jason, 1980). In this approach, appropriate transition behaviors are modeled, role-played, and rehearsed, and coping "self-talk" strategies are used. Illustratively, Bogat *et al.* developed a program for elementary-age children who were unexpectedly required to attend a public school following the closing of their parochial school. During a 2-day preventive orientation program, children were provided tours of the new school, peer-led discussion groups, and information concerning school rules and regulations. Specific strategies involving cognitive restructuring and modeling were used to assist the children throughout the orientation. Children exposed to this program were later assessed and found to score significantly higher than control children in terms of self-esteem related to peer relationships, knowledge of school rules, and teachers' conduct ratings. The findings suggested that this brief intervention was successful in helping the transfer students adjust to their new school environment. Whether or not the development of school phobia *per se* was prevented in these children is not reported; nonetheless, these results appear encouraging.

In summary, the development of learning-based strategies for the primary prevention of school phobia appears highly promising, though largely untested

at this time. As we have noted elsewhere in a more general treatment of preventive efforts:

> Whether or not approaches based on a primary prevention model actually prevent
> behavior problems from occurring remains to be empirically demonstrated. To
> date, claims of prevention have been based more on the intuitive appeal of the
> model than on actual, demonstrable effects. Considerably more research is needed
> to evaluate both the short- and long-term effects of such intervention. Until such
> time, primary prevention remains an admirable goal in need of empirical verifi-
> cation. (Ollendick & Cerny, 1981, p. 296)

This conclusion applies equally well to prevention of school phobia.

Nonetheless, we must conclude our discussion of school phobia by restating that primary prevention strategies derived from learning-based principles
show considerable promise. Not discounting the demonstrated efficacy of learning-based procedures in treating school phobia once it is evident, our future
efforts might productively be directed toward the development, refinement, and
evaluation of integrated prevention strategies based upon learning principles.

SUMMARY AND CONCLUSIONS

Although there have been some encouraging findings in both the treatment and prevention of school phobia, we must conclude this review by
acknowledging that our understanding of school phobia at present is rudimentary and clearly in need of additional refinement and articulation. Little systematic work has been conducted; rather, investigations in this area are for the
most part sporadic and vary with individual investigators' interest, enthusiasm
and persistence.

As previously noted, school phobia is a complex syndrome which, historically and even into the present, has been subject to definitional and diagnostic
confusion. Although the operational guidelines set forth by Berg *et al.* (1969)
are straightforward and seem useful, a majority of studies have not adhered to
them—nor for that matter have they adhered to any consistent set of criteria.
Moreover, efforts to distinguish between "subtypes" of school phobia have
encountered major difficulties and are characterized by inconsistent findings.
In addition, etiological factors remain poorly understood. As we have noted,
the etiology of school phobia varies from child to child; heterogeneity rather
than homogeneity prevails. Children evince school phobia for a number of reasons, including separation anxiety, fear of some aspect of the school situation,
anticipating anxiety following an illness, or some combination of these as well
as other yet unspecified factors.

From a behavioral perspective, school phobia is acquired according to the
specific principles of classical, vicarious, and operant conditioning. Once
acquired, it is likely that the phobic behavior is maintained by a complex inter-

active process involving each of these principles. Sorting out the relevant contributing factors is not an easy task. Nonetheless, assessment designed to ferret out these processes is important, since efficacious treatment is oftentimes dependent on the information obtained. In this pursuit, we have suggested the utility of a multimethod approach, involving behavioral interviews, self-report and other-report test data, and detailed behavioral observations. Based on this information, treatment strategies such as systematic desensitization, participant modeling, and contingency contracting have been recommended and, in general, found to be successful. Still, most of these investigations have been uncontrolled case studies. Although results are promising, they remain to be empirically validated by well controlled research strategies. Initial findings suggest that integrative treatments combining elements of operant, vicarious, and classical conditioning would be the most efficacious and hold the most promise.

Finally, although preventive efforts are in their infancy, they too show considerable promise. Given the possible "link" between school phobia and agoraphobia, the development of such programs assumes even added importance. We must be cautious, however, against blindly endorsing such programs; very little research is available to support their large-scale implementation, regardless of their intuitive appeal.

In summary, our review of school phobia raises as many questions as it purports to answer. Much remains to be accomplished. Even though "the whining schoolboy with his satchel and shining morning face creeping like a snail unwillingly to school" (Shakespeare, *As You Like It,* Act II) has been with us for a long time, we know very little about him. For us, this remains an exciting challenge; the area appears to be fertile soil for systematic and parametric research.

REFERENCES

Allen, G. J., Chinsky, J. M., Larcen, S. W., Lochman, J. E., & Selinger, H. V. *Community psychology and the schools: A behaviorally oriented approach.* Hillsdale, N.J.: Lawrence Erlbaum & Associates, 1976.

Ayllon, T., Smith, D., & Rogers, M. Behavioral management of school phobia. *Journal of Behavior Therapy and Experimental Psychiatry,* 1970, *1,* 125–138.

Baker, H., & Willis, U. School phobia: Classification and treatment. *British Journal of Psychiatry,* 1978, *132,* 492–499.

Barrios, B. A., Hartmann, D. B., & Shigetomi, C. Fears and anxieties in children. In E. J. Mash & L. G. Terdal (Eds.), *Behavioral assessment of childhood disorders.* New York: Guilford, 1981.

Bauer, D. Childhood fears in developmental perspective. In L. Hersov & I. Berg (Eds.), *Out of school.* New York: Wiley, 1980.

Berg, I. School phobia in the children of agoraphobic women. *British Journal of Psychiatry,* 1976, *128,* 86–89.

Berg, I., Nichols, K., & Pritchard, C. School phobia—its classification and relationship to dependency. *Journal of Child Psychology and Psychiatry,* 1969, *10,* 123–141.

Berg, I., Marks, I., McGuire, R., & Lipsedge, M. School phobia and agoraphobia. *Psychological Medicine,* 1974, *4,* 428–434.

Bogat, G. A., Jones, J. W., & Jason, L. A. School transitions: Preventive intervention following an elementary school closing. *Journal of Community Psychology,* 1980, *8,* 343–352.

Broadwin, I. T. A contribution to the study of truancy. *American Journal of Orthopsychiatry,* 1932, *2,* 253–259.

Brown, R. E., Copeland, R. E., & Hall, R. V. School phobia: Effects of behavior modification treatment applied by an elementary school principal. *Child Study Journal,* 1974, *4,* 125–133.

Caplan, G. *The theory and practice of mental health consultation.* New York: Basic Books, 1970.

Castaneda, A., McCandless, B. R., & Palermo, D. S. The children's form of the Manifest Anxiety Scale. *Child Development,* 1956, *27,* 317–326.

Chapel, J. L. Treatment of a case of school phobia by reciprocal inhibition. *Canadian Psychiatric Association Journal,* 1967, *12,* 25–28.

Chazan, M. School phobia. *British Journal of Educational Psychology,* 1962, *32,* 200–217.

Chess, S., Thomas, A., & Birch, H. G. Distortions in developmental reporting made by parents of behaviorally disturbed children. *Journal of the American Academy of Child Psychiatry,* 1966, *5,* 226–236.

Ciminero, A. R., & Drabman, R. S. Current developments in the behavioral assessment of children. In B. B. Lahey & A. E. Kazdin (Eds.), *Advances in clinical child psychology* (Vol. 1). New York: Plenum, 1977.

Coolidge, J. C., Hahn, P. B., & Peck, A. L. School phobia: Neurotic crisis or way of life. *American Journal of Orthopsychiatry,* 1957, *27,* 296–306.

Cooper, J. A. Application of the consultant role to parent–teacher management of school avoidance behavior. *Psychology in the Schools,* 1973, *10,* 259–262.

Cowen, E. L., Dorr, D., Izzo, L. D., Madonia, A., & Trost, M. A. The primary mental health project: A new way to conceptualize and deliver school mental health service. *Psychology in the Schools,* 1971, *8,* 216–225.

Davids, A. (Ed.), *Issues in abnormal child psychology.* Monterey, Cal.: Brooks/Cole, 1973.

Doleys, D. M., & Williams, S. C. The use of natural consequences and a make-up period to eliminate school phobic behavior: A case study. *Journal of School Psychology,* 1977, *15,* 44–50.

Edlund, C. A. A reinforcement approach to the elimination of a child's school phobia. *Mental Hygiene,* 1971, *38,* 433–436.

Eisenberg, L. School phobia: A study in the communication of anxiety. *American Journal of Psychiatry,* 1958, *114,* 712–718.

Estes, H. R., Haylett, C. H., & Johnson, A. M. Separation anxiety. *American Journal of Orthopsychiatry,* 1956, *10,* 682–695.

Evans, T. M., & Nelson, R. O. Assessment of child behavior problems. In A. R. Ciminero, K. S. Calhoun, & H. E. Adams (Eds.), *Handbook of behavioral assessment.* New York: Wiley-Interscience, 1977.

Franks, C. M., & Susskind, D. J. Behavior modification with children: Rationale and technique. *Journal of School Psychology,* 1968, *4,* 75–86.

Garvey, W. P., & Hegrenes, J. R. Desensitization techniques in the treatment of school phobia. *American Journal of Orthopsychiatry,* 1966, *36,* 147–152.

Gelfand, D. M. Behavioral treatment of avoidance, social withdrawal, and negative emotional states. In B. B. Wolman, J. Egan, & A. O. Ross (Eds.), *Handbook of treatment of mental disorders in childhood and adolescence.* Englewood Cliffs, N.J.: Prentice-Hall, 1978.

Gittelman-Klein, R., & Klein, D. School phobia: Diagnostic considerations in the light of imipramine effects. *Journal of Nervous and Mental Disease,* 1973, *156,* 199–215.

Gittelman-Klein, R., & Klein, D. Separation anxiety in school refusal and its treatment with drugs. In. L. Hersov & I. Berg (Eds.), *Out of school*. New York: Wiley, 1980.

Goldfried, M. R., & Kent, R. N. Traditional versus behavioral personality assessment: A comparison of methodological and theoretical assumptions. *Psychological Bulletin*, 1972, *77*, 409–420.

Graham, P., & Rutter, M. The reliability and validity of the psychiatric assessment of the child. II: Interview with the parent. *British Journal of Psychiatry*, 1968, *114*, 581–592.

Graziano, A. M., & DeGiovanni, I. S. The clinical significance of childhood phobias: A note on the proportion of child-clinical referrals for the treatment of children's fears. *Behaviour Research and Therapy*, 1979, *17*, 161–162.

Graziano, A. M., DeGiovanni, I. S., & Garcia, K. A. Behavioral treatment of children's fears: A review. *Psychological Bulletin*, 1979, *86*, 804–830.

Hagman, E. A study of fears of children of preschool age. *Journal of Experimental Education*, 1932, *1*, 110–130.

Hallam, R. S. Agoraphobia: A critical review of the concept. *British Journal of Psychiatry*, 1978, *133*, 314–319.

Hatzenbuehler, L. C., & Schroeder, H. E. Desensitization procedures in the treatment of childhood disorders. *Psychological Bulletin*, 1978, *85*, 831–844.

Herjanic, B., Herjanic, M., Brown, F., & Wheatt, T. Are children reliable reporters? *Journal of Abnormal Child Psychology*, 1975, *3*, 41–48.

Hersen, M. Behavior modification approach to a school phobia case. *Journal of Clinical Psychology*, 1970, *26*, 128–132.

Hersen, M. The behavioral treatment of school phobia. *Journal of Nervous and Mental Disease*, 1971, *153*, 99–107.

Hersen, M., & Barlow, D. H. *Single case experimental designs*. New York: Pergamon, 1976.

Hersov, L. A. Refusal to go to school. *Child Psychology and Psychiatry*, 1960, *1*, 137–145.

Hodgman, C. H., & Braiman, A. "College phobia": School refusal in university students. *American Journal of Psychiatry*, 1965, *12*, 801–805.

Jaremko, M. E. A component analysis of stress innoculation: Review and prospectus. *Cognitive Therapy and Research*, 1979, *3*, 35–45.

Jason, L. A. Prevention in the schools. In R. H. Price, R. F. Ketterer, B. C. Bader, & J. Monahan (Eds.), *Prevention in mental health: Research, policy, and practices*. Beverly Hills, Cal.: Sage Publications, 1980.

Jersild, A. T., & Holmes, F. B. Children's fears. *Child Development Monographs*, 1935, No. 20.

Johnson, A. M., Falstein, E. I., Szurek, S. A., & Svendsen, M. School phobia. *American Journal of Orthopsychiatry*, 1941, *11*, 702–711.

Johnson, S. B. Children's fears in the classroom setting. *School Psychology Digest*, 1979, *8*, 382–396.

Johnson, S. M., & Bolstad, O. D. Methodological issues in naturalistic observation: Some problems and solutions for field research. In L. A. Hamerlynck, L. C. Handy, & E. J. Mash (Eds.), *Behavior change: Methodology, concepts, and practice*. Champaign, Ill.: Research Press, 1973.

Jones, M. C. A laboratory study of fear: The case of Peter. *Pedagogical Seminary*, 1924, *31*, 308–315.

Jones, R. T., & Kazdi., A. E. Childhood behavior problems in the school. In S. M. Turner, K. S. Calhoun, & H. E. Adams (Eds.), *Handbook of clinical behavior therapy*. New York: Wiley-Interscience, 1981.

Kahn, J. H., & Nursten, S. P. School refusal: A comprehensive view of school phobia and other failures of school attendance. *American Journal of Orthopsychiatry*, 1962, *32*, 707–718.

Kazdin, A. E. Situational specificity: The two-edged sword of behavioral assessment. *Behavioral Assessment*, 1979, *1*, 57–75.

Kazdin, A. E. *Research design in clinical psychology.* New York: Harper & Row, 1980.

Kazdin, A. E. Drawing valid inferences from case studies. *Journal of Consulting and Clinical Psychology,* 1981, *49,* 183–192.

Kennedy, W. A. School phobia: Rapid treatment of fifty cases. *Journal of Abnormal Psychology,* 1965, *70,* 285–289.

Kennedy, W. A. A behavioristic community-oriented approach to school phobia and other disorders. In H. C. Richards (Ed.), *Behavioral intervention in human problems.* Oxford: Pergamon, 1971.

Lapouse, R., & Monk, M. A. Fears and worries in a representative sample of children. *American Journal of Orthopsychiatry,* 1959, *29,* 223–248.

Lazarus, A. A. The elimination of children's phobias by deconditioning. In H. J. Eysenck (Ed.), *Behavior therapy and the neuroses.* Oxford: Pergamon, 1960.

Lazarus, A. A. *Behavior therapy and beyond.* New York: McGraw Hill, 1971.

Lazarus, A. A., & Abramovitz, A. The use of "emotive imagery" in the treatment of children's phobias. *Journal of Mental Sience,* 1962, *108,* 191–195.

Lazarus, A. A., Davison, G. C., & Polefka, D. A. Classical and operant factors in the treatment of a school phobia. *Journal of Abnormal Psychology,* 1965, *70,* 225–229.

Lick, J. R., & Katkin, E. S. Assessment of anxiety and fear. In M. Hersen & A. S. Bellack (Eds.), *Behavioral assessment.* New York: Pergamon, 1976.

Linehan, M. M. Issues in behavioral interviewing. In J. D. Cone & R. P. Hawkins (Eds.), *Behavioral assessment: New directions in clinical psychology.* New York: Brunner/Mazel, 1977.

MacFarlane, J. W., Allen, L., & Honzik, M. P. *A developmental study of the behavioral problems of normal children between 21 months and 14 years.* Berkeley: University of California Press, 1954.

Marks, I. *Fears and phobias.* New York: American Press, 1969.

Matese, F., Shorr, S., & Jason, L. A. Behavioral and community interventions during transition to parenthood. In A. Jeger & R. Slotnick (Eds.), *Community mental health and a behavioral-ecology.* New York: Plenum, 1982.

Melamed, B. G., & Siegel, L. J. Reduction of anxiety in children facing hospitalization and surgery by use of filmed modeling. *Journal of Consulting and Clinical Psychology,* 1975, *43,* 511–521.

Miller, L. C., Barrett, C. L., Hampe, E., & Noble, H. Revised anxiety scales for the Louisville Behavior Checklist. *Psychological Reports,* 1971, *29,* 503–511.

Miller, L. C., Barrett, C. L., Hampe, E., & Noble, H. Comparison of reciprocal inhibition, psychotherapy, and waiting list control for phobic children. *Journal of Abnormal Psychology,* 1972, *79,* 269–279. (a)

Miller, L. C., Barrett, C. L., Hampe, E., & Noble, H. Factor structure of childhood fears. *Journal of Consulting and Clinical Psychology,* 1972, *39,* 264–268. (b)

Miller, L. C., Barrett, C. L., & Hampe, E. Phobias of childhood in a prescientific era. In A. Davids (Ed.), *Child personality and psychopathology: Current topics.* New York: Wiley, 1974.

Miller, P. M. The use of visual imagery and muscle relaxation in the counterconditioning of a phobic child: A case study. *Journal of Nervous and Mental Disease,* 1972, *154,* 457–460.

Mischel, W. Toward a cognitive social learning reconceptualization of personality. *Psychological Review,* 1973, *80,* 252–283.

Morganstern, K. P. Behavioral interviewing: The initial stages of assessment. In M. Hersen & A. S. Bellack (Eds.), *Behavioral assessment: A practical handbook.* New York: Pergamon, 1976.

Neisworth, J. T., Madle, R. A., & Goeke, K. E. "Errorless" elimination of separation anxiety: A case study. *Journal of Behavior Therapy and Experimental Psychiatry,* 1975, *6,* 79–82.

Ney, P. G. Combined therapies in a family group. *Canadian Psychiatric Association Journal,* 1967, *12,* 379–385.

Ollendick, T. H. *The revised fear survey schedule for children.* Unpublished manuscript, Indiana State University, 1978.

Ollendick, T. H. Fear reduction techniques with children. In M. Hersen, R. M. Eisler, & P. M. Miller (Eds.), *Progress in behavior modification* (Vol. 8). New York: Academic Press, 1979. (a)

Ollendick, T. H. Success and failure: Implications for child psychopathology. In A. J. Finch, Jr. & P. C. Kendall (Eds.), *Clinical treatment and research in child psychopathology.* New York: Spectrum, 1979. (b)

Ollendick, T. H., & Cerny, J. A. *Clinical behavior therapy with children.* New York: Plenum, 1981.

Ollendick, T. H., & Gruen, G. E. Treatment of a bodily injury phobia with implosive therapy. *Journal of Consulting and Clinical Psychology,* 1972, *38,* 389–393.

Ollendick, T. H., & Hersen, M. An historical introduction to child psychopathology. In T. H. Ollendick & M. Hersen (Eds.), *Handbook of child psychopathology.* New York: Plenum, 1983.

Ollendick, T. H., & Ollendick, D. G. Anxiety disorders in the mentally retarded. In J. L. Matson & R. P. Barrett (Eds.), *Psychopathology of the mentally retarded.* New York: Grune & Stratton, 1982.

Olsen, I. A., & Coleman, H. S. Treatment of school phobia as a case of separation anxiety. *Psychology in the School,* 1967, *4,* 151–154.

Partridge, J. M. Truancy. *Journal of Mental Science,* 1939, *85,* 45–81.

Patterson, G. R. A learning theory approach to the treatment of a school phobic child. In L. P. Ullman & L. Krasner (Eds.), *Case studies in behavior modification.* New York: Holt, Rinehart & Winston, 1965.

Patterson, G. R. *Families: Application of social learning to family life.* Champaign, Ill.: Research Press, 1971.

Poser, E. G. Toward a theory of "behavioral prophylaxis." *Journal of Behavior Therapy and Experimental Psychiatry,* 1970, *1,* 39–43.

Poser, E. G., & King, M. C. Strategies for the prevention of maladaptive fear responses. *Canadian Journal of Behavioral Science,* 1975, *1,* 279–294.

Price, R. H., Bader, B. C., & Ketterer, R. F. Prevention in community mental health: The state of the art. In R. H. Price, R. F. Ketterer, B. C. Bader, & J. Monahan (Eds.), *Prevention in mental health: Research, policy, and practice.* Beverly Hills, Cal.: Sage Publications, 1980.

Quay, H. C., & Werry, J. S. (Eds.). *Psychopathological disorders of childhood* (2nd ed.). New York: Wiley, 1979.

Rachman, S. *Phobias: Their nature and control.* Springfield, Ill.: Charles C Thomas, 1968.

Rachman, S., & Costello, C. G. The etiology and treatment of children's phobias: A review. *American Journal of Psychiatry,* 1961, *118,* 97–105.

Rimm, D. C., & Masters, J. C. *Behavior therapy: Techniques and empirical findings.* New York: Academic, 1974.

Rines, W. B. Behavior therapy before institutionalization. *Psychotherapy: Theory, Research, and Practice,* 1973, *10,* 281–283.

Ross, A. O. *Psychological disorders of children: A behavioral approach to theory, research, and therapy.* New York: McGraw Hill, 1980.

Rutter, M., & Graham, P. The reliability and validity of the psychiatric assessment of the child. I: Interview with the child. *British Journal of Psychiatry,* 1968, *114,* 563–579.

Ryall, M. R., & Dietiker, K. E. Reliability and clinical validity of the Children's Fear Survey Schedule. *Journal of Behavior Therapy and Experimental Psychiatry,* 1979, *10,* 303–309.

Scherer, M. W., & Nakamura, C. Y. A fear survey schedule for children (FSS-FC): A factor analytic comparison with manifest anxiety (CMAS). *Behaviour Research and Therapy,* 1968, *6,* 173–182.

Smith, R. E., & Sharpe, T. M. Treatment of a school phobia with implosive therapy. *Journal of Consulting and Clinical Psychology,* 1970, *35,* 239–243.

Smith, S. L. School refusal with anxiety: A review of sixty-three cases. *Canadian Psychiatric Association Journal,* 1970, *15,* 257–264.

Spielberger, C. D. *Manual for the state-trait anxiety inventory for children.* Palo Alto, Cal.: Consulting Psychologists Press, 1973.

Spivack, G., & Shure, M. B. *Social adjustment of young children.* San Francisco: Jossey-Bass, 1974.

Stampfl, T. G., & Levis, D. J. The essentials of implosive therapy: A learning-theory based psychodynamic behavioral therapy. *Journal of Abnormal Psychology,* 1967, *72,* 496–503.

Tahmisian, J. A., & McReynolds, W. T. Use of parents as behavioral engineers in the treatment of a school phobic girl. *Journal of Counseling Psychology,* 1971, *18,* 225–228.

Truax, C. B., & Carkhuff, R. R. *Toward effective counseling and psychotherapy: Training and practice.* Chicago: Aldine, 1967.

Vaal, J. J. Applying contingency contrasting to a school phobic: A case study. *Journal of Behavior Therapy and Experimental Psychiatry,* 1973, *4,* 371–373.

van der Ploeg, H. M. Treatment of frequent urination by stories competing with anxiety. *Journal of Behavior Therapy and Experimental Psychiatry,* 1975, *6,* 165–166.

Waldfogel, S., Coolidge, J. C., & Hahn, P. Development and management of school phobia. *American Journal of Orthopsychiatry,* 1957, *27,* 754–780.

Waldron, S., Jr. The significance of childhood neurosis for adult mental health: A follow-up study. *American Journal of Psychiatry,* 1976, *133,* 532–538.

Waller, D., & Eisenberg, L. School refusal in childhood—a psychiatric-pediatric perspective. In L. Hersov & I. Berg (Eds.), *Out of school.* New York: Wiley, 1980.

Weinberger, G., Leventhal, T., & Beckman, G. The management of chronic school phobia through the use of consultation with school personnel. *Psychology in the School,* 1973, *10,* 83–88.

Weiss, M., & Cain, B. The residential treatment of children and adolescents with school phobia. *American Journal of Orthopsychiatry,* 1964, *34,* 103–114.

Wolpe, J. *Psychotherapy by reciprocal inhibition.* Stanford, Cal.: Stanford University Press, 1958.

Yarrow, M. R., Campbell, J. D., & Burton, R. V. Recollections of childhood: A study of the retrospective method. *Monographs of the Society for Research in Child Development,* 1970, *35,* (5, Serial No. 138).

Yates, A. J. *Behavior therapy.* New York: Wiley, 1970.

Yule, W. Behavioural approaches. In M. Rutter & L. Hersov (Eds.), *Child psychiatry: Modern approaches.* Oxford: Blackwell Scientific Publications, 1977.

Yule, W., Hersov, L., & Treseder, J. Behavioural treatments of school refusal. In L. Hersov & I. Berg (Eds.), *Out of school.* New York: Wiley, 1980.

Zeligs, R. Children's worries. *Sociology and Social Research,* 1939, *24,* 22–32.

10

Anxiety Disorders in Childhood

KAREN C. WELLS and
LAWRENCE A. VITULANO

DEFINITIONS

Throughout childhood, fears and anxieties are common occurrences and are generally considered to be a component of normal development (Miller, Barrett, & Hampe, 1974). Nevertheless, these reactions are often brought to the attention of professionals because of their severity and negative influence on the functioning of children and families. While the child who shrieks at the sight of a large snake at the city zoo may be quite acceptable, the child who refuses to go outdoors for fear of encountering a number of ferocious animals is another matter.

This chapter is focused on the concepts and techniques involved in the behavioral assessment and treatment of children's anxieties. Although a significant amount of effort has been directed toward fear reduction in adults, the comparable problem of childhood fears has remained a relatively neglected area of research (Graziano, DeGiovanni, & Garcia, 1979).

Perhaps this neglect can be attributed to the statistics that describe even multiple childhood fears as frequently occurring in non-clinic-referred child populations. In the 6- to 12-year-old age group, for example, Lapouse and Monk (1959) found that 43% of the children displayed seven or more fears as reported by their mothers. However, it is the opinion of these authors that

KAREN C. WELLS ● Department of Psychiatry, Children's Hospital National Medical Center, George Washington University School of Medicine, Washington, D.C. 20010.   LAWRENCE A. VITULANO ● Greater Bridgeport Children's Services Center, Bridgeport, Connecticut 06610.

many such childhood reactions are often not transient in nature but rather so disturbing to children and families that they warrant the attention and treatment of professionals.

Children's fears are commonly described as reactions to real or imagined threats in the environment. When these fears intensify and persist, they can develop into phobias. At the severe level of fear, three response systems are typically involved: (a) overt behavioral avoidance, (b) covert or subjective feelings and thoughts, and (c) physiological activity (Graziano et al., 1979). At moderate or mild levels of fear, one or two of these response systems may be reactive. Although the distinction between fears and phobias is somewhat unclear, the designation of phobia is commonly attributed when one or more response systems becomes excessively reactive. Phobia has been defined by Marks (1969) as a fear which "is out of proportion to demands of the situation, cannot be explained or reasoned away, is beyond voluntary control, and leads to avoidance of the feared situation" (p. 3). Miller, Barrett, and Hampe (1974) further refined the definition of phobia to include the criteria that it also "persists over an extended period of time, is unadaptive, and is not age or stage specific" (p. 90). Thus, phobias are most easily distinguished from fears as being non-age- or stage-specific, more persistent and less appropriate in response (Ollendick, 1979). If one accepts Marks's (1969) definition, they always involve the first component in the tripartite model mentioned above, overt behavioral avoidance of the feared situation.

Furthermore, it has been emphasized by Graziano et al. (1979) that intensity and duration be utilized to distinguish mild from clinical fears. These authors suggest that "clinical fears be defined as those with a duration of over two years or an intensity that is debilitating to the client's routine life-style" (p. 805). It is extremely important that the distinction between normal and clinical fears or phobias be clearly established for purposes of both treatment and research. If treatment outcome studies are to set reliable standards for the various disturbances of childhood, then the initial definitions and diagnoses must first be clearly and reliably established. In the following sections of this chapter, assessment techniques will be described and the specific recommendations for clinical treatment of the major childhood fears will be reviewed.

ETIOLOGY

Behavioral formulations of the etiology of fears have assumed that fears and anxiety are acquired through processes of conditioning. Conditioning can occur directly through actual experiences of the child, or vicariously when children observe other children or adults undergoing frightening experiences, or experiencing positive consequences from fearful behavior. There are two basic conditioning paradigms through which fears are assumed to develop. In respondent or classical conditioning, stimuli present at the time of frightening experiences acquire the capacity to elicit fear, particularly if the pairing is repeated several times or if he frightening stimulus is extremely aversive. In operant conditioning, fearful behavior is shaped and maintained by the positive consequences it generates for the child. For example, parents or teachers may reinforce expressions of fear or avoidance behavior by excessive sympathizing with the child or by allowing special circumstances contingent upon expressions of fear and avoidance (e.g., staying home from school with the mother or special play time with the teacher for a child who expresses discomfort with peers). As indicated above, social learning theory predicts that fear can also be conditioned when children merely observe other children or adults in conditioning situations (see Bandura 1969; 1977, for a full explanation of conditioning theories of fear).

In recent years, it has been increasingly apparent that conditioning theories may be only a partial explanation for the etiology of fears and anxiety in children, and several authors have speculated that other variables may also contribute to fearful behavior. Rachman (1977) and Bandura (1977) have emphasized the potential importance of cognitive transmission of fears from parents to children through instructions, information giving, and verbal admonishment. In addition, Rachman (1977) speculates that there is almost certainly a genetic contribution to the general level of fearfulness or the propensity to develop fears. These speculations coincide with developmental data suggesting that emotional reactivity may represent a fundamental individual difference in temperament in children upon which experience builds (Thomas & Chess, 1977; Werry & Aman, 1980).

While it is clear that direct conditioning theories of fear and anxiety do not completely account for the genesis of these disorders, other cognitive and/or biological variables are just beginning to be hypothesized and very little research has been conducted on the contribution of these variables to fear acquisition. Such research is extremely important to our understanding of anxiety disorders and will lead to a more adequate theoretical model of fears in children. (See Chapter 1 for a full discussion of behavioral theories of fears.)

ASSESSMENT

The motor, cognitive, and physiological response components of childhood fears and anxiety reactions have all been assessed by various behavioral techniques. It is essential, however, to recognize which component or components of fear are being assessed during any evaluation. Without this distinction in mind, confusion often occurs at the later comparative and interpretive stages of data analysis. In addition, assessment of only one component or by means of only one assessment method may be an inadequate evaluation of the complete construct of childhood fear. Following the tripartite model of fear and anxiety (Lang, 1968), assessment instruments and techniques will be categorized into three groups: questionnaires and inventories, behavioral measures, and physiological measures.

Questionnaires and Inventories

Self-report questionnaires and behavior checklist inventories are the most common techniques employed in the assessment of childhood fears and anxieties. The Children's Manifest Anxiety Scale (Castaneda, McCandless, & Palermo, 1956) is a 53-item questionnaire which provides a general trait measure of anxiety in children. This scale has good test–retest reliability for a normal population, $r = .70$ to $r = .94$ (Castaneda, McCandless, & Palermo, 1956; Holloway, 1958), and moderate reliability for an emotionally disturbed population, $r = .77$ (Finch, Montgomery, & Deardorff, 1974a). A high score on this test is reflective of general learning-task errors and behavior problems, but lacks any reference to specific environments or stimuli associated with the anxiety. Rather, it provides a measure of three major anxiety factors: (1) worry and oversensitivity, (2) physiological concerns, and (3) concentration problems (Finch, Kendall, & Montgomery, 1974). Good normative data have been established for the test (Castaneda, McCandless, & Palermo, 1956; Coleman, Mackay, & Fidell, 1972; Finch & Nelson, 1974; Holloway, 1961; Scherer & Nakamura, 1968; Ziv & Luz, 1973). A revision of the test, the Children's Manifest Anxiety Scale—Revised, was published by Reynolds and Richmond (1978). This newer 37-item edition is quicker to administer and requires a lower reading level which makes it quite suitable for children in the primary grades.

The Test Anxiety Scale for Children is a 41-item questionnaire which is read aloud to a child who records yes or no answers on an answer sheet. This scale was developed by Sarason, Davidson, Lighthall, Waite and Ruebush (1960) and offers a measure of test anxiety in children. It has moderate test–retest reliability, $r = .67$ (Sarason, Davidson, Lighthall, Waite & Ruebush, 1960), and high split–half reliability, $r = .88$ to $.90$ (Mann, Taylor, Proger & Morrell, 1968) to $r = .72$ (Finch, Kendall, Montgomery, & Morris, 1975). However, correlations with other instruments have been inconsistent (Johnson & Melamed, 1979) and the validity of the A-State and A-Trait scales with an emotionally disturbed population is in question (Finch & Kendall, 1979).

Behavioral Measures

The Behavioral Avoidance Test (BAT) is the most commonly employed direct behavioral measure of specific fears. The standard procedure was first outlined by Lang and Lazovik (1963) and includes instructing the subject to enter a room wherein lies the feared object and then to approach and pick up or handle the object. Subjects are typically scored on their proximity to the feared object and the amount of time spent in contact with it. Although the BAT is administered in a standard and controlled setting, each researcher varies the measure with his own style and number of instructions to the subject. Kelly (1976) warned that the BAT is very sensitive to demand characteristics and results are easily changed by simply instructing children to try harder. Also, there is little reliability and validity data available on the BAT used with children (Barrios, Hartmann, & Shigetomi, 1981).

Observational coding systems are frequently utilized to assess behaviors associated with anxiety. Typically a checklist of behaviors is developed for an observer who rates the frequency of behaviors present in the subject for specified time-sampling periods in a designated environment. Paul's (1966) Timed Behavior Checklist which was originally developed to assess public-speaking anxiety in adults is currently being used with children and yielding encouraging results (Cradock, Cotler, & Jason, 1978). Melamed and Siegel's (1975) Observer Rating Scale of Anxiety is a popular scale which codifies and records behaviors associated with anxiety related to surgery. The Behavior Profile Rating Scale (Melamed, Weinstein, Hawes, & Katin-Borland, 1975) is another useful system which can be utilized in the study of dental anxiety. Many other coding systems have been developed for the assessment of separation anxiety (Glennon & Weisz, 1978; Neisworth, Madle, & Goeke, 1975) and various other fears (Barrios, Hartmann, & Shigetomi, 1981).

Physiological Measures

The physiological response component of anxiety in children is an understudied area for many reasons. Technically, it can require a high level of mechanical sophistication and expensive equipment. In addition, the behavioral researcher must also be adept in the area of psychophysiology in order to accurately record and interpret the data. Nevertheless, this is an important component of childhood fear and should be incorporated into clinical assessment and treatment whenever possible.

Heart rate and electrodermal responses are currently the most common physiological measures utilized in the study of childhood anxiety. Several studies have demonstrated increased heart rates in the dental setting (Melamed, Yurcheson, Fleece, Hutcherson, & Hawes, 1978; Stricker & Howitt, 1965) but one cannot assume that an increase in heart rate necessarily indicates an increase in anxiety. Such increases in physiological arousal can also be associated with other subjective states such as anger or excitement. Furthermore, poor correlations are reported between heart rate and self-report measures of anxiety (Darley & Katz, 1973; Sternbach, 1962). Electrodermal responses such as palmar sweat prints are currently under investigation as sensitive physiological indicators of changes in anxiety levels related to situational stress (Johnson & Stockdale, 1975; Melamed & Siegel, 1975; Melamed, Hawes, Heiby, & Glick, 1975; Venham, Bengston, & Cipes, 1977).

The tripartite model of fear and anxiety was first proposed by Lang (1968) and most of the confirmatory research has been conducted with adult populations. Although few studies with children have been conducted which include three-channel assessment, most authors agree that the tripartite model has heuristic, theoretical, and clinical value for study and treatment of children as well. The present authors will argue throughout this chapter that clinical treatment planning with anxious and phobic children is dependent upon information gathered in physiological, motor, and cognitive response systems using measuring techniques such as those described in this section.

TREATMENT OF ANXIETY DISORDERS IN CHILDREN

Next, the authors will review the relevant empirical literature evaluating outcome of various treatment approaches and, based on these studies, provide clinical recommendations regarding assessment and treatment of individual children presenting to a clinic with anxiety disorders. First, however, it is necessary to review and describe the various treatment techniques that have been applied to children. As Graziano *et al.* (1979) have pointed out, there is such a profusion of concepts and methods in studies of anxiety in children that it becomes difficult to organize these studies for discussion. Oftentimes, different authors will employ the same term (e.g., *desensitization*) to describe techniques which appear quite dissimilar; conversely, different labels have been used to describe treatment approaches which casual observation would indicate to be technically identical. For the sake of clear communication with the reader in the present discussion, it is necessary to review each of these treatment approaches briefly, along with the procedural variations which distinguish them from one another.

Systematic Desensitization

First developed by Wolpe for treatment of anxiety and phobic disorders in adults, this technique is based upon the Reciprocal Inhibition Principle which states that "if a response inhibiting anxiety can be made to occur in the presence of anxiety-evoking stimuli, it will weaken the bond between these stimuli and anxiety" (1973, p. 17). Thus, a basic requirement of this technique is use of a response incompatible with anxiety.

As it is typically employed with adults and with some children, systematic desensitization employs muscle relaxation as the response incompatible with anxiety. In this procedure, the child is first trained in deep muscle relaxation by sequentially tensing and then relaxing various muscle groups as instructed by the therapist (Bernstein & Borkovec, 1973; Cautela & Groden, 1981). A fear hierarchy is constructed with fear-eliciting scenes arranged in order from least to most anxiety provoking. In subsequent sessions the child is relaxed and the therapist presents the scenes verbally to the child with instructions to imagine each scene as clearly as possible. Treatment continues until the child has been presented with each scene in the fear hierarchy, with no more than three or four scenes presented in any session. (See Wolpe, 1973 for a detailed presentation of systematic densensitization.)

A few studies have applied systematic desensitization to children exactly as it is used with adults (e.g., MacDonald, 1975; Miller, Barrett, Hampe, & Noble, 1972; Tasto, 1975). In other studies, adaptations of the basic procedure have occurred due to the limited attention spans and cognitive abilities of young children or their difficulty following complex instructions. For example, a variety of procedures has been employed to induce relaxation in children for whom muscle exercises were difficult or impossible. These include emotive imagery (Lazarus & Abramowitz, 1962), music (Lazarus, 1959; Wish, Hasazi & Jurgeal, 1973), anxiolytic medication, feeding (Lazarus, 1959), and toy play and body contact with the mother (Bentler, 1962). Miklich (1973) employed reinforcement for remaining relaxed during imaginal presentation of phobic stimuli with a hyperactive boy who had difficulty sitting still. Similarly, candy, social praise or other reinforcers have been used with children to reinforce in session relaxation (Miller, 1972).

A variety of terms has been used to label the basic treatment strategy described above including *deconditioning* (Lazarus, 1959), *in vitro desensitization* (Ultee, Griffioen, & Schellekens, 1982), *counterconditioning* (Miller, 1972) and *reciprocal inhibition therapy* (Bentler, 1962). Excepting the minor adapations described above, the procedures described in these studies are essentially the same.

In Vivo *Desensitization*

This technique is similar to *in vitro* systematic desensitization with the exception that hierarchically arranged scenes are presented directly to the relaxed child rather than in imagination. This procedure is often used for very young children or for children who have a limited capacity for imagination (Croghan & Musante, 1975; Pomerantz, Peterson, Marholin, & Stern, 1977).

Contact Desensitization or Participant Modeling

This technique differs from *in vivo* desensitization in several important respects. The anxious child first observes a model (an adult or another child) directly approach and interact with the phobic stimulus in a series of graduated steps. The model then encourages the child to place his or her hand on the model's hand while the model manipulates the phobic stimuli. Then the child interacts with the phobic stimuli while the model observes. Ritter (1968) has employed the term *contact desensitization* because the child comes into direct contact with a model as well as with the phobic stimuli. Thus, contact desensitization appears to consist of graduated *in vivo* exposure to a phobic stimulus with modeling and guided practice. In contrast to *in vivo* desensitization procedures, no attempt is made to teach or induce relaxation prior to modeling, exposure, and guided practice. Perhaps for this reason, some authors have referred to this technique as "participant modeling" (e.g., Ollendick, 1979).

The present authors tend to agree that "participant modeling" is the more appropriate label to describe this strategy since the use of an anxiety-inhibiting response is fundamental to the reciprocal inhibition principle on which desensitization treatments are based.

Modeling

In this treatment approach, the child observes a model engaged in increasingly more intimate or more active contact with phobic stimuli. In some studies, the child also observes the model experiencing positive consequences after contact with the phobic stimulus or situation. Two variations of the basic modeling paradigm have been used: (1) *symbolic modeling* in which the child observes a film or videotape of other children interacting with the phobic stimulus, and (2) *in vivo modeling* in which the child observes a live model interacting directly with the phobic stimulus. Ritter (1968) has referred to *in vivo* modeling as vicarious desensitization.

Reinforced Practice

One study has investigated the effects of a procedure labeled "reinforced practice" with children. In this technique, the child is instructed to enter the phobic situation and remain in contact until such time that he or she becomes afraid. Repeated practice trials occur in each session and the child is reinforced for remaining in contact with the feared situation for longer and longer periods of time. Feedback is given to the children via a visual "thermometer" which displays the exact number of minutes the child remains in contact with the phobic stimulus. In reinforced practice, no model is used, no response incompatible with anxiety is employed, and no attempt is made to present phobic stimuli to children in graduated fashion. Thus, the active therapeutic ingredients in this procedure are practice, feedback, and reinforcement (Leitenberg & Callahan, 1973).

Cognitive Strategies

Speculations regarding the clinical usefulness of cognitive treatment strategies for anxious children have recently appeared in the behavioral literature. Although there is currently little confirmatory experimental evidence, we will briefly describe these strategies since it is our belief that cognitive treatments will increasingly be used with anxious children. The Three treatment strategies which emphasize the importance of cognitive variables in mediating behavior change, or which attempt to modify cognitions directly have been discussed for use with children: (1) stress inoculation training, (2) covert modeling and (3) direct training in verbal controlling responses.

Stress inoculation training involves three training phases. In the education phase the child is provided with a conceptual framework for the relationship between his thoughts and his feelings of fearfulness in words that he can understand. In the rehearsal phase, the child and therapist generate lists of coping self-statements that the child can rehearse during different stages of confrontation with a phobic stimulus. Separate cognitive statements are developed for preparing for a stressor, confronting a stressor, coping with feelings of being overwhelmed, and finally, reinforcing self-statements. In the application training phase, the child practices his newly learned cognitive coping skills in actual fearful situations (see Meichenbaum, 1977 for a detailed explanation of stress inoculation training).

One study has investigated the effects of covert modeling with anxious children (Chertock & Bornstein, 1979). In this study, children were first asked to imagine a series of hierarchically arranged scenes relevant to the phobic situation, and further, to imagine one or more models interacting in the phobic situation. Scenes of models coping in phobic situations are described to children, who are asked to clearly imagine the therapist's descriptions, but children never actually observe live or filmed models.

A final cognitive strategy involves direct training in verbal controlling or coping responses. In these strategies, children are read statements designed to emphasize their competence in coping with phobic situations, or to reduce the aversiveness of the phobic situation.

After practicing these statements with the therapists, children are then instructed to employ the statements in actual feared situations. This strategy is similar to stress inoculation training in its emphasis on providing children with self-statements to rehearse in feared situations.

TREATMENT OUTCOME

Desensitization

Desensitization treatment approaches are based largely on a classical conditioning model of fear acquisition and inhibition (see section on etiology of anxiety). In this model, fear and avoidance behavior are thought to be mediated by high anxiety. Desensitization treatment approaches employ what Wolpe (1973) refers to as the *counterconditioning* or *reciprocal inhibition* principle to decrease anxiety and eliminate avoidance behavior; that is, by repeatedly pairing anxiety-incompatible responses with anxiety-evoking stimuli, anxiety will be decreased via a counterconditioning mechanism. Thus, desensitization is designed to decrease avoidance behavior by directly influencing anxiety.[1]

Several studies, ranging from case reports to group outcome studies, have attempted to evaluate the effects of systematic desensitization and its variants on phobic children. Many of these case studies involved children referred to clinics for treatment of phobias significantly interfering with their adaptive functioning. While these studies have reported positive outcome using variants of systematic and/or *in vivo* desensitization, and have the advantage of reporting treatment for clinic-referred populations, they have all the problems attendant on the case-study approach for drawing valid conclusions regarding effects of treatment (see Hersen & Barlow, 1976).

One single-case design study has been reported which has adequate internal validity as well as the advantage of evaluating treatment outcome for a clinically phobic child (Van Hasselt, Hersen, Bellack, Rosenblum, & Lamparski, 1979). In this study systematic desensitization in imagination was applied to three phobias (blood, heights, and test-taking) in an 11-year-old multiphobic child. Treatment was applied to each phobia in multiple baseline fashion (see Hersen & Barlow, 1976).

In addition, consistent with the tripartite nature of anxiety (Borkovec, Weerts, & Bernstein, 1977), the authors measured motoric, cognitive and physiological components of anxiety for each of the boy's three phobias. Results indicated that relaxation alone had no appreciable effect on the three channels of anxiety, whereas desensitization significantly reduced motoric and cognitive aspects of anxiety when treatment was applied in sequence to each of the child's phobias. Physiological measures (heart rate, finger pulse volume) showed no systematic changes with treatment.

Several analogue studies of systematic desensitization with children have been reported (Barabasz, 1973; 1975; Kelly, 1976; Kondas, 1967; Mann & Rosenthal, 1969). Four of these studies have been reviewed carefully by Ollendick (1979) and we will not repeat methodological details here. These four studies were considered analogue studies because they involved mild or nonreferred subject populations and/or because they involved a less than adequate trial of systematic desensitization (e.g., three sessions).

Nevertheless, three of these four studies (Barabasz, 1973; 1975; Kondas, 1967; Mann & Rosenthal, 1969) demonstrated significant improvement with desensitization treatment, whereas one study showed no impovement (Kelly, 1976). One of the positive studies (Barabasz, 1973) is particularly interesting because it is among the limited number of desensitization treatment studies with children in which a physiological index of anxiety was obtained. Children in this study were divided into high and low fear groups on the basis of GSR

---

[1]The views presented here are those of Wolpe (1973). It should be noted that the theoretical model of which desensitization treatments are based has been widely criticized (Leitenberg, 1976; Yates, 1975).

responses to fear-relevant stimuli. Children in the high-fear systematic desensitization group showed significant reductions in GSR following treatment compared to the high-fear no-treatment control group. This study stands in contrast to the Van Hasselt *et al.* (1979) study in which no effects on heart rate and finger pulse volume were found following systematic desensitization, and suggests that GSR may be a more sensitive physiological measure of the effects of treatment in children. The one negative analogue study (Kelly, 1976) significantly departed from the standard method for systematic desensitization by presenting graduated stimuli to children in play rather than imaginally or *in vivo,* and by failing to employ relaxation or other counterconditioning agents.

A recent analogue study not reported in previous reviews compared the effects of systematic desensitization, delivered to children in imagination versus *in vivo* (Ultee, Griffioen, & Schellekens, 1982). Results indicated that systematic desensitization delivered *in vivo* resulted in significantly greater improvement on behavioral, and teacher observation measures as compared to imaginal desensitization or no-treatment control. Interestingly, there was no difference between imaginal desensitization and no treatment in this study of 5- to 10-year-old children.

The authors conclude that younger children do not improve with imaginal desensitization, because they are developmentally incapable of cognitive processes necessary for the therapeutic use of imagination. While this conclusion is logically appealing, its validity is obfuscated by the methodology of the study; namely, the use of mildly anxious, non-referred children as subjects, the failure to train children in relaxation or other anxiety-antagonistic responses, and the fact that experimental comparisons were made after only four sessions of treatment. Thus, while this study is suggestive, the final answer to the question of comparative efficacy of imaginal versus *in vivo* desensitization on clinical phobias, and the effects of age on outcome of these two treatments, awaits further investigation.

One group comparative-outcome study has been conducted with clinically phobic children. This study compared imaginal systematic desensitization, psychotherapy, and no treatment in 67 6- to 15-year-old phobic children. Parent counseling also occurred in both treatment groups and was identical for the two groups. Comparing the groups as a whole, results indicated significant improvement on parent report measures for both treatment conditions relative to no treatment. The two treatments did not differ with respect to their relative efficacy on parent report. However, clinician evaluations failed to confirm parental reports. No differences were found on clinician ratings among the three groups (desensitization, psychotherapy, no treatment) at posttreatment or at a 6-week follow-up (Miller, Barrett, Hampe & Noble, 1972). However, when the authors evaluated the effect of age on clinician evaluations of treatment outcome, some interesting results were obtained. For younger children (i.e., those aged 6–10 years) both treatments were found to be significantly and equally effective compared to no treatment. For older children (i.e., those aged 11–15), no effects for either treatment were found. Again, the treatments were found to be significantly and equally effective for both age groups on parent report measures.

Based on the above review, the present authors find themselves in disagreement with Graziano *et al.* (1979) who concluded that "there exists no convincing evidence that approaches developed on respondent-based systematic desensitization ... are effective methodologies for reducing children's fears" (p. 824). One single-case experimental design with adequate internal validity and three analogue studies which reported positive effects of desensitization approaches compared to no-treatment control groups were not included in the Graziano *et al.* (1979) review.

The existing literature elucidates neither the theoretical mechanisms nor the active therapeutic component(s) responsible for change in desensitization treatments, nor does it clarify the effect of age on treatment outcome. Several case histories and analogue studies suggest that *in vivo* desensitization may be more effective than imaginal desensitization with children, particularly younger children, whereas the one group clinical outcome study (Miller *et al.,* 1972) suggests exactly the opposite in reporting that a younger age group improved significantly with imaginal desensitization whereas an older group of children did not. It may be of interest that 69% of the children in the Miller *et al.* (1972) study were school-phobic, whereas all the other phobias reported in studies in this section were other clinical phobias. Because several authors have indicated that school phobia may be a distinct clinical entity with a much poorer prognosis in the older child, it is possible that the poor outcome for the older age group in the Miller *et al.* (1972) study was contributed by the school-phobic members of the sample. In conclusion then, we find ourselves in agreement with Ollendick (1979) that there is currently some evidence to support the use and continued investigation of systematic desensitization treatment approaches with phobic children. What is needed now is research to clarify the theoretical mechanism, active therapeutic elements(s) and effect of subject characteristics on this treatment strategy.

Modeling

Modeling approaches are based on principles of social learning theory which predict that just as fears can be acquired through vicarious conditioning processes, they can also be inhibited through vicarious extinction. O'Connor (1969) proposed a three-fold theory to account for modeling effects in children. According to O'Connor, modeling brings about decreases in fear and avoidance behavior by extinction effects which derive from observing models interact with the phobic stimulus with no aversive consequences ensuing; by the facilitation of approach and interaction responses which may be present in the child's repertoire; and/or by acquisition of new skills for interacting with phobic stimuli not previously in the child's behavioral repertoire. All of these effects are presumed to occur through processes of vicarious conditioning and extinction since in the basic modeling paradigm the phobic child merely observes models interacting with phobic stimuli. However Bandura and his colleagues (Bandura, 1969; Bandura, Grusec, & Menlove, 1967) have suggested that while modeling may be sufficient for emotional extinction and response acquisition, reinforcement procedures may be necessary for response performance, particularly durable performance. In addition, in later papers Bandura has increasingly emphasized the potential importance of cognitive variables influenced in the modeling process. That is, in addition to vicarious extinction and response facilitation effects, modeling may also provide accurate information, and may correct misconceptions regarding fear-inducing stimuli (Bandura, 1977; Bandura & Barab, 1973). This may be particularly relevant for children who may have large gaps in their understanding of the objective dangers and proper mode of interacting with feared objects.

In comparison with literature on systematic desensitization approaches with children, studies on the effects of modeling have been more restricted in the range of experimental methodologies used for investigation. Most modeling studies have been analogue investigations of non-clinic-referred children conducted in controlled laboratory situations. Three variations of modeling have been investigated: (1) *in vivo* modeling, (2) symbolic (filmed) modeling, and (3) participant modeling.

Ollendick (1979) has recently reviewed the extant literature on the three types of modeling mentioned above and presents these studies in tabular form. Examining the percentage of subjects improving with treatment in studies of symbolic modeling, *in vivo* modeling, and participant modeling, a 25% to 50% improvement rate was found for symbolic modeling, 50% to 60% for live modeling, and 80% to 92% for participant modeling (Ollendick, 1979). This ordering of treatment effectiveness has essentially been confirmed in studies directly comparing these treatment approaches. In a comparison of symbolic modeling, participation alone and modeling plus participation, Lewis (1974) found that modeling plus participation was most effective and symbolic modeling least effective in reducing avoidance behavior in 5- to 12-year-old children. Ritter (1968) found that participant modeling was significantly more effective than *in vivo* modeling in her sample of 5- to 11-year-old children. In this study 80% of children performed the terminal approach response following participant modeling treatment whereas 53% of children did so following *in vivo* modeling treatment. These figures correspond to those reported by Ollendick (1979) in his cross-study analysis. The extent to which the apparent ordering of treatment effects from symbolic modeling (least effective) to participant modeling (most effective) would hold for clinically phobic populations is unknown but results of these analogue studies are certainly suggestive.

A number of studies have suggested parameters of modeling which may enhance the effectiveness of these treatments. These include use of multiple models instead of only one model (Bandura & Menlove, 1968); use of models similar in age and sex to the phobic child (Kornhaber & Schroeder, 1975); use of coping models (i.e., models who initially display fear but subsequently master their fear) rather than fearless models (Meichenbaum, 1971); and the use of multiple phobic stimuli rather than a single phobic stimulus (Bandura & Menlove, 1968). Likewise, it has been suggested that certain subject characteristics may affect treatment outcome. For example, Bandura and Menlove (1968) found that in treatment involving multiple models, high emotional proneness in the subject (defined by the range and intensity of anxiety responsiveness) was inversely related to behavioral improvement. That is, the children with greater pre-treatment emotional arousal showed less improvement with treatment. Bandura and Menlove (1968) suggested that for such persons, relaxation training prior to model exposure may be necessary. This is of great importance to clinicians since it is precisely these children who are most likely to be referred to clinics for treatment.

In conclusion, the analogue studies on effects of modeling treatment suggest that these approaches can produce significant decreases in anxiety and avoidance behavior in children. It seems probable, based on the analogue research, that modeling strategies which include the active participation of the phobic child, and exposure to a wide range of models as well as phobic stimuli will be most beneficial to children likely to be referred to outpatient clinics. However, the validity of these speculations awaits confirmatory evidence collected from studies of clinically phobic populations.

Reinforced Practice

Although a few case studies exist utilizing aspects of reinforced practice in treatment of phobic children (e.g., Pomerantz, Peterson, Marholin, & Stern, 1977), only one experimental evaluation of this technique has been conducted with a child population (Leitenberg & Callahan, 1973). This technique is based on the notion that phobic avoidance in children can be treated directly without first decreasing subjectively experienced anxiety. Leitenberg and Callahan (1973) do not discount the contribution of cognitive and physiological components of fear, but suggest that these aspects of the fear response may often be reduced as a consequence of prior behavioral change. This approach stands in contrast to systematic desensitization as well as all the psychotherapies of anxiety which are based on the assumption that cognitive and physiological parameters of anxiety must be decreased before changes can occur in behavior.

The Leitenberg and Callahan (1973) study has many of the problems already mentioned regarding generalization of conclusions from analogue studies to clinical populations. Subjects were nonreferred kindergarten and nursery school children with a fear rather common for children this age, fear of darkness. Following eight sessions of treatment with reinforced practice (consisting of practice, visual feedback and reinforcement) experimental subjects improved significantly in their ability to stay in a dark room alone as compared to no-treatment control subjects whose ability to tolerate a dark room actually deteriorated. Unfortunately, no physiological or self-report measures of anxiety were collected in this study. The extent to which experimental children experienced a decrease in subjective anxiety is, therefore, not known. It would seem that collection of these measures in future research is mandatory, not only from a theoretical but also from a clinical point of view. This is particularly true in studies of clinic-referred phobic children whose initial levels of cognitive and physiological anxiety are likely to be much higher than in non-referred children. Conclusions regarding effectiveness of reinforced practice with phobic children are tentative, and must await further research.

Cognitive Strategies

The current experimental evidence for effectiveness of cognitive treatment strategies with phobic children is very weak. No experimental outcome studies of stress inoculation training with anxious children have been published, although there is increasing speculation that these strategies, developed for use with adults, may be applicable to anxious children as well (Meichenbaum, 1977). Likewise, the one study investigating covert modeling with children found no evidence for differential effectiveness of covert modeling compared to simple exposure in imagination with no model (Chertock & Bornstein, 1979), although methodological problems with this study prevent a clearcut conclusion at present (Tearnan & Graziano, 1980).

The one cognitive strategy which has received some support is the simple, direct training of verbal controlling or coping self-statements. Kanfer, Karoly, and Newman (1975) found that repeating to children sentences emphasizing the child's active control or coping significantly improved darkness tolerance in children afraid of the dark. In a more recent comparative outcome study, Peterson and Shigetomi (1981) found that cognitive coping strategies combined with filmed modeling were more effective than either modeling alone or coping alone in children facing hospitalization and surgery. The extent to which these treatment strategies would reduce true phobias in clinic-referred populations is, of course, unknown.

In summary, there is currently only weak support for cognitive training strategies in phobic children. The authors have presented these strategies primarily for clinical and heuristic purposes. In our opinion, it is only a matter of time before experimental investigations of cognitive training strategies for anxious children begin to proliferate. Although we must withhold judgment on these strategies at the present time, the adult literature indicates that treatment aimed at directly modifying the cognitive component of anxiety in children may represent an important addition to the clinician's treatment armamentarium.

CLINICAL RECOMMENDATIONS

There are several conceptual approaches to assessment that might be kept in mind when formulating a treatment plan for a given child presenting to a clinic with anxiety or phobic disorders. Firstly, perusal of the literature indicates that there are no clear recommendations that can be made dependent upon the type of anxiety or phobia experienced by the child.

Fears of natural and supernatural dangers (e.g., snakes, dogs, the dark, loud noises, water) have been treated by virtually all of the techniques discussed in this chapter with no clear indications that one may be more effective than another. Fears of physical injury and interpersonal or performance fears have been most likely treated by either imaginal desensitization, *in vivo* desensitization, or a combination of the two, perhaps because these fears often involve rather complex stimuli difficult to arrange in modeling treatments. Social withdrawal has been most often treated with filmed modeling often followed by live modeling and/or participation with reinforcement. However, there is no theoretical or empirical rationale for treating particular phobias with particular techniques at present.

Some authors (e.g., Barrios *et al.*, 1981) have indicated that treatment should be dependent upon idiosyncratic, tripartite assessment of the child, including assessment of motor, physiological, and cognitive components of anxiety. Selection of the most appropriate treatment strategy would then be dependent upon which channel(s) of anxiety is most reactive in a given child. For example, in a child who displays avoidance behavior (motor component) with very little physiological or cognitive reactivity, reinforced practice would be most appropriate. For a child with high cognitive anxiety (reflected in self-report) but little physiological or motor reactivity, a cognitive, self-control strategy might be selected. For a child who experiences all three channels of fear, a complex treatment strategy designed to address each component would be indicated (e.g., relaxation followed by training in coping self-statements which can be practiced during participant modeling).

The recommendations of Barrios *et al.* (1981), while logically appealing, are based primarily on research with adult populations. Studies involving three-channel assessment of anxiety in children are practically nonexistent, and there are no studies evaluating the interaction of treatment with type of reactivity (motor, physiological, cognitive). However, until appropriate research with children occurs, clinicians should be guided by the notion that individual children probably differ in their anxiety patterning (i.e., which channel(s) is most reactive), and this can only be discovered after a three-channel assessment (Johnson & Melamed, 1979, Wells, 1981). Treatments would then be chosen which most directly address the most reactive channel.

Treatment planning is most complicated for children displaying reactivity in two or more channels of anxiety, and we suggest that an empirical approach to case management must be followed in these cases (Wells, 1981). For example, with children displaying cognitive anxiety and motor avoidance one might begin with a modeling or reinforced practice treatment program. Repeated measures of avoidance behavior and cognitive anxiety should be taken both during a pretreatment baseline phase and during treatment to assess the effects of modeling on both anxiety channels. In some cases cognitive anxiety may change directly with changes in avoidance behavior, or may lag slightly behind. In other cases, however, cognitive changes may not occur or may lag so far behind behavioral changes as to be clinically unmeaningful. In these cases, a second strategy might then be implemented to modify cognitive aspects of anxiety directly.

A final area of consideration is the influence of skills deficits in phobic children. Several authors (e.g., Graziano *et al.*, 1979; Rimm & Masters, 1974) have pointed out that children may often lack the necessary skills for interacting in the feared situation. This point is most obvious in socially anxious children whose anxiety may be secondary to a social skills deficit (Wells, 1981), but is equally salient for children with specific phobias. This is especially true the younger the child, since children who become phobic at an early age may successfully avoid all contact with the phobic object at a time when their peers are learning interaction skills. MacDonald (1975) nicely illustrated this point in her study of a clinic-referred dog-phobic child who had no skills for petting and controlling dogs. A component of treatment for this child involved dog management skills training. Assessment of skills deficits should occur for all phobic children and a treatment strategy selected which includes modeling, practice and reinforcement in appropriate skills.

In summary, our recommendations regarding treatment planning for phobic children derive from the tripartite model of anxiety (Lang, 1968) developed in studies of adults. Treatment should be designed to modify the idiosyncratic anxiety pattern displayed by the individual child, and treatments (e.g., modeling) which impart new skills for interacting in the feared situation should be used for children with skills deficits. Strategies involving relaxation training and treatment in imagination preceding *in vivo* treatment may be necessary for children whose anxiety is so intense or pervasive that they can not tolerate even minimal contact with phobic stimuli initially. The reader is referred to MacDonald (1975) and Ross, Ross, and Evans, (1971) for excellent case examples of clinically phobic children treated with multi-component treatment strategies designed to address all relevant areas of anxiety response.

REFERENCES

Bandura, A. *Principles of behavior modification*. New York: Holt, Rinehart & Winston, 1969.

Bandura, A. *Social learning theory*. Englewood Cliffs, N.J.: Prenctice-Hall, 1977.

Bandura, A., & Menlove, F. L. Factors determining vicarious extinction of avoidance behavior through symbolic modeling. *Journal of Personality and Social Psychology*, 1968, *8*, 99–108.

Bandura, A., & Barab, P. G. Processes governing disinhibitory effects through symbolic modeling. *Journal of Abnormal Psychology*, 1973, *82*, 1–9.

Bandura, A., Grusec, J. E., & Menlove, F. L. Vicarious extinction of avoidance behavior. *Journal of Personality and Social Psychology*, 1967, *5*, 16–23.

Barabasz, A. F. Group densensitization of test anxiety in elementary school. *Journal of Psychology*, 1973, *83*, 295–301.

Barabasz, A. F. Classroom teachers as paraprofessional therapists in group systematic desensitization of test anxiety. *Psychiatry*, 1975, *38*, 388–392.

Barrios, B., Hartmann, D., & Shigetomi, C. Fears and anxieties in children. In E. J. Mash and L. G. Terdal (Eds.), *Behavioral assessment of childhood disorders*. New York: Guilford, 1981.

Bentler, P. M. An infant's phobia treated with reciprocal inhibition therapy. *Journal of Child Psychology and Psychiatry*, 1962, *3*, 185–189.

Bernstein, D. A., & Borkovec, T. D. *Progressive relaxation training: A manual for the helping professions*. Champaign, Ill.: Research Press, 1973.

Borkovec, T. D., Weerts, T. C., & Bernstein, D. A. Assessment of anxiety. In A. R. Ciminero, K. S. Calhoun, & H. E. Adams (Eds.), *Handbook of behavioral assessment*. New York: Wiley, 1977.

Castaneda, A., McCandless, B., & Palermo, D. The children's form of the Manifest Anxiety Scale. *Child Development*, 1956, *27*, 317–326.

Cautela, J. R., & Groden, J. *Relaxation: A comprehensive manual for adults, children and children with special needs*. Champaign, Ill., Research Press, 1981.

Chertok, S. L., & Bornstein, P. H. Covert modeling treatment of children's dental fears. *Child Behavior Therapy*, 1979, *1*, 249–255.

Coleman, S., Mackay, D., & Fidell, B. English normative data on the Children's Manifest Anxiety Scale. *British Journal of Social and Clinical Psychology*, 1972, *11*, 85–87.

Cradock, C., Cotler, S., & Jason, L. A. Primary prevention: Immunization of children for speech anxiety. *Cognitive Therapy and Research*, 1978, *2*, 389–396.

Croghan, L., & Musante, G. J. The elimination of a boy's high building phobia by *in vivo* desensitization and game playing. *Journal of Behavior Therapy and Experimental Psychiatry*, 1975, *6*, 87–88.

Darley, S., & Katz, I. Heart rate changes in children as a function of test versus game instructions and text anxiety. *Child Development*, 1973, *44*, 784–789.

Finch, A., & Kendall, P. The measurement of anxiety in children: Research findings and methodological problems. In A. J. Finch & P. C. Kendall (Eds.), *Clinical treatment and research in child psychopathology*. New York: Spectrum, 1979.

Finch, A., & Nelson, W. Anxiety and locus of conflict in emotionally disturbed children. *Journal of Abnormal Child Psychology*, 1974, *2*, 33–37.

Finch, A., Kendall, P., & Montgomery, L. Multidimensionality of anxiety in children: Factor structure of the Children's Manifest Anxiety Scale. *Journal of Abnormal Child Psychology*, 1974, *2*, 331–335.

Finch, A., Montgomery, L., & Deardorff, P. Children's Manifest Anxiety Scale: Reliability with emotionally disturbed children. *Psychological Reports*, 1974, *34*, 658. (a)

Finch, A., Montgomery, L., & Deardorff, P. Reliability of state-trait anxiety with emotionally disturbed children. *Journal of Abnormal Child Psychology*, 1974, *2*, 67–69. (b)

Finch, A., Kendall, P., Montgomery, L., & Morris, T. Effects of two types of failure on anxiety. *Journal of Abnormal Psychology*, 1975, *84*, 583–586.

Glennon, B., & Weisz, J. R. An observational approach to the assessment of anxiety in young children. *Journal of Consulting and Clinical Psychology*, 1978, *46*, 1246–1257.

Graziano, A. M., DeGiovanni, I. S., & Garcia, K. A. Behavioral treatment of children's fears: A review. *Psychological Bulletin*, 1979, *86*, 804–830.

Hersen, M., & Barlow, D. H. *Single case experimental designs: Strategies for studying behavior change.* New York: Pergamon, 1976.

Holloway, H. Reliability of the Children's Manifest Anxiety Scale at the rural third grade level. *Journal of Educational Psychology*, 1958, *49*, 193–196.

Holloway, H. Normative data on the Children's Manifest Anxiety Scale at the rural third grade level. *Child Development*, 1961, *32*, 129–134.

Johnson, P., & Stockdale, D. Effects of puppet therapy on palmar sweating of hospitalized children. *Johns Hopkins Medical Journal*, 1975, *137*, 1–5.

Johnson, S. B., & Melamed, B. G. The assessment and treatment of children's fears. In B. B. Lahey & A. E. Kazdin (Eds.), *Advances in clinical child psychology* (Vol 2). New York: Plenum, 1979.

Kanfer, F. H., Karoly, P., & Newman, A. Reduction of children's fear of the dark by competence related and situational threat-related verbal cues. *Journal of Consulting and Clinical Psychology*. 1975, *43*, 251–258.

Kelly, C. K. Play desensitization of fear of darkness in preschool children. *Behaviour Research and Therapy*, 1976, *14*, 79–81.

Kondas, O. Reduction of examination anxiety and stage fright by group desensitization and relaxation. *Behaviour Research and Therapy*, 1967, *5*, 275–281.

Kornhaber, R. C., & Schroeder, H. E. Importance of model similarity on the extinction of avoidance behavior in children. *Journal of Consulting and Clinical Psychology*, 1975, *43*, 601–607.

Lang, P. J. Fear reduction and fear behavior: Problems in treating a construct. In J. M. Shlien (Ed.), *Research in Psychotherapy* (Vol. 3). Washington, D.C.: American Psychological Association, 1968.

Lang, P., & Lazovik, A. Experimental desensitization of a phobia. *Journal of Abnormal and Social Psychology*, 1963, *66*, 519–525.

Lapouse, R., & Monk, M. A. Fears and worries in a representative sample of children. *American Journal of Orthopsychiatry*, 1959, *29*, 803–813.

Lazarus, A. A. The elimination of children's phobias by deconditioning. *Medical Proceedings* (South Africa), 1959, *5*, 261–265.

Lazarus, A. A. The elimination of children's phobias by deconditioning. In H. J. Eysenck (Ed.), *Behavior therapy and the neuroses.* New York: Pergamon, 1960.

Lazarus, A. A., & Abramowitz, A. The use of "emotive imagery" in the treatment of children's phobias. *Journal of Mental Science*, 1962, *108*, 191–195.

Leitenberg, H. Behavioral approaches to treatment of neuroses. In H. Leitenberg (Ed.), *Handbook of behavior modification and behavior therapy.* Englewood Cliffs, N.J.: Prentice-Hall, 1976.

Leitenberg, H., & Callahan, E. J. Reinforced practice and reduction of different kinds of fears in adults and children. *Behaviour Research and Therapy*, 1973, *11*, 19–30.

Lewis, S. A. A comparison of behavior therapy techniques in the reduction of fearful avoidance behavior. *Behavior Therapy*, 1974, *5*, 648–655.

MacDonald, M. L. Multiple impact behavior therapy in a child's dog phobia. *Journal of Behavior Therapy and Experimental Psychiatry*, 1975, *6*, 317–322.

Mann, J., & Rosenthal, T. L. Vicarious and direct counterconditioning of test anxiety through individual and group desensitization. *Behaviour Research and Therapy,* 1969, *7,* 359–367.

Mann, L., Taylor, R., Proger, B., & Morrell, J. Test anxiety and defensiveness against admission of test anxiety induced by frequent testing. *Psychological Reports,* 1968, *23,* 1283–1286.

Marks, I. M. *Fears and phobias.* New York: Academic, 1969.

Meichenbaum, D. Examination of model characteristics in reducing avoidance behavior. *Journal of Personality and Social Psychology,* 1971, *17,* 298–307.

Meichenbaum, D. *Cognitive-behavior modification: An integrative approach.* New York: Plenum, 1977.

Melamed, B., & Siegel, L. Reduction of anxiety in children facing hospitalization and surgery by use of filmed modeling. *Journal of Consulting and Clinical Psychology,* 1975, *43,* 511–521.

Melamed, B., Hawes, R., Heiby, E., & Glick, J. Use of filmed modeling to reduce uncooperative behavior of children during dental treatment. *Journal of Dental Research,* 1975, *54,* 797–801.

Melamed, B., Weinstein, D., Hawes, R., & Katin-Borland, M. Reduction of fear-related dental management problems with use of filmed modeling. *Journal of the American Dental Association,* 1975, *90,* 822–826.

Melamed, B., Yurcheson, R., Fleece, E., Hutcherson, S., & Hawes, R. Effects of filmed modeling in the reduction of anxiety-related behaviors in individuals varying in level of previous experience in the stress situation. *Journal of Consulting and Clinical Psychology,* 1978, *46,* 1357–1367.

Miklich, D. R. Operant conditioning procedures with systematic desensitization in a hyperkinetic asthmatic boy. *Journal of Behavior Therapy and Experimental Psychiatry,* 1973, *4,* 177–182.

Miller, L C., Barrett, C. L., Hampe, E., & Noble, H. Comparison of reciprocal inhibition, psychotherapy, and waiting list control for phobic children. *Journal of Abnormal Psychology,* 1972, *79,* 269–279.

Miller, L. C., Barrett, C. L., & Hampe, E. Phobias of childhood in a prescientific era. In A. Davids (Ed.), *Child personality and psychopathology: Current topics.* New York: Wiley, 1974.

Miller, P. M. The use of visual imagery and muscle relaxation in the counterconditioning of a phobic child: A case study. *Journal of Nervous and Mental Diseases,* 1972, *154,* 457–460.

Neisworth, J., Madle, R., & Goeke, K. "Errorless" elimination of separation anxiety: A case study. *Journal of Behavior Therapy and Experimental Psychiatry,* 1975, *6,* 79–82.

O'Connor, R. D. Modification of social withdrawal through symbolic modeling. *Journal of Applied Behavior Analysis,* 1969, *2,* 15–22.

Ollendick, T. H. Fear reduction techniques with children. In M. Hersen, R. M. Eisler & P. M. Miller (Eds.), *Progress in behavior modification* (Vol. 8). New York: Academic, 1979.

Paul, G. *Insight vs. desensitization in psychotherapy.* Stanford, Cal.: Stanford University Press, 1966.

Peterson, L., & Shigetomi, C. The use of coping techniques to minimize anxiety in hospitalized children. *Behavior Therapy,* 1981, *12,* 1–14.

Pomerantz, P. B., Peterson, N. T., Marholin, D., & Stern, S. The *in vivo* elimination of a child's water phobia by a paraprofessional at home. *Journal of Behavior Therapy and Experimental Psychiatry,* 1977, *8,* 417–421.

Rachman, S. The conditioning theory of fear acquisition: A critical examination. *Behaviour Research and Therapy,* 1977, *15,* 375–387.

Reynolds, C. R., & Richmond, B. O. What I think and feel: A revised measure of children's manifest anxiety. *Journal of Abnormal Child Psychology,* 1978, *6,* 271–280.

Rimm, D. C., & Masters, J. C. *Behavior therapy: Techniques and empirical findings.* New York: Academic, 1974.

Ritter, B. The group desensitization of children's snake phobias using vicarious and contact desensitization procedures. *Behaviour Research and Therapy,* 1968, *6,* 1–6.

Ross, D., Ross, S., & Evans, T. A. The modification of extreme social withdrawal by modification with guided practice. *Journal of Behavior Therapy and Experimental Psychiatry,* 1971, *2,* 273–279.

Sarason, S., Davidson, K., Lighthall, F., Waite, R., & Ruebush, B. *Anxiety in elementary school children.* New York: Wiley, 1960.

Scherer, M., & Nakamura, C. A fear survey schedule for children (FSS-FC): A factor analytic comparison with manifest anxiety (CMAS). *Behaviour Research and Therapy,* 1968, *6,* 173–182.

Sternbach, R. Assessing differential autonomic patterns in emotions. *Journal of Psychosomatic Research,* 1962, *6,* 87.

Stricker, G., & Howitt, J. Physiological recording during simulated dental appointments. *New York State Dental Journal,* 1965, *31,* 204–213.

Tasto, D. Systematic desensitization, muscle relaxation and visual imagery in the counterconditioning of a four year old phobic child. *Behaviour Research and Therapy,* 1969, *7,* 409–411.

Tearnan, B. H., & Graziano, W. G. Covert modeling and children's fears: A methodological critique of Chertock and Bornstein. *Child Behavior Therapy,* 1980, *2,* 73–77.

Thomas, A., & Chess, S. *Temperament and development.* New York: Brunner/Mazel, 1977.

Ultee, C. A., Griffioen, D., & Schellekens, J. The reduction of anxiety in children: A comparison of the effects of systematic desensitization *in vitro* and systematic desensitization in vivo. *Behaviour Research and Therapy.* 1982, *20,* 61–67.

Van Hasselt, V., Hersen, M., Bellack, A. S., Rosenblum, N., & Lamparski, D. Tripartite assessment of the effects of systematic desensitization in a multi-phobic child: An experimental analysis. *Journal of Behavior Therapy and Experimental Psychiatry,* 1979, *10,* 51–56.

Venham, L., Bengston, D., & Cipes, M. Children's responses to sequential dental visits. *Journal of Dental Research,* 1977, *56,* 454–459.

Wells, K. C. Assessment of children in outpatient settings. In M. Hersen & A. S. Bellack (Eds.), *Behavioral assessment: A practical handbook* (Second ed.) New York: Pergamon, 1981.

Werry, J. S., & Aman, M. G. Anxiety in children. In G. D. Burrows & B. M. Davies (Eds.), *Handbook of studies on anxiety.* Amsterdam: ASP Biological and Medical Press, 1980.

Wish, P. A., Hasazi, J. E., & Jurgela, A. R. Automated direct deconditioning of a childhood phobia. *Journal of Behavior Therapy and Experimental Psychiatry,* 1973, *4,* 279–283.

Wolpe, J. *The practice of behavior therapy.* New York: Pergamon, 1973.

Yates, A. S. *Theory and practice in behavior therapy.* New York: Wiley, 1975.

Ziv, A., & Luz, M. Manifest anxiety in children of different socioeconomic levels. *Human Development,* 1973, *16,* 224–232.

Index

435